The Religious Traditions of Asia

Religion, History, and Culture
Readings from The Encyclopedia of Religion

Mircea Eliade
EDITOR IN CHIEF

EDITORS

Charles J. Adams
Joseph M. Kitagawa
Martin E. Marty
Richard P. McBrien
Jacob Needleman
Annemarie Schimmel
Robert M. Seltzer
Victor Turner

ASSOCIATE EDITOR

Lawrence E. Sullivan

ASSISTANT EDITOR

William K. Mahony

The Religious Traditions of Asia

EDITED BY
Joseph M. Kitagawa

Religion, History, and Culture
Readings from The Encyclopedia of Religion

Mircea Eliade
EDITOR IN CHIEF

MACMILLAN PUBLISHING COMPANY
New York
COLLIER MACMILLAN PUBLISHERS
London

MACMILLAN PUBLISHING COMPANY
866 Third Avenue, New York, N.Y. 10022

Collier Macmillan Canada, Inc.

Library of Congress Catalog Card Number: 89-8129

Printed in the United States of America

printing number
1 2 3 4 5 6 7 8 9 10

Library of Congress Cataloging-in-Publication Data

The Religious traditions of Asia.

(Religion, history, and culture)
Includes readings from the Encyclopedia of religion.
1. Asia—Religion. ~~I. Kitagawa, Joseph Mitsuo~~,
1915– . ~~II. Series~~. ~~III. Encyclopedia of religion~~.
BL1032.R47 1989 291′.095 89-8129
ISBN 0-02-897211-2

CONTENTS

MAPS

INTRODUCTION

Books on the religions of Asia are many and varied, written from diverse perspectives. Inasmuch as the articles in the present volume came out of *The Encyclopedia of Religion*, a few words at this point about the perspectives of the encyclopedia may be in order.

Although such notions as the global community and the encounter between the West and the non-Western world are taken for granted by many of us today, these are relatively recent notions in the history of the human race. To be sure, Europeans have felt the presence of Muslim peoples since the religion's birth in the seventh century of the common era, but they did not come into direct contact with most other peoples in the non-Western world until Columbus's voyage to the Americas in 1492 and Vasco da Gama's voyage to the Indian Ocean in 1498. As Mircea Eliade often reminded us, the discovery of non-Western peoples, languages, religions, and cultures was as significant an experience for the West as the invention of the telescope; both radically changed the way the West perceived itself and its place in the universe. Understandably, the initial response of Europeans to non-Western peoples and their traditions was to measure them against their own value systems. For example, many Europeans assumed that all non-Western traditions revealed structures similar to those found in Christianity. If these structures proved to be different, European missionaries were expected to correct the non-Christians by converting them to "eternal" (Christian) truth. It was only after the Renaissance in the fourteenth century that Europeans came to recognize the existence of other religions as different but genuine traditions in their own right. In the course of time, especially after the Enlightenment, many Europeans began to interpret non-Western religions, not through the eyes of Christianity but on their own terms. Even then it was Europe—and not the non-Western peoples—who classified and interpreted non-Western religious traditions, for which were invented such designations as "primitive religions" (obviously a value judgment made from a modern European perspective), Hinduism, Buddhism, and Confucianism. (Of course, no Chinese had ever called K'ung Fu-tzu by the latinized name Confucius.)

Although we must give credit to the many European intellectuals who from the time of the Enlightenment have tried to appreciate non-Western religions and cultures on their own terms, it remains the case that from the Enlightenment up to World War II, it was assumed that non-Western peoples would present their religions and cultures primarily as data for Westerners to analyze and interpret from their own perspectives, perspectives they claimed were objective, neutral, and universal. Two things must be said in this connection. First, we are not trying to belittle the achievements of these perspectives and methods, methods that produced such great works as the Sacred Books of the East (edited by Friedrich Max Müller) and the *Encyclopaedia of Religion and Ethics* (edited by James Hastings.) This kind of approach to non-Western religions, often characterized as "Orientalism"—concocted in the *mundus imaginalis* of Western minds—is still influential in some circles today, as is evidenced by the fact that so many books on the religions of Asia are still written from this perspective. Second, to make matters more complicated, many intellectuals in Asia before World War II naively accepted the "autobiographical" statements of Westerners concerning their perspectives and approaches, claiming for them objectivity, neutrality, and universality. The reasons for this kind of intellectual twist in Asia are obvious. In those days, it was fairly fashionable to appropriate things Western in conformity with the program of westernization of Asia promoted by colonial regimes. To adopt Western modes of scholarship, moreover, was the only *entrée* into the global academy. Thus, a strange phenomenon took place in modern Asia. These westernized Asian intellectuals started writing about the religions and cultures of Asia as though they were Western scholars approaching them from the outside.

This analysis may help explain the confusing state of today's scholarship regarding the religions of Asia. It may also account for Mircea Eliade's astute observation that "the Western world has not yet, or not generally, met with authentic representatives of the 'real' non-Western traditions" (*Myths, Dreams and Mysteries,* Harper, 1960, pp. 8–9). Accordingly, under Eliade's editorship, those who contributed articles on the religions of Asia to the encyclopedia made serious efforts to overcome the falsely assumed universality of a Western provincial stance.

To be sure, Western concepts and symbols have become deeply ingrained in our scholarship on religion, which, as a result, is almost incurably influenced by Western ways of perceiving the texture of human experience. We have the sobering suspicion that our best efforts in trying to interpret the nature of human experience may still not enable us to deal adequately with the depth of non-Western peoples' religious traditions, traditions based on different ways of perceiving and organizing human experience. So in a way, our efforts to refine our scholarly approach and to overcome the false conviction of the universality of our methods may be somewhat analogous to the mariners' attempts to rebuild their ships on the high seas. We do not claim finality for our endeavor, but our encyclopedia indicates, at least, the best efforts of contemporary scholars. We hope that our readers will appreciate the ever-tentative character of scholarship as such, but also rejoice that we have come this far.

It is impossible to acknowledge our indebtedness to the many people who made *The Encyclopedia of Religion,* and also our present volume indirectly, a reality. But we would be terribly remiss if we did not recall the memory of Mircea Eliade, editor in chief of the encyclopedia, and also express our profound appreciation to Charles E. Smith, president and publisher of Macmillan Reference Division, Macmillan Publishing Company, and to Mark Cummings, who has served as the managing editor for the Religion, History, and Culture series.

February, 1989 Joseph Mitsuo Kitagawa

ONE

SOUTH AND SOUTHEAST ASIA

1 HINDUISM

Alf Hiltebeitel

Hinduism is the religion followed by about 70 percent of the roughly seven hundred million people of India. Elsewhere, with the exception of the Indonesian island of Bali, Hindus represent only minority populations. The geographical boundaries of today's India are not, however, adequate to contour a full account of this religion. Over different periods in the last four or five millennia, Hinduism and its antecedents have predominated in the adjacent areas of Pakistan and Bangladesh and have been influential in such other regions as Afghanistan, Sri Lanka, Southeast Asia, and Indonesia. But in these areas Hindu influences have been superseded or overshadowed by the influences of other religions, principally Buddhism and Islam. This account will treat only of Hinduism as it has taken shape historically in the "greater India" of the Indian subcontinent. [*For discussion of Hinduism outside the Indian subcontinent, see* Southeast Asian Religions.]

INDUS VALLEY RELIGION

There are good reasons to suspect that a largely unknown quantity, the religion of the peoples of the Indus Valley, is an important source for determining the roots of Hinduism.

The Indus Valley civilization arose from Neolithic and Chalcolithic village foundations at about the middle of the third millennium BCE as a late contemporary of Egyptian and Mesopotamian riverine civilizations. It engaged in trade with both, though mostly with Mesopotamia. Reaching its apogee around 2000 BCE, it then suffered a long period of intermittent and multifactored decline culminating in its eclipse around 1600 BCE, apparently *before* the coming of the Aryan peoples and their introduction of the Vedic religious current. At its peak, the Indus Valley civilization extended over most of present-day Pakistan, into India as far eastward as near Delhi, and southward as far as the estuaries of the Narmada River. It was apparently dominated by the two cities of Mohenjo-Daro, on the Indus River in Sind, and Harappa, about 350 miles to the northwest on a former course of the Ravi River, one of the tributaries to the Indus. Despite their distance from each other, the two cities show remarkable uniformity in material and design, and it has been supposed that they formed a pair of religious and administrative centers.

The determination of the nature of Indus Valley religion and of its residual impact upon Hinduism are, however, most problematic. Although archaeological sites have yielded many suggestive material remains, the interpretation of such finds is conjectural and has been thwarted especially by the continued resistance of the Indus Valley script, found on numerous steatite seals, to convincing decipherment. Until it is deciphered, little can be said with assurance. The content of the inscriptions may prove to be minimal, but if the language (most likely Dravidian) can be identified, much can be resolved.

At both Harappa and Mohenjo-Daro, the cities were dominated on the western side by an artificially elevated mound that housed a citadel-type complex of buildings. Though no temples or shrines can be identified, the complex probably served both sacred and administrative functions. A "great bath" within the Mohenjo-Daro citadel, plus elaborate bathing and drainage facilities in residences throughout the cities, suggests a strong concern for personal cleanliness, cultic bathing, and ritual purity such as resurface in later Hinduism. Indeed, the "great bath," a bitumen-lined tank with steps leading into and out of it from either end, suggests not only the temple tanks of later Hinduism but the notion of "crossing" associated with them through their Sanskrit name, *tīrtha* ("crossing place, ford").

A granary attached to the citadel may also have involved high officials in ceremonial supervision of harvests and other agricultural rituals. Terra-cotta female figurines with pedestal waists, found especially at village sites, reveal at least a popular cultic interest in fertility. They are probably linked with worship of a goddess under various aspects, for while some portray the figure in benign nurturing poses, others present pinched and grim features that have been likened to grinning skulls: these are likely foreshadowings of the Hindu Goddess in her benign and destructive aspects.

But most controversial are the depictions on the seals, whose inscriptions remain undeciphered. Most prominently figured are powerful male animals. They are often shown in cultic scenes, as before a sort of "sacred manger," or being led by a priestly ministrant before a figure (probably a deity and possibly a goddess) in a peepul tree, one of the most venerated trees in Hinduism. Male animals also frequently figure in combination with human males in composite animal-human forms. With female figures seemingly linked to the Goddess and males associated with animal power, it has been suggested that the two represent complementary aspects of a fertility cult with attendant sacrificial scenarios such as are found in the animal sacrifice to the Goddess in post-Vedic Hinduism. In such sacrifices the Goddess requires male offerings, and the animal represents the human male sacrificer. Most interesting and controversial in this connection is a figure in a yogic posture who is depicted on three seals and a faience sealing. Though features differ in the four portrayals, the most fully defined one shows him seated on a dais with an erect phallus. He has buffalo horns that enclose a treelike miter headdress, possibly a caricatured buffalo face, wears bangles and necklaces or torques, and is surrounded by four wild animals. Some of these associations (yoga, ithyphallicism, lordship of animals) have suggested an identification with the later Hindu god Śiva. Other traits (the buffalo-man composite form, association with wild animals, possible intimations of sacrifice) have suggested a foreshadowing of the buffalo demon Mahiṣāsura, mythic antagonist and sacrificial victim of the later Hindu goddess Durgā. Possibly the image crystallizes traits that are later associated with both of these figures.

The notion that features of Indus Valley religion form a stream with later non-Aryan religious currents that percolate into Hinduism has somewhat dismissively been called the substratum theory by opponents who argue in favor of treating the development of Hinduism as derivable from within its own sacred literature. Though this "substratum" cannot be known except in the ways that it has been structured within Hinduism (and no doubt also within Jainism and Buddhism), it is clear that a two-way process was initiated as early as the Vedic period and has continued to the present. [*For further discussion, see* Indus Valley Religion.]

VEDISM

The early sacred literature of Hinduism has the retrospective title of Veda ("knowledge") and is also known as *śruti* ("that which is heard"). Altogether it is a prodigious body of literature, originally oral in character (thus "heard"), that evolved into its present form over nine or ten centuries between about 1400 and 400 BCE. In all, four types of texts fall under the Veda-*śruti* heading: Saṃhitās, Brāhmaṇas, Āraṇyakas, and Upaniṣads. At the fount of all later elaborations are the four Saṃhitās ("collections"): the *Ṛgveda Saṃhitā* (Veda of Chants, the oldest), the *Sāmaveda* and *Yajurveda Saṃhitā*s (Vedas of Melodies and Sacrificial Formulas, together known as the "liturgical" Saṃhitās), and the *Atharvaveda Saṃhitā* (the youngest, named after the sage Atharvan). These constitute the four Vedas, with some early sources referring to the "three Vedas" exclusive of the last. [*See* Vedas.] The material of the four was probably complete by 1000 BCE, with younger parts of the older works overlapping older parts of the younger ones chronologically. The Saṃhitās, or portions of them, were preserved by different priestly schools or "branches" (*śākhā*s) through elaborate means of memorization. Many of these schools died out and their branches became lost, but others survived to preserve material for literary compilation and redaction. The subsequent works in the categories of Brāhmaṇa, Āraṇyaka, and Upaniṣad are all linked with one or another of the Vedic schools, and thus with a particular Vedic Saṃhitā, so that they represent the further literary output of the Vedic schools and also the interests of the four types of priests who came to be associated differentially with the ritual uses of the four Saṃhitās. It is from the *Ṛgveda* that Vedic religion in its earliest sense must be reconstructed.

Although the urban civilization of the Indus Valley had run its course by the time of the arrival of the Aryans in about 1500 BCE, the newcomers met heirs of this civilization in settled agricultural communities. The contrast between cultures was striking to the Aryans, who described the indigenous population as having darker skin, defending themselves from forts, having no gods or religious rituals but nonetheless worshiping the phallus. As small stone phallic objects have been found at Indus Valley sites, this is probably an accurate description of a cult continued from pre-Vedic Indus Valley religion that prefigures the later veneration of the *liṅga* (phallus) in the worship of Śiva. In contrast to this predominantly agricultural population, the invading Aryans were a mobile, warlike people, unattached to cities or specific locations, entering Northwest India in tribal waves probably over a period of several centuries. Moreover, their society inherited an organizing principle from its Indo-European past that was to have great impact on later Indian civilization in the formation of the caste system. The ideal arrangement, which myths and ritual formulas propounded and society was to reflect, called for three social "functions":

the priests, the warriors, and the agriculturalist-stockbreeders. Early Vedic hymns already speak of three such interacting social groups, plus a fourth—the indigenous population of *dāsa*, or *dasyu* (literally, "slaves," first mythologized as demon foes of the Aryans and their gods). By the time of the late *Ṛgveda,* these peoples were recognized as a fourth "class" or "caste" in the total society and were known as *śūdras*.

Most crucial to the inspiration of the early Vedic religion, however, was the interaction between the first two groups: the priesthood, organized around sacerdotal schools maintained through family and clan lines, and a warrior component, originally led by chieftains of the mobile tribal communities but from the beginning concerned with an ideal of kingship that soon took on more local forms. Whereas the priests served as repositories of sacred lore, poetry, ritual technique, and mystical speculation, the warriors served as patrons of the rites and ceremonies of the priests and as sponsors of their poetry. These two groups, ideally complementary but often having rival interests, crystallized by late Vedic and Brahmanic times into distinct "classes": the *brāhmaṇas* (priests) and the *kṣatriyas* (warriors).

Although the *Ṛgveda* alludes to numerous details of ritual that soon came to be systematized in the religion of the Brāhmaṇas, it brings ritual into relief only secondarily. The primary focus of the 1,028 hymns of the *Ṛgveda* is on praising the gods and the cosmic order *(ṛta),* which they protect. But insofar as the hymns invoke the gods to attend the sacrifice, there is abundant interest in two deities of essentially ritual character: Agni and Soma. Agni (Fire) is more specifically the god of the sacrificial fire who receives offerings to the gods and conveys them heavenward through the smoke. And Soma is the divinized plant of "nondeath" *(amṛta),* or immortality, whose juices are ritually extracted in the *soma* sacrifice, a central feature of many Vedic and Brahmanic rituals. These two gods, significantly close to mankind, are mediators between men and other gods. But they are especially praised for their capacity to inspire in the poets the special "vision" *(dhī)* that stimulates the composition of the Vedic hymns. Agni, who as a god of fire and light is present in the three Vedic worlds (as fire on earth, lightning in the atmosphere, and the sun in heaven), bestows vision through "illumination" into the analogical connections and equivalences that compose the *ṛta* (which is itself said to have a luminous nature). *Soma,* the extracted and purified juice of the "plant of immortality," possibly the hallucinogenic fly agaric mushroom, yields a "purified" vision that is described as "enthused" or "intoxicated," tremulous or vibrant, again stimulating the inspiration for poetry. The Vedic poet *(kavi, ṛṣi,* or *vipra)* was thus a "see-er," or seer, who translated his vision into speech, thus producing the sacred *mantras*, or verse-prayers, that comprise the Vedic hymns. Vedic utterance, itself hypostatized as the goddess Vāc (Speech), is thus the crystallization of this vision.

Vedic religion is decidedly polytheistic, there being far more than the so-called thirty-three gods, the number to which they are sometimes reduced. Though the point is controversial, for the sake of simplification we can say that at the core or "axis" of the pantheon there are certain deities with clear Indo-European or at least Indo-Iranian backgrounds: the liturgical gods Agni and Soma (cf. the Avestan deity Haoma) and the deities who oversee the three "functions" on the cosmic scale: the cosmic sovereign gods Varuṇa and Mitra, the warrior god Indra, and the Aśvins, twin horsemen concerned with pastoralism, among other things. Intersecting this structure is an opposition of Indo-Iranian background between *devas* and *asuras*. In the *Ṛgveda* both terms may refer to ranks among the gods, with *asura* being higher and more primal. But *asura* also has the Vedic meaning of "demon," which it retains in later Hinduism, so that the *deva-asura* opposition also takes on dualistic overtones. Varuṇa is the *asura par excellence,* whereas Indra is the leader of the *devas*. These two deities are thus sometimes in opposition and sometimes in complementary roles: Varuṇa being the remote overseer of the cosmic order (*ṛta*) and punisher of individual human sins that violate it; Indra being the dynamic creator and upholder of that order, leader of the perennial fight against the collective demonic forces, both human and divine, that oppose it. It is particularly his conquest of the *asura* Vṛtra ("encloser")—whose name suggests ambiguous etymological connections with Varuṇa—that creates order or being *(sat,* analogous to *ṛta)* out of chaos or nonbeing *(asat)* and opens cosmic and earthly space for "freedom of movement" *(varivas)* by gods and men. Considerable attention is also devoted to three solar deities whose freedom of movement, thus secured, is a manifestation of the *ṛta,* a prominent analogy for which is the solar wheel: Sūrya and Savitṛ (the Sun under different aspects) and Uṣas (charming goddess of the dawn). Other highly significant deities are Yama, god of the dead, and Vāyu, god of wind and breath. It is often pointed out that the gods who become most important in later Hinduism—Viṣṇu, Śiva (Vedic Rudra), and the Goddess—are statistically rather insignificant in the Veda, for few hymns are devoted to them. But the content rather than the quantity of the references hints at their significance. Viṣṇu's centrality and cosmological ultimacy, Rudra's destructive power and outsiderhood, and the this-worldly dynamic aspects of several goddesses are traits that assume great proportions in later characterizations of these deities.

Although it is thus possible to outline certain structural and historical features that go into the makeup of the Vedic pantheon, it is important to recognize that these are obscured by certain features of the hymns that arise from the type of religious "vision" that inspired them, and that provide the basis for speculative and philosophical trends that emerge in the late Veda and continue into the early Brahmanic tradition. The hymns glorify the god they address in terms generally applicable to other gods (brilliance, power, beneficence, wisdom) and often endow him or her with mythical traits and actions particular to other gods (supporting heaven, preparing the sun's path, slaying Vṛtra, and so on). Thus, while homologies and "connections" between the gods are envisioned, essential distinctions between them are implicitly denied. Speculation on what *is* essential—not only as concerns the gods, but the ritual and the *mantras* that invoke them—is thus initiated in the poetic process of the early hymns and gains in urgency and refinement in late portions of the *Ṛgveda* and the subsequent "Vedic" speculative-philosophical literature that culminates in the Upaniṣads. Most important of these speculations historically were those concerning the cosmogonic sacrifices of Puruṣa in *Ṛgveda* 10.90 (the *Puruṣa-sūkta,* accounting for, among other things, the origin of the four castes) and of Prajāpati in the Brāhmaṇas. Each must be discussed further. In addition, speculations on *brahman* as the power inherent in holy speech and on the *ātman* ("self") as the irreducible element of personal experience are both traceable to Vedic writings (the latter to the *Atharvaveda* only). We shall observe the convergence of all these lines of speculation in the Upaniṣads and classical Hinduism.

RELIGION OF THE BRĀHMAṆAS

The elaboration of Vedic religion into the sacrificial religion of the Brāhmaṇas is largely a result of systematization. The first indication of this trend is the compilation of the liturgical Saṃhitās and the development of the distinctive priestly schools and interests that produced these compendiums. Thus, while the *Ṛgveda* became the province of the *hotṛ* priest, the pourer of oblations and invoker of gods through the *mantras* (the term *hotṛ*, "pourer," figures often in the *Ṛgveda* and has Indo-Iranian origins), the newer collections developed around the concerns of specialist priests barely alluded to in the *Ṛgveda* and serving originally in subordinate ritual roles. The *Sāmaveda* was a collection of verses taken mostly from the *Ṛgveda,* set to various melodies (*sāman*s) for use mainly in the *soma* sacrifice, and sung primarily by the *udgātṛ* priest, who thus came to surpass the *hotṛ* as a specialist in the sound and articulation of the *mantras*. And the *Yajurveda* was a collection of *yajus*, selected sacrificial *mantra*s, again mostly from the *Ṛgveda,* plus certain complete sentences, to be murmured by the *adhvaryu* priest, who concerned himself not so much with their sound as with their appropriateness in the ritual, in which he became effectively the master of ceremonies, responsible for carrying out all the basic manual operations, even replacing the *hotṛ* priest as pourer of oblations. A fourth group of priests, the *brāhmaṇa*s, then claimed affiliation with the *Atharvaveda* and assumed the responsibility for overseeing the entire ritual performance of the other priests and counteracting any of their mistakes (they were supposed to know the other three Vedas as well as their own) by silent recitation of *mantra*s from the *Atharvaveda*. As specialization increased, each priest of these four main classes took on three main assistants.

The Brāhmaṇas—expositions of *brahman,* the sacred power inherent in *mantra* and more specifically now in the ritual—are the outgrowth of the concerns of these distinctive priestly schools and the first articulation of their religion. Each class of priests developed its own Brāhmaṇas, the most important and comprehensive being the *Śatapatha Brāhmaṇa* of one of the *Yajurveda* schools. The ritual system was also further refined in additional manuals: the Śrautasūtras, concerned with "solemn" rites, first described in the Brāhmaṇas and thus called *śrauta* because of their provenance in these *śruti* texts, and the Gṛhyasūtras, concerned with domestic rites (from *gṛha,* "home"), justified by "tradition" *(smṛti)* but still having much of Vedic origins. The Śrautasūtras were compiled over the period, roughly, from the Brāhmaṇas to the Upaniṣads, and the Gṛhyasūtras were probably compiled during Upaniṣadic times.

The domestic rites take place at a single offering fire and usually involve offerings of only grain or ghee (clarified butter). Along with the maintenance of the household fire and the performance of the so-called Five Great Sacrifices—to *brahman* (in the form of Vedic recitation), to ancestors, to gods, to other "beings," and to humans (hospitality rites)—the most prominent *gṛhya* ceremonies are the sacraments or life-cycle rites (*saṃskāra*s). Of these, the most important are the rites of conception and birth of a male child; the Upanayana, or "introduction," of boys to a *brāhmaṇa* preceptor or *guru* for initiation; marriage; and death by cremation (Antyeṣṭi, "final offering"). The Upanayana, involving the investiture of boys of the upper three social classes (*varṇa*s) with a sacred thread, conferred on them the status of "twice-born" *(dvija,* a term first used in the *Atharvaveda),* and their "second birth" permitted them to hear the Veda and thereby participate in the *śrauta* rites that, according to the emerging Brahmanic orthodoxy, would make it possible to obtain immortality.

The *śrauta* rites are more elaborate and are representative of the sacrificial system in its full complexity, involving ceremonies that lasted up to two years and enlisted as many as seventeen priests. Through the continued performance of daily, bimonthly, and seasonal *śrauta* rites one gains the year, which is itself identified with the sacrificial life-death-regeneration round and its divine personification, Prajāpati. In sur- passing the year by the Agnicayana, the "piling of the fire altar," one gains immortality and needs no more nourishment in the otherworld (see *Śatapatha Brāhmaṇa* 10.1.5.4).

Śrauta rites required a sacrificial terrain near the home of the sacrificer *(yajamāna),* with three sacred fires (representing, among other things, the three worlds) and an upraised altar, or *vedī.* Nonanimal sacrifices of the first varieties mentioned involved offerings of milk and vegetable substances or even of *mantras*. Animal sacrifices *(paśubandhu)*—which required a more elaborate sacrificial area with a supplemental altar and a sacrificial stake *(yūpā)*—entailed primarily the sacrifice of a goat. Five male animals—man, horse, bull, ram, and goat—are declared suitable for sacrifice. It is likely, however, that human sacrifice existed only on the "ideal" plane, where it was personified in the cosmic sacrifices of Puruṣa and Prajāpati. The animal *(paśu)* was to be immolated by strangulation, and its omentum, rich in fat, offered into the fire. *Soma* sacrifices, which would normally incorporate animal sacrifices within them plus a vast number of other subrites, involved the pressing and offering of *soma.* The most basic of these was the annual Agniṣṭoma, "in praise of Agni," a four-day rite culminating in morning, afternoon, and evening *soma* pressings on the final day and including two goat sacrifices. Three of the most ambitious *soma* sacrifices were royal rites: the Aśvamedha, the horse sacrifice; the Rājasūya, royal consecration; and the Vājapeya, a *soma* sacrifice of the "drink of strength." But the most complex of all was the aforementioned Agnicayana.

A thread that runs through most *śrauta* rituals, however, is that they must begin with the "faith" or "confidence" *(śraddhā)* of the sacrificer in the efficacy of the rite and the capacity of the officiating priests to perform it correctly. This prepares the sacrificer for the consecration *(dīkṣā)* in which, through acts of asceticism *(tapas),* he takes on the aspect of an embryo to be reborn through the rite. As *dīkṣita* (one undergoing the *dīkṣā*), he makes an offering of himself (his *ātman*). This then prepares him to make the sacrificial offering proper (the *yajña,* "sacrifice") as a means to redeem or ransom this self by the substance (animal or otherwise) offered. Then, reversing the concentration of power that he has amassed in the *dīkṣā,* he disperses wealth in the form of *dakṣiṇā*s (honoraria) to the priests. Finally, the rite is disassembled (the ritual analogue to the repeated death of Prajāpati before his reconstitution in another rite), and the sacrificer and his wife bathe to disengage themselves from the sacrifice and reenter the profane world.

In the elaboration of such ceremonies and the speculative explanation of them in the Brāhmaṇas, the earlier Vedic religion seems to have been much altered. In the religion of the Brāhmaṇas, the priests, as "those who know thus" (*evamvid*s), view themselves as more powerful than the gods. Meanwhile, the gods and the demons (*asura*s) are reduced to representing in their endless conflicts the recurrent interplay between agon-istic forces in the sacrifice. It is their father, Prajāpati, who crystallizes the concerns of Brahmanic thought by representing the sacrifice in all its aspects and processes. Most notable of these is the notion of the assembly or fabrication of an immortal self *(ātman)* through ritual action *(karman),* a self constructed for the sacrificer by which he identifies with the immortal essence of Prajāpati as the sacrifice personified. And by the same token, the recurrent death (*punarmṛtyu*, "redeath") of Prajāpati's transitory nature (the elements of the sacrifice that are assembled and disassembled) figures in the Brāhmaṇas as the object to be avoided for the sacrificer by the correct ritual performance. This Brahmanic concept of Prajāpati's redeath, along with speculation on the ancestral *gṛhya* rites (*śrāddhas*) focused on feeding deceased relatives to sustain them in the afterlife, must have been factors in the thinking that gave rise to the Upaniṣadic concept of reincarnation (*punarjanman*, "rebirth"). The emphasis on the morbid and transitory aspects of Prajāpati and the sacrifice, and the insistence that asceticism within the sacrifice is the main means to overcome them, are most vigorously propounded in connection with the Agnicayana.

In the Brāhmaṇas' recasting of the primal once-and-for-all sacrifice of Puruṣa into the recurrent life-death-regeneration mythology of Prajāpati, a different theology was introduced. Though sometimes Puruṣa was identified with Prajāpati, the latter, bound to the round of creation and destruction, became the prototype for the classical god Brahmā, personification of the Absolute *(brahman)* as it is oriented toward the world. The concept of a transcendent Puruṣa, however, was not forgotten in the Brāhmaṇas. *Śatapatha Brāhmaṇa* 13.6 mentions Puruṣa-Nārāyaṇa, a being who seeks to surpass all others through sacrifice and thereby become the universe. In classical Hinduism, *Nārāyaṇa* and *Puruṣa* are both names for Viṣṇu as the supreme divinity. This Brāhmaṇa passage neither authorizes nor disallows an identification with Viṣṇu, but other Brāhmaṇa passages leave no doubt that sacrificial formulations have given Viṣṇu and Rudra-Śiva a new status. Whereas the Brāhmaṇas repeatedly assert that "Viṣṇu is the sacrifice"—principally in terms of the organization of sacrificial space that is brought about through Viṣṇu's three steps through the cosmos, and his promotion of the order and prosperity that thus accrue—they portray Rudra as the essential outsider to this sacrificial order, the one who neutralizes the impure forces that threaten it from outside as well as the violence that is inherent within. Biardeau (1976) has been able to show that the later elevation of Viṣṇu and Śiva through yoga and *bhakti* is rooted in oppositional complementarities first formulated in the context of the Brahmanic sacrifice. [*For further discussion, see* Brāhmaṇas and Āraṇyakas; *see also* Vedism and Brahmanism.]

THE UPANIṢADS

Several trends contributed to the emergence of the Upaniṣadic outlook. Earlier speculations on the irreducible essence of the cosmos, the sacrifice, and individual experience have been mentioned. Pre-Upaniṣadic texts also refer to various forms of ascet- icism as performed by types of people who in one way or another rejected or inverted conventional social norms: the Vedic *muni, vrātya,* and *brahmacārin,* to each of whom is ascribed ecstatic capacities, and, at the very heart of the Brahmanic sacrifice, the *dīkṣita* (the sacrificer who performs *tapas* while undergoing the *dīkṣā,* or consecration). These speculative and ascetic trends all make contributions to a class of texts generally regarded as intermediary between the Brāhmaṇas and Upaniṣads: the Āraṇyakas, or "Forest Books." The Āraṇyakas do not differ markedly from the works that precede and succeed them (the *Bṛhadāraṇyaka Upaniṣad* is both an Āraṇyaka and an Upaniṣad), but their transitional character is marked by a shift in the sacrificial setting from domestic surroundings to the forest and a focus not so much on the details of ritual as on its interiorization and universalization. Sacrifice, for instance, is likened to the alternation that takes place between breathing and speaking. Thus correspondences are established between aspects of sacrifice and the life continuum of the meditator.

An *upaniṣad* is literally a mystical—often "secret"—"connection," interpreted as the teaching of mystical homologies. Or, in a more conventional etymology, it is the "sitting down" of a disciple "near to" (*upa,* "near"; *ni,* "down"; *sad,* "sit") his spiritual master, or *guru.* Each Upaniṣad reflects the Vedic orientation of its priestly school. There are also regional orientations, for Upaniṣadic geography registers the further eastern settlement of the Vedic tradition into areas of the Ganges Basin. But the Upaniṣads do share certain fundamental points of outlook that are more basic than their differences. Vedic polytheism is demythologized, for all gods are reducible to one. Brahmanic ritualism is reassessed and its understanding of ritual action *(karman)* thoroughly reinterpreted. *Karman* can no longer be regarded as a positive means to the constitution of a permanent self. Rather, it is ultimately negative: "the world that is won by work *(karman)*" and "the world that is won by merit *(puṇya)*" only perish (*Chāndogya Upaniṣad* 8.1.6). The "law of karma" (*karman)* or "law of causality" represents a strict and universal cause-effect continuum that affects any action that is motivated by desire *(kāma),* whether it be desire for good or for ill. Thus even meritorious actions that lead to the Vedic heaven "perish," leaving a momentum that carries the individual to additional births or reincarnations. The result is perpetual bondage to the universal flow-continuum of all *karman,* or *saṃsāra* (from *saṃ,* "together" and *sṛ,* "flow"), a term that the Upaniṣads introduce into the Vedic tradition but that is shared with Jainism and Buddhism. As with these religions, the Upaniṣads and Hinduism henceforth conceive their soteriological goal as liberation from this cycle of *saṃsāra:* that is, *mokṣa* or *mukti* ("release").

Mokṣa cannot be achieved by action alone, since action only leads to further action. Thus, though ritual action is not generally rejected and is often still encouraged in the Upaniṣads, it can only be subordinated to pursuit of the higher *mokṣa* ideal. Rather, the new emphasis is on knowledge *(vidyā, jñāna)* and the over- coming of ignorance *(avidyā).* The knowledge sought, however, is not that of ritual technique or even of ritual-based homologies, but a graspable, revelatory, and experiential knowledge of the self as one with ultimate reality. In the early Upaniṣads this experience is formulated as the realization of the ultimate "connection," the oneness of *ātman-brahman,* a connection knowable only in the context of communication from *guru* to disciple. (Herein can be seen the basis of the parable context and vivid, immediate imagery of many Upaniṣadic teachings.) The experience thus achieved is variously described as one of unified consciousness, fearlessness, bliss, and tranquillity.

Beyond these common themes, however, and despite the fact that Upaniṣadic thought is resistant to systematization, certain different strains can be identified. Of the thirteen Upaniṣads usually counted as *śruti,* the earliest (c. 700–500 BCE) are those in prose, headed by the *Bṛhadāraṇyaka* and the *Chāndogya.* Generally, it may be said that these Upaniṣads introduce the formulations that later Hinduism will develop into the *saṃnyāsa* ideal of renunciation (not yet defined in the Upaniṣads as a fourth stage of life) and the knowledge-path outlook of nondualistic *(advaita)* Vedānta. Even within these early Upaniṣads, two approaches to realization can be distinguished. One refers to an all-excluding Absolute; the self that is identified with *brahman,* characterized as *neti neti* ("not this, not this"), is reached through a paring away of the psychomental continuum and its links with *karman.* Such an approach dominates the *Bṛhadāraṇyaka Upaniṣad. Avidyā* here results from regarding the name and form of things as real and forming attachment to them. The other approach involves an all-comprehensive Absolute, *brahman-ātman,* which penetrates the world so that all forms are modifications of the one; ignorance results from the failure to experience this immediacy. In the *Chāndogya Upaniṣad* this second approach is epitomized in the persistent formula "Tat tvam asi" ("That thou art").

The later Vedic Upaniṣads (c. 600–400 BCE) register the first impact of theistic devotional formulations, and of early Sāṃkhya and Yoga. Most important of these historically are two "yogic" Upaniṣads, the *Śvetāśvatara* and the *Kaṭha,* the first focused on Rudra-Śiva and the second on Viṣṇu. Each incorporates into its terminology for the absolute deity the earlier term *puruṣa.* As Biardeau has shown in *L'hindouisme* (1981), they thus draw on an alternate term for the Absolute from that made current in the *brahman-ātman* equation. The Puruṣa of *Ṛgveda* 10.90 (the *Puruṣasūkta*) is sacrificed to create the ordered and integrated sociocosmic world of Vedic man. But only one quarter of this Puruṣa is "all beings"; three quarters are "the immortal in heaven" (*RV* 10.90.3). This transcendent aspect of Puruṣa, and also a certain "personal" dimension, are traits that were retained in the characterization of Puruṣa-Nārāyaṇa in the *Śatapatha Brāhmaṇa* and reinforced in the yogic characterizations of Rudra-Śiva and Viṣṇu in the previously mentioned Upaniṣads. The Upaniṣadic texts do not restrict the usage of the term *puruṣa* to mean "soul," as classical Sāṃkhya later does; rather, it is used to refer to both the soul and the supreme divinity. The relation between the soul and the Absolute is thus doubly defined: on the one hand as *ātman-brahman,* on the other as *puruṣa*-Puruṣa. In the latter case, the *Kaṭha Upaniṣad* describes a spiritual itinerary of the soul's ascent through yogic states to the supreme Puruṣa, Viṣṇu. This synthesis of yoga and *bhakti* will be carried forward into the devotional formulations of the epics and the Purāṇas. But one must note that the two vocabularies are used concurrently and interrelatedly in the Upaniṣads, as they will be in the later *bhakti* formulations. [*For further discussion, see* Upaniṣads.]

THE CONSOLIDATION OF CLASSICAL HINDUISM

A period of consolidation, sometimes identified as one of "Hindu synthesis," "Brahmanic synthesis," or "orthodox synthesis," takes place between the time of the late Vedic Upaniṣads (c. 500 BCE) and the period of Gupta imperial ascendancy (c. 320–467 CE). Discussion of this consolidation, however, is initially complicated by a lack of historiographical categories adequate to the task of integrating the diverse textual, inscriptional, and archaeological data of this long formative period. The attempt to cover as much of this span as possible with the name "epic period," because it coincides with the dates that are usually assigned to the formation and completion of the Hindu epics (particularly the *Mahābhārata*), is misleading, since so much of what transpires can hardly be labeled "epic." On the other hand, attempts to define the period in terms of heterogeneous forces operating upon Hinduism from within (assimilation of local deities and cults, geographical spread) and without (heterodox and foreign challenges) either have failed to register or have misrepresented the implications of the apparent fact that the epics were "works in progress" during the whole period. The view one takes of the epics is, in fact, crucial for the interpretation of Hinduism during this period. Here, assuming that the epics already incorporated a *bhakti* cosmology and theology from an early point in this formative period, I shall try to place them in relation to other works and formulations that contributed to the consolidation of classical Hinduism.

The overall history can be broken down into four periods characterized by an oscillation from disunity (rival regional kingdoms and tribal confederacies on the Ganges Plain) to unity (Mauryan ascendancy, c. 324–184 BCE, including the imperial patronage of Buddhism by Aśoka) to disunity (rival foreign kingdoms in Northwest India and regional kingdoms elsewhere) back to unity (Gupta ascendancy, c. 320–467 CE). The emerging self-definitions of Hinduism were forged in the context of continued interaction with heterodox religions (Buddhists, Jains, Ājīvikas) throughout this whole period, and with foreign peoples (Yavanas, or Greeks; Śakas, or Scythians; Pahlavas, or Parthians; and Kūṣāṇas, or Kushans) from the third phase on. In this climate the *ideal* of centralized Hindu rule attained no practical realization until the rise of the Guptas. That this ideal preceded its realization is evident in the rituals of royal paramountcy (Aśvamedha and Rājasūya) that were set out in the Brāhmaṇas and the Śrautasūtras, and actually performed by post-Mauryan regional Hindu kings.

When we look to the component facets of the overall consolidation, these four periods must be kept in mind, but with the proviso that datings continue to be problematic: not only datings of texts, but especially of religious movements and processes reflected in them, and in surviving inscriptions. Most scholars ordinarily assume that when a process is referred to in a text or other document, it has gone on for some time.

Śruti and Smṛti. Fundamental to the self-definition of Hinduism during this period of its consolidation is the distinction it makes between two classes of its literature: *śruti* and *smṛti. Śruti* is "what is heard," and refers to the whole corpus of Vedic literature (also called Veda) from the four Vedas to the Upaniṣads. *Smṛti,* "what is remembered" or "tradition," includes all that falls outside this literature. Exactly when this distinction was made is not certain, but it is noteworthy that the six Vedāṅgas or "limbs of the Veda" (writings on phonetics, metrics, grammar, etymology, astronomy, and ritual) are *smṛti* texts that were composed at least in part during the latter half of the Vedic or *śruti* period. [*See* Vedāṅgas.] The ritual texts (Kalpasūtras) are subdivided into three categories: Śrautasūtras, Gṛhyasūtras, and Dharmasūtras. Whereas the first two (discussed above under Brahmanic ritual) pertain to concerns developed in the Vedic period, the Dharmasūtras focus on issues of law (*dharma*) that become characteristic of the period now under discussion. [*See* Dharma, *article on* Hindu Dharma.] Dates given for the composition of these texts run from 600 to 300 BCE for the earliest (*Gautama Dharmasūtra*) to 400 CE for the more recent works. Both Gṛhyasūtras and Dharmasūtras were sometimes called Smārtasūtras (i.e., *sūtra*s based on *smṛti*), so it seems that their authors regarded them as representative of the prolongation of Vedic orthodoxy (and orthopraxy) that the *smṛti* category was designed to achieve. As the term *smṛti* was extended in its use, however, it also came to cover numerous other texts composed in the post-Upaniṣadic period. [*See* Sūtra Literature.]

This *śruti/smṛti* distinction thus marks off the earlier literature as a unique corpus that, once the distinction was made, was retrospectively sanctified. By the time of the *Mānava Dharmaśāstra,* or *Laws of Manu* (c. 200 BCE–100 CE; see *Manu* 1.23), and probably before this, *śruti* had come to be regarded as "eternal." Its components were thus not works of history. The Vedic *ṛṣis* had "heard" truths that are eternal, and not only in content—the words of the Vedas are stated to have eternal connection with their meanings—but also in form. The works thus bear no stamp of the *ṛṣis*' individuality. Such thinking crystallized in the further doctrine that the Vedas (i.e., *śruti*) are *apauruṣeya,* not of personal authorship (literally, "not by a *puruṣa*"). They thus have no human imperfection. Further, it was argued that they are even beyond the authorship of a divine "person" *(Puruṣa).* Though myths of the period assert that the Vedas spring from Brahmā at the beginning of each creation (as the three Vedas spring from Puruṣa in the *Puruṣasūkta*), the deity is not their author. Merely reborn with him, they are a self-revelation of the impersonal *brahman.* In contrast to *śruti, smṛti* texts were seen as historical or "traditional," passed on by "memory" *(smṛti),* and as works of individual authors *(pauruṣeya),* even though mythical authors—both human and divine—often had to be invented for them.

Smṛti texts of this period thus proclaim the authority of the Veda in many ways, and nonrejection of the Veda comes to be one of the most important touchstones for defining Hinduism over and against the heterodoxies, which rejected the Veda. In fact, it is quite likely that the doctrines of the eternality and impersonality of the Veda were in part designed to assert the superiority of the Veda over the "authored" and "historical" works of the heterodoxies, whose teachings would thus be on a par with *smṛti* rather than *śruti.* But it is also likely that the *apauruṣeya* doctrine is designed to relativize the "personal" god of *bhakti.* In any case, these doctrines served to place a considerable ideological distance between *śruti* and *smṛti,* and to allow *smṛti* authors great latitude in interpreting *śruti* and extending Hindu teachings into new areas. *Smṛti* thus supposedly functioned to clarify the obscurities of the Veda. But the claim that *smṛti* texts need only not contradict the Veda left their authors great freedom in pursuing new formulations.

Varṇāśramadharma ("Caste and Life-stage Law"). The most representative corpus of *smṛti* literature, and the most closely tied to the continued unfolding orthodox interests of the Vedic priestly schools, is that concerned with *dharma* ("law" or "duty"). As a literary corpus, it consists of two kinds of texts: the Dharmasūtras (600/300 BCE–400 CE), already mentioned in connection with the *śruti/smṛti* distinction, and the Dharmaśāstras. The most important and earliest of the latter are the *Mānava Dharmaśāstra,* or *Laws of Manu* (c. 200 BCE–100 CE), and the *Yājñavalkya Smṛti* (c. 100–300 CE). But other Dharmaśāstras were composed late into the first millennium, to be followed by important commentaries on all such texts. The main focus of these two classes of texts is fundamentally identical: the articulation of norms for all forms of social interaction, thus including but going far beyond the earlier Sūtras' concern for ritual. Four differences, however, are noteworthy. (1) Whereas the Dharmasūtras are in prose, the Dharmaśāstras are in the same poetic meter as the epics, *Manu* in particular having much material in common with the *Mahābhārata.* (2) Whereas the Sūtras are still linked with the Vedic schools, the Śāstras are not, showing that study and teaching of *dharma* had come to be an independent discipline of its own. (3) The Śāstra legislation is more extended and comprehensive. (4) The Śāstras are more integrated into a mythic and cosmological vision akin to that in *bhakti* texts, but usually ignoring *bhakti* as such, with references to duties appropriate to different *yugas* (ages), and the identification of north central India as the "middle region" *(madhyadeśa)* where the *dharma* is (and is to be kept) the purest. [*See* Śāstra Literature.]

The theory of *varṇāśramadharma,* the law of castes and life stages, was worked out in these texts as a model for the whole of Hindu society. There is little doubt that it was stimulated by the alternate lay/monastic social models of the heterodoxies, and no doubt that it was spurred on by the incursions of barbarian peoples—frequently named in these texts as *mlecchas* (those who "jabber")—into the Northwest. The model involves the working out of the correlations between two ideals: first, that society conform to four hierarchical castes, and second, that a person should pass through four life stages *(āśramas)*: student *(brahmacārin),* householder *(gṛhasthin),* forest dweller *(vānaprasthin),* and renunciant *(saṃnyāsin).* The first ideal is rooted in the *Puruṣasūkta.* The second presupposes the *śruti* corpus, since the four life stages are correlated with the four classes of *śruti* texts. Thus the student learns one of the Vedas, the householder performs domestic and optimally also *śrauta* rituals of the Brāhmaṇas, the forest dweller follows the teachings of the Āraṇyakas, and the *saṃnyāsin* follows a path of renunciation toward the Upaniṣadic goal of *mokṣa.* But although all the life stages are either mentioned (as are the first two) or implied in the *śruti* corpus, the theory that they should govern the ideal course of individual life is new to the Dharmasūtras. Together, the *varṇa* and *āśrama* ideals take on tremendous complexity, since a person's duties vary according to caste and stage of life, not to mention other factors like sex, family, region, and the quality of the times. Also, whereas a person's development through one life ideally is regulated by the *āśrama* ideal, the passage through many reincarnations would involve birth into different castes, the caste of one's birth being the result of previous *karman.* A further implication is that the life stages can be properly pursued only by male members of the three twice-born *varṇas*, as they alone can undergo the Upanayana ritual that begins the student stage and allows the performance of the rites pertinent to succeeding stages.

Each of these formulations has persisted more on the ideal plane than the real. In the case of the four *āśramas*, most people never went beyond the householder stage, which the Sūtras and Śāstras actually exalt as the most important of the four, since it is the support of the other three and, in more general terms, the mainstay of the society. The forest-dweller stage may soon have become more legendary than real: in epic stories it was projected onto the Vedic *ṛṣis*. The main tension, however, that persists in orthodox Hinduism is that be-tween the householder and the renunciant, the challenge being for anyone to integrate into one lifetime these two ideals, which the heterodoxies set out for separate lay and monastic communities.

As to the four *varṇas*, the ideal represents society as working to the reciprocal advantage of all the castes, each one having duties necessary to the proper functioning of the whole and the perpetuation of the hierarchical principle that defines the whole. Thus *brāhmaṇas* are at the top, distinguished by three duties that they share with no other caste: teaching the Veda, assisting in sacrifice, and accepting gifts. They are said to have no king but Soma, god of the sacrifice. In actual fact the traditional *śrauta* sacrifice counted for less and less in the *brāhmaṇa* householder life, and increasing attention was given to the maintenance of *brāhmaṇa* purity for the purpose of domestic and eventually temple rituals which, in effect, universalized sacrifice as the *brāhmaṇa*'s *dharma,* but a sacrifice that required only the minimum of impure violence. This quest for purity was reinforced by *brāhmaṇas*' adoption into their householder life of aspects of the *saṃnyāsa* ideal of renunciation. This was focused especially on increasing espousal of the doctrine of *ahiṃsā* (nonviolence, or, more literally, "not desiring to kill") and was applied practically to vegetarianism, which becomes during this period the *brāhmaṇa* norm. *Brāhmaṇa*s thus retain higher rank than *kṣatriya*s, even though the latter wield temporal power *(kṣatra)* and have the specific and potentially impure duties of bearing weapons and protecting and punishing with the royal staff (*daṇḍa).* The subordination of king to *brāhmaṇa* involves a subordination of power to hierarchy that is duplicated in contemporary rural and regional terms in the practice of ranking *brāhmaṇa*s above locally dominant castes whose power lies in their landed wealth and numbers. *Vaiśya*s have the duties of stock breeding, agriculture, and commerce (including money lending). Certain duties then distinguished the three twice-born castes as a group from the *śūdra*s. All three upper *varṇa*s thus study the Veda, perform sacrifices, and make gifts, whereas *śūdra*s are permitted only lesser sacrifices *(pākayajña*s) and simplified domestic rituals that do not require Vedic recitation.

Actual conditions, however, were (and still are) much more complex. The four-*varṇa* model provided the authors of the *dharma* texts with Vedic "categories" within which to assign a basically unlimited variety of heterogeneous social entities including indigenous tribes, barbarian invaders, artisan communities and guilds *(śreṇi*s), and specialists in various services. Susceptible to further refinement in ranking and regional nomenclature, all such groups were called *jāti*s, a term meaning "birth" and in functional terms the proper word to be translated "caste." Thus, although they are frequently called subcastes, the *jāti*s are the castes proper that the law books classified into the "categories" of *varṇa.*

To account for this proliferation of *jāti*s, the authors asserted that they arose from cross-breeding of the *varṇa*s. Two possibilities were thus presented: *anuloma* ("with the grain") unions, in which the husband's *varṇa* was the same as his wife's or higher (in anthropological terms, hypergamous, in which women are "married up"), and *pratiloma* ("against the grain") unions, in which the wife's *varṇa* would be higher than the husband's (hypogamous, in which women are "married down"). Endogamous marriage (marriage within one's own *varṇa*) set the highest standard and was according to some authorities the only true marriage. But of the other two, whereas *anuloma* marriages were permitted, *pratiloma* unions brought disgrace. Thus the *jāti*s supposedly born from *anuloma* unions were less disgraced than those born from *pratiloma* unions. Significantly, two of the most problematic *jāti*s were said to have been born from the most debased *pratiloma* connections: the Yavanas (Greeks) from *śūdra* males and *kṣatriya* females (similar origins were ascribed to other "barbarians") and the *caṇḍāla*s (lowest of the low, mentioned already in the Upaniṣads, and early Buddhist literature, as a "fifth caste" of untouchables) from the polluting contact of *śūdra* males and *brāhmaṇa* females. It should be noted that a major implication of the prohibition of *pratiloma* marriage is the limitation for *brāhmaṇa* women to marriages with only *brāhmaṇa* men. This established at the highest rank an association of caste purity with caste endogamy (and the purity of a caste's women) and thus initiated an endogamous standard that was adopted by all castes—not just *varṇa*s but *jāti*s—by the end of the first millennium.

This accounting of the emergence of *jāti*s was integrated with further explanations of how society had departed from its ideal. One is that "mixing of caste"—the great abomination of the *dharma* texts and also of the *Bhagavadgītā*—increases with the decline of *dharma* from *yuga* to *yuga*, and is especially pernicious in this Kali age. Another is the doctrine of *āpad dharma*, "duties for times of distress" such as permit inversion of caste roles when life is threatened. A third doctrine developed in the Dharmaśāstras identifies certain duties *(kalivarjyas)* as once allowed but now prohibited in the *kaliyuga* because people are no longer capable of performing them purely. Through all this, however, the ideal persists as one that embraces a whole society despite variations over time and space. [*For a more detailed treatment of the system of varṇāśramadharma, see* Rites of Passage, *article on* Hindu Rites; *see also* Varṇa and Jāti.]

The Four Puruṣārthas (Goals of Man). The theory that the integrated life involves the pursuit of four goals (*artha*s) is first presented in the Dharmaśāstras and the epics, in the latter cases through repeated narrative illustrations. The development of distinctive technical interpretations of each *artha,* or facets thereof, can also be followed during the period in separate manuals: the *Arthaśāstra,* a manual on statecraft attributed to Candragupta Maurya's minister Kauṭilya but probably dating from several centuries later, on *artha* (in the sense now of "material pursuits"); the Kāmasūtras, most notably that of Vātsyāyana (c. 400 CE), on *kāma* ("love, desire"); the already discussed Dharmasūtras and Dharmaśāstras on *dharma;* and the Sūtras of the "philosophical schools" (*darśana*s) insofar as they are concerned with the fourth goal, *mokṣa.* Early sources often refer to the first three goals as the *trivarga,* the "three categories," but this need not imply that the fourth goal is added later. The Dharmaśāstra and epic texts that mention the *trivarga* are focused on the concerns of the householder—and, in the epics, particularly of the royal householder—these being the context for the pursuit of the *trivarga.* The fourth goal, *mokṣa,* is to be pursued throughout life—indeed, throughout all lives—but is especially the goal of those who have entered the fourth life stage of the *saṃnyāsin.* The *trivarga-mokṣa* opposition thus replicates the householder-renunciant opposition. But the overall purpose of the *puruṣārtha* formulation is integrative and complementary to the *varṇāśramadharma* theory. From the angle of the householder, it is *dharma* that integrates the *trivarga* as a basis for *mokṣa.* But from the angle of the *saṃnyāsin,* it is *kāma* that lies at the root of the *trivarga,* representing attachment in all forms, even to *dharma.* Paths to liberation will thus focus on detachment from desire, or its transformation into love of God.

Philosophical "Viewpoints" (Darśanas) and Paths to Salvation. As an expression of Hinduism's increasing concern to systematize its teachings, the fourth goal of life *(mokṣa)* was made the subject of efforts to develop distinctly Hindu philosophical "viewpoints" (*darśana*s, from the root *dṛś,* "see") on the nature of reality and to recommend paths to its apprehension and the release from bondage to *karman.* Six Hindu *darśana*s were defined, and during the period in question each produced fundamental texts—in most cases *sūtras*—that served as the bases for later commentaries.

In terms of mainstream developments within Hinduism, only two schools have ongoing continuity into the present: the Mīmāṃsā and the Vedānta. And of these, only the latter has unfolded in important ways in the postsynthesis period. Nonetheless, all six have made important contributions to later Hinduism. It must thus suffice to discuss them all briefly at this point in terms of their basic features and major impact, and reserve fuller discussion of the Vedānta alone for the period of its later unfolding.

Of the six schools, two—Mīmāṃsā and Vedānta—are rooted primarily in the Vedic *śruti* tradition and are thus sometimes called *smārta* schools in the sense that they develop *smārta* orthodox currents of thought that are based, like *smṛti,* directly on *śruti.* The other four—Nyāya, Vaiśeṣika, Sāṃkhya, and Yoga—claim loyalty to the Veda, yet are quite independent of it, their focus instead being on rational or causal explanation. They are thus sometimes called *haituka* schools (from *hetu,* "cause, reason").

Of the *smārta* schools, the Mīmāṃsā is most concerned with ritual traditions rooted in the Vedas and the Brāhmaṇas, whereas the Vedānta is focused on the Upaniṣads. It is notable that both sustain Vedic orientations that reject (Mīmāṃsā) or subordinate (Vedānta) *bhakti* until the Vedānta is devotionalized in its post-Śaṅkara forms. Beginning with Jaimini's *Mīmāṃsā Sūtra* (c. 300–100 BCE), Mīmāṃsā ("reflection, interpretation") provides exegesis of Vedic injunctive speech, in particular as it concerns the relationship between intentions and rewards of sacrifice. Great refinement is brought to bear on issues relating to the authority and eternalness of the Veda and the relationship between its sounds, words, and meanings. Vedic injunctions are taken literally, the many Vedic gods are seen as real although superfluous to salvation (there is an anti-*bhakti* stance here), and it is maintained that the proper use of injunctions is alone enough to secure the attainment of heaven (not a higher release, or *mokṣa,* as propounded by all the other systems, including *bhakti*). Mīmāṃsā persists in two subschools, but only in small numbers among brahman ritualists.

As to the Vedānta ("end of the Veda," a term also used for the Upaniṣads), the foundational work is Bādarā- yaṇa's *Vedānta Sūtra*, or *Brahma Sūtra* (c. 300–100 BCE), an exegesis of various Upaniṣadic passages in aphoristic style easily susceptible to divergent interpretations. These it received in the hands of later Vedantic thinkers.

The *haituka* schools are notable for their development, for the first time within Hinduism, of what may be called maps and paths: that is, maps of the constituent features of the cosmos, and paths to deliverance from bondage. Emerging within Hindusim at this period, and particularly in the schools least affiliated with the Vedic tradition, such concerns no doubt represent an effort to counter the proliferation of maps and paths set forth by the heterodoxies (not only Buddhism and Jainism, but the Ājīvikas). They allow for a somewhat more open recognition of the deity of *bhakti* (Sāṃkhya excepted) than do the *smārta* schools, though none of the *haituka* schools makes it truly central.

Nyāya and Vaiśeṣika, systems first propounded in Gautama's *Nyāya Sūtra* (c. 200 BCE–150 CE) and Kaṇāda's *Vaiśeṣika Sūtra* (c. 200 BCE–100 CE), were quickly recognized as a hyphenated pair: Nyāya-Vaiśeṣika. Nyāya ("rule, logic, analysis"), emphasizing logic and methods of argumentation as means to liberation, was viewed as complementary to Vaiśeṣika ("school of distinct characteristics"), which advanced a theory of atom- ism and posited seven categories to explain such things as atomic aggregation and dualistic distinction between soul and matter. At least by about the fifth century, when the two schools had conjoined, Nyāya logic and Vaiśeṣika cosmology served to provide influential arguments from design for the existence of God as the efficient cause of the creation and destruction of the universe and liberator of the soul from *karman.*

Far more influential, however, were the pair Sāṃkhya ("enumeration") and Yoga. The foundational texts of these schools may be later than those of the others, but they are clearly distillations of long-continuing traditions, datable at least to the middle Upaniṣads, that had already undergone considerable systematization. Thus Patañjali's *Yoga Sūtra* is from either about 200 BCE or 300–500 CE, depending on whether or not one identifies the author with the grammarian who lived at the earlier date. And Īśvarakṛṣṇa's *Sāṃkhyakārikās* probably date from the fourth century CE. Even though Sāṃkhya's "atheism" and its soteriology of the isolation *(kaivalya)* of the soul *(puruṣa)* from matter *(prakṛti)* have been modified or rejected in other forms of Hinduism (both doctrines may link Sāṃkhya with Jainism), Sāṃkhya's cosmology and basic terminology have become definitive for Hinduism at many levels: not only in the Vedānta, but in *bhakti* and Tantric formulations as well. In fact, given the preclassical forms of theistic Sāṃkhya founded in the Upaniṣads and the *Mahābhārata* and their use in *bhakti* cosmologies, it may well be that the atheism of the classical Sāṃkhya results from a rejection of *bhakti* elements from a fundamentally theistic system. Sāṃkhya thus posits *puruṣa* without a transcendent, divine Puruṣa, and its *prakṛti* is also abstract and impersonal.

In any case, a number of Saṃkhya concepts became basic to the Hindu vocabulary, only to be integrated and reinterpreted from different theological and soteriological perspectives by other schools. These include the concepts of the evolution and devolution of *prakṛti,* the sexual polarity of *puruṣa* as male and *prakṛti* as female, the enumeration of twenty-three substances that evolve from and devolve back into the *prakṛti* "matrix," the concept of matter as a continuum from subtle psychomental "substances" to gross physical ones (in particular the five elements), and the notion of the three "strands" or "qualities" called *guṇa*s (*sattva,* goodness, lucidity; *rajas,* dynamism; *tamas,* entropy), which are "braided" together through all matter from the subtle to the gross.

Meanwhile, whereas Sāṃkhya provides the map to be "known," Yoga defines the path by which *puruṣa* can extricate itself from *prakṛti.* The "eight limbs" of Yoga (an answer to the Eightfold Path of Buddhism?) represent the most important Hindu formulation of a step-by-step (though also cumulative) path to liberation. The first two "limbs" involve forms of restraint *(yama)* and observance *(niyama).* The next three involve integration of the body and senses: posture *(āsana),* breath control *(prāṇāyāma),* and withdrawal of the senses from the dominance of sense objects *(pratyāhāra).* The last three achieve the integration of the mind or the "cessation of the mental turmoil" that is rooted in the effects of *karman:* "holding" *(dhāraṇā)* to a meditative support, meditative fluency *(dhyāna),* and integrative concentration *(samādhi)* through which the freedom of *puruṣa* can be experienced.

The classical Yoga of Patañjali, known as *rājayoga* ("royal yoga"), diverges from the Sāṃkhya in acknowledging the existence of God (Īśvara). But Īśvara is a focus of meditation, not an agent in the process of liberation. The use of the term *rāja-*

yoga, however, suggests that by Patañjali's time the term *yoga* had already been used to describe other disciplines or paths, resulting in a situation where the terms *yoga* ("yoke") and *mārga* ("path") had become interchangeable. One will thus find *rājayoga* mentioned later along with the more generalized "yogas", or "paths," that become definitive for Hinduism through their exposition in the *Bhagavadgītā* (c. 200 BCE): the paths (or yogas) of *karman* ("action"), *jñāna* ("knowledge"), and *bhakti* ("devotion"). [*Each of the six Hindu* darśanas *is the subject of an independent entry. See also* Indian Philosophies.]

Classical Bhakti Hinduism. The consolidation of Hinduism takes place under the sign of *bhakti.* And though Mīmāṃsā ritualism and Vedantic and other "knowledge" trends continue to affiliate with an "orthodox" strain that resists this synthesis, or attempts to improve upon it, classical *bhakti* emerges as constitutive henceforth of mainstream Hinduism, including forms of devotional sectarianism. [*See* Bhakti.]

Intimations of *bhakti* developments are registered as early as the late Vedic Upaniṣads, and in inscriptions and other records of syncretistic worship of Hindu deities (Viṣṇu and Śiva) alongside foreign and heterodox figures in the early centuries of the common era. However, the heterogeneity and scattered nature of the nontextual information available on the emergence of *bhakti* during this period have allowed for conflicting interpretations of the salient features of the process. But rather than reweave a fragile developmental web from supposedly separate sectarian and popular strands, it is better to look at the texts themselves to see what they attempted and achieved. We should note, however, that to the best of our knowledge it was achieved relatively early in the period of consolidation, for the *Bhagavadgītā*—the text that seals the achievement—seems to be from no later than the first or second century BCE (it is cited by Bādarāyaṇa in the *Vedānta Sūtra*), and possibly earlier. Of course, continued unfolding occurred after that.

The achievement itself is a universal Hinduism that, following Biardeau's discussion of *bhakti* in "Études de mythologie hindoue" (1976), we may designate as *smārta.* [*For discussion of the* smārta *tradition, see* Vedism and Brāhmaṇism.] It inherits from the Brahmanic sacrificial tradition a conception wherein Viṣṇu and Śiva are recognized as complementary in their functions but ontologically identical. The fundamental texts of this devotional *smārta* vision are the two epics—the *Mahābhārata* (c. 500 BCE–400 CE) and the *Rāmāyaṇa* (c. 400–200 BCE)—and the *Harivaṃśa* (c. 300–400 CE?). These works integrate much Puranic mythic and cosmological material, which later is spun out at greater length in the classical Purāṇas ("ancient lore"), of which there are said to be eighteen major and eighteen minor texts. The epics and Purāṇas are thus necessarily discussed together. But it should be recognized that whereas the *smārta* vision of the epics and the *Harivaṃśa* is fundamentally integrative and universal in intent, the Purāṇas are frequently dominated by regional and particularistic interests, including in some cases the strong advocacy of the worship of one deity (Śiva, Viṣṇu, or the Goddess) over all others. It is thus tempting to think of the period of Purāṇa composition (c. 400–1200 CE?) as one that extends the integrative vision of the fundamental texts but develops it in varied directions. Still, as it is not clear that instances of Puranic theological favoritism are motivated by distinct sects, it is misleading to speak of "sectarian" Purāṇas. [*See* Purāṇas.]

Taken together, then, the *Harivaṃśa* and the *Mahābhārata* (which includes the *Bhagavadgītā*) present the full biography of Kṛṣṇa, and the *Rāmāyaṇa* that of Rāma. The *Harivaṃśa* (Genealogy of Hari—i.e., Kṛṣṇa), the more recent of the texts concerning Kṛṣṇa, presents the stories of his birth and youth, in which he and his brother Balarāma take on the "disguise" *(veṣa)* of cowherds. Thus they engage in divine "sport" *(līlā)* with the cowherd women (*gopī*s), until finally they are drawn away to avenge themselves against their demonic uncle Kaṃsa, who had caused their exile [*See* Līlā]. The *Mahābhārata* (Story of the Great Bhārata Dynasty) focuses on Kṛṣṇa's assistance to the five Pāṇḍava brothers in their conflicts with their cousins, the hundred Kauravas, over the "central kingdom" of the lunar dynasty (the Bhārata dynasty) at Hāstinapura and Indraprastha near modern Delhi. Both texts incorporate telling allusions to the other "cycle," and since both stories must have circulated orally together before reaching their present literary forms, any notions of their separate origins are purely conjectural. The *Rāmāyaṇa* (Exploits of Rāma) tells the story of Rāma, scion of the solar dynasty and embodiment of *dharma,* who must rescue his wife Sītā from the demon *(rākṣasa)* Rāvaṇa. Though each of these texts has its special flavor and distinctive background, they become in their completed forms effectively a complementary triad. Indeed, in the "conservative" South, popular performances of Hindu mythology in dramas and temple recitations are still dominated by three corresponding specializations: *Mahābhārata, Rāmāyaṇa,* and *Bhāgavata Purāṇa,* the latter (c. 800–900 CE?) enriching the devotional themes of the *Harivaṃśa* in its tenth and eleventh books and in effect replacing it as representing the early life of Kṛṣṇa. [*See* Mahābhārata; Bhagavadgītā; *and* Rāmāyaṇa.]

The *smārta* universe in these texts is structured around Viṣṇu, and more particularly around his two heroic incarnations, Rāma and Kṛṣṇa. Thus other deities are frequently represented as subordinated to or subsumed by these figures. But there is also recognition of Viṣṇu's complementarity with Śiva: some passages that stress mutual acknowledgment of their ontological unity, others that work out the interplay between them through stories about heroic characters who incarnate them, and scenes in which Viṣṇu's incarnations do homage to Śiva. It should be clear that efforts to find "tendencies toward monotheism" in such texts involve the reduction of a very complex theology to distinctly Western terms. The same applies to those Purāṇas that are structured around Śiva or the Goddess rather than Viṣṇu but are still framed within the same cosmology and the same principles of theological complementarity and subordination.

This *smārta* vision is not, however, limited to one theological conundrum, for it extends to encompass Śiva and Viṣṇu's interaction with other major figures: the god Brahmā, masculine form of the impersonal Absolute (*brahman*), now subordinated to the higher "personal" deities; the Goddess in her many forms; Indra and other *deva*s (now "demigods"); their still perennial foes, the demons (*asura*s); and of course humans, animals, and so on. It also presents an overarching *bhakti* cosmology in which the yogic supreme divinity (Śiva or Viṣṇu) encompasses the religious values of *saṃnyāsa, tapas,* knowledge, and sacrifice, and introduces the view that taken by themselves, without *bhakti,* these values may be incomplete or even extreme "paths." Further, it incorporates the *smārta* social theory of the Dharmasūtras and the Dharmaśāstras, and works out its implications within the cosmology. The details of this *smārta* vision are best discussed, however, in relation to the Hindu chronometric theory that is presumed and first articulated in these texts and then further developed in the Purāṇas. [*See also* Cosmology, *article on* Indian Cosmologies.]

Time is structured according to three main rhythms, hierarchically defined, the longer encompassing the lesser. Most down-to-earth is the series of four *yuga*s named after four dice throws, which define a theory of the "decline of the *dharma*": first a *kṛtayuga* ("perfect age"), then a *tretāyuga* and a *dvāparayuga,* and finally a degenerate *kaliyuga* ("age of discord"). A *kṛtayuga* lasts 4,000 years, a *tretāyuga* 3,000, a *dvāparayuga* 2,000, and a *kaliyuga* 1,000, each supplemented by a dawn and twilight of one-tenth its total. A full four-*yuga* cycle thus lasts 12,000 years and is called a *mahāyuga* ("great *yuga*"). These are not human years, however, but divine years, which are 360 times as long as human years. Thus a *mahāyuga* equals 360 times 12,000, or 4,320,000 human years, and a *kaliyuga* is one-tenth of that total. A thousand *mahāyuga*s (4,320 million human years) is a *kalpa,* the second major time unit, which is also called a "day of Brahmā." Brahmā's days are followed by nights of equal duration. Brahmā lives a hundred years of 360 such days and nights, or 311,040 billion human years, all of which are sometimes said to pass in a wink of the eye of Viṣṇu. The period of a life of Brahmā, called a *mahākalpa,* is the third major temporal rhythm.

Working backward now, we may observe the *modus operandi* of Viṣṇu and Śiva (and of course others) as it is envisioned in the *smārta* Hinduism of our texts.

First, at the highest level, Viṣṇu and Śiva are great yogins, interacting with the rhythms of the universe in terms of their own oscillations between activity and yogic concentration *(samādhi).* At the *mahāpralaya* ("great dissolution"), the deity (usually Viṣṇu in these early texts, but just as often Śiva or the Goddess in later Puranic ones) oversees the dissolution of the universe into the primal *prakṛti* in accord with the cosmological theory of Sāṃkhya-Yoga. This ends the life of Brahmā, but it is also to be noted that it marks the restoration to its primordial unity of *prakṛti,* which—as feminine—is regarded mythologically as the ultimate form of the Goddess. From a Śaiva standpoint, the male (the deity as Puruṣa) and the female (the Goddess as Prakṛti) are reunited at the great dissolution of the universe, a theme that is depicted in representations of the deity as Ardhanārīśvara, "the Lord who is half female." Their union is nonprocreative and represents the unitive experience of the bliss of *brahman.* Creation then occurs when the deity (whether Śiva or Viṣṇu) emerges from this *samādhi* and instigates the renewed active unfolding of *prakṛti.*

The coincidence of the death of Brahmā with not only the dissolution of the universe but the reintegration of the Goddess and her reunion with Śiva is highly significant. The Goddess is an eternal being, worthy of worship because—like Viṣṇu and Śiva—she outlasts the universe and can bestow *mokṣa.* Brahmā, ultimately mortal and bound to temporality, is worshiped not for *mokṣa* but rather—and mostly by demons—for earthly power and lordship. Stories that portray Śiva's severing of Brahmā's fifth head and refer to the "head of Brahmā" *(brahmaśiras)* as the weapon of doomsday, are perhaps mythic echoes of this ultimate cosmological situation wherein the coming together of Puruṣa and Prakṛti coincide with his death.

The primary creation has as its result the constitution of a "cosmic egg," the *brahmāṇḍa* ("egg of Brahmā"). Further creation, and periodic re-creations, will be carried out by Brahmā, the personalized form of the Absolute *(brahman).* Insofar as the *brahman* is personalized and oriented toward the world, it is thus subordinated to the yogin Puruṣa, the ultimate as defined through *bhakti.* Moreover, the activity of Brahmā—heir in his cosmogenic role of the earlier Prajāpati—is conceived in terms of sacrificial themes that are further encompassed by *bhakti.*

It is at this level that the three male gods cooperate as the *trimūrti,* the "three forms" of the Absolute: Brahmā the creator, Śiva the destroyer, and Viṣṇu the preserver. Within the *brahmāṇḍa,* Brahmā thus creates the Vedic triple world of earth, atmosphere, and heaven (or alternatively heaven, earth, and underworld). These three samsaric worlds are surrounded by four ulterior worlds, still within the *brahmāṇḍa,* for beings who achieve release from *saṃsāra* but still must await their ultimate liberation. These ulterior worlds are not henceforth created or destroyed in the occasional creations or destructions. As to the triple world, Brahmā creates it by becoming the sacrificial boar *(yajñavarāha)* who retrieves the Vedas and the earth from the cosmic ocean. The destruction of the triple world is achieved by Śiva. As the "fire of the end of time," he reduces it to ashes, thus effecting a cosmic funerary sacrifice. And Viṣṇu, the god whom the Brāhmaṇas identify as "the sacrifice," maintains the triple world while it is sustained by sacrifices, and also preserves what is left of it after the dissolution when he lies on the serpent Śeṣa ("remainder") whose name indicates that he is formed of the remnant of the previous cosmos, or more exactly of the "remainder" of the cosmic sacrifice. This form of Viṣṇu, sleeping on Śeṣa, is called Nārāyaṇa, a name that the *Śatapatha Brāhmaṇa* already connects with the Vedic Puruṣa, the "male" source of all beings. When Viṣṇu-Nārāyaṇa awakens, Brahmā—who in some fashion awakens with him—re-creates the universe. Through all these myths the earth is a form of the Goddess, indeed the most concretized form she takes as a result of the evolution of *prakṛti* (earth being the last of the evolutes emitted and the first to dissolve).

Thus the greater universe whose rhythms are integrated within the divine yoga of Viṣṇu and Śiva encompasses an egg of Brahmā, which encloses a triple world whose rhythms form a round sustained by the divine sacrificial acts of the *trimūrti.* This pattern is transposed onto the third temporal rhythm, that of the *yuga*s. Thus the characteristic religious virtues of the *yuga*s are as follows: *dhyāna* ("meditation") or *tapas* ("asceticism") in the *kṛtayuga*; *jñāna* ("knowledge") in the *tretāyuga*; *yajña* ("sacrifice") in the *dvāparayuga*; and *dāna* ("the gift") in the *kaliyuga.* Thus the two *śruti*-based ideals of knowledge and sacrifice are enclosed within a framework that begins with yogic meditation as a divine *kṛtayuga* activity and ends in the *kaliyuga* with the devotional gift. *Bhakti* thus encompasses knowledge and sacrifice.

The distinctive feature of the rhythm of the *yuga* cycle is that it is calibrated by the rise and fall of *dharma* in the triple world. Beings who have achieved release from the triple world oscillate between the four higher worlds, enduring periodic destructions of the triple world and awaiting the great dissolution of the universe that will dissolve the egg of Brahmā (coincident with his death) and result in a vast collective ultimate liberation of reabsorption into the supreme Puruṣa. Needless to say, this is to occur only after an almost incalculable wait. But beings who have attained these ulterior worlds are no more affected by *dharma* than the yogic deity beyond them. The maintenance of *dharma* within the triple world thus engages the deities in their third level of activity, that of "descent." In classical terms this is the theory of the *avatāra.* Though the term is not used in the epics or the *Harivaṃśa* in its later, specialized sense, these texts are suffused by the concept and its *bhakti* implications, which include narrative situations wherein the divinity looks to all concerned, and sometimes even to himself, as a mere human. The programmatic statement of the *avatāra* concept (without mention of the term itself) is thus stated by Kṛṣṇa in the *Bhagavadgītā:* "For whenever the Law [*dharma*] languishes, Bhārata, and lawlessness flourishes I create myself. I take on existence from eon to eon [*yuga* to *yuga*], for the rescue of the good and the destruction of evil, in order to establish the Law" (4.7–8; van Buitenen, trans.).

The classical theory of the ten *avatāras*—most of whom are mentioned in the epics and the *Harivaṃśa,* but not in a single list—is worked out in relation to Viṣṇu. One thus has the following "descents" of Viṣṇu in order of appearance: Fish (Matsya), Tortoise (Kūrma), Boar (Varāha), Man-Lion (Narasiṃha), Dwarf (Vāmana), Rāma with the Ax (Paraśurāma), Rāma of the *Rāmāyaṇa,* Kṛṣṇa, the Buddha, and the future *avatāra* Kalki, who will rid the earth of barbarian kings and reestablish the *dharma* at the end of the *kaliyuga.* There are various attempts to correlate appearances of the *avatāra*s with distinct *yuga*s and even *kalpa*s, but the one feature that is consistently mentioned in these formative texts is that Kṛṣṇa appeared at the interval between the last *dvāparayuga* and *kaliyuga,* and thus at the beginning of our present age. It is likely that the theory was first formulated around Kṛṣṇa and Rāma along with the Dwarf (the only form to be associated with Viṣṇu in the *śruti* literature) and the apocalyptic Kalki. But in actuality, the *avatāra* theory is more complex. In the epics and in living Hinduism, Viṣṇu does not descend alone. In the literature, his incarnations take place alongside those of other deities, including most centrally Vāyu, Indra, Sūrya, the Goddess, and—at least in the *Mahābhārata*—Śiva. And in localized temple mythologies throughout India, one hears of *avatāra*s of Śiva and the Goddess as well as of Viṣṇu. In devotional terms, the *avatāra* is thus a form taken on earth (or, better, in the three worlds) by any one of the three deities we find at the ultimate level of cosmic absorption, where all that remains beside the liberated beings who join them are the eternal yogic deities Viṣṇu and Śiva and the primal Goddess. [*See* Avatāra.]

The classical concept of the *avatāra,* structured around Viṣṇu, remains, however, the chief Hindu use of the term. Its formulation in the epics and the *Harivaṃśa* is thus constitutive for succeeding eras of Hinduism, in which it will only be enriched but not essentially changed by later *bhakti* theologies. Looking at these texts comprehensively, then, with the *Gītā* as our main guide, we can outline its main contours. Against the background of the vast, all-embracing *bhakti* cosmology, the involvement of the yogic divinity on earth takes place completely freely, as "sport" or "play" *(līlā).* Still, the god takes birth to uphold the *dharma* and to keep the earth from being unseasonably inundated in the waters of dissolution under the weight of adharmic kings. The *avatāra* thus intercedes to uphold the system of *varṇāśrama-dharma* and to promote the proper pursuit of the four *puruṣārtha*s. Since he appears in times of crisis, a central concern in the texts is with the resolution of the conflicts between ideals: renunciation versus householdership, *brāhmaṇa* versus *kṣatriya,* killing versus "not desiring to kill" *(ahiṃsā), dharma* versus *mokṣa, dharma* versus *kāma* and *artha,* and conflicts between different *dharma*s (duties) such as royal duty and filial duty. But though the texts focus primarily on the two upper castes, the full society is represented by singular depictions of figures who evoke the lowest castes and tribal groups. It is also filled in with figures of real and reputed mixed caste.

Confusion of caste is a particularly prominent issue in the *Mahābhārata,* where it is raised by Kṛṣṇa in the *Gītā* as the worst of ills. Most significantly, the *Mahābhārata* and the *Harivaṃśa* identify a particularly per- nicious form of caste confusion among the barbarian *(mleccha)* peoples of the Northwest (the Punjab), mentioning Yavanas, Śakas, and Pahlavas among others as enemies of the *dharma* and causes for such "mixing." The fact that events of the period from 300 BCE to 300 CE are projected into the distant past indicates that part of the *bhakti* synthesis was the articulation of a mythical theory of historical events. One may thus look at these *smṛti* texts as posing a model for the revival of Hinduism in accord with "eternal" Vedic models, with the descent of the *avatāra*—and indeed of much of the Vedic pantheon along with him—guaranteeing the periodic adjustment of the sociocosmic world to these eternal norms. Furthermore, the tracing of all Hindu dynastic lines back to the defunct if not mythical "lunar" and "solar" dynasties provided the model for the spatial extension of this ideal beyond the central lands of Āryavarta where the *dharma,* according to both *Manu* and the *Mahābhārata,* was the purest.

But the focus of the *avatāra* is not solely on the renovation of the *dharma.* He also brings to the triple world the divine grace that makes possible the presence, imagery, and teachings that confer *mokṣa.* The epics and the *Harivaṃśa* are full of *bhakti* tableaux: moments that crystallize the realization by one character or another of the liberating vision *(darśana)* of the divine. Most central, however, is the *Bhagavadgītā,* which is both a *darśana* and a teaching.

The *Bhagavadgītā* (Song of the Lord) takes place as a dialogue between Kṛṣṇa and Arjuna just before the outbreak of the *Mahābhārata* war. Although he is the third oldest of the five Pāṇḍavas, Arjuna is their greatest warrior, and Kṛṣṇa's task in the *Gītā* is to persuade him to overcome his reluctance to fight in the battle. Fundamental to the argument is Arjuna's requirement to fulfill his *dharma* as a *kṣatriya* rather than adopt the ideal—unsuitable for him in his present life stage—of the renouncer. Thus the *Gītā* champions the theory of *varṇāśramadharma* as upholding the sociocosmic order.

Kṛṣṇa presents his teaching to Arjuna by revealing a sequence of "royal" and "divine" mysteries that culminate in his granting a vision of his "All-Form" *(Viśvarūpa-darśana)* as God, creator and destroyer of the universe. In this grand cosmic perspective, Arjuna is told that he will be but the "mere instrument" of the deaths of his foes, their destruction having now come to ripeness through Viṣṇu's own agency in his form as cosmic time, or *kāla* (*Bhagavadgītā* 11.32–33). Arjuna thus recognizes this omniform deity as Viṣṇu in this climactic scene.

On the way to this revelation, however, Kṛṣṇa acknowledges the three paths (*yogas*) to salvation: action, knowledge, and devotion. These are presented as instructions by which Arjuna can gain the resolute clarity of insight *(buddhi)* and yogic discipline by which to recognize the distinctions between soul and body, action and inaction, and thus perform actions—including killing—that are unaffected by desire. Ritual action and knowledge are set forth as legitimate and mutually reinforcing paths, but incomplete unless integrated within and subordinated to *bhakti.* Kṛṣṇa thus presents himself as the ultimate *karmayogin,* acting to benefit the worlds out of no personal desire. He thus bids his devotees (*bhaktas*) to surrender all actions to him as in a sacrifice, but a sacrifice *(karman)* no longer defined in Vedic-Mīmāṃsā terms as a means to fulfill some personal desire. Kṛṣṇa also presents himself as the object of all religious knowledge, the highest *puruṣa (uttamapuruṣa)* and supreme self *(paramātman),* beyond the perishable and the imperishable, yet pervading and supporting all worlds (15.16–17).

One other facet of the *bhakti* synthesis to which the *Gītā* alludes is the transition from traditional Vedic sacrifice *(yajña)* to new forms of offering to the deity (*pūjā,* literally, "honoring"). [*See* Pūjā, *article on* Hindu Pūjā.] This corresponds to the theory that the "gift" is the particularly appropriate religious practice for the *kaliyuga.* Thus Kṛṣṇa says: "If one disciplined soul proffers to me with love [*bhakti*] a leaf, a flower, fruit, or water, I accept this offering of love from him. Whatever you do, or eat, or offer, or give, or mortify, make it an offering to me, and I shall undo the bonds of *karman*" (9.26–27; van Buitenen, trans.). The passage probably refers to domestic worship of the "deity of one's choice" *(iṣṭadevatā).* But it is also likely to allude to temple worship, for it is known from inscriptions and literary sources from the third to first century BCE that sanctuaries existed for Vāsudeva and Keśava (presumably as names for Kṛṣṇa and Viṣṇu), as well as for other deities. By the beginning of the Gupta period, around 320 CE, temple building was in full swing, with inscriptions showing construction of temples for Viṣṇu, Śiva, and the Goddess. Temples were built at sites within cities, as well as at remote holy places, and sanctuaries at both such locations became objectives along pilgrimage routes that are first mentioned in the *Mahābhārata.* From very early if not from the beginning of such temple worship, the deities were represented by symbols and/or iconic images.

Certain aspects of temple construction and worship draw inspiration from the Vedic sacrifice. The plan of the edifice is designed on the ground as the Vāstupuruṣamaṇḍala, a geometric figure of the "Puruṣa of the Site" *(vāstu),* from whom the universe takes form. The donor, ideally a king, is the *yajamāna.* The *sanctum sanctorum,* called the *garbhagṛha* ("womb house"), continues the symbolism of the Vedic *dīkṣā* hut: here again the *yajamāna* becomes an embryo so as to achieve a new birth, now taking into his own being the higher self of the deity that he installs there in the form of an image. The temple as a whole is thus a Vedic altar comprising the triple world, but also an expanded image of the cosmos through which the deity manifests himself from within, radiating energy to the outer walls where his (or her) activities and interactions with the world are represented. [*See* Temple, *article on* Hindu Temples.]

But the use of the temple for ordinary daily worship involves radically non-Vedic objectives. The Vedic sacrifice is a means for gods and men—basically equals—to fulfill reciprocal desires. *Pūjā* rites are means for God and man to interact on a level beyond desire: for man to give without expectation of reward, or, more exactly, to get back nothing tangible other than what he has offered but with the paradoxical conviction that the deity "shares" (from the root meaning of *bhakti*) what is given and returns it as an embodiment of his or her grace *(prasāda).* God is thus fully superior, served as a royal guest with rites of hospitality. Basically four moments are involved: offerings, taking sight *(darśana)* of the deity, receiving this *prasāda,* and leave-taking by circumambulation of the *garbhagṛha* and the image within. The offerings are the *pūjā* proper and comprise a great variety of devotional acts designed to please the deity, some of which may be worked into a daily round by the temple priests, who offer on behalf of others.

Finally, one last element of the consolidation of Hinduism achieved by early Gupta times is the emergence of the Goddess as a figure whose worship is recognized alongside that of Viṣṇu and Śiva and is performed with the same basic rites. Indeed, it is possible that aspects of *pūjā* ceremonialism are derived from non-Vedic *śūdra* and village rites in which female deities no doubt figured highly, as they do in such cults today. The two epics, the *Mahābhārata* and the *Rāmāyaṇa,* reflect themes associated with the Goddess in the portrayals of their chief heroines, Draupadī and Sītā, but the *Harivaṃśa* is probably the first text to acknowledge the Goddess as such. There she takes birth as Kṛṣṇa and Balarāma's "sister" (actually she and Kṛṣṇa exchange mothers). Some of her future demon enemies are mentioned, and there is also reference to her having numerous places of worship and a cult that apparently included animal sacrifice. Thus the Goddess is integrated even within the texts of the early *smārta* Hinduism that are centered on Viṣṇu. But the text that registers her full emergence is the *Devīmāhātmyam* (Glorification of the Goddess). Probably from about 400–600 CE, it was included in the *Mārkaṇḍeya Purāṇa.* Here the Goddess is recognized under all her major aspects, as primal matter embodied in the universe yet beyond it, incarnate in many forms, cause of the joys and miseries of this world and of liberation from it, the power *(śakti)* enabling the roles of the *trimūrti,* yet higher than the gods and their last resort in the face of certain demons, most notably the buffalo demon Mahiṣāsura, her most dedicated and persistent foe through cults and myths both ancient and current. This emergence of the Goddess is registered more fully in the development of Tantric Hinduism. [*See* Goddess Worship, *article on* The Hindu Goddess.]

TANTRIC HINDUISM

Tantra is literally "what extends." In its Hindu form it may be taken, according to its name, as a movement that sought to extend the Veda (whose pedigree it loosely claimed) and more particularly to extend the universalistic implications of *bhakti* Hinduism. However, although it was quick to integrate *bhakti* elements and to influence *bhakti* in nearly all its forms (late Puranic, popular, and sectarian), its earliest and most enduring forms "extend" Hinduism in ways that were directly opposed to the epic-Puranic *bhakti* synthesis. Nonetheless, it is still formulated within the same cosmology.

Early Tantrism developed most vigorously, from the fourth to sixth centuries CE, in areas where Brahmanic penetration had been weakest: in the Northwest, in Bengal and Assam in the East, and in the Andhra area of the South. These are areas where one must assume non- Aryan influences in general, and more particularly probably also tribal and folk practices involving shamanism, witchcraft, and sorcery, and, at least in the East and South, a cult of the Goddess. As Tantrism gained currency in succeeding centuries throughout India, the shamanistic and magical features were assimilated to yogic disciplines, while the elevation of the Goddess gave full projection on a pan-Indian scale to roles and images of the Goddess that had been incorporated, but allowed only minimal scope, in the early orthodox *bhakti* and even earlier Vedic sacrificial traditions. The earliest extant Tantric texts are Buddhist, from about the fourth to sixth centuries. [*See* Buddhism, Schools of, *article on* Esoteric Buddhism.] Hindu Tantric texts include Vaiṣṇava Saṃhitās, Śaivāgamas from a slightly later period, and Śākta Tantras (exalting the Goddess as Śakti, or Power) from perhaps the eleventh century on. But from its start Tantrism represented a style and outlook that placed the Goddess at the center of its "extensions" and to a certain extent cut across sectarian and religious distinctions, whether Hindu, Buddhist, or even Jain.

Though Hindu Tantra thus asserts its Vedic legitimacy, its stance is intentionally anti-Brahmanic. It was especially critical of Brahmanic concepts of hierarchy, purity, and sexual status, all of which had been reinforced by the orthodox *bhakti* synthesis and which were in particular bound up with a theology that viewed the supreme divinity as a male (a Puruṣa, whether Śiva or Viṣṇu) whose ultimate form was accessible only beyond the rhythms of the cosmos and its hierarchy of impure and pure, gross and subtle worlds. For Tantrics, dualities were artificial and their experience was the result of delusion. On the analogy of the union between Śiva and Śakti, which in Puranic devotional terms is conceivable only at the end of the *mahāpralaya,* or great dissolution of the universe, Tantric practice *(sādhana)* addresses itself to experiencing the unity of *puruṣa* and *prakṛti* (*puruṣa* being both "soul" and deity, *prakṛti* being both "matter" and Goddess), male and female, pure and impure, knowledge and action, and so on. Most important, all this takes place here and now, not only in this world, where *prakṛti* and *puruṣa* on the macrocosmic scale are one, but in the human body, where their microcosmic embodiments can be experienced. The body thus becomes the ultimate vehicle for liberation, the dissolution of opposites taking place within the psychophysical continuum of the experience of the living adept, who realizes beyond duality the oneness of *brahman.*

In terms of practice, Tantra's rejection of Hindu orthopraxy is even more decisive. And practice is clearly exalted above theological or philosophical formulation. Two types of Tantra are mentioned: "left-hand" and "right-hand." The Tantric rejection and indeed inversion of orthopraxy is most pronounced in the former, as the right-hand Tantra interprets the most anti-Brahmanic practices of the left metaphorically, and also includes under its heading a wide variety of ceremonial rituals assimilated into *bhakti* Hinduism that are simply non-Vedic. These include the use of non-Vedic *mantras* as well as *yantras* and *maṇḍalas*, aniconic and non-Vedic geometric devices used for visualization and integration of divine-cosmic forces. Adepts come from all castes, but low-caste and even tribal practitioners and teachers are especially revered. The goal of liberation within the body takes the specific form of seeking magical powers (*siddhis*), which in orthodox forms of Hinduism are regarded as hindrances to spiritual achievement. Under the tutelage of a guru, who embodies the fulfillment sought and its transmission and who is thus all-important, the *siddhis* are sought through yoga disciplines that show the impact of Tantra through their anatomical analysis of the "subtle body" (*liṅga śarīra).* First practiced is *haṭhayoga,* the "yoga of exertion or violence," that is, rigorous physical discipline geared to coordinating the body's "ducts" or "channels" (*nāḍīs*) and "energy centers" (*cakras*). This is followed by *kuṇḍalinīyoga,* which awakens the dormant *śakti,* conceived as a coiled-up "serpent power" in the lowest *cakra* between the genitals and the anus, so that it (or she) can pierce and transform all the *cakras* (usually six) and unite with Śiva in the "thousand-petaled *cakra*" in the region of the brain.

Beyond these practices, "left-handed" Tantrics pursue in literal fashion the ceremonial of the "five *m*'s" *(pañcamakārapūjā).* That is, they incorporate into their cultic practice five "sacraments" beginning with the syllable *ma:* fish *(matsya),* meat *(māṃsa),* parched grain (*mudrā,* regarded as an aphrodisiac), wine *(madya),* and finally sexual intercourse *(maithuna).* It is likely that most if not all of these practices involve the incor-poration of elements of the cult and mythology of the Goddess, who already in the *Devīmāhātmyam* delights in meat and wine and is approached by lustful demons for sexual intercourse. Tantric texts stress that these practices are to be carried out within a circle of adepts and supervised by a male and female pair of "lords of the circle" who insist on strict ritual conventions that guard against an orgiastic interpretation. Classically, the male is to retain his semen at the point of orgasm, this being a sign not only of profound dispassion but an actualization of the nonprocreative union of Śiva and Śakti at the dissolution of the universe of dualities.

It is interesting to note that, although their historical validity is debated by scholars, there are strong Indian traditions suggesting that Śaṅkara's philosophical nondualism had practical Tantric repercussions. [*See also* Tantrism *and* Hindu Tantric Literature.]

ŚAṄKARA'S ADVAITA VEDĀNTA AND SMĀRTA ORTHODOXY

The Advaita (nondualist) interpretation of the Vedānta can be traced back at least to Gauḍapāda (c. 600 CE), but it is Śaṅkara (c. 788–820) who established this viewpoint as the touchstone of a revived *smārta* orthodoxy. Born in a small Kerala village, Śaṅkara spent his alleged thirty-two years as a vigorous champion of the unity of Hinduism over and against intra-Hindu divisions and the inroads of Buddhism and Jainism. He toured India, setting up monasteries (*maṭhas*) near famous temples or holy places at each of the four compass directions, and appointed a disciple at each center to begin a line of renunciant "pontiffs." And he wrote works of great subtlety and persuasiveness, including commentaries on the Upaniṣads, the *Brahma Sūtra,* and the *Bhagavadgītā* that inspired contemporaries, disciples, and authors of later generations to write additional important works from the perspective that he developed. [*See the biography of Śaṅkara.*]

An essential feature of Śaṅkara's argumentation is that lower views of reality must be rejected as they are contradicted or "sublated" by higher experiences of the real. Finally, all dichotomous formulations must be abandoned upon the nondual experience of the self *(ātman)* as *brahman.* The world of appearance is sustained by ignorance *(avidyā),* which "superimposes" limitations on reality. *Māyā* ("illusion" or "fabrication"), itself neither real nor unreal, is indescribable in terms of being or nonbeing. It appears real only so long as *brahman* is not experienced. But it is empirically real relative to things that can be shown false from the standpoint of empirical observation. *Māyā* is thus said to be more mysterious and unknowable than *brahman,* which is experienced as being, consciousness, and bliss *(sat-cit-ānanda).*

As philosophy, Advaita is thus a guide to *mokṣa,* which is experienced when the ignorance that results from superimposing *māyā* on *brahman* is overcome. Liberation arises with knowledge *(jñāna),* but from a perspective that recognizes relative truth in the paths of both action and *bhakti.* Practically, Śaṅkara fostered a rapprochement between Advaita and *smārta* orthodoxy, which by his time had not only continued to defend the *varṇāśramadharma* theory as defining the path of *karman,* but had developed the practice of *pañcāyatanapūjā* ("five-shrine worship") as a solution to varied and conflicting devotional practices. Thus one could worship any one of five deities (Viṣṇu, Śiva, Durgā, Sūrya, Gaṇeśa) as one's *iṣṭadevatā* ("deity of choice"). As far as *varṇāśramadharma* was concerned, Śaṅkara left householder issues largely aside and focused instead on founding ten orders of *saṃnyāsis* (the *daśanāmi,* "ten names"), each affiliated with one of the four principle *maṭhas* he founded. But traditional orthodox views of caste were maintained. According to Śaṅkara, as *śūdras* are not entitled to hear the Veda, they cannot pursue knowledge of *brahman* as *saṃnyāsis*; rather they may seek *mokṣa* through hearing the *Mahābhārata* and the Purāṇas. Four of the ten *saṃnyāsi* orders were thus restricted to *brāhmaṇas*, and it does not seem that any accepted *śūdras* until long after Śaṅkara's death. *Bhakti* sectarian reformers were generally more liberal on this point. As to the god (or gods) of *bhakti,* Śaṅkara views the deity (Īśvara) as essentially identical with *brahman* and real relative to empirical experience. But by being identified "with qualities" *(saguṇa),* God can be no more than an approach to the experience of *brahman* "without qualities" *(nirguṇa).* Viewed from the experience of the self as *nirguṇa brahman,* which "sublates" all other experiences, the deity is but the highest form of *māyā.* Clearly, *bhakti* traditions could not rest with this solution. But it should be noted that in opposing Śaṅkara and abandoning the universalist vision of the epic-Puranic devotional synthesis, the sects turned their backs on the main impulses that had attempted to sustain the unity of Hinduism.

SECTARIAN HINDUISM

The elaboration of *bhakti* Hinduism continued to unfold in the later Purāṇas, linking up with the temple and pilgrimage cultus and with local and regional forms of worship. It thus established itself until the time of Śaṅkara as the main expression of Brahmanic orthodoxy and the main shaping force of popular Hinduism. But though it proclaimed a universal Hinduism, it gave little weight to the problem of the immediate accessibility of salvation. While caste hierarchy was to remain in effect on earth to assure, among other things, the pure temple worship of the gods by the *brāhmaṇas*, the ultimate release that the Purāṇas promised was almost infinitely postponed. It is possible that their postponement of a collective liberation was a kind of purification process for liberated souls and thus a prolongation of the concern for *brāhmaṇa* purity on earth. In any case, the remoteness of salvation and the defense of caste purity and hierarchy in the Puranic devotionalism of Brahmanic orthodoxy were probably incentives for the development of alternate forms of *bhakti.* These emerged in sectarian traditions, in movements led by saint-singers who inspired vernacular forms of *bhakti* revivalism, and more generally in local and regional forms of Hinduism. [*For further discussion of sectarian movements, see* Vaiṣṇavism; Kṛṣṇaism; *and* Śaivism.]

Sectarian Traditions. Sectarianism and *bhakti* revivalism are movements of separate origins that converge for the first time in the eleventh and twelfth centuries in the Tamil-speaking area of South India. There the fusion was accomplished in the traditions of the Śrī Vaiṣṇavas and the Śaiva Siddhānta, sects whose names indicate their distinctive theological preferences for Viṣṇu and Śiva. Henceforth, sectarianism and *bhakti* revivalism continued to interact and produce hybrid forms as they spread over all of India.

Generally speaking, sects followed a reformist impulse, and in most of them one can identify the emergence of the *guru* as a new type of figure: not the transmitter of an "impersonal" Vedic teaching, but one who takes inspiration from the personal deity of the sect, with whom he may even be identified. Traditional hierarchy was generally respected, but with the proviso that within the sect divine grace was not limited by caste boundaries. Nonetheless, as groups formed around masters and their teachings, they took on many of the characteristics and functions of castes (endogamy, interior ranking), and certain sects formulated their stands with particularly positive attitudes (the northern school of Śrī Vaiṣṇavas) or negative attitudes (Liṅgāyats and Vīraśaivas) toward *brāhmaṇas*. Sects distinguish themselves over and against each other by many means, and often quite passionately: by bodily markings, forms of yoga discipline, worship, theology, and in particular by their choice of supreme deity, whether Śiva, Viṣṇu, Śakti, or, in the North, Kṛṣṇa or Rāma. Nonetheless, they generally participate in wider Hindu activities such as pilgrimage, festival, and temple worship (the Liṅgāyats are an exception) and draw upon fundamental Hindu belief structures. Thus most sects acknowledge other deities as subordinate to the supreme deity of the sect. In particular, most have worked out ways of encompassing the relation of the God and the Goddess at some fundamental theological level. Persistently the supreme deity is identified both as the ultimate *brahman* and also as in some way personal. The sects also frequently define various stages of divine descent or interaction with the world, various stages of the soul's ascent, and various types of relation between the soul and God. Thus the sects elaborate upon the epic-Puranic cosmology while modifying and refining the theological and soteriological terms. It is only against this background that their formulations are intelligible.

From the historical vantage point, one may note that the consolidation of the separate strands of sectarianism and *bhakti* revivalism occurs after, and is no doubt in part a response to, the growing success of Śaṅkara's Advaita Vedānta. Prior to Śaṅkara, sectarian groups had centered primarily around distinctive ritual traditions that were increasingly influenced by Tantrism: not only in forms of worship and theological formulation, but also, in some Śaiva sects, in actual practice. Thus the Vaiṣṇava Pāñcarātras and Vaikhānasas and the Śaiva Pāśupatas (all mentioned first in the late *Mahābhārata*) between the fifth and tenth centuries produced their Saṃhitās and Āgamas to regularize the construction of temples, iconography, and *pūjā* ceremonialism. Some Pāśupatas and Kāpālikas (a Tantric Śaiva sect) also incorporated forms of abrupt anticonventional behavior modeled on Śiva's character as the great yogin ascetic. With the exception of the Pāñcarātras, who elaborated an influential doctrine of the emanations (*vyūhas*) of Viṣṇu that paralleled the cosmogonic theory of evolution in the Sāṃkhya system, the theological formulations of these movements were apparently among their secondary concerns.

Saint-singer Tradition. Whereas the early sectarian movements were able to spread their impact from north to south using Sanskrit as their medium, the *bhakti* revivalist movement began in the South, drawing on Tamil. Like the sectarian movements, the saint-singers developed their traditions along Vaiṣṇava and Śaiva lines. The sixty-three Nāyaṉmār (or Nāyaṉārs) promoted the worship of Śiva, while the twelve Āḻvārs similarly honored Viṣṇu. Part of the revivalist motivation was provided by the earlier spread of Buddhism and Jainism in the South, both of which lost considerable following as a result of the efforts of the Nāyaṉmār and Āḻvārs, as well as those of their contemporary Śaṅkara.

Some of the most renowned among these two companies of saint-singers have left songs that they composed at the temples of Viṣṇu and Śiva, praising the form and presence of the deity therein, the place itself as his manifestation, and the communal attitude of worship generated there through pilgrimage and festival. Though they honor the deities in terms familiar from Puranic myths, the stories are set in the local terrain. The emotional side of *bhakti* thus draws from deep Tamil traditions, including a revival of classical Tamil poetic conventions involving the correlations between different types of landscape, different divinities, and different types of male-female love. In the hands of the saint-singers, erotic love in particular was drawn on as a metaphor for devotional feelings that stressed the feminine character of the soul in relation to the deity and idealized a softening of the mind or heart that could take the forms of "melting" into the divine, ecstatic rapture, divine madness, and possession.

Following the advent of Śaṅkara, most of the sectarian and revivalist movements found common cause in their devotionalist stance against Advaita nondualism and continued to develop for the most part interdependently. Thus, most formatively, the songs of the Āḻvārs were collected in the ninth century for eventual use by the Śrī Vaiṣṇavas. And the poems of the Nāyaṉmār—supplemented by the songs of Māṇikkavācakar, who apparently lived just after the list of sixty-three Nāyaṉmār had been set (ninth century)—were collected to form parts of the canon of the Śaiva Siddhānta. However, the revivalist and sectarian strains could also at times follow somewhat independent courses. The saint-singer tradition continued to take Śaiva and Vaiṣṇava forms among the Liṅgāyats and the Haridāsas of Karnataka, and also to be associated there with sects (the Liṅgāyats themselves and the Brāhma Saṃpradāya or Dvaita Vedānta tradition of Madhva, respectively). But its spread through Maharashtra, the Hindi-speaking areas of North India, and through Bengal was most focused on Viṣṇu, or more accurately on his forms as Rāma and Kṛṣṇa, who in turn, in the Hindi and Bengali areas, became the deities of different sects. In the case of Kṛṣṇa, erotic devotional poetry opened new dimensions on the theme of Kṛṣṇa's love-play with his "new" consort, Rādhā (her name does not appear before the twelfth-century Sanskrit *Gītāgovinda* by the Bengali court poet Jayadeva). In Hindi and Bengali poems, not only are the emotions of motherly love for the baby Kṛṣṇa and erotic love for the youthful Kṛṣṇa explored, but they are tied in with a classical theory of aesthetic appreciation *(rasa)*.

As to the sects, the impact of Śaṅkara's Advaita is evident at many points. Although Śaiva monasticism may predate Śaṅkara by about a century, his establishment of *maṭhas* around India was highly influential. Certain post-Śaṅkara sects thus adopted institutionalized forms of "monastic" renunciation, either like Śaṅkara setting their *maṭhas* alongside the temples (Śrī Vaiṣṇavas, Dvaita Vedāntins, Śaiva Siddhāntins) or in opposition to the whole temple cultus (Lingāyats). Vaiṣṇava sects also assume henceforth the mantle of new "Vedāntas" in order to seek Vedic authority for their advocacy of *bhakti* theologies over and against Śaṅkara's nondualism and in their efforts to subordinate the path of knowledge to that of *bhakti*.

Most distinctive and most important theologically among the Vaiṣṇava schools are those of Rāmānuja (c. 1017–1137) and Madhva (1238–1317), both of whom attempted to refute Saṅkara's interpretations of the Upaniṣads, the *Brahma Sūtra,* and the *Bhagavadgītā* with their own commentaries on those texts. The more prolific Madhva also wrote commentaries on the *Ṛgveda* and the epics. Rāmānuja, drawing

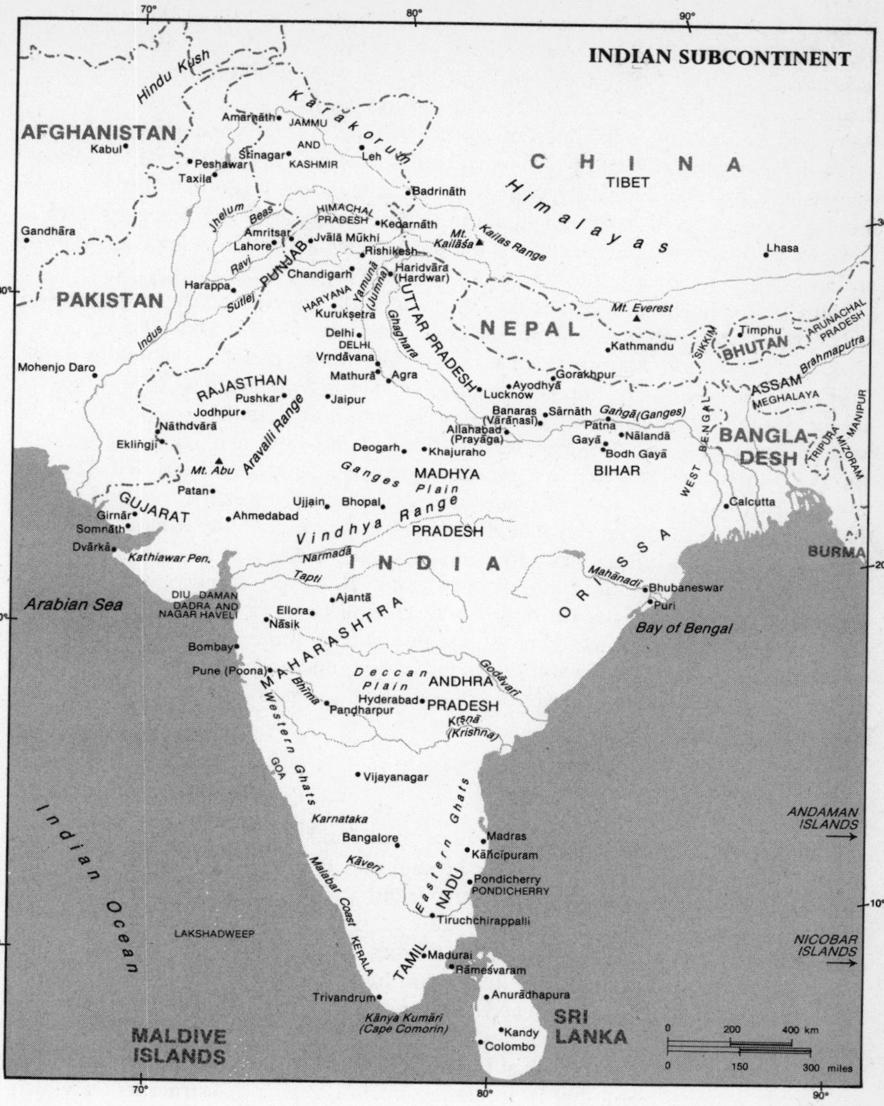

on the ceremonialism and theological formulations of the Pāñcarātra sect as well as on the revivalist poetry of the Āḻvārs, developed for the Śri Vaiṣṇavas the first *bhakti* sectarian repudiation of the Advaita. In his "qualified nondualistic Vedānta" *(viśiṣṭādvaita vedānta),* he argued that Viṣṇu-Nārāyaṇa is the ultimate *brahman,* his relation to the world and souls being "qualified" as substance to attribute. World and souls are thus real, as of course is God—all in opposition to Śaṅkara's view that there is no reality other than *brahman.* For Rāmānuja the three paths not only culminate in *bhakti* but are crowned by *prapatti,* "surrender" to God or "falling forward" at his feet. Criticizing both Śaṅkara and Rāmānuja, Madhva's "dualistic Vedānta" *(dvaita vedānta)* stressed the absolute sovereignty of God and the fivefold set of absolute distinctions between God and souls, God and the world, souls and souls, souls and the world, and matter in its different aspects—all of which are real and not illusory.

On the Śaiva side, the most distinctive sect is the Kashmir Śaiva, or Trika, school, established in the ninth century, with possibly earlier roots. It is nondualist, but from the standpoint that all is essentially Śiva. As pure being and consciousness, Śiva is aware of himself through reflection in the universe, which he pervades as the *ātman* and in which he is manifest through his *śakti* (power, or female energy, personified as the Goddess). The universe is thus an expression of Śiva's aesthetic experience of his creative awareness as self and his delight in unity with his Śakti. "Recognition" of Śiva as the *ātman,* and experience of the self through *spanda* ("vibration")—an attunement to the blissful throbbing waves of divine consciousness in the heart—are among the means to liberation. One of the foremost systematizers of this school was Abhinavagupta (c. 1000 CE), who developed the view that states of aesthetic appreciation (*rasa*s, "tastes") are modes of experiencing the divine Self. Though favoring *śāntarasa* (the *rasa* of peacefulness), Abhinavagupta's theories influenced the North Indian medieval devotional poetry that explored *bhakti* itself as a state of *rasa,* with such powerfully evocative modes as love of Kṛṣṇa in the relationships of servant-master, parent-child, and lover-beloved. This type of devotional intensity reached its peak in the person of the Bengali saint Caitanya (1486–1533), founder of the Gauḍiya Vaiṣṇava sect, whose ecstatic dancing and singing enabled him to experience the love of Rādhā and Kṛṣṇa. Popular tradition regards him as an *avatāra* of Kṛṣṇa, a form assumed by Kṛṣṇa to experience in one body his union with his Śakti.

POPULAR HINDUISM

The main current of living Hinduism is popular Hinduism. It has been affected by every change the tradition has gone through and may fairly be assumed to have ancient roots, in some aspects traceable to Indus Valley religion, in others to *śūdra,* village, and tribal forms of religion that were never more than alluded to—and then negatively—in the ancient and classical sources. *Bhakti* and Tantra are two movements within Hinduism that draw inspiration from this broad current, and popular Hinduism today remains dominated by *bhakti* and Tantric expressions. [*See also* Indian Religions, *article on* Rural Traditions.]

It is, however, perilous to look at popular Hinduism from the perspective of what it might have once been: that is, to attempt to isolate or reconstruct its Dravidian, pre-Aryan, or non-Brahmanic components. Although hypotheses about pre-Aryan and non-Aryan forms of popular Hinduism are certainly worth pursuing, they must be informed and restrained by a sound understanding of the comprehensive structures through which both popular and Brahmanic forms of Hinduism are integrated at the popular level. Aspects of popular religion that might look non-Aryan turn out on closer examination to involve Vedic prolongations. Nor are recent constructs like sanskritization, brahmanization, or kṣatriyazation—all useful up to a point, but stressing only the adoption by low-caste groups of high-caste models—adequate to account for the multivectored process that must have occurred for a long time as it continues to occur today.

Amid the bewildering variety of popular Hindu rites, customs, and beliefs, two broad structures can be identified that clarify this overall integration. One involves the working out of the implications of *bhakti* in relation to temple worship; the other involves the working out of the implications of the caste system in relation to local forms of worship more generally. As they function, the two structures are intimately related.

Generally speaking, whether one defines a locality in large terms (a region, a former kingdom) or small terms (a city, town, or village), one will find two types of divinities: pure and impure. The pure divinities are forms taken locally—*avatāras*—of the great gods Viṣṇu and Śiva. Sometimes the Goddess is also purified to this rank, often with a myth explaining her change from violent to peaceful habits (as with the alleged conversion of the goddess Kāmākṣī at Kanchipuram, Tamil Nadu, by Śaṅkara). And in certain regions Śiva's sons Murukaṉ/Skanda (in Tamil Nadu) and Gaṇeśa (in Maharashtra) also assume this role. In their temples, these gods are offered pure vegetarian food by brahmans. Today, all castes can worship in such temples, thanks to temple entry legislation by the postindependence government; formerly, low castes were excluded. These castes still maintain their own temples where impure gods are served with nonvegetarian offerings, that is, sacrifices of male animals, usually cocks and goats but occasionally water buffalo. Legislation prohibiting buffalo sacrifices has so far had mixed results.

Whereas worship of pure gods—especially at remote pilgrimage sites—is focused ultimately on renunciation and liberation, that of impure gods is dominated by down-to-earth concerns. One thus finds among the general category of impure gods lineage deities (*kuladevatā*s), caste deities, and village deities (*grāmadevata*s). The first are usually but not always male, and some are deities for brahman as well as low-caste lineages. Caste deities and village deities are usually female, and the category may overlap where the deity of a locally dominant caste becomes also the village deity. Where the village deity (usually a goddess) is the deity of a vegetarian caste or has had her cult purified to bring it into accord with high-caste standards, she frequently has one or more male assistants—impure demons converted to her cause and frequently lineage gods themselves—who handle the animal sacrifice (real or symbolic) for her, often out of her line of sight.

Nonetheless, though opposing principles are each given their play, it is their overlap and interrelation that is most striking. Low castes worship the pure gods in their temples. And high castes acknowledge the power of the impure deities, not only as *kuladevatā*s, but through selective (pure) means of participation in festivals sponsored by lower castes. Through the universalization of *bhakti,* the impure gods are sometimes also the prototypes for the demons whose deaths at the hands of the pure deities transform them into their devotees. These local myths have their roots in Puranic mythologies, and the sacrificial practices they evoke involve at least in part prolongations and reinterpretations of the Vedic animal sacrifice.

The second issue—working out of the implications of the caste system in relation to local forms of worship—has thus already been touched upon, but with the focus of issues of purity and impurity as defined by brahman and low-caste involvements. There remains the issue of the role of the *kṣatriya,* or more particularly the king, as the ruler of the land. The caste system has traditionally functioned in locally defined territories, "little kingdoms," where the local ruler had certain roles to perform. No matter what his actual caste, whether high or low, pure or impure, he had to function as a *kṣatriya.* In his ceremonial status, he performed the role of *jajmān,* engaging him at the core of a system of prestations and counterprestations with other castes as a sort of patron for those who perform services for him. Most significantly, this title derives from the Vedic *yajamāna,* "sacrificer," and prolongs not only the *yajamāna's* function as patron of other castes (particularly brahmans, who offer sacrifices for him), but that of "sacrificer" itself. The model of the king as *jajmān* on the regional territorial level has its counterpart in the village in the person(s) of the leader(s) of the locally dominant caste, who assumes the role of *yajamāna* at village festivals. When, as was until recently widely the case, the village festival involves the sacrifice of a buffalo, it thus occurs within a continuum that includes the royal buffalo sacrifice traditionally performed in connection with the pan-Hindu festival of Dussera, and the mythology of the goddess Durgā and the buffalo demon Mahiṣāsura that is traceable to the *Devīmāhātmyam* in the *Mārkaṇḍeya Purāṇa.* There are many local and regional transformations of this pattern, but a basic theme is that the Goddess, who personifies victory, acts for the *yajamāna* and the kingdom or village in her conquest over demonic forces (impure barbarians, drought, diseases) that threaten the welfare of the local terrain over which she, as goddess, presides.

HINDU RESPONSES TO ISLAM AND WESTERNIZATION

Self- conscious Hindu responses to influences from the West were first worked out in the classical period in the epics, the Dharmaśāstras, and the Purāṇas. It seems that military dominance by "barbarian" peoples in that period provided one of the incentives for the articulation of Hindu orthodoxy. Islamic rule and Western rule in India have provided similar incentives, but this often goes unmentioned as historians place their emphasis on what is supposedly new. A full accounting of the impact of almost ten centuries of Islam and five centuries of Western presence in India would have to deal not only with their distinctive new influences but also with the ways in which traditional Hindu models have been revived and applied in new and adaptive ways, often on the folk and popular level. That, however, can only be alluded to here.

Islamic influence on Hinduism has many dimensions, all difficult to assess. From the time of the raids of Mahmud of Ghazni into Northwest India (977–1030) into the period of Mughal dominance, Hindus had to deal periodically with outbreaks of violence and iconoclastic zeal. Regional defense of Hindu traditions against Islam—first by the Rajputs in Rajasthan, then by the Vijayanagar rulers and their successors in South India (1333–eighteenth century), and finally by the Marathas in Maharashtra and the South (late sixteenth century–1761)—clearly fostered the Hindu ideal of the territorial kingdom, big or "little," as a model for the protection of ongoing Hindu values. Under the Muslim rulers, in fact, many Hindu chiefs and petty rajas were left in control of their local realms so long as they paid tribute and supplied military support. In these circumstances, conservative and puritanical tendencies seem to have gained momentum in orthodox Hinduism, particularly in regard to caste and the purity of women. Nonetheless, one finds numerous cases where Muslim themes and figures have been integrated into popular Hindu myth and ritual, but usually in ways that indicate Muslim subordination to a local or regional Hindu deity.

While orthodox, popular, and domestic forms of Hinduism thus drew in on themselves, however, Hindu sectarian traditions multiplied, particularly in the period of the breakup of the Delhi sultanate (1206–1526). Notable at this time were Caitanya in Bengal, and two exemplars of the North Indian *sant* (holy man) tradition: Kabīr (c. 1440–1518, from Banaras) and Nānak (1469–1539, from the Punjab). These two latter figures both preached a path of loving devotion to one God that combined aspects of Islamic Sufism and Hindu *bhakti.* They thus formulated probably for the first time in terms partly Hindu an exclusivist monotheism like that found in the Abrahamic traditions of Islam, Christianity, and Judaism. Over and against the direct experience of this one God, all else was mediate and external, whether the practice were Muslim or Hindu. Thus not only caste but idol worship was rejected by these teachers. But though their syncretistic poetry remained highly popular, it did little to change the Hindu practices it criticized. Nānak's work in particular provided the foundation for the Sikh tradition, an increasingly non-Hindu and non-Muslim movement on its own. Nor did the syncretistic interests of the great Mughal emperor Akbar (ruled 1555–1605) do much to encourage theological synthesis, despite the popularity of his, for the most part, religiously tolerant rule. Akbar's successors on the Mughal throne abandoned his policies and pursued expansionist goals that aroused resistance from the heirs of the Vijayanagar and the Rajput kingdoms, and especially from the Sikhs and the new power of the Marathas. The seeds of a nationalist vision of Hinduism may be traced through these movements and back to the imperial ideal of the epics.

Under the British, certain reform tendencies initiated under Muslim rule were carried forward, freshly influenced by Christian missionary activity and Western education. Most notable were the reform movements of the nineteenth century. The Brāhmo Samāj was founded in 1828 by Raja Ram Mohan Roy (1772–1833, from Calcutta). In an early treatise Roy wrote an attack on idolatry that showed Muslim influence, but by the time he founded the Samāj he had been more affected by Christianity, and particularly by the Unitarians. Roy thus introduced a kind of deistic monotheism and a form of congregational worship to go along with a rejection of idolatry, caste, sacrifice, transmigration, and *karman.* The Ārya Samāj, founded in 1875 by Swami Dayananda Sarasvati (1824–1883, from Kathiawar), denied authenticity to Puranic Hinduism and attempted a return to the Vedas. Showing that the Vedas lent no support to image worship and various social practices, he went further to assert that they were monotheistic. As regards caste, he championed the *varṇa* theory as an ancient social institution but denied that it was religious. Both movements split into rival camps. [*See* Brāhmō Samāj *and* Ārya Samāj.]

The Ramakrishna Mission, established on the death of its founder Ramakrishna (1834–1886) and carried forward by his disciples, most notably Vivekananda (1863–1902), is more representative of traditional Hindu values. Strong *bhakti* and Tantric strains converged in the mystical experiences of Ramakrishna and were held in conjunction with an initiation into Advaita Vedānta and experiences of the oneness of all religions through visions not only of Hindu deities but of Jesus and Allāh. For many followers, this humble priest of Kālī has thus come to be regarded as an *avatāra,* in the tradition of Caitanya. Vivekananda, Western-educated and keenly intellectual, attended the World's Parliament of Religions in Chicago in 1893, lectured widely, and established the Vedānta Society of New York. When he returned to India as a recognized champion of Hindu self-pride, he helped to organize the disciples of Ramakrishna into the pan-Indian Ramakrishna Mission. The first such teacher to gain prominence in India by popularity gained abroad, he thus inadvertently set up a pattern that has been followed by many prominent gurus and swamis in the twentieth century. Notable among them are Swami A. C. Bhaktivedanta (1896–1977), founder of the Hare Krishna movement (ISKCON) as an outgrowth of the Bengal Caitanya tradition [*see* International Society for Krishna Consciousness], and Swami Muktananda (1908–1982), exponent of *siddhayoga* teachings that draw on Kashmir Śaivism.

An earlier figure, one who attracted a large Western following without ever leaving India, was Śrī Aurobindo (1872–1950), whose career spanned nationalist political activism in Bengal (up to 1908), followed by the establishment of an ashram (hermitage) in Pondicherry for the teaching of a type of integral yoga that stressed the "evolutionary" progress of the soul toward the divine. One must also mention Mohandas K. Gandhi (1869–1948), whose reputation upon returning to India in 1915 after twenty-one years in England and Africa was not that of a guru but a champion of Indian causes against social and economic discrimination. As he took on more and more ascetic and saintly aspirations, however, Gandhi sought to combine an ideal of dispassioned and nonviolent service to humanity, modeled on the *Bhagavadgītā*'s doctrine of *karmayoga,* with work for Indian *svarāj* ("self-rule").

Although sometimes referred to as a Hindu renaissance, the effect of the various reformers since the nineteenth century has been to a certain extent more ideological than religious. Where they founded religious movements, these attracted only small followings. But their religious views—that Hinduism is essentially monotheistic, that caste is not essentially Hindu, that Hindu tolerance does not deny the truths of other religions, that Hinduism is in accord with modern science, and so on—have had major influence on a Western-educated, largely urban elite that, at least for now, controls the media and the educational processes of contemporary India. It remains to be seen how this new vision of unity will square with the traditionally diverse Hinduism of the vast population of the countryside.

[*For surveys of regional religious traditions in India, see* Bengali Religions; Hindi Religious Traditions; Marathi Religions; *and* Tamil Religions. *For Hindu cultic life, see under* Worship and Cultic Life; *see also* Domestic Observances, *article on* Hindu Practices; Hindu Religious Year; *and* Priesthood, *article on* Hindu Priesthood. *The religious dimension of Indian artistic expression is treated in* Drama, *article on* Indian Dance and Dance Drama; Music, *article on* Music and Religion in India; Iconography, *article on* Hindu Iconography; *and* Poetry, *article on* Indian Religious Poetry. *Many of the technical terms and many of the personalities, both mythic and historical, mentioned herein are the subject of independent entries.*]

BIBLIOGRAPHY

Three introductions to the whole Hindu tradition deserve recommendation: Thomas J. Hopkins's *The Hindu Religious Tradition* (Encino, Calif., 1971) is strongest in the early period (a second edition is expected); Madeleine Biardeau's *L'hindouisme: Anthropologie d'une civilisation* (Paris, 1981) is strongest on the classical period and popular traditions; and J. L. Brockington's *The Sacred Thread: Hinduism in Its Continuity and Diversity* (New York, 1981) is strongest on medieval and modern Hinduism. On Indus Valley religion, a balanced and visually informative presentation is found in Robert E. Mortimer Wheeler's *Civilizations of the Indus Valley and Beyond* (New York, 1966). On pre-Upaniṣadic Vedic religion as a whole, see Jan Gonda's *Vedic Literature: Saṃhitās and Brāhmaṇas* (Wiesbaden, 1975), vol. 1, no. 1 of his *History of Indian Literature.* On Indo-European continuations in early Indian religion, see Georges Dumézil's *The Destiny of the Warrior,* translated by Alf Hiltebeitel (Chicago, 1970). On Ṛgvedic religion, see Wendy Doniger O'Flaherty's *The Rig Veda: An Anthology* (Harmondsworth, England, 1982) for a selection of important hymns; Jan Gonda's *The Vision of the Vedic Poets* (The Hague, 1963), for an account of the Vedic poetic process; Arthur A. Macdonell's *Vedic Mythology* (1897; reprint, New York, 1974), for the classic account of Vedic myth; and R. Gordon Wasson's *Soma: Divine Mushroom of Immortality* (New York, 1968), for his interpretation of the *soma* plant. On the Brāhmaṇas and Vedic ritual, see Sylvain Lévi's *La doctrine du sacrifice dans les Brâhmaṇas,* 2d ed. (Paris, 1966), for a classic study focused on the mythology; Madeleine Biardeau and Charles Malamoud's *Le sacrifice dans l'Inde ancienne* (Paris, 1976), especially the essay by Malamoud on the place of the ritual honoraria (*dakṣiṇās*) in the sacrificial round; and Arthur Berriedale Keith's *The Religion and Philosophy of the Veda and Upanishads,* 2d ed. (Westport, Conn., 1971), for a solid overview. On the Upaniṣads, Paul Deussen's *The Philosophy of the Upanishads,* 2d ed., translated by A. S. Gelden (New York, 1966), is still the standard comprehensive study. On the classical Hindu period as a whole, Madeleine Biardeau's study in *Le sacrifice* (cited above) and *Cosmogonies purāṇiques,* (Paris, 1981), vol. 1 of her *Études de mythologie hindoue*, are indispensable for their integrative treatment. On *dharma* literature, see Pandurang Vaman Kane's monumental *A History of Dharmaśāstra,* 5 vols. (Poona, 1930–1962), which covers far more besides, and Robert Lingat's *The Classical Law of India,* translated by J. D. M. Derrett (Berkeley, Calif., 1973), an invaluable overview. On caste, see Louis Dumont's *Homo Hierarchicus,* translated by Marc Sainsbury, rev. ed. (Chicago, 1970), discussing his own and others' theories. On the six philosophical systems, for the most authoritative overview see Surendranath Dasgupta's *A History of Indian Philosophy,* 5 vols. (Cambridge, 1922–1955). On classical *bhakti* and its mythology in the epics and Purāṇas, in addition to the works above by Biardeau, see also her important "Études de mythologie hindoue," parts 1 and 2, *Bulletin de l'École Française d'Extrême Orient* 63 (1976): 111–263, and 65 (1978): 87–238. My own *The Ritual of Battle: Krishna in the "Mahābhārata"* (Ithaca, N.Y., 1976) and Jacques Scheuer's *Śiva dans le Mahābhārata* (Paris, 1982) explore complementary roles of the major deities in the *Mahābhārata;* see also the classic study of E. Washburn Hopkins, *Epic Mythology* (1915; reprint, New York, 1969). On Puranic materials, see *Classical Hindu Mythology: A Reader in the Sanskrit Purāṇas,* translated and edited by Cornelia Dimmitt and J. A. B. van Buitenen (Philadelphia, 1978), a representative selection with interpretative introductions; and Wendy Doniger O'Flaherty's *Śiva: The Erotic Ascetic* (Oxford, 1973), on major themes in the mythology of Śiva, and *Women, Androgynes, and Other Mythical Beasts* (Chicago, 1980), on relations between the sexes and between humans, gods, and animals in the myths. On temple architecture and symbolism, see Stella Kramrisch's *The Hindu Temple,* 2 vols. (Calcutta, 1946). For a sound and highly readable translation of the *Bhagavadgītā,* and an important introduction, see *The Bhagavadgītā in the Mahābhārata* translated and edited by J. A. B. van Buitenen (Chicago, 1981). On Tantra, see Agehananda Bharati's *The Tantric Tradition* (London, 1965) and Sanjukta Gupta, Dirk Jan Hoens, and Teun Goudriaan's *Hindu Tantrism* (Leiden, 1979). For an incisive presentation of Śaṅkara's nondualism, see Eliot Deutsch's *Advaita Vedānta: A Philosophical Reconstruction* (Honolulu, 1969). On Yoga and asceticism, see Mircea Eliade's *Yoga: Immortality and Freedom,* 2d ed. (Princeton, 1969); see also G. S. Ghurye's *Indian Sadhus,* 2d ed. (Bombay, 1964) with discussion of monastic orders. On sectarian

Hinduism, see R. G. Bhandarkar's *Vaiṣṇavism, Śaivism, and Minor Religious Systems* (1913; reprint, Varanasi, 1965), still a classic overview. On *bhakti* revivalism, see V. Raghavan's *The Great Integrators: The Saint-Singers of India* (Delhi, 1966). On popular Hinduism, Henry Whitehead's *The Village Gods of South India,* 2d ed., rev. & enl. (Delhi, 1976), is the essential documentary introduction; Marie-Louise Reiniche's *Les dieux et les hommes: Étude des cultes d'un village du Tiruṇelveli Inde du Sud* (New York, 1979) and Lawrence A. Babb's *The Divine Hierarchy: Popular Hinduism in Central India* (New York, 1975) are important regional studies with significant anthropological insights; David D. Shulman's *Tamil Temple Myths: Sacrifice and Divine Marriage in the South Indian Śaiva Tradition* (Princeton, 1980) discusses local temple versions and inversions of the classical *bhakti* myths. On reform movements and modern Hinduism, see John N. Farquhar's *Modern Religious Movements in India* (New York, 1915), on nineteenth-century figures, and Agehananda Bharati's *Hindu Views and Ways and the Hindu-Muslim Interface* (Delhi, 1981), for an interesting inside-outside anthropological view.

2 BUDDHISM IN INDIA

LUIS O. GÓMEZ

A contemporary visitor to the South Asian subcontinent would find Buddhism flourishing only outside the mainland, on the island of Sri Lanka. This visitor would meet small pockets of Buddhists in Bengal and in the Himalayan regions, especially in Ladakh and Nepal, and as the dominant group in Bhutan and Sikkim. Most of the latter Buddhists belong to the Mahāyāna and Vajrayāna forms of Buddhism and represent denominations and orders of Tibetan and Nepalese origin. Buddhists may also be found in the subcontinent among Tibetan refugees (mostly in Himachal Pradesh and Bangalore), among the Ambedkar Buddhists of Maharashtra, and among pilgrims and missionaries flocking to the sacred sites of India. The diversity of manifestations is not new, but the specific forms are not representative of what Indian Buddhism was in the past.

Origins

Approximately twenty-five hundred years ago the founder of the Buddhist religion was born into the Śākya tribe in a small aristocratic republic in the Himalayan foothills, in what is today the kingdom of Nepal. In his youth he descended to the Ganges River valley in search of spiritual realization. After several years of study at the feet of spiritual masters he underwent a profound religious experience that changed his life; he became a teacher himself, and lived for the rest of his adult life as a mendicant peripatetic. His worldview and personal preoccupations were shaped in the cultural milieu of India of the sixth century BCE; the religious communities that trace their origin to him developed their most distinctive doctrines and practices in Indian soil.

SOURCES AND SETTING

Unfortunately, we do not possess reliable sources for most of the history of Buddhism in its homeland; in particular, we have precious little to rely on for its early history. Textual sources are late, dating at the very least five hundred years after the death of the Buddha. The archaeological evidence, abundant as it is, is limited in the information it can give us. A few facts are nevertheless well established. The roots of Indian Buddhism are to be found in the "shramanic" movement of the sixth century BCE, which owes the name to its model of religious perfection, the *śramaṇa,* or wandering ascetic. The *śramaṇa*s set religious goals that stood outside, and in direct opposition to, the religious and social order of the *brāhmaṇa*s (brahmans), who represented the Indo-Aryan establishment. Most of the values that would become characteristic of Indian, and therefore Hindu, religion in general were shaped by the interaction of these two groups, especially by a process of assimilation that transformed the Brahmanic order into Hindu culture. [*See* Vedism and Brahmanism.]

The appearance of two major shramanic religions, Buddhism and Jainism, marked the end of the Vedic-Brahmanic period and the beginning of an era of cross-fertilization between diverse strata of Indian culture. This new age, sometimes called the Indic period, was characterized by the dominant role of "heterodox" or non-Hindu religious systems, the flourishing of their ascetic and monastic orders, and the use of the vernaculars in preference to Sanskrit.

We can surmise that this new age was a time of social upheaval and political instability. The use of iron had changed radically the character of warfare and the nature of farming. The jungle was cleared, farmland could support a court bureaucracy, and palaces and city walls could be built. A surplus economy was created that made possible large state societies, with concentrated populations and resources, and consequently with heightened political ambition.

The Buddha must have been touched directly by these changes: shortly before his death the republic of the Śākyas was sacked by the powerful kingdom of Kośala, which in turn would shortly thereafter fall under the power of Magadha. At the time of the Buddha sixteen independent states existed in North Central India, a century later only one empire would rule in the region, and in another hundred years this empire, Magadha, would control all of northern India and most of the South. The unity of the empire was won at a price: political and social systems based on family or tribal order crumbled; the old gods lost their power.

As the old order crumbled, the brahmans claimed special privileges that other groups were not always willing to concede. Those who would not accept their leadership sought spiritual and moral guidance among the *śramaṇa*s. Although recent research has shown that the interaction between these two groups was more complex than we had previously imagined, it is still accepted that the shramanic movement represented some of the groups displaced by the economic and political changes of the day, and by the expansion of Brahmanic power. The *śramaṇas,* therefore, were rebels of sorts. They challenged the values of lay life in general, but especially the caste system as it existed at the time. Thus, what appeared as a lifestyle designed to lead to religious realization may have been at the same time the expression of social protest, or at least of social malaise.

The shramanic movement was fragmented: among the shramanic groups, Buddhism's main rival was Jainism, representing an ancient teaching whose origin dated to at least one or two generations before the Buddha. A community of mendicants reformed by Vardhamāṇa Mahāvīra (d. around 468 BCE) shortly before the beginning of Buddha's career, Jainism represented the extremes of world denial and asceticism that Buddhism sought to moderate with its doctrine of the Middle Way. Buddhists also criticized in Jainism what they saw as a mechanistic conception of moral responsibility and liberation. Another school criticized by early Buddhists was that of

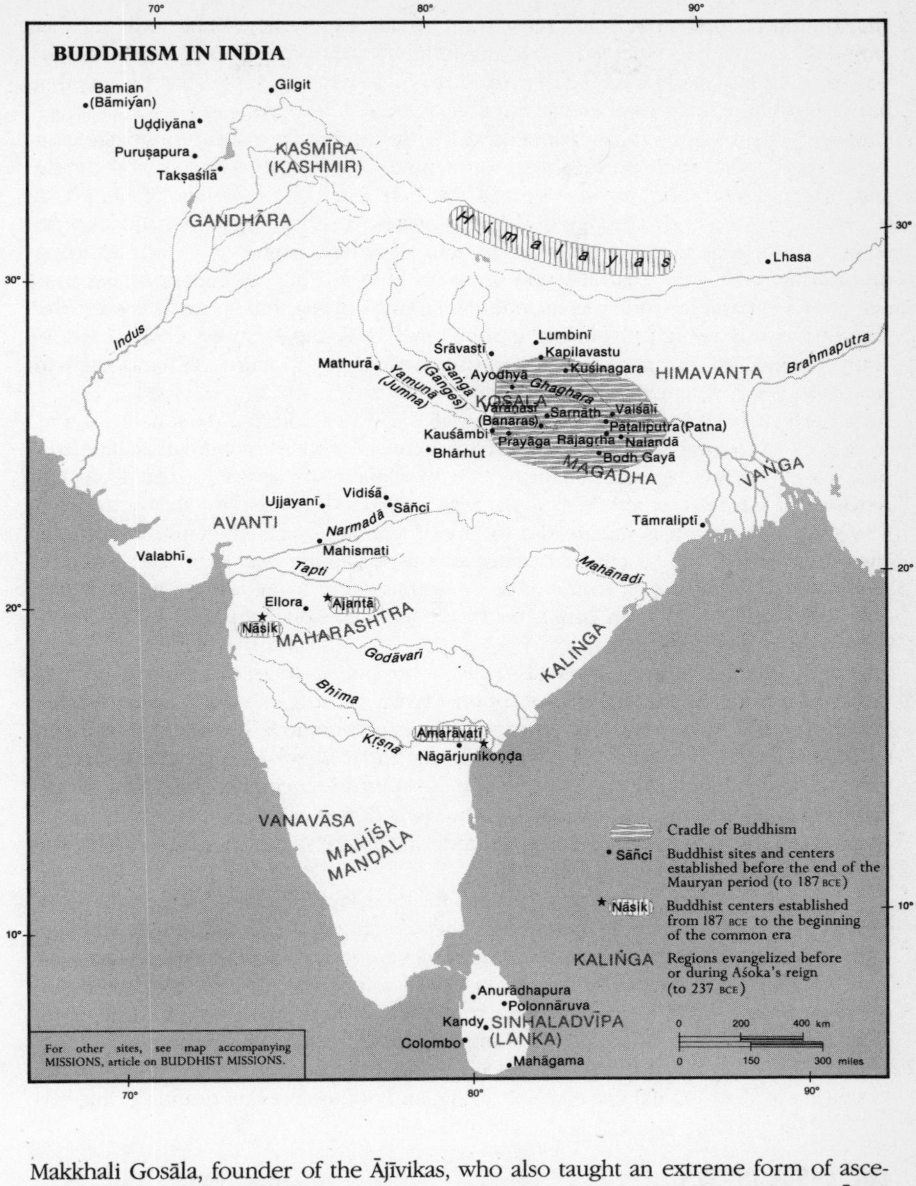

Makkhali Gosāla, founder of the Ājīvikas, who also taught an extreme form of asceticism that was based, strangely, on a fatalistic doctrine. [*See* Jainism; Mahāvīra; Ājīvikas; *and the biography of Gośāla.*]

We have to understand the shramanic movements as independent systems and not as simple derivations or reforms of Brahmanic doctrine and practice. One can find, nevertheless, certain elements common to all the movements of the age: the *śramaṇas*, called "wanderers" (*parivrājakas*), like the forest dwellers of Brahmanism, retired from society. Some sought an enstatic experience; some believed that particular forms of conduct led to purity and liberation from suffering; others sought power through knowledge (ritual or magical) or insight (contemplative or gnostic); but most systems contained elements of all of these tendencies.

Among the religious values formed during the earlier part of the Indic age, that is, during the shramanic period, we must include, above all, the concept of the cycle and bondage of rebirth *(saṃsāra)* and the belief in the possibility of liberation *(mokṣa)* from the cycle through ascetic discipline, world renunciation, and a moral or ritual code that gave a prominent place to abstaining from doing harm to living beings *(ahiṃsā)*. This ideal, like the quest for altered states of consciousness, was not always separable from ancient notions of ritual purity and spiritual power. But among the shramanic movements it sometimes took the form of a moral virtue. Then it appeared as opposition to organized violence—political, as embodied in war, and religious, as expressed in animal sacrifice.

The primary evil force was no longer envisioned as a spiritual personality, but as an impersonal moral law of cause and effect *(karman)* whereby human actions created a state of bondage and suffering. In their quest for a state of rest from the activities of *karman,* whether the goal was defined as enstasy or knowledge, the new religious specialists practiced a variety of techniques of self-cultivation usually known as *yoga*s. The sustained practice of this discipline was known as a "path" *(mārga),* and the goal was a state of peace and freedom from passion and suffering called *nirvāṇa*. [*See* Karman, *article on* Hindu and Jain Concepts; Mokṣa; Yoga; Saṃsāra; Ahiṃsā; *and* Saṃnyāsa.]

As a shramanic religion, Buddhism displayed similar traits but gave to each of these its unique imprint. The conception of rebirth and its evils were not questioned, but suffering was universalized: all human conditions lead to suffering, suffering has a cause, and that cause is craving, or "thirst" *(tṛṣṇā)*. To achieve liberation from the cycle of rebirth one must follow the spiritual discipline prescribed by the Buddha, summarized in the Eightfold Path. The follower of Buddhism was expected to renounce the lay life and become a wandering ascetic, an ideal epitomized by the spiritual career of the founder.

Most shramanic groups made provisions for their lay supporters, essentially members of the community who by circumstance or choice could not follow the wanderer's path. Buddhist laymen could begin moving in the right direction—with the hope of being able to renounce the world in a future birth—by "taking refuge" *(śaraṇa-gamana),* that is, by making a confession of faith in the Buddha, his teachings, and his monastic order, and by adopting five fundamental moral precepts *(pañcaśīla):* not to deprive a living thing of life, not to take what is not given to you, not to engage in illicit sexual conduct, not to lie, and not to take intoxicating drinks.

THE THREE JEWELS

Perhaps all we can say with certainty about the roots of Buddhist doctrine and doctrinal continuity in Buddhism is that the figure of the Buddha and his experience dominate most of Buddhist teachings. If we wish to understand Buddhism as a doctrinal system, we can look at its oral and written ideology—including its scriptures—as the effort of diverse Buddhist communities to explore and define the general issues raised by the Buddha's career. These include questions such as the following:

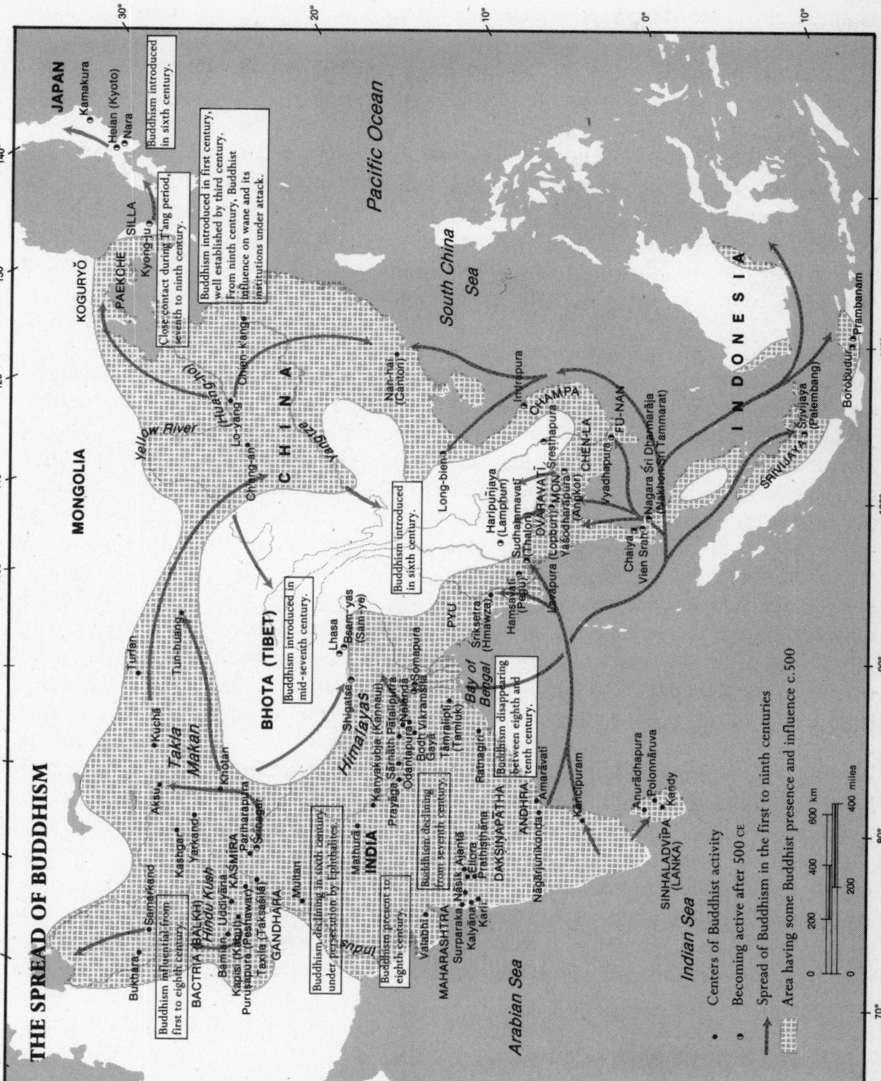
THE SPREAD OF BUDDHISM
MONGOLIA
JAPAN
Kamakura
Heian (Kyoto)
Nara
KOGURYŎ
PAEKCHE
SILLA
Kyong-ju
Buddhism introduced in sixth century.
Close contact during T'ang period, seventh to ninth century.
Buddhism introduced in first century, well established by third century. From ninth century, Buddhist influence on wane and its institutions under attack.
Pacific Ocean
South China Sea
Yellow River
Lo-yang
Ch'ang-an
C H I N A
Yangtze
Nan-hai (Canton)
Buddhism introduced in sixth century.
BHOTA (TIBET)
Buddhism introduced in mid-seventh century.
Lhasa
Turfan
Kucha
Tun-huang
Takla Makan
Aksu
Khotan
Kashgar
Yarkand
Bukhara
Samarkand
Buddhism influential from first to eighth century.
BACTRIA (BALKH)
Hindu Kush
Bamiyan
Uddiyana
KASMIRA
GANDHARA
Multan
Buddhism declining in sixth century under persecution by Ephthalites.
Indus
Himalayas
INDIA
Mathura
Kanyakubja (Kannauj)
Nalanda
Bodh Gaya
Buddhism present to eighth century.
Buddhism declining from seventh century.
MAHARASHTRA
Valabhi
Ajanta
Ellora
Karli
Bay of Bengal
Tamralipti (Tamluk)
Ratnagiri
Buddhism disappearing between eighth and tenth century.
ANDHRA
Amaravati
DAKSINAPATHA
Nagarjunikonda
Kancipuram
PYU
Sriksetra (Hmawza)
Hamsavati (Pegu)
DVARAVATI
MON
Haripunjaya (Lamphun)
Long-bien
CHAMPA
Indrapura
FU-NAN
CHEN-LA
Yasodharapura (Angkor)
Vyadhapura
Chaiya
Nagara Sri Dharmaraja (Nakhon Sri Tammarat)
SRIVIJAYA
Srivijaya (Palembang)
Borobudur
Prambanam
I N D O N E S I A
Arabian Sea
Indian Sea
SINHALADVIPA (LANKA)
Anuradhapura
Polonnaruva
Kandy
Centers of Buddhist activity
Becoming active after 500 CE
Spread of Buddhism in the first to ninth centuries
Area having some Buddhist presence and influence c.500

Does the Buddha "exist" after liberation? Is the experience of awakening ineffable? Which of the two experiences, awakening or liberation, is the fundamental one?

On the other hand, if we wish to understand Buddhism as a religion rather than as a system of doctrines, its focus or fulcrum must be found in the religious communities and their objects of veneration. The early community was represented primarily by the gathering of mendicants or monks called the *saṃgha,* held together by ascetic or monastic codes *(prātimokṣa)* attributed to the Buddha himself, and by the objects of worship represented by (1) the founder himself as the "Awakened One" *(buddha);* (2) his exemplary and holy life, his teachings and his experience *(dharma);* and (3) the community *(saṃgha)* itself, sustained by the memory of his personality and teaching. These objects of veneration are known as the "Three Treasures" *(triratna),* and the believer's trust in these ideals is expressed, doctrinally and ritually, in the "Three Refuges" (to rely on the Buddha, the Dharma, and the Sangha). To this day, this formula serves at once as an indication of the meaning of monastic ordination and a lay confession of faith.

Buddha. No Western scholar today would claim to know the exact details of the founder's biography, or for that matter the exact content of his teachings. The above is merely an educated guess based on formulations from a time removed by several centuries from their origins. Scholars agree, nevertheless, on the historicity of the founder. That is to say, though they may doubt the accuracy of the information transmitted in traditional "biographies" (beginning with his personal name, Siddhārtha Gautama) or in legends about the Buddha's sermons, Western scholars accept the existence of an influential religious figure, called Śākyamuni ("the sage of the Śākya tribe") by his disciples, who at some point in the sixth century BCE founded in the Ganges River valley the community of wandering mendicants that would eventually grow into the world religion we now call Buddhism.

Scholars generally tend to accept the years 563 to 483 BCE as the least problematic, if not the most plausible, dating for the life of Gautama Buddha. (Other dating systems exist, however, that place his life as much as a century later.) Assuming, moreover, that the legend is reliable in some of its details, we can say that the history of the religion begins when Śākyamuni was thirty-five (therefore, in about 528), with his first sermon at Sārnāth (northeast of the city of Vārāṇasī).

Before and after his enlightenment, Śākyamuni followed the typical career of a wanderer. At twenty-nine he abandoned the household and sought a spiritual guide. An early legend claims that Śākyamuni actually studied under two teachers of the age, Āḷāra Kālāma and Udraka Rāmaputra. From such teachers the young ascetic learned techniques of meditation that he later rejected, but the imprints of which remain in Buddhist theories of meditation. Dissatisfied with what he had learned, he tried the life of the hermit. Finally, after six years of struggle, he "awakened" under a pipal tree *(Ficus religiosa)* near the border town of Uruvilvā (Bodh Gayā).

His first sermon was followed by forty-five years of wandering through the Ganges River valley, spreading his teachings. Although tradition preserves many narratives of isolated episodes of this half century of teaching, no one has been able to piece together a convincing account of this period. For the tradition this was also a time for the performance of great miracles, and historical accuracy was never an important consideration.

At the age of eighty (c. 483), Siddhārtha Gautama, the Buddha Śākyamuni, died near the city of Kuśināgara. To his immediate disciples perhaps this fading away of the Master confirmed his teachings on impermanence, but the Buddha's death would soon come to be regarded as a symbol of his perfect peace and renunciation: with death he had reached his *parinirvāṇa,* that point in his career after which he would be reborn no more. His ashes, encased in a reliquary buried in a cairn, came to stand for the highest achievement of an awakened being, confirming his status as the one who had attained to truth, the Tathāgata—an epithet that would come to denote ultimate truth itself. [*See* Buddha *and* Tathāgata.]

Dharma. The first preaching, known as the "First Turning of the Wheel of Dharma" (or, in the West, the "Sermon at Banaras" or the "Deer Park Sermon"), symbolizes the appearance in history of the Buddhist teaching, whereas Śākyamuni's enlightenment experience, or "Great Awakening" *(mahābodhi),* which occurred in the same year, represents the human experience around which the religion would develop its practices and ideals. This was the experience whereby Śākyamuni became an "Awakened One" *(buddha).* His disciples came to believe that all aspects of Buddhist doctrine and practice flow from this experience of awakening *(bodhi)* and from the resultant state of freedom from passion, suffering, and rebirth called *nirvāṇa.* The teachings found in the Buddha's sermons can be interpreted as definitions of these two experiences, the spiritual practices that lead to or flow from them, and the institutions that arose inspired by the experience and the human beings who laid claim to it. [*See* Nirvāṇa.]

However, it is difficult, if not impossible, to surmise which, if any, among the many doctrines attributed by tradition to the founder are veritably his. Different Buddhists, even when they can agree on the words, will interpret the message differently. Although most would find the nucleus of Śākyamuni's teachings in the "First Sermon," especially in the doctrine of the Four Noble Truths allegedly preached therein, a host of other doctrinal statements compete for the central position throughout the history of Buddhism in India and beyond. Moreover, a number of texts that can claim great antiquity are not only silent about the Four Noble Truths but actually do not seem to presuppose them in any way. The same can be said about other doctrines that would become central to the development of Buddhist doctrinal speculation, for instance, the principle of conditioned arising *(pratītya-samutpāda)* and the analysis of the human personality into its constituent parts (*skandha*s, etc.).

It is difficult to determine to what extent early Buddhism had an accompanying metaphysics. Some of the earliest strata of Buddhist literature suggest that the early community may have emphasized the joys of renunciation and the peace of abstention from conflict—political, social, and religious—more than a philosophical doctrine of liberation. Such are the ascetic ideals of one of the earliest texts of the tradition, the *Aṭṭhakavagga (Suttanipāta).* The mendicant abstains from participating in the religious and metaphysical debates of brahmans, *śramaṇa*s, and sages. He is detached from all views, for

> Purity is not [attained] by views, or learning,
> by knowledge, or by moral rules, and rites.
> Nor is it [attained] by the absence of views,
> learning, knowledge, rules or rites.

> Abandoning all these, not grasping at them,
> he is at peace; not relying, he would not
> hanker for becoming. (*Suttanipāta* 839)

There is in this text a rejection of doctrine, rule, and rite that is a critique of the exaggerated claims of those who believed they could become pure and free through ritual, knowledge, or religious status. The lonely ascetic seeks not to become one thing or the other and avoids doctrinal disputes.

If such statements represent some of the earliest moments in the development of the doctrine, then the next stage must have brought a growing awareness of the need for ritual and creed if the community was to survive. This awareness would have been followed in a short time by the formation of a metaphysic, a theory of liberation, and a conscious system of meditation. In the next strata of early Buddhist literature these themes are only surpassed in importance by discussions of ascetic morality. The ascetic ideals of the early community were then expanded and defined by doctrine—as confession of faith, as ideology, and as a plan for religious and moral practice. The earliest formulations of this type are perhaps those of the Eightfold Path, with its triple division into wisdom, moral practice, and mental concentration. The theoretical or metaphysical underpinnings are contained in the Four Noble Truths and in the Three Marks (impermanence, sorrow, and no-self), both traditionally regarded as the subject matter of the Buddha's first sermons. [*See* Four Noble Truths; Eightfold Path; Karman, *article on* Buddhist Concepts; Soul, *article on* Buddhist Concepts; *and* Dharma, *article on* Buddhist Dharma and Dharmas.]

Saṃgha. With the first sermon the Buddha began a ministry that would last forty-five years. During this period he established a religious order—perhaps only a mendicant order in its beginnings—and trained a number of distinguished disciples who would carry on the teaching after the founder's death. Tradition preserves the names of many of his disciples and immediate heirs to his teaching: Kauṇḍinya, the first convert to be admitted into the Buddha's religious order *(saṃgha);* Yasa, the first householder to receive full lay initiation with the Three Refuges; Śāriputra, the master of wisdom; Maudgalyāyana, the great thaumaturge; Upāli, the expert in the monastic code; Ānanda, the Buddha's cousin and beloved disciple; Mahāprajāpati, the first woman admitted into the monastic order; and Mahākāśyapa, who undertook to preserve the Buddha's teaching and organized the First Council. The Buddha's disciples represented a wide spectrum of social classes. Yasa was the son of a wealthy gild master; Upāli, a humble barber; Śāriputra, a brahman; Ānanda, a member of the nobility *(kṣatriya).* Among the early followers we find not only world renouncers but believers from a variety of walks of life; King Bimbisāra, the wealthy banker Anāthapiṇḍika, the respectable housewife Viśākhā, and the courtesan Amrapālī, for instance.

Although the Buddhist monastic community was an integral part of Indian society, serving as an instrument of legitimation and cohesion, it also served on occasions as a critic of society. Especially in its early development, and in particular during the period of the wandering mendicants, the *saṃgha* was a nonconformist subgroup. The variety of social classes represented by the roster of early disciples in part reflects the fluid state of Indian society at the time; but it also reflects the Buddha's open opposition to the caste system as it existed then. Although the challenge was religious and political as well as social, the Buddha's critique of Brahmanism made his order of mendicants an alternative community, where those who did not fit in the new social order could find a sense of belonging, acceptance, and achievement. Buddhist reforms and institutions would waver in their function as rebels and supporters of social order until Buddhism ultimately became absorbed into Hinduism during the centuries following the first millennium of the common era.

We can surmise that the earliest community did not have a fixed abode. During the dry season the Buddhist *śramaṇa*s would sleep in the open and wander from village to village "begging" for their sustenance—hence their title *bhikṣu,* "mendicant" (fem., *bhikṣuṇī*). They were persons who had set forth *(pravrajyā)* from the household to lead the life of the wanderer *(parivrājaka).* Only during the rainy season would they gather in certain spots in the forest or in special groves provided by lay supporters. There they would build temporary huts that would be dismantled at the end of the rainy season, when they would set out again in their constant wandering to spread the Buddha's Dharma.

The main ideals of the mendicant life of the "wanderers" is expressed in a passage that is presented as the creed or code (the Prātimokṣa) recited by the followers of the "former Buddha" Vipaśyin when they interrupted the wandering to meet and renew their common ideals:

> Enduring patience is the highest austerity,
> *nirvāṇa* is the highest condition—say the Buddhas.
> For he who injures another is not a true renouncer,
> He who causes harm to others is not a true ascetic.
> Not to do any evil, to practice the good,
> to purify one's own mind:
> This is the teaching of the Buddhas.
>
> Not to speak against others, not to harm others,
> and restraint according to the rule *(prātimokṣa),*
> Moderation in eating, secluded dwelling,
> and the practice of mental cultivation *(adhicitta):*
> This is the teaching of the Buddhas.
>
> *(Mahāpadāna Suttanta)*

These verses outline important aspects of the early teaching: the centrality of *ahiṃsā,* the two aspects of morality—abstention and cultivation—and the practice of meditation, all in the context of a community of ascetics for whom a life of solitude, poverty, and moderation was more important than the development of subtle metaphysics. [*For a discussion of ascetic practices, see* Soteriology, *article on* Buddhist Soteriology.]

Probably—and the earliest scriptures suggest this—the first aspect of Buddhist teachings to be systematized was the rule, first as a confession of faith for dispersed communities of mendicants, soon as a monastic rule for sedentary ascetics. Also at an early stage, the community sought to systematize its traditions of meditation, some of which must have been pre-Buddhistic (the Buddha himself having learned some of these from his teachers). Thus, Buddhist techniques of meditation represent a continuation of earlier processes of *yoga,* though we cannot be certain as to the exact connection, or the exact content of the early practices.

The first of these developments brought the community closer together by establishing a common ritual, the recitation of the rule *(prātimokṣa)* at a meeting held on the full and new moon and the quarter moons *(uposatha).* The second development confirmed an important but divisive trait of the early community: the primary source of authority remained with the individual monk and his experience in solitude. Thus, competing systems of meditation and doctrine probably developed more rapidly than differences in the code. [*See* Saṃgha, *especially the overview article.*]

The Cenobium

As India moved into an age of imperial unity under the Maurya (322–185) and Śuṅga dynasties (185–73), the Buddhist community reached its point of greatest unity. Although the *saṃgha* split into schools or sects perhaps as early as the fourth century BCE, differences among Buddhists were relatively minor. Transformed into a monastic brotherhood, Buddhism served a society that shared common values and customs. Unity, however, was shortlived, and Buddhism, like India, would have to adapt rapidly to new circumstances as the first invasions from Central Asia would put an end to the Śuṅga dynasty in 175. Until then, however, during the approximately three hundred years from the death of the founder to the beginning of the age of foreign invasions, Buddhist monks and laymen began the process of systematization that defined the common ground of Indian Buddhism in practice, scripture, and doctrine.

The primary element of continuity became the Prātimokṣa, the rules for the maintenance of the community and the liturgical recitation thereof; differences in this regard would be more serious than differences of doctrine. Thus the Second Council, which is supposed to have caused the most serious split in the history of the community, is said to have been called to resolve differences in the interpretation and formulation of minor details in the monastic regulations. In order to justify and clarify the rules that held the community together a detailed commentary of the Prātimokṣa rules had to be developed. The commentary, attributed to the Buddha himself, eventually grew into the Vinaya, an extensive section of the canon.

But the full development of the monastic code presupposes a sedentary *saṃgha.* We can surmise that not long after the Buddha's death the retreat for the rainy season began to extend into the dry season, perhaps at the invitation of the lay community, perhaps owing to dwindling popular support for the mendicant wanderers. Soon the temporary huts were replaced by more or less permanent structures built of wood, and the community of wanderers became a cenobium. The stone and gravel foundation of one of the earliest monasteries remains in the vicinity of Rājagṛha (Bihar). These are the ruins of the famous "Jivaka's Mango Grove" (Jivakāmravaṇa) Monastery, built on a plot of land donated to the order at the time of the Buddha. In its early history it may have been used only during the rainy season, but it already shows the basic structure of the earliest monasteries: living quarters for the monks and a large assembly hall (perhaps for the celebration of the Uposatha).

As the community settled down, rules and rituals for regulating monastic life became a necessity. At least some of the items in the *Prātimokṣa* section of the Vinaya and some of the procedural rules discussed in the *Karmavācanā* may go back to the time of the Buddha. The rule and the procedures for governing the *Saṃgha* are clearly based on republican models, like the constitution of the Licchavis of Vaiśālī, which is praised in the canonical texts. If this admiration goes back to the founder, then we can say that the Buddha ordered his community of wandering mendicants on the political model provided by the disappearing republics of North India. Such a rule would encourage order and harmony on the one hand, and peaceful disagreement and individual effort on the other. It provided for mutual care and concern in matters of morals, but lacked a provision for a central authority in political or doctrinal matters. [*See* Vinaya *and* Monasticism, *article on* Buddhist Monasticism.]

THE COMMON DOCTRINAL GROUND

The Buddha realized the true nature of things, their "suchness" *(tathatā),* and therefore is one of those rare beings called *tathāgata*s. Yet, whether there is a *tathāgata* to preach it or not, the Dharma is always present, because it is the nature of all things *(dharmatā).* Four terms summarize this truth known by the *tathāgata*s: impermanence, sorrow, no-self, *nirvāṇa.* The first implies the second, for attachment to what must change brings sorrow. Our incapacity to control change, however, reveals the reality of no-self—nothing is "I" or "mine." The experience of no-self, on the other hand, is liberating; it releases one from craving and the causes of sorrow; it leads to peace, *nirvāṇa.*

These principles are summarized also in a doctrine recognized by all schools, that of the Four Noble Truths: sorrow, its cause, its cessation, and the path leading to cessation. Buddhist tradition, therefore, will spend much of its energy in understanding the causes of suffering and the means to put an end to it, or, in doctrinal shorthand, "arising" and "cessation." Since cessation is in fact the obverse of arising, a proper understanding of arising, or causation, becomes central to Buddhist speculation in India. The most important doctrine for this aspect of the religion is the principle of dependent arising *(pratītya-samutpāda):* everything we regard as "the self" is conditioned or compounded; everything conditioned depends on causes and conditions; by understanding the causes of our idea of the self and of the sorrow that this idea brings to us we can become free of suffering. [*See* Pratītya-samutpāda.] This doctrine is summarized in a stanza that has become one of the best known Buddhist creeds throughout Asia:

> The Tathāgata has proclaimed the cause,
> as well as the cessation,
> of all things *(dharma)* arising from a cause.
> This is the Great *Śramaṇa's* teaching.
> (*Mahāvastu* 2.62; Pali *Vinaya* 1.40)

Abstract theories of causation were perceived as having an ultimately soteriological meaning or function, for they clarified both the process of bondage (rebirth forced upon us as a consequence of our actions) and the process of liberation (freedom from rebirth by overcoming our ignorance and gaining control over the causes of bondage). Liberation was possible because the analysis of causation revealed that there was no reincarnating or suffering self to begin with.

Impermanence and causation were explained by primitive theories of the composition of material reality (the four elements) and mental reality (the six senses, the six types of sense objects, etc.) and, what is more important, by the theory of the constituents *(skandhas)* of human personality. These notions would become the main focus of Buddhist philosophy, and by the beginning of the common era they were being integrated into systematic treatments of the nature of ultimately real entities *(dharma)*. [*See* Dharma, *article on* Buddhist Dharma and Dharmas.]

Although the themes of impermanence and causation will remain at the heart of Buddhist philosophical speculation for several centuries, from the religious point of view the question of no-self plays a more important role. At first seen as an insightful formulation of the meaning of awakening and liberation, the doctrine of no-self raised several difficulties for Buddhist dogma. First, it was not at all obvious how moral (or karmic) responsibility could be possible if there was no continuous self. Second, some Buddhists wondered what was the meaning of liberation in the absence of a self.

Closely related to these issues was the question of the nature and status of the liberated being. In other words, what sort of living being is a *tathāgata?* Some Buddhists considered the *tathāgata* as a transcendent or eternal being, while others saw him as someone who by becoming extinct was nonexistent; still others began to redefine the concept of liberation and no-self in an attempt to solve these questions and in response to changes in the mythological or hagiographic sphere. These issues are an essential part of the changes in doctrine and practice that would take place during the age of invasions, culminating in the emergence of Mahāyāna Buddhism.

WORSHIP AND RITUAL

The most important ritual of the monastic community continued to be Upavasatha or Uposatha, a gathering of the *saṃgha* of a given locality or "parish" *(sīmā)* to recite the rules of the Prātimokṣa. These meetings were held at every change in the moon's phase. A similar ceremony, but with greater emphasis on the public confession of individual faults, was held at the end of the rainy season. At this time too was held the *kaṭhina* ceremony, in which the monks received new robes from the lay community. Other rituals, such as the ordination ceremony, had a more limited impact on the community at large, but were nevertheless important symbols of the status of the religious specialist in society at large.

Above all other rituals, one of Shramanic origin offered continued reinforcement of the ties that bound the religious order with the laity. The *bhikṣu,* as his title indicates, was expected to receive his sustenance from the charity *(dāna)* of pious laymen and laywomen. Accordingly, the monks would walk the villages every morning to collect alms. By giving the unsolicited gift the layperson was assured of the merit *(puṇya)* necessary to be reborn in a state of being more favorable for spiritual or material progress. According to some traditions, the monk received the benefits of helping others gain merit; but some believed the monk could not gain merit except by his own virtue.

In the early stages lay followers were identified by their adherence to the fivefold moral precept *(pañcaśīla)* and the formal adoption of the Three Refuges. These practices continued throughout the history of Indian Buddhism. It is also likely that participation of lay members in Upavasatha meetings with the *saṃgha* was also an early and persistent practice.

At first the cenobitic life of the monks probably had no room for explicit acts of devotion, and the monk's religion was limited to a life of solitude and meditation. The early monastic ruins do not show evidence of any shrine room. It was essential to have the cells open onto a closed courtyard, to keep out the noise of the world; it was essential to have an assembly hall for teaching and the recitation of the Prātimokṣa; a promenade *(caṅkrama)* for walking meditation was also necessary. But there were no shrine rooms.

With the institutionalization of Buddhism, however, came new forms of lay and monastic practice. The monastic brotherhood gradually began to play a priestly role; in tandem with the lay community, they participated in nonmonastic rituals, many of which must have been of pre-Buddhist origin. [*See* Priesthood, *article on* Buddhist Priesthood.] One practice that clearly was an important, nonascetic ritual, yet characteristic of Buddhism, was the worship of the relics of the Buddha and his immediate disciples. The relics were placed in a casket, which was then deposited in a cairn or tumulus *(stūpa, caitya),* to which the faithful would come to present their offerings. Already by the time of Aśoka (mid-third century BCE) we find evidence of a flourishing cult of the relics, often accompanied by the practice of pilgrimage to the sacred sites consecrated by their role in the life of Śākyamuni—especially the birth place, the site of the Great Awakening, the site of the First Sermon, and the spot where the Buddha was believed to have died. [*See also* Pilgrimage, *article on* Buddhist Pilgrimage in South and Southeast Asia.] Following an ancient custom, tumuli were built on these spots—perhaps at first as reliquaries, later as commemorative monuments. Monasteries near such sites assumed the role of shrine caretakers. Eventually, most monasteries became associated with stupas.

Aśoka erected columns and stupas (as many as eighty thousand, according to one tradition) marking the localities associated with the life of the Buddha as well as other ancient sacred sites, some associated with "former Buddhas," that is, mythical beings believed to have achieved Buddhahood thousands or millions of lives before the Buddha Śākyamuni. The latter practice and belief indicates the development of a new form of Buddhism, firmly based on the mythology of each locality, that expanded the concept of the Three Treasures to include a host of mythical beings who would share in the sanctity of Śākyamuni's experience and virtue and who were therefore deserving of the same veneration as he had received in the past.

The cairn or tumulus eventually became sacred in itself, whether there was a relic in it or not. Chapels were built to contain the *caitya.* The earliest surviving examples of these structures are built in stone and date from the first or second century BCE, but we can surmise that they existed in wood from an earlier date. These "*caitya* halls" became the standard shrine room of the monastery: a stylized memorial tumulus built in stone or brick, housed in an apsidal hall with a processional for the ritual circumambulation of the tumulus. [*See* Temple, *article on* Buddhist Temple Compounds.]

Reliefs at the *caitya* hall at Bhājā in Western India (late Śuṅga, c. end of the second century BCE) suggest various aspects of the cult: the main form of worship was the ritual of circumambulation *(pradakṣiṇa),* which could be carried out individually or in groups. The stupa represented the sacred or cosmic mountain, at whose center was found the *axis mundi* (now represented by the Buddha's royal parasol); thus the rite of circumambulation expressed veneration for the Buddha and his teaching, while at the same time it served as a symbolic walking of the sun's path around the cosmic mountain.

Stupas were often erected at ancient sacred sites, hills, trees, the confluence of streams, which in many cases were sacred by virtue of non-Buddhist belief. Thus, pre-Buddhist practice, if not belief, survived side by side, and even within, Buddhist liturgy and belief. There is ample evidence of a coexisting cult of the tree (identified with the "Tree of Awakening"), of forest spirits *(yakṣas)* and goddesses *(devatā),* and the persistence of Vedic deities, albeit in a subordinate role, beside a more austere, and presumably monastically inspired, cult of aniconic symbolizations of Buddhahood: the tree and the throne of enlightenment standing for the Great Awakening, the stupa representing the *nirvāṇa,* the wheel representing the doctrine of the Buddha. But one must not assume that the implied categories of "high tradition" and popular cult were mutually exclusive. [*See* Stupa Worship *and* Nāgas and Yakṣas. *For a discussion of Buddhist/local syncretism, see* Folk Religion, *article on* Folk Buddhism. *See also* Worship and Cultic Life, *article on* Buddhist Cultic Life in Southeast Asia.]

THE COUNCILS AND THE BEGINNING OF SCRIPTURAL TRADITION

The First Council, or Council of Rājagṛha, if a historical fact, must have served to establish the Buddhist *saṃgha* and its doctrine for the community of the Magadhan capital. In all probability the decisions of the Council were not accepted by all Buddhists. Further evidence of disagreement, and geographical fragmentation is found in the legend of the Second Council, one hundred years after the Buddha's death.

Since the early community of wanderers, there had been ample room for disagreement and dissension. But certain forces contributed to maintaining unity: the secular powers, for instance, had much at stake in preserving harmony within the *saṃgha,* especially if they could maintain some kind of control over it. Thus, as the legends have it, each of the three major councils were sponsored by a king: Ajātaśatru, Kālāśoka, and Aśoka, respectively. Within the *saṃgha,* there must have been interests groups, mainly conservative, seeking to preserve the religion by avoiding change—two goals that are not always conciliable. There must have been, therefore, a strong pressure to recover the ideal unity of the early community (as we have seen, probably a fantasy), by legislation. These efforts took two forms: in the first place, there was the drive to establish a common monastic code, in the second place, there was the drive to fix a canon of scriptures. Both tendencies probably became stronger toward the beginning of the common era, when a number of political factors recreated a sense of urgency and a yearning for harmony and peace similar to the one that had given rise to the religion. [*See* Councils, *article on* Buddhist Councils.]

The most important result of the new quest for harmony was the compilation and redaction of scriptures. Transmitted and edited through the oral tradition, the words of the Buddha and his immediate disciples had suffered many transformations before they came to be compiled, to say nothing of their state when they were eventually written down. We have no way of determining which, if any, of the words contained in the Buddhist scriptures are the words of the founder: in fact we have no hard evidence for the language used by the Buddha in his ministry. Scholars have suggested an early form of Māgadhī, since this was probably the lingua franca of the kingdom of Magadha, but this is at best an educated guess. If it is correct, then none of the words of the Buddha have come to us in the original language.

Although the Theravādin tradition claims that the language of its canon, Pali, is the language spoken by the Buddha, Western scholars disagree. Evidently, the Pali canon, like other Buddhist scriptures, is the creation, or at least the compilation and composition, of another age and a different linguistic milieu. As they are preserved today, the Buddhist scriptures must be a collective creation, the fruit of the effort of several generations of memorizers, redactors, and compilers. Some of the earliest Buddhist scriptures may have been translations from logia or sayings of the Buddha that were transmitted for some time in his own language. But even if this is the case, the extant versions represent at the very least redactions and reworkings, if not creations, of a later age.

Since the *saṃgha* was from the beginning a decentralized church, one can presume that the word of the Buddha took many forms. Adding to this the problem of geographical isolation and linguistic diversity, one would expect that the oral transmission would have produced a variegated textual tradition. Perhaps it is this expectation of total chaos that makes it all the more surprising that there is agreement on so many points in the scriptures preserved to this day. This is especially true of the scriptures of the Theravāda school (preserved in Pali), and fragments of the canon of the Sarvāstivāda school (in the original Sanskrit or in Chinese translation). Some scholars have been led to believe, therefore, that these two traditions represent the earliest stratum of the transmission, preserving a complex of pericopes and logia that must go back to a stage when the community was not divided: that is, before the split of the Second Council. Most scholars tend to accept this view; a significant minority, however, sees the uniformity of the texts as reflecting a late, not an early stage, in the redaction of the canon.

The early canon, transmitted orally, must have had only two major sections, Dharma and Vinaya. The first of these contained the discourses of the Buddha and his immediate disciples. The Vinaya contained the monastic rules. Most Western scholars agree that a third section, Abhidharma, found in all of the surviving canons, could not have been included in early definitions of canonicity, though eventually most schools would incorporate it in their canon with varying degrees of authority.

Each early school possessed its own set of scriptural "collections" (called metaphorically "baskets," *piṭaka*). Although eventually the preferred organization seems to have been a tripartite collection of "Three Baskets," the Tripiṭaka, divided into monastic rules, sermons, and scholastic treatises (Vinaya, Sūtra, Abhidharma), some schools adopted different orderings. Among the collections that are now lost there were fourfold and fivefold subdivisions of the scriptures. Of the main surviving scriptural collections, only one is strictly speaking a Tripiṭaka, the Pali corpus of the Theravādins. (The much later Chinese and Tibetan collections have much more complex subdivisions and can be called Tripiṭakas only metaphorically.) [*See* Buddhist Literature, *article on* Canonization.]

The Age of Foreign Invasions

The decline and fall of the Maurya dynasty (324–187) brought an end to an age of assured support for Buddhist monastic institutions. Political circumstances unfavorable to Buddhism began with persecution under Puṣyamitra Śuṅga (r. about 187–151). The Śuṅga dynasty would see the construction of some of the most important Buddhist sites of India: Bhārhut, Sāñcī, and Amarāvatī. But it also foreshadowed the beginning of Hindu dominance. The rising cult of Viṣṇu seemed better equipped to assimilate the religion of the people and win the support of the ruling classes. Although Buddhism served better as a universal religion that could unite Indians and foreign invaders, the latter did not always choose to become Buddhists. A series of non-Indian rulers—Greek, Parthian, Scythian (Saka), Kushan—would hesitate in their religious allegiances.

Among the Greek kings, the Buddhist tradition claims Menander (Milinda, c. 150 BCE) as one of its converts. The Scythian tribe of the Sakas, who invaded Bactriana around 130 BCE, roughly contemporaneous with the Yüeh-chih conquest of the Tokharians, would become stable supporters of Buddhism in the subcontinent. [*See* Inner Asian Religions.] Their rivals in South India, the Tamil dynasty of the Śātavāhana (220 BCE–236 CE), sponsored in Andhra the construction of major centers of worship at Amarāvatī and Nāgārjunīkoṇḍa. The Yüeh-chih (Kushans) also supported Buddhism, though perhaps less consistently. The most famous of their rulers, Kaṇiṣka, is represented by the literature as a pious patron of Buddhism (his dates are uncertain; proposed accession in 78 or 125 CE). During the Kushan period (c. 50–320 CE) the great schools of Gandhāra and Mathurā revolutionized Indian, especially Buddhist, art. Both the northern styles of Gandhāra and Mathurā and the southern school of Andhra combined iconic and ani-conic symbolization of the Buddha: the first Buddha images appeared around the third century of the common era, apparently independently and simultaneously in all three schools.

THE APPEARANCE OF SCHOOLS AND DENOMINATIONS

Any understanding of the history of composition of the canons, or of their significance in the history of the religion, is dependent on our knowledge of the geographic distribution, history, and doctrine of the various sects. Unfortunately, our knowledge in this regard is also very limited. [*See* Buddhism, Schools of, *overview article*.]

Developments in Doctrine and in Scholastic Speculation. As the original community of wandering mendicants settled in monasteries, a new type of religion arose, concerned with the preservation of a tradition and the justification of its institutions. Although the "forest dweller" continued as an ideal and a practice—some were still dedicated primarily to a life of solitude and meditation—the dominant figure became that of the monk-scholar. This new type of religious specialist pursued the study of the early tradition and moved its doctrinal systems in new directions. On the one hand, the old doctrines were classified, defined, and expanded. On the other hand, there was a growing awareness of the gap that separated the new developments from the transmitted creeds and codes. A set of basic or "original" teachings had to be defined, and the practice of exegesis had to be formalized. In fact, the fluidity and uncertainty of the earlier scriptural tradition may be one of the causes for the development of Buddhist scholasticism. By the time the canons were closed the degree of diversity and conflict among the schools was such, and the tradition was overall so fluid, that it was difficult to establish orthodoxy even when there was agreement on the basic content of the canons. In response to these problems Buddhists soon developed complicated scholastic studies.

At least some of the techniques and problems of this early scholasticism must go back to the early redactions of the Sūtra section of the canon, if not to precanonical stage. The genre of the *mātṛkā*, or doctrinal "matrices," is not an uncommon form of Sūtra literature. It is suggested in the redaction of certain sections of the Pali and Sarvāstivādin canons, is found in early Chinese translations (e.g., the *Dharmaśarīraka Sūtra* and the *Daśottara Sūtra*), and continues in Mahāyāna Sūtra literature. It is a literary form that probably represents not only an exegetic device but an early technique of doctrinal redaction—a hermeneutic that also served as the basis for the redaction of earlier strata of the oral transmission.

The Early Sects. Given the geographical and linguistic diversity of India and the lack of a central authority in the Buddhist community one can safely speculate that Buddhist sects arose early in the history of the religion. Tradition speaks of a first, but major, schism occurring at (or shortly after) the Second Council in Vaiśālī, one hundred years after the death of the founder. Whether the details are true or not, it is suggestive that this first split was between the Sthaviras and the Mahāsāṃghikas, the prototypes of the two major divisions of Buddhism: "Hīnayāna" and Mahāyāna.

After this schism new subdivisions arose, reaching by the beginning of the common era a total of approximately thirty different denominations or schools and subschools. Tradition refers to this state of sectarian division as the period of the "Eighteen Schools," since some of the early sources count eighteen groups. It is not clear when these arose. *Faut de mieux*, most Western scholars go along with classical Indian sources albeit with a mild skepticism, and try to sort out a consistent narrative from contradictory sources. Thus, we can only say that if we are to believe the Pali tradition, the Eighteen Schools must have been in existence already in the third century BCE, when a legendary Moggaliputtatissa compiled the *Kathāvatthu*. But such an early dating raises many problems. [*See the biography of Moggaliputtatissa.*]

In the same vein, we tend to accept the account of the Second Council that sees it as the beginning of a major split. In this version the main points of contention were monastic issues—the exact content and interpretation of the code. But doctrinal, ritual, and scholastic issues must have played a major role in the formation of separate schools. Many of the main points of controversy, for instance, centered on the question of the nature of the state of liberation and the status of the liberated person. Is the liberated human *(arhat)* free from all moral and karmic taint? Is the state of liberation *(nirvāṇa)* a condition of being or nonbeing? Can there be at the same time more than one fully awakened person *(samyaksaṃbuddha)* in one world system? Are persons already on their way to full awakening, the *bodhisattvas* or future Buddhas, deserving of worship? Do they have the ability to descend to the hells to help other sentient beings?

Among these doctrinal disputes one emerges as emblematic of the most important fissure in the Buddhist community. This was the polemic surrounding the exalted state of the *arhat* (Pali, *arahant*). Most of the Buddhist schools believed that only a few human beings could aspire to become fully awakened beings *(samyaksaṃbuddha),* others had to content themselves with the hope of becoming free from the burden of past *karman* and attaining liberation in *nirvāṇa,* without the extraordinary wisdom and virtue of Buddhahood. But the attainment of liberation was in itself a great achievement, and a person who was assured of an end to rebirth at the end of the present life was considered the most saintly, deserving of the highest respect, a "worthy" *(arhat).* Some of the schools even attributed to the *arhat* omniscience and total freedom from moral taint. Objections were raised against those who believed in the faultless wisdom of the *arhat,* including obvious limitations in their knowledge of everyday, worldly affairs. Some of these objections were formalized in the "Five Points" of Mahādeva, after its purported proponent. These criticisms can be interpreted either as a challenge to the belief in the superhuman perfection of the *arhat* or as a plea for the acceptance of their humanity. Traditionally, Western scholars have opted for the first of these interpretations. [*See* Arhat.]

The controversies among the Eighteen Schools identified each group doctrinally, but it seems unlikely that in the early stages these differences lead to major rifts in the community, with the exception of the schism between the two trunk schools of the Sthavira and the Mahāsāṃghika; and even then, there is evidence that monks of both schools often lived together in a single monastic community. Among the doctrinal differences, however, we can find the seeds of future dissension, especially in the controversies relating to ritual. The Mahīśāsakas, for instance, claimed that there is more merit in worshiping and making offerings to the *saṃgha* than in worshiping a stupa, as the latter merely contains the remains of a member of the *saṃgha* who is no more. The Dharmaguptakas replied that there is more merit in worshiping a stupa, because the Buddha's path and his present state (in *nirvāṇa*) are far superior to that of any living monk. Here we have a fundamental difference with both social and religious consequences, for the choice is between two types of communal hierarchies as well as between two types of spiritual orders. [*For further discussion of sectarian splits in early Buddhism, see* Buddhism, Schools of, *article on* Hīnayāna Buddhism. *For specific* nikāyas, *see* Sarvāstivāda; Sautrāntika; Mahāsāṃghika; *and* Theravāda.]

DEVELOPMENTS IN THE SCRIPTURAL TRADITION

Apart from the Theravāda recension of the Pali canon and some fragments of the Sarvāstivādin Sanskrit canon nothing survives of what must have been a vast and diverse body of literature. For most of the collections we only have the memory preserved in inscriptions referring to *piṭaka*s and *nikāya*s and an occasional reference in the extant literature.

According to the Pali tradition of Sri Lanka, the three parts of the Tripiṭaka were compiled in the language of the Buddha at the First Council. The Second Council introduced minor revisions in the Vinaya, and the Third Council added Moggaliputtatissa's *Kathāvatthu.* A few years later the canon resulting from this council, and a number of extracanonical commentaries, were transmitted to Sri Lanka by Mahinda. The texts were transmitted orally *(mukhapāṭhena)* for the next two centuries, but after difficult years of civil war and famine, King Vaṭṭagāmaṇī of Sri Lanka ordered the texts written down. This task was carried out between 35 and 32 BCE. In this way, it is said, the canon was preserved in the original language. Although the commentaries were by that time extant only in Sinhala, they continued to be transmitted in written form until they were retranslated into Pali in the fifth century CE.

Modern scholarship, however, questions the accuracy of several points in this account. Pali appears to be a literary language originating in Avantī, western India; it seems unlikely that it could be the vernacular of a man who had lived in eastern India all his life or, for that matter, the lingua franca of the early Magadhan kingdom. The Pali texts as they are preserved today show clear signs of the work of editors and redactors. Although much in them still has the ring of oral transmission, it is a formalized or ritualized oral tradition, far from the spontaneous preaching of a living teacher. Different strata of language, history, and doctrine can be recognized easily in these texts. There is abundant evidence that already at the stage of oral transmission the tradition was fragmented, different schools of "reciters" *(bhāṇaka)* preserving not only different corpuses (the eventual main categories of the canons) but also different recensions of the same corpus of literature. Finally, we have no way of knowing if the canon written down at the time of Vaṭṭagāmaṇī was the Tripiṭaka as we know it today. There is evidence to the contrary, for we are told that the great South Indian scholar Buddhaghosa revised the canon in the fifth century when he also edited the commentaries preserved in Sinhala and translated them into Pali, which suggests that Pali literature in general had gone through a period of deterioration before his time.

Most scholars, however, accept the tradition that would have the Pali canon belong to a date earlier than the fifth century; even the commentaries must represent an earlier stratum. However late may be its final recension, the Pali canon preserves much from earlier stages in the development of the religion.

Of the Sanskrit canon of the Sarvāstivāda school we only possess a few isolated texts and fragments in the original, mostly from Central Asia. However, extensive sections survive in Chinese translation. This canon is supposed to have been written down at a "Fourth Council" held in Jālandhara, Kashmir, about 100 CE, close to the time when the same school systematized its Abhidharma in a voluminous commentary called the *Mahāvibhāṣa*. If this legend is true, two details are of historical interest. We must note first the proximity in time of this compilation to the date of the writing down of the Pali canon. This would set the parameters for the closing of the "Hīnayāna" canons between the first century BCE and the first century CE. Second, the close connection between the closing of a canon and the final formulation of a scholastic system confirms the similar socioreligious function of both activities: the establishing of orthodoxy.

DEVELOPMENTS IN PRACTICE

The cult at this stage was still dominated by the practice of pilgrimage and by the cult of the *caitya*, as described above. However, we can imagine an intensification of the devotional aspect of ritual and a greater degree of systematization as folk belief and "high tradition" continued to interact. Sectarian differences probably began to affect the nature of the liturgies, as a body of liturgical texts became part of the common or the specific property of different groups of Buddhists. Among the earliest liturgical texts were the hymns in praise of the Buddha, especially the ones singing the many epithets of the Awakened One. Their use probably goes back to the earliest stages in the history of monastic ritual and may be closely connected with the practice of *buddhānusmṛti,* or meditation on the attributes of the Buddha. [*See also* Nien-fo.]

Pilgrimage Sites and Stupas. Many Buddhist practices and institutions remain apparently stable in the subcontinent until the beginnings of the common era. The monuments of Bhārhut and Sāñcī, for example, where we find the earliest examples of aniconic symbolism, represent a conservative Buddhism. Other signs of conservatism, however, confirm a continuous nonliterary cult. The oldest section at Sāñcī, the east gateway, dating from perhaps 90 to 80 BCE, preserves, next to the illustrated Jātakas, the woman and tree motifs, *yakṣa*s and *yakṣī*s (with the implied popular cult of male and female fertility deities), and the aniconic representations of the wheel, the footprint, the throne, and the tree.

The most advanced or innovative trait is the increasing iconographic importance of the previous lives of the Buddha, represented in the reliefs of Jātakas. These indicate a developed legend of the Buddha's past lives, a feature of the period that suggests the importance of past lives in the cult and in the future development of Mahāyāna. The most important cultic development of the pre-Mahāyāna period, however, was the shift from the commemorative ritual associated with the stupa and the aniconic symbol to the ritual of worship and devotion associated with the Buddha image.

After the beginning of the Christian era major developments in practice reflect outside influence as well as new internal developments. This is the time when the sects were beginning to commit to writing their sacred literature, but it is also the time of foreign invasions. These may have played a major role in the development of the Buddha image. Modern scholarship has debated the place of origin of this important cultic element and the causal factors that brought it about. Some, following Foucher, proposed a northwestern origin, and saw the Buddhas and *bodhisattva*s created under the influence of Greco-Roman art in Gandhāra (Kushan period) as the first images. Others, following Coomaraswamy, believed the first images were created in Andhra, as part of the natural development of a South Indian cult of the *yakṣa*s, and in the north central region of Mathurā. Be that as it may, the Buddha image dominates Buddhist iconography after the second century CE; stupas and Jātaka representations remain but play a secondary role.

There seems to be, especially in Mathurā art, an association between the Buddha image and solar symbolism, which suggests Central Asian or Iranian influences on Buddhism and may be closely related to the development of the new doctrinal conceptions, such as those that regarded the Buddha as "universal monarch" *(cakravartin)* and lord of the universe, and Buddhas and *bodhisattva*s as radiant beings. [*See* Cakravartin.] The abundance of *bodhisattva* images in Gandhāra, moreover, suggests the beginning of a gradual shift towards a conception of the ideal being as layman, or at least a shift in the way the *bodhisattva* was conceived (from merely an instance of a Buddha's past to the central paradigm of Buddhahood). [*See* Iconography, *article on* Buddhist Iconography.]

As a balance to the growing importance of the past lives of the Buddha, the process of redacting the scriptures also brought about the necessity of formulating a biography of the Buddha. The first "biographies" appear at the beginning of the common era, perhaps as late as the second century CE. Partial biographies appear in the literature of the Sarvāstivādins *(Lalitavistara)* and Lokottaravādins *(Mahāvastu)*. The first complete biography is a cultured poem in the *kāvya* style, the *Buddhacarita* of Aśvaghoṣa.

This is also a time when noncanonical literature flourished. Poets wrote Buddhist dramas and poetical recastings of canonical parables and legends. Aśvaghoṣa, for instance, wrote a drama on the life of Śāriputra, and a poem narrating the conversion of Nanda *(Saundarānanda)*. Developments in the literary tradition perhaps should be seen as reflecting other strata of the living tradition. Thus, the vitality of the Jātaka tradition is seen in its appearance as a literary genre in the *Jātakamālā* of Āryaśūra (fl. c. 150 CE). This classical poet is sometimes identified with Mātṛceṭa, who in his works (e.g., *Śatapañcaśatka*) gives us a highly cultured reflection of the hymns of praise (*stotras*) that must have been a regular part of the Buddhist cult of the day. In these hymns we already see the apotheosis of the Buddha figure, side by side with the newly redefined *bodhisattva* ideal.

Mystics and Intellectuals. The development of devotional Buddhism did not obscure the ascetic and contemplative dimensions of the religion. The system of meditation contained in the Nikāyas probably achieved its final form during this period. Diverse techniques for the development of enstasy and insight were conflated first in the canonical Sūtra literature, then in the Abhidharmic texts.

Side by side with the development of popular and monastic cults a new elite of religious specialists appeared, seeking to follow the Buddha's path through systematic study into the scriptures. They belonged to the tradition of the *mātṛkās* and composed treatises purporting to treat the "higher" Dharma *(abhidharma)*—or, what is perhaps the more correct etymology, treatises "on the Dharma." Although the analysis of meditational categories was an important aspect of these traditions, the scholar-monks were not always dedicated meditators. In fact, many of them must have made scholarship the prime objective of their religious life, leaving the practice of meditation to the forest monks. For the scholars, the goal was to account for the whole of Buddhism, in particular, the plethora of ancient doctrines and practices found in the canon. Above all, they sought to define and explain the ultimately real components of reality, the *dharmas*, into which one could analyze or explode the false conception of the self.

This critique was not without soteriological implications. The goal was conceived at times as ineffable, beyond the ken of human conception. Thus canonical literature describes the liberated person, the *arhat*, as follows:

> When bright sparks fly
> as the smith beats red-hot iron,
> and fade away,
> one cannot tell where they have gone.

> In the same way, there is no way of knowing
> the final destination of those who are truly free,
> who have crossed beyond the flood, bondage, and desire,
> obtaining unshakable bliss. (*Udāna*, p. 93)

But side by side with the tradition of ineffability, there was a need to define at the very least the process of liberation. For the gradual realization of selflessness was understood as personal growth. Accordingly, a set of standard definitions of liberation was accompanied by accepted descriptions of the stages on the path to liberation, or of degrees of spiritual achievement. The canonical collections already list, for instance, four types of saints *(āryapudgala):* the one who will be reborn no more *(arhat);* the one who will not come back to this world, the "non-returner" *(anāgamin);* the one who will return only once more *(sakṛdāgamin);* and the one who has entered the path to sainthood, the "stream-enterer" *(srotāpanna).* [*See also* Soteriology, *article on* Buddhist Soteriology.]

Canonical notions of levels or hierarchies in the path to liberation became the focus of much scholastic speculation—in fact, the presence of these categories in the canons may be a sign of scholastic influence on the redaction of the scriptures. The construction of complex systems of soteriology, conceived as maps or detailed descriptions of the path, that integrated the description and analysis of ethical and contemplative practices with philosophical argumentation, characterized the Abhidharmic schools. This activity contributed to the definition of the doctrinal parameters of the sects; but it also set the tone for much of future Buddhist dogmatics. The concerns of the Abhidharmists, ranging from the analysis of enstasy and the contemplative stages to the rational critique of philosophical views of reality, had a number of significant doctrinal consequences: (1) scholars began devising "maps of the path," or theoretical blueprints of the stages from the condition of a common human being *(pṛthag-jana)* to the exalted state of a fully awakened being *(samyaksaṃbuddha);* (2) Buddhist scholars engaged other Indian intellectuals in the discussion of broad philosophical issues; (3) various orthodox apologetics were developed, with the consequent freezing of a technical terminology common to most Buddhists; (4) the rigidity of their systems set the stage for a reaction that would lead to the creation of new forms of Buddhism.

The Sects and the Appearance of Mahāyāna

Most of the developments mentioned above overlap with the growth of a new spirit that changed the religion and eventually created a distinct form of Buddhist belief and practice. The new movement referred to itself as the "Great Vehicle" (Mahāyāna) to distinguish itself from other styles of Buddhism that the followers of the movement considered forms of a "Lesser Vehicle" (Hīnayāna). [*See* Buddhism, Schools of, *article on* Mahāyāna Buddhism.]

THE EARLY SCHOOLS OUTSIDE INDIA

If we accept the general custom of using the reign of Aśoka as the landmark for the beginning of the missionary spread of Buddhism, we may say that Buddhism reached the frontiers of India by the middle of the second century BCE. By the beginning of the common era it had spread beyond. In the early centuries of the era Mahāyāna and Hīnayāna spread in every direction; eventually certain areas would become predominantly Mahāyāna, others, predominantly Hīnayāna. [*See* Missions, *article on* Buddhist Missions, *and the biography of Aśoka.*]

Mahāyāna came to dominate in East and Central Asia—with the exception of Turkistan, where Sarvāstivādin monasteries flourished until the Muslim invasion and conversion of the region. Hīnayāna was slower to spread, and in some foreign lands had to displace Mahāyāna. It lives on in a school that refers to itself as the Theravāda, a Sinhala derivative of the Sthavira school. It spread throughout Southeast Asia where it continues to this day.

THE GREAT VEHICLE

The encounter of Buddhism with extra-Indian ethnic groups and the increasing influence of the laity gradually transformed the monastic child of shramanic Buddhism into a universal religion. This occurred in two ways. On the one hand, monasticism adapted to the changing circumstances, strengthened its ties to the laity and secular authorities, established a satisfactory mode of coexistence with nonliterary, regional forms of worship. Both Mahāyāna and Hīnayāna schools participated in this aspect of the process of adaptation. But Buddhism also redefined its goals and renovated its symbols to create a new synthesis that in some ways may be considered a new religion. The new style, the Mahāyāna, claimed to be a path for the many, the vehicle for the salvation of all sentient beings (hence its name, "The Great Vehicle"). Its distinctive features are: a tilt toward world affirmation, a laicized conception of the human ideal, a new ritual of devotion, and new definitions of the metaphysical and contemplative ideals.

The Origins of Mahāyāna. The followers of Mahāyāna claim the highest antiquity for its teachings. Their own myths of origin, however, belie this claim. Mahāyāna recognizes the fact that its teachings were not known in the early days of Buddhism by asserting that Śākyamuni revealed the Mahāyāna only to select *bodhisattvas* or heavenly beings who kept the texts hidden for centuries. One legend recounts that the philosopher Nāgārjuna had to descend to the underworld to obtain the Mahāyāna texts known as the "Perfection of Wisdom" (Prajñāpāramitā).

Western scholars are divided on the question of the dates and location of the origins of Mahāyāna. Some favor an early (beginning of the common era) origin among Mahāsāṃghika communities in the southeastern region of Andhra. Others propose a northwestern origin, among the Sarvāstivādins, close to the second and third centuries CE. It may be, however, that Mahāyāna arose by a gradual and complex process involving more than one region of India. It is clear that Mahāyāna was partly a reform movement, partly the natural development of pre-Mahāyāna Buddhism; still in another sense, it was the result of new social forces shaping the Indian subcontinent.

The theory of a southern origin assumes that the Mahāsāṃghika monastic centers of Andhra continued to develop some of the more radical ideals of the school, until some of these communities saw themselves as a movement completely distinct from other, so-called Hīnayāna schools. This theory also recognizes external influences: the Iranian invaders as well as the non-Aryan substratum of southern India, the first affecting the mythology of the celestial *bodhisattvas*, the second incorporating non-

Aryan concepts of the role of women into the mainstream of Buddhist religious ideals.

For the sake of clarity one could distinguish two types of causes in the development of Mahāyāna: social or external, and doctrinal or internal. Among the first one must include the Central Asian and Iranian influences mentioned above, the growing importance of the role of women and the laity, especially as this affected the development of the cultus, and the impact of the pilgrimage cycles. The foreign element is supposed to have introduced elements of light symbolism and solar cults, as well as a less ascetic bent.

Doctrinal factors were primarily the development of the myth of the former lives of Śākyamuni and the cult of former Buddhas, both of which contributed to a critique of the *arhat* ideal. The mythology of the Buddha's former lives as a *bodhisattva* led to the exaltation of the *bodhisattva* ideal over that of the *arhat*. The vows of the *bodhisattva* began to take the central role, especially as they were seen as an integral part of a developing liturgy at the center of which the dedication of merit was transformed as part of the exalted *bodhisattva* ideal.

It seems likely, furthermore, that visionaries and inspired believers had continued to compose *sūtras*. Some of these, through a gradual process we can no longer retrace, began to move away from the general direction of the older scholastic traditions and canonical redactors. Thus it happened that approximately at the time when the older schools were closing their canons, the Mahāyāna was composing a set of texts that would place it in a position of disagreement with, if not frank opposition to, the older schools. At the same time, the High Tradition began to accept Mahāyāna and therefore argue for its superiority; thus, a Mahāyāna *śāstra* tradition began to develop almost at the same time as the great Sarvāstivādin synthesis was completed.

In the West, the gap between Mahāyāna and Hīnayāna is sometimes exaggerated. It is customary to envision Mahāyāna as a revolutionary movement through which the aspirations of a restless laity managed to overcome an oppressive, conservative monastic establishment. Recent research suggests that the opposition between the laity and the religious specialists was not as sharp as had hitherto been proposed. Furthermore, it has become apparent that the monastic establishment continued to be a powerful force in Indian Mahāyāna. It seems more likely that Mahāyāna arose gradually and in different forms in various points of the subcontinent. A single name and a more or less unified ideology may have arisen after certain common aspirations were recognized. Be that as it may, it seems evident that the immediate causes for the arising of this new form of Buddhism were the appearance of new cultic forms and widespread dissatisfaction with the scholastic tradition.

Merit, Bodhisattvas, and the Pure Land. Inscriptional evidence shows that the doctrine of merit transference had an important role in the cultus even before the appearance of Mahāyāna. Although all Buddhists believe that virtuous thoughts and actions generate merit, which leads to a good rebirth, it appears that early Buddhists believed that individuals could generate merit only for themselves, and that merit could only lead to a better rebirth, not to liberation from the cycle of rebirth. By the beginning of the common era, however, some Buddhists had adopted a different conception of merit. They believed that merit could be shared or transferred, and that it was a factor in the attainment of liberation—so much so that they were offering their own merit for the salvation of their dead relatives.

Dedication of merit appears as one of the pivotal doctrines of the new Buddhism. Evidently, it served a social function: it made participation in Buddhist ritual a social encounter rather than a private experience. It also contributed to the development of a Buddhist high liturgy, an important factor in the survival of Buddhism and its assimilation of foreign elements, both in and outside India. [*See* Merit, *article on* Buddhist Concepts.]

This practice and belief interacted with the cult of former Buddhas and the mythology of the former lives to create a Buddhist system of beliefs in which the primary goal was to imitate the virtue of Śākyamuni's former lives, when he was a *bodhisattva* dedicated to the liberation of others rather than himself. To achieve this goal the believer sought to imitate Śākyamuni not as he appeared in his last life or after his enlightenment, when he sought and attained *nirvāṇa,* but by adopting a vow similar to Śākyamuni's former vow to seek awakening *(bodhi)* for the sake of all sentient beings. On the one hand, this shift put the emphasis on insight into the world, rather than escape from it. On the other hand, it also created a new form of ideal being and object of worship, the *bodhisattva*. [*See* Bodhisattva Path.]

Contemporary developments in Hindu devotionalism *(bhakti)* probably played an important role in the development of Buddhist liturgies of worship *(pūjā)*, but it would be a mistake to assume that the beginnings of Mahāyāna faith and ritual can be explained adequately by attributing them merely to external theistic influences. [*See* Bhakti.] For instance, the growth of a faith in rebirth in "purified Buddha fields," realms of the cosmos in which the merit and power of Buddhas and *bodhisattva*s create an environment where birth without suffering is possible, can be seen as primarily a Buddhist development. The new faith, generalized in India through the concept of the "Land of Bliss" (the "Pure Land" of East Asian Buddhism), hinged on faith in the vows of former *bodhisattva*s who chose to transfer or dedicate their merit to the purification of a special "field" or "realm." The influence of Iranian religious conceptions seems likely, however, and one may have to seek some of the roots of this belief among Central Asian converts. [*See* Pure and Impure Lands *and* Amitābha.]

Formation of a New Scriptural Tradition. With the new cult and the new ideology came a new body of scriptures. Mahāyāna *sūtra*s began to be composed probably around the beginning of the Christian era, and continued to be composed and redacted until at least the fifth or sixth century CE. Unlike the canons of the earlier schools, the Mahāyāna scriptures do not seem to have been collected into formal, closed canons in the land of their origin—even the collections edited in China and Tibet were never closed canons.

In its inception Mahāyāna literature is indistinguishable from the literature of some of the earlier schools. The *Prajñāpāramitā* text attributed to the Pūrvaśailas is probably an earlier version of one of the Mahāyāna texts of the same title; the *Ratnakūṭa* probably began as part of a Mahāsāṃghika canon; and the now lost *Dhāraṇī Piṭaka* of the Dharmaguptaka school probably contained prototypes of the *dhāraṇī-sūtra*s of the Mahāyāna tradition. The Mahāyānist monks never gave up the pre-Mahāyāna Vinaya. Many followed the Dharmaguptaka version, some the Mahāsāṃghika. Even the Vinaya of a school that fell squarely into the Hīnayāna camp, the Sarvāstivāda, was used as the basis for Mahāyāna monastic rule.

Still, the focus of much Mahāyāna rhetoric, especially in the earlier strata of the literature, is the critique of non-Mahāyāna forms of Buddhism, especially the ideal of the *arhat*. This is one of the leading themes of a work now believed to represent an early stage in the development of Mahāyāna, the *Raṣṭrapālaparipṛcchā,* a text of the *Ratnakūṭa* class. In this text, the monastic life is still exalted above all other forms of spiritual life, but the *bodhisattva* vows are presented for the first time as superior to the mere monastic vows.

It is difficult, if not impossible, to establish with any degree of certainty the early history of Mahāyāna literature. It seems, however, that the earliest extant Mahāyāna *sūtra* is the *Aṣṭasāhasrikāprajñāpāramitā,* or its verse rendering, the *Ratnaguṇa-saṃcayagāthā*. Both reflect a polemic within Buddhism, centering on a critique of the "low aspirations" of those Buddhists who chose not to take the vows of the *bodhisattvas*. The *Ratnaguṇa* defines the virtues of the *bodhisattva,* emphasizing the transcendental insight or "perfect wisdom" *(prajñāpāramitā)* that frees him from all forms of attachment and preconceived notions—including notions of purity and world renunciation. An important aspect or complement of this wisdom is skill in means *(upāya-kauśalya)*—defined here as the capacity to adapt thought, speech, and action to circumstances and to the ultimate purpose of Buddhist practice, freedom from attachment. This virtue allows the *bodhisattva* to remain in the world while being perfectly free from the world.

The *Aṣṭasāhasrikā* treats these same concepts, but also expands the concept of merit in at least two directions: (1) dedication of merit to awakening means here seeing through the illusion of merit as well as applying merit to the path of liberation; and (2) dedication of merit is an act of devotion to insight (wisdom, *prajñā*). As the goal and ground of all perfections *(pāramitā)*, Perfection of Wisdom is personified as the Mother of All Buddhas. She gives birth to the mind of awakening, but she is present in concrete form in the Sacred Book itself. Thus, the *Aṣṭasāhasrikāprajñāpāramitā Sūtra* is at the same time the medium expressing a sophisticated doctrine of salvation by insight and skill in means, the rationalization of a ritual system, and the object of worship. [*See* Pāramitās; Prajñā; *and* Upāya.]

Another early Mahāyāna text, the *Saddharmapuṇḍarīka* (Lotus Sutra), also attacks the *arhat* ideal. This *sūtra* is considered the paradigmatic text on the developed Buddhology of the Mahāyāna: the Buddha is presented as a supernatural being, eternal, unchanging; at the same time he is Buddha by virtue of the fact that he has become free from all conceptions of being and nonbeing. The Buddha never *attained* awakening or *nirvāṇa*—because he *is* Buddhahood, and has been in awakening and *nirvāṇa* since eternity, but also because there is no Buddhahood or *nirvāṇa* to be attained.

The widespread, but clearly not exclusively popular, belief in the Land of Bliss (Sukhāvatī) finds expression in two texts of the latter part of the early period (c. first to second century CE). The two *Sukhāvatī sūtras* express a faith in the saving grace of the *bodhisattva* Dharmākara, who under a former Buddha made the vow to purify his own Buddha field. The vows of this *bodhisattva* guarantee rebirth in his Land of Bliss to all those who think on him with faith. Rebirth in his land, furthermore, guarantees eventual enlightenment and liberation. The Indian history of these two texts, however, remains for the most part obscure.

The attitude of early Mahāyāna *sūtras* to laity and to women is relatively inconsistent. Thus, the *Ugradattaparipṛcchā* and the *Upāsakaśīla,* while pretending to preach a lay morality, use monastic models for the householder's life. But compared to the earlier tradition, the Mahāyāna represents a significant move in the direction of a religion that is less ascetic and monastic in tone and intent. Some Mahāyāna *sūtras* of the early period place laypersons in a central role. The main character in the *Gaṇḍavyūha,* for instance, is a young lay pilgrim who visits a number of *bodhisattvas* in search of the teaching. Among his teachers we find laymen and laywomen, as well as female night spirits and celestial *bodhisattvas*. The *Vimalakīrtinirdeśa* is more down-to-earth in its exaltation of the lay ideal. Although not without its miraculous events, it represents the demythologizing tendencies of Mahāyāna, which are often carried out to the extreme of affirming that the metaphoric meaning of one doctrine is exactly its opposite.

The Development of Mahāyāna

Although Buddhism flourished during the classical age of the Guptas, the cultural splendor in which it grew was also the harbinger of Hindu dominance. Sanskrit returned as the lingua franca of the subcontinent, and Hindu devotionalism began to displace the ideals of the Indic period. Mahāyāna must have been a divided movement even in its inception. Some of the divisions found in the Hīnayāna or pre-Mahāyāna schools from which Mahāyāna originated must have carried through into Mahāyāna itself. Unfortunately, we know much less of the early sectarian divisions in the movement than we know of the Eighteen Schools. It is clear, for instance, that the conception of the *bodhisattva* found among the Mahāsāṃghikas is different from that of the Sarvāstivādins. It appears also that the Prajñaptivādins conceived of the unconditioned *dharmas* in a manner different from other early schools. However, though we may speculate that some of these differences influenced the development of Mahāyāna, we have no solid evidence.

As pre-Mahāyāna Buddhism had developed a scholastic system to bolster its ideological position, Mahāyāna developed special forms of scholarly investigation. A new synthesis, in many ways far removed from the visionary faith underlying the religious aspects of Mahāyāna, grew in the established monasteries partly as a critique of earlier scholastic formulations, partly due to the need to explain and justify the new faith. Through this intellectual function the monastery reasserted its institutional position. Both monk and layman participated in giving birth to Mahāyāna and maintaining its social and liturgical life, but the intellectual leadership remained monastic and conservative. Therefore, Mahāyāna reform brought with it an element of continuity—monastic institutions and codes—that could be at the same time a cause for fossilization and stagnation. The monasteries would eventually grow to the point where they became a burden on society, at the same time that, as institutions of conservatism, they failed to adapt to a changing society.

Still, from the beginning of the Gupta dynasty to the earlier part of the Pāla dynasty the monasteries were centers of intellectual creativity. They continued to be supported under the Guptas, especially Kumāra Gupta I (414–455), who endowed a major monastery in a site in Bihar originally consecrated to Śāriputra. This monastic establishment, called Nālandā after the name of a local genie, probably had been active as a center of learning for several decades before Kumāra Gupta decided to give it special recognition. It would become the leading institution of higher learning in the Buddhist world for almost a thousand years. Together with the university of Valabhī in western India, Nālandā represents the scholastic side of Mahāyāna, which coexisted with a nonintellectual (not necessarily "popular") dimension, the outlines of which appear through archaeological remains, certain aspects of the Sūtra literature, and the accounts of Chinese pilgrims.

Some texts suggest a conflict between forest and city dwellers that may in fact reflect the expected tension between the ascetic and the intellectual, or the meditator and the religious politician. But, lest this simple schema obliterate important aspects of Buddhist religious life, one must note that there is plentiful evidence of intense and constant interaction between the philosopher, the meditator, and the devotee—often all three functions coinciding in one person. Furthermore, the writings of great philosophical minds like Asaṅga, Śāntideva, and Āryadeva suggest an active involvement of the monk-*bodhisattva* in the social life of the community. The nonintellectual dimensions of the religion, therefore, must be seen as one aspect of a dialectic that resolved itself in synthesis as much as rivalry, tension, or dissonance.

Mahāyāna faith and devotion, moreover, was in itself a complex phenomenon, incorporating a liturgy of the High Tradition (e.g., the *Hymn to the Three Bodies of the Buddha,* attributed to Aśvaghoṣa) with elements of the nonliterary and non-Buddhist religion (e.g., pilgrimage cycles and the cult of local spirits, respectively), as well as generalized beliefs such as the dedication of merit and the hope of rebirth in a purified Buddha Land.

DEVELOPMENTS IN DOCTRINE

In explaining the appearance of Mahāyāna, two extremes should be avoided carefully. On the one hand, one can exaggerate the points of continuity that link Mahāyāna with pre-Mahāyāna Buddhism; on the other, one can make a distinction so sharp that Mahāyāna appears as a radical break with the past, rather than a gradual process of growth. The truth lies somewhere between these two extremes: although Mahāyāna can be understood as a logical expansion of earlier Buddhist doctrine and practice, it is difficult to see how the phenomenon could be explained without assuming major changes in the social fabric of the Indian communities that provided the base for the religion. These changes, furthermore, are suggested by historical evidence.

The key innovations in doctrine can be divided into those that are primarily critiques of early scholastic constructs and those that reflect new developments in practice. In both types, of course, one should not ignore the influence of visionary or contemplative experience; but this aspect of the religion, unfortunately, cannot always be documented adequately. The most important doctrine of practical consequence was the *bodhisattva* doctrine; the most important theoretical development was the doctrine of emptiness *(śūnyatā)*. The first can be understood also as the result of a certain vision of the concrete manifestation of the sacred; the second, as the expression of a new type of mystical or contemplative experience.

The Bodhisattva. In pre-Mahāyāna Buddhism the term *bodhisattva* referred primarily to the figure of a Buddha from the time of his adoption of the vow to attain enlightenment to the point at which he attained Buddhahood. Even when used as an abstract designation of an ideal of perfection, the value of the ideal was determined by the goal: liberation from suffering. In the teachings of some of the Hīnayāna schools, however, the *bodhisattva* became an ideal with intrinsic value: to be a *bodhisattva* meant to adopt the vow *(praṇidhāna)* of seeking perfect awakening *for the sake of living beings;* that is, to follow the example set by the altruistic dedication of the Buddha in his former lives, when he was a *bodhisattva,* and not to aspire merely to individual liberation, as the *arhat*s were supposed to have done. The Mahāyāna made this critique its own, and the *bodhisattva* ideal its central religious goal.

This doctrinal stance accompanied a shift in mythology that has been outlined above: the belief in multiple *bodhisattva*s and the development of a complex legend of the former lives of the Buddha. There was likewise a change in ritual centered around the cult of the *bodhisattva,* especially of mythical *bodhisattva*s who were believed to be engaged in the pursuit of awakening primarily, if not exclusively, for the sake of assisting beings in need or distress. Closely allied with this was the increasing popularity of the recitation of *bodhisattva* vows.

Whereas the *bodhisattva* of early Buddhism stood for a human being on his way to become a liberated being, the *bodhisattva* that appears in the Mahāyāna reflects the culmination of a process of change that began when some of the Hīnayāna schools extended the apotheosis of the Buddha Śākyamuni to the *bodhisattva*—that is, when they idealized both the Buddha and the spiritual career outlined by the myth of his previous lives. Mahāyāna then extended the same religious revaluation to numerous mythical beings believed to be far advanced in the path of awakening. Accordingly, in its mythology Mahāyāna has more than one object of veneration. Especially in contrast to the more conservative Hīnayāna schools (the Sarvāstivāda and the Theravāda, for instance), Mahāyāna is the Buddhism of multiple Buddhas and *bodhisattva*s, residing in multiple realms, where they assist numberless beings on their way to awakening. [*See* Celestial Buddhas and Bodhisattvas.]

Accordingly, the early ideal of the *bodhisattva* as future Buddha is not discarded; rather it is redefined and expanded. As a theory of liberation, the characteristic position of Mahāyāna can be summarized by saying that it emphasizes *bodhi* and relegates *nirvāṇa* to a secondary position. Strictly speaking, this may represent an early split within the community rather than a shift in doctrine. One could speculate that it goes back to conflicting notions of means to liberation found among the shramanic religions: the conflict between enstasy and insight as means of liberation. But this analysis must be qualified by noting that the revaluation of *bodhi* must be seen in the context of the *bodhisattva* vow. The unique aspiration of the *bodhisattva* defines awakening as "awakening for the sake of all sentient beings." This is a concept that cannot be understood properly in the context of disputes regarding the relative importance of insight.

Furthermore, one should note that the displacement of *nirvāṇa* is usually effected through its redefinition, not by means of a rejection of the basic concept of "freedom from all attachment." Although the formalized texts of the vows often speak of the *bodhisattva* "postponing" his entrance into *nirvāṇa* until all living beings are saved, and the Buddha is asked in prayer to remain in the world without entering *nirvāṇa,* the central doctrine implies that a *bodhisattva* would not even consider a *nirvāṇa* of the type sought by the *arhat*. The *bodhisattva* is defined more by his aspiration for a different type of *nirvāṇa* than by a rejection or postponement of *nirvāṇa* as such. The gist of this new doctrine of *nirvāṇa* can be summarized in a definition of liberation as a state of peace in which the liberated person is neither attached to peace not attached to the turmoil of the cycle of rebirth. It is variously named and defined: either by an identity of *saṃsāra* and *nirvāṇa* or by proposing a *nirvāṇa* in which one can find no support *(apratiṣṭhita-nirvāṇa)*. [*See* Soteriology, *article on* Buddhist Soteriology.]

As noted above, in the early conception a *bodhisattva* is a real human being. This aspect of the doctrine is not lost in Mahāyāna, but preserved in the belief that the aspiration to perfect awakening (the *bodhicitta*) and the *bodhisattva* vow should be adopted by all believers. By taking up the vow—by conversion or by ritual repetition—the Mahāyāna Buddhist, monk or layperson, actualizes the *bodhicitta* and progresses toward the goal of becoming a *bodhisattva*. Also uniquely Mahāyāna is the belief that these human aspirants to awakening are not alone—they are accompanied and protected by "celestial *bodhisattva*s," powerful beings far advanced in the path, so perfect that they are free from both rebirth and liberation, and can now choose freely if, when, and where they are to be reborn. They engage freely in the process of rebirth only to save living beings.

What transforms the human and ethical ideal into a religious ideal, and into the object of religious awe, is the scale in which the *bodhisattva* path is conceived. From the first aspiration to awakening *(bodhicitta)* and the affirmation of the vow to the attainment of final enlightenment and liberation, countless lives intervene. The *bodhisattva* has to traverse ten stages *(bhūmi)*, beginning with the intense practice of the virtue of generosity (primarily a lay virtue), passing through morality in the second stage, patience in the third, then fortitude, meditation, insight, skill in means, vows, powers, and the highest knowledge of a Buddha. The stages, therefore, correspond with the ten perfections *(pāramitā)*. Although all perfections are practiced in every stage, they are mastered in the order in which they are listed in the scheme of the stages, suggesting at one end of the spectrum a simple and accessible practice for the majority of believers, the human *bodhisattva*, and at the other end a stage clearly unattainable in the realm of normal human circumstances, reserved for semidivine Buddhas and *bodhisattva*s, the object of worship. Although some exceptional human beings may qualify for the status of advanced *bodhisattva*s, most of these ideal beings are the mythic objects of religious fervor and imagination.

Among the mythic or celestial *bodhisattva*s the figure of Maitreya—destined to be the next Buddha of this world system after Śākyamuni—clearly represents the earliest stage of the myth. His cult is especially important in East Asian Buddhism. Other celestial *bodhisattva*s include Mañjuśrī, the *bodhisattva* of wisdom, the patron of scripture, obviously less important in the general cultus but an important *bodhisattva* in monastic devotion. The most important liturgical role is reserved for Avalokiteśvara, the *bodhisattva* of compassion, whose central role in worship is attested by archaeology. [*See also* Maitreya; Mañjuśrī; *and* Avalokiteśvara.]

Emptiness. The doctrine of emptiness *(śūnyatā)* represents a refinement of the ancient doctrine of no-self. In some ways it is merely an extension of the earlier doctrine: the denial of the substantial reality of the self and what belongs to the self, as a means to effect a breaking of the bonds of attachment. The notion of emptiness, however, expresses a critique of our common notions of reality that is much more radical than the critique implicit in the doctrine of no-self. The Mahāyāna critique is in fact unacceptable to other Buddhists, for it is in a manner of speaking a critique of Buddhism. Emptiness of all things implies the groundlessness of all ideas and conceptions, including, ultimately, Buddhist doctrines themselves.

The doctrine of emptiness was developed by the philosophical schools, but clearly inspired by the tradition of the Mahāyāna *sūtras*. Thus we read: "Even *nirvāṇa* is like a magical creation, like a dream, how much more any other object or idea *(dharma)*. . . ? Even a Perfect Buddha is like a magical creation, like a dream. . ." (*Aṣṭasāhasrikā*, p. 40). The practical correlate of the doctrine of emptiness is the concept of "skill in means" *(upāya):* Buddhist teachings are not absolute statements about reality, they are means to a higher goal beyond all views. In their cultural context these two doctrines probably served as a way of making Buddhist doctrine malleable to diverse populations. By placing the truth of Buddhism beyond the specific content of its religious practices, these two doctrines justified adaptation to changing circumstances and the adoption of new religious customs.

But emptiness, like the *bodhisattva* vows, also reflects the Mahāyāna understanding of the ultimate experience of Buddhism—understood both as a dialectic and a meditational process. This experience can be described as an awareness that nothing is self-existent. Dialectically, this means that there is no way that the mind can consistently think of any thing as having an existence of its own. All concepts of substance and existence vanish when they are examined closely and rationally. As a religious experience the term *emptiness* refers to a direct perception of this absence of self-existence, a perception that is only possible through mental cultivation, and which is a liberating experience. Liberation, in fact, has been redefined in a way reminiscent of early texts such as the *Suttanipāta*. Liberation is now the freedom resulting from the negation of all assumptions about reality, even Buddhist assumptions.

> The cessation of grasping and reifying,
> calming the plural mind—this is bliss.
> The Buddha never taught any thing/doctrine [*dharma*]
> to anyone anywhere.
> (*Madhyamakakārikā* 25.24)

Finally, emptiness is also an affirmation of the immanence of the sacred. Applied to the turmoil of the sphere of rebirth *(saṃsāra)*, it points to the relative value and reality of the world and at the same time transforms it into the sacred, the experience of awakening. Applied to the sphere of liberation *(nirvāṇa)*, emptiness is a critique of the conception of liberation as a religious goal outside the world of impermanence and suffering. [*See* Śūnyam and Śūnyatā.]

Other Views of the Absolute. Mahāyāna developed early notions of the supernatural and the sacred that guaranteed an exalted status to the symbols of its mystical and ethical ideals. Its notion of extraordinary beings populating supernal Buddha fields and coming to the aid of suffering sentient beings necessitated a metaphysic and cosmology that could offer concrete images of a transcendent sacred. Accordingly, the abstract, apophatic concept of emptiness was often qualified by, or even rejected in favor of, positive statements and concrete images.

Pre-Mahāyāna traditions had emphasized impermanence and no-self: to imagine that there is permanence in the impermanent is the most noxious error. Mahāyāna introduced the notion of emptiness, urging us to give up the notion of permanence, but to give up the notion of impermanence as well. Within the Mahāyāna camp others proposed that there was something permanent within the impermanent. Texts like the [*Mahāyāna*] *Mahāparinirvāṇa Sūtra* asserted that the Buddha himself had taught a doctrine of permanence: the seed of Buddhahood, innate enlightenment, is permanent, blissful, pure—indeed, it is the true self, present in the impermanent mind and body of sentient beings.

The Tathāgata as object of worship was associated with "suchness" *(tathatā)*, his saving actions were seen as taking effect in a world formed in the image of the Dharma and its ultimate truth *(dharmadhātu)*, and his form as repository of all goodness and virtue represented his highest form. [*See* Tathatā.]

A doctrine common to all Mahāyānists sought to establish a link between the absolute and common human beings. The Tathāgata was conceived of as having several aspects to his person: the human Buddha or "Body of Magical Apparition" *(nirmāṇakāya)*, that is, the historical persons of Buddhas; the transcendent sacred, the Buddha of the paradises and Buddha fields, who is also the form that is the object of worship *(saṃbhogakāya)*; and the Buddha as Suchness, as nonduality, the *tathāgata* as embodiment of the *dharmadhātu*, called the "Dharma Body" *(dharmakāya)*.

DEVELOPMENTS IN PRACTICE

The practice of meditation was for the Mahāyānist part of a ritual process beginning with the first feelings of compassion for other sentient beings, formulating the vow, including the expression of a strong desire to save all sentient beings and share one's merit with them, followed by the cultivation of the analysis of all existents, reaching a pinnacle in the experience of emptiness but culminating in the dedication of these efforts to the salvation of others.

Worship and Ritual. The uniquely Mahāyāna aspect of the ritual is the threefold service *(triskandhaka)*. Variously defined, this bare outline of the essential Mahāyāna ritual is explained by the seventh-century poet Śāntideva as consisting of a confession of sins, formal rejoicing at the merit of others, and a request to all Buddhas that they remain in the world for the sake of suffering sentient beings. A pious Buddhist was expected to perform this threefold ritual three times in the day and three times in the night.

A text known as the *Triskandhaka,* forming part of the *Upālipariprcchā,* proves the central role of confession and dedication of merit. The act of confession is clearly a continuation of the ancient Prātimokṣa ritual. Other elements of continuity include a link with early nonliterary tradition (now integrated into scripture) in the role of the dedication of merit, and a link with the general Buddhist tradition of the Three Refuges.

More complicated liturgies were in use. Several versions remain in the extant literature. Although many of them are said to be "the sevenfold service" *(saptavidhānuttarapūjā)*, the number seven is to be taken as an abstract number. The most important elements of the longer liturgies are the salutation to the Buddhas and *bodhisattvas*, the act of worship, the act of contrition, delight in the merit of others, and the dedication of merit. Hsüan-tsang, the seventh-century Chinese pilgrim to India, describes, albeit cursorily, some of the liturgies in use in the Indian monasteries of his time.

Most common forms of ritual, however, must have been less formalized and less monkish. The common rite is best represented by the litany of Avalokiteśvara, preserved in the literature and the monuments. In its literary form it is a solemn statement of the *bodhisattva*'s capacity to save from peril those who call on his name. But in actual practice, one can surmise, the cult of Avalokiteśvara included then, as it does today in East Asia, prayers of petition and apotropaic invocations.

The basic liturgical order of the literary tradition was embellished with elements from general Indian religious custom, especially from the styles of worship called *pūjā*. These included practices such as bathing the sacred image, carrying it in procession, offering cloth, perfume, and music to the icon, and so forth. [*See* Pūjā, *especially the article on* Buddhist Pūjā.]

Ritual practices were also expanded in the monastic tradition. For instance, another text also going by the title *Triskandhaka* (but preserved only in Tibetan translation) shows an intimate connection between ritual and meditation, as it integrates—like many monastic manuals of meditation—the typical daily ritual cycle with a meditation session.

Meditation. The practice of meditation was as important in the Mahāyāna tradition as it had been before. The maps of the path and the meditation manuals of Mahāyāna Buddhists give us accounts, if somewhat idealized ones, of the process of meditation. Although no systematic history of Mahāyāna meditation has been attempted yet, it is obvious that there are important synchronic and diachronic differences among Mahāyāna Buddhists in India. Considering, nevertheless, only those elements that are common to the various systems, one must note first an element of continuity with the past in the use of a terminology very similar to that of the Mahīśāsakas and the Sarvāstivāda, and in the acceptance, with little change, of traditional lists of objects and states of contemplation. [*See* Meditation, *article on* Buddhist Meditation.]

The interpretation of the process, however, and the definition of the higher stages of contemplation differed radically from that of the Hīnayāna schools. The principal shift is in the definition of the goal as a state in which the object of contemplation *(ālambana)* is no longer present to the mind *(nirālambana)*. All the mental images (or "marks," *nimitta, saṃjñā*) that form the basis for conceptual thought and attachment must be abandoned through a process of mental calm and analysis, until the contemplative reaches a state of peaceful concentration free of mental marks *(ānimitta)*, free of conceptualizations *(nirvikalpa-samādhi)*.

These changes in contemplative theory are closely connected to the abandonment of the *dharma* theory and the doctrine of no-self as the theoretical focus of speculative mysticism. One may say that the leading theme of Mahāyāna contemplative life is the meditation on emptiness. But one must add that the scholastic traditions are very careful to define the goal as constituted by both emptiness and compassion *(karuṇā)*. The higher state of freedom from conceptions (the "supramundane knowledge") must be followed by return to the world to fulfill the vows of the *bodhisattva*—the highest contemplative stage is, at least in theory, a preparation for the practice of compassion. [*See* Karuṇā.]

The New Ethics. The *bodhisattva* ideal also implied new ethical notions. Two themes prevail in Mahāyāna ethical speculation: the altruistic vow and life in the world. Both themes reflect changes in the social context of Buddhism: a greater concern, if not a stronger role for, lay life and its needs and aspirations and a cultural context requiring universal social values. The altruistic ideal is embodied in the *bodhisattva* vows and in the creation of a new set of ethical rules, commonly known as the "Bodhisattva Vinaya." A number of Mahāyāna texts are said to represent this new "Vinaya." Among these, the *Bodhisattvaprātimokṣa* was especially important in India. It prescribes a liturgy for the ritual adoption of the *bodhisattva* vows, which is clearly based on the earlier rites of ordination *(upasaṃpadā)*. Although the Mahāyāna Vinaya Sūtras never replaced in India the earlier monastic codes, they preserved and transmitted important, and at times obligatory, rites of monastic and lay initiation, and were considered essential supplements to traditional monastic Vinaya. [*See also* Buddhist Ethics.]

The High Tradition and the Universities

The most important element in the institutionalization of Mahāyāna was perhaps the establishment of Buddhist universities. In these centers of learning the elaboration of Buddhist doctrine became the most important goal of Buddhist monastic life. First at Nālandā and Valabhī, then, as the Pāla dynasty took control of East Central India (c. 650), at the universities of Vikramaśīla and Odantapurī, Mahāyāna scholars trained disciples from different parts of the Buddhist world and elaborated subtle systems of textual interpretation and philosophical speculation.

THE MAHĀYĀNA SYNTHESIS

Although eventually they would not be able to compete with more resilient forms of Buddhism and Hinduism, the Mahāyāna scholars played a leading role in the creation of a Mahāyāna synthesis that would satisfy both the intelligentsia and the common believers for at least five hundred years. Devotion, ritual, ethics, metaphysics, and logic formed part of this monument to Indian philosophical acumen. Even as the ruthless Mihirakula, the Ephthalite ("White") Hun, was invading India from the northwest (c. 500–528) and the Chalukya dynasty was contributing to a Hindu renaissance in the southwest (c. 550–753), India allowed for the development of great minds—such distinguished philosophical figures as Dignāga and Sthiramati, who investigated subtle philosophical issues. Persecution by Mihirakula (c. 550) was followed by the reign of one of the great patrons of Buddhism, Harṣa Vardhana (c. 605–647). Once more Buddhism was managing to survive on the seesaw of Indian politics.

SCHOOLS

The scholastic tradition of Mahāyāna can be divided into three schools: Mādhyamika (Madhyamaka), Yogācāra, and the school of Sāramati. The first two dominated the intellectual life of Mahāyāna in India. The third had a short-lived but important influence on Tibet, and indirectly may be considered an important element in the development of East Asian Buddhism.

Mādhyamika. The founder of this school can also be regarded as the father of Mahāyāna scholasticism and philosophy. Nāgārjuna (fl. c. 150 CE) came from South India, possibly from the Amarāvatī region. Said to have been the advisor to one of the Śātavāhana monarchs, he became the first major philosopher of Mahāyāna and a figure whose ideas influenced all its schools. The central theme of his philosophy is emptiness *(śūnyatā)* understood as a corollary of the pre-Mahāyāna theory of dependent origination. Emptiness is the Middle Way between affirmations of being and nonbeing. The extremes of existence and nonexistence are avoided by recognizing certain causal relations (e.g., the path and liberation) without predicating a self-existence or immutable essence *(svabhāva)* to either cause or effect. To defend his views without establishing a metaphysical thesis, Nāgārjuna argues by reducing to the absurd all the alternative philosophical doctrines recognized in his day. For his own "system," Nāgārjuna claims to have no thesis to affirm beyond his rejection of the affirmations and negations of all metaphysical systems. Therefore, Nāgārjuna's system is "the school of the Middle" *(madhyamaka)* both as an ontology (neither being nor nonbeing) and as a logic (neither affirmation nor negation). In religious terms, Nāgārjuna's Middle Way is summarized in his famous statement that *saṃsāra* and *nirvāṇa* are the same. [*See the biography of Nāgārjuna.*]

Three to four centuries after Nāgārjuna the Mādhyamika school split into two main branches, called Prāsaṅgika and Svātantrika. The first of these, represented by Buddhapālita (c. 500) and Candrakīrti (c. 550–600), claimed that in order to be faithful to the teachings of Nāgārjuna, philosophers had to confine themselves to the critique of opposing views by *reductio ad absurdum*. The Svātantrikas, on the other hand, claimed that the Mādhyamika philosopher had to formulate his own thesis; in particular, he needed his own epistemology. The main exponent of this view was Buddhapālita's great critic Bhāvaviveka (c. 500–550). The debate continued for some time but was eclipsed by other philosophical issues; for the Mādhyamika school eventually assimilated elements of other Mahāyāna traditions, especially those of the logicians and the Yogācārins. [*See the biographies of Buddhapālita, Bhāvaviveka, and Candrakīrti.*]

Mādhyamika scholars also contributed to the development of religious literature. Several hymns *(stava)* are attributed to Nāgārjuna. His disciple Āryadeva discusses the *bodhisattva*'s career in his *Bodhisattva-yogācāra-catuḥśataka*, although the work deals mostly with philosophical issues. Two anthological works, one attributed to Nāgārjuna, the *Sūtrasamuccaya,* and the other to the seventh-century Śāntideva, the *Śikśāsamuccaya,* became guides to the ritual and ethical practices of Mahāyāna. Śāntideva also wrote a "guide" to the *bodhisattva*'s career, the *Bodhicaryāvatāra,* a work that gives us a sampling of the ritual and contemplative practices of Mādhyamika monks, as well as a classical survey of the philosophical issues that engaged their attention. [*See also* Mādhyamika *and the biographies of Āryadeva and Śāntideva.*]

Yogācāra. Approximately two centuries after Nāgārjuna, during the transition period from Kushan to Gupta power, a new school of Mahāyāna philosophy arose in the northwest. The founders of this school, the brothers Asaṅga (c. 310–390) and Vasubandhu (c. 320–400), had begun as scholars in the Hīnayāna schools. Asaṅga, the elder brother, was trained in the Mahīśāsaka school. Many important features of the Abhidharma theories of this school remained in Asaṅga's Mahāyāna system. Vasubandhu, who converted to Mahāyāna after his brother had become an established scholar of the school, began as a Sautrāntika with an extraordinary command of Sarvāstivādin theories. Therefore, when he did become a Mahāyānist he too brought with him a Hīnayāna scholastic grid on which to organize and rationalize Mahāyāna teachings.

The school founded by the two brothers is known as the Yogācāra, perhaps following the title of Asaṅga's major work, the *Yogācārabhūmi* (sometimes attributed to Maitreya), but clearly expressing the centrality of the practice of self-cultivation, especially through meditation. In explaining the experiences arising during the practice of yoga, the school proposes the two doctrines that characterize it: (1) the experience of enstasy leads to the conviction that there is nothing but mind *(cittamātratā)*, or the world is nothing but a perceptual construct *(vijñaptimātratā)*; (2) the analysis of mind carried out during meditation reveals different levels of perception or awareness, and, in the depths of consciousness, the basis for rebirth and karmic determination, a storehouse consciousness *(ālaya-vijñāna)* containing the seeds of former actions. Varying emphasis on these two principles characterize different modes of the doctrine. The doctrine of mind-only dominates Vasubandhu's *Viṃśatikā* and *Triṃśikā*; the analysis of the *ālaya-vijñāna* is more central to Asaṅga's doctrine. Since both aspects of the doctrine can be understood as theories of consciousness *(vijñāna)*, the school is sometimes called Vijñānavāda.

One of the first important divisions within the Yogācāra camp reflected geographical as well as doctrinal differences. The school of Valabhī, following Sthiramati (c. 500–560), opposed the Yogācārins of Nālandā, led by Dharmapāla (c. 530–561). The point at issue, whether the pure mind is the same as the storehouse consciousness, illustrates the subtleties of Indian philosophical polemics but also reflects the influence of another school, the school of Sāramati, as well as the soteriological concerns underlying the psychological theories of Yogācāra. The debate on this point would continue in the Mādhyamika school, involving issues of the theory of perception as well as problems in the theory of the liberated mind. [*See also* Yogācāra; Vijñāna; Ālaya-vijñāna; *and the biographies of Asaṅga, Vasubandhu, Sthiramati, Dharmapāla, and Śīlabhadra.*]

Tathāgata-garbha Theory. Another influential school followed the tendency—already expressed in some Mahāyāna *sūtras*—toward a positive definition or description of ultimate reality. The emphasis in this school was on the ontological basis for the experience and virtues of Buddhahood. This basis was found in the underlying or innate Buddhahood of all beings. The school is known under two names; one describes its fundamental doctrine, the theory of *tathāgata-garbha* (the presence of the Tathāgata in all beings), the other refers to its purported systematizer, Sāramati (c. 350–450). The school's emphasis on a positive foundation of being associates it closely with the thought of Maitreyanātha, the teacher of Asaṅga, to whom is often attributed one of the fundamental texts of the school, the *Ratnagotravibhāga*. It may be that Maitreya's thought gave rise to two lines of interpretation—*tathāgata-garbha* and *cittamātratā*.

Sāramati wrote a commentary on the *Ratnagotravibhāga* in which he explains the process whereby innate Buddhahood becomes manifest Buddhahood. The work is critical of the theory of emptiness and describes the positive attributes of Buddhahood. The *bodhisattva*'s involvement in the world is seen not so much as the abandonment of the bliss of liberation as it is the manifestation of the Absolute *(dharmadhātu)* in the sphere of sentient beings, a concept that can be traced to Mahāsāṃghika doctrines. The *dharmadhātu* is a positive, metaphysical absolute, not only eternal, but pure, the locus of ethical, soteric, and epistemological value. This absolute is also the basis for the *gotra,* or spiritual lineage, which is a metaphor for the relative potential for enlightenment in living beings. [*See also* Tathāgatagarbha.]

The Logicians. An important development in Buddhist scholarship came about as a result of the concern of scholastics with the rules of debate and their engagement in philosophical controversies with Hindu logicians of the Nyāya school. Nāgārjuna and Vasubandhu wrote short treatises on logic, but a creative and uniquely Buddhist logic and epistemology did not arise until the time of Dignāga (c. 480–540), a scholar who claimed allegiance to Yogācāra but adopted a number of Sautrāntika doctrines. The crowning achievement of Buddhist logic was the work of Dharmakīrti (c. 600–650), whose *Pramāṇavārttika* and its *Vṛtti* revised critically the whole field. Although his work seems on the surface not relevant for the history of religion, it is emblematic of the direction of much of the intellectual effort of Mahāyāna scholars after the fifth century. [*See the biographies of Dignāga and Dharmakīrti.*]

Yogācāra-Mādhyamika Philosophers. As India moved away from the security of the Gupta period, Mahāyāna Buddhist philosophy gradually moved in the direction of eclecticism. By the time the university at Vikramaśīla was founded in the eighth century the dominant philosophy at Nālandā was a combination of Mādhyamika and Yogācāra, with the latter as the qualifying term and Mādhyamika as the core of the philosophy. This movement had roots in the earlier Svātantrika Mādhyamika and like its predecessor favored the formulation of ontological and epistemological theses in defense of Nāgārjuna's fundamental doctrine of emptiness. The most distinguished exponent of this school was Śāntirakṣita (c. 680–740); but some of his theories were challenged from within the movement by his contemporary Jñānagarbha (c. 700–760). The greatest contribution to religious thought, however, came from their successors. Kamalaśīla (c. 740–790), a disciple of Śāntirakṣita who continued the latter's mission in Tibet, wrote a number of brilliant works on diverse aspects of philosophy. He traveled to Tibet, where he wrote three treatises on meditation and the *bodhisattva* path, each called *Bhāvanākrama,* which must be counted among the jewels of Indian religious thought. [*See the biographies of Śāntirakṣita and Kamalaśīla.*]

NEW SCRIPTURES

The philosophers found their main source of inspiration in the Mahāyāna *sūtras,* most of which did not advocate clearly defined philosophical theories. Some *sūtras,* however, do express positions that can be associated with the doctrines of particular schools. Although scholars agree that these compositons are later than texts without a clear doctrinal affiliation, the connection between the *sūtras* and the schools they represent is not always clear.

For instance, some of the characteristic elements of the school of Sāramati are clearly pre-Mahāyānic, and can also be found in a number of *sūtras* from the *Avataṃsaka* and *Ratnakūṭa* collections. However, Sāramati appealed to a select number of Mahāyāna *sūtras* that clustered around the basic themes of the school. Perhaps the most famous is the *Srīmālādevīsiṃhanāda*, but equally important are the [*Mahāyāna*] *Mahāparinirvāṇa Sūtra*, the *Anūnatvāpūrṇatvanirdeśa*, and the *Dhāraṇīrāja*.

A number of Mahāyāna *sūtras* of late composition were closely associated with the Yogācāra school. Although they were known already at the time of Asaṅga and Vasubandhu, in their present form they reflect a polemic than presupposes some form of proto-Yogācāra theory. Among these the *Laṅkāvatāra* and the *Saṃdhinirmocana* are the most important from a philosophical point of view. The first contains an early form of the theory of levels of *vijñāna.*

DECLINE OF MAHĀYĀNA

It is difficult to assess the nature and causes of the decay of Mahāyāna in India. Although it is possible to argue that the early success of Mahāyāna led to a tendency to look inward, that philosophers spent their time debating subtle metaphysical, logical, or even grammatical points, the truth is that even during the period of technical scholasticism, constructive religious thought was not dormant. But it may be that as Mahāyāna became more established and conventional, the natural need for religious revival found expression in other vehicles. Most likely Mahāyāna thinkers participated in the search for new forms of expression, appealing once more to visionary, revolutionary and charismatic leaders. But the new life gradually would adopt an identity of its own, first as Tantric Buddhism, eventually as Hinduism. For, in adopting Tantric practices and symbols, Mahāyāna Buddhists appealed to a symbolic and ritual world that fit naturally with a religious substratum that was about to become the province of Hinduism. [*For Hindu Tantrism, see* Tantrism *and* Hindu Tantric Literature.]

The gradual shift from Mahāyāna to Tantra seems to have gained momentum precisely at the time when Mahāyāna philosophy was beginning to lose its creative energy. We know of Tantric practices at Nālandā in the seventh century. These practices were criticized by the Nālandā scholar Dharmakīrti but apparently were accepted by most distinguished scholars of the same institution during the following century. As Tantra gained respectability, the Pāla monarchs established new centers of learning, rivaling Nālandā. We may say that the death of its great patron, King Harṣa, in 657 signals the decline of Mahāyāna, whereas the construction of the University of Vikramaśīla under Dharmapāla about the year 800 marks the beginning of the Tantric period. [*For Buddhist Tantrism, see* Buddhism, Schools of, *article on* Esoteric Buddhism.]

Tantric Innovations

As with Mahāyāna, we must assume that Tantra reflects social as well as religious changes. Because of the uncertainties of the date of its origin, however, few scholars have ventured any explanation for the arising of Tantra. Some advocate an early origin for Tantra, suggesting that the literature existed as an esoteric practice for many centuries before it ever came to the surface. If this were the case, then Tantra must have existed as some kind of underground movement long before the sixth century. But this theory must still explain the sudden appearance of Tantrism as a mainstream religion.

In its beginnings, Buddhist Tantra may have been a minority religion, essentially a private cult incorporating elements from the substratum frowned upon by the Buddhist establishment. It echoed ancient practices such as the critical rites of the *Atharvaveda* tradition, and the initiatory ceremonies, Aryan and non-Aryan, known to us from other Brahmanic sources. Starting as a marginal phenomenon, it eventually gained momentum, assuming the same role Mahāyāna had assumed earlier; a force of innovation and a vehicle for the expression of dissatisfaction with organized religion. The followers of Tantra became the new critics of the establishment. Some asserted the superiority of techniques of ritual and meditation that would lead to a direct, spontaneous realization of Buddhahood in this life. As wandering saints called *siddhas* ("possessed of *siddhi*," i.e., realization or magical power), they assumed the demeanor of madmen, and abandoned the rules of the monastic code. [*See* Mahāsiddhas.] Others saw Tantra as the culmination of Mahāyāna and chose to integrate it with earlier teachings, following established monastic practices even as they adopted beliefs that challenged the traditional assumptions of Buddhist monasticism.

The documented history of Tantra, naturally, reveals more about the second group. It is now impossible to establish with all certainty how the substratum affected Buddhist Tantra—whether, for instance, the metaphoric use of sexual practices preceded their explicit use, or vice versa. But is seems clear that the new wandering ascetics and their ideology submitted to the religious establishment even as they changed it. Tantra followed the pattern of cooperation with established religious institutions set by Mahāyāna in its relationship to the early scholastic establishment. Tantric monks would take the *bodhisattva* vows and receive monastic ordination under the pre-Mahāyāna code. Practitioners of Tantra would live in the same monastery with non-Tantric Mahāyāna monks. Thus Tantric Buddhism became integrated into the Buddhist high tradition even as the *siddhas* continued to challenge the values of Buddhist monasticism.

Although it seems likely that Tantric Buddhism existed as a minority, esoteric practice among Mahāyāna Buddhists before it made its appearance on the center stage of Indian religion, it is now impossible to know for how long and in what form it existed before the seventh century. The latter date alone is certain because the transmission of Tantra to China is marked by the arrival in the Chinese capitals of Tantric masters like Śubhākarasiṃha (arrives in Ch'ang-an 716) and Vajrabodhi (arrives in Lo-yang 720), and we can safely assume that the exportation of Tantra beyond the Indian border could not have been possible without a flourishing activity in India. [*See the biographies of Vajrabodhi, Śubhākarasiṃha, and Amoghavajra.*] Evidence for an earlier origin is found in the occasional reference, critical or laudatory, to *mantras* and *dhāraṇīs* in the literature of the seventh century (Dharmakīrti, Śāntideva) and the presence of proto-Tantric elements in Mahāyāna *sūtras* that must date from at least the fourth century *(Gaṇḍavyūha, Vimalakīrtinirdeśa, Saddharmapuṇḍarīka).*

Tantra in general makes use of ritual, symbolic, and doctrinal elements of earlier form of Buddhism. Especially the apotropaic and mystical formulas called *mantras* and *dhāraṇis* gain a central role in Tantrayāna. [*See* Mantra.] The *Mahāmāyūrī*, a proto-Tantric text of the third or fourth century, collects apotropaic formulas associated with local deities in different parts of India. Some of these formulas seem to go back to *parittas* similar to those in the Pali canonical text *Āṭānātiya Suttanta* (*Dīgha Nikāya* no. 32). Although one should not identify the relatively early, and pan-Buddhist, genre of the *dhāraṇī* and *paritta* with the Tantrayāna, the increased use of these formulas in most existing forms of Buddhism, and the appearance of *dhāraṇī-sūtras* in late Mahāyāna literature perhaps marks a shift towards greater emphasis on the magical dimension of Buddhist faith. The Mahāyāna *sūtras* also foreshadow Tantra with their doctrine of the identity of the awakened and the afflicted minds *(Dharmasaṅgīti, Vimalakīrtinirdeśa)*, and innate Buddhahood (Tathāgata-garbha *sūtras*).

VARIETIES OF TANTRA

Whatever may have been its prehistory, as esoteric or exoteric practice, the new movement—sometimes called the third *yāna*, Tantrayāna—was as complex and fragmented as earlier forms of Buddhism. A somewhat artificial, but useful classification distinguishes three main types of Tantra: Vajrayāna, Sahajayāna, and Kālacakra Tantra. The first established the symbolic terminology and the liturgy that would characterize all forms of the tradition. Many of these iconographic and ritual forms are described in the *Mañjuśrīmūlakalpa* (finished in its extant form c. 750), the *Mahāvairocana Sūtra,* and the *Vajraśekhara* (or *Tattvasaṃgraha*) *Sūtra*, which some would, following East Asian traditions, classify under a different, more primitive branch of Tantra called "Mantrayāna." The Sahajayāna was dominated by long-haired, wandering *siddhas*, who openly challenged and ridiculed the Buddhist establishment. They referred to the object of their religious experience as "the whore," both as a reference to the sexual symbolism of ritual Tantra and as a challenge to monastic conceptions of spiritual purity, but also as a metaphor for the universal accessibility of enlightenment. The Kālacakra tradition is the farthest removed from earlier Buddhist traditions, and shows a stronger influence from the substratum. It incorporates concepts of messianism and astrology not attested elsewhere in Buddhist literature.

Unfortunately, the history of all three of these movements is clouded in legend. Tibetan traditions considers the Mantrayāna a third "turning of the wheel [of the Dharma]" (with Mahāyāna as the second), taking place in Dhānyakaṭaka (Andhra) sixteen years after the enlightenment. But this is patently absurd. As a working hypothesis, we can propose that there was an early stage of Mantrayāna beginning in the fourth century. The term *Vajrayāna* could be used then to describe the early documented manifestations of Tantric practice, especially in the high tradition of the Ganges River valley after the seventh century.

Sahajayāna is supposed to have originated with the Kashmirian yogin Lūi-pa (c. 750–800). The earliest documented Sahajayānists are from Bengal, but probably from the beginning of the ninth century. Regarding the Kālacakra, Western scholarship would not accept traditional views of its ancient origins in the mythic land of Shambhala. It must be dated not earlier than the tenth century, probably to the beginning of the reign of King Mahīpāla (c. 974–1026). Its roots have been sought in the North as well as in the South.

The Vajrayāna. The Vajrayāna derives its name from the centrality of the concept of *vajra* in its symbolism. The word *vajra* means both "diamond" and "cudgel." It is therefore a metaphor for hardness and destructiveness. Spiritually, it represents the eternal, innate state of Buddhahood possessed by all beings, as well as the cutting edge of wisdom. The personification of this condition and power is Vajrasattva, a deity and an abstract principle, which is defined as follows:

> By *vajra* is meant emptiness;
> *sattva* means pure cognition.
> The identity of these two is known
> as the essence of Vajrasattva.
> (*Advayavajra Saṃgraha*, p. 24)

Behind this definition is clearly the metaphysics of Yogācāra-Mādhyamika thought. Vajrasattva stands for the nondual experience that transcends both emptiness and pure mind. In religious terms this principle represents a homology between the human person and the essence of *vajra*: in the human body, in this life, relative and absolute meet.

The innate quality of the nondual is also represented by the concept of the "thought of awakening" *(bodhicitta)*. But innate awakening in Vajrayāna becomes the goal: enlightenment is present in its totality and perfection in this human body; the thought of awakening *is* awakening:

> The Thought of Awakening is known to be
> Without beginning or end, quiescent,
> Free from being and nonbeing, powerful,
> Undivided in emptiness and compassion.
> (*Guhyasamāja* 18.37)

This identity is established symbolically and ritually by a series of homologies. For instance, the six elements of the human body are identified with different aspects of the body of Mahāvairocana, the five constituents of the human personality *(skandhas)* are identified with the five forms of Buddha knowledge.

But the most characteristic aspect of Tantric Buddhism generally is the extension of these homologies to sexual symbolism. The "thought of awakening" is identified with semen, dormant wisdom with a woman waiting to be inseminated. Therefore, wisdom *(prajñā)* is conceived as a female deity. She is a mother *(jananī)*, as in the Prajñāpāramitā literature; she is the female yogi *(yoginī)*; but she is also a low-caste whore *(ḍombī caṇḍālī)*. Skillful means *(upāya)* are visualized as her male consort. The perfect union of these two *(prajñopāya-yuganaddha)* is the union of the nondual. Behind the Buddhist interpretation, of course, one discovers the non-Aryan substrantum, with its emphasis on fertility and the symbolism of the mother goddess. [*See* Goddess Worship, *article on* The Hindu Goddess.] But one may also see this radical departure from Buddhist monkish prudery as an attempt to shock the establishment out of self-righteous complacency.

Because the sexual symbolism can be understood metaphorically, most forms of Buddhist Tantra were antinomian only in principle. Thus, Vajrayāna was not without its vows and rules. As *upāya,* the symbols of ritual had as their goal the integration of the Absolute and the relative, not the abrogation of the latter. Tantric vows included traditional monastic rules, the *bodhisattva* vows, and special Tantric rules—some of which are contained in texts such as the *Vinayasūtra* and the *Bodhicittaśīlādānakalpa.*

The practice of the higher mysteries was reserved for those who had mastered the more elementary Mahāyāna and Tantra practices. The hierarchy of practice was established in systems such as the "five steps" of the *Pañcakrama* (by the Tantric Nāgārjuna). Generally, the order of study protected the higher mysteries, establishing the dividing line between esoteric and exoteric. Another common classification of the types of Tantra distinguished external daily rituals (Kriyā Tantra), special rituals serving as preparation for meditation, (Caryā Tantra), basic meditation practices (Yoga Tantra), and the highest, or advanced meditation Tantras (Anuttarayoga Tantra). This hermeneutic of sorts served both as an apologetic and a doctrinal classification of Tantric practice by distinguishing the audience for which each type of Tantra was best suited: respectively *śrāvakas, pratyekabuddhas,* Yogācārins, and Mādhyamikas.

Elements of Tathāgata-garbha theory seem to have been combined with early totemic beliefs to establish a system of Tathāgata families or clans that also served to define the proper audience for a variety of teachings. Persons afflicted by delusion, for instance, belonged to Mahāvairocana's clan, and should cultivate the homologies and visualizations associated with this Buddha—who, not coincidentally, represents the highest awakening. This system extends the homologies of *skandhas*, levels of knowledge, and so forth, to personality types. This can be understood as a practical psychology that forms part of the Tantric quest for the immanence of the sacred.

The Sahaja (or Sahajiyā) Movement. Although traditional Sahaja master-to-disciple lineages present it as a movement of great antiquity, the languages used in extant Sahaja literature belong to an advanced stage in the development of New Indic. These works were written mostly in Apabhrāṃśa (the *Dohākośa*) and early Bengali (the *Caryāgīti*). Thus, although their dates are uncertain, they cannot go as far back as suggested by tradition. Scholars generally agree on a conjectural dating of perhaps eighth to tenth century.

Works attributed to Sahaja masters are preserved not only in New Indian languages (Saraha, c. 750–800, Kaṇha, c. 800–850, Ti-lo-pa, c. 950–1000); a few commentaries exist in Sanskrit. The latter attest to the influence of the early wandering *siddhas* on the Buddhist establishment.

The basic doctrinal stance of the Sahaja movement is no different from that of Vajrayāna: *sahaja* is the innate principle of enlightenment, the *bodhicitta,* to be realized in the union of wisdom and skillful means. The main difference between the two types of Tantra is in the life-style of the adept. The Sahajiyā was a movement that represented a clear challenge to the Buddhist establishment: the ideal person was a homeless madman wandering about with his female consort, or a householder-sorcerer—either of which would claim to practice union with his consort as the actualization of what the high tradition practiced only in symbolic or mystical form. The Vajrayāna soon became integrated into the curriculum of the universities, controlled by the Vinaya and philosophical analysis. It was incorporated into the ordered program of spiritual cultivation accepted in the monasteries, which corresponded to the desired social and political stability of the academic institutions and their sponsors. The iconoclastic staints of the Sahaja, on the other hand, sought spontaneity, and saw monastic life as an obstacle to true realization. The force of their challenge is seen in quasi-mythic form in the legend that tells of the bizarre tests to which the *siddha* Ti-lo-pa submitted the great scholar Nā-ro-pa when the latter left his post at Vikramaśīla to follow the half-naked madman Ti-lo-pa.

This particular Tantric tradition, therefore, best embodied the iconoclastic tendencies found in all of Tantra. It challenged the establishment in the social as well as the religious sphere, for it incorporated freely practices from the substratum and placed women and sexuality on the level of the sacred. In opposition to the bland and ascetic paradises of Mahāyāna—where there were no women or sexual intercourse—Tantrism identifies the bliss of enlightment with the great bliss *(mahāsukha)* of sexual union.

The Kālacakra Tantra. This text has several features that separate it from other works of the Buddhist tradition: an obvious political message, suggesting an alliance to stop the Muslim advance in India, and astrological symbolism and teachings, among the others. In this work also we meet the concept of "Ādibuddha," the primordial Buddha, whence arises everything in the universe.

The high tradition, however, sees the text as remaining within the main line of Buddhist Tantrism. Its main argument is that all phenomena, including the rituals of Tantra, are contained within the initiate's body, and all aspects of time are also contained in this body. The concept of time *(kāla)* is introduced and discussed and its symbolism explained as a means to give the devotee control over time and therefore over the impermanent world. The *Sekoddeśaṭīkā,* a commentary on part of the *Kākacakra* attributed to Nā-ro-pa (Nāḍapāda, tenth century), explains that the time *(kāla)* of the *Kālacakra* is the same as the unchanging *dharmadhātu,* whereas the wheel *(cakra)* means the manifestations of time. In *Kālacakra* the two, absolute and relative, *prajñā* and *upāya,* are united. In this sense, therefore, in spite of its concessions to the substratum and to the rising tide of Hinduism, the *Kālacakra* was also integrated with mainline Buddhism.

TANTRIC LITERATURE

The word *tantra* means "thread" or "weft" and, by extension, "text." The sacred texts produced as the new dispensation, esoteric or exoteric, were called Tantras, and formed indeed a literary thread interwoven with the secret transmission from master to disciple. Some of the most difficult and profound Tantras were produced in the early period (before the eighth century); the *Mahāvairocana, Guhyasamāja,* the earlier parts of the *Mañjuśrīmūlakalpa,* and the *Hevajra.* By the time Tantra became the dominant system and, therefore, part of the establishment, a series of commentaries and authored works had appeared. Nāgārjuna's *Pañcakrama* is among the earliest. The Tantric Candrakīrti (ninth century) wrote a commentary on the *Guhyasamāja,* and Buddhaguhya (eighth century) discussed the *Mahāvairocana.* Sanskrit commentaries eventually were written to fossilize even the spontaneous poems of Sahaja saints.

TANTRA AND THE HIGH TRADITION

Thus, Tantra too, like its predecessors, eventually become institutionalized. What arose as an esoteric, intensely private, visionary and iconoclastic movement, became a literary tradition, ritualized, often exoteric and speculative.

We have abundant evidence of a flourishing Tantric circle at Nālandā, for instance, at least since the late seventh century. Tantric masters were by that time established members of the faculty. Especially during the Pāla dynasty, Tantric practices and speculation played a central role in Buddhist universities. This was clearly the period of institutionalization, a period when Tantra became part of the mainstream of Buddhism.

With this transformation the magical origins of Tantra were partly disguised by a high Tantric liturgy and a theory of Tantric meditation paralleling earlier, Mahāyāna theories of the path. Still, Tantric ritual and meditation retained an identity of their own. Magic formulas, gestures, and circles appeared transformed, respectively, into the mystical words of the Buddhas, the secret gestures of the Buddhas, and charts *maṇḍalas)* of the human psyche and the path.

The mystical diagram *(maṇḍala)* illustrates the complexity of this symbolism. It is at the same time a chart of the human person as it is now, a plan for liberation, and a representation of the transfigured body, the structure of Buddhahood itself. As a magic circle it is the sphere in which spiritual forces are evoked and controlled, as religious symbol it is the sphere of religious progress, experience, and action. The primitive functions remain: the *maṇḍala* is still a circle of power, with apotropaic functions. For each divinity there is an assigned meaning, a sacred syllable, a color, and a position within the *maṇḍala.* Spiritual forces can thus be evoked without danger. The sacred syllable is still a charm. The visualization of Buddhas is often inseparable from the evocation of demons and spirits. New beings populated the Buddhist pantheon. The Buddhas and *bodhisattvas* are accompanied by female consorts—these spiritual sexual partners can be found in explicit carnal iconographic representations. [*See* Maṇḍala, *article on* Buddhist Maṇḍalas.]

Worship and Ritual. Whereas the esoteric ritual incorporated elements of the substratum into a Buddhist doctrinal base, the exoteric liturgies of the Tantric high tradition followed ritual models from the Mahāyāna tradition as well as elements that evince Brahmanic ritual and Hindu worship. The daily ritual of the Tantric Buddhist presents a number of analogies of Brahmanic *pūjā* that cannot be accidental. But the complete liturgical cycle is still Buddhist. Many examples are preserved, for instance, in the Sanskrit text *Ādikarmapradīpa.* The ritual incorporates Tantric rites (offering to a *maṇḍala*, recitation of *mantras*) into a structure composed of elements from pre-Mahāyāna Buddhism (e.g., the Refuges), and Mahāyāna ritual (confession, vows, dedication of merit).

More complex liturgies include rites of initiation or consecration *(abhiṣeka)* and empowerment *(adhiṣṭhāna)*, rites that may have roots going as far back as the *Atharvaveda.* The burnt-offering rites *(homa)* also have Vedic and Brahmanic counterparts. Elements of the substratum are also evident in the frequent invocation of *yakṣas* and *devatās*, the propitiation of spirits, and the underlying sexual and alchemical symbolism.

Meditation. The practice of Tantric visualization *(sādhana)* was even more a part of ritual than the Mahāyāna meditation session. It was always set in a purely ritual frame similar to the structure of the daily ritual summarized above. A complete *sādhana* would integrate pre-Mahāyāna and Mahāyāna liturgical and contemplative processes with Tantric visualization. The meditator would first go through a gradual process of purification (sometimes including ablutions) usually constructed on the model of the Mahāyāna "sevenfold service." He would then visualize the mystical syllable corresponding to his chosen deity. The syllable would be transformed into a series of images that would lead finally to clear visualization of the deity. Once the deity was visualized clearly, the adept would become one with it. But this oneness was interpreted as the realization of the nondual; therefore, the deity became the adept as much as the adept was turned into a deity. Thus, the transcendent could be actualized in the adept's life beyond meditation in the fulfillment of the *bodhisattva* vows.

Tantric Doctrine. Tantric symbolism was interpreted in the context of Mahāyāna orthodoxy. It is therefore possible to explain Tantric theoretical conceptions as a natural development from Mahāyāna. The immanence of Buddhahood is explicitly connected with the Mahāyāna doctrine of the identity of *saṃsāra* and *nirvāṇa* and the teachings of those Yogācārins who believed that consciousness is inherently pure. The magical symbolism of Tantra can be traced—again through explicit references—to the doctrine of the *bodhisattva* as magician: since the world is like a dream, like a magical apparition, one can be free of it by knowing the dream as dream—knowing and controlling the magical illusion as a magician would control it. The *bodhisattva* (and therefore the *siddha*) is able to play the magical trick of the world without deceiving himself into believing it real.

One should not forget, however, that what is distinctively Tantric is not limited to the externals of ritual and symbolism. The special symbolism transforms its Mahāyāna context because of the specifically Tantric understanding of immanence. The Buddha is present in the human body innately, but the Buddha nature is manifested only when one realizes the "three mysteries," or "three secrets." It is not enough to be free from the illusion of the world; one becomes free by living *in* illusion in such a way that illusion becomes the manifestation of Buddhahood. Tantra seeks to construct an alternative reality, such that a mentally constructed world reveals the fundamental illusion of the world and manifests the mysterious power of the Buddha through illusion. The human body, the realm of the senses, is to be transformed into the body of a Buddha, the senses of a Buddha.

The body, mind, and speech of the Buddha (the Three Mysteries) have specific characteristics that must be recognized and reproduced. In ritual terms this means that the adept actualizes Buddhahood when he performs prostrations and ritual gestures (*mudrās*); he speaks with the voice of the Buddha when he utters *mantras*; his mind is the mind of the Buddha when he visualizes the deity. The magical dimension is evident: the power of the Buddha lives in the formalized "demeanor of a Buddha." But the doctrine also implies transforming the body by a mystical alchemy (rooted in substratum sexual alchemy) from which is derived the soteriological meaning of the doctrine: the ritual changes the human person into a Buddha, all his human functions become sacred. Then this person's mind is the mind of an awakened being, it knows all things; the body assumes the appearance appropriate to save any living being; the voice is able to speak in the language of any living being needing to be saved. [*See also* Soteriology, *article on* Buddhist Soteriology.]

The Decline of Buddhism in India

With Harṣa's death Indian Buddhism could depend only on the royal patronage of the Pāla dynasty of Bihar and Bengal (c. 650–950), who soon favored the institutions they had founded—Vikramaśīla (c. 800), Odantapurī (c. 760). The last shining lights of Nālandā were the Mādhyamika masters Śāntirakṣita and Kamalaśīla, both of whom participated actively in the conversion of Tibet. Then the ancient university was eclipsed by its rival Vikramaśīla, which saw its final glory in the eleventh century.

Traditionally, the end of Indian Buddhism has been identified with the sack of the two great universities by the troops of the Turk Muḥammad Ghūrī: Nālandā in 1197 and Vikramaśīla in 1203. But, although the destruction of Nālandā put an end to its former glory, Nālandā lingered on. When the Tibetan pilgrim Dharmasvāmin (1197–1264) visited the site of the ancient university in 1235 he found a few monks teaching in two monasteries remaining among the ruins of eighty-two others. In this way Buddhism would stay on in India for a brief time, but under circumstances well illustrated by the decay witnessed by Dharmasvāmin—even as he was there, the Turks mounted another raid to further ransack what was left of Nālandā.

For a long time scholars have debated the causes for the decline of Buddhism in India. Although there is little chance of agreement on a problem so complex—and on which we have precious little evidence—some of the reasons adduced early are no longer widely accepted. For instance, the notion that Tantric Buddhism was a "degenerate form" of Buddhism that contributed to or brought about the disappearance of Buddhism is no longer entertained by the scholarly community. The image of a defenseless, pacifist Buddhist community annihilated by invading hordes of Muslim warriors is perhaps also a simplification. Though the Turkish conquerors of India were far from benevolent, the Arabs who occupied Sindh in 711 seem to have accepted a state of peaceful coexistence with the local population. Furthermore, one must still understand why Jainism and Hinduism survived the Muslim invasion while Buddhism did not.

Buddhist relations with Hindu and Jain monarchs were not always peaceful—witness the conquest of Bihar by the Bengali Śaiva king Śaśīṅka (c. 618). Even without the intervention of intolerance, the growth of Hinduism, with its firm roots in Indian society and freedom from the costly institution of the monastery, offered a colossal challenge to Buddhism. The eventual triumph of Hinduism can be followed by a number of landmarks often associated with opposition to Buddhism: the spread of Vaiṣṇavism (in which the Buddha appears as a deceptive *avatāra* of Viṣṇu); the great Vaiṣṇava and Śaiva saints of the South, the Āḻvārs and Nāyaṉārs, respectively, whose Hindu patrons were openly hostile to Buddhism and Jainism; the ministry of Śaṅkara in Mysore (788–850), a critic of Buddhism who was himself accused of being a "crypto-Buddhist"; and the triumph of Śaivism in Kashmir (c. 800). [*See* Vaiṣṇavism, *overview article;* Āḻvars; Śaivism, *overview article and article on* Nāyaṉārs; Kṛṣṇaism; Avatāra; *and the biography of Śaṅkara*.]

But the causes for the disappearance of Buddhism were subtle: the assimilation of Buddhist ideas and practices into Hinduism and the inverse process of the Hinduization of Buddhism, with the advantage of Hinduism as a religion of the land and the locality. More important than these were perhaps the internal causes for the decline: dependence on monastic institutions that did not have broad popular support but relied exclusively on royal patronage; and isolation of monasteries from the life of the village community, owing to the tendency of the monasteries to look inward and to lose interest in proselytizing and serving the surrounding communities.

The disappearance of Buddhism in India may have been precipitated by the Muslim invasion, but it was caused primarily by internal factors, the most important of which seems to have been the gradual assimilation of Buddhism into Hinduism. The Muslim invasion, especially the Turkish conquest of the Ganges Valley, was the *coup de grace;* we may consider it the dividing line between two eras, but it was not the primary cause for the disappearance of Buddhism from India. [*See* Islam, *articles on* Islam in Central Asia *and* Islam in South Asia.]

Buddhist Remnants and Revivals in the Subcontinent

After the last days of the great monastic institutions (twelfth and thirteenth centuries) Indian Buddhism lingered on in isolated pockets in the subcontinent. During the period of Muslim and British conquest (thirteenth to nineteenth century) it was almost completely absorbed by Hinduism and Islam, and gave no sign of creative life until modern attempts at restoration (nineteenth and twentieth centuries). Therefore, a hiatus of roughly six hundred years separates the creative period of Indian Buddhism from its modern manifestations.

BUDDHISM OF THE FRONTIER

As the Turk occupation of India advanced, the last great scholars of India escaped from Kashmir and Bihar to Tibet and Nepal. But the flight of Buddhist talent also responded to the attraction of royal patronage and popular support in other lands. The career of Atīśa (Dīpaṃkara Śrījñāna, 982–1054), who emigrated to Tibet in 1042, is emblematic of the great loss incurred by Indian Buddhism in losing its monk-scholars. He combined extensive studies in Mahāyāna philosophy and Tantra in India with a sojourn in Sumatra under the tutorship of Dharmakīrti. He had studied with Bodhibhadra (the successor of Nā-ro-pa when the latter left Vikramaśīla to become a wandering ascetic), and was head master *(upādhyāya)* of Vikramaśīla and Odantapurī at the time of King Bheyapāla. He left for Tibet at the invitation of Byaṅ-chub-'od, apparently attracted by a large monetary offer. [*See the biography of Atiśa.*]

The migration of the Indian scholars, and a steady stream of Tibetan students, made possible the exportation of Buddhist academic institutions and traditions to Tibet, where they were preserved until the Chinese suppression of 1959. The most learned monks were pushed out to the Himalayan and Bengali frontiers in part because the Indian communities were no longer willing to support the monasteries. Certain forms of Tantra, dependent only on householder priests, could survive, mostly in Bengal and in the Himalayan foothills. But some Theravādin Buddhists also survived in East Bengal—most of them taking refuge in India after the partition, some remaining in Bangladesh and Assam. [*See* Bengali Religions.]

Himalayan Buddhism of direct Indian ancestry remains only in Nepal, where it can be observed even today in suspended animation, partly fused with local Hinduism, as it must have been in the Gangetic plain during the twelfth century. Nepalese Buddhists produced what may very well be considered the last major Buddhist scripture composed in the subcontinent, the *Svayaṃbhū Purāṇa* (c. fifteenth century). This text is an open window into the last days of Indian Buddhism. It reveals the close connection between Buddhist piety and non-Buddhist sacred localities, the formation of a Buddhist cosmogonic ontology (the Ādibuddha), and the role of Tantric ritual in the incorporation of religious elements from the substratum. Nepalese Buddhism survives under the tutelage of married Tantric priests, called *vajrācāryas*. It is therefore sometimes referred to as "Vajrācārya Buddhism."

Buddhism of Tibetan origin survives in the subcontinent mostly in Ladakh, Sikkim, and Bhutan, but also in Nepal. [*See* Himalayan Religions.] Perhaps the most significant presence in modern India, however, is that of the Tibetan refugee communities. The Tibetan diaspora includes about eighty thousand persons, among which are several thousand monks. Some have retained their monastic robes and have reconstructed in India their ancient Buddhist academic curricula, returning to the land of origin the disciplines of the classical universities. So far their impact on Indian society at large has been insignificant and their hope of returning to Tibet dwindles with the passing of time. But the preservation, on Indian soil, of the classical traditions of Nālandā and Vikramaśīla is hardly a trivial accomplishment.

ATTEMPTED REVIVAL: THE MAHĀBODHI SOCIETY

Attempts to revive Buddhism in the land of its origin began with the Theosophical Society, popularized in Sri Lanka in the early 1880s by the American Henry S. Olcott. Although the society eventually became the vehicle for broader and less defined speculative goals, it inspired new pride in Buddhists after years of colonial oppression. [*See* Theosophical Society.] The Sinhala monk Anagārika Dharmapāla (1864–1933; born David Hewavitarane) set out to modernize Buddhist education. He also worked untiringly to restore the main pilgrimage sites of India, especially the temple of Bodh Gayā, which had fallen in disrepair and had been under Hindu administration for several centuries. To this end he founded in 1891 the Mahābodhi Society, still a major presence in Indian Buddhism.

AMBEDKAR AND "NEO-BUDDHISM"

The most significant Buddhist mass revival of the new age was led by Dr. Bhimrao Ramji Ambedkar (1891–1956). He saw Buddhism as the gospel for India's oppressed and read in the Buddhist scriptures ideals of equality and justice. After many years of spiritual search, he became convinced that Buddhism was the only ideology that could effect the eventual liberation of Indian outcastes. On 14 October 1956 he performed a mass "consecration" of Buddhists in Nagpur, Maharashtra. The new converts were mostly from the "scheduled caste" of the *mahār*s. Although his gospel is in some way on the fringes of Buddhist orthodoxy, Buddhist monks from other parts of Asia have ministered to the spiritual needs of his converts, and inspired Indian Buddhists refer to him as "Bodhisattva Ambedkar." [*See* Marathi Religions *and the biography of Ambedkar*.]

OTHER ASPECTS OF MODERN BUDDHISM

The most fruitful and persistent effort in the rediscovery of Indian Buddhism has been in the West, primarily among Western scholars. The achievements of European scholars include a modern critical edition of the complete Pali canon, published by the Pāli Text Society (founded in London in 1881), and the recovery of original texts of parts of the canon of the Sarvāstivāda. The combined effort of Indian, North American and European historians, archaeologists, and art historians has placed Indian Buddhism in a historical and social context, which, though still only understood in its rough outlines, allows us to see Buddhism in its historical evolution.

Japanese scholarship has also made great strides since the beginning of the twentieth century. The publication in Japan of three different editions of the Chinese canon between 1880 and 1929 may be seen as the symbolic beginning of a century of productive critical scholarship that has placed Japan at the head of modern research into Indian Buddhism. [*See* Buddhist Studies.]

Another interesting phenomenon of the contemporary world is the appearance of "neo-Buddhists" in Europe and North America. Although most of these groups have adopted extra-Indian forms of Buddhism, their interest in the scriptural traditions of

India has created an audience and a demand for research into India's Buddhist past. The Buddhist Society, founded in London in 1926, and the Amis du Bouddhisme, founded in Paris in 1928, both supported scholarship and encouraged the Buddhist revival in India.

In spite of the revived interest in India of the last century, the prospects of an effective Buddhist revival in the land of Śākyamuni seem remote. It is difficult to imagine a successful living Buddhism in India today or in the near future. The possibility of the religion coming back to life may depend on the reimportation of the Dharma into India from another land. It remains to be seen if Ambedkar and Anagārika Dharmapāla had good reasons for hope in a Buddhist revival, or if in fact the necessary social conditions for the existence of Indian Buddhism disappeared with the last monarchs of the Pāla dynasty.

[*See also* Indian Religions.]

BIBLIOGRAPHY

Bareau, André. "Le bouddhisme indien." In *Les religions de l'Inde,* vol. 3, pp. 1–246. Paris, 1966. In addition to this useful survey, see Bareau's "Le bouddhisme indien," in *Histoire des religions,* edited by Henri-Charles Puech vol. 1, (Paris, 1970), pp. 1146–1215. Bareau has written the classical work on the question of the dating of the Buddha's life, "La date du Nirvāṇa," *Journal asiatique* 241 (1953): 27–62. He surveys and interprets classical documents on the Hīnayāna schools in "Les sectes bouddhiques du Petit Véhicule et leurs Abhidharmapiṭaka." *Bulletin de l'École Française d'Extrême-Orient* 50 (1952): 1–11; "Trois traités sur les sectes bouddhiques dus à Vasumitra, Bhavya et Vinitadeva," *Journal asiatique* 242–244 (1954–1956); *Les premiers conciles bouddhiques* (Paris, 1955); *Les sectes bouddhiques de Petit Véhicule* (Saigon, 1955); "Les controverses rélatives à la nature de l'arhant dans le bouddhisme ancien," *Indo-Iranian Journal* 1 (1957): 241–250. Bareau has also worked extensively on the "biography" of the Buddha: *Recherches sur la biographie du Bouddha,* 3 vols. (Paris, 1970–1983); "Le parinirvāṇa du Bouddha et la naissance de la religion bouddhique," *Bulletin de l'École Française d'Extrême-Orient* 61 (1974): 275–300; and, on a more popular but still scholarly bent, *Le Bouddha* (Paris, 1962).

Basham, A. L. *The Wonder That Was India.* London, 1954. This is the most accessible and readable cultural history of pre-Muslim India. A more technical study on the religious movements at the time of the Buddha is Basham's *History and Doctrine of the Ājīvikas* (London, 1951).

Beal, Samuel. *Travels of Fa-hian and Sung-Yun, Buddhist Pilgrims from China to India (400 A.D. and 518 A.D.).* London, 1869. The travel records of two early pilgrims. See also Beal's *Si-yu-ki: Buddhist Records of the Western World,* 2 vols. (London, 1884). Translation of Hsüan-tsang's accounts of his travels to India.

Bechert, Heinz. "Zur Frühgeschichte des Mahāyāna-Buddhismus." *Zeitschrift der Deutschen Morgenländischen Gesellschaft* 113 (1963): 530–535. Summary discussion of the Hīnayāna roots of Mahāyāna. On the same topic, see also "Notes on the Formation of Buddhist Sects and the Origins of Mahāyāna," in *German Scholars on India,* vol. 1 (Varanasi, 1973), pp. 6–18; "The Date of the Buddha Reconsidered," *Indologica Taurinensia* 10 (1982): 29–36; "The Importance of Aśoka's So-called Schism Edict," in *Indological and Buddhist Studies in Honour of Prof. J. W. de Jong* (Canberra, 1982), pp. 61–68; and "The Beginnings of Buddhist Historiography," in *Religion and Legitimation of Power in Sri Lanka,* edited by Bardwell L. Smith (Chambersburg, Pa., 1978), pp. 1–12. Bechert is also the editor of the most recent contribution to the question of the language of Buddha and early Buddhism, *Die Sprache der ältesten buddhistischen Überlieferung / The Language of the Earliest Buddhist Tradition* (Göttingen, 1980).

Bechert, Heinz, and Georg von Simson, eds. *Einführung in die Indologie: Stand, Methoden, Aufgaben*. Darmstadt, 1979. A general introduction to Indology, containing abundant materials on Indian history and religion, including Buddhism.

Bechert, Heinz, and Richard Gombrich, eds. *The World of Buddhism*. London, 1984. This is by far the most scholarly and comprehensive survey of Buddhism for the general reader. Indian Buddhism is treated on pages 15–132 and 277–278.

Demiéville, Paul. "L'origine des sectes bouddhiques d'après Paramārtha." In *Mélanges chinois et bouddhiques,* vol. 1, pp. 14–64. Brussels, 1931–1932.

Demiéville, Paul. "A propos du Concile de Vaiśālī." *T'oung pao* 40 (1951): 239–296.

Dutt, Nalinaksha. *Aspects of Mahāyāna Buddhism and Its Relation to Hīnayāna.* London, 1930. Although Dutt's work on the development of the Buddhist sects is now largely superseded, there are no comprehensive expositions to replace his surveys. His *Mahāyāna Buddhism* (Calcutta, 1973) is sometimes presented as a revision of *Aspects,* but the earlier work is quite different and far superior. Most of Dutt's earlier work on the sects, found hidden in various journals, was compiled in *Buddhist Sects in India* (Calcutta, 1970). See also his *Early Monastic Buddhism*, rev. ed. (Calcutta, 1960).

Dutt, Sukumar. *The Buddha and Five After-Centuries*. London, 1957. Other useful, although dated, surveys include *Early Buddhist Monachism* (1924; new ed., Delhi, 1960) and *Buddhist Monks and Monasteries in India* (London, 1962).

Fick, R. *The Social Organization in Northeast India in the Buddha's Time*. Calcutta, 1920.

Frauwallner, Erich. "Die buddhistische Konzile." *Zeitschrift der Deutschen Morgenländischen Gesellschaft* 102 (1952): 240–261.

Frauwallner, Erich. *The Earliest Vinaya and the Beginnings of Buddhist Literature*. Rome, 1956.

Frauwallner, Erich. "The Historical Data We Possess on the Person and Doctrine of the Buddha." *East and West* 7 (1956): 309–312.

Fujita Kotatsu. *Genshi jōdoshisō no kenkyū*. Tokyo, 1970. The standard book on early Sukhāvatī beliefs.

Glasenapp, Helmuth von. "Zur Geschichte der buddhistischen Dharma Theorie." *Zeitschrift der Deutschen Morgenländischen Gesellschaft* 92 (1938): 383–420.

Glasenapp, Helmuth von. "Der Ursprung der buddhistischen Dharma-Theorie." *Wiener Zeitschrift für die Kunde des Morgenlandes* 46 (1939): 242–266.

Glasenapp, Helmuth von. *Buddhistische Mysterien*. Stuttgart, 1940. Discusses most of the theories on early Brahmanic influence on Buddhist doctrine.

Glasenapp, Helmuth von. *Buddhismus und Gottesidee*. Mainz, 1954.

Gokhale, Balkrishna Govind. *Buddhism and Aśoka*. Baroda, 1948. Other of this author's extensive writings on the social and political contexts of early Buddhism include "The Early Buddhist Elite," *Journal of Indian History* 43 (1965): 391–402; "Early Buddhist View of the State," *Journal of the American Oriental Society* 89 (1969): 731–738; "Theravāda Buddhism in Western India," *Journal of the American Oriental Society* 92 (1972): 230–236; and "Early Buddhism and the Brāhmaṇas," in *Studies in History of Buddhism,* edited by A. K. Narain (Delhi, 1980).

Gómez, Luis O. "Proto-Mādhyamika in the Pāli Canon." *Philosophy East and West* 26 (1976): 137–165. This paper argues that the older portions of *Suttanipāta* preserve a stratum of the tradition that differs radically from the dominant themes expressed in the rest of the Pali canon, especially in its Theravāda interpretation. The question of dedication of merit in the

Mahāyāna is discussed in "Paradigm Shift and Paradigm Translation: The Case of Merit and Grace in Buddhism," in *Buddhist-Christian Dialogue* (Honolulu, forthcoming). On Mahāyāna doctrine and myth, see also my "Buddhism as a Religion of Hope: Polarities in the Myth of Dharmākara," *Journal of the Institute for Integral Shin Studies* (Kyoto, in press).

Grousset, René. *The Civilizations of the East,* vol. 2, *India*. London, 1931. One of the best surveys of Indian history. See also his *Sur les traces du Bouddha* (Paris, 1957) for a modern expansion and retelling of Hsüan-tsang's travels.

Hirakawa Akira. *Indo bukkyōshi*. 2 vols. Tokyo, 1974–1979. A valuable survey of Indian Buddhism from the perspective of Japanese scholarship (English translation forthcoming from the University Press of Hawaii). The development of the earliest Vinaya is discussed in *Ritsuzō no kenkyū* (Tokyo, 1960) and in *Shoki daijō bukkyō no kenkyū* (Tokyo, 1969). The author's "The Rise of Mahāyāna Buddhism and Its Relationship to the Worship of Stupas," *Memoirs of the Research Department of the Tōyō Bunko* 22 (1963): 57–106, is better known in the West and summarizes some of the conclusions of his Japanese writings.

Horner, I. B. *Early Buddhist Theory of Man Perfected*. London, 1936. A study of the *arhat* ideal in the Pali canon. See also Horner's translation of the dialogues between King Menander and Nāgasena, *Milinda's Questions* (London, 1964), and *Women under Primitive Buddhism* (1930; reprint, Delhi, 1975).

Horsch, P. "Der Hinduismus und die Religionen der primitivstämme Indiens." *Asiatische Studien / Études asiatiques* 22 (1968): 115–136.

Horsch, P. "Vorstufen der Indischen Seelenwanderungslehre." *Asiatische Studien / Études asiatiques* 25 (1971): 98–157.

Jayatilleke, K. N. *Early Buddhist Theory of Knowledge*. London, 1963. Discusses the relationship between early Buddhist ideas and śramaṇic and Upaniṣadic doctrines.

Jong, J. W. de. "A Brief History of Buddhist Studies in Europe and America." *Eastern Buddhist* 7 (May 1974): 55–106, (October 1974): 49–82. For the most part these bibliographic surveys, along with the author's "Recent Buddhist Studies in Europe and America: 1973–1983," *Eastern Buddhist* 17 (1984): 79–107, treat only the philological study of Indian Buddhism. The author also tends to omit certain major figures who are not in his own school of Buddhology. These articles are nonetheless the most scholarly surveys available on the field, and put forth truly excellent models of scholarly rigor.

Joshi, Lal Mani. *Studies in the Buddhistic Culture of India*. Delhi, 1967. Indian Buddhism during the middle and late Mahāyāna periods.

Kajiyama Yūichi. "Women in Buddhism." *Eastern Buddhist* 15 (1982): 53–70.

Kajiyama Yūichi. "Stūpas, the Mother of Buddhas, and Dharma-body." In *New Paths in Buddhist Research,* edited by A. K. Warder, pp. 9–16. Delhi, 1985.

Kimura Taiken. *Abidammaron no kenkyū*. Tokyo, 1937. A survey of Sarvāstivāda Abhidharma, especially valuable for its analysis of the *Mahāvibhāṣā*.

Lamotte, Étienne. "Buddhist Controversy over the Five Propositions." *Indian Historical Quarterly* 32 (1956). The material collected in this article is also found, slightly augmented, in Lamotte's *magnum opus, Histoire du bouddhisme indien des origines à l'ère Śaka* (Louvain, 1958), pp. 300–319, 542–543, 575–606, 690–695. This erudite work is still the standard reference tool on the history of early Indian Buddhism (to circa 200 CE). Unfortunately, Lamotte did not attempt a history of Indian Buddhism for the middle and late periods. He did, however, write an article on the origins of Mahāyāna titled "Sur la formation du Mahāyāna," in *Asiatica: Festschrift Friedrich Weller* (Leipzig, 1954), pp. 381–386; this is the definitive statement on the northern origin of Mahāyāna. See also *Der Verfasser des Upadeśa und seine Quellen* (Göttingen, 1973). On early Buddhism, see "La légende du Buddha," *Revue de l'histoire des religions* 134 (1947–1948): 37–71; *Le bouddhisme de Śākyamuni* (Göttingen, 1983); and *The Spirit of Ancient Buddhism* (Venice, 1961). Lamotte also translated a vast amount of Mahāyāna literature, including *Le traité de la grande vertu de sagesse,* 5 vols. (Louvain, 1944–1980); *La somme du Grand Véhicule d'Asaṅga,* 2 vols. (Louvain, 1938); and *L'enseignement de Vimalakīrti* (Louvain, 1962), containing a long note on the concept of Buddha field (pp. 395–404).

La Vallée Poussin, Louis de. *Bouddhisme: Études et matériaux*. London, 1898. One of the most productive and seminal Western scholars of Buddhism, La Vallée Poussin contributed to historical studies in this and other works, as *Bouddhisme: Opinions sur l'histoire de la dogmatique* (Paris, 1909), *L'Inde aux temps des Mauryas* (Paris, 1930), and *Dynasties et histoire de l'Inde depuis Kanishka jusqu'aux invasions musulmanes* (Paris, 1935). Contributions on doctrine include *The Way to Nirvāṇa* (London, 1917); *Nirvāṇa* (Paris, 1925); "La controverse du temps et du pudgala dans la *Vijñānakāya,*" in *Études asiatiques, publiées à l'occasion du vingt-cinquième anniversaire de l'École Française d'Extrême-Orient*, vol. 1 (Paris, 1925), pp. 358–376; *La morale bouddhique* (Paris, 1927); and *Le dogme et la philosophie du bouddhism* (Paris, 1930). On Abhidharma, see "Documents d'Abhidharma," in *Mélanges chinois et bouddhiques,* vol. 1 (Brussels, 1931–1932), pp. 65–109. The Belgian scholar also translated the most influential work of Abhidharma, *L'Abhidharmakośa de Vasubandhu*, 6 vols. (1923–1931; reprint, Brussels, 1971). His articles in the *Encyclopaedia of Religion and Ethics,* edited by James Hastings, are still of value. Especially useful are "Bodhisattva (In Sanskrit Literature)," vol. 2 (Edinburgh, 1909), pp. 739–753; "Mahāyāna," vol. 8 (1915), pp. 330–336; and "Councils and Synods (Buddhist)," vol. 7 (1914), pp. 179–185.

Law, B. C. *Historical Gleanings*. Calcutta, 1922. Other of his numerous contributions to the early history of Buddhism include *Some Kṣatriya Tribes of Ancient India* (Calcutta, 1924), *Tribes in Ancient India* (Poona, 1943), and *The Magadhas in Ancient India* (London, 1946).

Law, B. C., ed. *Buddhistic Studies*. Calcutta, 1931. A collection of seminal essays on the history and doctrines of Indian Buddhism.

Legge, James. *A Record of Buddhist Kingdoms*. Oxford, 1886. English translation of Fa-hsien's accounts.

Majumdar, R. C., ed. *History and Culture of the Indian People,* vols. 2–5. London, 1951. A major survey of the periods of Indian history when Buddhism flourished.

Masson, Joseph. *La religion populaire dans le canon bouddhique Pāli*. Louvain, 1942. The standard study on the interactions of high tradition Buddhism with the substratum, not superseded yet.

Masuda Jiryō. "Origins and Doctrines of Early Indian Buddhist Schools." *Asia Major* 2 (1925): 1–78. English translation of Vasumitra's classical account of the Eighteen Schools.

May, Jacques. "La philosophie bouddhique de la vacuité." *Studia Philosophica* 18 (1958): 123–137. Discusses philosophical issues; for historical survey, see "Chūgan," in *Hōbōgirin,* vol. 5 (Paris and Tokyo, 1979), pp. 470–493, and the article coauthored with Mimaki (below). May's treatment of the Yogācāra schools (including the school of Sāramati), on the other hand, is both historical and doctrinal; see "La philosophie bouddhique idéaliste," *Asiatische Studien / Études asiatiques* 25 (1971): 265–323.

Mimaki Katsumi and Jacques May. "Chūdō." In *Hōbōgirin*, vol. 5, pp. 456–470. Paris and Tokyo, 1979.

Mitra, Debala. *Buddhist Monuments*. Calcutta, 1971. A handy survey of the Buddhist archaeological sites of India.

Mitra, R. C. *The Decline of Buddhism in India*. Calcutta, 1954.

Nagao Gadjin. "The Architectural Tradition in Buddhist Monasticism." In *Studies in History of Buddhism*, edited by A. K. Narain, pp. 189–208. Delhi, 1980.

Nakamura Hajime. *Indian Buddhism: A Survey with Bibliographical Notes*. Tokyo, 1980. Disorganized and poorly edited, but contains useful information on Japanese scholarship on the development of Indian Buddhism.

Nilakanta Sastri, K. A. *Age of the Nandas and Mauryas*. Varanasi, 1952. See also his *A History of South India from Prehistoric Times to the Fall of Vijayanagar* (Madras, 1955) and *Development of Religion in South India* (Bombay, 1963).

Oldenberg, Hermann. *Buddha, sein Leben, seine Lehre, seine Gemeinde* (1881). Revised and edited by Helmuth von Glasenapp. Stuttgart, 1959. The first German edition was translated by W. Hoey as *Buddha, His Life, His Doctrine, His Order* (London, 1882).

Paul, Diana. *The Buddhist Feminine Ideal: Queen Śrīmālā and the Tathāgatagarbha*. Missoula, Mont., 1980. See also her *Women in Buddhism* (Berkeley, 1980).

Prebish, Charles S. "A Review of Scholarship on the Buddhist Councils." *Journal of Asian Studies* 33 (February 1974): 239–254. Treats the problem of the early schools and the history and significance of their Vinaya. Other works on this topic include Prebish's "The Prātimokṣa Puzzle: Facts Versus Fantasy," *Journal of the American Oriental Society* 94 (April–June 1974): 168–176; and *Buddhist Monastic Discipline: The Sanskrit Prātimokṣa Sūtras of the Mahāsāṅghikas and the Mūlasarvāstivādins* (University Park, Pa., 1975).

Prebish, Charles S., and Janice J. Nattier. "Mahāsāṅghika Origins: The Beginning of Buddhist Sectarianism." *History of Religions* 16 (1977): 237–272. An original and convincing argument against the conception of the Mahāsāṃghika as "liberals."

Rhys Davids, T. W. *Buddhist India*. London, 1903. A classic, although its methodology is questionable. Also of some use, in spite of its date, is his "Sects (Buddhist)," in the *Encyclopaedia of Religion and Ethics,* edited by James Hastings, vol. 11 (Edinburgh, 1920), pp. 307–309.

Robinson, Richard H. "Classical Indian Philosophy." In *Chapters in Indian Civilization,* edited by Joseph Elder, vol. 1, pp. 127–227. Dubuque, 1970. A bit idiosyncratic, but valuable in its attempt to understand Buddhist philosophy as part of general Indian currents and patterns of speculative thought. Robinson's "The Religion of the Householder Bodhisattva," *Bharati* (1966): 31–55, challenges the notion of Mahāyāna as a lay movement.

Robinson, Richard H., and Willard L. Johnson. *The Buddhist Religion: A Historical Introduction*. 3d rev. ed. Belmont, Calif., 1982. A great improvement over earlier editions, this book is now a useful manual, with a good bibliography for the English reader.

Ruegg, David S. *The Study of Indian and Tibetan Thought*. Leiden, 1967. The most valuable survey of the main issues of modern scholarship on Indian Buddhism, especially on the early period. The author has also written the definitive study of the Tathāgata-garbha doctrines in *La théorie du tathāgatagarbha et du gotra* (Paris, 1969). See also on the Mādhyamika school his "Towards a Chronology of the Madhyamaka School," in *Indological and Buddhist Studies in Honour of J. W. de Jong* (Canberra, 1982), pp. 505–530, and *The Literature of the Madhyamaka School of Philosophy in India* (Wiesbaden, 1981).

Schayer, Stanislaus. "Precanonical Buddhism." *Acta Orientalia* 7 (1935): 121–132. Posits an early Buddhism not found explicitly in the canon; attempts to reconstruct the doctrines of Buddhism antedating the canon.

Schopen, Gregory. "The Phrase '*sa pṛthivīpradeśaś caityabhūto bhavet*' in the *Vajracchedikā*: Notes on the Cult of the Book in Mahāyāna." *Indo-Iranian Journal* 17 (1975): 147–181. Schopen's work has opened new perspectives on the early history of Mahāyāna, emphasizing its religious rather than philosophical character and revealing generalized beliefs and practices rather than the speculations of the elite. See also "Sukhāvatī as a Generalized Religious Goal in Sanskrit Mahāyāna Sūtra Literature," *Indo-Iranian Journal* 19 (1977): 177–210; "Mahāyāna in Indian Inscriptions," *Indo-Iranian Journal* 21 (1979): 1–19; and "Two Problems in the History of Indian Buddhism: The Layman/Monk Distinction and the Doctrines of the Transference of Merit," *Studien zur Indologie und Iranistik* 10 (1985): 9–47.

Schlingloff, Dieter. *Die Religion des Buddhismus*. 2 vols. Berlin, 1963. An insightful exposition of Buddhism, mostly from the perspective of canonical Indian documents.

Snellgrove, David L., ed. *Buddhist Himālaya*. Oxford, 1957. Although the context of this study is modern Himalayan Buddhism, it contains useful information on Buddhist Tantra in general. Snellgrove's two-volume *The Hevajra Tantra: A Critical Study* (London, 1959) includes an English translation and study of this major Tantric work. In *The Image of the Buddha* (Tokyo and London, 1978) Snellgrove, in collaboration with other scholars, surveys the history of the iconography of the Buddha image.

Stcherbatsky, Theodore. *The Central Conception of Buddhism and the Meaning of the Word "Dharma"* (1923). Reprint, Delhi, 1970. A classic introduction to Sarvāstivādin doctrine. On the Mādhyamika, Stcherbatsky wrote *The Conception of Buddhist Nirvana* (Leningrad, 1927). On early Buddhism, see his "The Doctrine of the Buddha," *Bulletin of the School of Oriental Studies* 6 (1932): 867–896, and "The 'Dharmas' of the Buddhists and the 'Gunas' of the Sāṃkhyas," *Indian Historical Quarterly* 10 (1934): 737–760. Stcherbatsky categorized the history of Buddhist thought in "Die drei Richtungen in der Philosophie des Buddhismus," *Rocznik Orjentalistyczny* 10 (1934): 1–37.

Takasaki Jikidō. *Nyoraizō shisō no keisei—Indo daijō bukkyō shisō kenkyū*. Tokyo, 1974. A major study of Tathāgata-garbha thought in India.

Thapar, Romila. *Asoka and the Decline of the Mauryas*. London, 1961. Controversial study of Aśoka's reign. Her conclusions are summarized in her *History of India*, vol. 1 (Baltimore, 1965). Also relevant for the study of Indian Buddhism are her *Ancient Indian Social History: Some Interpretations* (New Delhi, 1978), *Dissent in the Early Indian Tradition* (Dehradun, 1979), and *From Lineage of State* (Bombay, 1984).

Thomas, Edward J. *The Life of the Buddha as Legend and History* (1927). New York, 1960. Still the only book-length, critical study of the life of Buddha. Less current, but still useful, is the author's 1933 work *The History of Buddhist Thought* (New York, 1975).

Varma, V. P. *Early Buddhism and Its Origins*. New Delhi, 1973.

Vetter, Tilmann. "The Most Ancient Form of Buddhism." In his *Buddhism and Its Relation to Other Religions*. Kyoto, 1985.

Warder, A. K. *Indian Buddhism*. 2d rev. ed. Delhi, 1980. One of the few modern surveys of the field, this work includes a bibliography of classical sources (pp. 523–574). Unfortunately, the author does not make use of materials available in Chinese and Tibetan translation.

Watanabe Fumimaro. *Philosophy and Its Development in the Nikāyas and Abhidhamma*. Delhi, 1983. The beginnings of Buddhist scholasticism, especially as seen in the transition from Sūtra to Abhidharma literature.

Watters, Thomas. *On Yuan Chwang's Travels in India*. 2 vols. London, 1904–1905. Extensive study of Hsüan-tsang's travels.

Wayman, Alex. *The Buddhist Tantras: Light on Indo-Tibetan Esotericism*. New York, 1973. Not a survery or introduction to the study of Indian Tantra, but a collection of essays on specific issues and problems. Chapter 1.2 deals with the problem of the early history of Tantra. See also Wayman's *Yoga of the Guhyasamājatantra: The Arcane Lore of Forty Verses; A Buddhist Tantra Commentary* (Delhi, 1977). In his "The Mahāsāṅghika and the Tathāgatagarbha (Buddhist Doctrinal History, Study 1)," *Journal of the International Association of Buddhist*

Studies 1 (1978): 35–50, Wayman discusses possible connections between the Mahāsāṃghika subsects of Andhra and the development of Mahāyāna. His "Meditation in Theravāda and Mahīśāsaka," *Studia Missionalia* 25 (1976): 1–28, is a study of the doctrine of meditation in two of the leading schools of Hīnayāna.

Winternitz, Moriz. *Geschichte der indischen Literature*, vol. 2. Leipzig, 1920. Translated as *A History of Indian Literature* (Delhi, 1983). Largely dated but not superseded.

Zelliot, Eleanor. *Dr. Ambedkar and the Mahar Movement.* Philadelphia, 1969.

3 JAINISM

Colette Caillat

Jainism (or Jinism) is the name given to the religious movement of the Jains, whose community follows the religious path established by Vardhamāna Mahāvīra, a prophet also known as the Jina, or "Victor." Born in northern Bihar, India, Mahāvīra is alleged to have preached in the sixth century BCE. Thus, according to tradition, he lived in the same area, and at approximately the same time as the Buddha. The earliest developments of Buddhism and Jainism are comparable to some extent. In later centuries, however, their destinies diverged. While Buddhism was progressively suppressed in India, the Jains remained in their homeland where, today, they form an admittedly small but nonetheless influential and comparatively prosperous community of 2,604,837 people (1981 census).

HISTORY

There remains no objective document concerning the beginnings of Jainism. The date of Mahāvīra's death ("entry into *nirvāṇa*"), which is the starting point of the traditional Jain chronology, corresponds to 527/526 BCE, but some scholars believe it occurred about one century later. In any case, the Jain community was probably not "founded" solely by Mahāvīra. Rather, his adherents merged with the followers of a previous prophet (Pārśva); reorganizations and reforms ensued and a fifth commandment was added to the older code, as was the practice of confession and repentance; nakedness came to be recommended to those among the believers who took the religious vows, although apparently it was not imposed on Pārśva's disciples.

Some differences in the monks' behavior were accepted, but disputes appear to have arisen at the end of the fourth century BCE, allegedly after a famine forced several religious groups, led by the eminent patriarch Bhadrabāhu, to migrate south. Finally, in 79 CE, the community split into two main churches—the Digambara, "sky-clad" (and thus naked), and the Śvetāmbara, "white-clad." By the time of the separation, however, the doctrine had been fixed for the whole community; this accounts for the fundamental agreement in the main tenets professed by the Śvetāmbaras and the Digambaras. On the other hand, epigraphic and literary records prove that religious "companies" *(gaṇa)* already existed, subdivided into *śākhās* ("branches") and *kulas* ("families" or "schools"). The remarkable organization of Mahāvīra's church has proved a firm foundation for the welfare and survival of his followers. The community of the monks and nuns is said to have been entrusted by Mahāvīra to eleven chief disciples, or *gaṇadharas* ("company leaders"). The chief among them was Gautama Indrabhūti, while his colleague Sudharman allegedly taught his own pupil Jambū the words spoken by the Jina. Thus the canon of the Śvetāmbaras goes back to Sudharman through uninterrupted lines of religious masters *(ācāryas)*.

The history of the sacred texts is further marked by the efforts made to preserve them from oblivion. To this effect, about two centuries after Mahāvīra, a synod was held in Pāṭaliputra (modern-day Patna). A great role was then played by Bhadrabāhu—whom the Jain traditions unanimously consider to be the last person who knew the Pūrvas (the "ancient" texts).

Other councils were later held by the Śvetāmbaras. The most important met in the middle of the fifth century in Valabhī (in Kathiawar, Gujarat), and at its close numerous manuscripts of the authoritative texts were copied and widely distributed in the community. However, the Digambaras deny the authenticity of this corpus and instead recognize the authority of "procanonical" treatises.

After Mahāvīra's time the Jain community spread along the caravan routes from Magadha (Bihar) to the west and south. They claim to have enjoyed the favor of numerous rulers. Notwithstanding possible exaggerations, they probably were supported by a number of princes, including King Bimbisāra of Magadha (a contemporary of the Jina), and later the Maurya emperor Candragupta Maurya (who, they say, fasted unto death on one of the hillocks overlooking the village of Śravaṇa Beḷgoḷa, following Bhadrabāhu's example). By the fifth century (or earlier), the Digambaras were influential in the Deccan, especially in Karnataka. Under the Gaṅga, Rāṣṭrakūṭa, and other dynasties Jain culture undoubtedly flourished. Numerous sects were founded, among them the brilliant Yāpanīya, now extinct. In the tenth century, however, Vaiṣṇavism and Śaivism crushed Jainism in the Tamil area, and in the twelfth century they triumphed over Jainism in Karnataka as well.

As for the Śvetāmbaras, they were especially successful in Gujarat where one of their famous pontifs, Hemacandra (1089–1172), served as minister to the Cālukya king Kumārapāla (1144–1173) and enforced some Jain rules in the kingdom. Decline was to follow soon after his death, which was hastened by the Muslim invasions. Jain activities did not cease with his demise, however. Elaborate sanctuaries were erected, such as that on Mount Abu, now in Rajasthan. The rise of several reformist sects testifies to the vitality of the Śvetāmbaras, who even succeeded in interesting the Moghul emperor Akbar (r. 1555–1605) in the Jain doctrine. Some of those sects have survived: the Sthānakvāsins (founded 1653) and Terāpanthins (founded 1761), who are known for their strong opposition to idols and temple worship, and the present Anuvrata movement, which was founded in 1949 by the Terāpanthin monk Acarya Sri Tulsi.

Although the Jain community never regained its former splendor, it did not disappear entirely; nowadays, the Digambaras are firmly established in Maharashtra and Karnataka and the Śvetāmbaras in Panjab, Rajasthan, and Gujarat. Jain businessmen are generally active in all the main cities of India, and many also outside India.

LITERATURE

From early times the Jains have been engaged in a variety of literary activities. Their works, whether intended for their own adherents or composed with rival groups in view, generally have an edifying, proselytizing, or apologetic purpose. The languages used vary to suit the audience and the epoch.

All of the oldest texts are composed in varieties of Prakrits (i.e., Middle Indo-Aryan), more or less akin to the languages in current use among the people of northern India at the time of the first sermons. Later, the Jains turned to local vernaculars such as Old Gujarati in the North, and Tamil and Kannaḍa in the Dravidian South. In the Middle Ages, however, they also adopted the use of Sanskrit (i.e., Old Indo-Aryan), which had become the normal idiom for all scholarly debates.

The Jain traditions, while considering that the fourteen Pūrvas have been lost, contend that part of the material they included was incorporated into later books. The Digambaras boldly assert that some sections are the immediate basis of two of their early treatises (c. first century CE) whereas, according to the Śvetāmbaras, the teachings of the Pūrvas were embedded in the so-called twelfth Aṅga of their canon, now considered lost. The earliest extant documents are the canonical scriptures of the Śvetāmbaras and the systematic treatises *(prakaraṇa*s) of the Digambaras.

The Śvetāmbara canon (variously called *āgama,* "tradition," *siddhānta,* "doctrine," etc.) is composed of forty-five treatises (according to the Sthānakvāsins, only thirty-two) grouped in six sections: the Aṅgas ('limbs"), Upāṅgas ("sub-*aṅgas*"), Prakīrṇakas ("miscellanea"), Chedasūtras ("treatises on cutting" [partially] religious authority; these mostly concern disciplinary technicalities), Cūlikāsūtras ("appendixes"; two propaedeutic texts), and Mūlasūtras ("basic" texts). As systematic as this arrangement appears to be, the canon is in fact mostly a compilation of texts of different origin, age, and importance, focusing on a wide range of topics; an entire subculture is reflected in its books. The oldest parts are written in a Prakrit characterized by several eastern (i.e., Gangetic) features, whereas a westernized idiom prevails in the later portions. Moreover, the preservation and traditional interpretation of the canonical texts has been ensured by an enormous mass of scholastic exegesis, written first in Prakrit and later (beginning with Haribhadra in the mid-eighth century) in Sanskrit.

The Digambaras rely on *prakaraṇa*s, of which the oldest are written in a third variety of Prakrit. Their authors, who lived around the first century of the common era, are: Vaṭṭakera, author of the *Mūlācāra* (Basic Conduct; approximately 1,250 stanzas); Kundakunda, a prolific writer and much admired mystic, and author of *Samayasāra,* (Essence of the Doctrine) and of *Pravacanasāra* (Essence of the Teaching); and Śivārya, who wrote *Ārādhana* (Accomplishment), which has more than 2,000 stanzas.

These books mark the beginning of an important literary genre that was also cultivated by the Śvetāmbaras. One of the fundamental treatises in this category is by Umāsvāti (c. second century; most likely a Śvetāmbara): with small variants, both churches accept the authority of his *Tattvārthādhigama Sūtra* (Sūtra for Attaining the Meaning of the Principles), a doctrinal synthesis composed of 350 aphorisms written in Sanskrit. This linguistic selection shows that the Jains were prepared to engage in polemics with other schools of thought and to engage the brahmans with Brahmanic terminology and words of discourse.

At this stage, the canonical collections and procanonical writings have been supplemented by many new compositions, often termed *anuyoga,* or "exposition." From the first to the fifteenth century CE an enormous mass of literature was produced, covering a wide range of topics: dialectics and logic, politics and religious law, grammar, scientific subjects, epico-lyric poems devoted to "universal history," *dharmakathās* ("narratives on the [Jain] law"), *kathānakas* ("short stories" illustrating the doctrinal teachings), gnomic poetry, and hymns. Although Jain literary activity has never ceased, since the fourteenth and fifteenth centuries it has often lacked its earlier force and originality.

RELIGIOUS PRACTICES

The practices observed among the Jains are dependent on two main factors: specific Jain convictions and the general Indian environment. They reflect, in fact, many parallels with the rules and observances of Brahmanic ascetics and Buddhist monks.

All Jains are members of the four-fold congregation *(saṃgha),* composed of monks and nuns, laymen and laywomen. They share a common belief in the *triratna* ("three jewels"): *samyagdarśana* ("right faith"), *samyagjñāna* ("right knowledge"), and *samyakcaritra* ("right conduct"). Observance of the "three jewels" provides the conditions for the attainment of the goal, that is, liberation from bondage. Deliverance can be attained only by the *nirgrantha,* the Jain monk "free from bonds" both external and internal. The ideal practices therefore are those in force in the (male) religious community. Nevertheless, householders are permitted certain ceremonies (such as the worship of images, a practice borrowed from Hinduism), though they do actually break some of the restraints clearly accepted by all. Both the lay and the monastic followers must take solemn vows (*vratas*), which form the basis of Jain ethics and will guide the pious believers' lives.

The monks and nuns take the five "great vows" *(mahāvratas*), pledging to abstain from (1) injuring life, (2) false speech, (3) taking what is not given, (4) unchastity, and (5) appropriation. A sixth *vrata* ("vow") consists of abstaining from taking food and drink at night: it is evidently aimed at avoiding injury to insects, which might go unnoticed in the darkness, and thus is a consequence of the first *mahāvrata.*

The life of Mahāvīra is regarded as an ideal model. But despite the fact that he is depicted as living in solitude, ordinary monks and nuns live in a "company" *(gaṇa, gaccha),* where they benefit from the advice of their superiors and from the active solidarity of their brethren. The *gaṇa* is further subdivided into smaller units.

Religious age and hierarchy play a great role: elders look to the material and spiritual welfare of the company; the *upādhyāya* is a specialist in teaching the scriptures; the *ācārya* acts as spiritual master. Full ordination takes place after a short novitiate that lasts approximately four months. Admission as a novice is subject to prior examination. At his departure from home, the novice abandons all property and his head is shaved. He then receives the equipment of a monk (alms bowl, broom, napkin, loincloths), and is taught the basic formulas or "obligations" *(āvaśyakas*). Full admission entails taking the five great vows mentioned above. The *nirgranthas* (monks) are also called *bhikṣu* ("mendicant") or *sādhu* ("pious"); the *nigranthīs* (nuns) are called *bhikṣuṇī,* or *sādhvī.* Monks and nuns must observe the utmost reserve. The nun's status, however, is always inferior to that of the monk.

Right religious conduct is minutely defined, giving rules for habitation and wandering, begging, study, confession, and penances. During the four months of the rainy season the religious groups remain in one locality; nowadays fixed places of shelter *(upāśrayas)* are prepared for them, often near a temple, where householders visit, ask advice, and listen to teachings. During the rest of the year members of the order wander from place to place, walking with circumspection indefatigably on the long Indian roads. Day and night are each divided into four equal parts *(pauruṣīs)* with prescribed occupations: the first and fourth *pauruṣīs* of both day and night are reserved for study, the second of both day and night for meditation, the third of the night for sleep, and the third of the day for alms-begging (*Uttarajjhāyā* 22.11–12; 17–18).

The begging tour is important in a community where the religious members have no possessions: it is therefore minutely codified. As always in India, the prescriptions concerning food are rigorous: to be "pure and acceptable," food should not be prepared especially for the monk and should contain absolutely no living particle. The monk—and the layman—are thus constrained to be strictly vegetarian, to the point that they should take only sterile water. Because of the importance attached to food, many of the "external" ascetic practices (which include difficult postures, etc.) consist of restrictions in the number, abundance, and seasoning of the meals. Fasting can even be prolonged unto death *(saṃlekhanā),* which is regarded as "the wise man's death."

Begging and fasting must be conducted with great care and preceded by confession *(ālocanā)* and repentance *(pratikramaṇa),* which are deemed essential activities. These two also take place at regular intervals (each fortnight), and, ideally, every day. They are prominent in the list of the ten penances which, together with good education, service, study, mental concentration, and abandonment, form the six "internal" austerities. These have been specified since the earliest tradition and are so perfectly integrated in the doctrine that the intellectual and spiritual aspirations of Jainism cannot be doubted.

Called *śrāvakas* ("listeners") or *upāsakas* ("servants"), the lay believers also take five main vows, similar to (but milder than) the *mahāvratas*, and hence termed *aṇuvratas* ("lesser vows"). These include *ahiṃsā* ("nonviolence") and *satya* ("truthfulness"). They are complemented by three "strengthening vows" and four "vows of spiritual discipline," of which the last, but not the least, is *dāna* ("charity"). *Dāna* has a wide range of connotations; in its more restricted sense the term naturally refers to almsgiving—which ensures the ascetics' existence, and therefore the transmission of the doctrine; the laity should further visit and venerate the mendicant teachers. Following the example set by monks, householders observe the six "obligatory" duties, cultivate the right state of mind (often by taking part in pilgrimages to holy places), regularly practice meditation, observe fasts on the eighth and fourteenth days of the moon's waxing and waning periods, and confess their faults: a popular ceremony is the Sāṃvatsarī ("the annual"), performed for an eight- to ten-day period during the rainy season, when a general admission of sins and pleas for forgiveness are directed toward all.

These practices are evidently relevant in a doctrine that emphasizes individual exertion, and that considers the Jinas to be inaccessible, liberated souls. On the other hand, the Jain church has not been able to ignore the devotional aspirations of the laity, who are also attracted by Hindu ritual. Hence, although temple worship (with the burning and waving of lamps, plucked flowers and fruit, preparation of sandal paste, etc.) implies violence, cultic practices are tolerated, being considered ultimately of help to the worshiper's progress. Most sects (though not the Sthānakvāsins) allow the *upāsaka* to visit the temples and participate in rituals, including solemn celebrations such as the Digambara anointing of the head of Bāhubali's statue in Śravaṇa Beḷgoḷa, which every twelve years attracts enormous crowds. (Bāhubali was the son of the prince who later became the first *tīrthaṃkara* of the present *avasarpiṇī* period.) All these practices are believed to lead the soul to achieve its own "perfection" *(siddhi),* acting as vehicles through which one crosses the stream of the innumerable rebirths one must face in the immensity of the cosmos during the course of many eons.

MYTHOLOGY AND COSMOLOGY

The Jain representation of the cosmos *(loka)* is akin to (though not identical with) the standard Brahmanical descriptions. [*See* Cosmology, *article on* Hindu and Jain Cosmologies.] The cosmos is composed of three main parts: the lower, middle, and upper worlds. It is often represented as a colossal upright human figure, the enormous base of which is formed by seven hells (populated by beings whose past actions were violent and cruel and who consequently suffer terrible torments).

Compared with the other two, the "middle world" (Madhyaloka) is extremely small and resembles a thin disk. Though small, it has a great importance: there, in a few circumscribed areas, time and the law of retribution prevail, different kinds of men live (among them the civilized *āryas*), and spiritual awakening and perfection can be achieved. This is possible in some of its innermost parts, especially in the circular *dvīpa* ("island") situated in the middle of the Madhyaloka: this is Jambūdvīpa ("continent of the rose-apple tree"), with Mount Mandara (or Meru) rising exactly in its center and Bhārata (India) in its southern part. It is surrounded by numerous alternating rings of oceans and island-continents.

Occasionally, divinities come from the other two worlds to visit the Madhyaloka. Others belong to it: at various heights far above its surface those stellar gods (suns, moons, planets, constellations, and stars) who overlook the two and a half inner continents revolve around Meru. In twenty-four hours the suns and moons accomplish half the circuit, so that there are two of each, at a distance of 180 degrees from one another.

Beginning far above the stars, the upper world appears as a gradually purer and purer counterpart of the lower world. Finally, near the top of the *loka* lies the place, shaped like an inverted umbrella (or the crescent moon) where the *siddhas* ("perfected ones," i.e., liberated souls) are assembled.

Divinities are found in the three worlds, and fall into four main classes. Only mankind, however, can give birth to the Jain prophets, who are called *tīrthaṃkaras*, literally, "ford-makers" across the ocean of rebirths.

Like other Indian systems, Jainism compares the cyclic course of time *(kāla)* to the movement of a wheel, and divides it into recurring periods called *kalpas* ("eons"). Each *kalpa* has two phases, each further divided into six eras. In the first, descending phase *(avasarpiṇī)* a progressive decline leads from great prosperity to utter misery, which in the second, ascending phase *(utsarpiṇī)* progressively recedes until great prosperity is reached again. The first Jina of each phase is born in the course of the third era, which is characterized by prosperity mixed with sorrow. We are at present in the fifth era of an *avasarpiṇī* whose first Jina was Ṛṣabha and whose next twenty-three *tīrthaṃkaras* lived in the fourth era, which ended seventy-five years and eight and one-half months after the death of Mahāvīra (i.e., according to the Jains, 527/526 BCE).

DOCTRINE

The tenets of Jainism are well delineated in the Śvetāmbara canon and the Digambara procanonical books, and are systematically presented in the *Tattvārthādhigama Sūtra.* Jain logic (for the most part elaborated somewhat later, probably to meet the needs of controversy) will here be sketched first, together with the Jain theory of knowledge.

Knowledge *(jñāna),* of which the Jains distinguish five kinds, is an essential attribute of the soul *(jīva).* It culminates in *kevala-jñāna,* absolute and perfect omniscience. [*See also* Jñāna.]

The Jain system of logic is characterized by the complementary theories of *syādvāda* ("[different] possibilities") and of *nayavāda* ("[method of] approach"). The first affirms that a statement about an object is valid not absolutely but under one of "several conditions" (hence its other name, *anekāntavāda*); considering that an object "can be" *(syād)* such, not such, and so forth, seven modes of assertion are distinguished. The *nayavāda* defines seven main points of view (generic, specific, etc.) from which to consider an object. The Jains adopt an empirical standpoint.

Jainism is a pluralist substantialism that insists on the reality of change. The world and non-world are basically constituted from five *astikāyas* ("masses of being"): the *jīva* ("life" or soul, a real, spiritual monad), and, on the other hand, the inanimate substances: matter, space, movement, and rest. To these, several schools add time. All these factors are eternal and infinite in number. Matter furnishes to the souls a body in which to be incorporated and the possibility of corporeal functions. There are five kinds of bodies, each having different functions. All corporeal beings possess at least two of them, the "karmic" and the "fiery" (the latter for digestion). The karmic body results from previous actions; it is intimately attached to the *jīva,* for whom it causes servitude: hence arise incarnation and transmigration, that is, the law of the universe. [*See also* Karman, *article on* Hindu and Jain Concepts.]

Bondage occurs because the subtle matter resulting from anterior intentions and volitions is attracted to the soul through the vibration of its "soul-points"; this attraction (called *yoga*) is exercised by means of the material elements of speech, body, and mind. The subtle matter that has been so attracted becomes *karman* when entering the soul. The pious Jain strives to rid the latter of these material extrinsic elements. When life ends, the *jīva,* if it has recovered its essential nature, immediately rejoins the other *siddhas* at the pinnacle of the universe. If not, it passes to its new place of rebirth (determined by its *karman*); there are four "ways" of destiny: human, divine, animal, and infernal.

The process of bondage and liberation, then, may be summarized in the following table of seven categories: (1) *jīva;* (2) *ajīva;* (3) influx of karmic matter into the *jīva;* (4) bondage; (5) stoppage of karmic influx *(saṃvara);* (6) expulsion *(nirjarā)* of previously accumulated karmic matter; and (7) total liberation, to which (8) merit and (9) demerit are sometimes added. This table is both ontological and moral, thus leading to Jain ethics.

ETHICS

The essentials of Jain ethics are contained in the sets of vows to be taken by the monks and nuns on the one hand, and by the lay believers on the other. Monks and householders further observe other series of prohibitions and engagements that are meant to favor spiritual progress.

The monks cultivate *saṃvara,* the spiritual path defined by the cessation of karmic influx, by means of established ethical and behavioral practices that are usually enumerated in stock lists, as follows:

1. the triple "supervision" of mental, verbal, and bodily activities
2. the fivefold "care" not to hurt living beings when walking, acting, speaking, begging, or performing excretory functions
3. the "tenfold righteousness," or *daśa-dharma:* patience, humility, uprightness, purity, truthfulness, restraint, austerity, renunciation, voluntary poverty, and spiritual obedience
4. the twelve mental "reflections," or *anuprekṣā*s, including reflection on the impermanence of things, the helplessness of man, the course of transmigration *(saṃsāra),* the unmitigated solitude of each being in this cycle, the fundamental difference between body and soul, the impurity of the body, the presence of karmic influx, the means by which such influx may be stopped, the ways in which one may rid oneself of karmic matter, the fact that each person is responsible for his own salvation without the assistance of a deity, the rarity of enlightenment, and the truth (i.e., of the teachings presented by the Jinas, especially that of *ahiṃsā*)
5. the twenty-two "trials" (ranging from hunger to confusion) imposed by the pains inherent in religious life.

The monk finally sheds the residues of *karman* by means of steadfast and thorough asceticism *(tapas).*

Lists of the virtues required of the householder have received much attention in Jain tradition and literatures. Some lists include as many as thirty-five ethical imperatives incumbent on the nonclerical Jain, but all include five *aṇuvrata*s ("small vows," as opposed to the monks' *mahāvrata*s, or "great vows"): *(ahiṃsā),* truthfulness and honesty in all business affairs *(satya),* that material wealth be gained only through legitimate transactions (*asteya,* lit., "non-stealing"), restraint from all illicit sexual activities *(brahma),* and renunciation of one's attachment to material wealth *(aparigraha).* Moreover, the householder or business person should progress through the higher stages of renunciation involving increasingly complete performance of these vows. Thus, he can come closer and closer to fulfilling the monk's vows as well, and ultimately can attain the purity of the "wise man's death," the fast-unto-death *(saṃlekhanā).*

The actual path to liberation *(mokṣa)* is described by Jains as one that includes fourteen "stages of qualification" *(guṇa-sthāna).* Leaving the state characterized by "wrong views," the path leads ultimately to the elimination of all passions and culminates in omniscience. [*See also* Mokṣa.]

CULTIC STRUCTURES

It is a specific aspect of the householder's religious life that he is allowed to take part in temple rituals and to worship temple images. In fact, abundant amounts of money are spent on the construction of new temples and in the restoration or reproduction of ancient monuments, a source of prestige as well as a meritorious act.

The structure of the Jain temple is on the whole similar to the Hindu temple. [*See* Temple, *article on* Hindu Temples.] The distinctive feature of the Jain shrine is the image of the *tīrthaṃkara* to whom it is dedicated and the idols of the prophets who flank him or occupy the various surrounding niches. Secondary divinities are frequently added (and are very popular); there are also auspicious and symbolic diagrams: the wheel of the Jain law, and the "Five Supreme Ones": *arhat*s, *siddha*s, *ācārya*s, *upādhyāya*s, and *sādhu*s. There are also conventional representations of continents, of holy places, and of the great festive congregation *(samavasaraṇa)* in the middle of which the Jina is said to have delivered his sermon for the benefit of all creatures. In effect, the Jain temple is often said to be a sort of replica of this assembly. The offerings placed on the offering plates or planks by the faithful with the rice grains he has brought to the shrine are symbols of the three jewels (three dots), which provide escape from the cycle of bondage (the *svastika*) and lead to *siddhi* (a crescent at the top of the figure).

The example set by great men other than the *tīrthaṃkara*s is also commemorated: homage is paid to the "footprints" (*pādukā*s) in stone of the great teachers. Above all, Bāhubali is a source of inspiration to the Digambaras: "sky-clad" on the crest of the Indragiri hill in Śravaṇa Beḷgoḷa, his colossal monolithic statue (fifty-seven feet high, erected c. 980) attracts streams of pilgrims, and has been reproduced at several other sites.

The two main churches differ on some other points of varying importance, such as the lists of auspicious objects and the cognizances of certain *tīrthaṃkara*s. The question of nudity has been controversial for centuries: nowadays in the Śvetāmbara shrines the *tīrthaṃkara*s are partly clothed and even decorated, with silver inlay in their eyes.

ICONOGRAPHY

As is to be expected, Jain art is essentially religious. The earliest preserved specimens apparently date back to the age of the Mauryas (third century BCE), and though the Jains' artistic activities have never ceased, their most impressive masterpieces date from the fifth to the fifteenth century CE. These were produced in central and southern India, and above all in the west and in Karnataka.

Stupas were among the first monuments erected by the Jain community, but very soon the Buddhists alone continued this tradition, so that in effect, the Jains have two main types of architectural masterpieces: rock-cut and structural temples. Caves had been used as habitations for monks from very early times in many parts of India. Many were altered, particularly in the Deccan and Tamil Nadu, to make them suitable as shrines. Some are comparatively simple, as, for example, in Sittanavasal. In the Cāḷukya kingdom caverns have been elaborately carved in the cliffs of Vātāpi (Badami) and in Aihole, where the carvings date to the seventh century; under the Rāṣṭrakūṭas (eighth to tenth centuries) the activity shifted to Ellora, where the Jains chiseled out of the rock a monolithic shrine called the Choṭā ("little") Kailāsa.

Structural temples are the most common. The earliest were probably made of wood; later, brick and masonry were used. Building in stone became extremely popular, and thus many architectural monuments have been preserved from as early as the sixth and seventh centuries. The general structure of the Jain temple resembles that of the Brahmanic shrine. The basic ground plan is comparatively simple: several halls in an axial line lead to the sanctum; the number of these *maṇḍapa*s can be increased and the decorative features multiplied. On the other hand, the Jains have favored a variant of the axial hall plan, the so-called *catur-mukha* ("four-faced") type, with a pivotal square at the center and four doors opening in the four directions giving access to a quadruple *tīrthaṃkara* image. Many of the shrines are built in an enclosed courtyard.

Some sites are famous: in the Deccan, Śravaṇa Beḷgoḷa and Aihole (from the ninth century); in southern Karnataka, Mudbidri ("Jain Kāśī," fourteenth century); in Tamil Nadu, Tirupparuttikkunram ("Jain Kāñcī," eleventh century). In the North, temple building began early in Osia near Jodhpur in Rajasthan (from the seventh century onward). In central India, Deogarh has comparatively simple shrines (beginning in the seventh or eighth century), whereas in Khajuraho several temples (such as Pārśvanāth temple, constructed in 954) rival the Brahmanic monuments.

It is probably in western India, however, that the Jain temples are the most numerous and impressive. Many have contributed to the fame of the "Caulukyan style." A number are in Mount Abu, where one of the earliest was erected in 1032, and several are built of delicately polished white marble. Another celebrated complex is in the Aravalli hills, at Ranakpur, where the main shrine (constructed in 1439) is of the *catur-mukha* type. Finally, in the Kathiawar Peninsula famous temple cities have been built in holy pilgrimage places: on the Girnar hill (900 meters above sea level), and south of Palitana, where, 600 meters above sea level, they cover two ridges, each some 320 meters long, of the Śatruñjaya mountain (from the sixteenth century onward).

For all these monuments a large quantity of statues and bas-reliefs (sometimes of enormous dimensions) was prepared in various sorts of stone and metal. Metal casting was well developed in the Caulukya period; a statue of the first *tīrthaṃkara* in one of the Abu temples weighs more than 4,000 kilograms. Smaller pieces have been constantly and abundantly carved and molded for home shrines and temples. For poorer people terra-cotta has been used.

The most characteristic carvings are the hieratic sculptures of the *tīrthaṃkara*s (and Bāhubali); they conform to strict canons that probably came into existence around the beginning of the common era (though two torsos found near Patna are older and are perhaps Mauryan). The Jains have also represented lesser divinities, whose carvings are not as hieratic as those of the *tīrthaṃkara*s. Moreover, decorative pillars, ceilings, brackets, friezes, and panels adorn many shrines (in Khajuraho, Abu, and Ranakpur) and contrast by their exuberance with the mystic concentration, renouncement, and serenity of the prophets. The *tīrthaṃkara* figures (sitting or standing erect in meditation) are now renowned worldwide: innumerable statues are installed in the shrines, and bas-reliefs are carved on the walls of a number of caves and cells. Many carvings of all sizes can also be seen in the open, chiseled on cliffs and boulders. Perhaps some of the best known are the huge images engraved in rows on the Gwalior cliffs; others, on the contrary, are extremely delicate.

Though only a few mural paintings have been well preserved there is no doubt that many shrines were embellished by painted panels. Nevertheless it is owing to the numerous illustrated manuscripts left by the Jains that their painting has come to be appreciated. The earliest miniatures are on palm leaves (Śvetāmbara, 1060 CE; Digambara, c. 1110); the largest dimensions of paper manuscripts afforded new facilities to the Śvetāmbara artists of Gujarat, especially in the fourteenth and fifteenth centuries. They popularized a typical "western Indian style," with many stereotypes and conventional figures (characterized by protruding eyes). The manner is linear, the colors bright (red, blue, white, green), placed directly beside one another. Altogether, in the five centuries preceding Akbar's reign, the quantity of Jain miniature painting was considerable: in this field no Indian community has matched the profuseness of the Śvetāmbaras.

The Jains have also been very successful in woodcutting, as can still be seen in Rajasthan and Gujarat: this artistic technique flourished particularly from the seventeenth to the nineteenth century. In and around Patan (Gujarat) it is not rare to see window frames and door lintels carved with *tīrthaṃkara* images or auspicious signs, as well as screen doors, lattice windows, and decorated pillars supporting the upper stories in private homes. Other masterpieces of which the preserved specimens are comparatively recent (from the fifteenth century onward), although the first models are certainly older, are the fine wooden temples (whether public or home shrines), still numerous in Gujarat. Given by wealthy individuals of the middle class, these sanctuaries are of modest proportions but exquisitely carved and decorated, sometimes with motifs influenced by the Mughal style. Built on the same pattern, the home shrines of the Gujarati Jains (some dating from the fifteenth century) are also elegantly embellished, as were the homes of the wealthy householders of such centers as Ahmedabad, Patan, Palitana, and Cambay. Though not as widespread as those mentioned earlier, these include perfect masterpieces of Jain art.

PROMINENT JAIN PERSONALITIES

Jain achievements are due to the energy and courage of a comparatively united community. Certain brilliant and outstanding individuals, however, have influenced the movement, such as Devarddhi, president of the Valabhī council, or Haribhadra (eighth century), a great Śvetāmbara commentator and writer, in both Prakrit and Sanskrit. Others, such as Kundakunda and Hemacandra, embodied some or most of its tendencies or brilliantly represented it, as did Hīravijaya at Akbar's court. More recently, Mohandas Gandhi himself paid homage to the Jain jeweller and poet Raychandbhai Mehta (1868–1901). [*See also the biography of Mohandas Gandhi.*] This is the epoch when, after two to three centuries of relative stagnation, a reawakening took place thanks to enlightened monks and householders. Among those who took part in this renewal, Vijaya Dharma Suri (1868–1922) is one of the best known, both in India and in the West. Among the many others who deserve mention are two Digambara scholars, Hiralal Jain (1898–1973) and A. N. Upadhye (1906–1975), or, on the Śvetāmbara side, those whose collaboration made the foundation of the Lalbhai Dalpatbhai Institute of Indology in Ahmedabad possible: the Muni Puṇyavijaya (1895–1971), Kasturbhai Lalbhai, and Pandit D. M. Malvania (a pupil of the philosopher Sukhlalji, 1880–1978).

Through the ages the Jains, though a minority, have clearly occupied a major place in Indian history. Their culture is both original and influenced by the Brahmanic society surrounding them. Conversely, their presence has probably encouraged certain tendencies of Hinduism, perhaps the most outstanding of which are the high value set on asceticism, and, certainly, the faith in *ahiṃsā.*

[*For further discussion of specific Jain topics, see* Tīrthaṃkaras *and the biography of Mahāvīra. For the Jain influence on Hindu and Buddhist thought, see* Ahiṃsā.]

BIBLIOGRAPHY

Interest in Jainism was awakened and placed on a sound basis by the pioneering works of Albrecht Weber and Ernst Leumann, editors of *Indische Studien,* vols. 16–17 (1883; reprint, Hildesheim, 1973), and Hermann Jacobi, editor of *The Kalpasūtra of Bhadrabāhu* (Leipzig, 1879) and translator of four basic canonical books in the series "Sacred Books of the East," vols. 22, 45 (1884, 1895; reprint, Delhi, 1968), all preceded by very important introductions in English.

Excellent presentations of Jainism are Helmuth von Glasenapp's *Der Jainismus* (1925; reprint, Hildesheim, 1964) and Padmanabh S. Jaini's *The Jaina Path of Purification* (Berkeley, 1979), the latter emphasizing (somewhat unusually) the Digambara point of view. A comprehensive Hindi dictionary of Jainism is Jinendra Jaini's *Jainendra Siddhānta Kosá,* 4 vols. (New Delhi, 1970–1973). A social survey has been presented by Vilas A. Samgave, *Jaina Community,* 2d rev. ed. (Bombay, 1980). The history of Jainism in the different parts of India is the object of numerous monographs; a more general account is given in Jyoti Prasad Jain's *The Jaina Sources of the History of Ancient India, 100 B.C.–A.D. 900* (Delhi, 1964).

Given the considerable literature of the Jains, philological studies are of prime importance. Ludwig Alsdorf has provided a general survey of the scholarly achievements and desiderata in this field in his *Les études jaina: État présent et tâches futures* (Paris, 1965); the same scholar has made many other illuminating contributions.

The doctrine is presented in a masterly book by Walther Schubring, *Die Lehre der Jainas, nach den alten Quellen dargestellt* (Berlin, 1935), based mostly, but not exclusively, on the Śvetāmbara canon (with an important bibliography up to 1935); it has been translated into English from the revised German edition by Wolfgang Beurlen as *The Doctrine of the Jainas, Described after the Old Sources* (Delhi, 1962), but the above-mentioned bibliography is not included. Schubring has also edited and translated several canonical texts and is the author of basic monographs; see his *Kleine Schriften,* edited by Klaus Bruhn (Wiesbaden, 1977).

The fifth Aṅga can be regarded as a summary of Jainism: it is very well analyzed in Jozef Deleu's *Viyāhapannatti (Bhagavaī): The Fifth Aṅga of the Jaina Canon. Introduction, Critical Analysis, Commentary, and Indexes* (Brugge, 1970). It is impossible to quote all the editions (critical or uncritical) and translations of the original books. A convenient edition of the canon is the two-volume version published in Gurgaon (1954; being by Sthānakvāsins, it includes only thirty two texts). Important editorial series have also been created in recent years, the edited texts being often preceded by important introductions, and specialized journals have been published. Excellent English translations of selected Jain texts by A. L. Basham are included in *Sources of Indian Tradition,* compiled by Wm. Theodore de Bary et al. (New York, 1958).

Specialized studies are numerous. Several catalogues of manuscript collections (in India and in Europe) have been published, and contribute to our knowledge of Jain history, literature, and "manuscriptology" (a very important activity of the community); the most recent by Chandrabhāl Tripāṭhī, is the *Catalogue of the Jaina Manuscripts at Strasbourg* (Leiden, 1975), scrutinizing the systematic collection assembled there by Ernst Leumann.

Jain polemics against other schools of thought (as well as the commentators' methods) are studied in Willem B. Bollée's *Studien zum Sūyagaḍa: Die Jainas und die anderen Weltanschauungen vor der Zeitwende* (Wiesbaden, 1977). Monastic discipline is examined in Shantaram Bhalchandra Deo's *History of Jaina Monachism from Inscriptions and Literature* (Poona, 1956), and by many other scholars. The rules laid down for the laity are well analyzed in R. Williams's *Jaina Yoga* (London, 1963; reprint, Delhi, 1983). Jain cosmology is one of the three main parts of Willibald Kirfel's *Die Kosmographie der Inder* (1920; reprint, Bonn, 1967). See also my *La cosmologie jaïna* (Paris, 1981), which has been translated into English by K. R. Norman as *The Jain Cosmology* (Basel, 1981).

For the history of Jain literature (apart from good contributions in Hindi) reference can be made to Maurice Winternitz's *History of Indian Literature,* vol. 2 (Calcutta, 1933; reprint, Delhi, 1963). Attention has rightly been focused on some of the literary genres cultivated by the Jains; see, for example, Jagdishchandra Jain's *Prakrit Narrative Literature* (in fact, more or less completely Jain; New Delhi, 1981); see also the proceedings of the International Symposium on Jaina Canonical and Narrative Literature (Strasbourg, 1981), an edited version of which can be found in *Indologica Taurinensia* 11 (Turin, 1984).

Many books on Jain art and architecture have been published as a contribution to the celebration of the twenty-five hundredth anniversary of Mahāvīra's *nirvāṇa.* A comprehensive survey, edited by Amalananda Ghosh, is *Jaina Art and Architecture,* 3 vols. (New Delhi, 1974–1975), and very good monographs are collected in *Jaina Art and Archaeology,* edited by Umakant Premanand Shah and M. A. Dhaky (Ahmedabad, 1975).

Iconography is the subject of Brindavan Chandra Bhattacharyya's *The Jaina Iconography,* 2d rev. ed. (Delhi, 1974), and has inspired numerous important studies by Umakant Premanand Shah, whose *Studies in Jaina Art* (Varanasi, 1955) should also be mentioned. Illustrated manuscripts have been studied by W. Norman Brown in *A Descriptive and Illustrated Catalogue of Miniature Paintings of the Jaina Kalpasūtra* (Washington, D.C., 1934); on this subject, there exist many books, by Umakant Premanand Shah, for example, *Treasures of Jaina Bhaṇḍāras* (Ahmedabad, 1978), as well as Moti Chandra, Sarabhai Manilal Nawab, and others; they include many plates.

4 THE SIKHS

Khushwant Singh

The word *Sikh* is derived from the Pali *sikkha* and the Sanskrit *śiṣya,* meaning "disciple." The Sikhs are the disciples of ten *gurūs* (Skt., *guru*), beginning with Nānak (b. 1469 CE) and ending with Gobind Singh (d. 1708). A Sikh has been defined as "one who believes in the ten *gurūs* and the *Granth Sahib,*" a scripture compiled by their fifth *gurū,* Arjun Dev, in 1604.

Sikhism was a later offshoot of the *bhakti* (devotional) cult of Vaiṣṇava Hinduism, which developed in Tamil Nadu and was based upon the teachings of Āḻvār and Adiyar saints. Its chief propagators were Ādi Śaṅkara (eighth century), who expounded *kevalādvaita* (pure monism), and, later, Rāmānanda (1360–1470) and Kabir (1398–1518), who were influenced by Islam and accepted Muslim disciples. The fifteenth and sixteenth centuries saw the spread of *bhakti* throughout India: Caitanya in Bengal; Jñaneśwar, Nāmdev, and Tukarām in Maharashtra; Mīrā Bāī in Rajasthan; Sādhana in Sindh. The *bhakti* tradition taught that God is the one and only reality; the rest is *māyā,* or "illusion." The best way to serve God is by absolute submission to his will. The best way to find his will is through the guidance of a spiritual mentor, a *gurū*. The best way to approach God is by meditating and singing hymns of love and praise. [*See also* Bhakti *and* Poetry, *article on* Indian Religious Poetry.]

FOUNDATION

Nānak, the founder of Sikhism, was the Punjab's chief propounder of the *bhakti* tradition. Born in April 1469, Nānak was the son of a revenue official in the village of Talwandi, about forty miles from Lahore (in present-day Pakistan). A member of the *kṣatriya,* or warrior class, and of the *bedi* (one versed in the Vedas) subsect, he received elementary education in Sanskrit, Persian, and Punjabi. Many of his boyhood years were spent taking the family cattle to pasture or in the company of itinerant *sādhus*. He married at age thirteen and was the father of two sons. For a while Nānak worked as an accountant in the office of the nawab of Sultanpur, where he met a Muslim minstrel named Mardana. The two began to organize community meetings where hymns written by Nānak and set to music by Mardana were sung. These hymns were later incorporated into the Sikhs' sacred hymnology and are to this day sung in musical measures (*rāgas*) prescribed at the time.

A mystical experience at age twenty-nine was the turning point in Nānak's life. While bathing in a nearby rivulet, he disappeared from view and was given up as drowned. According to the Janamsakhis ("life stories"), he was summoned by God and charged with his mission in the following words: "Nānak, I am with thee. Through thee will my name be magnified. . . . Go in the world to pray and to teach mankind how to pray. Be not sullied by the ways of the world. Let your life be one of praise of the 'word' [*nām*], 'charity' [*dān*], 'ablution' [*ishnān*], 'service' [*sevā*], and 'prayer' [*simran*]." It is reported that Nānak was missing for three days and nights but reappeared on the fourth day. The opening pronouncement of his mission was, "There is no Hindu; there is no Muslim."

Abandoning worldly pursuits, Nānak undertook four long voyages. On the first, he went eastward as far as Assam, visiting Hindu places of pilgrimage and meeting and discussing spiritual problems with ascetics and holy men. It was either on this journey or on the final one that the famous offering of water to the dead took place at Hardwar. The pilgrims were throwing palmfuls of water to the rising sun as an offering to their ancestors in heaven. Nānak, however, threw it in the opposite direction. When questioned, he answered simply: "If you can send water to your dead ancestors in heaven, surely I can send it to my fields in the Punjab." Nānak thereby demonstrated what he considered to be the futility of meaningless ritual.

He returned to his home for a short time before setting out on another long tour. This time he went southward, through Tamil Nadu and as far as Sri Lanka. Upon his return to India, he spent a few years with his family in a new township he built and named Kartarpur ("abode of the creator"). His third journey was to the northern regions of the Himalayas; his fourth and last of the long journeys began in 1518. This time he went westward to Mecca, Medina, and as far as Basra and Baghdad. It was on this journey that a now-famous incident took place. Nānak unwittingly fell asleep with his feet pointing toward the Kaʿbah. An enraged mullah rudely woke him and told him of the indignity he had committed by having his feet toward the house of God. "Then turn my feet in some other direction where God does not exist," answered Nānak.

By the time Nānak returned home, he was too old to undertake any more strenuous journeys. He decided to settle down at Kartarpur and instruct people who came to him. Large numbers of peasants—both Hindus and Muslims—flocked to hear him. Many became his disciples, or *śisyas*, from which the Punjabi word *Sikh* is derived. His death came on 22 September 1539 at age sixty-nine. The legend goes that both Hindus and Muslims clamored for his body: the former wanted to cremate him as a Hindu, the latter to bury him as a Muslim.

Nānak accepted most of the traditional beliefs of Hinduism pertaining to the origin of creation and its dissolution. For example, his version of the genesis of life, *arbad narbad dhundu kāra*, follows the Ṛgvedic hymn of creation: "Nonbeing then existed not, nor being. . . . Desire then entered the one in the beginning; it was the earliest seed, of thought, the product. . . . Creative force was there and fertile power: below was energy, above was impulse." Nānak likewise accepted the theory of *saṃsāra*—of birth, death, and rebirth. He describes this process with a picturesque simile: "Just as the pots of a Persian wheel go down, fill with water as they come up, empty and go down again, so is this life—a pastime of our Lord."

According to Nānak, God changed his own nature and function after the creation of the world—and God is himself the author of duality and delusion. In the *Āsā-di-*

Vār (The Dawn Hymns), he writes, "Āpīnai ap sājio, āpīnai raceo nāu / Duyī qudrat sāj kai kar āsan ditho chāu" ("He himself created creation and gave currency to the Name / And then assumed a second nature and with pleasure regarded his creation seated on his prayer mat"). It is this God who, having set the world as well as life in motion, threw in it, as it were, *moh thagauli:* an opiate used by thugs to drug their victims before robbing them. "Amal galola koor kā dittā devan hār," writes Nānak ("The Great Giver himself gave us the pill of falsehood. We forget death and for four short days indulge in pleasure. The temperate abstain, find truth and the court of God"). Thus both good and evil emanate from God; man's role is to choose the one and avoid the other, to follow the ordinances of God *(hukum Rajāī chalnā)* and earn his grace *(nadar).*

The opening lines of *Japjī,* the Sikhs' morning prayer, clearly state Nānak's concept of God:

There is one God.
He is the supreme truth.
He, the creator,
Is without fear and without hatred.
He, the omnipresent,
Pervades the universe.
He is not born,
Nor does he die to be born again.
By his grace shalt thou worship him.

Before time itself
There was truth.
When time began to run its course
He was the truth.
Even now, he is the truth,
And evermore shall truth prevail.

Nānak's God was one, omnipotent, and omniscient.

Nānak also believed that God was *sat* (both "truth" and "reality"), as opposed to *asat* ("falsehood") and *mithya* ("illusion"). He thus not only made God a spiritual concept but also based principles of social behavior on this concept. In other words, if God is truth, to speak an untruth is to be ungodly. Untruthful conduct not only hurts one's neighbors; it is also irreligious. A good Sikh, therefore, must not only believe that God is the only reality, but he must also not harm his fellow beings, for hurtful conduct—lying, cheating, fornicating, trespassing on a person or his property, and so on—does not conform to the truth that is God.

Nānak's God is ineffable because he is *nirankār,* or "formless." The best one can do is to admit the impossibility of defining him. But the fact that God cannot be defined should not inhibit us from learning about truth and reality. This we can do by following the path of righteousness.

God is the Father (Pitā), the Lover (Pritam), the Master (Khasam, Mālik, or Sāhib), and the Great Giver (Dātā) of all gifts. He is good, but evil also emanates from him, perhaps to purify us or to test our faith. He is known as Rab, Rahim, Rām, Govinda, Murāri, and Hari. Nānak first called God Aumkāra, a name familiar to readers of the

Vedas and the Upaniṣads, but later referred to him as Sat Kartār ("the true creator") or Sat Nām ("the true name").

The Sikh word for "god" is *wah gurū*. It started as an exclamation of praise meaning "Hail *gurū*!" (just as the Muslim's "Subhan Allāh," or "Allāh be praised," came into use). Later it was used to personify God. Every chapter of the *Ādi Granth* begins with the invocation "Ek Onkar Satgurūparśād," which translates as, "The one God—by the grace of *gurū*—worship." Gurū Nānak took other aspects of God from the Vedas, such as the concept that God was *nirguṇa* (without quality) and in *śūnya samādhi* (a state of profound meditation) before creation. After creation, however, he became the repository of all qualities *(saguṇa)*. Likewise, the symbolic representation of God as the mystic syllable or sound *oṃ* (in the *Māṇḍūkya* and the *Prasna Upaniṣad*), which "contains all that is past, present, and future"—"Bhutam, bhavad, bhaviśyad iti sarvam auṃkār evaḥ"—is found in the *gurū*'s *Dakhni Onkar*. He writes in this work that God is "the creator of Brahmā, of consciousness, of time and space, of the Vedas, the emancipator, the essence of the three worlds." The concept of *oṃ,* which is somewhat elusive in Hinduism, is crystallized in Sikh theology and given the status of a symbol—the symbol of God. It invariably emphasizes his singularity, expressed in the saying "Ik Aumkar" ("There is one God").

In equating God with the abstract principle of truth, Nānak bypasses the difficult questions encountered by religious leaders who describe God only as the creator or the Father: If God created the world, who created God? If he is the Father, who was his father? But Nānak's system had its own problems. It raised such questions as, If God is truth, what is the truth? Nānak's answer was that in situations in which believers cannot decide for themselves, they should let the *gurū* guide them.

Nānak made the institution of "guruship" the pivot of his religious system. Without the *gurū* as a guide, he insisted, no one can attain *mokṣa* ("release"). The *gurū* keeps his followers on the path of truth; he acts as a goad stick, keeping man, who is like a rogue elephant, from running amok. He applies the "salve of knowledge" *(gyān anjan)* to a follower's eyes so he can see the truth that is God; he is the divine ferryman who takes him across the fearful "ocean of life" *(bhava sāgar)*. The *gurū* or the *satgurū* ("true guru") is just a shade below God.

Nānak insisted on the separation of God and the *gurū*. The *gurū* is to be consulted, respected, and cherished—but not worshiped. He is a teacher, not a reincarnation of God, an *avatāra*, or a messiah. Nānak constantly referred to himself as the bard *(dhādi),* slave, and servant of God.

Nānak describes the qualities one should look for in a *gurū:* "Take him as guru who shows the path of truth, who tells you of the one of whom nothing is known, who tells you of the divine word." The *gurū* was not only man's bridge to union with God but also his mentor. The *gurū* taught a man how to conduct himself toward his fellow men and what general pattern of living he should follow.

Nānak strongly disapproved of asceticism, of penance, and of torturing the flesh as a step toward enlightenment. "Be in the world but not worldly," he said.

Although Nānak abandoned his family when he first launched his spiritual quest and often left it when he was away on his travels, he always came back to it. He propagated the *gṛhastha dharma*—the religion of the householder. He advocated the company of holy men *(sādh sangat)* as an essential requisite of righteous living. And although he equated truth with God, he put righteous behavior above truth.

Because Nānak advocated associating with righteous people, he rejected the social class system, which not only vitiated the relationship between people but also ran counter to the ordinances of God, who was the embodiment of truth. He refused to grant audiences to people unless they first broke bread in the community kitchen *(gurū kā langar),* where the brahman and the untouchable, the Muslim and the Hindu sat alongside one another as equals. He was just as critical of concepts of purity and impurity that had sprung out of notions of higher and lower categories of human beings.

Human birth, said Nānak, is a priceless gift. It is the opportunity that God gives us to escape the cycle of birth, death, and rebirth. The aim of life should be *yoga,* or union with God. Salvation lies in the blending of our light with the Light Eternal. The *Bhagavadgītā* advocates three alternative paths to salvation: that of action *(karmamārga),* of knowledge *(jñānamārga),* and of devotion *(bhaktimārga).* Nānak accepted the path of *bhakti,* emphasizing the worship of the name of God *(nāmamārga).* "I have no miracles except the name of God," he said.

Nānak believed that by repetition of the *nām,* one can conquer the greatest of all evils: the ego, or *haumain* ("I am"). So great is the power of the ego, said Nānak, that those who conquer it attain salvation while still alive; they become *jīvanmuktas.* [*See also* Jīvanmukti.] According to Nānak, the ego carries within itself the seed of salvation, which can be fully nurtured by the repetition of the *nām.* Once the power of the ego is properly channeled, the conquest of the other five sins—lust, anger, greed, attachment, and pride—follows as a matter of course. The wanderings of the restless mind stop, and it attains a state of divine bliss *(vismād).* It is in this state of superconscious stillness *(divya dṛṣṭi)* that the tenth gate, the *dasam dvār* (the body having only nine natural orifices), is opened. One then receives a vision of God and merges one's light with the Light Eternal. "Nām japo" ("Worship the name of the Lord") was Nānak's constant exhortation. But this meant more than a parrotlike repetition of "Rāma, Rāma, Rāma." To Nānak, *nām* implied not only prayer but also the understanding of the words of that prayer and the acceptance of them as the rules of life. The path of *nāma (nāmamārga)* required three things: realization of the truth within the heart *(hriday gyān),* its expression in prayer *(mukh bhakti),* and detachment from worldly things *(vartan vairāg).* Nānak believed that a man's real battle in life is fought with himself. "Mansa mār mano seo lujhai" ("Overcome the base desires and battle with the mind"), he wrote, adding, "Gyān Kharag lai man seo lujhai mansā manah samāi" ("Use knowledge as a double-edged dagger, then will base desires subside within the mind"). He who conquers these desires ends the cycle of birth, death, and rebirth and attains salvation.

Nānak believed in the triumph of human will over fate and predestination. He believed that all human beings have a basic fund of goodness that, like the pearl in the oyster, only awaits the opening of the shell to emerge and enrich them. But most human beings are as ignorant of the goodness in them as the deer is of the aromatic *kasturi* in its navel; and just as the deer wanders about in the woods and falls into the snares of poachers or becomes a victim of the hunter's darts, so man falls into the snares of *māyā* (illusion). The chief task of the guru is to make man aware of the treasure within him and then help him unlock the jewel box.

A method advocated by Nānak was the gentle one of *sahaj.* Just as a vegetable cooked on a gentle fire tastes best because its own juice gives it the proper flavor, so a gradual training of the body and mind will bring out the goodness that is inherent in all human beings. There is no general rule applicable to everyone; each person should discipline himself according to physical capacity and temperament. Ascetic austerity, penances, celibacy, and other such measures have no place in Nānak's religion. In addition to self-imposed discipline of the mind, he advocated listening to and participating in *kīrtan* (hymn singing). Nānak's verses were put to music in *rāgas* (modes) that were best suited to convey their meaning. He advised his followers to rise well before dawn and listen to the soft strains of music under the light of the stars. He believed that one was best able to have communion with God in the stillness of the ambrosial hours *(amritvela)*.

Gurū Nānak believed in prayer and in *kīrtan* to focus one's mind on God. He did not believe in pilgrimages, and to this day no place of pilgrimage is sanctified by the Sikh scriptures. He also did not believe in the profession of priesthood (as distinct from that of the *gurū* or the teacher), and the class has not been able to establish itself firmly in the Sikh community.

DEVELOPMENT

Nānak had founded the town of Kartarpur and built a *dharamsāla* (abode of faith) where his disciples went to congregate and chant the many beautiful hymns he had composed. This congregational worship was formalized by his successor, the second *gurū,* Angad (1504–1552), who used the *gurmukhī* script to compile a hymnal. Apparently Angad also tried to collect information on the earlier life and travels of Nānak. In addition, Angad put the *gurū-kā-langai*—the *gurū*'s kitchen—on a regular footing in order to feed the disciples who came to the *dharamsāla*. Thus began the drift away from the parent communities—the Hindus, from whom the majority of disciples were drawn, and the Muslims. The process was carried a step further by the third *gurū,* Amar Das (1479–1574), who organized the Sikhs into twenty-two *manjis,* or bishoprics, for the purpose of collecting the *dasvandh* ("the tenth"), a tax to defray the expenses of the *gurū*'s establishment and of the communal welfare. He also built another *dharamsāla* at Goindwal.

The fourth *gurū,* Ram Das (1534–1581), carried the process still further. He bought land, set up a new town, and had a large tank dug that came to be known as Amritsar, the "pool of immortality." Amritsar was in the heart of the country populated by Hindu peasants, who had begun to join the Sikh movement in large numbers. It soon developed into the most important trading center of the Punjab. Goods from distant Bukhara, Kabul, and Kashmir were exchanged there for products from eastern and southern India. In addition, Ram Das was held in esteem by Emperor Akbar. This not only helped him to build temples and towns but also to assume leadership of the Hindus of the Punjab. His most important innovation, which gave a sort of continuity to guruship, was making the office of *gurū* hereditary: thereafter it remained in one family, the Sodhis. This gave a sense of expectancy to the community as well as a sort of sanctity to the family.

The fifth *gurū,* Arjun (1563–1606), freed the Sikhs of the tutelage of the parent communities—the Hindus and the Muslims—and launched them on their own. One of his most important accomplishments was the compilation of the *Ādi Granth,* a collection of the writings of the first four *gurūs,* the works of Hindu and Muslim saints from all over northern India, and his own compositions. He installed it as the sacred scripture of the Sikhs, a step that had most important consequences. The Sikhs, who understood neither Sanskrit nor Arabic, stopped turning to the Hindu or Muslim scriptures for inspiration and, instead, looked to the *gurus'* hymns, which were couched in a language intelligible to them. Moreover, Arjun had been judicious in his choice of hymns, taking only the very best compositions by the saints of northern India. The poetic excellence, the spiritual content, and the haunting, lilting melodies of the hymns of the *Ādi Granth* are Sikhism's greatest attraction to this day. Arjun also gave Amritsar a permanent place in Sikh religious geography by building a new temple on the site of the temple his father had built. It is believed that he had the Muslim divine, Mian Meer of Lahore, lay the foundation stone of the new temple. This was not just another Sikh *dharamsāla* but the Hari Mandir (temple of God); it was the Sikh counterpart of the Haridwar or Banaras of the Hindus and the Mecca of the Muslims. Arjun built another temple at Taran Taran, a few miles from the city, to cater to the peasantry, which by now had turned Sikh.

Gurū Arjun was fully conscious of the new role he was planning for his community. In a passage from the *Ādi Granth,* he mentions the separate identity the Sikhs had acquired in their hundred years of existence:

> I do not keep the Hindu fast nor the Muslim Ramaḍān.
> I serve Him alone who is my refuge.
> I serve the one Master, who is also Allāh.
> I have broken with the Hindu and the Muslim,
> I will not worship with the Hindu, nor like the Muslim
>   go to Mecca;
> I shall serve Him and no other.
> I will not pray to idols nor heed the Muslim's *azān*;
> I shall put my heart at the feet of the one supreme being,
> For we are neither Hindus nor Muslims.

Arjun was probably most responsible for the growth of the Sikh church. He organized a revenue system, appointed tax collectors, and tapped other sources of income. He sent his followers across the northwest frontier to Afghanistan, Persia, and Turkey to trade goods and to sell Indian silks and spices and buy horses. These ventures brought the Sikhs money and, above all, set up a tradition of good horsemanship among them. Although Arjun was a devoutly religious man, his varied activities to promote the well-being of his following made him an important merchant-prince and radically changed the status of the *gurū*. The *gurū* was no longer a recluse who devoted himself exclusively to prayer and preaching; he had become a *sachā pādshāh,* the true emperor of the nebulous kingdom of the Sikhs. He had come to wield secular power. He held court and received emissaries from rulers of states.

But Arjun's rising importance, as well as the support he gave to Emperor Jehangir's rebellious son Prince Khusro, brought the wrath of the emperor on his head and led to his downfall. He was arrested and tortured in Lahore Prison, where he died in June 1606. Before his incarceration, Arjun named his son Hargobind as the sixth *gurū* and girded him with two swords that symbolized spiritual and temporal power. "Let him sit upon the throne and maintain an army to the best of his ability," he ordered.

Temperamentally, Hargobind (1595–1644) was inclined to the role his father had outlined for him. Fond of hunting and martial exercises, he abandoned the vegetarianism of his predecessors and enjoined his followers to eat meat and build their physique. He maintained a cavalry and a bodyguard of three hundred Sikhs. He was in and out of favor with Emperor Jehangir and had to spend some years as a prisoner in the fort of Gwalior. This new temporal role of the *gurū* was not well received by all disciples; some complained that he was "too much Mohammadan and military exercises." The role, however, had come to stay. On his release from the fort, Hargobind raised an army and became an important military leader in the Punjab. He fought and won three battles against the Mughals.

The next two *gurūs*—Har Rai (1630–1661) and Hari Kishan (1656–1664)—maintained peace with the authorities. When Emperor Aurangzeb secured the throne, he tried to take action against Har Rai, who had espoused the cause of the emperor's brother Dara Shikoh, by summoning Har Rai's infant son, Hari Kishan, to Delhi. But Hari Kishan escaped the emperor's vindictiveness by becoming a victim of smallpox. Aurangzeb's wrath had to fall on the successor—the ninth *gurū,* Tegh Bahadur (1621–1675), a devout man with ascetic habits who emerged from the seclusion of a hermit's life to assume the guruship. When the Hindus asked him to face Aurangzeb, he did so with complete disregard of the fate that he knew awaited him. He came to Delhi and was promptly put in prison and charged with criminal extortion. It is believed that he was offered his life if he would abjure his faith. On his refusal to do so he was beheaded. It is also said that he was asked to perform a miracle and, in response, he wrote some words on a piece of paper and strung it around his neck, saying that it would be a charm against death. After his execution, the paper was opened. It read: "Sīs diyā par sirr nā diya" ("I gave my head but not my faith"). The final transformation of Sikhism from a pacifist sect to a militant fraternity came with Tegh Bahadur's son Gobind Singh, who succeeded him as the tenth and last of the Sikh's *gurūs*.

[*For further discussion of the main figures of Sikhism, see the biographies of Nānak and Gobind Singh. The Sikh scriptures are further discussed in* Ādi Granth *and* Dasam Granth. *For the development of Sikhism in the context of other North Indian religious movements, see* Hindi Religious Traditions.]

BIBLIOGRAPHY

The classic work on the history of the Sikhs from the inception of the faith to the fall of the Sikh kingdom remains Joseph Davey Cunnigham's *A History of the Sikhs* (1849; reprint, Delhi, 1966). Subsequent histories of the Sikhs have largely accepted Cunnigham's interpretation of Sikh religion, the transformation of the community from pacificist sect to a militant fraternity, its rise to power as rulers of the Panjab, and the collapse of their empire. However, for a fuller understanding of the teachings of the Sikh *gurūs* and translations of the Sikh scripture, Max Arthur Macauliffe's *The Sikh Religion: Its Gurus, Sacred Writings and Authors,* 6 vols. in 3 (Oxford, 1909), and W. H. Mcleod's *Guru Nanak and the Sikh Religion* (Oxford, 1968) can be recommended. In addition I would recommend my *A History of the Sikhs,* 2 vols. (Princeton, 1963) and its subsequent paperback editions published by the Oxford University Press (Delhi, 1979–1983), which brings the history of the Sikhs to the year 1977.

5 BUDDHISM IN SOUTHEAST ASIA

Donald K. Swearer

Conventional wisdom labels the Buddhism of Southeast Asia as Theravāda. Indeed, customarily a general distinction pertains between the "southern," Theravāda, Buddhism of Southeast Asia, whose scriptures are written in Pali, and the "northern," Sanskrit Mahāyāna (including Tantrayāna), Buddhism of Central and East Asia. A Thai or a Burmese most likely thinks of the Buddhism of his country as a continuation of the Theravāda tradition, which was allegedly brought to the Golden Peninsula (Suvaṇṇabhūmi) by Aśoka's missionaries Soṇa and Uttara in the third century BCE. But modern scholarship has demonstrated that prior to the development of the classical Southeast Asian states, which occurred from the tenth or eleventh century to the fifteenth century CE, Buddhism in Southeast Asia—the area covered by present-day Burma, Thailand, Vietnam, Cambodia (Kampuchea), and Laos—defies rigid classification. Both archaeological and chronicle evidence suggest that the religious situation in the area was fluid and informal, with Buddhism characterized more by miraculous relics and charismatic, magical monks than by organized sectarian traditions. In short, the early period of Buddhism in Southeast Asia was diverse and eclectic, infused with elements of Hindu Dharmśāstra and Brahmanic deities, Mahāyāna Buddhas such as Lokeśvara, Tantric practices, Sanskrit Sarvāstivādin texts, as well as Pali Theravāda traditions.

The classical period of Southeast Asian Buddhism, which lasted from the eleventh to the fifteenth century, began with the development of the monarchical states of Śrīvijaya in Java, Angkor in Cambodia, Pagan in Burma, Sukhōthai in Thailand, and Luang Prabang in Laos, and culminated in the establishment of a normative Pali Theravāda tradition of the Sinhala Mahāvihāra monastic line. Hence, by the fourteenth and fifteenth centuries the primary, although by no means exclusive, form of Buddhism in Burma, Thailand, Laos, and Cambodia was a Sinhala orthodoxy that was dominated doctrinally by "the commentator" (Buddhaghosa) but enriched by various local traditions of thought and practice. By this time, what is now Malaysia and Indonesia, with the exception of Bali, had been overrun by Islam, and the popular religion there was an amalgamation of animism, Brahmanic deities, and the religion of the Prophet. The colonial interregnum, which infused Western and Christian elements into the religious and cultural milieu of Southeast Asia, gradually challenged the dominance of the Indian Buddhist worldview and its symbiotically related institutional realms of kingship *(dhammacakka)* and monastic order *(sāsanacakka)*. From the nineteenth century onward Buddhism in Southeast Asia has faced the challenges of Western science; provided cultural and ideological support for modern nationalist movements; offered idiosyncratic, sometimes messianically flavored, solutions to the stresses and strains of political, economic, and social change; and formulated doctrinal innovations challenging the Abhidammic orthodoxy of Buddhaghosa that characterizes the Sinhala Theravāda.

The following essay will examine Buddhism in Southeast Asia in terms of its early development, the establishment of a normative Theravāda orthodoxy, and the diverse responses of this tradition to the challenges of the modern period. The future of Buddhism in Southeast Asia may not hang in the balance; nevertheless, it does appear to be problematic. Political events in Cambodia (Kampuchea) and Laos have threatened the very foundations of institutional Buddhism in those countries. Thailand's rapid and widespread modernization and secularization have undermined many traditional aspects of the religion *(sāsana)*, and internal political strife in Burma has had severe, detrimental effects on the *sangha* (Skt., *saṃgha*). Our attention to Southeast Asian Buddhism should not ignore its fragility or its potential contribution to the continuing self-definition and self-determination of these civilizations.

EARLY DEVELOPMENT

From its earliest beginnings to the establishment of the major monarchical states, Buddhism in Southeast Asia can only be characterized as diverse and eclectic. Its presence was felt as part of the Indian cultural influence that flourished throughout the area. During these early centuries Buddhism competed successfully with indigenous forms of magical animism and Brahmanism, undoubtably becoming transformed in the process. Its propagation probably followed the same pattern that was seen in Central and East Asia, with which we are more familiar: Padmasambhava-type monks subjugating territorial guardian spirits; monks accompanying traders and bringing in objects of power and protection, such as relics and images, as well as a literary tradition in the forms of magical chants in sacred languages and also written texts. We glean something of this pattern from Buddhist chronicles in Pali and in Southeast Asian vernacular languages of a later time. When the *Sāsanavaṃsa* of Burma or the *Mūlasāsana* of Thailand relates the story of the Buddha's visit to these countries to establish the religion, we interpret myth in historical terms, reading "the Buddha" to mean "unnamed Buddhist monks" who were bearers of a more advanced cultural tradition. While the chronicles, more so than the early inscriptions, paint a picture of dubious historical accuracy, they correctly associate Buddhism with a high continental way of life in contrast to the less sophisticated life of tribal peoples. Buddhism, then, abets the development of a town or urban culture, provides symbols of translocal value, and articulates a worldview in which diverse communities can participate and find a new identity, a language in which they can communicate, and institutions in which an organized religious life can be pursued and systematically taught.

Such a general description of the early centuries of Buddhism in Southeast Asia does not preclude the establishment of identifiable Buddhist traditions in the area.

These include not only strong Pali Theravāda tradition but also other Buddhist sects and schools representing Mahāyāna and Tantric traditions. Pali inscriptions found in Hmawza, the ancient Pyu capital of Śrīkṣetra in lower Burma, indicate the existence of Theravāda Buddhism by the fifth or sixth century CE. Their Andhra-Kadamba script points to connections with Kāñcīpuram, Negapatam, and Kāverīpaṭṭanam in South India. The Chinese traveler I-ching, who visited Shih-li-cha-to-lo (Śrīkṣetra, or Prome) in the seventh century, mentions the presence of not only Theravādins (Āryasthaviras) but also the Āryamahāsāṃghika, Āryamūlasarvāstivāda, and Āryasammatīya schools. We know of the Mahāsāṃghikas as among the forerunners of the Mahāyāna tradition. While their original home was in Magadha, their tradition established itself in parts of northern, western, eastern, and southern India. The Amarāvatī and Nāgārjunikoṇḍa inscriptions, for instance, mention the Mahāsāṃghikas and state that their canon was written in Prakrit. The three other sects are Hīnayāna schools. The Mūlasarvāstivāda, according to one tradition, was one of the seven branches of the Sarvāstivādin tradition and was widespread in India, although it was especially strong in the north, whence it was propagated under the aegis of King Kaniṣka during the late first century CE. Its canon was written in a Buddhist Hybrid Sanskrit. The Sammatīya sect, also known as the Vātsīputrīya or Vajjipattaka, came from Avanti, but inscriptions point to its presence in Sārnāth during the fourth century and in Mathurā during the fifth century. The great early seventh-century ruler Harṣavardhana is thought to have supported the Sammatīyas in the early part of his reign. Hence, the four sects whose presence in the Prome area was attested to by I-ching are all associated with important Indian Buddhist centers and with the reigns of powerful monarchs reputed to have been supporters of various Buddhist sectarian traditions.

Evidence of the diverse nature of sectarian Buddhism during the formative period of Southeast Asian history comes from Burmese and other sources in both mainland and insular Southeast Asia. The T'ang dynastic chronicles (seventh to tenth century CE) state that Buddhism flourished in the P'iao (Pyu) capital of Shih-li-cha-to-lo (Śrīkṣetra) in the eighth and ninth centuries. Archaeological and sculptural evidence of the same period from Prome and Hmawza portray the Buddha in scenes from the Jātakas and from popular commentarial stories. Terra-cotta votive tablets depicting scenes from the life of the Buddha and of the Mahāyāna *bodhisattva*s have also been found, as well as inscriptions written in Sanskrit, Pali, mixed Pali and Sanskrit, and Pyu written in South Indian alphabets. Evidence from ruined stupas in Hmawza, which date from the fifth to the eighth centuries, reinforce the claim to a strong but diverse Buddhist presence.

The Mon, or Talaing, lived south of the Pyu, occupying the coastal area of lower Burma, with flourishing centers at Pegu (Haṃsavatī) and Thaton (Sudhammavatī). This region, known as Rāmaññadesa in Burmese and Thai chronicles, extended over much of present-day Thailand; one major Mon center was as far north as Haripuñjaya (present-day Lamphun). In Nakorn Prathom, thirty miles southwest of Bangkok, archaeological evidence points to a flourishing Mon Buddhist culture in the region known as Dvāravatī, in which forms of both Hīnayāna and Mahāyāna Buddhism were present. Amarāvatī-style Buddha images in the vicinity of Nakorn Prathom and Pong Tuk date from the fourth to fifth century CE, and images of both early and late Gupta are also found there. While Mon-Dvāravatī Buddhism in Thailand and lower Burma lacked the homogeneity attributed to it by later chroniclers, both archaeological and textual evidence suggest a strong Pali Theravāda presence, especially in comparison to that found in Pagan.

Pagan, near the sacred Mount Popa on the Irrawaddy Plains of upper Burma, had become the locus of power of the Mrammas, a Tibeto-Dravidian tribe who eventually dominated and consequently named the entire region. During the tenth and eleventh centuries, the Buddhism present among people of the Pagan-Irrawaddy River basin seems to have been dominated by an eclectic form of Mahāyāna Tantrism similar to that found in esoteric Śaivism or in animistic *nāga* cults. According to the Burmese chronicles, the monks of this sect, who are referred to as Ari, rejected the teachings of the Lord Buddha. They believed in the efficacy of magical *mantra*s over the power of *karman* and propagated the custom of sending virgins to priests before marriage. In addition to numerous figures of Mahāyāna *bodhisattva*s, such as Avalokiteśvara and Mañjuśrī, findings include remnants of murals that depict deities embracing their consorts.

According to the *Hmannān mạha yazạwintawkyī* (Glass Palace Chronicle, begun 1829) of Burma, the country's political and religious history was changed by the effect of Shin Arahan, a charismatic Mon Theravāda monk from Thaton, on the Burmese ruler Aniruddha (Anawratha), who ascended to power in Pagan in 1044 CE. According to this account, Shin Arahan converted Aniruddha to a Theravāda persuasion, advising him to secure relics, *bhikkhu*s (monks), and Pali texts from Manuha (Manohari), the king of Thaton. Manuha's refusal became the excuse for Aniruddha's invasion of Thaton, the eventual subjugation of the Mons in lower Burma, and the establishment of Theravāda under Kyanzittha (fl. 1084–1113) as the dominant, although by no means exclusive, Buddhist sect.

As part of the Indian cultural expansion into "greater India," Mahāyāna, Tantric, and Hīnayāna forms of Buddhism were established in other parts of mainland and insular Southeast Asia from the fifth century onward. Guṇavarman is reputed to have taken the Dharmaguptaka tradition from northern India to Java in the fifth century, and by the seventh century Buddhism was apparently flourishing in the Sumatra of Śrīvijaya. An inscription from 684 CE, for instance, refers to a Buddhist monarch named Jayanāsā. I-ching, who spent several months in Java on his return to China in order to copy and translate Buddhist texts, indicates that both Hīnayāna and Mahāyāna forms of Buddhism were present at that time. Indonesia was also visited by Dharmapāla of Nālandā University and by two prominent South Indian monks, Vajrabodhi and Amoghavajra, both adherents of a Tantric form of Buddhism. Two inscriptions from the late eighth century refer to the construction, under the aegis of Śailendra rulers, of a Tārā temple at Kalasan and an image of Mañjuśrī at Kelunak. The Śailendras were great patrons of the North Indian Pāla form of Mahāyāna Buddhism. [*See the biographies of Dharmapāla, Vajrabodhi, and Amoghavajra. Evidence for the flourishing of Tantric forms of Buddhism in Southeast Asia is treated in* Buddhism, Schools of, *article on* Esoteric Buddhism.]

The rulers of Champa, in southern Annam (Vietnam), also patronized Buddhism. According to I-ching, the dominant tradition in Champa was that of the Āryasammatīya *nikāya*, but the Sarvāstivādins were also present. Amarāvatī-style Buddha images and monastery foundations from the ninth century have been discovered in Quang Nam Province, and an inscription of the same period from An-Thai records the erection of a statue of Lokanātha and refers to such Mahāyāna deities as Amitābha and Vairocana.

Although Hinduism was initially the dominant religion in Cambodia, there is some evidence of Buddhism from the fifth century CE. Jayavarman of Fu-nan sent representatives to China in 503 CE, who took as gifts a Buddha image; and an inscription by Jayavarman's son, Rudravarman, invokes the Buddha. In the eleventh century Sūryavarman was given the posthumous Buddhist title of Nirvāṇapada, and Jayavarman VII, the Khmer empire's greatest monarch and builder of Angkor Thom, patronized Buddhism of the Mahāyāna variety. A Pali inscription from 1308, during the reign of Śrīndravarmadeva, refers to a Hīnayāna form of Buddhism, and a Chinese source from about the same time refers to Hīnayāna Buddhism as flourishing in Cambodia at that time.

The evidence cited supports the contention that throughout much of Southeast Asia Buddhism was present as part of the larger Indian cultural influence. Various sources, ranging from testimony of Chinese and indigenous chronicles, diaries of Chinese monk-travelers, as well as a large amount of archaeological and inscriptional evidence, support the contention that both Mahāyāna and Hīnayāna forms of Buddhism existed side by side, dependent on such factors as the particular regional Indian source and the predilection of a given ruler. Clearly, before the emergence of the major classical Southeast Asian states, no standard form of Buddhism existed.

It is also true that various types of Buddhism in this period competed with autochthonous forms of animism as well as Brahmanic cults. Were the early states in Burma, Cambodia, Thailand, and Indonesia—such as Fu-nan, Champa, Śrīkṣetra, Dvāravatī, and so on—Buddhist or Hindu? Or were these great traditions themselves so accommodated and transformed by the Southeast Asian cultures that they qualified the labels "Buddhist" and "Hindu" almost beyond recognition? Although rulers in these preclassical states may be characterized as Hindu or Buddhist and their brand of Buddhism defined by a given sect or school, in all probability they supported a variety of priests, monks, and religious institutions and worshiped various gods and spirits ranging from territorial guardians to Viṣṇu, Śiva, and Vairocana. In some cases we are prone to assign labels when, in reality, the diversity of the situation makes labeling a problematic enterprise at best. Such a qualification does not mean that we are unable to make certain claims about the nature of Buddhism in Southeast Asia in the formative period; however, evidence supporting the presence of particular Buddhist schools and sects should be understood within the general framework of the varied and eclectic nature of Buddhism in this era.

CLASSICAL PERIOD

While diversity and eclecticism continue to mark the character of Buddhism during the period of the foundation of the classical Southeast Asian monarchical states, homogeneity of form and institutional orthodoxy began to emerge during this period. On the one hand, Buddhism and Hinduism contributed to the development of the nature and form of Southeast Asian kingship. On the other hand, the symbiotic relationship that developed between the monarchy and the Buddhist *sangha* tended to support a loose religious orthodoxy. Historically, this orthodoxy follows the Sinhala Theravāda tradition and accompanies the ascendancy of the Burmese and the Tai in mainland Southeast Asia. Vietnam, Malaysia, and Indonesia, however, depart from this pattern: Vietnamese culture was strongly influenced by China, and Malaysia and Indonesia were affected by the advent and spread of Islam during the thirteenth century. We shall first examine Buddhism at the level of the nature and form of classical Southeast Asian kingship and then trace the emergence of Sinhala Theravāda Buddhism as the normative tradition in Burma, Thailand, Cambodia, and Laos after the thirteenth century.

Buddhism and Monarchy. The relationship between Buddhism and the rise of the monarchical states in the classical period of Southeast Asian history is customarily referred to as symbiotic, that is, one of mutual benefit. Rulers supported Buddhism because it provided a cosmology in which the king was accorded the central place and a view of society in which the human community was dependent on the role of the king. Ideologically, Buddhism legitimated kingship, providing a metaphysical rationale and moral basis for its existence. The Buddhist *sangha,* in turn, supported Southeast Asian monarchs because the material well-being, success, and popularity of institutional Buddhism depended to a significant degree on the approval, support, and largess of the ruling classes.

The Theravāda picture of the cosmos, set forth classically in the *Aggañña Suttanta* of the *Dīgha Nikāya,* depicts the world as devolving from a more perfect, luminous, undifferentiated state to a condition of greater opacity and differentiation. Imperfection results because differences in sex, comeliness, size of rice fields, and so on engender desire, greed, lust, and hatred, which, in turn, lead to actions that destroy the harmony and well-being of the inhabitants of the world. Recognizing the need to correct the situation, the people select a person whose comeliness, wisdom, virtue, and power enable him to bring order to this disharmonious, chaotic situation. That person, the ruler or king, is referred to in the text as *mahāsammata* because he is chosen by the people. He is *rāja* (king) because he rules by the Dhamma, and he is also *khattiya,* or lord of the fields, responsible for maintaining the economic and political order. Social order is dependent upon the righteous ruler, who creates and maintains the fourfold social structure (the traditional Indian *varṇa* hierarchy). Such a peaceful and harmonious situation also allows for the sustenance of *bhikkhu*s, who seek a higher, nonmundane end, that is, *nibbāna* (Skt., *nirvāṇa*). The ruler, then, is responsible for the peace, harmony, and total well-being of the people, which includes the opportunity to pursue a religious or spiritual life.

Buddhism's contribution to the classical conception of Southeast Asian kingship is particularly noteworthy in its emphasis on Dhamma and on the role of the ruler as a moral exemplar. The king is a *cakkavattin,* one whose rule depends upon the universal Dhamma of cosmic, natural, and moral law. His authority stems from the place he assumes in the total cosmic scheme of things. But his power and, hence, his effectiveness rest on his virtue. While the king rules by strength of arms, wealth, intellect, able ministers, and the prestige of his own status, his embodiment of the Dhamma and, hence, his ability to rule depend on his maintenance of the ten *rājadhamma*s: liberality, good conduct, nonattachment, straightforwardness, mildness, austerity, suppression of anger, noninjury, patience, and forbearance. The ideal king should cleanse his mind of all traces of avarice, ill will, and intellectual confusion and eschew the use of force and weapons of destruction. These moral virtues represent the highest ideals of Theravāda Buddhism, an overlapping of two "wheels" *(cakka),* or realms: the mundane *(ānācakka, lokiya)* and the transmundane *(sāsanacakka, lokuttara),* or the ideals of the political leader *(cakkavattin)* and the religious exemplar (Buddha).

This symbiotic relationship between political and religious leadership roles takes a particular mythic pattern in many of the classical Southeast Asian chronicles, such as the *Jinakālamālipakaraṇaṃ,* (The Sheaf of Garlands of the Epochs of the Conqueror), a pattern also present in the Pali chronicles of Sri Lanka (e.g., the *Mahāvaṃsa*). Essentially, the chroniclers hold that the Budda sacralizes a region by visiting it. He frequently converts the indigenous populations and teaches them the Dhamma. To be sure, the monastic authors had a vested interest in establishing the precedence of Buddhism in the land, but the Buddha's visits to such places as the Tagaung kingdom of Burma and Haripuñjaya in northern Thailand serve the additional purpose of grounding a later interrelationship between Buddhism and kingship. In the northern Thai chronicles, for example, when the Buddha visits the Mon-Lava state of Haripuñjaya in the Chiangmai Valley, he predicts that his bone relic will be discovered by King Ādicca (Āditarāja), one of the principal twelfth-century monarchs of this state. This tale not only points to royal support of the *sāsana,* it makes the king the symbolic actualizer of the tradition, which he celebrates by building a *cetiya* for the relic. Furthermore, the Buddha in effect engenders the monarch with the power necessary to rule, a magical potency inherent in the relic. The *cetiya* reliquary mound thus functions as a magical center, or *axis mundi,* for the kingdom. In Haripuñjaya, alliances between the northern Tai kingdom of Lānnā and other states were sealed in front of the magical center. The Emerald Buddha image has played a similar role in Lao and Tai religious history, with various princes of the kingdom swearing fealty to the reigning monarch who possessed it.

The nature of the interrelationship between Buddhism and classical monarchical rule in Southeast Asia manifests itself architecturally in the great *cetiya* or stupa (Skt., *stūpa*) monuments of Borobudur, Angkor, Pagan, and other ancient capitals. The earliest of these, Borobudur, was constructed on the Kedu Plain outside of present-day Jogjakarta on the island of Java in the mid-eighth century CE under a dynasty known as the Śailendras, or "kings of the mountain." The monument's strong Mahāyāna influence is reflected in bas-reliefs that depict stories from the *Lalitavistara*, *Divyāvadāna*, *Jātakamālā*, and *Gaṇḍavyūha.* The seventy-two perforated, hollow stupas on the top of three circular platforms cover seated images of the Buddha Vairocana. Scholars have argued that the monument, as a cosmic mountain, connects royal power with the Dharma, the basis of all reality; it may also synthesize an autochthonous cult of "kings of the mountain" with the Ādibuddha, or universal Buddha nature. In support of this connection it is speculated that Śailendra inscriptions use the Sanskrit term *gotra* to signify both "line of the ancestors" as well as "family of the Buddha," thereby identifying the Śailendra ancestral line with that of the Tathāgata.

Angkor, in Cambodia, has been even more widely studied as a source for understanding the interrelationships between Southeast Asian kingship and religion, especially regarding the *devarāja* (god-king) concept. It may be that this concept originated in Fu-nan, a Chinese term derived from the Mon-Khmer *bnam*, meaning "mountain" and possibly referring to a cult of a national guardian spirit established by the founder of the state. In the early ninth century the Khmer ruler Jayavarman II built on this background, adopting Śaivism as the state religion and thus requiring that the king be worshiped as a manifestation of Śiva. This identification was symbolized by a *liṅga* that was set upon the central altar of a pyramidal temple as an imitation of Mount Meru and the center of the realm. The *devarāja* cult took on

Mahāyāna Buddhist forms under Sūryavarman I in the early eleventh century and under Jayavarman VII (1181–1218), who constructed the great Bayon Temple, in which Jayavarman and Lokeśvara appear to be identified, at Angkor Thom at the end of the twelfth century. It can be inferred that in the tradition of the *devarāja*, Sūryavarman and Jayavarman became *buddharājas*, or incarnate Buddhas.

Other classical Southeast Asian capitals and major royal and religious monuments exhibit the influence of both Hindu and Buddhist worldviews. The remains of over five thousand stupas can be seen at the site of ancient Pagan, an area covering sixteen square miles. It was unified by Aniruddha (1040–1077) and the commander of his forces and successor, Kyanzittha (fl. 1084–1113). The Schwezigon Pagoda, possibly begun by Aniruddha but certainly completed by Kyanzittha, enshrines three sacred Buddha relics, symbolizing the power of the *cakkavattin* as the defender of the sacred order of things *(dhamma)*. Other stupas, such as the Mingalazedi, which was completed in the late thirteenth century, reflect the basic macro-micro cosmological symbolism of Borobudur; it has truncated pyramidal and terraced bases and a central stairway on each side. The Ānanda Temple, the stupa that dominated Pagan, was constructed by Kyanzittha in the late eleventh century and combines both cosmic mountain and cave symbolism: an ascetic's cave in which the Buddha meditates and a magical *axis mundi* that empowers the entire cosmos. A small kneeling image facing the large Buddha image in the temple is thought to represent Kyanzittha, corroborating inscriptional claims that he saw himself as a *bodhitsatta* and *cakkavattin*.

The mythic ideal of the *cakkavattin* is embodied in the moral example of Aśoka Maurya. Similarly, the *cakkavattin* of the Suttas provides the legendary charter for the idealized kingly exemplar of the Southeast Asian Theravāda chronicles. Aśoka was the moral exemplar *par excellence*, in whose footsteps, so say the chronicles and inscriptions, the monarchs of Burma, Thailand, and Laos follow. Aśoka's conversion divides his biography into two halves—the first tells of warring, wicked Aśoka (Pali, Caṇḍāsoka) and the second of the just, righteous Aśoka (Pali, Dhammāsoka). Similarly Aniruddha kills his brother to become the ruler of Pagan but then becomes a patron of Buddhism, and Tilokarāja (1441–1487) of Chiangmai revolts against his father but then devotes much of his attention to the prosperity of the Buddhist *sangha*. Southeast Asian rulers are also reputed to have called councils, as did Aśoka, in order to purify the *sangha* and regularize the Tipiṭaka. These activities, which supported Buddhism, represented ways the monarch could uphold his reputation for righteousness in ruling the state and in his dealings with the people. In his famous 1292 inscription, Rāma Khamhaeng (Ramkhamhaeng) of Sukhōthai says that the king adjudicates cases of inheritance with complete impartiality, does not kill or beat captured enemy soldiers, and listens to the grievances of his subjects. This paternalistic model of the dhammically righteous king is obviously indebted to the Aśoka model. [*See* Kingship, *article on* Kingship in Southeast Asia; Cakravartin; *and the biography of Aśoka.*]

Dominance of Sinhala Theravāda Buddhism. The shift to a Sinhala Theravāda orthodoxy in what became, in the true sense, Buddhist Southeast Asia (Burma, Thailand, Laos, and Cambodia) took place gradually from the late eleventh to the early thirteenth century and onward. This development reflected several factors: the decline of Buddhism in parts of Asia that had influenced the Southeast Asian mainland;

the rising influence of Sri Lanka under Vijayabāhu I (1055–1110) and Parākramabāhu I; the consolidation of power by the Burmese and Tai; an increasing interrelationship among Sri Lanka, Burma, and Thailand; and the spread of popular Theravāda practice among the general population of mainland Southeast Asia. The general outline of the story of the establishment of Sinhala Theravāda Buddhism in Southeast Asia is reasonably clear, although disparities between epigraphic and chronicle sources make historical precision difficult. Consequently, scholars disagree on dates, and historical reconstructions keep on changing.

Pali Theravāda and Sanskrit Hīnayāna forms of Buddhism were present at a relatively early time. Pali inscriptions found in central Thailand and lower Burma and associated with Mon culture support this claim, as does chronicle testimony, such as the story of Aniruddha's excursion into Rāmaññadesa to secure Pali scriptures. Inscriptional evidence makes it reasonable to assume that the roots of Mon Theravāda lay in the Kāñcīpuram area along the east coast of India. Even the popular Burmese tradition that holds that Buddhaghosa, who has been associated with Kāñcī, either came from Thaton or went there after visiting Sri Lanka may contain a kernel of historical truth, namely, the spread of Kāñcī Theravāda Buddhism into the Mon area. The presence of Pali Theravāda Buddhism among the Mon, who strongly influenced both the Burmese and Tai, provides the religio-cultural backdrop to the eventual consolidation of Sri Lankan forms of Theravāda Buddhism. As we shall see, both the Burmese and the Tai assimilated elements of Mon culture: its religion, legal traditions, artistic forms, and written script. Mon Theravāda, in effect, mediated Sinhala Theravāda. On the one hand, Theravāda Buddhism from Sri Lanka provided continuity with Mon religio-cultural traditions; on the other, it enabled the Burmese and Tai to break away from a Mon religio-cultural dominance. We must now explore some of the details of this story of cultural transformation and religious consolidation.

Burma. Contact between Burma and Sri Lanka dates from the establishment of the Pagan era by Aniruddha. Because of the disruption of Sri Lanka caused by wars with the Cōḻas in the mid-eleventh century, Vijayabāhu I, knowing of the strength of the Mon Theravāda traditions, sought help from Aniruddha to restore valid ordination. Aniruddha responded by sending a group of monks and Pali scriptures to Sri Lanka. In turn, Aniruddha requested, and was sent, a replica of the Buddha's tooth relic and a copy of the Tipiṭaka with which to check the copies of the Pali scriptures acquired at Thaton. The tooth relic was enshrined in Pagan's Schwezigon Pagoda, which became Burma's national palladium. Although archaeological evidence calls into question the chronicler's claim regarding the acquisition of the entire Pali Tipiṭaka, the tale might well be interpreted to indicate the growing importance of Sinhala Buddhism, not simply because the texts were more authoritative, but because the alliance between the king and the new sectarian tradition legitimated his authority over the Mon religio-cultural tradition.

Sinhala Buddhism flourished during the reign of Narapatisithu (1173–1210), and the Mahāvihāra tradition became normative at this time. Sinhala Buddhism, in particular the Mahāvihāra tradition, gained position partly through visits of distinguished Burmese monks to Sri Lanka. Panthagu, successor to Shin Arahan as the nominal head of the Pagan Buddhist *sangha*, visited the island in 1167. The Mon monk Uttarajīva Mahāthera followed in his predecessor's footsteps by journeying to Sri Lanka in 1180 with a group of monks that included a Mon novice named Chapaṭa, who was to figure most prominently in establishing the precedent authority of the Mahāvihāra. Chapaṭa and four others remained in Sri Lanka for ten years and were reordained as Mahātheras in the Mahāvihāra lineage. Their return to Burma marked the permanent establishment of Sinhala Buddhism in mainland Southeast Asia and brought about a schism in the Burmese Buddhist *sangha* between the Theravāda school of Thaton and Kāñcī, characterized by Shin Arahan's orthodoxy; and the Sinhala Theravāda tradition. When Chapaṭa returned to Pagan, Narapatisithu requested that he and the other four Mahātheras reordain Burmese monks of the Shin Arahan tradition, thereby establishing the superior legitimacy of the Sinhala orthodoxy over the Mon form of Theravāda. The chronicles refer to the Shin Arahan tradition as the "early school" *(purimagaṇa)* and to Chapaṭa's Sīhaḷa Sangha simply as the "late school" *(pacchāgaṇa)*. Owing to disciplinary and personal reasons, the *pacchāgaṇa* was to divide into several branches each loyal to one or another of the Mahātheras who had returned from Sri Lanka. One point of dispute among the branches was whether gifts could be given to particular monks or to the *sangha* at large.

The Sīhaḷa order was introduced to lower Burma at Dala, near Rangoon, by Sāriputta, who bore the title Dhammavīlasa, meaning a scholar of great repute. This tradition is referred to as the Sīhaḷapakkhabhikkhu Sangha, in contrast with the Ariyārahantapakkhabhikkhu Sangha, which represents the Mon Theravāda tradition. The chronicles also call this school the Kambojasanghapakka on the grounds that it was headquartered near a settlement of Kambojans (Cambodians). This title may reflect historical fact or refer to the earlier Theravāda of the Mon-Khmer areas to the east (i.e., Dvāravatī), which found its way into lower Burma. The Sīhaḷa Sangha was also introduced to Martaban by two Mon monks, Buddhavaṃsa Mahāthera and Mahāsāmi Mahāthera, who had been reordained in Sri Lanka. According to the Kalyāṇī inscriptions of Pegu, by the thirteenth century six Buddhist schools—the Mon Ariyārahanta and five Sīhaḷa sects—existed in Martaban. Sectarianism in Burmese Theravāda has continued into the modern period and contrasts with the relative homogeneity of Theravāda Buddhism in Thailand.

Buddhism prospered during the reign of Narapatisithu (1173–1210). Many beautiful temples were built under his sponsorship (e.g., Sulamani, Gawdawpalin), and Pali scholarship flourished. For example, Chapaṭa (also known as Saddhammajotipāla) wrote a series of famous works dealing with Pali grammar, discipline (Vinaya), and higher philosophy (e.g., *Suttaniddesa, Sankhepavaṇṇanā, Abhidhammatthasangha)*, and Sāriputta wrote the first collection of laws composed in Rāmaññadesa, known as the *Dhammavīlasa* or *Dhammathāt*. The shift away from a dominant Mon influence that occurred during Narapatisithu's reign is also reflected in the architectural style and the use of Burmese in inscriptions.

Thailand. The development of Buddhism among the Tai followed roughly the same pattern as in Burma. As the Tai migrated from southwestern China into the hills east of the Irrawaddy (home of the Shans), the upper Menam Plain (the Siamese), and farther east to the Nam U (the Lao), and as they gradually moved into the lowland area dominated by the Mons and the Khmers, they came into contact with Theravāda and Mahāyāna forms of Buddhism as well as with Brahmanism. After Khubilai Khan's conquest of Nan-chao in 1254 caused ever greater numbers of Tai to push south, they began to establish domination over the Mon and Khmer and to absorb elements of these more advanced cultures. As was the case in Burma, Mon Buddhism in particular became a major influence on the Tai as they extended their sway over much of what we now know as modern Thailand. This influence is seen in the establishment of two major Tai states in the late thirteenth and fourteenth centuries, Sukhōthai and Chiangmai.

Both Sukhōthai and Chiangmai became powerful centers of Tai settlement under the leadership of the able rulers Rāma Khamhaeng (r. c. 1279–1299) and Mengrai respectively. Sukhōthai, which had been a Khmer outpost from at least the time of Jayavarman VII, became an independent Tai state in the middle of the thirteenth century. Two Tai chieftains, Phe Mu'ang and Bang Klang Hao, seized Śrī Sajanalāya and drove the Khmer governor from Sukhōthai. Bang Klang Hao, was installed as ruler of Sukhōthai with the title Indrāditya. Indrāditya's third son, Rāma Khamhaeng, was to become Sukhōthai's greatest monarch and one of the exemplary Buddhist kings of Tai history. During his reign, which extended over the last two decades of the century, Rāma Khamhaeng asserted his sway over a large area extending from Haṃsavatī (Pegu) to the west, Phrae to the north, Luang Prabang to the east, and Nakorn Sri Dhammaraja (Nagara Śrī Dharmarāja; Ligor or Tambraliṅga) to the south. Nakorn Sri Dhammaraja, although dominated by Śrīvijaya from the eighth to the twelfth century and later by the Khmer, was an important center of Theravāda Buddhism by the eleventh century. Prior to Rāma Khamhaeng's ascendance to power in Sukhōthai, Chandrabhānu of Nagara Śrī Dharmarāja had sent a mission to Sri Lanka, and the *Cūlavaṃsa* reports that Parākramabāhu II invited Dhammakitti Mahāthera, a monk from Nagara Śrī Dharmarāja, to visit Sri Lanka. Rāma Khamhaeng, who was well aware of the strength of Theravāda Buddhism at Nagara Śrī Dharmarāja, invited a Mahāthera from the forest-dwelling tradition *(araññaka)* there to reside in Sukhōthai. Rāma Khamhaeng's famous 1292 stela inscription refers to various religious sanctuaries in Sukhōthai, including the *araññaka* monastery (Wat Taphan Hin), a Khmer temple (Wat Phra Phai Luang), and a shrine to the guardian spirit of the city, Phra Khaphung. In short, while we have definitive evidence that Rāma Khamhaeng supported Theravāda Buddhism, religion in thirteenth-century Sukhōthai was varied and eclectic.

During the reigns of Rāma Khamhaeng's successors—his son Lö Tai (1298–1347), and his grandson Lü Thai (1347–1368/74?)—Sinhala Buddhism became normative. According to the *Jīnakālamāli,* a Sukhōthai monk named Sumana studied under, and received ordination from, a Sinhala Mahāthera, Udumbara Mahāsāmi, who was resident in Martaban. Sumana returned to Sukhōthai to establish the Sīhaḷa Sangha there, and, along with his colleague Anōmadassī, he proceeded to spread the Sīhaḷa order throughout much of Thailand (Ayuthayā, Pitsanulōk, Nān, Chiangmai, and Luang Prabang). King Lü Thai, in particular, was noted for his piety and his support of Buddhism. He brought Buddha relics and images and established Buddha "footprints" *(buddhapada)* in an effort to popularize Buddhist practice throughout his realm. A Buddhist scholar of note, he was particularly known as the author of the *Traibhūmikathā* (Verses on the Three Worlds), thought to be the first systematic Theravāda cosmological treatise.

About the same time that Sinhala Buddhism was coming into its own in Sukhōthai, it was also being spread to Tai states to the north and northeast, namely, Chiangmai and Luang Prabang. Chiangmai was established as the major Tai state in northern Thailand by Mengrai, who expanded his authority from Chiangsaen to encompass

Chiangrai, Chiangkhong, and Fāng. He subjugated the Mon-Lava center of Haripuñjaya in 1291 before founding Chiangmai in 1296. According to both inscriptional and chronicle evidence, Sumana Mahāthera brought the Sinhala Buddhism he had learned from his preceptor in Martaban to Chiangmai in 1369 at the invitation of King Küna (1355–1385). Küna built Wat Suan Dọk to house the Buddha relic brought by Sumana, and Sinhala Buddhism gained favored status over the Mon Theravāda traditions of Haripuñjaya. As in the case of Sukhōthai and Pagan, Sinhala Buddhism functioned not only as a means to build continuity with the Mon Theravāda tradition over which the Tai and the Burmese established their authority but also as a means to assert their unique religio-cultural traditions.

The apogee of the development of the Sīhaḷa order in Chiangmai was reached during the reigns of Tilokarāja, one of the greatest of the Tai monarchs, and Phra Mu'ang Kaew (1495–1526). Tilokarāja legitimated the overthrow of his father, Sam Fang Kaen, through the support of the Mahāvihāra order, which had been brought to Chiangmai in 1430. According to the Mūlasāsana of Wat Pa Daeng in Chiangmai, the center of this sect, this tradition was brought to Thailand by a group of thirty-nine monks from Chiangmai, Lopburi, and lower Burma who had visited Sri Lanka in 1423 during the reign of Parākramabāhu VI of Kotte. They returned to Ayutthayā, a Tai state that subjugated Sukhōthai under the Indrarāja in 1412, and dominated central Thailand until they were conquered by the Burmese at the end of the eighteenth century. According to the northern Tai chronicles, members of this mission spread throughout central and northern Thailand, reordaining monks into the new Sīhaḷa order. Tilokarāja made this Wat Pa Daeng-Mahāvihāra group the normative monastic tradition in Chiangmai at a general council in 1477. The Pa Daeng chronicles depict Tilokarāja as a great supporter of the *sangha* and as a righteous and exemplary monarch in the Aśokan mode. During the reign of Tilokarāja's successor, Phra Mu'ang Kaew, Pali Buddhist scholarship in Chiangmai flourished. The *Māṅgaladīpaṇi,* a Pali commentary on the *Māṅgala Sutta,* was written at this time and is still used as the basis of higher-level Pali studies, and the most important northern Tai chronicle, the *Jīnakālamālipakaraṇa,* also dates from this period.

Contemporaneous with the apogee of Buddhism in Chiangmai was the reign of Dhammaceti (1472–1492), who ruled Burma from Pegu, in the lower part of the country. According to the northern Tai and Burmese chronicles as well as the Kālyaṇī inscriptions, during Dhammaceti's reign there were several religious missions to Sri Lanka from Pegu and Ava, and Sīhaḷa monks, in turn, visited Burma. Burmese monks were reordained and visited sacred shrines on the island. Like Tilokarāja, Dhammaceti wanted to unify the *sangha* and used the new ordination to unite Buddhists in the Pegu kingdom. Monks from all over lower Burma, Ava, Tougoo, from the Shan kingdoms, Thailand, and Cambodia came to Pegu to be ordained during what the chronicles portray as the "golden age" of lower Burma.

Cambodia and Laos. Theravāda Buddhism was introduced to Cambodia by the Mon of the lower Menam Chaophraya River valley. In the eleventh and twelfth centuries, Theravāda also existed alongside Mahāyāna forms of Buddhism as well as Brahmanism. Mahāyāna Buddhism certainly received royal patronages in the eleventh century, and Jayavarman VII, the builder of the Bayon Temple at Angkor Thom, was identified with the Buddha Lokeśvara in the divine-royal symbiosis of the Khmer *devarāja/buddharāja* cult. Yet, typical of the classical Southeast Asian monarchs, Jayavarman's patronage of Mahāyāna Buddhism was not exclusive. According to the Kālyaṇī inscriptions and *The Glass Palace Chronicle,* a Cambodian monk, possibly Jayavarman's son, was part of the Burmese mission to Sri Lanka in the twelfth century. There was certainly an influx of Mon Buddhists from the Lopburi region in the face of Tai pressure in the thirteenth and early fourteenth centuries. Testimony of Chau Ta Kuan, a member of a late thirteenth century mission to Angkor, indicates that Theravāda monks were present in the Khmer capital during that period. The *Jīnakālamāli* account of the Chiangmai mission to Sri Lanka in 1423 CE includes reference to eight Khmer monks who brought the Sīhaḷa order of the Mahāvihāra to Cambodia.

The development of Buddhism in Laos was influenced by both Cambodia and Thailand. According to the Lao chronicles, Jayavarman Parmesvara (1327–1353) helped Phi Fa and Fa Ngum establish the independent kingdom of Lān Chāng, which earlier had been under the political hegemony of Sukhōthai. An inscription at Wat Keo in Luang Prabang refers to three Sinhala Mahātheras—including Mahāpasaman, Fa Ngum's teacher at Angkor—who went from Cambodia to Lān Chāng as part of a religious mission. Certainly, from the late fourteenth century onward, Buddhism in Laos and Cambodia was primarily influenced by the Tai as a consequence of their political dominance in the area. Even in the modern period, Theravāda sectarian developments in Thailand were reflected in Cambodia and Laos, and prior to the Communist revolution, monks from Cambodia and Laos studied in the Buddhist universities in Bangkok.

Summary. During the period that marks the rise of the classical Southeast Asian states, Buddhism existed in many guises. Pali Theravāda was introduced principally through the Mon of Dvāravatī and lower Burma and was considered a "higher" culture appropriated by the Burmese and the Tai. A strong Mahāyāna Buddhist presence is apparent not only in Śrīvijaya and Angkor but also in Pagan and the early Tai states. Furthermore, these forms of Buddhism competed with, and were complemented by, autochthonous animistic cults and Brahmanism. Buddhism made a decisive contribution to the conception of Southeast Asian kingship and monarchical rule through its ideal of the *dhammarāja,* who was not only represented by King Aśoka in India but by such Southeast Asian monarchs as Kyanzittha, Rāma Khamhaeng, and Tilokarāja.

Sri Lanka played the decisive role in the increasing dominance of Theravāda Buddhism in mainland Southeast Asia. Several factors contributed to this development, but I have singled out two: the rise to power of the Burmese and the Tai, who appropriated the Theravāda Buddhism of the Mon; and their subsequent adoption of Sinhala Buddhism as a way of establishing their own distinctive cultural and religious identity. While Sinhala influence can be traced to the eleventh century, the Sīhaḷa order only became dominant with the rise and development of the classical states from the mid-twelfth to the end of the fifteenth century. Sinhala Buddhism contributed to the legitimation of the ruling monarchies through its worldview, interpretation of history, monastic institution, education, and language; however, just as important, it became the religion of the masses through the worship of relics and sacred images and through the development of popular syncretic cults.

Vietnam has been largely excluded from the story of the development of the classical Buddhist Southeast Asian states because of the predominance of Hinduism among the Chams during early Vietnamese history and the overwhelming cultural influence of China on the country. Until the eleventh century the Vietnamese were effectively a group within the Chinese empire, and they looked to China for cultural inspiration even after they achieved independence under the Ly dynasty (1009–1224). Mahāyāna Buddhism was certainly part of the Chinese cultural influence, and the Ch'an (Viet., Thien) school, allegedly first established in 580 CE by Ti-ni-da-lu'u-chi, was the major Buddhist tradition in Vietnam. The elite eventually came to prefer Confucianism, but Buddhism continued to be important among the masses.

SOUTHEAST ASIAN BUDDHISM IN THE MODERN PERIOD

The classical Southeast Asian religio-cultural synthesis, of which Theravāda Buddhism has been a major component, has given the cultures of Burma, Thailand, Cambodia, Laos, and Vietnam a unique sense of identity and has sustained them to the present. Faced with Western imperialistic expansion from the seventeenth century onward and the challenge of modernity, the classical religious worldview, institutional structures, and cultural ethos have been changed, modified, and reasserted in a variety of ways. We shall examine how Buddhism has adapted to this challenge, its role in the development of the modern nation-state, and what the most recent trends suggest for the future of Buddhism in the region.

The condition of Southeast Asian Buddhism in the modern period reflects, to a large degree, the forces unleashed during the colonial period, especially during the nineteenth and twentieth centuries. Although modern religious histories of Burma, Thailand, and Indochina differ because of internal factors as well as the uniqueness of their colonial experiences—just as the Enlightenment fundamentally challenged the medieval synthesis of Christian Europe—the last century and a half has called into question the traditional Buddhist-Brahmanic-animistic synthesis of Southeast Asia and, consequently, the institutions and values associated with that worldview. The challenge to the classical worldview, and to the traditional moral community that was based on it, occurred on many fronts. Throughout the region the educational role of the *sangha* has been undermined by Western education. The status of the monk as one who was educated and as an educator and the significance of what was traditionally taught have also suffered. In Burma, the destruction of the institution of Buddhist kingship in 1885, as well as the relatively open posture of the British toward Buddhism, left the *sangha* in disarray, without the authority and direction the king traditionally provided. Thailand's rapid urbanization over the past fifty years has dramatically changed the village or town milieu that has historically informed and supported Buddhist religious practice. The communist revolutions in Laos, Cambodia, and Vietnam have displaced Buddhism as the fundamental mediator of cultural values. These are but a few of the challenges that Southeast Asian Buddhism has faced in the modern and contemporary periods.

Modernization and Reform. The eve of the assertion of colonial power in the Buddhist countries of Southeast Asia found them in differing states and conditions. The Burmese destruction of Ayutthayā in 1767 provided the Thai (the designation applied to Tai living in the modern nation-state) the opportunity to establish a new capital on the lower Chaophraya River at present-day Bangkok. Because of its accessibility to international commerce the new site was much better situated for the new era about to dawn; the new dynastic line was better able to cope with the increasing impact of Western influence and was also committed to building a new sense of national unity. The Burmese, on the other hand, tired of wars under Alaungpaya and his son, were beset by religious and ethnic fractionalism. They were disadvantaged by the more isolated location of their capital (Ava, Amarapura, and then Mandalay), and governed by politically less astute rulers such as King Bagyidaw, who lost the Arakan and lower Burma to the British in the Anglo-Burmese Wars. Cambodia, in the eighteenth and early nineteenth centuries, basically fell victim to either the Thai or the Vietnamese until the French protectorate was established over the country in the 1860s. The Lao kingdoms of Luang Prabang and Vientiane were subject to Thai dominance in the nineteenth century until King Norodom was forced to accept French protection in 1863. Only in the 1890s were the French able to pacify Cochin China, Annam, and Tongkin, which, together with Cambodia, were formed into the Union Indochinoise in 1887. With the rest of Buddhist Southeast Asia disrupted by the colonial policies of France and Great Britain, Thailand's independence and able leadership under Mongkut (Rama IV, 1851–1868) and Chulalongkorn (1868–1910) abetted religious modernization and reform, making Thailand the appropriate focus for this topic.

The classical Thai Buddhist worldview had been set forth in the *Traibhūmikathā* of King Lü Thai of Sukhōthai. In one sense this text must be seen as part of Lü Thai's program to reconstruct an administrative and political framework and to salvage the alliance structure that had collapsed under the policies of his predecessor. In laying out the traditional Buddhist stages of the deterioration of history, Lü Thai meant to affirm the meaningfulness of a karmically calculated human life within a given multitiered universe. As a Buddhist sermon it urges its listeners to lead a moral life and by so doing to reap the appropriate heavenly rewards. Within its great chain of being framework of various human, heavenly, and demonic realms, the text focuses on a central figure, the universal monarch, or *cakkavattin,* exemplified by the legendary king Dharmaśokarāja. Lü Thai's traditional picture of the world, the role of the king, the nature of karmic action, and the hope of a heavenly reward provide a rationale for Sukhōthai political, social, and religious order. That King Rama I (1782–1809), who reestablished the fortunes of the Thai monarchy, commissioned a new recension of the *Traibhūmi* testifies to its longevity and also to its utility as a charter for order and stability during yet another time of political and social disruption.

The worldview of the *Traibhūmi* was soon to be challenged by the West, however. European and American missionaries, merchants, and travelers came to Bangkok in the 1830s and 1840s, and by 1850 Thailand, or Siam, had signed commercial treaties with several Western nations. Led by Mongkut, who was crowned king in 1851, and by Chao Phraya Thiphakorawong, his able minister of foreign affairs, the Siamese noble elite proved to be interested in and open to Western technology and culture. A pragmatic type of scientific empiricism began to develop among them, leading even the devout Mongkut to articulate a demythologized Buddhism somewhat at odds with the traditional *Traibhūmi* worldview. This critique was formally set forth in 1867 in Chao Phraya Thiphakorawong's *Kitchanukit* (A Book Explaining Various Things), which explains events not in terms of traditional cosmological and mythological sources but using astronomy, geology, and medicine. For example, he argues that rain falls not because the rainmaking deities venture forth or because a great serpent thrashes its tail but because the winds suck water out of clouds; illness, he says, is caused not by a god punishing evil deeds but by air currents. Although the explanations were inaccurate, they were naturalistic rather than mythological or religious. The *Kitchanukit* presents Buddhism as primarily a system of social ethics; heaven and hell are not places but have a moral or pedagogical utility; *kamma* (Skt., *karman*) is not an actual causal force but a genetic principle that accounts for human diversity. Mongkut's successor, his son Chulalongkorn, moved even further from the mythic cosmology of the traditional Southeast Asian Buddhist worldview, declaring the *Traibhūmi* simply an act of imagination.

Modernization of the Thai Buddhist worldview was accompanied by a reform of the Buddhist *sangha,* led initially by Mongkut and continued during the reign of Chulalongkorn. Before his coronation in 1851 Mongkut had been a monk for twenty-five years. During that time his study of the Pali scriptures and his association with Mon monks of a stricter discipline convinced him that Thai Buddhism had departed from the authentic Buddhist tradition. He advocated a more serious study of Pali and Buddhist scripture as well as the attainment of proficiency in meditation. His efforts at religious reform resulted in an upgrading of monastic discipline in an effort to make it more orthodox. The group of monks who gathered around Mongkut at Wat Bovornives called themselves the Thammayut ("those adhering to the doctrine") and formed the nucleus of a new, stricter sect of Thai Buddhism. With its royal origins and connections, the Thammayut, or Dhammayuttika, sect has played a very influential role in the development of modern Thai Buddhism. In 1864 the Khmer royal family imported it to Cambodia, where it played a similar role. Its impact in Laos, however, was less significant. [*See the biography of Mongkut.*]

The development of a reformist Buddhist tradition that embodied Mongkut's ideals brought about further changes in the monastic order, especially as the *sangha* became part of the policies and programs of Mongkut's son Chulalongkorn. At the same time that he implemented reforms designed to politically integrate outlying areas into the emergent nation-state of Thailand, Chulalongkorn also initiated policies aimed at the incorporation of all Buddhists within the kingdom into a single national organization. As a consequence, monastic discipline, as well as the quality of monastic education, improved throughout the country. A standard monastic curriculum, which included three levels of study in Buddhist history, doctrine, and liturgy, and nine levels of Pali study, was established throughout the country. In addition, two Buddhist academies for higher studies were established in Bangkok.

The modernization and reform of Buddhism in Thailand in the late nineteenth and early twentieth centuries stand out, but the Thai case must be seen as part of a general trend in all the Southeast Asian Buddhist countries. In the area of text and doctrine a new scripturalism, epitomized by the new redaction of the Tipiṭaka in conjunction with the general Buddhist council held in Burma in 1956 and 1957, has emerged. Doctrinal reinterpretation has followed three major lines: an emphasis on the ethical dimensions of the tradition at the expense of the supernatural and mythical; a rejection of magical elements of popular thought and practice as incompatible with the authentic tradition; and a rationalization of Buddhist thought in terms of Western categories, along with an apologetic interest in depicting Buddhism as scientific. Some apologists, such as U Chan Htoon of Burma, have claimed that all modern scientific concepts preexisted in Buddhism. Others make less sweeping claims but cite specific correlations between such Buddhist doctrines as interdependent co-arising *(paṭicca samuppāda;* Skt., *pratītya-samutpāda)* and Einstein's relativity theory. Generally speaking, Buddhist apologists have attempted to prove that

Buddhism is more scientific than other religions, particularly Christianity; that the empirical approach or methodology of Buddhism is consistent with modern science; and that science proves or validates particular Buddhist teachings.

Institutional modernization and reform have also taken place along the lines that we have examined in some detail in regard to Thailand. Cambodia, for example, not only adopted the Dhammayuttika sect from Thailand but also reorganized the *sangha* along national lines. In Laos and Burma various Buddhist organizations and associations with reformist intent emerged, often under lay leadership.

Buddhism and the Modern Nation-state. Buddhism proved to be a crucial factor during the end of the colonial and the postcolonial periods, as Burma, Thailand, Cambodia, Laos, and Vietnam became modern nation-states. On the one hand, Buddhism contributed decisively to the development of the new nationhood; on the other, it resisted in various ways to changes forced upon traditional Buddhist thought and practice. We shall first examine the Buddhist contributions to the national independence movements and to the maintenance of national identity and unity; second, we shall explore Buddhist resistance to pressures put on the tradition by the organization of the modern nation-state.

Historically, Buddhism played an important role in the definition of the classical Southeast Asian states. It was inevitable, therefore, that it would be a crucial factor in the redefinition of these states. In those cases, for example, in which a country was dominated by a colonial power, nationalist movements grew out of, or were identified with, a religious base or context. Take Burma as a case in point. Buddhism provided the impetus for the independence movement that arose there during the first decades of the twentieth century. The YMBAs (Young Men's Buddhist Association) of Rangoon and elsewhere in Burma quickly assumed a political role. The first issue of major consequence was the "no footwear" controversy of 1918. The YMBAs argued that Europeans, in keeping with Burmese custom, should be prohibited from wearing shoes in all pagodas; accordingly, the British government allowed the head monk of each pagoda to decide the regulations applying to footwear. During the next decade the nationalist cause was led primarily by the General Council of Burmese Associations and by such politically active monks as U Ottama, who was imprisoned for urging a boycott of government-sponsored elections, and U Wisara, who became a martyr to the independence movement when he died during a hunger strike in a British jail.

When U Nu became prime minister in January 1948, following Aung San's assassination, he put Buddhism at the heart of his political program. Although he rejected Marxism, he espoused a Buddhist socialism. In essence, he believed that a national community could be constructed only if individuals are able to overcome their own self-acquisitive interests. Sufficient material needs should be provided for everyone, class and property distinctions should be minimized, and all should strive for moral and mental perfection. The state was to meet the material needs of the people and Buddhism their spiritual needs. To this end he created a Buddhist Sasana Council in 1950 to propagate Buddhism and to supervise monks, appointed a minister of religious affairs, and ordered government departments to dismiss civil servants thirty minutes early if they wished to meditate. In 1960 U Nu committed himself and his party to making Buddhism the state religion of Burma, an unpopular move with such minorities as the Christian Karens. This attempt was one of the reasons given for General Ne Win's coup in March 1962, which deposed U Nu as prime minister. While in many ways naive and politically unrealistic, U Nu's vision of Buddhist socialism harked back to an earlier vision of the political leader as one who ruled by *dhamma* and who would engender peace and prosperity by the power of his own virtue. But such a vision proved incompatible with the political realities of the 1960s.

Buddhism figured prominently in other Southeast Asian countries, both as a basis of protest against ruling regimes and as an important symbolic component of political leadership. In the 1960s politically active Vietnamese monks contributed to the downfall of the Diem regime, and afterward the United Buddhist Association, under the leadership of Thich Tri Quang and Thich Thien Minh, remained politically active. In Cambodia, Prince Sihanouk espoused a political philosophy based on Buddhist socialism and was the last Cambodian ruler to represent, although in an attenuated way, the tradition of classical Southeast Asian Buddhist rule.

In addition to providing the inspiration for political independence movements, contributing to a political ideology with uniquely Buddhist features, and being the motivating force challenging political power structures, Southeast Asian Buddhism has been used to promote political unity within the boundaries of the nation-state. U Nu's hope that making Buddhism the state religion would promote national unity was naive; it did not take into account the contending factions within the Buddhist *sangha* and the presence of sizable non-Buddhist minorities who feared they might be threatened by covert, if not overt, pressure from the Buddhist majority.

In Thailand the centralization of the Thai *sangha* under King Chulalongkorn and his able *sangharāja,* Vajirañāṇa, not only improved monastic discipline and education but also integrated the monastic order more fully into the nation-state. Chulalongkorn's successor, Vajiravudh (1910–1925), made loyalty to the nation synonymous with loyalty to Buddhism; in effect, he utilized Buddhism as an instrument to promote a spirit of nationalism. In particular, he glorified military virtues and identified nationalism with the support of Thai Buddhism. He founded the Wild Tigers Corps, resembling the British Territorial Army; the Tiger Cubs, a branch of the corps, was later assimilated into the Boy Scout movement. Both encouraged loyalty to nation, religion (i.e., Buddhism), and the king.

Buddhism has continued to be an important tool in the government's policy to promote national unity. In 1962 the Buddhist Sangha Act further centralized the organization of the monastic order under the power of the secular state. In the same year the government organized the Dhammadhuta program, and in 1965 the Dhammacarika program. The former supported Buddhist monks abroad and those working in sensitive border areas, especially the northeastern region of the country, while the latter has focused on Buddhist missions among northern hill tribes.

Buddhism, however, has not only functioned as a kind of "civil religion," contributing to the definition and support of the new Southeast Asian nation-states in the postcolonial period. It has also resisted the kind of accommodation and change brought on by the new nationalism. In some cases this resistance has been generated by the desire to maintain traditional religious practices and more local autonomy; in others, it has come in the form of armed rebellion and messianic, millenarian movements. As an example of the former we cite Khrūbā Sīwichai, a northern Thai monk of the early twentieth century, and of the latter we cite the Saya San rebellion (1930–1931) in Burma.

While the vast majority of the Buddhist *sangha* in Thailand cooperated with the central government's attempts in the early twentieth century to standardize monastic organization, discipline, and education, there were a few notable exceptions. Khrūbā Sīwichai of the Chiangmai region of northern Thailand was one of them. He ran into problems with the *sangha* hierarchy because he ordained monks and novices according to northern Thai custom although he had not been recognized as a preceptor by the national order. He also singlehandedly raised vast sums of money to rebuild monasteries that had fallen into disrepair and to construct a road, using manual labor, to the famous Mahādhātu Temple on Doi Sutēp Mountain, overlooking Chiangmai. Because of his success in these enterprises, miraculous powers were attributed to him. In 1919, however, he was ordered to report to Bangkok to answer charges of clerical disobedience and sedition, but high Thai officials, fearing the repercussions that punishment of Khrūbā Sīwichai might have, intervened on his behalf. Although eventually Sīwichai submitted to the laws of the Thai national monastic order, *sangha* officials tacitly agreed to permit the northern clergy to follow some of its traditional customs.

Other, more radical Buddhist responses to the emerging nation-state developed in various parts of Southeast Asia and usually centered on a charismatic leader who was sometimes identified as an incarnation of the *bodhisattva* Maitreya. In Burma several rebellions in the early twentieth century aimed to overthrow British rule and to restore the fortunes of both Burmese kingship and Burmese Buddhism. One of these was led by Saya San, who had been a monk in the Tharrawaddy district in lower Burma but disrobed to work in a more directly political way to overthrow the British. Saya San's movement had a strongly traditional religious and royal aura, and much of his support came from political monks associated with nationalistic associations *(wunthanu athin*s) that had formed in the 1920s. Saya San was "crowned" as "king" in a thoroughly traditional Burmese manner in a jungle capital on 28 October 1930. An armed group was trained and the rebellion launched toward the end of December. As the conflict spread throughout lower Burma and into the Shan States, the British army was called in to help the police forces repress the rebellion. Only after eight months of fighting did the warfare end.

Recent Trends. The chapter on Southeast Asian Buddhism's future within the context of the modern nation-state has yet to be closed. The disestablishment of the *sangha* in Cambodia and Laos has shaken, but by no means rooted out, the tradition, even though Pol Pot's genocidal regime attempted such wholesale destruction in the aftermath of American withdrawal from the war in Indochina. Laos and Cambodia, however, have experienced a breakdown of the traditional religio-cultural synthesis. This is taking place more slowly in Thailand and even in Burma, which has been much more isolated from Western influences since the early 1960s. The political and economic contexts of Southeast Asian Buddhism, in short, have obviously affected the state of Buddhism in Southeast Asia. The trends that have emerged seem paradoxical, if not contradictory. We shall examine three sets or pairs: increasingly active lay leadership and the veneration of monks to whom supernatural powers are ascribed; a revival of meditation practice and an emphasis on active political and social involvement; rampant magical, syncretic ritual practice and insistence on the purity of the authentic teaching.

The modern period has seen increased lay leadership at various levels of religious life. The YMBAs of Burma and the Buddhist "Sunday schools" that have arisen in Thailand have obviously been influenced by Western Christian models. Lay associations have developed for various purposes. For example, prior to the revolution Cambodia had the Buddhist Association of the Republic of Cambodia (1952), the Association of Friends of the Buddhist Lycée (1949), the Association of Friends of Religious Welfare Aid Centers, the Association of Religious Students of the Republic of Cambodia (1970), the Association of the Buddhist Youth of Cambodia (1971), and so on. Buddhist laity have also been actively involved in the worldwide Buddhist movement. Most notable of the laity groups are the World Fellowship of Buddhists, which has headquarters in Bangkok, and the World Council of Churches, which holds interreligious dialogue consultations.

The increasingly significant role of the laity in a religious tradition noted for the centrality of the monk reflects many developments in modern Southeast Asian countries, not the least of which is the spread of secular, Western education among the elites. Coupled with this phenomenon, however, we find a polar opposition—a persistent cult of the holy man to whom supernatural powers are attributed. In some instances the holy monk becomes a charismatic leader of a messianic cult (e.g., the Mahagandare Weikzado Apwegyoke in Burma), while in others the form of veneration is more informal and generalized (e.g., Phra Acharn Mun in Thailand). In many cases the holy monk makes few, if any, miraculous or supernatural claims, but these will be ascribed to him by his followers. Hagiographic literature, describing cosmic portents of the monk's birth, extraordinary events during his childhood, and other characteristics of this genre, will often emerge. While the monk as miracle worker is not a new phenomenon in Theravāda Buddhism, it has persisted to the present time and, some observers claim, has been on the upswing in the contemporary period.

Meditation has always been the *sine qua non* of Buddhist practice, but traditionally it was the preserve of the forest-dwelling *(araññavāsī)* or meditating *(vipassana dhura)* monk. In the modern period, meditation has been more widely practiced as part of the routines of ordinary Buddhist temples and, more particularly, in meditation centers that either include or are specifically for lay practice. The lay meditation movement was especially strong in Burma under the leadership of such meditation masters as U Ba Khin and Ledi Sayadaw (1856–1923). Westerners have been particularly attracted to some of Southeast Asia's renowned meditation teachers, such as Acharn Cha of Wat Pa Pong in Ubon Ratchathani. Some meditating monks have also gained reputations not only for their method of meditation or for holiness but for the attainment of extraordinary powers as well.

While meditation has become a lay as well as monastic practice in contemporary Southeast Asian Buddhism, this development has not precluded a movement to formulate a strong, activist social ethic. The Vietnamese Zen monk Thich Nhat Hahn attempted to work out a Buddhist solution to the military conflict in his country during the 1960s, and there has been a widespread interest in formulating a Buddhist theory of economic development that is critical of Western capitalism but not necessarily indebted to Marxism. Buddhists have also acted to solve particular social problems, such as drug addiction, and have spoken out strongly against the proliferation of nuclear arms. Southeast Asian Buddhists have also joined with members of other religious groups, both within their own countries as well as in international organizations, to work for such causes as world peace and basic civil rights for all peoples. Buddhist interpreters, such as the Thai monk Bhikkhu Buddhadāsa, have referred to Buddhism as a practical system of personal and social morality.

Buddhadāsa has also been strongly critical of conventional Thai Buddhist religious practice, which has stressed merit-making rituals. These are aimed at obtaining personal benefit and propitiating various supernatural powers for protection or good luck. In his writings and at his center in Chaiya, southern Thailand, he emphasizes the importance of overcoming greed and attachment. *Nibbāna,* for Buddhadāsa, is the state that is achieved when egoism is overcome. This is the goal of all Buddhists, not just monks. Indeed, he argues, this is the purpose of all religions. Buddhadāsa's critique reflects the magical nature of popular Buddhist ritual practice not only in Thailand but, more generally, in Southeast Asian Buddhism, the goal of which is to improve one's life materially through the mechanism of gaining merit or improving one's karmic status. Buddhadāsa's proposal that such teachings as *nibbāna* and *anatta* (not-self), which represent the essence of the Buddha's teachings, must be part of every Buddhist's religious practice exemplifies an interest on the part of many contemporary Buddhist thinkers to restore the kernel of the authentic tradition, which has often been hidden beneath layers of cultural accretions. Thus, while the popular religious ethos is syncretic and emphasizes the attainment of worldly goals, various apologists in Burma and Thailand are attempting to make the core of the tradition a part of the understanding and practice of the Buddhist populace at large. Some critical observers have referred to this trend as a "protestantizing" of Southeast Asian Buddhism.

The contemporary ethos of Buddhism in Southeast Asia reflects an ancient heritage but also points in new directions. It is difficult to predict how the *sangha* will fare under the Marxist regimes in Laos and Cambodia or, for that matter, in the urban and increasingly materialistic environment of Bangkok and Chiangmai. Can the Theravāda monk maintain his place in society when his education cannot compare with that of the elite? Can Buddhism effectively address problems of overpopulation, prostitution, malnourishment, and economic exploitation? To what extent can the tradition change with the times and retain its identity? These and other questions face a religion that has not only been fundamental in the identity of the Burmese, Thai, Laotians, Cambodians, and Vietnamese but has also contributed much to world culture.

[*For a discussion of the institutional history of the Buddhist order in Southeast Asia, see* Theravāda. *An examination of the relationship between the* saṃgha *and the larger societies of which it is a part can be found in* Saṃgha, *article on* Saṃgha and Society. Southeast Asian Religions, *article on* Mainland Cultures *treats local Buddhist traditions in Southeast Asia. See also* Buddhism, *article on* Folk Buddhism; Pilgrimage, *article on* Buddhist Pilgrimage in South and Southeast Asia; Worship and Cultic Life, *article on* Buddhist Cultic Life in Southeast Asia; Burmese Religion; Khmer Religion; Lao Religion; Thai Religion; *and* Vietnamese Religion.]

BIBLIOGRAPHY

Works on Buddhism in Southeast Asia include text translations and doctrinal studies, histories of the development of Buddhism in various Southeast Asian countries, anthropological treatments of popular, village Buddhism, and studies of Buddhism and political change.

Georges Coedès's studies, *The Indianized States of Southeast Asia,* edited by Walter F. Vella and translated by Susan Brown Cowing (Canberra, 1968), and *The Making of South-East Asia,* translated by H. M. Wright (Berkeley, 1966), are standard treatments of the region, as is Reginald Le May's *The Culture of South-East Asia* (London, 1954). The classic study of Southeast Asian religion and kingship is Robert Heine-Geldern's *Conceptions of State and Kingship in Southeast Asia* (Ithaca, N.Y., 1956). A readable, general study of the history of Theravāda Buddhism in Southeast Asia and its present teachings and practices is Robert C. Lester's *Theravada Buddhism in Southeast Asia* (Ann Arbor, 1973). My *Buddhism and Society in Southeast Asia* (Chambersburg, Pa., 1981) is an analysis of Theravāda Buddhism in terms of the themes of syncretism, political legitimation, and modernization. The theme of Buddhism and political legitimation is discussed in several seminal articles in *Buddhism and Legitimation of Power in Thailand, Laos, and Burma,* edited by Bardwell L. Smith (Chambersburg, Pa., 1978).

The monumental work on the early Pagan period is Gordon H. Luce's *Old Burma—Early Pagán,* 3 vols. (Locust Valley, N.Y., 1969–1970). Two of the important Burmese chronicles have been translated: *Hmannān maha yazawintawkyī: The Glass Palace Chronicle of the Kings of Burma,* translated by Pe Maung Tin and G. H. Luce (London, 1923); and Pannasami's *The History of the Buddha's Religion (Sāsanavaṁsa),* translated by B. C. Law (London, 1952). Standard treatments of both Pali and Sanskritic Buddhism in Burma are Nihar-Ranjan Ray's *An Introduction to the Study of Theravāda Buddhism in Burma* (Calcutta, 1946), and his *Sanskrit Buddhism in Burma* (Calcutta, 1936). A more recent study is Winston L. King's *A Thousand Lives Away* (Cambridge, Mass., 1964). Two standard anthropological studies are Melford E. Spiro's *Buddhism and Society: A Great Tradition and its Burmese Vicissitudes,* 2d. ed. (Berkeley, 1982), and Manning Nash's *The Golden Road to Modernity* (New York, 1965). Nash was also the general editor of *Anthropological Studies in Theravada Buddhism* (New Haven, 1966), which contains valuable articles on Burmese and Thai Buddhism by Nash, David E. Pfanner, and Jasper Ingersoll. E. Michael Mendelson's *Sangha and State in Burma,* edited by John P. Ferguson (Ithaca, N.Y., 1965), although difficult going is a mine of information. Buddhism and the early nationalist period are studied in Emanuel Sarkisyanz's *Buddhist Backgrounds of the Burmese Revolution* (The Hague, 1965), and Donald E. Smith's *Religion and Politics in Burma* (Princeton, 1965).

The standard Thai history with much information about Thai Buddhism is David K. Wyatt's *Thailand: A Short History* (New Haven, 1984); Kenneth E. Wells's *Thai Buddhism: Its Rites and Activities* (Bangkok, 1939), while somewhat dated and rather dry is still very useful. One of the major northern Thai chronicles, Ratanapanya's *Jinakālamālīpakaranam,* has been translated by N. A. Jayawickrama as *The Sheaf of Garlands of the Epochs of the Conqueror* (London, 1968). Frank E. Reynolds and Mani B. Reynolds have translated the major Thai cosmological treatise, *Trai Phūmi Phra Rūang,* as *Three Worlds according to King Ruang* (Berkeley, 1982). Prince Dhani-Nivat's *A History of Buddhism in Siam,* 2d ed. (Bangkok, 1965), provides a brief historical overview of the development of Buddhism in Thailand. Much recent, significant work on Thai Buddhism has been done by anthropologists; see especially Stanley J. Tambiah's *World Conqueror and World Renouncer* (Cambridge, 1976) and several articles by Charles F. Keyes, for example, "Buddhism and National Integration in Thailand," *Journal of Asian Studies* 30 (May 1971): 551–567. Historians of religion have also contributed to our knowledge of Thai Buddhism. Frank E. Reynolds has written several articles including, "The Holy Emerald Jewel: Some Aspects of Buddhist Symbolism and Political Legitimation in Thailand and Laos," in *Religion and Legitimation of Power in Thailand, Laos, and Burma,* edited by Bardwell L. Smith (Chambersburg, Pa., 1978), pp. 175–193. I have analyzed a major northern Thai monastery in

Wat Haripuñjaya: A Study of the Royal Temple of the Buddha's Relic, Lamphun, Thailand (Missoula, Mont., 1976).

French scholars have made the major contribution to the study of Buddhism in Laos, Cambodia, and Vietnam. Louis Finot's "Research sur la littérature laotienne," *Bulletin de l'École Française d'Extrême-Orient* 17 (1917) is an indispensable tool in the study of Lao Buddhist literature. Marcel Zago's *Rites et cérémonies en milieu bouddhiste lao* (Rome, 1972) provides a comprehensive treatment of Lao religion, although Charles Archaimbault's "Religious Structures in Laos," *Journal of the Siam Society* 52 (1964): 57–74, while more limited in scope is very useful. Lawrence Palmer Brigg's "The Syncretism of Religions in Southeast Asia, especially in the Khmer Empire," *Journal of the American Oriental Society* 71 (October–December 1951): 230–249, provides a survey of the development of religion in Cambodia. Adhémard Leclère's classic study, *Le bouddhisme au Cambodge* (Paris, 1899) remains the standard work. The classic study of Vietnamese religion is Leopold Michel Cadière's *Croyances et pratiques religieuses des Viêtnamiens,* 3 vols. (Saigon, 1955–1958), but more accessible is the brief sketch in the trilingual volume by Chanh-tri Mai-tho-Truyen, *Le bouddhisme au Vietnam, Buddhism in Vietnam, Phat-giao Viet-nam* (Saigon, 1962). Thich Thien-An's *Buddhism and Zen in Vietnam in Relation to the Development of Buddhism in Asia,* edited by Carol Smith (Los Angeles, 1975), studies the development of Buddhist schools from the sixth to the seventeenth century. Thich Nhat-Hanh's *Vietnam: Lotus in a Sea of Fire* (New York, 1967) puts the Buddhist situation in the 1960s into historical perspective.

Interested readers may also wish to consult the following works: Heinz Bechert's three-volume study, *Buddhismus, Staat und Gesellschaft in den Ländern Theravāda-Buddhismus* (Frankfurt, 1966–1973); *Religion in South Asia,* edited by Edward B. Harper (Seattle, 1964), especially the articles by Michael Ames and Nur Yalman; and *Religion and Progress in Modern Asia,* edited by Robert N. Bellah (New York, 1965).

6 ISLAM IN SOUTH ASIA

PETER HARDY

As Islam in South Asia has, in its twelve-hundred-year history, manifested most of the varieties of response to the proclamations of the Qur'ān and the life of the prophet Muḥammad that are found in other parts of the Islamic world, "South Asia" might appear to be merely geographers' shorthand for a physically distinct region inhabited by large populations (approaching 240 million) of professing Muslims. The temper of their religious responses has ranged, as elsewhere, from the violent, pietist, and assured to the pacific, introspective, and tentative; and the setting of those responses has been, as elsewhere, the individual conscience and conduct, the life of the sect, order, or community, the courts of kings, the councils of legislators, or the conferences of politicians.

But perhaps it is the very protean character of Islam in South Asia that constitutes its distinctive "South-Asian-ness." So too perhaps is the sense of disappointment and uneasy wariness among the Muslims of the region at having, after so many centuries, some witnessing great Muslim kingdoms and empires, still to live in close proximity with a majority of neighbors whose Hindu culture can be seriously assaulted but not seriously wounded. Muslims throughout the world have lived as minorities surrounded by eavesdropping neighbors, but only Muslims in South Asia have succeeded in registering successfully the claim that members of a minority Muslim culture must have their own state to protect their culture. This must be regarded as a distinctively South Asian Muslim contribution to world Islam; so too must the openness of the theological, ethical, and jurisprudential debates occurring among the Muslims of the Republic of India on how best to obey God in their present situation. If a patterned and lively confusion is characteristic of Hinduism, so too is it characteristic of Islam in South Asia.

THE ARRIVAL OF MUSLIMS IN SOUTH ASIA

Muslims came to South Asia to earn a living, to conquer, to teach their religion, and to seek refuge. According to tradition, within a generation of the Prophet's death, the western coastal peoples first encountered Muslims as Arab settler-traders. In the following centuries, Arab Muslim traders were to be found in most of the ports on the east and west coasts of South India. By the tenth century (fourth century AH),

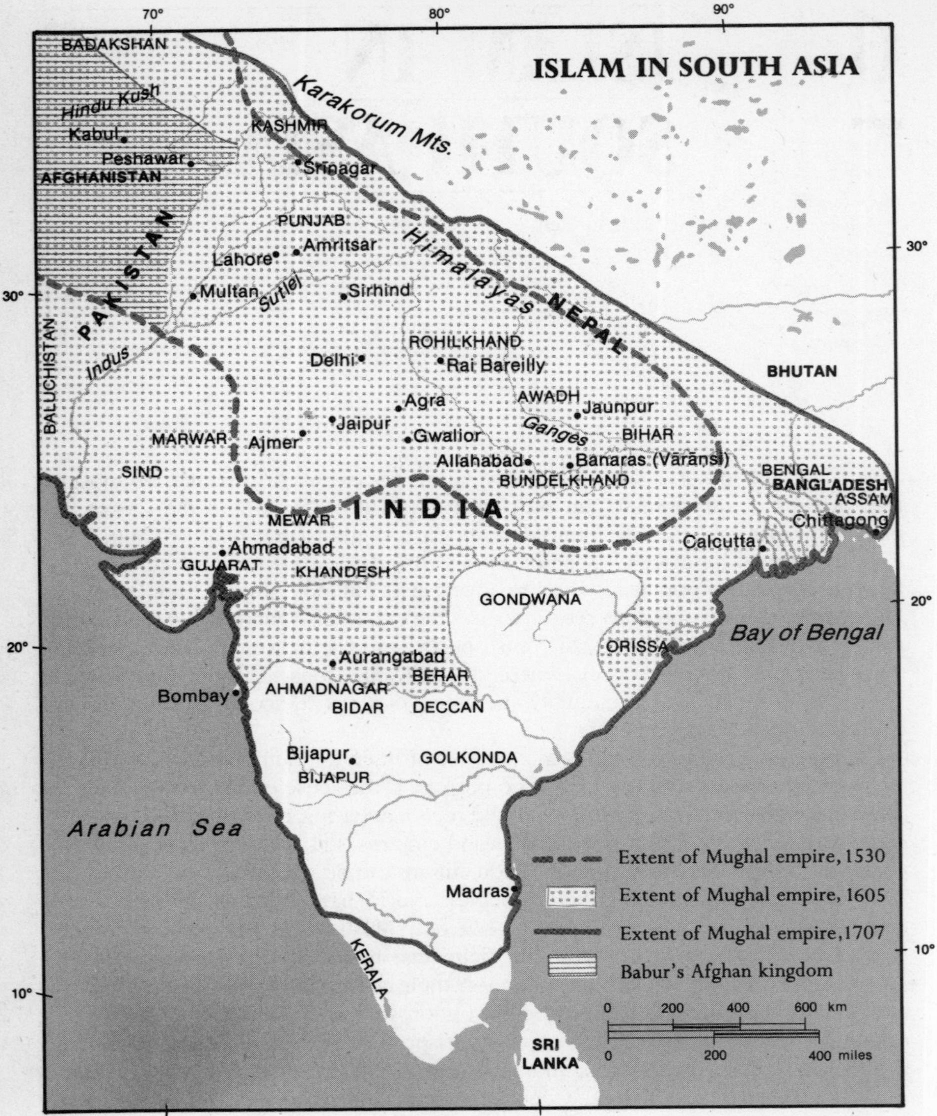

Muslim merchants had settled in major cities of the Deccan and the North Indian plain. In the eleventh century, Ismāʿīlī missionaries from the Yemen were active in Gujarat. As raiders, then as conquerors, Muslims penetrated the Indo-European areas of western Afghanistan toward the end of the seventh century. The Arabs conquered Sind from 711 on. Ghaznah became the Muslim headquarters in 962 and from the time of Sebüktigin (977–997) Muslims from Central Asia were using force to penetrate the North Indian plain. Inland areas of Bengal were conquered at the beginning of the thirteenth century, and Muslims invaded Assam and Orissa about the same time. Muslim Turks were probably first seen in Kashmir in the eleventh century, while from the fourteenth century Muslims from northern India penetrated the Terai plain at the foot of the mountains of Nepal. Muslim settlements in the central and western areas of Nepal date from the seventeenth century. Major Muslim settlement in the interior of the Deccan and the south (as distinct from settlements of resident traders) began with raids by the forces of the sultan of Delhi between 1295 and 1323. There are traditional accounts of the penetration of parts of Bengal and Bijapur by Muslim saints before the main Muslim military thrusts occurred in those regions, but there is no scholarly consensus that such traditions represent actual historical events.

ISLAMIC EDUCATION IN SOUTH ASIA

There has been no overarching framework or set of constraints in South Asia within which Islam has spread. Scholar, Ṣūfī, piously inclined ruler, creator of a *waqf* ("trust, inalienable endowment"), *qalandār,* or wandering holy man, Ismāʿīlī *dāʿī* ("propangandist"), and, in modern times, teacher of Islamic studies in a government college in Pakistan—all have remained remarkably free to make their own contributions as they wished. Certainly, in more modern times, coincident with Muslim loss of political supremacy, scholars have gathered under the umbrellas of such teaching institutions as Farangī Maḥall (founded 1694), Dār al-ʿUlūm at Deoband (founded 1867), and Nadwat al-ʿUlamā' (founded 1891) to follow a common syllabus for study and to award formal qualifications, but these began and continued as wholly voluntary associations of like-minded scholars. For the greater part of Islam's history in South Asia, the only hierarchy among religious communicators was one of esteem. Perhaps the most formal organization was to be found among members of the Ṣūfī *ṭā'ifah*s, or orders, with their formal ceremonies of initiation and successorship and their hierarchy of tyros, accepted disciples, and spiritual directors. But there was no bar to the introduction of orders new to South Asia and little inhibition of the formation of sub-branches of the main orders (as, for example, the Ṣābirīyah branch of the Chishtī order) with their own regional focuses and modified disciplines.

Sunnī Scholars. Little is known of the coming of Sunnī Muslim *ʿulamā',* or religious scholars, to the Muslim trading settlements on the southwest coast of India: the sixteenth-century Malayali author Zayn al-Dīn al-Maʿbarī suggests in his *Tuḥfat al-mujāhidīn* (Gift to the Holy Warriors) that missionaries from Arabia founded the first mosques in Kerala. In 1342, the Moroccan Arab traveler Ibn Baṭṭūṭah found mosques, *qāḍī*s ("judges") following the Shāfiʿī school of law, and students being supported by gifts from Muslim seamen and merchants. Sebüktigīn and Maḥmūd, the Ghaznavid rulers of eastern Afghanistan and the Punjab, patronized *ʿulamā'* of the Karrāmīyah sect (said by opponents to hold that God has a body). The Shāfiʿī school was strong under the later Ghaznavids and the Ghurids, but by the middle of the thirteenth century, the Ḥanafī school was dominant in northern India. The presence of the scholar-Ṣūfī Shaykh ʿAlī al-Hujwīrī in Lahore, where he died between 1072 and 1077, the travels of Fakhr al-Dīn al-Rāzī (1149–1209), the famous theologian and exegete, in the Ghurid territories, archaeological remains in Lahore from the eleventh and twelfth centuries, and the praises of Muslim historians for the Muslim rulers' zeal in founding mosques and encouraging scholars to move to India all indicate that the *'ulamā'* were firmly established in the Punjab by the beginning of the thirteenth century. Under the Delhi sultan Iltutmish (1211–1236) and his successors, a considerable migration of scholars from the Mongol-devastated lands of Islam to India eased the task of appointing *qāḍī*s to the increasing number of strongholds of Muslim rule in the north. Gujarat and the Deccan drew scholars more from the Yemen and the Hejaz, but as Shī'ī ideas found rulers' favor from the middle of the fifteenth century, more scholars migrated to the Deccan from southern Iran.

Under the Delhi sultanate the teaching centers of the Sunnī *'ulamā'* appear to have been informal schools attached to mosques rather than separate *madrasah*s, or religious colleges. Under the Bahmani sultanate in the Deccan, the Persian minister Maḥmūd Gāwān founded a *madrasah* at Bidar in 1472. In Bengal, inscriptions of the thirteenth to fifteenth centuries refer to *madrasah*s attached to mosques. But it was not until the last years of the rule of Awrangzīb (d. 1707) that *madrasah*s that were to acquire a far-reaching reputation made their appearance: in addition to the Farangī Maḥall already mentioned, Shāh 'Abd al-Raḥīm, Shāh Walī Allāh's father, founded at Delhi the Madrasah-i Raḥīmīyah, which the son was to make famous. The nineteenth century was the age of the *madrasah* in South Asia, with foundations affiliated to Deoband being established at Muradabad, Saharanpur, and Darbhanga, for example. Colleges founded in such widely separated centers as Madras, Peshawar, and Chittagong regarded themselves as Deobandi. In this century, *madrasah*s have multiplied in Kerala.

The Sunnī *'ulamā'* obtained material support from a variety of sources. All Muslim rulers in South Asia, sultans of Delhi, "provincial" sultans, and Mughal *pādshāh*s ("emperors") appointed *qāḍī*s, royal tutors, *khaṭīb*s ("mosque preachers"), and *imām*s ("mosque prayer-leaders") and paid them in cash or by income from revenue-free land. Others received an income from *waqf*s. *'Ulamā'* who did not enter service (and were often the more respected for that) lived from gifts from the faithful, from fees in money or kind for private tuition, or sometimes from cultivation or trade, though this was uncommon. Sometimes a noted scholar would accept a royal pension or a subvention from a government official, without the obligation to perform a public function. The *'ulamā'* of the Dār al-'Ulūm at Deoband broke new ground under British rule: they opened subscription lists and drew regular voluntary contributions from Muslims at all social levels, though chiefly from the better-off. Deoband today is a flourishing institution, while Farangī Maḥall, which drew much of its income from large landholders, is defunct.

The social status of the *'ulamā'* was high. Indeed, at all times, though not in all places, a good proportion of them belonged to families with a record of high position under the rulers of the day. As sayyids and shaykhs, many claimed an ancestry reaching outside South Asia and back to seventh- or eighth-century Arabia. In the nineteenth century some *'ulamā'* openly despised the indigenous convert. In later nineteenth-century Bengal, some disliked efforts to communicate Islam to rural Muslims in Bengali, partly because Bengali was not to them an "Islamic" language, but also partly because it was not an educated Muslim gentleman's language. The *'ulamā'* maintained their status by marrying within the family or at least within the circle of the so-called *ashrāf,* the honorable, who claim descent from the Prophet, or from his companions, or from the former Pathan and Mughal ruling elite. But acceptance by other *'ulamā'* through the following of a recognized course of study according to recognized methods could gain entry to the body of the *'ulamā'* for the lowly, even for the recent convert to Islam. Such social mobility is more fully documented in modern than in medieval times: for example, the family of Sayyid Ḥusayn Aḥmad Madanī of Deoband was thought to have been weavers; Mawlānā 'Ubayd Allāh Sindhī, also a prominent Deobandi *'ālim,* was born a Sikh. Of course, the high status of an *'ālim* might have a very local recognition: the rural mullah and *mawlawī* in Bengal, Bengali-speaking and able only to imitate the sounds of the Qur'ān, would not be recognized outside his neighborhood as an equal of the scholar with Arabic, Persian, and Urdu at his command.

Shī'ī Scholars. Although in South Asia reverent respect for the Prophet's family was strong, public communication of the Twelver Shī'ī tradition waited on favorable political and social developments, both in the outside Muslim world and in parts of South Asia. In the fifteenth century, following marked immigration to the Deccan Bahmani sultanate from the area of southern Iran, where Twelver Shī'ī sentiment was growing, the Bahmani sultan Aḥmad I (1422–1436) was himself "converted," but the dynasty's public position continued to be ambiguous. Of the successor sultanates to the Bahmanis, Bijapur supported the Twelver Shī'ī position from about 1510 to 1534 and again between 1558 and 1580; Golkonda's Quṭb-Shāhī dynasty was Shī'ī from its beginning under Qulī Quṭb al-Mulk (1496–1543); and from the reign of Burhān I (1509–1553), the sultanate of Aḥmadnagar supported Twelver Shiism. The establishment of Mughal rule made northern India a safer place for Shī'ī scholars. The Shī'ī Safavid shah, Ṭahmāsp (1524–1576), helped Humāyūn to reestablish the Mughal position in eastern Afghanistan by 1550, and Shī'ī Persians formed an important proportion of the Muslim elite of the Mughal empire from its creation under Akbar. In the eighteenth century, under the nawabs of Awadh, Lucknow became the Twelver Shī'ī cultural and educational capital in South Asia.

The Ismā'īlī Shī'ī communities in South Asia present, by contrast, a hierarchical model for conveying Islam as they understood it. Regarded as subversive by the Abbasid caliphs and by the Sunnī warlords who took effective control of the eastern Muslim world by the middle of the ninth century CE, they managed in the tenth century to establish a stronghold in the fringe area of Multan and, in the following century, a community in the Hindu-ruled area of Gujarat. In 1094, the Ismā'īlīyah split, over the succession of the Fatimid imamate, into the Musta'līyah and the Nizārīyah. In South Asia this split gave rise to the Bohora and the Khoja communities, respectively. Bohora communities were probably in existence in Gujarat by the middle of the twelfth century and certainly before the conquest of Gujarat by the Delhi sultan that began in 1299. The Khojas probably formed communities in Sind in the twelfth century and were well established in Gujarat by the fifteenth century. In the 1840s, the living imam of the Nizārīyah, the Aga Khan, Ḥasan 'Alī Shāh, moved to India from Iran and asserted his leadership over the Khoja community. Among the Bohoras, the *dā'ī muṭlaq,* or untrammeled summoner, acting for the imam believed to be in occlusion, has full religious knowledge and controls all activities of the community, assisted by shaykhs, mullahs, and *'āmil*s ("agents"), who are, however, only executive functionaries and do not participate in the formulation of doctrine and right conduct. Among the Khojas, the Aga Khan has an absolute power of decision over belief and practice, but in the running of the day-to-day affairs of the community, he is assisted by a hierarchy of central, provincial, and local councils. Among both Bohoras and Khojas, there have been opponents of the claims to supremacy of the *dā'ī muṭlaq* and of the imam, respectively.

THE ṢŪFĪ ORDERS

The authority of the *'ulamā',* of whatever persuasion, as "mediums" of Islam flows from recognition of learning; the authority of the mystics, the spiritualists of Islam, the seekers of the wisdom of the heart, flows from recognition that they have had (or are preparing themselves and others to have) direct, intuitive experience of the divine realities, and that divine grace might endow them with special efficacies. These efficacies have often been believed to continue after physical death. By the twelfth century, seekers had developed distinct spiritual disciplines and formed themselves into fraternities organized around *khāngāh*s ("hospices") headed by a shaykh responsible for investing a successor, appointing deputies, admitting novices to full discipleship, and perhaps controlling a network of centers.

The Arrival of the Orders. Although Shaykh 'Alī al-Hujwīrī, the Ṣūfī author of a textbook on Sufism, *Kashf al-maḥjūb* (The Unveiling of the Veiled), settled and died in Lahore, the arrival of members of orders in South Asia was broadly contemporary with the Ghurid invasions at the end of the twelfth century. Khwājah Mu'īn al-Dīn of the Chishtī order, founded in Afghanistan, settled in Ajmer (Rajasthan) in the 1290s. His successor, Quṭb al-Dīn Bakhtiyār Kākī (d. 1235) spread Chishtī influence to Delhi, while his successor Farīd al-Dīn, called Ganj-i Shakar ("store of sweetness," d. 1265), who left Delhi for Pākpattan by the Sutlej, consolidated a Chishtī position in the Punjab. During the lifetimes of the two great shaykhs of fourteenth-century Delhi, Niẓām al-Dīn Awliyā' (1238–1325) and Nāṣir al-Dīn Maḥmūd Chirāgh-i Dihlī ("lamp of Delhi," 1276–1356), the Chishtī order was spread to Bengal by Shaykh Sirāj al-Dīn (d. 1357), to Daulatabad by Burhān al-Dīn (d. 1340), and to Gulbarga by Sayyid Muḥammad Gīsū Dārāz ("of the long locks," 1321–1422). Other Chishtī mystics settled in Malwa and Gujarat. The other principal order in sultanate South Asia, the Suhrawardīyah, was strong in the southwest Punjab, at Multan in the person of Shaykh Bahā' al-Dīn Zakarīyā' (1182–1262), and, at Uchch, of Sayyid Jalāl al-Dīn Surkhpush ("red-dressed") Bukhārī (d. 1292) and his grandson Jalāl al-Dīn Makhdūm-i Jahāniyān ("lord of the mortals," 1308–1384). In Bengal a leading Suhrawardī saint was Shaykh Jalāl al-Dīn Tabrīzī (thirteenth century, dates uncertain). In Bihar, an offshoot of the Kubrawīyah order, the Firdawsīyah, attained fame through Sharaf al-Dīn ibn Yaḥyā Manērī (1263–1381). In Kashmir, the intellectually influential Kubrawīyah order gained a foothold through a visit by Sayyid 'Alī Hamadānī between about 1381 and 1384.

From about the middle of the fifteenth century, other Ṣūfī orders made their appearance in South Asia, notably the Qādirīyah, the Shaṭṭārīyah, and the Naqshbandīyah. Muḥammad Ghawth (d. 1517), claiming to be tenth in succession to the founder 'Abd al-Qādir al-Jīlānī (1077–1176), settled at Uchch, but before that, Qādirī Ṣūfīs had settled at Bidar about the time it became the capital of the Bahmani sultanate in 1422. The Bijapur sultanate later became a major center for the Qādirīyah. Another order that, as with the Qādirīyah, became influential in the Deccan as well as in North India, was the Shaṭṭārīyah, introduced from Iran by Shaykh 'Abd Allāh al-Shaṭṭār (d. 1485). Under Muḥammad Ghawth of Gwalior (1485–1562/3), the order spread to Gujarat and caught the attention of the Mughal emperors Humāyūn and Akbar. A Central Asian order which, after its introduction into South Asia, was to challenge the direction which Sufism had hitherto taken was the Naqshbandīyah, principally introduced by Khwājah Bāqī Billāh (1563/4–1603), who initiated in his last years the most influential member of the order in South Asia, Shaykh Aḥmad Sirhindī (1564–1624).

The Social Role of the Mystics. Members of the mystic orders in Islam have been, according to some scholars, "bridge-people" adjusting the demands and the proclamations of Islam to the psychology of different populations and, in the reverse direction, introducing new emphases and rites into the central tradition of Islam. Certainly, by the period that the orders came to South Asia, Sufism had become more a devotional than a mystical movement, embracing a collection of cult associations which centered on the pir or shaykh, a figure more approachable than that of the Arabian prophet or the *ʿālim* for many in South Asia. Not that the Chishtī saints of the earlier period did not emphasize the grounding of their spiritual teaching in the scriptural and jurisprudential disciplines of the *ʿulamāʾ:* they and their fellow Ṣūfīs of the Suhrawardī order preferred to reassure their followers that, as much as the *ʿulamāʾ* and their pupils, they belonged to *dār al-Islām* (the "abode of Islam").

Discussions of more speculative and philosophical formulations of Sufism were not taken up until the middle of the fourteenth century. However, by the later fifteenth and early sixteenth centuries, possibly as an outcome of the growth of an indigenous Muslim convert population, the shaykh or the pir was being seen as a charismatic figure with special personal efficacies, rather than as a teacher and guide along a path to personal experience of the truths of God. The *dargāh,* or tomb, was beginning to supplant the *khāngāh* in the popular imagination. Membership in, or allegiance to, particular orders became less important—indeed some adepts now belonged to more than one order. Some orders gained in appeal; others diminished. Perhaps this was related to the way in which members of particular orders responded to the local environment. Traditionally, Muʿīn al-Dīn Chishtī is represented as having gained many followers after allowing music in his *khāngāh.* No doubt, too, willingness to use the local vernacular would enhance a shaykh's appeal. Ṣūfīs belonging to the *ṭāʾifah*s appear to have been more willing than the *ʿulamāʾ* to found *khāngāh*s away from the principal centers of political power and thus to have drawn more of the rural and small-town populations to themselves. Certain orders, notably the Qādirīyah and Shaṭṭārīyah in Bijapur, were more urban-based. Rulers of the day early recognized the popular appeal of the shaykhs among Muslims and wished to turn that appeal to their own advantage. Shaykhs were offered pensions and revenue-free lands. The Chishtīyah would have none of this and relied upon voluntary offerings *(futūḥ),* while Suhrawardī saints were willing to accept royal largesse, and the Shaṭṭārī order cultivated Mughal rulers. In Bijapur in the seventeenth century, Qādirī and Shaṭṭārī Ṣūfīs accepted land grants. It is difficult therefore to accept fully the contention that the Ṣūfī orders represented an organized religious establishment in medieval India independent of the different Muslim political establishments.

Qalandārs. Closest to the common people as mediums of Islam were a variety of wandering mendicants distinguished from orthodox or "respectable" Ṣūfīs by scantiness of dress, the wearing of bizarre iron insignia, indifferent performance of prescribed religious obligations, and, sometimes, aggressive attitudes toward Ṣūfīs belonging to the mainstream orders. They went under a variety of names—*qalandār*s, Ḥaydarīs, Madārīs among them. Certain great shaykhs of the orders, notably the Chishtī, recognized men of genuine intuitive experience among these *qalandār*s and sometimes looked to them to reach those classes of Muslims that the regular orders did not reach. On the other hand, the Madārīs (so called after a Jewish convert, Shāh Madār, who migrated to South Asia from Syria), who sometimes went naked, smeared themselves with ashes, used hashish, and ignored the duty to fast and pray, and who possessed no property, went far toward Hindu religious idioms. Just because the *qalandār*s and others were footloose and so evidently outside the Muslim "establishment," it is possible to regard them as being important in communicating some identifiable Islamic religious motifs to the non-Muslim country-dweller.

RELIGIOUS THOUGHT BEFORE THE NINETEENTH CENTURY

The extended register of relationships between Muslim and non-Muslim in South Asia, ranging from a wary and frigid intimacy to a warm and indulgent segregation, did not, in the premodern period, give rise to a body of religious thought dramatically different in its concerns from those of other regions of the contemporary Islamic world. True, in Bengal, the fifteenth- and sixteenth-century poems of Shaykh Zāhid and Sayyid Sulṭān express such Hindu ideas as creation through the union of the male and female principles and the human body as a microcosm of the cosmos, with descriptions of its psycho-physiological processes in a Nath idiom, but the Lord being sought is the God of Islam; the problem was to convey that Lord to would-be Muslims using a language and living in an environment charged with non-Islamic nuances. If the agenda of religious discussion among Muslims in South Asia is much the same as that elsewhere, the timing and emphases of discussion, however, appear related to the regional situation. For example, the emphatic discussion of the status of the shaykh and spiritual director (a general Muslim concern) among the Chishtīyah and by Sharaf al-Dīn Yaḥyā Manērī seems especially relevant for Muslims needing reassurance about the authority of their preceptors in a plural religious world.

No doubt the intuition that, in a colonial society, stability and self-assurance lay in adhering to the established religious and intellectual disciplines prompted the *'ulamā'*'s use of the works of the assured authorities of the parent culture: for *ḥadīth,* the selections called *Mashāriq al-anwār* (Lights of the East) by Mawlānā Rāzī al-Dīn Ḥasan Saghānī (from Badā'ūn, d. 1225); for Qur'anic commentary, the *Kashshāf* (Unveiler) by Abū al-Qāsim al-Zamakhsharī (d. 1143/4), and for jurisprudence, the *Hidāyah* (Guidance) by Burhān al-Dīn al-Marghināni (d. 1197). Until the middle of the fourteenth century, the religious literature of the mystics points to the Chishtī and Suhrawardī orders' concentration, in partnership with the *'ulamā',* on the teaching of a basic piety that Muslim immigrants to South Asia would find acceptably Islamic.

The Influence of Ibn al-'Arabī. From that time on, however, theoretical discussion was awakened by the reception, somewhat delayed, of the ideas of the Spanish Ṣūfī Ibn al-'Arabī (1165–1240), mediated to South Asia by the poet Fakhr al-Dīn

ʿIrāqī (d. 1287) in his *Lamaʿāt* (Flashes), a poetic interpretation of Ibn al-ʿArabī's *Fuṣūṣ al-ḥikam* (Bezels of Wisdom). Ibn al-ʿArabī's work provided, against the background of Islam's commitment to monotheism, a spiritually enriching statement of the experience of absorption in unity that finally overcame the seeker. At the end of the mystical path only God is found because only he, at the end, is there to be found: since creatures only exist as reflections of the divine attributes, and since God becomes a mirror in which humans contemplate their reality, and humans become a mirror in which God contemplates his names and qualities, there is but one substantively real being, namely God, with which the mystic becomes identical.

The doctrine of *waḥdat al-wujūd,* the unity of being (or rather the nonexistence of all other than God), has preoccupied Ṣūfīs and others in South Asia until modern times. Possibly drawing upon ʿAlā' al-Dawlah alSimnānī of Khorasan (1261–1336), who argued that the being of God was an attribute distinct from his essence and that the final degree of reality attainable by the mystic was *ʿubūdīyah* or servanthood, the Chishtī saint Gīsū Dārāz voiced his opposition; Sharaf al-Dīn Manērī, in his *Maktūbāt-i sadī* (One Hundred Letters), also disassociated himself from *waḥdat al-wujūd.* Shaykh Aḥmad Sirhindī in the Punjab, probably also indebted to ʿAlā al-Dawlah al-Simnānī, offered a formulation of mystical experience which, Sirhindī claimed, was the correct interpretation of Ibn al-ʿArabī's ideas. Sirhindī was concerned lest the mystics' experience of oneness should be so described as to put in question the distinction, essential to Islam, between the creator and the created. *Waḥdat al-wujūd* or, in Sirhindī's Persian terminology, *tawḥīd-i wujūdī,* is merely an intellectual perception. At the level of experience, with the sight rather than the knowledge of certitude, the mystic becomes aware that God is manifesting his Oneness *(tawḥīd-i shuhūdī),* but not that nothing else exists at that moment. In an image similar to one used by Manērī, Sirhindī argues that the light of the sun may blind one to the light of the stars, but they continue to exist nevertheless. In an effort to grant the world of phenomena a kind of independent but derivative existence, Sirhindī holds that the divine attributes are reflected in their opposite not-beings, and these reflections are the world as humans know it, a shadow of the perfections of the only Necessary Being, namely God.

The Challenge to Prophetic Islam. In the late fifteenth and sixteenth centuries, Muslims in South Asia appeared to be pushing the figure of the prophet Muḥammad into the background and to be challenging the principle that the *ijmāʿ,* or consensus of the *ʿulamā',* represented in practice the authoritative interpretation of divine command. Around this time in Gujarat, Sayyid Muḥammad of Jaunpur (1443–1505) claimed to be the Mahdi ("guided one") of Sunnī tradition, who will lead the world to order and justice before the day of resurrection. His followers claimed for him a rank equal to that of the Prophet and clustered around him as though around a pir. Bāyazīd Anṣārī (1525–1572/3), born at Jallandhar in the Punjab, was a Pathan who claimed to be the *pīr-i kāmil* ("perfect preceptor") in direct communication with God, who shone his divine light upon him. Bāyazīd himself combined the perfections of the paths of law, mysticism, and wisdom attaining to gnosis of God. In the last stage of his disciples' spiritual ascent, they might exempt themselves from some of the obligations of the *sharīʿah.* Gathering support from among the Pathan tribesmen of the northwest, he and his followers clashed with the Mughals.

Shaykh Aḥmad Sirhindī, too, claimed to enjoy some of the perfections of prophethood and not to need, as ordinary believers do, prophetic mediation in order to reach God. His disciples acclaimed him as *mujaddid-i alf-i thānī,* "renewer of the second millennium" (of Islam). The Mughal emperor Akbar's friend Abū al-Faẕl (1551–1602), in his *Akbar-nāmah* (Book of Akbar) and *Āʾīn-i Akbarī* (Institutes of Akbar), drew heavily upon Ṣūfī concepts of the perfect man as a microcosm of the divine perfections, indeed a divine epiphany; upon Illuminationist ideas of light, perhaps transmitted through a divinely illumined figure, making knowledge of the real possible; upon Twelver Shīʿī beliefs in inner spiritual meanings of the text of revelation and of the universe; upon Ismāʿīlī theories of a secret knowledge communicated in each cycle of time by specially endowed people; upon philosophical ideas of the ruler maintaining an organic society, and upon Sunnī ideas of the caliph and the just sultan and all of this to present Akbar as the earthly homologue and symbol of God. The Prophet, where he appears at all, is limited to giving a name to one religion among many.

Sunnī Muslims reacted to this submergence of prophetic Islam with a reassertion both of Muḥammad's role and of the paradigmatic character of his companions' lives. ʿAbd al-Ḥaqq Dihlāwī (1551–1642) devoted himself to the study of *ḥadīth* and wrote on prophethood. Mindful of a strong Shīʿī presence among the Mughal elite by reason of immigration from Iran, where the Safavids had established Twelver Shiism as the state religion, Shaykh Aḥmad Sirhindī wrote his *Radd-i rawāfiḍ* (On the Refutation of the Shīʿah) against the Shīʿī practice of cursing some of the companions. In his *Najāt al-rashīd* (The Orthodox Way of Deliverence), written in 1591, the historian Badāʾūnī condemned innovation, idol worship, and time-serving *ʿulamāʾ*. He upheld the duty of the Muslim ruler to enforce the *sharīʿah* as understood by the consensus of the Sunnī scholars. But all these writers—together with the admiring commentator on Ibn al-ʿArabī, Shāh Muḥibb Allāh of Allahabad (1587–1648), and the emperor Shāh Jahān's eldest son Dārā Shikūh (1615–1659), a follower of the Qādirī order who attempted a comparative study of technical terms in Vedanta and Sufism, the *Majmaʿ al-baḥrayn* (Confluence of the Two Seas), and a Persian translation of fifty-two Upaniṣads, and who was executed on pretext of heresy by his brother and rival for the throne, Awrangzīb—treated *taṣawwuf,* the personal quest for God, as the fulfillment of Islam.

Shāh Walī Allāh. *Taṣawwuf* continued its hold over the Muslim religious imagination in South Asia into the eighteenth century, but in the encyclopedic scholarship of the Delhi *ʿālim* Shāh Walī Allāh (1703–1762), there are signs of a sea-change. Although he wrote much on mysticism, trying to show that the differences between *waḥdat al-wujūd* and *waḥdat al-shuhūd* are only verbal in that for both, God's imagination of himself is the only real existent, he believed himself called by God to demonstrate, over the whole range of the Islamic sciences, in *fiqh* (jurisprudence), *tafsīr* (Qurʾān commentary), *falsafah* (philosophy), that a harmony of apparently different views in fact exists, or could be achieved. In jurisprudence he is concerned to argue that more emphasis on rulings supported by *ḥadīth* from the Prophet which had been carefully examined for authenticity would tend to bring the four schools of Sunnī jurisprudence together, and that indeed it is permissible for rulings to be sought outside one's usual school. In theology he tries to reconcile doctrines of creation from nothing with those of the unity and changelessness of God by claiming an overflow of divine power which brings the universe into being from potential not-being (because the source of everything is not-being, there is no duality in the one divine being, and because potentiality was already an aspect of the divine being, there was no change in the divine being when that potentiality was manifested). In his *Ḥujjat Allāh al-bālighah* (The Mature Proof of God), Shāh Walī Allāh argues that, although the divine truths and commandments do not originate in a reason comprehensible to humans, nevertheless they are not an affront to that reason.

Concerned with the growing divisions between Sunnī and Shīʿī Muslims in his time (following, probably, more Shīʿī immigration in the 1740s and the growing influence of the Shīʿī nawabs of Awadh), Shāh Walī Allāh wrote a defense of the actual line of succession of the Sunnī caliphs after the Prophet's death, entitled *Izālat al-khafāʾ ʿan khilāfat al-khulafāʾ* (Clarification of Tenets Regarding the Successorship of the Successors). Furthermore, although Shāh Walī Allāh was an *ʿālim* writing mainly for *ʿulamāʾ* (indeed, he wrote much in Arabic), he did write a number of letters calling for political action by Muslim rulers to curb the power of non-Muslims by waging *jihād* (war for the supremacy of Islam). Shāh Walī Allāh's work provided an epitome of Sunnī scholarship for South Asia to which later generations of *ʿulamāʾ,* and indeed of other educated Muslims, have resorted for instruction and inspiration. But more than that, his work was an assertion that the individual commitment to Islam might now need widespread public action in its support.

THE VERNACULAR ISLAM OF THE REGIONS: THE EXAMPLE OF BENGAL

In South Asia, Islam as commitment and praxis spread to those for whom Arabic, Persian, and Urdu (the new North Indian vernacular with a large Arabic and Persian vocabulary capable of conveying scriptural and Middle Eastern Islam) remained impenetrable. Only if Islamic values and cultural images were expressed in the regional languages would human beings with a nurture greatly removed from that in the Arabic- and Persian-speaking lands be able to make the Islamic perception of reality both meaningful and their own. In Bengal, where developed the second largest total (after Indonesia) of rural Muslims in the Islamic world, between the fifteenth and eighteenth centuries, many Muslim cultural mediators, writing in Bengali, expressed Islam in the local cultural idiom, an idiom greatly enriched in the same period by translations of the great Hindu epics, the *Rāmāyaṇa* and the *Mahābhārata,* into Bengali, and the expression of Nath and Vaiṣṇava teachings.

For example, in his *Nabīvaṃśa,* Sayyid Sulṭān (sixteenth–seventeenth centuries) depicted the prophet Muḥammad as an *avatāra* of God, as worshiped by members of the Hindu pantheon and as struggling against Hindu enemies in an Arabia portrayed as Bengal. He assimilated Hindu ideas of the four *yugas* in a cosmogonical myth which treated the four ages as periods of gestation for the divine messenger, Muḥammad. Sayyid Murtaẓā (dates uncertain) identified stages and stations of *taṣawwuf* with the *cakras* or nerve plexuses of Tantric yoga. Other Bengali Muslim writers apotheosize their preceptors as gurus. Muḥammad the Prophet is able to bring the blessings of *siddhi* (fulfillment) and *mukti* (liberation) to his devotees. The spiritual guide, guru, or pir should be served as the Lord himself. Folk literature endowed the pir, sometimes addressed as a historical figure and sometimes as a personified spirit, with supernatural and thaumaturgic powers. In the nineteenth century, the manifestations of such efforts to make Islam a religion of, as well as for, Bengali-speakers, were attacked by scripturalist-minded reformers drawing inspiration from outside Bengal.

ISLAMIC RENEWAL

By 1800 an irreversible change in the temporal setting of Islamic faith and practice in South Asia first gradually, and then dramatically, transformed the assumptions of debate and action among the communicators of Islam. Marathas, Sikhs, and the English East India Company had overborne Mughal military power and become the effective rulers, even in the territory of Delhi itself. Muslim ruling elites were not rudely supplanted nor did they all immediately suffer hardship; indeed some of their members quickly made themselves, with personal profit, indispensable to the new masters. But they were no longer confidently in charge, under Muslim rulers, of their future. By 1803 the East India Company had occupied Delhi and Agra, the historical centers of Mughal imperial power, and had begun to control the application of Islamic law to Muslim society. In their savage repression of mutiny and rebellion in 1857–1858, the British demonstrated that any future Muslim success and prosperity must be on terms laid down by British rulers. Moreover, Muslims were obliged to live under censorious rulers who made it possible for Christian missionaries publicly to attack their religion and for anyone to allege that Muslims were behind in the race of progress because they were Muslim. Infidels had conquered Muslims before but had often surrendered to Islam later. Now Western imperialism, intellectual and moral as well as political, seemed to proclaim that either God was not omnipotent or that he was punishing his would-be servants for failing to be true and faithful servants.

Today, in South Asia, few openly claim that they are Muslim by culture only—"census Muslims." Most would-be Muslims proclaim the reality of Allāh, the authenticity of the Qur'ān as his revelation and of Muḥammad the Prophet as his messenger, and the truth of the existence of heaven and hell for which life on earth is a selective examination by continuous assessment. Some Muslims in South Asia (as in other regions of the Islamic world) have tried to restore strength and, sometimes, sincerity to their convictions by seeking in scripture—variously defined as the Qur'ān only or as the Qur'ān and the authentic collections of Muḥammad's *ḥadīth*—norms and the authority for norms appropriate to modern needs and situations in the belief that in scripture those needs and situations had been, if not foreseen, then provided for, in other words, that change is good and Islamic or could be rendered so. Other Muslims have wished instead to reproduce exactly the patterns of a past period of human life, a period deemed to be ideal, usually that of the Prophet's own lifetime and of that of his companions. Change, it is implied, has been for the worse, and should be reversed. Muslim debate over the future has swayed between these two positions.

Muslim experience and understanding of British rule and of intrusive Western cultures have shaped decisively such debate. Temporal success, associative social action, community identity, and intracommunity and group cooperation have moved to the center of Muslims' preoccupations. British assumptions that law was a corpus of rules made mandatory by a sovereign power, that in medieval times Muslims had been governed by such law, the *sharīʿah,* indeed had been defined as a community by such governance, and that their law was essentially a law directed to extraterrestrial ends, fostered, in some Muslims, convictions that without the ability to enforce such law upon themselves, they could not be true Muslims. As the *sharīʿah* was seen more as legal rules to be enforced and less as ethical and moral aspirations to be satisfied (it embraces, of course, both), so the issues of authoritative interpretation of the *sharīʿah* and of the identity and character of its enforcers grew more insistent.

Early Revivalist Movements. With the loss of ground in the eighteenth century, Muslims shifted their vision away from the pir in medieval South Asia to the Prophet in seventh-century Arabia. Khwājah Mīr Dard (1721–1785) places the spiritual perfections of Muḥammad above those of imam and saint. Shāh Walī Allāh's son, Shāh ʿAbd al-ʿAzīz (1746–1824), depicts Muḥammad as a figure radiating light, of which all the protectors and teachers of Islam are but reflections. Shāh ʿAbd al-ʿAzīz criticizes some of the practices of Sufism in South Asia as innovations without foundation in the Prophet's *ḥadīth.* Sayyid Aḥmad of Rai Bareilly (1786–1831) led a militant movement, some of whose adherents migrated, in 1826, from British India to the Pathan borderlands, where they waged *jihād* against the Sikhs, creating an imitation of the first Muslim community of Mecca among the Pathans before being killed by the Sikhs at the Battle of Balakot. The ideology of the movement, expressed in *Ṣirāṭ-i mustaqīm* (The Straight Path) and *Taqwiyat al-īmān* (The Strengthening of Faith in God), compiled and written by Shāh Muḥammad Ismāʿīl (1779–1831), grandson of Shāh Walī Allāh, took the form of a *ṭarīqah-i muḥammadī* ("Muhammadan way"), a Sufism reformed of polytheistic practices (such as expecting the spirits of dead saints to grant boons). It was advocated that the Prophet should be regarded as the seeker's pir. The urge to recreate the earliest days of Islam is signaled by Sayyid Aḥmad's refusal to initiate *jihād* in British India without first making *hijrah* ("emigration"). (The hold of the Prophet's Hijrah over Muslim sentiment was to be further demonstrated in 1920 when, on the urging of mosque imams and pirs, about thirty thousand Muslims from Sind and the Frontier Province migrated to Afghanistan as their *dār al-Islām.*)

In Bengal, Ḥājjī Sharīʿat Allāh (1781–1840) founded the Farā'iḍī movement. He had earlier lived in the Hejaz for about eighteen years. He sought to teach Bengali Muslims to observe the obligatory duties *(farā'iḍ)* of Islam, to abandon reverence for pirs, and to forsake "hinduized" life ceremonies. On the ground that there were no properly constituted Muslim rulers and *qāḍī*s in nineteenth-century India, the Farā'iḍīs abandoned Friday and *ʿīd* ("holiday") prayers. Under Ḥājjī Sharīʿat Allāh's son Dudū Miyān (1819–1862) violence broke out between the movement's largely peasant following and the landlords. Throughout the nineteenth century, a variety of Sunnī scholars and teachers, including Mawlānā Karāmat Jawnpurī (d. 1873), a follower of Sayyid Aḥmad Barēlī willing to accept British rule, devoted themselves to trying to rid Islam in Bengal of polytheistic attitudes and practices, while disagreeing among themselves about the acceptability of *taṣawwuf,* or about which school of jurisprudence should be followed. In the far south, among the Māppiḷḷas, *ʿulamā'* such as Sayyid ʿAlawī (d. 1843/4) and his son Sayyid Faḍl (d. 1900), though creating no formal organization, perpetuated local Muslim traditions of *jihād* and martyrdom so that the violent Māppiḷḷa agrarian opposition to Hindu landlords, and to the British, which continued throughout the nineteenth century and during the Māppiḷḷa rebellion of 1921, was expressed in the idiom of a return to the earliest days of Islam.

The Deobandi ʿUlamāʾ. But renewal of Islam by attempts to relive the believed patterns of a model era occurred mainly as a peaceful process of education by the *ʿulamāʾ*. They progressively took over the religious leadership of Muslims in South Asia under non-Muslim rule. Shāh ʿAbd al-ʿAzīz had begun to assert that leadership by delivering rulings (*fatwā*s) to the many Muslims seeking assurance in a period of rapid change. The position of the *ʿulamāʾ* was strengthened in the course of Sunnī-Shīʿī controversy—Shāh ʿAbd al-ʿAzīz's *Tuḥfat al-Ithnā ʿAsharīyah* (An Offering to the Twelvers) was of major significance—and in public debate with Christian missionaries. After 1857, the *ʿulamāʾ* at Deoband proved adept at using the post, telegraph, railways, and the press to communicate their teachings to the Urdu-knowing Muslim public. Their leaders, Mawlānā Muḥammad Qāsim Nanawtawī (1832–1880) and Rashīd Aḥmad Gangohī (1828–1905) stood for the Ḥanafī school, subjecting local custom to a careful critique in the light of the model practice of the Prophet and seeking always to ensure that believers kept the divine *tawḥīd* (unity) before them. The Deobandi leaders assumed the status of Ṣūfī shaykhs and initiated disciples; but the special efficacies *(karāmāt)* that were attributed to them were depicted as being exercised to influence people to follow the *sunnah*. The Deobandis were opposed to treating the tombs of shaykhs as centers of worship or intercession. Since some leading Deobandis claimed initiation into all the main Ṣūfī orders in South Asia, Deoband encouraged comprehensiveness and consolidation of intellectual and experiential traditions. Although they accepted the British as rulers, the Deobandis (in *fatwā*s sought by anxious Muslims) weighed their culture and usually found it wanting. Muslims were not to accept their contemporary world on its own terms.

Other Groups. The Ahl-i Ḥadīth (People of the *Ḥadīth*) were another group of *ʿulamāʾ* aiming to reform custom and to purify convictions soiled by custom. Led by Ṣiddīq Ḥasan Khān (1832–1890) and Sayyid Nadhīr Ḥusayn (d. 1902), they derided the authority of the four schools of Islamic jurisprudence in favor of a literal interpretation of Qurʾān and *ḥadīth*. At the same time, they opposed the Sufism of the shrines. However, the Ahl-i Ḥadīth's treatment of the prophet Muḥammad's *ḥadīth* as an implicit revelation which elaborated authoritatively the explicit revelation of the Qurʾān exposed them to the charge of introducing a dualism into God's communication with humans. In reaction, the Punjab-based Ahl-i Qurʾān (People of the Qurʾān), founded in 1902 and led by ʿAbd Allāh Chakralawī, held that Muḥammad was the messenger for only the Qurʾanic mode of revelation and that Muslims should treat as divine commandment only what was specifically and exclusively enjoined in the Qurʾān. Hence, for example, the Ahl-i Qurʾān regarded the call to prayer and the performance of *ʿīd* and funerary prayers as not essential Islamic obligations. But other *ʿulamāʾ* accepted the customs and practices that had developed in medieval South Asia. Led by Aḥmad Riḍā Khān (1856–1921) with headquarters at Bareilly and Badāʾūn in Rohilkhand, they accepted a variety of mediators of Islam from the prophet Muḥammad to the saints and pirs of the shrines. The Barelwīs observed the birthdays of both the Prophet and the saints—a practice objected to by Deobandis and others on the ground that such celebrations implied that the dead were present. Some *'ulamā'* were less concerned with taking up militant stances toward the past of Islam in South Asia and devoted themselves to teaching a simple understanding of Islam to those whose knowledge was limited. In the later nineteenth century more *madrasahs* were founded in Bengal, and popular *naṣīhat-nāmahs* (books of admonition) in Bengali were published. In the twentieth century, Mawlānā Muḥammad Ilyās (1885–1944) traveled in Mewar (southwest of Delhi) preaching and encouraging those who were not *'ulamā'* to uphold the basic articles of faith. This "mass-contact" campaign was conducted with a minimum of formal organization.

Sayyid Ahmad Khan. The first major figure to argue that the changes Muslims were experiencing in the nineteenth century were Islamic was Sir Sayyid Ahmad Khan (1817–1898). The British suppression of the mutiny and rebellion of 1857–1858 convinced him that Muslims must accept a future shaped by British power. As a totally believing Muslim, he wished to demonstrate that God was not being mocked when Muslims, in hope of advancement, were being taught in British-influenced schools and colleges a natural science that appeared to contradict divine revelation and indeed to give, in supposedly immutable laws of nature, partners to God. He wished to assure Muslims that they were not disobeying divine commandments in search of worldly gain when they acted as though they had abandoned even the ideal of a public and social life controlled by the norms of the *sharī'ah*. Briefly, Sayyid Ahmad Khan argued that the word of God and the work of God, revelation and nature as understood by nineteenth-century Western science, are wholly in harmony. God is the cause of causes; the laws of nature are divine attributes, and any apparent discrepancies between the Qur'ān's account of the natural world and that of Western scientists are to be attributed to misunderstandings of the language of the Qur'ān. As for the Muslims' belief that their social arrangements and behavior must be obedient to God's command, Sayyid Ahmad Khan did not disagree. Muslims have, however, wrongly taken to be divine command what is not. Although each prophet in history has communicated the same *dīn,* or set of human obligations toward God, each has brought to his age a different *sharī'ah,* or set of detailed prescriptions for performing those obligations. Islam, then, accommodates historical change. Muslims must realize that only the manifestly declared injunctions of the Qur'ān are the commandments of religion and that much of the reported dicta and behavior of the Prophet is of doubtful authenticity.

Muhammad Iqbal. The poet-seer Muhammad Iqbal (1877–1938) offered a conception of a God-human relationship which he intended to inspire Muslims to action with the confidence that they would be innovating, but in a distinctively Islamic fashion. Reality is not a given, but a becoming. Thought is a potency which forms the very being of its material. The life of the individual ego is that of actualizing in thought and deed the infinite possibilities of the divine imagination. Men and women explore servanthood in acting as God's assistants in creation, but in accordance with the principle of unity that is the godhead. Iqbal's philosophy of "humanism with God" was intended to inspire Muslims to act as an association of participants in a common enterprise and to advance beyond the individual cultivation of a pious but passive sensibility. Iqbal called for a free *ijtihād,* a striving to discover the demands of Islam in changing circumstances, and he pointed out that Muslims would not be collectively free to exercise that *ijtihād* and to implement it unless they had their own independent polity free from the interference of non-Muslim legislators. His call in 1930 for an autonomous Muslim state embracing the northwestern areas of India expressed his confidence in Islam's ability to inspire a new social order for the twentieth century.

Abū al-Kalām Āzād. Abū al-Kalām Āzād (1888–1958) began by proclaiming, immediately before and immediately after World War I, that Indian Muslims should assert their distinctive collectivity by rallying around the symbol of the *khilāfat* (an office held, so he argued, by the Ottoman sultan) and organizing themselves voluntarily to obey the *sharī'ah*. Later, in his *Tarjumān al-Qur'ān* (Interpretation of the Qur'ān), first published in 1930 and 1936, Abū al-Kalām offers a personal reaction to the Qur'ān when approached directly without any intermediate commentary. Revelation interprets correctly the inward moral convictions planted in humans by God, who exercises his benevolent lordship over nature to human advantage. God lays upon all humankind the same obligations to recognize the real nature of the world he has created; at the root of all apparently distinctive religions is the same *dīn* ("religion"). People have disguised this truth by their "groupism" and attachment to group rites and rituals. They should gradually abandon their distinctions and recognize that only one group fulfills their true destiny—the group comprised of all humankind. In effect, Abū al-Kalām Āzād modifies a classical position, that God fashions all people to be Muslims were they but aware of it; the inference he draws, however, is not that some should coerce others to become so aware, but that all should cooperate peacefully (especially Hindus and Muslims in South Asia) until all voluntarily come to acknowledge the Muslim-ness within them. (There is an interesting analogy here with the Upaniṣadic idea of recognition of the reality of *brahman-ātman* within each person.)

Ghulām Aḥmad. In the nineteenth-century Punjab a movement arose from within Islam expressing the motif of renewal under a mahdi, this time a mahdi who prohibited *jihād* and whose followers were willing to adopt modern methods of propaganda, economic organization, and education, especially of women. Mīrzā Ghulām Aḥmad (1839?–1908), son of a doctor in Qādiyān, claimed to be a mahdi or *masīḥ* ("messiah"). He claimed also the status of a minor prophet, reminding people of revealed scripture, but not bringing a new scripture. After Ghulām Aḥmad's death, his adherents, the Aḥmadīyah, formed themselves into an exclusive community for emulating the believed standards, but not the particular mores, of the time of the first four Sunnī caliphs. [*See* Aḥmadīyah.]

ISLAM IN CONTEMPORARY SOUTH ASIA

Developments since the gaining, in 1947, of political independence for the subcontinent demonstrate that plasticity is the most widely shared characteristic of an Islam located, since 1971, in three separate states: India, Pakistan, and Bangladesh.

In the Republic of India there is no method other than voluntary cooperation for Muslims to express their aspirations to live as an *ummah,* or community in obedience to divine law. The Deobandi *'ulamā'* have taken full advantage of constitutional guarantees of freedom to run their religious institutions as before. The Indian branch of Mawdūdī's Jamā'at-i Islāmī (Islamic Society) has continued work in hope that all Indians will turn to Islam. Although a decreasing majority of Indian Muslims continues to resist any replacement of Muslim law (as interpreted by the Indian courts) by a wholly secular code for all the Republic's citizens, writers such as A. A. Fyzee (1899–1981) and Muhammad Mujeeb have questioned whether religious belief must be complemented by religious law. Meanwhile the personal quest for the divine realities in a Ṣūfī idiom and the teaching of Islamic ideals of right conduct continue.

In Pakistan, the integral Islam visualized by Iqbal and, later, by such supporters of the Pakistan movement as Mawlānā Shabbīr Aḥmad 'Uthmānī (1887–1949) in their different ways, has not come to pass. The constitutions of 1956, 1962, and 1972 all left the character and the pace of islamization under the control of largely Western-educated political, military, and bureaucratic elements. The only major legislative outcome of their *ijtihād* has been the Family Laws Ordinance of 1961, which made polygamy and male-pronounced divorce more difficult (but not illegal) and conferred rights of inheritance from grandparents upon orphaned grandchildren.

Something resembling the medieval ideal of a partnership between a pious ruling institution and qualified scholars was advocated by Sayyid Abū al-A'lā Mawdūdī (1903–1979), founder of the Jamā'at-i Islāmī in British India in 1940. [*See* Jamā'at-i Islāmī.] Opposed before 1947 to the creation of Pakistan because he believed it would not be governed by true Muslims in a truly Islamic mode, he subsequently migrated to Pakistan and advocated the establishment of an Islamic state by elective assemblies and by representative government. A more codified form of the *sharī'ah* as interpreted by properly qualified scholars would become the law of Pakistan. Mawdūdī would not have enforced all rulings in existing books of *fiqh* and would have allowed some interpretative decisions to be arrived at by majority vote. He was prepared for modern legislation where the Qur'ān and *sunnah* were silent, provided that the general objectives of the *sharī'ah* were served and no infringement of divine commandment could occur. Mawdūdī appreciated, more perhaps than the *'ulamā',* the need for clarity, certainty, and effectiveness of action in a fast-changing world of rising Muslim expectations.

Under the martial-law regime of General Ẓiyā alḤaqq (Zia al-Haq), *sharī'ah* courts have been established, *zakāt* (prescribed alms levy) introduced, and the intention of enforcing the Qur'anic penalties for crimes against God proclaimed. Attempts are being made to introduce interest-free forms of banking and commercial enterprise. Such measures, even though devised and applied at the discretion of a regime seeking popular consent, may awaken Muslim minds and hearts in Pakistan to the servanthood of God or may nourish national sentiment for meeting worldly needs. Perhaps that ambiguity is inherent in the situation of Islam in Pakistan today. In Bangladesh, since 1971, there has been little attempt to assert that public life is shaped by the demands of Islam; it is sometimes maintained that how Bangladesh is being governed is not out of kilter with Islam.

MUSLIM SOCIETY IN SOUTH ASIA

Until the partition and mass migrations of 1947, which brought about vast Muslim majorities in what are now Bangladesh and Pakistan (85 percent and 97 percent respectively as of 1977), all the Muslims of South Asia lived embedded in a non-

Muslim society. Muslim and non-Muslim alike had developed mutually dependent economic relationships—for example, in Calcutta Muslims paint images for Hindus, and in the villages, particularly, Muslims depend on Hindu astrologers, musicians, potters, and tinkers, whether by way of market exchange or through the traditional patron-client service relationship of *jajmani.* Before 1947 there were no distinct Muslim and non-Muslim economic orders. In patterns of social life, in kinship relationships, life cycles, forms of social stratification, and social avoidances, the surrounding non-Muslim environment has shaped Muslim behavior in modes that recent work has shown to be much more subtle than can be embraced by such concepts as filtration, syncretism, and synthesis.

The Role of the Sharīʿah. Despite the show by both *ʿulamāʾ* and "modernist" Muslim thinkers that the *sharīʿah* displays Islam as a religion of total guidance for human relationships, Islamic law tends to curb and regulate those relationships rather than to define or command them in all their minutiae. Islamic law requires the individual to act or not to act in certain ways; it does not offer a reticulation for society. For example, Islamic law imposes modest limits on the degrees of relationship within which marriages are forbidden, but it does not forbid the principle of endogamy; indeed, in that it requires Muslim women to marry only Muslim men, it enjoins that principle. Through its rules of succession, its compulsory alms tax *(zakāt),* and its rules for commercial partnerships, Islamic law takes individual property rights for granted, but it does not specify particular types of economic organization. The Muslim may lawfully take profit from an individual or from a collective enterprise so long as that profit is not usurious.

Reformist aspirations among the Muslims of South Asia in modern times have sometimes obfuscated comment on Muslim social behavior in South Asia by introducing the concept of "the spirit of Islam." Islamic law does not require a Muslim to marry any other lawfully available Muslim. Yet a strict regard for relative social position in the arrangement of a marriage is sometimes treated as a peculiarly South Asian infringement on Islamic norms perceived in the "egalitarian spirit of Islam." Again, although widows may remarry in Islamic law, they are not compelled to do so. Muslim behavior in South Asia, as doubtless elsewhere in the Islamic world, expresses an interplay between aspirations identifiable as Islamic and the experiences of daily life. Crucial is the aspiration: for example, Islamic authority for the matrilocal marriage and residence customs of the Māppiḷḷas of northern Kerala has been sought in the prophet Muḥammad's residing with his wife Khadījah's kin.

Succession is the principal area in Muslim social life in South Asia where *sharīʿah* requirements have often been ignored. Exclusion of women from inheritance of landed property is widespread. It is doubtful whether the Shariat Act of 1937 (and its subsequent extension in both India and Pakistan to cover succession to agricultural land), asserting the supremacy of Islamic law over custom, has had much effect. The Khojas may leave all their property by testamentary succession. Until the earlier years of the twentieth century, most Muslim Māppiḷḷas of northern Kerala lived in matrilocal joint family groups. Where joint family property was divided by common consent, shares devolved in the female lines. More recently, social change toward self-supporting patrilocal families and, since 1918, legislation by the Madras and Kerala legislatures empowering the courts to apply the Muslim rules of succession have weakened but not wholly removed the hold of customs so out of line with the *sharī'ah.*

Kinship and Class Systems. Muslim family and kinship systems in South Asia betray great variety within the general customs of endogamy and treating marriage as a form of social exchange between groups. Cross and parallel-cousin marriages are common, sometimes within the male descent group as with some Punjabi Muslims, sometimes not, as with some Bengali Muslims. Others such as the Meos and certain North Indian artisan groups reject cousin marriage. Among matrilocal Māppiḷḷas, cross- but not parallel-cousin marriages occur. In Nepal, the exogamous patrilineal lineage has nothing like the depth of neighboring Hindu lineages.

Muslim society is highly stratified. The division between *ashrāf* ("honorable") and *ajlāf* ("ignoble"), between those of supposedly immigrant descent and those of convert descent, is related more to styles of education, occupation, and leadership and may have no relevance to status in a particular local situation. Subgroups of the *ashrāf,* namely, sayyids, shaykhs, Mughals, and Pathans, are more ready to intermarry than are respectable *ajlāf* groups. The latter follow specialized and mainly manual occupations, forming graded endogamous groups named after a hereditary calling which each member does not now necessarily follow: gardener, potter, carpenter, blacksmith. Below them are weavers, cotton carders, tailors, bracelet-makers; much lower, considered unclean but not untouchable, are the barbers, the *faqīr*s ("mendicants"), butchers, oil-pressers, and washermen. At the bottom are the descendants of former untouchables: musicians, dancers, tanners, sweepers, and cesspool-emptiers. It is these Muslim groups who can suffer discrimination in Muslim public life—refusal of the use of common burial grounds and denial of an equal place in the mosque as well as commensality on festive occasions. At these lower levels of Muslim society similarities with caste are most evident—more rigid hereditary occupational specialization and sharp hierarchical distinctions based on the dichotomy of pure and impure.

Rites of Passage. Recent studies of Muslim social behavior in Nepal and Bengal suggest that that behavior may be, so to speak, an anagram of the behavior of the local Hindu society and that Hindu society, while magnetizing Muslim customs, does not dominate them completely. Life-cycle ceremonies in parts of Nepal and Bengal indicate the interplay that occurs. In Nepal, at birth, the *adhān* ("announcement of prayer") is shouted into the baby's ear. A period of impurity is then observed not only for the mother but for the whole patrilineage collectively—a deviation from scriptural Islam. The Cchaṭhī ("sixth day") ceremony follows, introducing the child to the community and placing it under the protection of the saint Shāh Madār, with singing and dancing by untouchable Hindus. The more canonical ceremony of *'aqīqah* (shaving of the child's head and animal sacrifice) is not performed. At six months the baby is fed solid food by unmarried girl relatives. The Islamic modes of initiation—circumcision and religious instruction—are followed. Forms of marriage are Islamic with *nikāḥ* ("marriage contract"), *mahr* ("bridal gift"), and officiating *qāḍī.* The accompanying ceremonies betray local attitudes: washing of the couple's feet by the bride's relatives and gifts from the bride's family suggest not the spirit of the canonical *nikāḥ* as a free exchange of consents, but the giving of a daughter to the bridegroom's kin-group. At death, burial ceremonies follow canonical rules, but the whole patrilineage of the deceased is affected by death-impurity, and ceremonies continue for forty days. In Nepal, rice balls used to be offered to the spirit of the deceased in the belief that if the death was not from old age or illness, the deceased would otherwise become an unquiet spirit speaking through a medium, usually a member of the deceased's patrilineage. In West Bengal, the placenta is buried in a clay pot for fear of attack by evil spirits, the mother's birth impurity lasts for forty days, and the mother's brother provides her with her first rice meal and the baby with its first solid food.

So a selective combination of canonical Islamic and local elements may occur: on the one hand, formal adherence to norms of Sunnī Islam, extending to ablutions and the killing of lawful animals in due form; on the other hand, extension of the Islamic rules for individual purity and impurity to a collectivity, the patrilineage. Local influence is betrayed in the role of young unmarried girls who are believed to be auspicious, in the emphasis on lineage solidarity (symbolized by the gifts of food by relatives and acts of deference by the bride's family toward the family of the bridegroom), and in the rites performed to pacify the spirit of the dead, which may otherwise wander.

South Asian Muslims present a truncated and reshuffled version of caste society, a simulacrum. The higher specialists, imam, *qāḍī,* and *ʿālim,* do not, as educated laymen, rank higher (as do the brahmans) than those who employ them; nor do they have ritual efficacy. The lower specialists who are essential to a Muslim way of life, the barbers who circumcise and the butchers who kill sacrificial animals, rank lower than those who employ them. The *faqīr* who receives *zakāt,* performs funeral ceremonies, officiates at shrines (notably at those dedicated to their patron saint Ghāzī Miyān), and organizes festivals dedicated to Ḥasan and Ḥusayn (the Prophet's grandsons), attended by both Sunnīs and Shīʿah, ranks low. Ṣūfī shaykhs, to whom some Muslims look for intercessory services and who rank high, are not analogous to brahmans, for they are made, not born, and their services are not indispensable. The proper ordering of Hindu society into functional classes, the maintenance of the dichotomy of ritual purity and ritual impurity, and the performance of rituals associated with the worship of gods, are necessary in Hinduism for the very functioning of the cosmos; for Islam, society is a situation in which individual Muslims perform acts of servanthood before their Lord; its proper ordering has no efficacy in the running of the world of the sacred.

ISLAMIZATION IN SOUTH ASIA

Non-Muslims became Muslims more through slow acculturation by reason of a change in social belonging than through a dramatic individual change of attitude and conviction. Muslim rulers' need in South Asia for political brokers between them and the rural population discouraged proselytism of Hindu chiefs by kingdom-builders, while, having discovered that Muslim rulers would employ brahmans and leave Hindu society to itself as long as it paid revenue, brahmans usually preferred to remain brahmans. In a ritually stratified society, conversion of a ruler did not lead to all in his kingdom undergoing conversion too, although tribes freer of ritual hierarchy might follow their leader into Islam. Muslim political power did, however, create an urban milieu where the providers for Muslim garrisons of goods and services socially depressing in Hindu society might find turning Muslim convenient if not advantageous. Deracination and enslavement of captives, male and female, might lead to conversion in hope of better treatment and in search of companionship. As the depressed classes of Hindu society often remained depressed in Muslim society too, and as there are sometimes large numbers of untouchables in villages where Muslim landholders are dominant, the hypothesis of conversion in order to enjoy the greater equality of Islam is challengeable. Some conversion among landholding groups in order to ensure Muslim rulers' support probably did occur.

Ṣūfī shaykhs probably made more converts after death than in life—through pilgrimage to their tombs by those seeking successful exercise of the shaykhs' believed efficacies. Some shaykhs would accept disciples without prior conversion; advance along a spiritual path under Muslim guidance led to acceptance of Islam as a necessary condition of further advance. Attaching oneself to a *qalandār* might not bring one close to scriptural Islam, but it would take one away from previous associations and open the way to further education by revivalists in Islam for descendants. British census reports created the "census Muslim" in the nineteenth century, a Muslim for whom the perception that identification with the "great tradition" of Islam could bring advantages has often spurred greater study and practice of that tradition. Except for the Ismā'īlīyah, Muslim missionary activity in South Asia has been directed more to awakening faith among those displaying some insignia of Islam than to converting adherents of another faith. It is interesting to speculate on the possible consequences for Islam in South Asia of the present, greatly increased opportunities for South Asian Muslims to acquire a knowledge of the language of the "great tradition" of Islam, namely Arabic. Large-scale migration to Arabia for employment and, especially in Pakistan, Arab aid for Arabic teaching, might transform existing structures of religious and cultural authority.

[*For further discussion of Sufism in India, see* Ṭarīqah *and the biographies of Khusraw, Niẓām al-Dīn Awliyā', and Sirhindī. For modern developments, see* Modernism, *article on* Islamic Modernism; Jamā'at-i Islāmī; *and the biographies of Ahmad Khan, Ameer Ali, Iqbal, Mawdūdī, and Walī Allāh.*]

BIBLIOGRAPHY

The most comprehensive and scholarly handbook is Annemarie Schimmel's *Islam in the Indian Subcontinent* (Leiden, 1980), which has full bibliographies. Muhammad Mujeeb's *The Indian Muslims* (London, 1967) is a sensitive interpretation of Muslim responses to the South Asian setting. Sufism in South Asia has attracted much attention and some grinding of axes. Athar Abbas Rizvi's *A History of Sufism,* 2 vols. (New Delhi, 1978–1983), draws on rich material in an impressionistic way. Yohanan Friedmann's *Shaykh Aḥmad Sirhindī: An Outline of His Thought and a Study of His Image in the Eyes of Posterity* (Montreal, 1971) aims, successfully, to correct modern misconceptions. Monographs analyzing Shah Walī Allāh's thought in its full historical setting have yet to appear, but G. N. Jalbani's *Teachings of Shah Waliyullah of Delhi,* 2d ed. (Lahore, 1973), and Athar Abbas Rizvi's *Shāh Wali-Allah and His Times* (Canberra, 1980), the latter with an exhaustive bibliography, are useful compendia. Richard Maxwell Eaton's *Sufis of Bijapur, 1300–1700: Social Roles of Sufis in Medieval India* (Princeton, 1978) is a pioneer work in its field. Asim Roy's *The Islamic Syncretistic Tradition in Bengal* (Princeton, 1984) is an original demonstration of how the exogenous religion of Islam was remolded as an effective appeal in a region with a vigorous autochthonous culture.

For modern developments, Aziz Ahmad's *Islamic Modernism in India and Pakistan 1857–1964* (London, 1967) is the standard survey. Also recommended is Wilfred Cantwell Smith's *Modern Islām in India,* rev. ed. (New York, 1972). Christian Troll's *Sayyid Ahmad Khan: A Reinterpretation of Muslim Theology* (New Delhi, 1978) is authoritative and contains original translations from Sayyid Ahmad Khan's writings. Annemarie Schimmel's *Gabriel's Wing: A Study into the Religious Ideas of Sir Muhammad Iqbal* (Leiden, 1963) is the essential work of reference. Barbara Metcalf's fine effort of scholarly empathy, *Islamic Revival in British India: Deoband, 1860–1900* (Princeton, 1982), in fact covers more than the Deobandi scholars. For a sample of Mawdūdī's writing, see Syed Abul ʿAla Maudoodi's *The Islamic Law and Constitution,* 2d ed., translated and edited by Khurshid Ahmad (Lahore, 1960).

Significant advances in the study of Muslim social behavior are reflected in three works edited by Imtiaz Ahmad: *Caste and Social Stratification among Muslims in India,* 2d rev. ed. (New Delhi, 1973), *Family, Kinship and Marriage among Muslims in India* (New Delhi, 1976), and *Ritual and Religion among Muslims in India* (Columbia, Mo., 1982). Valuable new insights are provided in two articles by Marc Gaborieau: "Life Cycle Ceremonies of Converted Muslims in Nepal and Northern India," in *Islam in Asia,* vol. 1, *South Asia,* edited by Yohanan Friedmann (Jerusalem, 1984), pp. 241–262, and "Typologie des spécialistes religieux dans le sous-continent indien: Les limites de l'islamisation," *Archives de sciences sociales des religions* 55 (1983): 29–51.

7 ISLAM IN SOUTHEAST ASIA

A. H. JOHNS

Southeast Asia is in some respects a forgotten world of Islam, for much the same reasons as its counterparts in West and East Africa. Neither its arrival nor its development there was spectacular, and the local languages that were to be adopted by Muslim communities did not become vehicles for works of universal and commanding stature as had Arabic, Persian, Turkish, and some of the vernaculars of the Indian subcontinent. Yet, Islam in Southeast Asia has its own styles and its own temper and intellectual traditions. Its sacral practices and folk beliefs that color and live alongside the profession of Islam no more invalidate that basic allegiance than do the sacral practices and folk beliefs of Arab Muslims. Indeed, Southeast Asia is the home of almost one-third of the world's Muslims. Indonesia alone, with over 130 million Muslims, is the largest such community in the world.

Historical Geography

Southeast Asia is best described as a great archipelago, a huge land mass that juts southward between the Indian subcontinent and China and then fragments at its extremity into a complex of thousands of islands, the largest of which are Sumatra, Borneo, and Java, while the smallest hardly registers on the map. Today this region is identified with the modern nation-states of Burma, Vietnam, Laos, Kampuchea, Thailand, Malaysia, Singapore, Brunei, Indonesia, and the Philippines. All of these nation-states have Muslim communities. In Burma, Kampuchea, and Vietnam they are insignificant minorities. In Thailand, the Muslim community, though still a minority, has a distinct profile. In Malaysia, Indonesia, and Brunei, on the other hand, Islam has an imposing position. Farther to the east, in the Philippines, it constitutes a significant cultural minority that is in some respects a part of the Philippine nation, but in others, the nucleus of a distinct national entity.

STRUCTURES IN TRANSITION

In seeking to understand the historical evolution and contemporary significance of these communities, it is necessary to distinguish between the modern period of nation-states, on the one hand, which derive from the growth of local nationalisms, and, on the other hand, the traditional distribution of centers of power in Southeast Asia. With the creation of nation-states such as Indonesia and Malaysia, the establishment of capital cities in Jakarta or Kuala Lumpur has made these centers a focus of the national personality of the political entities in which they are set. They are the gateway, the immediate point of identification, the seat of government, to which their inhabitants turn. They have a status that defines the other parts of the country as provinces.

Nevertheless, and although it might seem, from a contemporary perspective, that these nations have always existed in some form or another and that their present role derives simply from the expulsion of colonial powers and the recovery of national sovereignty, the reality is far more complex and the results more radical. In fact, the creation of such states has turned the traditional world of Southeast Asia on its head. The role of capital cities with a strong central authority dominating the political, economic, and religious life of the region is very recent.

Traditionally, centers of political power in Southeast Asia were distributed among a wide range of focal points that served as harbors for the exchange and transshipment of goods; these points became the sites of port cities, which from time to time grew strong enough to wield an extensive political authority. Such sites were diverse, discrete, numerous, scattered, and largely unstable centers of activity; they had relations with each other on the basis of rivalry and self-interest, without the direct hegemony of a central authority or any stable and continuing point of reference. Unlike the great cities of the Middle East and South Asia, which enjoyed stability over centuries, if not millennia (one need only mention Cairo, Alexandria, Damascus, Baghdad, or Delhi), centers of power in traditional Southeast Asia rarely maintained their position for more than a century, and the authority they enjoyed was very different from that of the modern capital cities of, for example, Kuala Lumpur and Jakarta. The historiography of the region, in its many languages, reflects this character in the emphasis that it lays on genealogy in its accounts of the origins of settlements.

These circumstances have important implications for an understanding of Islam and the processes of islamization in the region. On the one hand, its origins need to be seen in the planting of numerous local traditions of Islam at focal points in the archipelago. In the course of time, these traditions coalesced and emerged for a while as Islamic city-states or fissiparated and disappeared as significant entities, to be succeeded by new ones. On the other hand, the establishment of modern nation-states with single centers of authority has laid the foundation for a new kind of Islamic tradition with a national character, and these centers in turn have exercised a normative influence on the development of such traditions.

THE DIVERSITY OF SOUTHEAST ASIA

From earliest times, Southeast Asia has been a region with a variety of peoples, social structures, means of livelihood, cultures, and religions. Denys Lombard, admittedly writing of the modern period, puts it this way:

> *We are in fact dealing with several levels of mentality. . . . The thought processes of fringe societies in which "potlatch" is a prevailing custom (the Toraja); those of*

> *concentric agrarian societies (the Javanese states and their off-shoots at Jogja and Surakarta); those of trading societies (Malay towns,* pasisir *[Javanese coastal centers]); those of the societies living in large modern towns, and above all, the interplay of these various processes on each other, and their inter-relationships.*

If the first broad distinction to be made is temporal and political, between the constellation of modern nation-states and that of the traditional period, another is geographical: between continental (excluding the Malay Peninsula) and insular Southeast Asia. The former includes the states of Vietnam, Kampuchea, and Thailand; the latter, the Malay Peninsula and the islands of what are now Indonesia and the southern Philippines.

To be sure, each has economic and social elements in common—settled rice cultivation, slash-and-burn shifting cultivation, fishing and seafaring, trading and piracy, gold mining, along with elements of megalithic culture, ancestor worship, and the numerous rituals and beliefs associated with rice cultivation. Yet they are separated by a division into two great language families—the Austronesian, of which the most important representatives are Malay and Javanese, and the Mon Khmer, of which the most important are Thai and Burmese—and the communications barrier between these families is much greater than that between related members within one family or the other. Equally important, although both parts of the great archipelago received a tincture of Hindu influence well before the birth of Islam, in continental Southeast Asia, Theravāda Buddhism became dominant, whereas Mahāyāna Buddhism in one form or another was practiced in the southern regions, in particular, Srivijaya (seventh to fourteenth centuries) based on South Sumatra, and Majapahit (thirteenth to fifteenth centuries) in East Java. These great divisions correspond to those regions in which Islam secured a dominant position and those in which it did not.

SOUTHEAST ASIA IN WORLD TRADE

The great archipelago of Southeast Asia lies across the sea routes between the Indian Ocean and the China Sea. In both divisions of the region there were some points open to a range of contacts with the outside world, and others where access was more difficult and where a lifestyle conditioned by such remoteness was preserved.

For centuries before the Christian era, the Indian Ocean had been dominated by the Yemenis, who traded in gold, gums, spices, rhinoceros horn, and ivory from the east coast of Africa. For this early period, it is not possible to identify place names accurately, but it is known that the Yemenis brought their goods to the land of gold, *suvarna bhumi,* the term by which Southeast Asia was referred to in some Sanskrit texts.

In the beginning of the Christian era, both continental and insular Southeast Asia reacted to, and in a remarkable way were fecundated by, contact with Indian cultural influences carried to the focal trading centers referred to earlier, which were to be creative for over a millennium. A constant succession of Hindu and Buddhist influences was established in particular regions, with various phases carrying the different traditions, schools, and artistic styles of these great religions and modifying each other as they were adapted to the new environment.

The Coming of Islam

Up to the tenth century CE there is very little evidence of the presence of Islam in Southeast Asia. Indeed, although the Portuguese conquerors of Malacca in 1511 give us some important information about the progress of Islam in the region, apart from a few archaeological remains, reports by Chinese merchants, and the records of individual travelers such as Marco Polo and Ibn Baṭṭūṭah, both of whom give descriptions of North Sumatra, there is little concrete documentation until the seventeenth century. By that time, however, with the appearance of the Dutch and British trading companies in the region, the evidence of widespread islamization becomes overwhelming. The territories of the Islamic commonwealth in Southeast Asia were so vast that the process of their creation has been called "the second expansion of Islam," alluding to the original expansion from Arabia into North Africa and the Fertile Crescent. Unlike that first period of extraordinary growth in the seventh century, however, the spread of Islam in Southeast Asia was hesitant, modest, and discreet: what was achieved in one century in the Middle East took virtually a millennium in Southeast Asia.

There is too little evidence to document the beginnings of this process, yet a reasonable working hypothesis may be formulated as follows: as soon as there were Muslim sailors aboard ships sailing under whatever flag in the Indian Ocean trading system and disembarking goods or individuals at points in Southeast Asia, there was the possibility of a Muslim presence at those points. This could have been as early as the end of the seventh century. Hardly anything is known of the history of trading settlements along the littoral of Southeast Asia during this period; however, reliable evidence for the presence of Muslims in China from the beginning of the eighth century, if not before, suggests that Muslim seamen and merchants were already breaking their long voyages at one or another of the numerous natural harbors along the coasts of Sumatra, the Malay Peninsula, Borneo, and northern Java. The unloading of goods to await transshipment with the change of the monsoon, the establishment of warehouses and semipermanent settlements, and trading and intermarriage—and other relationships—with the local peoples were all factors that combined to establish small but viable Muslim communities.

Given the diversity and discontinuities of the region, the provenance of Southeast Asian Islam is not a practical topic for discussion, although hypotheses have located it anywhere from Egypt to Bengal. One thing is certain: all movement of ideas and peoples from West and South Asia to Southeast Asia is related to the maritime history of the Indian Ocean (although it is still possible that communities made part of the journey by land across the Indian subcontinent, or even the "great circle" route via the Silk Road through Central Asia, and then by sea from Canton to the islands). The greater the number of Muslims involved in the trading system, the greater the diversity of the Muslim tradition that became diffused, and the greater the probability of Muslims coming together in sufficient numbers to generate a critical mass—a Muslim community that could become stable through intermarriage with local women and play a distinctive role among other communities on equal terms. This community may have already included Arabs in the early years of the Islamic commonwealth; from that era, no information has survived. But the process of consolidation was slow. It is not until the thirteenth century that Islamic communities appear with a political profile, as port city-states ruled by sultans. The earliest of these sultanates

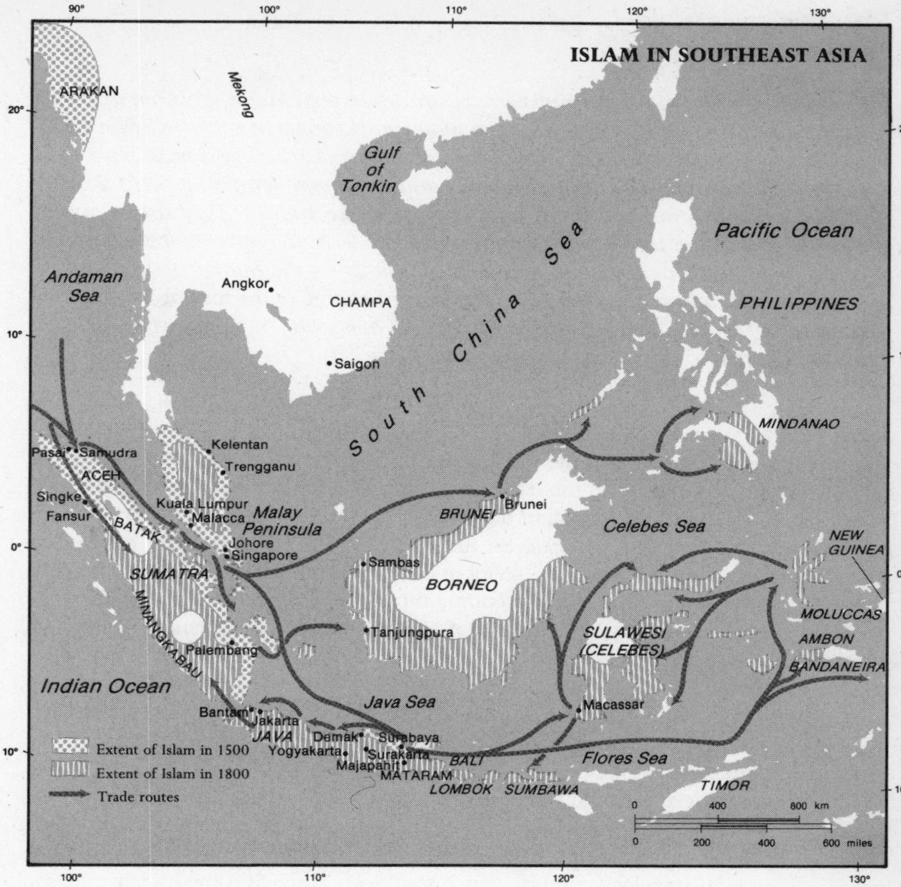

was that of Pasai, on the east coast of North Sumatra; it was succeeded by others. The appearance of such city-states must be seen as the culmination of a long period of Muslim presence with a rather lower profile, and a circumstance that has made the ethnic mix of the communities difficult to define.

Once Islam achieved a political presence in the region, further growth and the exercise of political powerbecame possible. By this time the trading system of the Indian Ocean was largely in Muslim hands; this assured economic power to Muslims, and Muslim mercantile law served to generate business confidence. The power and self-confidence of the Muslim states gave them a position as power brokers and allies. Marriage alliances that required a profession of Islam doubtless had a role as well.

FIRST TRACES

The earliest archaeological evidence is slight: a lone pillar in the region of Phanrang on the mid-east coast of Vietnam, inscribed in Arabic and dating from the tenth century. The French scholar Ravaisse (quoted by S. Q. Fatimi in *Islam Comes to Asia*) believes it to indicate that

> *there existed there in the eleventh century an urban population of whom we know little. They were very different from the indigenous people in race, belief and habits. Their ancestors must have come about a century earlier, and must have married native women. They were merchants and craftsmen living in a perfectly well-organized society mixing more and more with the natives. They asked one of themselves to act as their representative and defender with respect to the authorities of the place. He was called Shaikh al-Suq* ["*master of the market*"], *and was assisted by the Naqib (a merchant or craftsman in charge of the management of the community to which he belonged). Along with him were "notables who, enriched by their commerce, occupied an important place."*

Another piece of evidence from roughly the same period suggests that there was some kind of Muslim presence at Leren on the north coast of Java. This is a tombstone marking the grave of a merchant's daughter. It provides no certain evidence of a Muslim community; even the date cannot be taken for granted since tombstones were frequently imported long after a burial.

In Trengganu, an east-coast state on the Malay Peninsula, a fragment of a stone pillar inscribed in Malay in Arabic script and dating from between 1321 and 1380, suggests the presence of a Muslim community. By the fifteenth century there is sporadic but more substantial evidence of Muslims in the East Javanese empire of Majapahit, again from gravestones. Probably they belonged to communities of merchants, but this too is hardly more than surmise. Just as there were Muslims in Java, there is evidence that there were Muslims in the great Buddhist empire of Srivijaya (seventh to thirteenth centuries) based on South Sumatra, an empire that thrived on trade and maintained close relations with China and India.

The earliest evidence that substantiates not simply the presence of Muslims in the region but the existence of an Islamic maritime sultanate dates from the thirteenth century. This is a tombstone of the first Muslim ruler of Pasai, in North Sumatra, and reports of foreign travelers confirm that his subjects were Muslims. What circumstances enabled the Muslim community to achieve a critical mass and generate a state in which the ruler could style himself sultan, and what processes led to this event, we cannot tell. Likewise there is little evidence as to the ethnic composition of this state: to what extent was it local, to what extent foreign? (And even the term "foreign" at this time begs a number of questions.) Many of the titles and names attributed to the personalities of this sultanate in a local chronicle have a South Indian ring to them.

Nonetheless, from this point on, the documentation of Islam at the political level is relatively straightforward, and it is possible to chronicle the emergence of states with Islamic rulers. Even though internal records are sparse and their human and cultural dynamics remain in darkness, at the very least their names are recorded by foreign visitors.

THE SULTANATES

I have posited Pasai as the earliest Muslim state in the Malay world and its ruler as the first sultan there. The only evidence of his life comes from his tombstone. But

Pasai was at least referred to by Marco Polo and Ibn Baṭṭūṭah in the thirteenth and fourteenth centuries. Although the extent of its political authority is not known, it occupied a strategic position at the entrance to the straits of Malacca and was a convenient point for exchanging goods and taking on board supplies of water and firewood. Moreover, by making alliances with either pirates or nascent states on the other side of the straits, it was able to ensure that shipping did not go elsewhere, and that port taxes were paid.

Malacca. Malacca, on the west coast of the Malay Peninsula, inherited the mantle of Pasai. Far more is known of its history than that of Pasai, from both local and foreign sources. It became Muslim shortly after its foundation around 1400, and via its dependencies, both on the Malay Peninsula, where it established the dynasties of the Malay sultanates, and on the east coast of Sumatra, it served as a conduit for Muslim influence to other parts of the archipelago. Various factors were involved here: local traders from the neighboring islands were attracted to its emporium, Muslim traders from Bengal, India, and further afield found scope for business activities opened up in its trading partners and dependencies, and it attracted foreign *ʿulamāʾ* (religious scholars; sg., *ʿālim*), principally from India, although many of them may have had Arab blood and used this Arab descent to their advantage. Although Malacca held an important position, however, it was not unique. There were many smaller states that played an analogous role along the littoral of East Sumatra, the north coast of Java, Borneo, Sulawesi (Celebes), and later the Spice Islands (Moluccas) and the southern Philippines. In every case the same kind of processes that were illustrated at Malacca were taking place, perhaps on a smaller scale, perhaps on a larger scale, and they had been happening even before the birth of Malacca. It must be stressed that there is no "big bang" explanation for the coming of Islam to Southeast Asia; such claims as the Portuguese statement that Java was converted from Malacca must be regarded as hyperbole.

Smaller States. After Malacca fell to the Portuguese in 1511, it was such smaller states that were to grow to eminence: Aceh, Palembang, Banten, Ceribon, Demak, Surabaya, and Makassar, as well as smaller centers in the Spice Islands. Each of them became integrated into the Muslim trading system, each became a center of Islamic learning, and each, by a continuing process of osmosis, attracted people from the interior into contact with these cities. In every case, networks of family, Ṣūfī order *(ṭarīqah),* guild, and trade association relationships gradually served to diffuse Islam back into the interior, although it was transmitted at different levels of intensity and perceived in rather different ways according to the cultural backgrounds of the various communities.

Special attention should be drawn to Aceh, which first came to prominence in the 1520s and reached its apogee during the reign of Sultan Iskandar Muda (1607–1636). During the first half of the seventeenth century it was the dominant economic and political power of the region. It conquered the northern half of the Malay Peninsula and northern and parts of central Sumatra, gaining control of the pepper areas and enforcing a trading monopoly. Aceh was the first Muslim state in the region to have extended intercourse with Europe. It is also noteworthy for a surviving legacy of Islamic learning: for the first time we have historical information about a state in the region generating works of Islamic scholarship that remain accessible to us, some of which are used in schools throughout the Malay world even today. In addition, we are able to identify individual Acehnese scholars, both in Aceh and in the Arabian centers of Mecca and Medina, and the teachers with whom they studied. Indeed, of the great ministers of state between 1600 and 1630, Shams al-Dīn was a noted *ʿālim.* There are eyewitness reports from British, Dutch, and French sailors on the celebration of the conclusion of the fast of Ramaḍān (ʿĪd al-Fiṭr) and the festival of the sacrifice marking the climax of the pilgrimage rites in Mecca. It is also possible to establish and describe some of the relations between Aceh, the Mughal court, and the Ottoman empire. [*See* Acehnese Religion.]

The Islamic history of Aceh during this period is better known than that of any of its neighbors, but analogous centers of lesser political power played a major role elsewhere in the region as Islam moved inland during the seventeenth century. In Sumatra, for example, the inland highlands of the Minangkabau region, territories rich in gold and pepper and which for centuries had established this part of the island in a network of trading systems, became Muslim. This area was to put a distinctive stamp on its interpretation and realization of Islam by maintaining a matrilineal social structure alongside a commitment to Islam that was among the staunchest in the archipelago.

Another inland region where Islam became established was the state of Mataram in Central Java, which was, until its defeat by the United Dutch East India Company in 1629, the largest single state on the island. Even after the defeat, it maintained this status, a status that added special significance to the fact that its ruler, Susuhunan Agung (1613–1645), assumed the title of sultan and in 1633 established the Islamic calendrical system in Java.

THE COLONIAL ERA

The expansion of the United Dutch East India Company as a political power in the region and its increasing monopoly of international trade severely dislocated the traditional rhythm of the rise and fall of states in the region as well as the economic life. Company power continued to grow to the point that it was not simply a state among states but was virtually invulnerable. During this period of colonial expansion from the seventeenth century on, Islam, according to conventional wisdom, was in decline. Decline, however, is a word that conceals more than it reveals. Throughout the region more people were gradually drawn into the new religion, to the basic recognition of transcendence implicit in the confession "There is no god but God." To be sure, numerous cults survived alongside this confession, together with practices and rituals and the use of spells and magical formulas that derived from the Indic and megalithic traditions. Nevertheless there was a continuing momentum toward the subordination and finally the subsuming of the spiritual concepts of such traditions into the terminology of Islam: thus numerous Javanese spirits were largely included within the Islamic category of beings, the *jinn.* Doubtless the intensity of response to the more exclusive demands of Islam waxed and waned, yet amid all these communities where Islam had been planted, some degree of formal recognition was given to Islamic law, particularly in relation to diet, to burial of the dead, to marriage, to circumcision, and to the fast, even where the performance of the daily prayer was lax. Indeed it is striking how the pre-Islamic cult of the dead reflected in the building of great mausolea for the Javanese god-kings, and the extravagant sacrifices of buffaloes still carried on today in non-Muslim areas such as the Torajas (Central Sulawesi), completely disappeared with the acceptance of Islam.

The pilgrimage too was important; some individuals stayed to study for years in the Middle East; The Ṣūfī orders also played their role, and religious teachers, keeping on the circuit, gave fresh life to communities and religious schools and held the ear of local rulers. The constant retelling of stories of the prophets and the heroes of Islam and their cultural adaptation to local conditions gradually created a unitary and universalistic frame of reference for local and world history and established Islamic concepts—of the creation, of the sending of God's messengers culminating in Muḥammad, of the community, and eventually of the resurrection of the body—as the norm and benchmark by which all competing systems of ideas were to be measured and into which they were largely to be assimilated.

THE ERA OF REFORMS

This spread of sensitivity to and identification with an Islamic ethos, although at times mixed and not totally unequivocal, rendered such communities responsive to movements that caught the imagination and fired the enthusiasm of Muslims in other parts of the Muslim world. One such movement was the Wahhābī uprising in Arabia during the last quarter of the eighteenth century. Inspired by the ideal of cleansing Islam from accretions and practices that were held to be incompatible with *tawḥīd,* the oneness of God, it resorted to force to put Islamic law and ritual observances into effect.

The Wahhābī Legacy. The enthusiastic preaching of such doctrines by a group of scholars returning from Arabia in 1803 led to the rise of the Padri movement in the Minangkabau area of Sumatra. This movement set itself against the traditional elite, which it regarded as compromising with non-Islamic practices and values, whether reflected in the lifestyle of the traditional rulers or in the matrilineal descent system of the region. Their reaction was to lead to a civil war that gave the Dutch government an opportunity to intervene on the part of the traditionalists and to defeat the leader of the revolt, Imam Bondjol, in 1842.

It may well have been also that the Java War (1826–1830) between rival members of the royal court likewise took part of its energy from this ferment in Islam. It should not be imagined that the expansion of Islam was always peaceful, or that even the relationships among different traditions of Islam were without conflict. One need only recall the persecution and book burning in Aceh between 1637 and 1642, sometimes referred to as an attempt by the so-called Shuhūdīyah ("unity of witness") school of mysticism to suppress the Wujūdīyah ("unity of being") tradition; the wars waged by Sultan Agung's successor, Amangkurat I, in the 1660s against the legalistic Muslim communities of the north coast of Java; and the scatological diatribes written in Javanese to make fun of the professional *'ulamā'* in the nineteenth century.

The same channels that had brought the aftermath of the Wahhābī movement to the then-Dutch East Indies, were, about a century later, to bring the Islamic reformist movement to Sumatra, Java, and the Malay Peninsula, to be diffused from there to southern Thailand, and paradoxically, from Ḥaḍramī communities in Java back to southern Arabia.

The Impact of ʿAbduh and Rashīd Riḍā. In fact, appearance of the reform movement inspired by Jamāl al-Dīn al-Afghānī and pioneered by Muḥammad ʿAbduh soon fecundated a vigorous counterpart in Southeast Asia. In particular, students from the Malay world in the Middle East, especially those studying at al-Azhar University in Cairo, were inspired by ʿAbduh, Rashīd Riḍā, and their followers, and as they returned to Malaya and the Indies, they carried the new ideas with them. The effect that they had in their homeland was quite dramatic. ʿAbduh's reformist program was based on four main points: the purification of Islam from corrupting influences and practices; the reformation of Muslim education; the reformation of Islamic doctrine in the light of modern thought; and the defense of Islam. The establishment of the reformist journal *Al-manār* (The Lighthouse), published between 1898 and 1936 under the editorship of ʿAbduh and later that of Riḍā, directly inspired two counterparts in the Malay world. *Al-imām* (The Imam), published in Singapore between 1906 and 1908, transmitted the views of *Al-manār* and ʿAbduh's earlier journal, *Al-ʿurwah al-wuthqā* (The Strongest Bond), and published translations of their articles into Malay. Its layout followed that of *Al-manār*. *Al-munīr* (The Radiant), established in the major West Sumatran port town of Padang, was published between 1911 and 1916; it too referred regularly to *Al-manār* and published translations from the Egyptian journal.

Al-manār in turn reflected the great interest that it generated in Southeast Asia: from the very year of its founding, it included articles, in Arabic, either written by Southeast Asian Muslims studying in Cairo or sent from a wide range of places in the Indies, including Singapore, Batavia, Malang, Palembang, Surabaya, and Sambas (Borneo). A 1930 communication from Sambas was particularly important, for it requested Rashīd Riḍā to put to the famous writer Shakīb Arslān certain questions relating to reasons for the backwardness of Muslims and the progress of other peoples. The response to this request, first published in three parts in *Al-manār,* was to become Arslān's well-known book *Limādhā ta'akhkhara al-Muslimūn wa-taqaddama al-ākharūn* (Why Do the Muslims Stay Behind and the Others Progress?), which was in due course to be translated into Malay. The episode is important because it indicates the seriousness and care of the response of Egyptian scholars to the queries and difficulties of their Southeast Asian coreligionists.

There is an interesting range of Southeast Asia–related topics raised in *Al-manār*. An 1898 article, for example, reports on a request by some Javanese Muslims to the Dutch colonial government for them to be allowed to acquire Ottoman citizenship; other articles address complaints of Dutch harassment of Muslims, problems of marriages between sayyids (the Muslim elite) and Muslim commoners, and the humiliations of quarantine regulations imposed on Muslims making the pilgrimage. A 1909 article from Palembang tells how *Al-manār* had inspired the Muslims of the region to form associations and financial unions to support Islamic schools to teach Arabic, the religious disciplines, and secular subjects. Two years later, another interesting entry praises the periodical for creating an intellectual movement among Muslims and describes how a school director had been inspired by *Al-manār* to introduce the Berlitz method of teaching foreign languages in his school. [*See also* Modernism, *article on* Islamic Modernism.]

The educational dimension of the reform program quickly made itself felt. Here a few examples will suffice. The work of To'Kenali (1866–1933), a scholar from Kelantan, an east-coast state of the Malay Peninsula, is representative of many, including some who became famous in Patani and Cambodia (Kampuchea) at the turn of the century. He went to Mecca at the age of twenty and stayed in the Middle East for twenty-two years before returning to Kelantan in 1908. In 1903 he traveled to Egypt to visit al-Azhar and other educational institutions. It is possible that he met ʿAbduh on this occasion. There is no doubt, however, that he had absorbed the educational ideals of the movement. He quickly became famous as a teacher was appointed assistant to the *muftī* in Kelantan with responsibility for Islamic education in the state, and set up a network of schools. He introduced Malay textbooks in religious knowledge and devised a system of graded instruction in Arabic grammar. Indeed, one of his students (born in Mecca of Malay parents in 1895), on returning to Kelantan in 1910, was inspired by him to compile an Arabic-Malay dictionary with entries and definitions in part based on the Arabic classic *Al-munjid;* published in 1927, the Malay work is still popular.

The reform, however, was reflected not only in text- books, but also in classroom organization. The traditional method of teaching was known as the *ḥalaqah* ("study circle"), where students, irrespective of age, would sit in a circle around the teacher, who would present material to be learned by rote. The introduction of the classroom method, where the students sat in rows and used graded texts, together with the encouragement of active class participation, was a remarkable change of style. No less remarkable was the inclusion of secular subjects in the curriculum. Schools inspired by the reform movement multiplied in various parts of the archipelago, sometimes identified with individuals, sometimes initiated within the framework of an organization. Many sprang up and disappeared like mushrooms.

Of those founded by individuals, one that became important was the Sumatra Thawalib school founded in 1918. Another was the Sekolah Diniyah Putri in Padang Panjang, a religious school for girls founded in 1921 by a woman named Rahmah al-Yunusiyah. Designed to train students in the basic rules and practices of Islam and in the understanding of the principles and applications of Islamic law, particularly in matters of special concern to women, the school also set out to give girls an education in those matters that would enable them to run their homes efficiently and care for the health and education of their children. While from one standpoint the discipline of the institution was very strict and the scope for individual development narrow, it won the confidence of isolated village communities, and in fact, its students gained wider horizons than those girls who remained in the interior.

This school was a strikingly original institution (which was to inspire the founding of the Kullīyat al-Banāt within al-Azhar in 1957). Yet it was based on very simple premises: a universalistic interpretation of Islam, and the founder's determination to establish an institution that would present itself in every respect as an alternative to the Dutch system, from curriculum to the yearly cycle of festivals and the Islamic calendar (Friday was the day off) to student dress. It guarded its independence and refused offers of subsidy from the Dutch government. It still flourishes today and during the 1930s had branches in Java and the Malay Peninsula.

The Muhammadiyah. The most famous and long-lived of all socioreligious reformist movements in the Indies was the Muhammadiyah, founded in 1912 in Jogjakarta (Central Java) by Kiai H. A. Dahlan. One of the goals of its founder was to inculcate the ideas of the reformists concerning the purification of Islam from traditional accretions, in particular from the animistic beliefs that were so much part of the worldview of the Javanese peasantry, and from the religious attitudes and values of the upper classes, for whom the Hindu-Buddhist traditions of the pre-Islamic period—traditions embodied in the Javanese shadow theater—were still very much alive.

One particular target was the cult of saints' tombs. The movement consciously adopted the institutional structures of the Dutch, and its members made a careful study of the techniques of Christian missionary organizations. Carrying on vigorous missionary activities, it expanded into journalism and publishing and established mosques, religious endowments, orphanages, and clinics. But its central role was in education, where it set up an entire system from primary school to teacher training colleges. Like To'Kenali in Kelantan, the Muhammadiyah carried on the impulse generated by Muḥammad ʿAbduh to reform the traditional Islamic educational system—by grading teaching materials and classes, by sitting students at desks faced by teachers with blackboards, and by assessing their progress with formal examinations and the award of individual marks that determined when they could move from one grade to the next.

The Muhammadiyah's strict and responsible methods of organization and financial management ensured its stability, and by the 1930s it had established branches as far afield as North, Central, and South Sumatra, Borneo, and Sulawesi, thus taking on a protonational character.

Another aspect of the reformist movement was its campaign against the Ṣūfī *ṭarīqah*. For the reformers the *ṭarīqah* represented the one element in traditional Islam that most contributed to the backwardness of Muslims and the lack of respect they had in the world. They held that the *ṭarīqah* promoted a passive otherworldliness, that it discouraged initiative, and that the dedication to the shaykh, the head of the branch, overshadowed devotion to the Prophet and God himself. In addition, the ascetic exercises of members and their fondness for reciting sacred formulas were considered intellectually harmful, often paving the way for the absorption of non-Islamic practices. In short, the reformists took over and applied all the arguments marshaled against the *ṭarīqah* by the *Al-manār* tradition. There is a reasonable documentation of debates between the two sides on the issue. In the Dutch East Indies, the Ṣūfī orders appeared to be almost a spent force by the 1930s, with their followers to be found only in the remoter rural areas. The qualification is important, for of religious life in these remoter rural areas little is known. On the Malay Peninsula they fared better and still maintain a social role there. Indeed, one of the leading figures of religious reform and revival in Kelantan was Wan Musa, who, when he studied in Mecca with his father, was introduced to the theosophy of Muḥyī al-Dīn ibn al-ʿArabī and inducted into the Shādhilīyah *ṭarīqah*. He introduced the reforms of ʿAbduh and Rashīd Riḍā into Kelantan and rejected *taqlīd*, or unquestioning acceptance of precedent, yet defended the institutional role of the *ṭarīqah* and preserved the content of Ṣūfī doctrine, stressing in his instruction the role of intellect, intuition, and emotion. [*See also* Ṭarīqah.]

Some idea of the residual role of the Indonesian *ṭarīqah* at a public level by 1955 can be gained from the fact that an attempt to obtain representation for these movements in the national parliament at the first general election resulted in the election of one member, a Naqshbandī. This, of course, need mean nothing more than that many *ṭarīqah* members did not see the national parliament as a place for *ṭarīqah* representation.

There was, however, a response to the reform movement in the Indies, and this was the Nahdatul Ulama (lit., "revival of the *ʿulamāʾ*"), founded in 1926. This movement was not designed to defend the *ṭarīqah,* or even the mystical tradition, although in practice it did so. It stood for the traditional role of the *ʿulamāʾ* and opposed the reformists' reliance on the Qur'ān and *sunnah* alone. Adherence to one or another of the four schools of law as the basis for the application of *fiqh* was basic, and in Indonesia this meant, in practice, the Shāfiʿī school.

Postwar Politics. With the Japanese occupation, all Muslim associations were dissolved and then reconstituted into an umbrella organization encompassing both reformists and traditionalists, the Majlis Shura Muslimin Indonesia, or Consultative Assembly of Indonesian Muslims, known widely by its acronym Masyumi. After the war, the organization broke up into two main wings: the one that kept the name Masyumi became the political wing of the reformist movement and drew most of its strength from Sumatra and the large towns in Java, while the other, Nahdatul Ulama, now took a public role as a political party and derived most of its strength from the rural areas of East Java. An index to the standing of the parties, and therefore the distribution of attitudes, is furnished by the results of the 1955 elections, in which the Masyumi won 57 seats and the Nahdatul Ulama won 45 out of a total of more than 250. Even taking into account the seats held by minor religious parties, this meant that more than half of the Muslim electorate had cast its vote for nonreligious parties.

In Malaysia, up to the time of independence in 1957 religious parties did not have a high political profile: to be a Malay is, by definition, to be a Muslim, to live by Malay custom, and to speak the Malay language. In a country in which the native inhabitants were less than half the total population, had scarcely any urban presence or economic power, and could only manifest their identity in the persons and ceremonial role of the sultans and in the profession of Islam—a situation in which the Malay language and even survival of the Malay race was at stake—there was no scope for splitting up the components of the political package that became known as the United Malays National Organization into competing religious allegiances. Indeed, it is striking that with Malayan independence in 1957, Islam became a national religion without the creation of an Islamic state in Malaya (now Malaysia). The situation, however, is not quite what it seems, for this is at the national level. At the state level, under the rule of the hereditary sultans, Islamic law is enforced upon Muslims, and offenses such as breaking the fast are punishable by religious courts.

Islam in a Spiritual and Cultural Role

The modalities by which islamization established itself in the region and its subsequent cultural achievements are far richer in character than a purely political survey can communicate, although the political survey provides a necessary framework. Discussion of such issues must be based on the territories that are now Malaysia and Indonesia, the core Islamic areas of the region. Compared to these regions, and despite their intrinsic interest and importance, Thailand, the other mainland states, and the Philippines are fringe areas.

Let us consider in a little more detail the cases we have mentioned. The community at Phanrang lived and governed itself apart from its neighbors. Typologically this situation is difficult to account for. Thus the hypothesis that it was founded by descendants of a community of Shīʿī refugees who fled from a persecution by the Umayyad governor al-Ḥajjāj (d. 714) is plausible. It will be noted later that although today the region is Sunnī, there are some remnants of Shīʿī influence from the past, such as the commemoration of the martyrdom of Ḥasan and Ḥusayn in a coastal region of western Sumatra.

PROCESSES OF ISLAMIZATION

The descriptions of the sultanate of Pasai referred to earlier make a clear distinction between the Muslim community of the city itself and those people of the hinterland who were still unbelievers. This distinction suggests that an originally foreign community became settled over a number of years, and that an individual with sufficient charisma at one point proclaimed himself sultan. The coastal port of Malacca on the other hand presents an example of a mercantile state whose ruler professed Islam soon after its foundation. The case of Aceh is different again, in that it appears to have arisen after the amalgamation of two small Muslim states in the north of Sumatra into a single state that was to dominate the straits of Malacca for the greater part of the seventeenth century.

The importance of Aceh cannot be overstressed. It was known in popular parlance as the gateway to the Holy Land (Arabia). Aspiring pilgrims and scholars from all parts of the archipelago would make the journey in stages over a period of years. Aceh was the last port of work and residence and study that they would encounter before leaving their own region of the world and heading out across the Bay of Bengal. It was also the first place of call on their return journey. And the intensity of religious education, debate, and teaching in Aceh, as well as the constant movement of peoples of diverse ethnic groups, ensured a wide dissemination of religious ideas and, to some extent, a normalization of religious life through the distribution of networks of religious affiliations. (From the early days, it should be noted, there is evidence of the presence of *ṭarīqah*s.)

The acceptance of Islam by Sultan Agung of Mataram (r. 1613–1646) is a special case. His kingdom was not a port-state but was located in the interior and was based on wet rice cultivation rather than on trade. It was the prestigious heir to the great Śiva Buddha tradition of East Java and included in its territories the sites of the great Buddhist stupa, the Borobudur, and other Hindu and Buddhist shrines built during the seventh, eighth, and ninth centuries. Yet for Agung, this history was not enough, nor was his title of *susuhunan*. To all this he added the title of sultan, purchased from Mecca; thus he assumed a dignity which, although largely symbolic, had a major role in elevating the status of Islam in Java (although this activity should not be confused with the conversion of Java to Islam).

As C. C. Berg points out in a seminal article (1955), kings and princes operated as factors of acceleration and deceleration of the islamization process in Java. In this instance, Agung played a role of acceleration following his defeat by the Dutch East India Company in 1629. This event turned him toward whatever enemies of the Dutch could be found in the seas and islands of the archipelago: the Portuguese and communities of Muslim merchants. As a Muslim by profession, if not by passion, until 1629, he soon became a Muslim in search of authority and power. Whatever his psychological motivations, he changed the face of his kingdom and its cultural character by introducing the Muslim calendar with the announcement that from 1 Muḥarram 1043 AH, a date corresponding to 8 July 1633 CE, this calendrical system should operate in Java alongside the traditional Javanese system of Saka years. Symbolically this was an act of very great importance, because it meant that the advent of Islam became the event in relation to which other events in Javanese society were to be recorded.

In the last analysis, however, the creative achievement of a religion is to be seen in the lives of the individuals it inspires, the intellectual activity it generates, and the dimensions it adds to spiritual, cultural, and social life. But one of the difficulties in coping with the story of Islam in Southeast Asia is the absence of historical figures to whom one can attribute the early spread of the religion.

It is striking that, in the Malay texts at least, there are no historical figures to whom the primal conversion of a state to Islam can be attributed. The same holds true for the preaching of Islam in Java as presented by Javanese court chronicles. This is not to say that such figures are always nameless, or that they may not be based on individuals who did once exist, but certainly in the way they are presented, there is nothing that could be described as a personality base. In his contribution to Nehemia Levtzion's *Conversion to Islam* (1980), Jones gives an account of ten conversion myths from different parts of the archipelago. The account from the *Sejarah Malayu* (Malay Annals) is typical: the ruler of Malacca had a dream in which he saw Muḥammad, who ordered him to recite the Muslim Shahādah ("witnessing"): "There is no god but God, and Muḥammad is his Messenger." The prophet then told him that the following day, at the time of the afternoon prayer, a ship would arrive from Jidda with a religious teacher on board whom he was to obey. When the king awoke, he found he had been circumcised. At the time foretold on the following day the ship arrived, and the religious teacher came down from it. There and then he performed the afternoon prayer on the beach, and the bystanders gathered round asking: what is this bobbing up and down. The king, on hearing what was happening went down to the beach to welcome him, and together with all his courtiers and subjects embraced Islam.

An intriguing feature of this work is that most of the religious teachers described in its pages are presented as figures of fun. There is the eccentric who takes sling shots at kites flown over his house, and there is the religious teacher who is teased by a drunken court officer because he cannot pronounce Malay words correctly. There is also the mystically inclined teacher who refuses to accept the sultan as a religious disciple unless he leaves his elephant behind at the palace and comes humbly on foot.

Of these figures, one may possibly be identified: Sadar Jahan, the religious adviser to Sultan Ahmad Shah of Malacca. When Ahmad Shah came out on his elephant to face the Portuguese attack that destroyed the city in 1511, Sadar Jahan accompanied the sultan. Under a hail of musket shots he begged his master to retreat to a safer position with the words: "This is no place to discuss the mystical union." He has been identified with a scholar-jurist-diplomat Fayd Allah Bambari, known as Sadr-i Jahan, who was sent by King Ayaz from Gujarat via Jidda to negotiate a defensive wall from Hormuz to Malacca against the Portuguese incursion into the Indian Ocean. He arrived in Malacca by ship in 1509 to stiffen Malaccan resistance to the

Portuguese and is presumed to have been killed during the sack of the city. The identification is not wholly certain. Nevertheless, the evidence is sufficient to show that as early as the fifteenth century, religious teachers from various parts of the Muslim world took part in the religious life of the Southeast Asian sultanates. It is also worth noting that the religious figures in the Javanese chronicles are presented without the lightness of touch and irreverence that characterize the Malay figures. They are sometimes identified as numbering eight, but more often nine, a total that has more to do with cosmology than arithmetic, since the number nine indicates the eight points of the compass and the center. Their spheres of influence are distributed among different regions of Java, and they are associated with the origin of elements of Javanese culture such as the Javanese shadow theater and gamelan orchestra, which existed long before Islam. All of them are presented as figures with a mystical insight into the reality of things; they have a role in the founding of dynasties and are not subject to the laws of nature. One of them, Siti Jenar, was executed for uttering words that claimed identity between himself and God. It seems likely that this event—if indeed it occurred—is a doublet of the al-Ḥallāj story.

It is only from the late sixteenth century that it becomes possible to identify individuals among religious teachers, and so to have the foundations for an intellectual and spiritual history of Islam in this region. However, since the information available about such figures is very sparse—biography and, even more, autobiography are undeveloped art forms in Southeast Asia—it is not possible to do much more than situate them within a general framework of the intellectual and spiritual life of the region, as far as this can be established.

LANGUAGES

Southeast Asia is an area of great linguistic diversity: there are over three hundred languages in the Indonesian area alone. Of these languages, Malay was known throughout Southeast Asia as a lingua franca as early as the sixteenth century. During the period already discussed, it had also been established as a vernacular of Islam and as a language of the court forareas as far afield and diverse as Malacca, Aceh, and Makassar. It is this very early diffusion of the language, with its religious, economic, cultural, and chancellery roles, that led to its adoption in the twentieth century, in slightly different forms, as the national language of Malaysia and Indonesia, where it became known as Bahasa Malaysia and Bahasa Indonesia, respectively. Of course, other languages related to Malay were to become vehicles of Muslim learning and culture, in particular Javanese, Sundanese, Madurese, and some of the languages of southern Sulawesi. But although some of these, notably Javanese, had a far richer literary tradition than did Malay, none rivaled its widespread authority.

Its role as a language of Islam was also made clear by the well-nigh universal use of a form of the Arabic script for its written transmission, supplanting a script of Indic derivation that was used for inscriptions before the coming of Islam. Other languages that accepted the Arabic script include Taosug and Maranouw from the southern Philippines, and it was also used alongside (but never supplanted) scripts derived from Indian syllabaries for writing Javanese and Sundanese.

There is only one example of the use of an Indic script for an already islamized Malay. This is found on a tombstone from Minye Tujuh in Aceh marking the grave of a Queen Alalah, daughter of a Sultan Malik al-Zahir, who was a khan and a son of a khan (the title suggests a foreign origin). Dated in the equivalent of 1389 CE, it is written in an Indian script, and possibly in an Indian meter; if this is so, it shows a remarkable skill, even at this early period, in using Arabic loanwords within the requirements of Indic meters. The Malay inscription on the Trengganu stone (1320–1380), it will be recalled, was written in the Arabic script. The fact that there is a gap of almost two centuries between this tombstone and the survival of manuscripts simply emphasizes how arbitrary are the constellations of chance that provide material for knowledge of the region.

By the seventeenth century Malay had absorbed a rich stratum of Arabic loanwords and the acceptance of Arabic structures, along with some elements of Arabic morphology, provides striking evidence of the permeation of the region by an Islamic ethos and its modulation to the expression of Islamic ideas. Many of these ideas relate to religious matters, for example, those relating to the ritual prayer, marriage, divorce, and inheritance. Some Arabic words have undergone a narrowing: that is to say, they have lost a general meaning and kept only a religious one. Others range from technical terms, relating to religious matters and the administration of religious law, or terms of medicine, architecture, and the sciences, to the most common everyday expressions. Sometimes the words are so thoroughly assimilated that they would pass unrecognized unless one were able to identify them as Arabic by following through the patterns of sound change that Malay imposes on the loanwords it absorbs. Most remarkable is the adoption of an Arabic word to refer to local systems of culture, law, and traditional usage: *adat* (Arab., *ʿādah*). In fact, the concept identified by the word is so characteristically Malay that it would not be recognized as an Arabic word unless its origin were pointed out. The number of Arabic words in Malay—whether borrowed directly from Arabic or indirectly from other languages such as Persian—is well over a thousand.

Nor is it only Malay that has received a large corpus of Arabic loanwords; the same is true of many of the Malay-related languages in Sumatra, Java, and Borneo, notably Javanese, Sundanese, Madurese, Acehnese, and Minangkabau. The establishment of Muslim communities in the Philippines likewise brought numbers of loanwords to various Philippine languages. In Tagalog the number is relatively small, but in the southern Philippines, where Muslim communities are concentrated, they are most numerous.

LOCAL SCHOLARSHIP

This absorption of Arabic words in large measure derived from the study of Arabic works on the fundamental Islamic disciplines of Qur'anic exegesis, traditions, and jurisprudence, as well as Sufism (i.e., *tafsīr, ḥadīth, fiqh,* and *taṣawwuf*). There is no documentation of the early stages of the development of these studies, although there is no reason to doubt that the seeds were planted at least as early as the thirteenth century. Indeed, it should be stressed again that there were Islamic communities in the region long before the earliest evidence for Islamic states.

It is only from the seventeenth century that manuscripts from these traditions survive, whether in Arabic (mostly representing key works from the Islamic tradition) or in Malay or other regional languages such as Javanese. The Arabic manuscripts, some doubtless copied on the instructions of, or at least the permission of, a teacher in the Muslim Holy Land are of various levels of difficulty. Of works of *tafsīr,* that known as *Al-Jalālayn* is the most popular. Van Ronkel (1913) lists a significant number of manuscripts from various parts of the archipelago, some with interlinear translations, or at least annotations, in Malay or Javanese, sometimes with a dedication to a local ruler. There may be a temptation to look down on *Al-Jalalayn.* In fact it contains *multum in parvo* and is an excellent work for early levels of study, ideally suited for students who, though trained in an Islamic school, are not native speakers of Arabic. After *Al-Jalālayn,* al-Bayḍāwī's *Anwār al-tanzīl* takes pride of place, followed by al-Khāzin's *Lubāb al-ta'wīl fī ma'ānī al-tanzīl.* There are in addition fragments of Ṣūfī commentaries, including al-Bayhaqī's *Kitāb al-tahdhīb fī al-tafsīr* copied in 1652, which for a manuscript with a Southeast Asian provenance is very early indeed. There is even a work by al-Dānī on the seven recitations *(qirā'at)* of the Qur'ān. It should be stressed that these manuscripts represent the tip of the iceberg in relation to the number of those unknown from that period, or simply lost.

Collections of *ḥadīth,* especially those of al-Bukhārī, are numerous, and with them commentaries; the same collections of forty *ḥadīth (Al-arbā'īn),* especially that of al-Nawawī, were also popular. To these may be added a selection of works on history and biography, jurisprudence, astronomy, and *taṣawwuf.* A very popularṢūfī text, on the basis of the number of surviving manuscripts, is *Al-ḥikam al-'Aṭā'īyah* of Ibn 'Aṭā' Allāh; this work too is often accompanied by commentaries. There are treatises on the Shādhilī, Naqshbandī, and 'Alawī orders and a sprinkling of works in the Ibn al-'Arabī tradition, both by Ibn al-'Arabī himself and by his great commentator, al-Kāshānī. Of such manuscripts, one of the most striking contains the introduction to the commentary on Ibn al-Fāriḍ's poem *Al-tā'īyah al-kubrā* by Sa'īd ibn 'Alī al-Farghānī (d. 1299).

Given how scattered and arbitrary this list is, clearly, manuscripts have only survived by chance. Nevertheless, the evidence is sufficient to show that many basic Arabic works were accessible to scholars in this region, and that a variety of traditions was represented.

LOCAL AUTHORS

We have already mentioned interlinear translations, glosses, and annotations on Arabic manuscripts. These represent in embryonic form the tradition of works in Malay and other regional languages on the religious disciplines. How early this tradition began it is not possible to determine, nor do the extant manuscripts allow us to establish the order in which works of different categories were written.

Ḥamzah Fanṣūrī. The earliest Malay author known is Ḥamzah Fanṣūrī (d. 1600). The details of his life remain few, but some of his writings have been preserved. These suggest that in Mecca he came into contact with a particular formulation of Ṣūfī theosophy, apparently an Arabo-Iranian one based on the Ibn al-'Arabī tradition as it was reformulated and extended by al-Jīlī. It may have included Shī'ī elements; at least this would be consistent with the stories of Shī'ī heroes in Malay versions that were discovered in Aceh from the beginning of the seventeenth century.

A verse from one of the *sya'ir* (poems made up of end rhyming quatrains) of Ḥamzah Fanṣūrī gives a good example of the ascetic theology of the Ibn al-'Arabī school of mysticism:

Regard heat and cold as one and the same;
Abandon greed and avarice;
Let your will melt like wax in the flame
So that you will gain your difficult goal.

It should not be supposed that this is the earliest instance of Islamic writing in Malay. The technical skill in which religious ideas are handled in his quotations suggests that he represents a culminating point in a long tradition.

Shams al-Dīn. The next figure to emerge is Shams al-Dīn, the guide and teacher of Iskandar Muda, sultan of Aceh from 1607 to 1636. Shams al-Dīn reflects a tradition from North India, in which the system of emanations so characteristic of the Ibn al-ʿArabī tradition was reduced to a convenient seven, and this framework, which was rapidly adopted by the Naqshbandī, Shādhilī and Shaṭṭārī orders, soon became part of the stock-in-trade of the mystical tradition in all parts of the archipelago. An important figure of state, Shams al-Dīn was the author of a significant corpus of writings in both Arabic and Malay. The single most important work that he used as the basis for his teaching was a summary of the key ideas of Ibn al-ʿArabī's system set out in a framework of seven grades of being ranging between the Absolute and the Perfect Human Being. This system appears to have been inaugurated by development of a North Indian tradition of Islam that replaced the tradition of al-Jīlī.

This tradition of scholarly works on Islam written in Arabic has continued even up to the present. Many such works are minor tracts devoted to issues that became shibboleths, for example, whether the commencement of the fasting month was to be decided by the sighting of the moon or by calculation, or whether the formulation of intention before beginning a ritual prayer should be made aloud or mentally. Such material has only a local and historical importance. Occasionally, however, a substantial work appears and wins an established position. One such text was *Marāḥ labīd* (Rich Pasture), a two-volume Qur'ān commentary of about one thousand pages by a scholar from Banten, on the north coast of West Java, Muḥammad Nawawī al-Jāwī. He was born in 1815, went to study in the Muslim Holy Land in 1830, and died early in the twentieth century. Published in Cairo by the well-known firm of Ḥalabī in 1887, *Marāḥ labīd* is still available in the Middle East and remains very popular as an intermediate-level work in religious schools in many regions of Malaysia and Indonesia. The Arabic style, it may be remarked, is fluent and lucid, and among the author's acknowledged sources, Fakhr al-Dīn al-Rāzī's *Mafātīḥ al-ghayb* has an important position. It is also worth drawing attention to a large (thousand-page) commentary on al-Ghazālī's *Minhāj al-ʿābidīn ilā jannat rabb al-ʿālamīn* by an East Javanese scholar from the region of Kediri, which was recently republished in Surabaya. In addition to these major works, there are hundreds of minor ones issuing from Arabic printing presses scattered over Sumatra, Java, the Malay Peninsula, and Borneo, where both private and public schools have also been established.

ʿAbd al-Raʾūf. By the second half of the seventeenth century, ʿAbd al-Raʾūf (1615–1690) had prepared a full rendering of the Jalālayn *tafsīr* in Malay. It was extended by one of his students, Dāwūd al-Rūmī, by selections from the *qirāʾāt* literature and citations from the *tafsīrs* of al-Khāzin and al-Bayḍāwī. It is still reprinted with the cover title *Tafsīr al-Bayḍāwī.* The translation of this work into Malay means in effect that there was also a complete rendering of the Qur'ān in Malay before the end of the seventeenth century.

In addition to these works, others written in Malay include, for example, simple summaries of the Muslim creed, such as al-Sanūsī's *Umm al-barāhīn* (Mother of Proofs), and hundreds of works on topics such as the mystical practice of various *ṭarīqah*s (the Naqshbandīyah, Shaṭṭārīyah, and Shādhilīyah in particular), the twenty attributes of God, *tawḥīd* (the unity of God), the application of Islamic law on various topics, and eschatology. One example is a four-volume abridgement of al-Ghazālī's *Iḥyā' 'ulūm al-dīn* (The Revivification of the Religious Sciences) by an expatriate scholar, 'Abd al-Ṣamad of Palembang, who compiled it around 1780 in Ṭā'if, Arabia. It is still reprinted in various parts of Malaysia and Indonesia, and although there are now more academically prepared translations of the work in Malay published in the Roman script, they have not yet supplanted the earlier version.

The process of development from an understanding and explication of traditional texts to the preparation of original ones developed to meet local needs was slow and has not yet attained a commanding stature in this part of the Islamic world; this is largely due, no doubt, to the dominance of the oral tradition in the transmission of knowledge. From this standpoint, there is no comparison between the intellectual achievements of Southeast Asia and those to be found in Turkish, Persian, or Arabic language areas. This is only to say, however, that the achievements of Southeast Asia are of a different character—as in fact is also the case with India and sub-Saharan Africa—particularly when one considers how different the human ecology of monsoon Southeast Asia is from that of the Middle East, and how wide was the range of traditions and forms of social organization that had their home there.

Historiography. The Arabo-Muslim tradition also contributed to the development of a historiography in Malay. Certainly there is an influence of both Arabic and Persian historiography on the writing of Malay court chronicles. Such works were given an Arabic flavor by the use of words derived from Arabic, such as *sejarah* (Arab., *shajara*[*t al-nasab*]), meaning family line, chronicle, or history, and *silsilah,* or lineage, in the titles to indicate a genealogy or succession of rulers. The Malay chronicle of the kingdom of Malacca that purports to give an account of the antecedents and genealogy of the Malaccan sultanate (1400–1511), for example, is known as the *Sejarah Melayu.* Although popularly known in English as *The Malay Annals,* the title really means a genealogy of the Malays, who are in this case the Malay rulers of Malacca. The work, it may be noted, although it spans a century and the careers of rulers, has no dates, and its division into chapters may be a result of Persian influence.

There are numerous histories of the Malay states of the peninsula; despite Arabic words in their titles, however, they are more representative of the Malay folk tradition than of Arabic historiography. In fact, up to the late nineteenth century only in a few cases did works of this kind develop with the concern for date and fact that characterizes Muslim historiography as a whole. One such example is found in the historical writings of Nūr al-Dīn al-Rānīrī, an itinerant scholar of Gujarati origin (thus illustrating the continuing role of expatriate *'ulamā'* in the religious life of the region). Although only in Aceh between 1637 and 1642, he wrote copiously in Malay and compiled a universal history, including a book on the history of Aceh up to this day, but also contributed vigorously to polemics between adherents of different schools of Ṣūfī theosophy during this period. Another example is the *Tuhfat al-nafīs* by Raja Haji Ali of Riau, written in the wake of an Islamic revival toward the end of the nineteenth century.

Literature. Works more literary in character, although based on figures of the prophets, of people around the prophet, and of the heroes of Islam, likewise are known from the seventeenth century. The early stories that have been discovered include Malay renderings of the story of Joseph and Potiphar's wife, possibly from a Persian source that was copied in 1604, and alongside it versions of the story of Iskandar Dhū al-Qarnayn (Alexander the Great) and other stories of the prophets of Islam. The 1612 rescension of *The Malay Annals* opens with a version of the story of Alexander's invasion of India and presents him as the ultimate ancestor of the Malacca dynasty. Thus the story was well known, and the name was popular. Iskandar, it may also be remarked, was the name of the greatest ruler of Aceh (Iskandar Muda, r. 1607–1636).

Other stories that became popular from this period centered on the Prophet's uncle Amīr Ḥamzah and the Shīʿī hero Muḥammad ibn al-Ḥanafīyah. *The Malay Annals* suggests that versions of these stories were preserved in the Malacca library and as of 1511 were held in great esteem. The reference to them may be apocryphal: it indicates that they were to be recited to the Malaccan soldiers to give them courage for battle against the Portuguese on the following day, a battle that was to end in the Portuguese occupation of Malacca. Nevertheless, their symbolic role was well known at the time that the 1612 rescension of *The Malay Annals* was compiled. Equally important, the popularity of such works suggests at least the presence of a Shīʿī flavor to Islam in Aceh during this period. Shīʿī or not, there is certainly a strong Persian flavor in the literary works that were rendered into Malay, the most outstanding of which at this early period is a version of the *Ṭūṭī-nāmah* (Book of the Parrot) known in Malay as *Hikayat bayan budiman* (Story of the Wise Parrot).

Popular Storytelling. At the same time, a whole complex of the storytelling tradition of Islam has found its way into Malay and Javanese. Such stories derive more from the popular than the belletristic traditions, and more has come via the Indian subcontinent than directly from the Arab Middle East, although even here the distinction is not absolute. Arabic works have been recopied in India and transmitted, or passed through, a variety of Indian languages into the languages of the Indonesian archipelago.

It must be remembered that stories about the heroes of Islam, while having a role as religious instruction, were equally important as entertainment and became widely popular. As a result, these heroes became part of community education for all levels of society and all ages, and thus, by allowing popular audiences to share in the experience of other communities of these heroes, they served to create a general pan-Islamic consciousness. Manuscript catalogues include numerous copies of stories of Muḥammad ibn al-Ḥanafīyah and Amīr Ḥamzah; there are collections of stories of the prophets and tales of the individual prophets including Adam, Abraham, Noah, and Moses. In Java, the story of Joseph was especially popular.

To these, however, should be added stories quite divorced from these religious figures, but which derive from Islamic sources and which have an Islamic ethos. These include many tales that appear in collections such as *The 1,001 Nights,* and classics such as the *Tūṭī-nāmah* referred to earlier. Among other collections of stories are the *Kalīlah and Dimnah,* which was known as early as 1736, and the *Bakhtiyār-nāmah* (Book of Bakhtiyār), a kind of reversal of the *1,001 Nights* that is a grand story of a young prince who is accused by ten viziers of having an affair with a chambermaid, but who postpones his execution by telling stories until the truth is discovered. This theme, it may be noted, was famous in Persian and Turkish popular literature, as well as in medieval Latin.

How these tales were first rendered into Malay is not known: they may have been carried by the oral tradition and set down in writing by court scribes, according to established literary conventions, to be recited on royal occasions, or there may have been some kind of committee composed of reader, oral translator, and scribe. It is certain, however, that such stories were preserved in court libraries, that access to them was restricted to senior court officials, and that the sultan had the authority to declare which might be read.

This composite Islamic tradition, whether formed directly from Arabic sources or mediated through Indian vernaculars, remains popular throughout Muslim Southeast Asia in numerous retellings, adaptations, and even dramatizations. In West Java, a cycle of Amīr Ḥamzah stories has become part of the repertory of the puppet theater. Evidence of this past and present popularity, apart from observation, can be gleaned from the catalogues of Malay, Javanese, and Sundanese manuscripts, to mention only a few.

In view of this rich complex of traditions and wide popularity, it is striking that although some members of the Muslim educated elite pioneered the use of Malay in either its Malaysian or its Indonesian form, the greater part of the modern literary achievement has been produced by authors secular in orientation and secular in subject matter and theme.

Recent Times

With the proclamation of Indonesian independence on 17 August 1945, two days after the Japanese surrender, and with the transfer of sovereignty by the Dutch in 1950, Muslim groups exerted considerable pressure to have Indonesia declared an Islamic state, with the provisions of Muslims law binding on Muslims.

It was only after long and bitter debates between religious factions and the secular nationalists in the few months prior to the Japanese surrender that a compromise was reached, and the Pancasila ("five pillars"), a set of five principles devised largely by Sukarno, first president of the republic, were with certain qualifications accepted as the basis of the new state. Since the first of these principles was belief in one God, this formula made Indonesia a nonconfessional state without making it a secular one. A corollary of this charter was the establishment of a ministry of religion early in the republic's history. This ministry was to take care of the needs and interests of every religious community in the country (although later there were to be difficulties as to the terms under which the Hindu Balinese and the Javanese mystical groups might be included within its terms of reference).

RELIGIOUS REVOLTS

The compromise, however, did not last long. After the proclamation of independence, the secular nationalists dropped the references to the position of Islam in the state agreed to in it. For the hard-line Muslims, this was a confirmation of their worst fears. The disillusion and bitterness generated on the Muslim side led to three major risings against the republican government. The first and most dangerous broke out before independence from the Dutch had been secured. After several months of guerrilla activity, Kartosuwirjo (1923–1962), a former medical student, proclaimed the establishment of the Islamic state of Indonesia on 7 August 1949 in the mountainous regions of West Java and was inaugurated as imam of the state. He and his movement conducted a guerrilla war, the Darul Islam revolt, against the government until 1962, when Kartosuwirjo was captured, and he and five of his associates were executed. The movement, while at first idealistic and attracting at least tacit support among some members of the Muslim political parties, gradually degenerated into a terrorist group that caused great human and material damage over West Java for more than ten years. It plundered and destroyed farms and peasant holdings to get financial resources and was behind several attempts to assassinate President Sukarno.

Two other major religious revolts inspired by the ideal of making Indonesia an Islamic state and realizing in it a *dār al-Islām* (Arab., "abode of Islam"; Indon., *darul Islam*) were to break out. One was on the island of Sulawesi in 1952, with the leader of the movement, Kahar Muzakkar, accepting a commission from Kartosuwirjo in West Java as commander of the fourth division of the Islamic army of Indonesia. With varying levels of success he managed to maintain his movementuntil early 1965, when he was encircled and shot by republican forces. The other revolt, in late 1953, was led by Daud Beureu'eh in Aceh, a region already referred to on several occasions for the strength of its Islamic traditions. This rising too was associated with the West Javanese movement. Daud Beureu'eh proclaimed an Islamic state of Aceh and styled himself "Commander of the Faithful" (Amīr al-Mu'minīn, the historic title of the Muslim caliphs), but after nine years of struggle he made his peace with the central government in 1962. The details of these struggles belong more to political history than to that of Islam. It is important to observe, however, that these three very serious uprisings, costly in human lives and property, were put down by Muslim soldiers under a Muslim president of a national state based on an ideology, the Pancasila, that did not recognize exclusive claims on the part of any one religious tradition.

OPPOSITION POLITICS

On a predominantly political level, the years between 1950 and 1965 saw continued but decreasingly successful efforts by the Muslim parties to gain by political means the power required to make Indonesia an Islamic state. However they were never sufficiently strong to outnumber or wily enough to outmaneuver the alliance between the "secular" nationalists and the radical left-wing parties. In the last resort they could claim loyalty to the Indonesian state by recognizing the Pancasila as the state ideology. And this they did by claiming that only Muslims could supply an adequate content to its first principle: belief in one God.

The elimination of Sukarno as a political force in 1965 in the wake of an attempted communist coup, and the destruction of the Communist Party, led to a revival of

Muslim expectations of a positive Islamic stance in government. These expectations were again disappointed, although Muslim mass action succeeded in blocking a proposed civil marriage law in 1973.

By the last quarter of the twentieth century, the Muslim parties, although under secular names, had assumed the role of a political opposition to what was essentially a secular government and offered the only form of organized dissent. If in the 1950s the Islamic parties set as their goal the ideal of Indonesia as an Islamic state, their role was now to demand social and economic justice and to protest against corruption in government, against secularism, consumerism, and an open economy.

It should be stressed, however, that far from a majority of Indonesian Muslims support Islamic political movements. The majority live and work within the status quo, Javanese dominated though it is, and with Islamic norms of behavior and forms of worship tacitly accepted as the majority cultural religious tradition ofthe nation in much the same way as the Church of England fulfills such a role in Britain, although, let it be stressed, Islam is a majority, not an established, religion.

This however is not the whole story. There are systems of Islamic education alongside the government system, and there are state institutes of Islamic training designed to produce graduates in Islamic law, education, and preaching. There is a large number of smaller institutions that teach in Arabic and graduate hundreds of students who travel overseas for higher learning; sometimes these students attend secular institutes in Australia, Britain, and Canada, for example, but of course they go more often to religious ones in India, Pakistan, Saudi Arabia, and Egypt. Indeed, students from Indonesia and Malaysia have a very high profile at al-Azhar in Cairo, and at the celebration of the millennium of al-Azhar in April 1983, Southeast Asian students were the most prominent community of foreigners studying at the institution, as indeed they are on the pilgrimage to Mecca. Nevertheless, the diffusion of graduates of these institutions is uneven, and there is a significant number of Muslim thinkers who have developed an intellectual interest in the role of religion in the modern world, outside of the traditional Islamic disciplines of *fiqh* and *kalām*, some under the influence of the minority Lahore Aḥmadīyah, who have a small presence in Indonesia.

THE CONTINUUM OF ISLAMIC EXPERIENCE

There is therefore a great variety of intensity in the profession of Islam. To the superficial observer, many of the Javanese peasantry, for example, might not appear to be Muslims at all. Yet relatively few claim exclusive allegiance either to Buddhism, which is enjoying a revival, or to the mystical sects. For the great majority, what perception they have of transcendence is of Islamic transcendence. Even if this is the limit of their commitment, it is sufficient for them to be identified as Muslims. At the opposite extreme are groups of radical Muslims inspired by the ideals of Hasan al-Bannā', founder of the Ikhwān al-Muslimūn, or Muslim Brotherhood, and of Mawdūdī of Pakistan, or even by the Egyptian Takfīr wa-al-Hijrah ("denounce and abandon") groups. Despite internal differences, principally regarding tactics and strategy, they understand Islam as a revealed total way of life, with absolute demands. They reject the four schools of law and accept as their authorities the Qur'ān and *sunnah* alone. Theirs is a view that rejects the tradition of scholars who accept the authority of the four schools of law and the role of case law, precedent, and analogy.

Yet the divisions are not clear cut, and one has to do with a continuum rather than sharp discontinuities. For the ordinary members of the Muslim community, moreover, these issues do not arise. Community practice is as rhythmic as the act of breathing, whether the community places a high value on external observances such as the fast and the ritual prayer or a low one, and whatever the regional observances it chooses to decorate and enhance its Islamic practice. One cannot overstress, however, that for many, Islam is a matter of personal devotion, morality, marriage, divorce, and to an uncertain degree, depending on the region, inheritance.

The situation in Malaysia is complicated by the racial composition of the country. To be a Malay is to be a Muslim, and Islam is the means by which the Malays assert their identity and their rights against other races, the Chinese in particular; thus the danger of a kind of religious fascism is not altogether absent. There have been waves of Islamic enthusiasm since the early 1970s, and there is considerable pressure to islamize the government of the country. This has taken the form of moves to introduce Islamic banking; promulgation of rules for social behavior, especially in the form of *khalwat* laws, which prohibit situations of "suspicious proximity" between the sexes; and the imposition of conditions on the handling and selling of pork that virtually ban it from the menus of international hotels.

The government's response to these and various other pressures has been measured. To take the initiative away from extremists, it has committed itself to a policy of islamization, which, it explains, is directed exclusively toward making Muslims better Muslims. There are differences of opinion, however, on the degree to which non-Muslims should be made subject to the norms of an Islamic ethos. A minor crisis developed in the northern Borneo state of Sabah in 1985 because of the election of a Dyak Christian as chief minister.

Certainly during this period observers have noted a marked increase in religious fervor. This is particularly evident in the university campuses and among civil servants: it is reflected in the observance of daily prayers and the fast, in the numbers of Muslims making the pilgrimage to Mecca, and in women's dress. In addition, various religious associations have sprung up, all dedicated to spreading Islamic teachings, but with different emphases. Some have been infiltrated by Iranian or Libyan elements; others find their inspiration in Mawdūdī. One of particular interest is the Dār al-Arqam, an association that is establishing self-sufficient commune-type communities to which individuals and their families, often from the professional classes, can withdraw on a short- or long-term basis; there they are to live a life totally in accord with the *sunnah* of the Prophet and away from the distractions of the imperfect world, which, it is believed, will gradually learn from the fruit of their example.

To the superficial observer, there is little outward evidence of Southeast Asia's widespread Islamic allegiance. There is none of the exuberant architecture that so characterizes Muslim civilization in South and West Asia. Traditional forms of music and the dance, styles of dress, social structures, systems of inheritance, and personal and family law all suggest a complex of cultures that owes little to Islam. Observers coming from the Middle East, taking as a norm outward manifestations of Islam in the Arab world, where so much that was local custom at the time of the Prophet is now inseparable from the Islamic tradition, may be perplexed at the variety and distinctiveness of Southeast Asian Islam. They may even regard much of what they see as non-Islamic, forgetting that at one time much even in Middle Eastern Islam was non-Islamic.

Nevertheless, it has been shown that virtually every movement in the Islamic world and every emphasis and school has found a counterpart in Southeast Asia, and that there is a long tradition of expatriate local *'ulamā'* settling in the Middle East, either permanently or on a long-term basis, as well as a tradition of *'ulamā'* from the Middle East and South Asia becoming domiciled in Southeast Asia. Indeed, in the region today there is a strength and vitality in Islamic life expressed in a wide range of religious perceptions and enthusiasms both at individual and community levels. The potential is negative as well as positive. Either way, in the fifteenth century of the Hijrah, Islam in Southeast Asia can no longer be ignored, whether in the heartlands of Islam, where it still has an impact to make, or in the West.

[*For other perspectives on Islam in Southeast Asia, see* Javanese Religion *and* Southeast Asian Religions, *article on* Insular Cultures.]

BIBLIOGRAPHY

No single classic work on Islam in Southeast Asia exists, unfortunately. What follows should serve as a guide to the general reader and not as an exhaustive list. For the historical context within which Islam plays its various roles in Southeast Asia, John Sturgus Bastin and Harry J. Benda's exquisitely written and lucid *A History of Modern Southeast Asia: Colonialism, Nationalism, and Decolonization* (Englewood Cliffs, N.J., 1968) makes sense of the region as a whole, from Burma to the Philippines. D. G. E. Hall's *A History of South-East Asia,* 4th ed. (London, 1981), is still the basic work for a historical survey of Southeast Asia as a whole from the earliest times up to 1950. A very useful source book is *Readings on Islam in Southeast Asia,* edited by Ahmad Ibrahim (Singapore, 1985). See also Barbara Andaya and Leonard Andaya's *A History of Malaysia* (London, 1982) and M. C. Ricklefs's *A History of Modern Indonesia, c. 1300 to the Present* (Bloomington, Ind., 1981).

The Modern Period. C. van Dijk's *Rebellion under the Banner of Islam: The Darul Islam in Indonesia* (The Hague, 1981) is an admirably lucid analysis of revolts against the republican government in Indonesia between 1950 and 1965 directed toward the transformation of the nation into an Islamic state. Clifford Geertz's *The Religion of Java* (Chicago, 1976) is a masterpiece of sensitive ethnographic description, despite its somewhat mechanistic division of Javanese society into Santri (Muslim), *abangan* (peasant), and Prijayi (aristocratic bureaucrat), and its lack of depth in understanding the historical context of Javanese religion. Peter G. Gowing's *Muslim Filipinos: Heritage and Horizon* (Quezon City, Philippines, 1979), an excellent survey of the Muslim communities in the Philippines from the earliest days up to the 1970s, has a particularly useful bibliography. *The Crescent in the East: Islam in Asia Major,* edited by Raphael Israeli (London, 1982), includes chapters on Islam in Burma, Malaysia, Thailand, Indonesia, and the Philippines. *Islam in Public Life,* edited by John L. Esposito (New York, 1986), includes chapters on Islam in public life in Malaysia and Indonesia that give a reasonable account of the state of play in each nation. See also B. J. Boland's *The Struggle of Islam in Modern Indonesia* (The Hague, 1982); G. W. J. Drewes's "Indonesia: Mysticism and Activism," in *Unity and Variety in Muslim Civilization,* edited by Gustave E. von Grunebaum (Chicago, 1955), pp. 284–310; my "An Islamic System or Islamic Values?: Nucleus of a Debate in Contemporary Indonesia," in *Islam and the Political Economy of Meaning: Comparative Studies in*

Muslim Discourse, edited by W. R. Roff (Berkeley, 1986); and Astri Suhrke's "The Thai Muslims: Some Aspects of Minority Integration," *Pacific Affairs* 43 (Winter 1970–1971): 531–547.

Specialized Studies. S. Q. Fatimi's *Islam Comes to Malaysia* (Singapore, 1963) is a short, provocative, but delightfully written book that elaborates a role attributed to Ṣūfīs in the preaching of Islam in Southeast Asia, with a particularly interesting analysis of the inscribed pillar discovered at Phanrang. *Islam in South-East Asia,* edited by M. B. Hooker (Leiden, 1983), a collection of seven essays that add up to a fresh and vigorous approach to Islam in Southeast Asia, brings together perspectives derived from studies in ethnography, Islamic philosophy and law, and literature. Christiaan Snouck Hurgronje's *The Achehnese,* 2 vols., translated by A. W. S. O'Sullivan (Leiden, 1906), is a classic work of description of what from many aspects is the single most important Muslim community in Southeast Asia. *Islam in Asia,* vol. 2, *Southeast and East Asia,* edited by Raphael Israeli and myself (Boulder, 1984), includes such topics as a sociological analysis of islamization in Java,Qur'anic exegesis in Malaysia and Indonesia, and the reciprocal relationships between Islamic Southeast Asia and the heartlands of Islam. Clive S. Kessler's *Islam and Politics in a Malay State: Kelantan 1838–1969* (Ithaca, N.Y., 1978) is an excellent microstudy of a small town in a Malay state that has wide implications for all Malaysia. *Conversion to Islam,* edited by Nehemia Levtzion (New York, 1979), is a very useful collection of essays providing a foundation for a comparative study of conversion to Islam. *Kelantan: Religion, Society, and Politics in a Malay State,* edited by W. R. Roff (Kuala Lumpur, 1974), is a most useful collection of material on Islamic life and movements in Kelantan that also presents a convincing paradigm for other regions. See also Muhammed Abdul Jabbar Beg's *Arabic Loan-Words in Malay: A Comparative Study* (Kuala Lumpur, 1982); C. C. Berg's "The Islamisation of Java," *Studia Islamica* 4 (1955): 11–142; Christine E. Dobbin's *Islamic Revivalism in a Changing Peasant Economy: Central Sumatra, 1784–1847* (London, 1983); my "Islam in Southeast Asia: Reflections on New Directions," *Indonesia,* no. 19 (April 1975): 33–55; and Deliar Noer's *The Modernist Muslim Movement in Indonesia, 1900–1942* (Singapore, 1973).

Literature. For an introduction to Islamic writing in the regional vernaculars, C. C. Brown's *Sĕjarah Mĕlayu; or, Malay Annals* (Kuala Lumpur, 1970) is a somewhat mannered but readable translation of the 1612 rescension of the *Sejarah Melayu.* G. W. J. Drewes's *The Admonitions of Seh Bari* (The Hague, 1969) is an edition and translation of a manuscript of a Javanese Primbon (student notebook) brought back to Europe around 1598; his *Directions for Travellers on the Mystic Path* (The Hague, 1977) includes a very valuable index and bibliography. Richard Winstedt's *A History of Classical Malay Literature* (Kuala Lumpur, 1969) is a difficult book, but worthy of sympathetic, careful study. See especially those chapters dealing with Muslim legends, cycles of tales from Muslim sources, and Islamic theology, jurisprudence, and history. See also L. F. Brakel's *The Hikayat Muhammad Hanafiyyah* (The Hague, 1975).

TWO

INNER ASIA AND TIBET

8 THE RELIGIONS OF TIBET

PER KVAERNE

To the Western mind, Tibet has traditionally appeared as a remote yet uniquely fascinating country. Profoundly Buddhist in all aspects of its social, cultural, and religious life, it was, until 1959, dominated by a monastic hierarchy. In the imagination of some, the so-called Land of Snow (as the Tibetans style their country) has also been regarded as the home of mysterious, superhuman beings, *mahatmas*, who, from their secret abodes in the Himalayas, give mystic guidance to the rest of humanity.

As sources become more abundant, a more realistic and complex view of Tibetan history and religion is gaining ground. The following points, which make this clear, should be kept in mind.

First, Buddhism in Tibet is represented by several traditions, monastic "orders," or schools, which have certain basic traits in common but also differ in significant respects. This must be taken into account when working with written sources, since traditional Tibetan historiography (which invariably is religious historiography) tends to reflect the more or less partisan views of the authors.

Second, Buddhism is not the only religion that must be taken into account. Buddhism penetrated into Tibet relatively late—perhaps not before the eighth century CE—and only gradually succeeded in supplanting a well-established indigenous religion that is still only fragmentarily known. Furthermore, from the tenth or eleventh century onward, the various Buddhist orders have existed alongside a religion known as Bon, which, while claiming, certainly not without some justification, continuity with the pre-Buddhist religion, is nevertheless almost indistinguishable from Buddhism in many respects. Bon has retained its own identity to this day. In addition, there remains a vast area of rites and beliefs that are neither specifically Buddhist nor Bon but may be styled "popular religion" or "the religion without a name." There is also a small minority of Tibetan Muslims (who will, however, not be treated in this article).

Third, it should be recognized that *Tibet* is a somewhat ambiguous term. In the present context it can only be used in a meaningful way to refer to an ethnically defined area—including parts of India and Nepal—that shares a common culture and language, common religious traditions, and, to a large extent, a common history.

The so-called Tibetan Autonomous Region of China only comprises the western and central parts of Tibet, including the capital, Lhasa. The vast expanses of eastern and northeastern Tibet (Kham and Amdo) have since the 1950s been incorporated into China proper, but are ethnically and historically entirely Tibetan. Beyond Tibet (thus defined), Tibetan Buddhism is the official religion of Bhutan; until the early years of the twentieth century it reigned supreme in Mongolia; and it is still found among the Buriats and Tuvin in the Soviet Union. Its recent spread in the West will be discussed at the end of this article.

The term *Lamaism* is frequently used to refer to Tibetan religion. Tibetans often object to this term, as it could be taken to imply that Buddhism in Tibet is somehow basically different from Buddhism in other parts of Asia. To the extent that the term *Lamaism* points to the important role of the lama (Tib., *bla ma*), or religious guide and expert in Tibetan religion, it can be said to refer equally to Buddhism and Bon, and thus it retains a certain usefulness. However, as a term intended to describe Tibetan religion as a whole, it remains one-sided and hence misleading.

THE PRE-BUDDHIST RELIGION

When Buddhism was introduced into Tibet in the eighth century, it did not enter a religious vacuum. At present, however, it is not possible to arrive at an adequate understanding of the pre-Buddhist religion because of the incompleteness of the sources.

These sources fall into two categories: ancient and later. Ancient sources are those that predate the collapse of the royal dynasty in the middle of the ninth century. Archaeological sources are practically nonexistent, since only sporadic excavations have been undertaken to date. The royal tombs at 'Phyoṅ-rgyas in central Tibet are still prominently visible but were plundered at an early date. The vast majority of the written sources are later than the introduction of Buddhism and thus often show traces of syncretic beliefs. These sources include inscriptions on pillars and bells, manuscripts containing fragments of rituals and myths or of divinatory practices, Buddhist texts that refute the ancient religion, and Chinese chronicles from the T'ang dynasty (618–907). The language of these Tibetan texts, however, is archaic and all too often obscure, and the manuscripts themselves are not infrequently in a fragmentary condition.

The later sources date from the twelfth century onward and are found mainly in the historical writings of Buddhism and the Bon religion, which, between them, had by this time been completely successful in an institutional sense at least in replacing the ancient religion. Many indigenous beliefs and practices have persisted until today in the popular, nonmonastic religion, but as they are usually closely intermixed with elements of Buddhism (or, as the case may be, with Bon), it is an exceptionally delicate task to use folk religion as a basis for reconstructing the pre-Buddhist religion.

Thus the picture of pre-Buddhist religion that emerges on the basis of the ancient sources is, unfortunately, fragmentary. Certain rituals, beliefs, and parts of myths may be discerned, but the overall feeling of coherency is lacking. Those elements that are known focus largely on the person of the king. It is safe to assert that the Tibetans, at least from the sixth century onward, if not earlier, had a sacral kingship. The welfare of the country depended on the welfare of the king. Accordingly, rites of divination and sacrifice were performed to protect his life, guarantee his victory in battle, and ensure his supremacy in all things. It is said in the ancient sources that "his helmet is mighty" and his rule "great, firm, supreme," and "eternal." The king "does not change"; he is endowed with "long life."

The king was regarded not only as a vitally important personage but above all as a sacred being. According to a frequently encountered myth, the first king of Tibet descended from heaven ("the sky") and alighted on the summit of a mountain (according to later sources, he made the descent by means of a supernatural rope or ladder). At the foot of the mountain he was received by his subjects. The earliest kings were believed to have ascended bodily to heaven by the same means, thus leaving no corpse behind. Furthermore, the king was assimilated to the sacred mountain itself, just as in later popular religion the distinction between a sacred mountain and the deity residing on it was often blurred.

The myth relates that when the seventh king was killed, funerary rites had to be performed for the first time. In fact, in historical times (i.e., from the sixth century CE onward) huge funerary mounds were erected, assimilated both to the sacred mountains and to the kings, the tombs being given names that consisted of the same elements as those found in the names of the kings themselves. The death of a king was surrounded by elaborate rituals: processions, sacrifices, and the depositing on a lavish scale of all sorts of precious objects in the burial chamber. The officiating priests were known generically as *bon pos*, but apparently there were numerous specialized subgroups. Animals were sacrificed: in particular, sheep, horses, and yaks. The sacrificial sheep seem to have had an important role as guides for the deceased along the difficult road leading to the land of the dead—a land apparently conceived of in terms analogous to that of the living. Servants and officials, perhaps also members of the family, were assigned to the dead king as his "companions"; it is uncertain, however, whether they, too, actually accompanied him to the grave, or, as certain later sources suggest, only lived within the precincts of the tomb for a specified period.

A surviving early text outlines an eschatological cosmology that embodies a cyclical view of time. In a "golden age" plants and animals are transposed from their celestial home to the earth for the benefit of humanity. Virtue and "good religion" reign supreme. However, a demon breaks loose from his subterranean abode and causes a general decline in morals as well as in the physical world. Those who nevertheless follow the path of virtue and honor the gods are led after death to a land of bliss. In the meantime, the world rapidly reaches a point at which everything is destroyed, whereupon a new golden age begins in which the virtuous dead are reborn. Thus the cycle presumably—the text is not explicit—repeats itself.

Little is known of the pantheon of the pre-Buddhist religion. The universe was conceived of as having three levels: the world above (the sky), inhabited by gods *(lha);* the middle world (the earth), the abode of human beings; and the world below (the subterranean world, conceived of as aquatic), inhabited by a class of beings known as *klu* (and later assimilated to the Indian *nāgas*). [*See also* Nāgas and Yakṣas.]

According to some sources, the heavenly world above had thirteen levels, inhabited by a hierarchy of male and female deities. Both Chinese sources and epigraphic evidence speak of the sun, the moon, and the stars being invoked as guardians and guarantors of treaties. Sacrifices in the form of various animals were made at the conclusion of the treaty of 822 between China and Tibet. By this time, however, Buddhism had appeared on the scene and the Three Jewels of Buddhism (i.e., Buddha, Dharma, and Sangha) were also invoked. A Buddhist monk with the rank of minister was at the head of the Tibetan delegation.

The subterranean beings, the *klu,* posed a constant danger to humanity, since they were particularly prone to be annoyed by activities that interfered with the surface of the land, such as plowing and digging. The *klu* could cause the eruption of diseases, especially leprosy and dropsy, that could only be cured through rites of atonement and propitiation. However, in determining the details of these rites and in obtaining specific information about the host of demons presumably populating the supernatural world of the ancient Tibetans we are to a large extent reduced to speculation on the basis of later, popular religious practices. Likewise, we meet with the names of various types of deities that are of great importance in later, popular religion: warrior god *(dgra bla),* god of the fireplace *(thab lha),* life god *(srog lha),* god of the land *(yul lha),* and so on.

It is difficult to establish which elements in the pre-Buddhist religion are truly indigenous. The later sources insist that many of the Bon-po priests came from countries bordering Tibet, in particular, areas to the west. After Buddhism had triumphed, the Tibetans themselves speculated whether the Bon-pos were Śaiva adepts from Kashmir. Possible influences emanating from the Iranian world have also been the subject of speculation by Western scholars, so far without conclusive evidence. On the other hand, the importance of the Chinese influence, long ignored, has now been firmly established. The royal tombs have obvious Chinese prototypes, as does the sacredness of the king: he is "god son" *(lha sras),* corresponding to the Chinese emperor, the "Son of Heaven"; he is "sacred and divine" *('phrul gyi lha),* corresponding to the Chinese *sheng-shen.* This sacredness is manifested in a supernormal intelligence and in the power to act, politically as well as militarily. [*See* Kingship, *article on* East Asian Kingship.]

It has been suggested that the pre-Buddhist religion was transformed into a coherent political ideology in the seventh century, modeled on the Chinese cult of the emperor. This royal religion was, according to this view, referred to as *gtsug* or *gtsug lag,* a word that was defined as "the law of the gods." However, the later sources, Buddhist and Bon-po, unanimously refer to the ancient religion as Bon, a claim that is supported by recent research. In any case, the cult of the divine kings disappeared together with the organized priesthood.

BUDDHISM

Buddhism was established in Tibet under royal patronage in the eighth century. In the preceding century, Tibet had become a unified state and embarked upon a policy of military conquest resulting in the brief appearance of a powerful Central Asian empire. The introduction of Buddhism was certainly due to the need to provide this empire with a religion that enjoyed high prestige because of its well-established status in the mighty neighboring countries of India and China. The first Buddhist temple was built at Bsam-yas (Samyé) in approximately 779; soon afterward the first monks were ordained. From the very start, the Buddhist monks were given economic and social privileges.

When Buddhism was introduced, the Tibetans had a choice as to whether the new religion should be brought from India or China. Modern scholarship has established the important role that China played as a source of Buddhism in the early stages of its history in Tibet. Nevertheless, it was the Indian form of Buddhism that eventually predominated. According to later sources, the Tibetan kings were guided by spiritual considerations and the proponents of Indian Buddhism emerged victorious from a doctrinal debate with Chinese monks representing a form of Ch'an Buddhism. However, hard political motives were surely equally important: in military and political terms China was Tibet's main rival, and Chinese influence at the Tibetan court would be unduly increased if it gained control of the powerful Buddhist hierarchy.

In any case, Tibet turned to India for its sacred texts, philosophical ideas, and rituals, in the same way as it had adopted, in the seventh century, an Indian alphabet. Once set on its course, Buddhism rapidly became the dominant religion, suffering only a temporary setback after the collapse of the royal dynasty in 842. In several important respects, Buddhism in Tibet remained faithful to its Indian prototype. It must, of course, be kept in mind that this prototype was, by the seventh and eighth centuries, a form of Mahāyāna Buddhism that was, on the one hand, increasingly dependent on large monastic institutions, and on the other, permeated by Tantric rites and ideas. Both these features—vast monasteries and a pervasive Tantric influence—have remained characteristic of Buddhism in Tibet. Similarly, there has been little development in the realm of philosophical ideas; the Tibetans have, on the whole, been content to play the role of exegetes, commentators, and compilers. However, the political domination that the monasteries gradually obtained was without precedent. A uniquely Tibetan feature of monastic rule was succession by incarnation—the head of an order, or of a monastery, being regarded as the reincarnation (motivated by compassion for all beings) of his predecessor. In other cases, a religious figure might be regarded as the manifestation of a deity (or a particular aspect of a deity). In the person of the fifth Dalai Lama (1617–1682) both ideas were combined. Each Dalai Lama was already regarded as the incarnation of his predecessor; the fifth, who established himself as head of the Tibetan state, also came to be regarded as the emanation or manifestation of the great *bodhisattva* Avalokiteś-vara (Tib., Spyan-ras-gzigs), as have all subsequent Dalai Lamas down to the present, the fourteenth. [*See also* Dalai Lama *and* Avalokitśvara.]

The choice of Avalokiteśvara was not made at random. As early as the twelfth or thirteenth century, Avalokiteśvara had come to be regarded in a double respect as the divine protector of Tibet. In the form of an ape he had, in ancient times, assumed the role of progenitor of the Tibetan people in order that the teachings of the Buddha might flourish in Tibet in due course; in the form of the great Tibetan king Sroṅ-btsan-sgam-po, who created the Tibetan empire in the seventh century, Avalokiteśvara had established Buddhism—according to this retrospective view—in the Land of Snow. The Potala Palace in Lhasa, the ancient capital, was built in its present form by the fifth Dalai Lama and made his residence; situated on a hill, it symbolically reestablished the pre-Buddhist connection between the divine king and the sacred mountain.

POPULAR RELIGION

It would be illusory to draw a sharp line of demarcation between popular and monastic religion. Nevertheless, while the study of the Mahāyāna philosophical systems and the performance of elaborate Tantric rites take place within the confines of the monasteries, monks actively participate in a wide range of ritual activities outside the monasteries, and beliefs that do not derive from Buddhism are shared by monks and laypeople alike.

These rites and beliefs may be styled "popular religion," a term that only signifies that it is nonmonastic, traditional, and related to the concerns of laypeople. It does not imply a system representing an alternative to Buddhism (or the Bon religion). For the last thousand years, Buddhist ideas have provided a general cosmological and metaphysical framework for popular religion. In many cases one may also assume that there is continuity with the pre-Buddhist religion, but it is often a delicate task to determine this continuity in precise terms.

Turning, first of all, to elements inspired by Buddhism, the most important—and conspicuous—are undoubtedly the varied and ceaseless efforts to accumulate merit. [*See* Merit, *article on* Buddhist Concepts.] The law of moral causality *(karman)* easily turns into a sort of balance in which the effect of evil deeds in this life or in former lives may be annulled by multiplying wholesome deeds. While an act of compassion, such as ransoming a sheep destined to be slaughtered, theoretically constitutes the ideal act of virtue, the accumulation of merit generally takes a more mechanical form. Hence the incessant murmuring of sacred formulas (in particular the *mantra* of Avalokiteśvara, "Oṃ maṇi padme hūṃ"), the spinning of prayer wheels (ranging in size from hand-held wheels to enormous cylinders housed in special buildings), the carving of *mantra*s on stones (which may eventually grow into walls several miles in length, so-called *mani*-walls), and the hoisting of banners and strings of flags on which prayers are printed ("prayer flags"). Ritual circumambulation of holy places, objects, and persons is also a distinctly Buddhist, as well as truly popular, practice. Showing generosity toward monks and observing—lightly or scrupulously, as the case may be—the universal precepts of Buddhism (particularly the prohibition against taking the life of any living being, however small) are ethical norms that Tibetans share with all Buddhists. [*See also* Worship and Cultic Life, *article on* Buddhist Cultic Life in Tibet.]

Pilgrimages constitute an important religious activity: above all to the holy city of Lhasa—sanctified by its ancient temples and (since the seventeenth century) the presence of the Dalai Lama—but also to innumerable monasteries, shrines, and caves in which relics of holy men and women may be seen, honored, and worshiped. Sacred mountains, such as Mount Kailāśa in western Tibet, attract a stream of pilgrims who circumambulate, perhaps for weeks or months, the holy abode of the chosen deity. The supreme pilgrimage is the long journey to the sacred sites of Buddhism in India and Nepal (Bodh Gayā, Rājagṛha, Lumbinī, Sārnāth); although the flow of pilgrims to India virtually ceased after the thirteenth century, it has once more become possible in the twentieth century. [*See also* Pilgrimage, *article on* Tibetan Pilgrimage.]

Ritual practices, while generally having an overall Buddhist conceptual framework, often contain elements that point back to the pre-Buddhist religion. One such element, frequently met with, is the "ransom" *(glud)* in the form of a small human figurine that is offered as a gesture of propitiation to demons. In the New Year rituals as traditionally practiced in Lhasa, the *glud* was in fact a human scapegoat who was driven out of the city and who, in earlier times, was symbolically killed.

As in other Buddhist countries, regional and local deities have remained objects of worship, generally performed by laypeople. In particular, the deities connected with (or even identified with) sacred mountains, powerful gods of the land *(yul lha),* are worshiped during seasonal festivals with the burning of juniper branches that emit clouds of fragrant smoke; horse races; archery contests; drinking bouts; and songs extolling the might of the deity, the beauty of the land, the fleetness of its horses, and the valor of its heroes. These gods have a martial nature and are accordingly known as enemy gods *(dgra bla);* they are also known as kings *(rgyal po).* Usually they are depicted as mounted warriors, dressed in archaic mail and armor and wearing plumed helmets.

The house ideally reproduces the outside world, and it has its own guardian deities, such as the god of the fireplace *(thab lha).* Care must be taken to avoid polluting the fireplace in any way, as this angers the god. On the flat rooftops are altars dedicated to the "male god" *(pho lha)* and the "female god" *(mo lha)* and a banner representing the enemy god. The "male" and "female" gods are tutelary deities of the household, supervising the activities of its male and female members, respectively. The "enemy god" is —in spite of its name—a deity who protects the entire household or, as a member of the retinue of the local "god of the land," the district. The worship of these gods on the rooftops corresponds to that performed in their honor on mountaintops and in passes: spears and arrows dedicated to them are stacked by the altar and juniper twigs are burned amid fierce cries of victory and good luck.

The person, too, possesses a number of tutelary deities residing in different parts of the body. Every person is also accompanied, from the moment of birth, by a "white" god and a "black" demon whose task it is, after death, to place the white and the black pebbles—representing the good and evil deeds one has done in this life—on the scales of the judge of the dead. The basic opposition between "white" and "black," good and evil, is a fundamental concept in Tibetan popular religion and figures prominently in pre-Buddhist traditions as well. Iranian influences have been suggested, but it seems likely that the Chinese conceptual dichotomy of *yin* and *yang* lies closer at hand. [*See also* Yin-yang Wu-hsing.]

The ancient cosmological scheme of sky, earth, and underworld remains fundamental in popular religion. In particular, the cult of the *klu*—subterranean or aquatic beings easily irritated by activities such as house building or plowing, which provoke them to afflict people as well as animals with various diseases— remains widespread and provides a direct link to the pre-Buddhist religion.

An important aspect of popular religion (and, indeed, of the pre-Buddhist religion) is the emphasis on knowing the origins not only of the world but of all features of the landscape, as well as of elements of culture and society that are important to man. Tibetans have a vast number of myths centering on this theme of origins; while some of them have a purely narrative function, others serve to legitimate a particular ritual and must be recited in order that the ritual may become effective.

Rites of divination and of healing in which deities "descend" into a male or female medium (*lha pa,* "god-possessed," or *dpa' bo,* "hero") and speak through it are an important part of religious life, and such mediums are frequently consulted. Other, simpler means of divination are also extremely widespread.

A special kind of medium is the *sgruṅ pa,* the bard who in a state of trance can recite for days on end the exploits of the great hero Ge-sar. Regarded as an emanation of the *bodhisattva* Avalokiteśvara, Ge-sar has been approved by the Buddhist hierarchy; but essentially he is a popular, epic hero, a mighty king and warrior. His epic is a storehouse of myths, folklore, and pan-Eurasian narrative motifs, and is widespread outside Tibet in the Hindu Kush and, above all, among the Mongolians. [*See* Geser.] Other visionaries *('das log)* travel in trance to the Buddhist purgatories, their bodies lying as if dead; on awakening, they give detailed accounts of the punishment awaiting sinners beyond the grave. Still others find hidden "treasures" *(gter ma)* consisting of texts or sacred objects; indeed, this has remained until today an important way of adding to the body of authoritative texts translated from Sanskrit (and, to a lesser extent, from Chinese), for the "treasure-discoverers" *(gter ston)* claim to bring to light texts that have been hidden away (especially by the eighth-century Tantric master Padmasambhava) during times of persecution of Buddhism, to be rediscovered, usually with the assistance of supernatural beings, for the benefit of humanity when the time is ripe. Finally, ecstatics and visionaries point the way to earthly paradises such as the mythical kingdom of Shambhala or to hidden valleys, untouched by man, in the secret recesses of the Himalayas.

Summing up, Tibetan popular religion may perhaps be characterized as an infinitely varied attempt to circumvent, or at least mitigate, the mechanism of the law of moral causality. According to orthodox Buddhist doctrine, this law is inexorable and its justice cannot be avoided; however, since one cannot know what acts one has committed in the past for which one may have to suffer in the future, the intolerable rigor of the law of cause and effect is in practice modified by a religious worldview in which the destiny of the individual also depends on ritual acts and on spiritual beings—benevolent as well as malevolent—who may at least be approached and at best be manipulated.

BON

It has already been noted that a class of ritual experts in the pre-Buddhist religion were known as *bon-po*s and that certain early sources indicate that their religion was known as Bon. In any case, the later sources all agree that the pre-Buddhist religion was in fact known as Bon, and these sources tend to describe the struggle between Bon and Buddhism in dramatic terms. This is true not only of the later Buddhist sources but also of texts emanating from a religious tradition, explicitly styling itself Bon, that emerged in the eleventh century, if not before.

While virtually indistinguishable from Buddhism in such aspects as philosophy, monastic life, ritual, and iconographical conventions, this "later" Bon has always insisted that it represents the religion that prevailed in Tibet before the coming of Buddhism. In spite of occasional syncretic efforts on both sides, the Buddhists have tended to regard Bon as heretical, and not infrequently the term *bon-po* has been used in the sense of "heretic," "black magician," and so forth.

Two points about Bon must be made. First, the historical background of the Bon religion that emerged in the eleventh century is far from clear. There is a significant element of continuity with the pre-Buddhist religion, but nothing approaching identity. Second, it is seriously misleading to identify Bon with popular religion in general. On the level of popular religion, followers of Bon and Buddhism alike share the same beliefs and perform, to a very large extent, the same rituals, although details may differ (for example, the Bon-pos spin their prayer wheels and perform circumambulations in the opposite direction than the Buddhists do, i.e., counterclockwise; they worship different deities and hence use other *mantra*s, and so forth). These correspondences do not represent a case of "perversion," "contradiction," or the like (as has been too hastily suggested), for Bon and Buddhism share the same religious ideals and goals, and they approach them by essentially similar means.

TIBETAN RELIGION TODAY

An overview of Tibetan religion would be incomplete without an attempt to take stock of the situation in the mid-1980s. The most significant single fact is the downfall of monastic religion. Starting in the 1950s and culminating in the period of the Cultural Revolution in the 1960s and 1970s, the Chinese unleashed a violent antireligious campaign in Tibet that resulted in the total destruction of monastic life. A large number of monks were killed, and the rest were, without exception, defrocked. Most monasteries were razed to the ground, and others were converted into secular buildings such as granaries or army barracks. Vast libraries were destroyed, and ritual objects, Buddha images, and relics were systematically profaned. At the height of the campaign, even the most insignificant expression of religious faith would be severely punished by Chinese soldiers or Red Guards.

The new and more pragmatic policy in China began to take effect in Tibet around 1980. A number of buildings, officially regarded as historical monuments, have been carefully restored; a limited number of monks have been installed in a number of the largest monasteries: 'Bras-spuṅs (Drepung) near Lhasa, Bkra-śis-lhun-po (Tashilhunpo) outside Gźis-ka-rtse (Shigatse), and Bla-braṅ (Labrang) and Sku-'bum (Kumbum) in eastern Tibet; a few temples have been reopened for worship; and hundreds of other monasteries are being reconstructed on a voluntary basis by the Tibetans themselves. On the whole, religious activity seems to be tolerated as long as it does not interfere with economic policies. The 1980s have in fact seen a remarkable resurgence of religious fervor that finds outlet, among other things, in the reconstruction of monasteries and the traditional practices of the popular religion, including extended pilgrimages to sacred mountains and other sites throughout Tibet. Within the limits set by the political and economic conditions imposed on Tibet, it is clear that religious belief and practice remain a fundamental factor in the overall situation in the Land of Snow.

Among the Tibetan refugees in India and Nepal, religious life flourishes, to a large extent along traditional lines. There is a tendency to emphasize monastic life together with those aspects of Buddhism that are common to all Buddhists. In the West, a number of Tibetan lamas have become highly successful "gurus," and numerous Tibetan Buddhist centers have been established, generally focusing on the teachings of one particular order and emphasizing meditation and ritual rather than conventional, scholastic studies. In exile, the fourteenth Dalai Lama, Bstan-'dzin-rgya-mtsho (Tenzin Gyatsho; b. 1935), has become an internationally respected Buddhist figure, pointing out to a world in turmoil the Buddhist way to human happiness and world peace through the development of insight and compassion.

BIBLIOGRAPHY

Tibetan religion is a field in which quasi-esoteric literature abounds. However, there are also many works of serious scholarship available to the general reader. The following survey lists titles that are easily available.

General Studies. A classic and still useful introduction to the subject is Charles A. Bell's *The Religion of Tibet* (1931; reprint, Oxford, 1968). More recently, several excellent studies have been published: David L. Snellgrove and Hugh E. Richardson's *A Cultural History of Tibet* (1968; reprint, Boulder, 1980); Rolf A. Stein's *Tibetan Civilization,* translated by J. E. Stapleton Driver (Stanford, Calif., 1972) and republished in a revised French edition as *La civilisation tibétaine* (Paris, 1981); and Giuseppe Tucci's *The Religions of Tibet,* translated by Geoffrey Samuel (Berkeley, 1980). Tucci's monumental *Tibetan Painted Scrolls,* 2 vols., translated by Virginia Vacca (1949; reprint, Kyoto, 1980), remains a work of fundamental importance to the field. In the 1980 edition, the plates accompanying volume 2 are reproduced in the form of slides. A particularly lucid exposition is Anne-Marie Blondeau's "Les religions du Tibet," in *Histoire des religions,* edited by Henri-Charles Puech, vol. 3 (Paris, 1976), pp. 233–329.

Pre-Buddhist Religion. Most studies of the pre-Buddhist religion can be found only in specialized publications. The works of Snellgrove and Richardson, Stein, and Blondeau, however, all contain pertinent discussions based on their own research. The most recent study of the early inscriptions is H. E. Richardson's *A Corpus of Early Tibetan Inscriptions* (London, 1985).

Buddhism. Snellgrove and Richardson's work is particularly strong on the formation of the orders and the subsequent political history of the church. Tucci's *The Religions of Tibet* contains a most useful survey of Buddhist doctrine and monastic life. A concise presentation of Tibetan Buddhism is provided in Per Kvaerne's "Tibet: The Rise and Fall of a Monastic Tradition," in *The World of Buddhism: Buddhist Monks and Nuns in Society and Culture,* edited by Heinz Bechert and Richard F. Gombrich (London, 1984), pp. 253–270. For Tibetan art and symbols Tucci's *Tibetan Painted Scrolls* remains unsurpassed. A recent useful work by a Tibetan scholar is Loden S. Dagyab's *Tibetan Religious Art,* 2 vols. (Wiesbaden, 1977). For a discussion of ritual and meditation, see Stephan Beyer's *The Cult of Tārā: Magic and Ritual in Tibet* (Berkeley, 1973).

Popular Religion. General surveys of Tibetan popular religion are given by Stein in *Tibetan Civilization* and in Per Kvaerne's "Croyances populaires et folklores au Tibet" in *Mythes et croyances du monde entier,* edited by André Akoun, vol. 4 (Paris, 1985), pp. 157–169. A basic reference work is René de Nebesky-Wojkowitz's *Oracles and Demons of Tibet: The Cult and Iconography of the Tibetan Protective Deities* (1956; reprint, Graz, 1975). The reprint edition contains an introduction by Per Kvaerne in which numerous corrections and additions to the earlier edition are provided. A useful supplement to this work is Tadeusz Skorupski's *Tibetan Amulets* (Bangkok, 1983). A major study of ritual texts has been published by Christina Klaus, *Schutz vor den Naturgefahren: Tibetische Ritualtexte aus dem Rin chen gter mdzod ediert, Übersetzt und Kommentiert* (Wiesbaden, 1985). A discussion of Tibetan myths intended for the nonspecialist is provided by Per Kvaerne in a series of articles in *Dictionnaire des mythologies,* edited by Yves Bonnefoy (Paris, 1981), vol. 1, pp. 42–45, 249–252; vol. 2, pp. 194–195, 381–384, 495–497. A survey of the most important pilgrimages is provided in Anne-Marie Blondeau's "Les pèlerinages tibetains," in *Les pèlerinages,* edited by Anne-Marie Esnoul et al. (Paris, 1960), pp. 199–245. The most complete study of Tibetan festivals is Martin Brauen's *Feste in Ladakh* (Graz, 1980).

There is a considerable body of literature on the Ge-sar epic. The fundamental study is R. A. Stein's *L'épopée et le barde au Tibet* (Paris, 1959). Several translations of the text exist, mainly in the form of summaries. The most easily accessible is probably that of Alexandra David-Neel, *La vie surhumaine de Guésar de Ling* (Paris, 1931), translated with the collaboration of Violet Sydney as *The Superhuman Life of Gesar of Ling* (1933; rev. ed., London, 1959). More scholarly translations are R. A. Stein's *L'épopée tibétaine de Gesar dans la version lamaïque de Ling*

(Paris, 1956), and Mireille Helffer's *Les chants dans l'épopée tibétaine de Ge-sar d'après le levre de la course de cheval* (Geneva, 1977). On visionary journeys to Śambhala and related phenomena, see Edwin Bernbaum's *The Way to Shambhala: A Search for the Mythical Kingdom beyond the Himalayas* (New York, 1980).

Bon. An important translation of a Bon text is David L. Snellgrove's *The Nine Ways of Bon: Excerpts from the gZi-brjid* (1967; reprint, Boulder, 1980). Gamten G. Karmay surveys the Bon religion in "A General Introduction to the History and Doctrines of Bon," *Memoirs of the Research Department of the Tōyō Bunko,* no. 3 (1975): 171–218. On Bon literature, see Per Kvaerne's "The Canon of the Bonpos," *Indo-Iranian Journal* 16 (1975): 18–56, 96–144. See also the works of Snellgrove and Richardson, Stein, and Blondeau cited above.

Contemporary Religion. By far the best treatment of the subject is Peter H. Lehmann and Jay Ullai's *Tibet: Das stille Drama auf dem Dach der Erde,* edited by Rolf Winter (Hamburg, 1981). The book is remarkable not least for its photographic documentation of contemporary Tibet.

9 THE SCHOOLS OF TIBETAN BUDDHISM

David L. Snellgrove

The various sects or schools of Buddhism in Tibet are probably best referred to as "religious orders" in that most of them are in many ways analogous to Christian monastic orders in the West, namely Benedictines, Dominicans, and so forth. Thus, not only do they accept as fundamental the same Tibetan Buddhist canon (finally compiled in the thirteenth century and consisting almost entirely of works translated from Buddhist Sanskrit originals), but many of them were founded by outstanding men of religion, just as the various Christian orders were established, and so far as doctrine and religious practice is concerned there are no considerable differences between them. Conversely, the various sects or schools of Indian Buddhism were clearly distinguishable at two levels: first, they began to separate according to their various diverging versions of the traditional "monastic rule" (Vinaya), attributed by all of them to Śākyamuni Buddha himself; second, ever greater divergences developed from the early centuries CE onward as some communities adopted philosophical views and religious cults typical of the Mahāyāna, while other communities held to the earlier traditions.

Distinctions of these kinds do not exist in Tibetan Buddhism, since all Tibetan religious orders have accepted unquestioningly the monastic rule of one particular Indian Buddhist order, namely that of the Mūlasarvāstivādins, who happened to be particularly strong in Central Asia and in northern India, and it was in these circles that the Tibetans found their first Indian teachers. Moreover, the form of Buddhism which became established in Tibet represents Indian Buddhism in its late Mahāyāna and Vajrayāna form, with the result that the earlier sects, known collectively as Hīnayāna, have left no impression on Tibetan Buddhism and are known in Tibet only in a historical and doctrinal context. These considerations inevitably lent an overall unity to Tibetan Buddhism that was lacking in India. It follows, however, that such divergences as do exist between the various Tibetan orders are special to Tibet, being largely the result of the many historical vicissitudes which have conditioned the gradual introduction of Buddhism into Tibet—a long process which lasted from the seventh until the thirteenth century. Thus their differences, which from the Tibetan point of view may appear appreciable, can only be explained against a historical context. Moreover, having compared Buddhist religious orders with Christian ones, one must emphasize that whereas monastic orders are in a sense accidental to Christianity, which can operate quite well without them, monastic orders are fundamental to Buddhism in all its traditional forms. Once the monasteries have been destroyed or "laicized," it ceases to exist as a effective cultural and religious force.

Yet another distinction must be drawn, one which is important for an understanding of Tibetan religious life in general and which affects profoundly the relationships between one Tibetan religious order and another. The idea of a religious lineage, that is to say, of a particular religious tradition, usually involving special kinds of religious practice, which is passed in succession from master to pupil, is not altogether unknown in the West, but it is absolutely fundamental in Tibetan thought, and it is precisely this idea which gives coherence to their various religious orders and explains the many links which may exist between them. As distinct from a "lineage," which is bound up with the personal relationships of those involved in the various lines of transmission, who may often belong to different religious orders, we may define a "religious order" (or sect) as one which is to outward appearances a separate corporate body distinguished by its own hierarchy and administrative machinery, by the existence of its various monastic houses, and by its recognized membership. It is precisely in these respects, as well as in the manner of its foundation, that some Tibetan orders may be said to resemble Christian ones. However, religious lineage remains so important in Tibetan Buddhism that some supposed religious orders exist rather as a group of lineages than as an order in any understandable Western sense. This can be made clear only by dealing with them in a historical sequence.

From the time of the foundation of the first monastery in Tibet (Bsam-yas) toward the end of the eighth century until the mid-eleventh century there was no separately named religious order in the country. It had been ordained by royal decree that the Vinaya of the Mūlasarvāstivādins should be followed, and as more monasteries were founded there was no need in the early period for distinctions of any other kind to be made. However, the breakup of the Tibetan kingdom in 842 and the disappearance of any central control resulted in a kind of free-for-all in the matter of maintaining or winning the support of people in Tibet for the new religion, and the conditions of proselytization varied greatly from one part of the country to another. Contacts were certainly maintained with the Tun-huang region in eastern Central Asia, whence Chinese Buddhist influences had already made themselves felt during the royal period, while Indian teachers and Tantric yogins continued to remain easily available across the western and southern borders of the land. Through lack of aristocratic patronage many temples and monasteries fell into decay, but religious lineages were maintained and new ones initiated, and as circumstances became more favorable old monastic sites were brought to life again and fresh ones were founded. According to later Tibetan accounts, this period was one of almost total disruption; but if one judges by what emerged later, this is certainly not the whole truth.

Toward the end of the tenth century, a new royal dynasty began to assert its authority in western Tibet, and the rest of the country gradually became stabilized under the rule of local chieftains. There is now no sign of opposition to the new religion, which certainly made itself felt during the earlier period, and thanks to the royal and aristocratic support which became available once more, religious life began to be organized again under some semblance of control. The vast work of translating Sanskrit Buddhist literature into Tibetan was a continuing priority, and monasteries and literary centers began to flourish. It was in this context that the famous Indian scholar Atīśa (more properly, Atiśa) was invited to Tibet in 1042, remaining there until his death in 1054. He was one of many such teachers, but is especially important in the present context, because his chief Tibetan disciple, 'Brom-ston (1008–1064), established with his master's support the first distinctive Tibetan religious order with the founding of Rwa-sgreṅ Monastery in 1056. Known as the Bka'-gdams-pa ("bound to the [sacred] word"), this new order was intended to bring a proper measure of organized monastic discipline into the professed religious life. A few years later, in 1073, another monastery was founded in the principality of Sa-skya by Dkon-mchog Rgyal-po of the 'Khon family, who was one of the disciples of a remarkable scholar-traveler known as 'Brog-mi (a name meaning simply "the nomad," 992–1072).

This later period, from the later tenth century onward, is known as the "second diffusion" of Buddhism in Tibet; it differed from the earlier period in that the influences were now exclusively Indian, earlier contacts with Central Asia and China having been very largely forgotten. While the same level of scholarly activity, which typified the earlier royal period, was encouraged primarily by the religious rulers of western Tibet, much the same kind of free enterprise which had characterized the hundred years and more of the politically unstable period which had followed continued to account for much of the progress which was now made.

Another successful entrepreneur, who seems to have had no aristocratic support at all, was Mar-pa (1012–1096), who made several journeys to eastern India, studying with various Tantric yogins and especially with his chosen master, Nā-ro-pa (956–1040). The most famous of Mar-pa's pupils is Mi-la-ras-pa ("the cotton-clad Mila"), renowned for his life of extreme asceticism. It is interesting to note how the practice of sexual yoga, in which Mar-pa was adept, could be associated in this particular lineage with the strictest abstinence. Mi-la-ras-pa transmitted Mar-pa's teachings, derived from those of famous Indian sages and yogins, to Sgam-po-pa (1079–1153), who founded the monastery of Dwags-lha-sgam-po, where the teachings continued to be passed on, although it never became the center of a distinct religious order. However, Sgam-po-pa's direct disciples established six famous schools, which developed subsequently into the various branches of the now well-known Bka'-brgyud order,.all of whom trace their traditions back through Sgam-po-pa, Mi-la-ras-pa, and Mar-pa, to the Indian yogin Nā-ro-pa and his master Ti-lo-pa, who are placed in immediate succession beneath the supreme Buddha Vajradhara. The so-called Bka'-brgyud order therefore represents an interrelated group of suborders, which are effectively religious orders in their own right, in that they have developed from the start separate hierarchies and administrative organizations with some quite distinct traditions. [*See the biographies of Mi-la-ras-pa, Mar-pa, Nā-ro-pa, and Tilo-pa.*]

The greatest of Sgam-po-pa's disciples was probably the Lama Phag-mo-gru (1110–1170) who founded the first important Bka'-brgyud monastery, that of Gdan-sa-mthil. It is interesting to record that he started this later-flourishing establishment as a simple hut in which he lived, while disciples gathered around building huts of their own. It was soon transformed into a wealthy monastery, however, thanks to the patronage of the wealthy Rlaṅs family, which thereafter provided the religious head as well as the chief administrative officer. This close relationship between an important religious hierarchy and a local ruling family also has characterized the Sa-skya order. As may be expected, both of these religious orders have been involved in national politics, and they may be said to foreshadow in their organization the later religious form of government which became the Tibetan norm.

Special mention must also be made of the Karma-pa order, founded by another of Sgam-po-pa's disciples, namely Dus-gsum-mkhyen-pa (1110–1193), who founded the monastery of Mtshur-phu in 1185. This order is probably named after the monastery of Karma Gdan-sa, which he had earlier founded in eastern Tibet, whence he had come. This order has the distinction of being one of the first to use the reincarnation system for the discovery and identification of successive head lamas, and its hierarchy has continued right down to the present day. Other Bka'-brgyud-pa orders adopted the same system, especially those that were not subject to aristocratic patronage, in which cases the controlling family would normally keep the succession within its own ranks. The practice was presumably adopted by these early Bka'-brgyud-pas from the circles of Indian Tantric yogins, with whom they were so closely connected in their origins and where such reincarnations were traditionally believed to occur. Gradually, the practice was adopted in other religious orders, of which the best-known examples are the reincarnating heads of the Dge-lugs-pa order, the Dalai and Panchen lamas (see below), but they are but two of many later hundreds.

It should be added that the name *Karma-pa* is explained traditionally in another way. According to this interpretation, an assembly of gods and *ḍākinīs* is believed to have bestowed upon the founder of the order knowledge of the past, present, and future (viz., the whole chain of karmic effects) as well as a magical black miter, woven from the hair of a myriad of *ḍākinīs*. This has resulted in the nickname "Black Hats" for this order as distinct from the later "Red Hat" lineage, which branched off after a certain Grags-pat-seṅge received special honors, including a fine red hat from one of the Mongol emperors of China. We shall refer to such political involvements briefly below.

Returning to Sgam-po-pa's disciples, one recalls a third important one, Sgom-pa (1116–1169), who founded the suborder known as Mtshal-pa from the name of the district where his first monastery, Guṅ-thaṅ, was established. Three other Bka'-brgyud orders are second-generation foundations, in that they were started by disciples of the great lama Phag-mo-gru. These are the 'Bri-guṅ-pa, named after 'Bri-guṅ Monastery, which was founded by 'Jig-rten-mgon-po (1143–1212); the Stag-luṅ-pa, also named after its chief monastery; and the 'Brug-pa, named after the monastery of 'Brug in central Tibet, although it was Rwa-luṅ which became in effect its chief monastery. Whether one refers to these various Bka'-brgyud-pa branches as orders or suborders is a matter for choice, depending upon their later historical vicissitudes. Important ones surviving to this day are the Karma-pa, which is well established now in exile, the 'Bri-guṅ-pa, which survives in Ladakh, and the 'Brug-pa, which has been all-powerful in Bhutan since the seventeenth century and which is also well represented in Ladakh.

Noting that Bka'-brgyud (Śaṅs-pa-bka'-brgyud) has the more general meaning of "lineage of the (sacred) word," one may draw attention to the Śaṅs-pa-bka'-brgyud, a separate order founded by Khyuṅ-po-rnal-'byor around 1100 (dates uncertain). Having begun his religious life studying Bon and Rñiṅ-ma doctrines, this remarkable scholar later traveled in northern India, where his chief teacher was the extraordinary *yoginī* Ni-gu-ma, the sister of Nā-ro-pa. Having studied with her and other Tantric teachers, he established himself at Źaṅ-źuṅ in Śaṅs, after which his school was named. The lineage of his teachings has continued to the present, but internal dissensions later brought his school to an end as a separate order.

These various Bka'-brgyud traditions, whether linked as most were with Mar-pa's line of transmission or not, and also the traditions of the Sa-skya order, all have related origins in the late Mahāyāna and Tantric Buddhism of northeast India from the tenth to the early thirteenth century. It is exactly the same form of developed Indian Buddhism, which varies only insofar as their original Indian masters preferred slightly varying Tantric traditions. The Bka'-gdams-pa order differed only in its far stricter adherence to the monastic rule, while the others permitted noncelibate as well as monastic religious life. However, wherever there were monasteries, it was always the same ancient Indian Buddhist monastic rule, namely that of the Mūlasarvāstivādins, that was followed. High standards of scholarship were of the order of the day, for it was precisely during this period that the great enterprise of transferring all that remained of Indian Buddhism onto Tibetan soil was achieved. One should mention in particular the considerable works of translation of the great Rin-chen-bzaṅ-po (958–1055) of western Tibet and of his collaborators and successors, who may be associated with the Bka'-gdams-pa order from the time of its foundation, and later the impressive scholarship of the great Sa-skya lamas during the twelfth and thirteenth centuries. Scholars of all orders contributed in their various ways to the eventual formation of the Tibetan Buddhist canon, consisting of well over a hundred volumes of doctrine attributed to Śākyamuni Buddha himself or his accredited representatives and over twice as many volumes of commentaries and exegetical works by Indian masters.

THE RÑIṄ-MA-PA AND BON TRADITIONS

All the various orders so far discussed were founded during the eleventh and twelfth centuries in a country where Buddhist traditions had been more or less active since the eighth century, if not before. In the earlier period there had been religious lineages of the kind described above, but no religious orders with separate hierarchies and distinctive traditions as already defined. However, it is quite understandable that those who continued to represent the earlier teachings, which were still being transmitted, should begin to band together in order to protect them, the more so as the new orders tended more and more to challenge their orthodoxy. Thus, the "Old Order" (Rñiṅ-ma) and Bon as another clearly constituted order gradually appear on the scene from the twelfth century onward. The latest to achieve recognized existence, they preserve the oldest Buddhist as well as pre-Buddhist traditions, while at the same time benefiting from the teachings accumulated during the later period.

Neither the Rñiṅ-ma-pas nor the Bon-pos are religious orders in the precise sense defined above, but rather groupings of related lineages, where certain high lamas (like many other orders, they came to adopt the reincarnation system) have achieved particular eminence. By their very nature they have no clearly distinguishable historical founder, as do the later orders, although the Rñiṅ-ma-pas claim in retrospect the yogin-magician Padmasambhava, who visited Tibet in the later eighth century, as their founder, while the Bon-pos attribute their teachings to the mythical teacher

Gśen-rab, who came from the country of Ta-źig, a vague region beyond western Tibet (the same name occurs in Tadzhik S.S.R.) in the remote past. While they hold many religious teachings in common, there is one fundamental difference between them. Although the later orders rejected some of the teachings of the Rñiṅ-ma-pas as unorthodox (thus inducing them to make their own special collection of Rñiṅ-ma Tantras), they have never doubted their credibility as reliable Buddhist teachers; thus, they unquestioningly form part of the whole Tibetan Buddhist tradition.

On the other hand, the Bon-pos have put themselves beyond the acknowledged Buddhist pale by insisting that their teachings, very largely Buddhist in content as they undoubtedly are, have come not from India but from Ta-źig or Shambhala, a totally mythical land, and maintaining that while Gśen-rab is a genuine Buddha, Śākyamuni is a counterfeit one. I suspect that their earliest Buddhist traditions go back to the period before the seventh century, when Indian religious teachings were already penetrating ancient western Tibet from the far northwest of India and from Central Asia, and that subsequently they would never have accepted the undoubted historical origin of similar teachings when they were later imported into Tibet under royal patronage. Much pre-Buddhist Tibetan religion has been formally incorporated into their teachings, but their whole way of life from the time they appear in Tibet as an organized body from the twelfth century onward has been modeled on that of the recognized Buddhist orders and, in recent centuries, especially on the Dge-lugs-pa, in whose great monastic schools they had no hesitation in studying. Since the recognized Buddhist orders have also adopted many non-Buddhist cults at a popular level of practice, the Bon-pos have lost even that separate distinction. Seemingly unaware of the overwhelmingly Buddhist content of Bon-po teachings, orthodox Tibetan writers have identified them retrospectively with all those who opposed the introduction of the new religion into Tibet during the seventh and eighth centuries. All in all, the Bon-pos are a most curious religious phenomenon. They survive now in exile together with the other Tibetan religious orders that have succeeded in rebuilding their fortunes abroad after the organized destruction of religion in Tibet from 1959 onward.

In their transmitted teachings the Rñiṅ-ma-pas have much in common with the Bon-pos because they have preserved teachings which were developed in Tibet under Central Asian and Chinese Buddhist influence from the eighth century onward. Most distinctive of these is the Rdzogs-chen ("great fulfillment") tradition, which can be traced back through eighth-century Tibetan teachers to Central Asian and Chinese masters. The loss of contact with the Indian originals, inevitably involved in such long lines of transmission, led scholars of the later orders, who could so easily obtain Indian originals directly from Nepal and northern India, to challenge in good faith many Rñiṅ-ma-pa teachings, although it must be added that in some cases the Rñiṅ-ma claim has since been vindicated by the discovery of Sanskrit originals. At the same time, none of the later schools deny the great importance of Padmasambhava, often incorporating rituals that center upon him as a recognized Buddha emanation.

Both Rñiṅ-ma-pas and Bon-pos have resorted to the practice of rediscovering "hidden treasure" *(gter ma),* namely religious books, really or supposedly deposited in some secret place by an earlier renowned teacher, often in times of persecution, real or imagined, so that they might be rediscovered at an appropriate later date by those who are skilled in the task. Some of these works are in a prophetic form and (like the *Book of Daniel*) can be dated more or less by the later events to which they refer. The Rñiṅ-ma and the Bon traditions represent the most complex and interesting of Tibetan religious orders.

OTHER LATER RELIGIOUS ORDERS

We may refer briefly to later Tibetan orders of the fourteenth and fifteenth centuries, which were constituted after the completion of the formative period of Tibetan Buddhism described above and which are therefore more or less relatable to the already existing orders, although their leaders often appealed directly to Indian Buddhist sources in justification of their teachings. The Jo-naṅ-pas emerge as a distinct school in the fourteenth century as the result of the precise form given certain teachings on the nature of the absolute by a renowned scholar, Śes-rab-rgyal-mtshan of Dolpo (1292–1361), although similar views can be traced back to earlier teachers, certainly to the Indian Yogācārins to whom this Tibetan school appeals. It was named after the monastery of Jo-mo-naṅ, founded by Śes-rab-rgyal-mtshan's own teacher. It would seem to be a rare example of a Tibetan order of which the distinctive characteristic was a particular philosophical doctrine, namely the real existence of Buddhahood in an ontological sense. Like some of their Yogācārin forebears, they were accused of being "Buddhist brahmans," and the order was formally proscribed by the fifth Dalai Lama after he came to power in 1642, but probably more for political than philosophical motives.

Yet another totally innocuous order was started by the disciples of the great scholar Bu-ston (1290–1364), who had been largely responsible for bringing the work on the Tibetan canon to a successful conclusion. Named Źwa-lu-pa after his monastery Źwa-lu, this small order had close associations with the then powerful Sa-skya order. [*See the biography of Bu-ston.*] In the fifteenth century a great Sa-skya scholar, Kun-dga'-bzaṅ-po (1382–1444), founded the monastery of Nor E-vam-chos-ldaṇ, and based on this foundation there developed a new Sa-skya suborder known as Nor-pa, which, like other surviving Tibetan schools, exists nowadays in exile in India.

Left for final consideration is the very important order of the Dge-lugs-pa, nicknamed the "Yellow Hats," founded by the great scholar-reformer Tsoṅ-kha-pa (1357–1419). Having studied with teachers belonging to several of the already established orders, Mtshal, Sa-skya, Phag-mo-gru, Źwa-lu, and Jo-naṅ, he joined the great Bka'-gdams-pa monastery of Rwa-sgreṅ, founded by Atīśa's disciple 'Brom-ston. After he founded his first monastery of Dga'-ldan near Lhasa in 1409, his school was referred to as the "New Bka'-gdams-pa," since he insisted on the same strict monastic discipline as had his great predecessor Atīśa. His flourishing order certainly won early esteem on account of its superior moral virtues, but to the detriment of such qualities it eventually achieved political power during the reign of the fifth Dalai Lama by the same method of calling upon foreign aid as had been used earlier by other religious orders.

POLITICAL INVOLVEMENTS

The history of Tibet is so bound up with its religious orders and, prior to 1959, its form of government was so peculiarly religious in structure, that some brief summary of these political involvements is required. Tibet was strong and independent as a self-constituted united country of Tibetan-speaking peoples from approximately 600 CE until the fall of the last of the line of Yar-kluṅs kings in 842. Thereafter, although disunited it remained free from foreign interference until the Mongols, united under Chinggis Khan, took possession of it during the first half of the thirteenth century. Looking for a notable local representative whom they could hold responsible for Tibetan submissiveness, they lighted upon the grand lamas of Sa-skya as the most suitable in the absence of any obvious nonreligious choice. The Sa-skya order began to benefit greatly from this connection, especially when Khubilai Khan became the first Mongol emperor of China and established Peking as his capital (1263). Jealous of the wealth and power that Sa-skya enjoyed, other orders, the Karma-pa, the Mtshal-pa, and the 'Bri-guṅ-pa, also sought for Mongol patrons. Thus from 1267 until 1290 the monasteries of Sa-skya and 'Bri-guṅ waged war with one another, resulting in the destruction and burning of 'Bri-guṅ. However, the Karma-pas maintained a profitable interest at the Chinese court, lasting beyond the Mongol (Yüan) dynasty into the Ming without such untoward results.

Sa-skya preeminence was brought to an end by one of its own monks, Byaṅ-chub-rgyal-mtshan of the Rlaṅs family, which was affiliated with the Phag-mo-gru order, and for one hundred thirty years Tibet was ruled by him and his successors as an effectively independent country. Their rule was then replaced by that of their powerful ministers, the princes of Rin-spuṅ, and they in turn by the rulers of Gtsaṅ, both of these families being supporters of the Karma-pa order, which duly benefited. With the destruction of the supremacy of Gtsaṅ by the fifth Dalai Lama and his new Mongol supporters, the Karma-pas suffered most from his displeasure. It was probably as much due to the patronage which the Jo-naṅ-pas had also previously enjoyed as a result of their good relations with the Karma-pas, which led to their proscription by the fifth Dalai Lama, as to any unorthodox views which they may have held.

Scarcely any country throughout its history has been as tolerant in the religious sphere as Tibet, but vengeance has been terrible wherever political interests were involved. It is significant that the Rñiṅ-ma order, which might well be judged even more unorthodox, has survived more or less unscathed throughout the centuries, thanks to its lack of political involvement; the same is true of the Bon-pos, whose views must surely be interpreted as totally heretical so far as the person of Śākyamuni Buddha himself is concerned. The Karma-pas survived the displeasure of the fifth Dalai Lama and have since lived gentle lives remote from the political scene. However, their "Red Hat" incarnation came to a sad end in 1792 as a result of his treacherous involvement with the newly established Gorkha regime in Nepal. Largely at his personal instigation, the Gorkhas invaded Tibet in 1788 and sacked Bkra-śis-lhun-po, against which he harbored a particular grudge. When the Gorkhas were later defeated by a Chinese army he committed suicide and was duly forbidden by the Tibetan government to reincarnate in future.

The last victim of Tibetan political intrigue was the Incarnate Lama of Rwa-sgreṅ Monastery (the original Bka'-gdams-pa foundation) in 1947, an event that was surely disastrous for the whole country, just when it was threatened with foreign Communist occupation. Whatever benefits the Tibetans have gained in spiritual well-being from their religious orders, they have suffered correspondingly politically as a result of the built-in weaknesses of such a religious form of government. Quite apart from sectarian jealousies, the reincarnation system leaves long periods of interregnum between the decease of one ruling lama and the time when his successor becomes old enough to attempt to regain power from the regents who have been operating in his stead.

[*See also* Buddhism, *article on* Buddhism in Tibet; Tibetan Religions, *overview article*; Bon; Dge-lugs-pa; Mādhyamika; *and* Yogācāra.]

BIBLIOGRAPHY

Kapstein, Matthew. "The Shangs-pa bKa'-brgyud: An Unknown Tradition of Tibetan Buddhism." In *Tibetan Studies in Honour of Hugh Richardson*, edited by Michael Aris and Aung San Suu Kyi, pp. 136–143. Warminster, 1979.

Kvaerne, Per. "The Canon of the Bonpos." *Indo-Iranian Journal* 16 (1974): 18–56, 96–144.

Kvaerne, Per. "Who are the Bonpos?" *Tibetan Review* 11 (September 1976): 30–33.

Li An-che. "Rñin-ma-pa: The Early Form of Lamaism." *Journal of the Royal Asiatic Society* (1948): 142–163.

Li An-che. "The bKa'-brgyud-pa Sect of Lamaism." *Journal of the American Oriental Society* 69 (1949): 51–59.

Petech, Luciano. "The *'Bri-guṅ-pa* Sect in Western Tibet and Ladakh." In *Proceedings of the Csoma de Kőrös Memorial Symposium*, edited by Louis Ligeti. Budapest, 1978, pp. 313–325.

Richardson, Hugh E. "The Karma-pa Sect: A Historical Note." *Journal of the Royal Asiatic Society* (1958): 139–165 and (1959): 1–18.

Richardson, Hugh E. "The Rva-sgreng Conspiracy of 1947." In *Tibetan Studies in Honour of Hugh Richardson*, edited by Michael Aris and Aung San Suu Kyi. Warminster, 1979.

Ruegg, David S. "The Jo-naṅ-pas: A School of Buddhist Ontologists According to the *Grub-mtha' śel-gyi-me-loṅ*." *Journal of the American Oriental Society* 83 (1963): 73–91.

Sperling, Elliot. "The Fifth Karma-pa and Some Aspects of the Relationship between Tibet and the Early Ming." In *Tibetan Studies in Honour of Hugh Richardson*, edited by Michael Aris and Aung San Suu Kyi, pp. 280–287. Warminster, 1979.

Snellgrove, David L., and Hugh E. Richardson. *A Cultural History of Tibet* (1968). Reprint, Boulder, 1980.

Tarthang Tulku. *A History of the Buddhist Dharma*. Crystal Mirror, no. 5. Berkeley, 1977.

Tucci, Giuseppe. *The Religions of Tibet*. Translated by Geoffrey Samuel. Berkeley, 1980.

10 BON

Per Kvaerne

There are two organized religious traditions in Tibet: Buddhism and a faith that is referred to by its Tibetan name, Bon. Since its introduction into Tibet in the eighth century, Buddhism has been the dominant religion; in the person of the Dalai Lama, present-day Tibetan Buddhism has an articulate and internationally respected spokesman.

The Bon religion is much less well known, although the number of its adherents in Tibet is by all accounts considerable. In the West, the traditional view of Bon has been less than accurate. It has been characterized as "shamanism" or "animism," and as such, regarded as a continuation of what supposedly were the religious practices prevalent in Tibet before the coming of Buddhism. It has also been described in rather unfavorable terms as a perversion of Buddhism, a kind of marginal countercurrent in which elements of Buddhist doctrine and practice have either been shamelessly copied or inverted and distorted in a manner that has been somewhat imaginatively compared with satanic cults. It is only since the mid-1960s that a more accurate understanding of this religion has emerged (first and foremost thanks to the efforts of David L. Snellgrove), so that Bon is now recognized as closely related to the various Buddhist schools in Tibet (in particular the Rñiṅ-ma-pa order) and yet possessed of an identity of its own that justifies its status as a distinct religion.

PROBLEMS OF DEFINITION

An adherent of the Bon religion is called a Bon-po, again using the Tibetan term. A Bon-po is "a believer in *bon,*" and for such a believer the word *bon* signifies "truth," "reality," or the eternal, unchanging doctrine in which truth and reality are expressed. Thus *bon* has the same range of connotations for its believers as the Tibetan word *chos* (corresponding to the Indian word *dharma*) has for Buddhists.

A problem, however, arises when one is confronted with the fact that an important group of ritual experts in pre-Buddhist Tibet were likewise known as *bon-pos*. It is possible that their religious practices were styled Bon (although scholars are divided on this point); certainly they were so designated in the later, predominantly Buddhist historiographical tradition. Be that as it may, their religious system was essentially different not only from Buddhism, but also, in certain important respects, from the Bon religious tradition as practiced in later centuries. For example, the pre-Buddhist religion of Tibet gives the impression of being preoccupied with the continuation of life beyond death. It included elaborate rituals for ensuring that the soul of a dead person was conducted safely to a postmortem land of bliss by an appropriate animal—usually a yak, a horse, or a sheep—which was sacrificed in the course of the funerary rites. Offerings of food, drink, and precious objects likewise accompanied the dead. These rites reached their highest level of elaboration and magnificence in connection with the death of a king or a high nobleman; as was the case in China, enormous funerary mounds were erected, and a large number of priests and court officials were involved in rites that lasted for several years. The purpose of these rites was twofold: on the one hand, to ensure the happiness of the deceased in the land of the dead, and on the other, to obtain their beneficial influence for the welfare and fertility of the living.

The term *Bon* refers not only to these and other religious practices of pre-Buddhist Tibet, but also to the religion that apparently developed in close interaction with Buddhism from the eighth century onward and that still claims the adherence of many Tibetans. It is with the latter religion that this article is concerned. The Bon-pos claim that there is an unbroken continuity between the earlier and the later religion—a claim that, whatever its historical validity, is significant in itself.

The matter is further complicated by the fact that there has always existed a vast and somewhat amorphous body of popular beliefs in Tibet, including beliefs in various techniques of divination, the cult of local deities (connected, above all, with certain mountains), and conceptions of the soul. In Western literature, such beliefs are frequently styled "Bon," and reference is made to "Bon animism" and other supposedly typical Bon attributes. This has, however, no basis in Tibetan usage, and since this popular, unsystematized religion does not form an essential part of Buddhism or Bon (although it is, to a large extent, sanctioned by and integrated into both religions), an appropriate term for it is the one coined by Rolf A. Stein, "the nameless religion."

THE BON-PO IDENTITY

Although limited to Tibet, Bon regards itself as a universal religion in the sense that its doctrines are true and valid for all humanity. For this reason it styles itself G'yuṅ-druṅ Bon, "Eternal Bon." According to its own historical perspective, it was introduced into Tibet many centuries before Buddhism and enjoyed royal patronage until it was supplanted and expelled by the "false religion" (Buddhism) coming from India.

Before reaching Tibet, however, it is claimed that Bon prospered in a land known as Źaṅ-źuṅ and that this country remained the center of the religion until it was absorbed by the expanding Tibetan empire in the seventh century. There is no doubt as to the historical reality of Źaṅ-źuṅ, although its exact extent and ethnic and cultural identity are far from clear. It does, however, seem to have been situated in what today is, roughly speaking, western Tibet, with Mount Kailāśa as its center.

The ultimate homeland of Bon, is, however, to be sought farther to the west, beyond the borders of Źaṅ-źuṅ. The Bon-pos believe that their religion was first proclaimed in a land called Rtag-gzigs (Tazik) or 'Ol-mo Luṅ-riṅ. Although the former name suggests the land of the Tajiks (in present-day Soviet Central Asia), it has so far not been possible to identify this holy land of Bon in a convincing manner.

In Rtag-gzigs, so the Bon-pos claim, lived Ston-pa Gśen-rab (Tönpa Shenrap), a fully enlightened being who was, in fact, nothing less than the true Buddha of our world age. The Bon-pos possess a voluminous biographical literature in which his exploits are extolled. Without entering into details, or discussing the many problems connected with the historical genesis of this extraordinary figure, one may at least note that his biography is not closely related to the biographical traditions connected with Śākyamuni, the Buddha on whose authority the Buddhists base their doctrines. Ston-pa Gśen-rab was a layman, and it was as a prince that he incessantly journeyed from his capital in all directions to propagate Bon. It is remarkable that this propagation also included the institution of innumerable rituals, the supervision of the erection of temples and stupas, and the conversion of notorious sinners. His numerous wives, sons, daughters, and disciples also played a significant role (in a way for which there is no Buddhist parallel) in this soteriological activity. It was only late in his life that he was ordained as a monk, and at that point in his career he retired to a forest hermitage. On the other hand, Ston-pa Gśen-rab is considered to have been a fully enlightened being from his very birth, endowed with numerous supernatural powers. His importance in the Bon religion is crucial; it is he who—directly or indirectly—lends authority to the religious literature of the Bon-pos, and he is the object of their intense devotion.

RELIGIOUS BELIEFS AND PRACTICES

In the same way as the Buddhists of Tibet divide their sacred scriptures into two vast collections, the Bon-pos also—probably since the middle of the fourteenth century CE—possess their own Bka'-'gyur (Kanjur, texts considered to have been actually expounded by Ston-pa Gśen-rab) and Brten-'gyur (Tenjur, later commentaries and treatises), comprising in all approximately three hundred volumes. Since the middle of the nineteenth century wooden blocks for printing the entire collection have been available in the principality of Khro-bcu in the extreme east of Tibet, and printed copies of the canon were produced until the 1950s. (The blocks were destroyed during the Cultural Revolution). Large portions of the Bka'-'gyur and Brten-'gyur may be reconstituted on the basis of texts published by Bon-po exiles living in India, and it seems that a complete set of the printed edition has survived the ravages of war and of the Cultural Revolution in Tibet itself.

A common division of the Bon-po Bka'-'gyur is the fourfold one into Sūtras *(mdo),* Prajñāpāramitā texts *('bum),* Tantras *(rgyud),* and texts dealing with the higher forms of meditation (*mdzod,* lit. "treasurehouse"). The Brten-'gyur is divided into three basic textual categories: "External," including commentaries on the Vinaya, the Abhidharma, and the Sūtras; "Internal," comprising the commentaries on the Tantras and the rituals focusing on the major Tantric deities, as well as the cult of *ḍākinīs*, *dharmapālas*, and worldly rituals of magic and divination; and finally, "Secret," a section that treats meditation practices. A section containing treatises on grammar, architecture, and medicine is appended.

For the sake of convenience, the Indian (Buddhist) terms corresponding to the Tibetan have been used here, but it must be kept in mind that although the Bon-pos employ the same Tibetan terms as the Buddhists, they do not accept their Indian origin, since they trace, as explained above, their entire religious terminology to Źaṅ-źuṅ and, ultimately, to Rtag-gzigs.

As this review of Bon-po religious literature indicates, the doctrines they contain are basically the same as those of Buddhism. The concepts of the world as suffering, of moral causality and rebirth in the six states of existence, and of enlightenment and Buddhahood are basic doctrinal elements of Bon. Bon-pos follow the same path of virtue and have recourse to the same meditational practices as do Buddhist Tibetans.

In the early fifteenth century—and indeed even earlier—the Bon-pos began to establish monasteries that were organized along the same lines as those of the Buddhists, and several of these monasteries developed into large institutions with hundreds of monks and novices. The most prestigious Bon-po monastery, founded in 1405, is Sman-ri in central Tibet (in the province of Gtsaṅ, north of the Brahmaputra River). Fully ordained monks, corresponding to the Buddhist *dge-sloṇ* (Skt., *bhikṣu*), are styled *draṅ-sroṅ* (a term that in Tibetan otherwise translates *ṛṣi,* the semidivine "seers" of the Vedas). They are bound by all the rules of monastic discipline, including strict celibacy.

Over the centuries the monastic life of Bon has come increasingly under the influence of the tradition of academic learning and scholastic debate that characterize the dominant Dge-lugs-pa school, but the older tradition of Tantric yogins and hermits, constituting an important link between the Bon-pos and the Rñiṅ-ma-pas, has never been quite abandoned. [*See* Dge-lugs-pa.]

An important class of religious experts, which likewise finds its counterpart in the Rñiṅ-ma-pa tradition, consists of the visionaries—both monks and laymen—who reveal "hidden texts." During the Buddhist persecution of Bon in the eighth and ninth centuries, the Bon-pos claim, their sacred texts were hidden in caves, buried underground, or walled up in certain temples. Later (apparently from the tenth century onward) the texts were rediscovered—at first, it would seem, by chance, and subsequently through the intervention of supernatural beings who would direct the chosen *gter-ston* ("treasure finder") to the site. Later still, texts would be revealed in visions or through purely mental transference from divine beings. The greater part of the Bon-po Bka'-'gyur and Brten-'gyur consists of such "rediscovered" or supernaturally inspired texts. "Treasure finders" have been active until the present, and indeed may be said to play an important role in the revival of religious activities in Tibet today, as texts that were hidden for safekeeping during the systematic destruction of the 1960s and 1970s are once more being removed from their hiding places.

As is the case in Tibetan religion generally, these texts are particularly important in that they serve, in an almost literal sense, as liturgical scores for the innumerable and extremely complex rituals, the performance of which occupies much of the time and attention of the monks. Many of these rituals do not differ significantly from those performed by the Buddhists, except that the deities invoked—although falling into the same general categories as those that apply to the deities of Mahāyāna Buddhism—are different from the Buddhist ones. They have different names, iconographical characteristics, evocatory formulas (*mantras*), and myths. A systematic study of this pantheon remains, however, to be undertaken, and likewise, our knowledge of the rituals of the Bon-pos is still extremely incomplete.

The laypeople are confronted by many of these deities, impersonated by monks, in the course of mask dances. The lay Bon-pos have the same range of religious activities as Tibetan Buddhist laypeople: the practice of liberality toward monks and monasteries (in exchange for the performance of rituals); the mechanical multiplication of prayers by means of prayer flags and prayer wheels; and journeys of pilgrimage to the holy places of Bon, such as Mount Kailāśa in the western Himalayas, or Bon-ri ("mountain of Bon"), in the southeastern province of Rkoṅ-po.

THE DIFFUSION OF BON

Both Buddhists and Bon-pos agree that when Buddhism succeeded in gaining royal patronage in Tibet in the eighth and ninth centuries, Bon suffered a serious setback. By the eleventh century, however, an organized religious tradition, styling itself Bon and claiming continuity with the earlier, pre-Buddhist religion, appeared in central Tibet. It is this religion of Bon that has persisted to our own times, absorbing doctrines and practices from the dominant Buddhist religion but always adapting what it learned to its own needs and its own perspectives. This is, of course, not just plagiarism, but a dynamic and flexible strategy that has ensured the survival, indeed the vitality, of a religious minority.

Until recent years, much has been made in Western literature of the fact that the Bon-pos perform certain basic ritual acts in a manner opposite to that practiced by the Buddhists. Thus, when circumambulating sacred places and objects or when spinning their prayerwheels, the Bon-pos proceed counterclockwise rather than following the (Indian and Buddhist) tradition of *pradakṣiṇā,* or circumambulation "toward the right." For this reason, it has been said of Bon that "its essence lay largely in contradiction and negation," and Bon's "willful perversions and distortions" have been pointed out. The error of such views cannot be too strongly emphasized. The Bon-pos are conscious of no element of "contradiction and negation" in their beliefs and practices but regard their religion as the pure path to liberation from suffering and rebirth. It is true that down through the centuries Bon-po historiographers have generally regarded the introduction of Buddhism into Tibet as a catastrophe, which they have ascribed to the accumulated collective "evil karma" of the Tibetans. On the other hand, conciliatory efforts have not been lacking; thus one source suggests that Ston-pa Gśen-rab and Śākyamuni were really twin brothers.

It is difficult to assess just how large the Bon-po community of Tibet is. Certainly the Bon-pos are a not insignificant minority. Particularly in eastern Tibet, whole districts are populated by Bon-pos. Scattered communities are also to be found in central and western Tibet, particularly in the Chumbi Valley (bordering Sikkim) and among nomads. In the north of Nepal, too, there are Bon-po villages, especially in the district of Dol-po. At a point in history that remains to be determined precisely, Bon exerted a strong influence on the religion of the Na-khi people in Yunnan Province in southwestern China; with this exception, the Bon-pos do not seem to have engaged in missionary enterprises. In India, Bon-pos belonging to the Tibetan refugee community have established (since 1968) a large and well-organized monastery in which traditional scholarship, rituals, and sacred dances are carried on with great vigor. Since 1980, when religious life was revived in Tibet itself, the Bon-pos there have rebuilt several monasteries (albeit on a reduced scale), installed monks, and resumed—to the extent that prevailing conditions permit—many aspects of traditional religious life. It would thus seem that there is good reason to believe that Bon will continue to exist, and even, with certain limits, to flourish.

[*For further discussion of the religious traditions of Tibet and their relationship to Bon, see* Tibetan Religions, *overview article, and* Buddhism, Schools of, *article on* Tibetan Buddhism.]

BIBLIOGRAPHY

When it was published in 1950 and for many years thereafter, Helmut Hoffman's *Quellen zur Geschichte der tibetischen Bon-Religion* (Wiesbaden, 1950) was the most reliable and comprehensive study of Bon, based as it was on all sources available at the time. Since 1960, Tibetan Bon-po monks in exile have collaborated with Western scholars. The first major work to result from this entirely new situation was *The Nine Ways of Bon: Excerpts from the gZi-brjid,* edited and translated by David L. Snellgrove (1967; reprint, Boulder, 1980), in which doctrinal material from the important fourteenth-century Bon-po text *Gzi-brjid* was presented for the first time. In the following year, David L. Snellgrove and Hugh E. Richardson presented a historical framework for the development of Bon in *A Cultural History of Tibet* (1968; reprint, Boulder, 1980) that has since been generally accepted. An excellent and up-to-date presentation of Bon is also given by Anne-Marie Blondeau in her article "Les religions du Tibet," in *Histoire des religions,* edited by Henri-Charles Puech, vol. 3 (Paris, 1976), pp. 233–329.

An important survey of the Bon religion is Samten G. Karmay's "A General Introduction to the History and Doctrines of Bon," *Memoirs of the Research Department of the Tōyō Bunko,* no. 33 (1975): 171–218 (also printed as a separate booklet, *The M.T.B. Off-prints Series,* no. 3; Tokyo, 1975). The same scholar has also translated a history of Bon written by the Bon-po scholar Śar-rdza Bkra-śīs Rgyal-mtshan (1859–1935) in 1922 under the title *The Treasury of Good Sayings: A Tibetan History of Bon* (London, 1972).

On Bon literature, see Per Kvaerne's "The Canon of the Bonpos," *Indo-Iranian Journal* 16 (1975): 18–56, 96–144, and Samten G. Karmay's *A Catalogue of Bonpo Publications* (Tokyo, 1977). The monastic life of Bon (based on information from Sman-ri monastery) is outlined in Kvaerne's "Continuity and Change in Tibetan Monasticism," in *Korean and Asian Religious Tradition,* edited by Chai-shin Yu (Toronto, 1977), pp. 83–98. On meditational practices, see Kvaerne's "'The Great Perfection' in the Tradition of the Bonpos," in *Early Ch'an in China and Tibet,* edited by Whalen Lai and Lewis R. Lancaster (Berkeley, 1983), pp. 367–392.

A detailed description of a Bon-po ritual has been provided in Per Kvaerne's *Tibet, Bon Religion: A Death Ritual of the Tibetan Bonpos* (Leiden, 1984). The same book analyzes the extensive iconography connected with that particular ritual. General studies of Bon-po iconography are still lacking. Detailed descriptions of a few painted scrolls are, however, provided in Kvaerne's "Art Bon-po: Art du bouddhisme lamaïque," in *Dieux et démons de l'Himâlaya* (Paris, 1977), pp. 185–189; and in his "A Bonpo Version of the Wheel of Existence," in *Tantric and Taoist Studies in Honour of R. A. Stein,* edited by Michel Strickman (Brussels, 1981), vol. 1, pp. 274–289. The biography of Ston-pa Gśen-rab has been studied intensively on the basis of the *Gzi-rjid* and a series of paintings in Per Kvaerne's "Peintures tibétaines de la vie de *sTon-pa-gçen-rab,*" *Arts asiatiques* 41 (1986).

11 THE RELIGIONS OF INNER ASIA

Ruth I. Meserve

Inner Asia, essentially a historical concept, was that great land mass surrounded by the civilized worlds of Rome, Greece, Arabia, Persia, India, and China. Central Eurasia, the more scholarly term for the region, should not be confused with Central Asia, which, in the strict sense, comprises the modern-day Uzbek, Turkmen, Kirghiz, Kazakh, and Tajik republics in the Soviet Union; or, in a broader sense, adds Chinese Turkistan (Sinkiang). Until modern times, the boundaries that separated Inner Asia from the rest of the Eurasian land mass were in constant flux, expanding or contracting according to the relations of the peoples within Inner Asia toward the surrounding sedentary states.

Inner Asia is a vast area with a multitude of peoples, speaking a variety of languages, possessing distinct religious practices, yet culturally united in a unique civilization. The languages spoken in Inner Asia belong to a number of linguistic families, the largest of which is Altaic (comprising the Turkic, Mongol, and Tunguz languages), followed by Uralic (the Finno-Ugric and Samoyed languages), Paleosiberian or Paleo-Asiatic, Indo-Iranian, and the isolated languages of the Caucasus. The noninstitutionalized forms of religion in Inner Asia, as reported by early travelers and recorded by historians, were most evident in their myths of origin, in the ceremonial activities present in daily life, such as rituals performed before hunting or connected with funerals, and in art. Tolerance of outside religions was the norm, rather than the exception, and Buddhism, Islam, and Christianity all exerted great influence on the region.

Ecologically, Inner Asia is divided into four great longitudinal belts: the tundra in the far north, the forest (taiga), the steppe, and finally the desert in the south. The existence of these four separate zones has led to the inaccurate stereotyping of the economic activity practiced in the north by the Finno-Ugric, Samoyed, and Tunguz peoples as hunting, fishing, and gathering, and that practiced in the south by the Turkic and Mongol peoples as exclusively nomadic herding. However, just as hunting and limited agriculture were a part of Turkic and Mongol economies, so was animal husbandry a part of the economy of the more northern peoples. The prevailing climatic conditions severely limited agricultural potential without man-made changes in the environment, giving rise to one of the most important unifying features of Inner Asia: the relationship between horse and pasture. As the mainstay of Inner Asian economy, the horse, dependent only on pasture, was either traded for basic necessities, particularly armaments that could only be manufactured by the surrounding sedentary civilizations, or used for military conquest. It thus became the key to the rise of the great nomadic civilizations.

Major problems arise in dealing with the history of Inner Asia. Indigenous written material is extremely scant, existing only from the eighth century CE. Much of the Inner Asian tradition was preserved only orally, transmitted by storytellers, singers, shamans, and priests. Most often the early history of Inner Asia was recorded by the surrounding civilizations, eager to protect their own ways of life and highly critical of different customs and manners. Because the written records are in a variety of nonindigenous languages, the correct identification of names in Inner Asia presents problems. Ethnonyms and toponyms, not to mention personal names and titles, that appear, for example, in Chinese sources are extremely difficult to equate with names or terms given in Greek or Arabic sources. When a name such as *Scythian* or *Hun* or *Turk* first appeared, it meant a specific people; later, the name would often become a generic term applied to any barbarian people. Imprecise geographical knowledge only added to the problems; distances were exaggerated, and few people from the surrounding sedentary civilizations had actually visited Inner Asia. The history of the region therefore must be filtered from ideas and ways hostile to its peculiar civilization and drawn from the precious scraps of indigenous material—written fragments, archaeological data, art—often literally scraped out of the desert sands or the frozen soil of the tundra.

To most peoples of the so-called civilized world, Inner Asia was seen as one vast zone. The world, from the time of Homer (c. tenth century BCE) until the beginning of the Russian expansion into Asia in the late sixteenth century, saw Inner Asia as a land shrouded in mystery and myth, defined only by its barbarousness. It was the inhospitable land of the north, unfit for man or beast.

ANCIENT VIEWS OF INNER ASIA

Early Chinese and Classical Greek sources spoke of Inner Asia, but many of the peoples mentioned were imaginary and showed the civilized world's lack of real knowledge about the region. To the Greeks these were the peoples who inhabited such places as the City of Perpetual Mist or the Rhipaean Mountains. These regions and the peoples who lived there were removed, beyond the pale of Greek civilization, their barbarous nature, according to Hippocrates (460?–377? or 359?), directly determined by the environment in which they lived. The Greek geographer and historian Strabo (c. 63 BCE–23 CE) reminded his readers that before the Black Sea was navigable the barbarous tribes surrounding it as well as the fierce storms on it caused it to be called Axine ("inhospitable"); not until the Ionians established cities on its shores did it become known as Euxine ("hospitable"). This case is an example of one of the myths perpetuated about Inner Asia by external historians: the lack of cities was equated with a lack of civilization. On the other side of Inner Asia, the Chinese held similar views. The Inner Asian lived in the "submissive wastes," the "great wilderness," the region of the "floating sands," in the barren lands "where frost came early." The "five grains" would not grow there. Chinese emperors were often challenged by their ministers on the wisdom of trying to expand Chinese

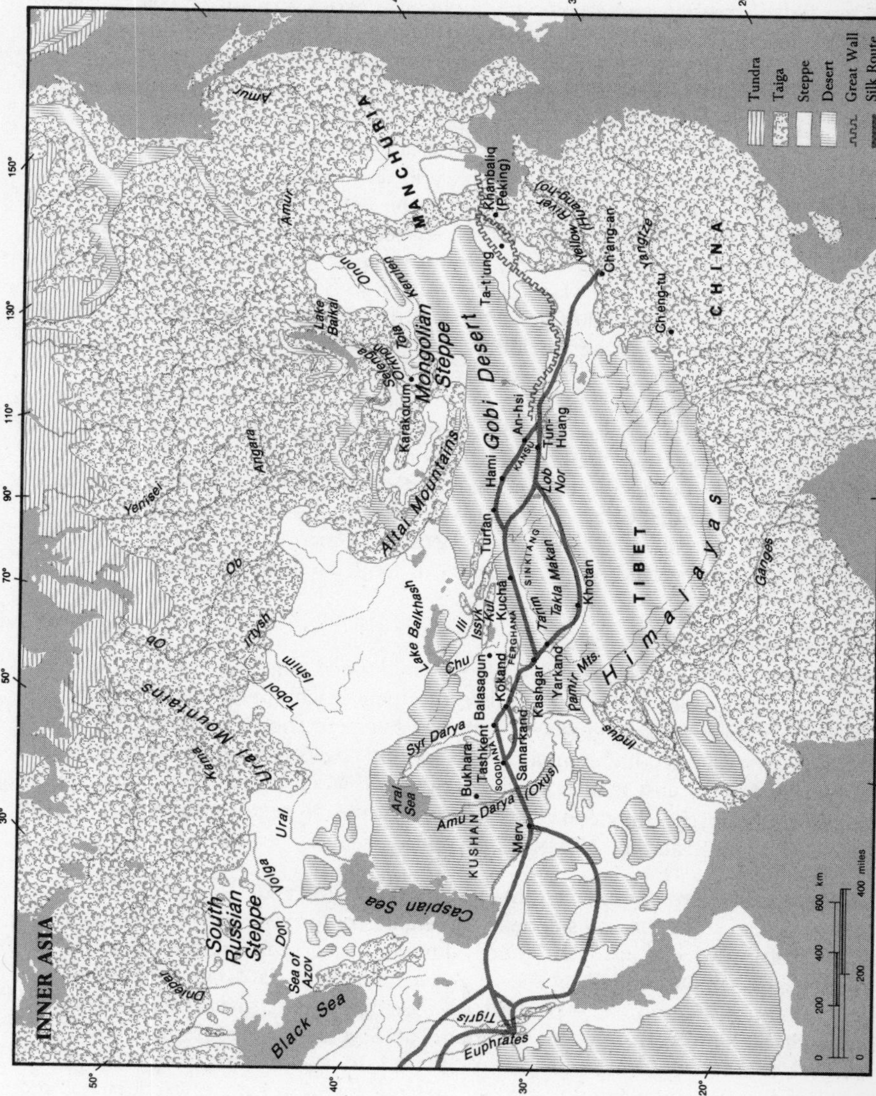
INNER ASIA
Tundra
Taiga
Steppe
Desert
Great Wall
Silk Route
0 200 400 600 km
0 200 400 miles
MANCHURIA
Amur
Khanbaliq (Peking)
Yellow River (Huang-ho)
Ta-t'ung
Ch'ang-an
Yangtze
Ch'eng-tu
CHINA
Onon
Kerulen
Lake Baikal
Selenga
Orkhon
Tola
Mongolian Steppe
Karakorum
Gobi Desert
An-hsi
Tun-Huang
KANSU
Hami
Lob Nor
Altai Mountains
Angara
Yenisei
Turfan
SINKIANG
Takla Makan
Tarim
Khotan
TIBET
Himalayas
Ganges
Ob
Irtysh
Ishim
Tobol
Lake Balkhash
Ili
Issyk Kul
Kucha
Chu
Balasagun
FERGHANA
Kokand
Kashgar
Yarkand
Pamir Mts.
Indus
Syr Darya
Tashkent
SOGDIANA
Samarkand
Bukhara
Aral Sea
Amu Darya (Oxus)
KUSHAN
Merv
Ural Mountains
Kama
Ural
Volga
South Russian Steppe
Don
Dnieper
Sea of Azov
Caspian Sea
Black Sea
Tigris
Euphrates
50°
40°
30°
20°
30°
50°
70°
90°
110°
130°
150°
70°
90°
110°

territory into these wastelands. This attitude perpetuated another myth: the lack of agriculture meant the people were uncivilized.

EARLY MEDIEVAL JUDAIC, CHRISTIAN, AND ISLAMIC VIEWS

In the Judeo-Christian and Islamic traditions, the peoples of Inner Asia had been driven into the barren, desolate lands of the north, to the hidden, dark regions of the world—to the land of Gog and Magog. When Jeremiah was asked by the Lord what he saw, he answered, "I see a seething pot; and the face thereof is toward the north" (*Jer.* 1:13). Within this "seething pot" were the unknown kingdoms of the north, which, at the end of time, would rise and the contents spill upon the land, bringing death and destruction. Classical Arab and Persian geographers (ninth to eleventh century) located Gog and Magog in the fifth and sixth climes and warned of their cold, bestial nature, but others recognized their brave, warriorlike qualities. To al-Kāshgharī (fl. eleventh century) they were an army, the army of the prophet Muḥammad, to be sent out when he was angry with a people. This army, called Turk, would come at the end of time. The fear that medieval man had regarding the peoples of the north was also manifest in the *Roman d'Alexandre,* in which the hordes of Gog and Magog are sealed off behind an iron gate.

The armies of Inner Asia did not exist in myth alone; the fears of medieval man had been justified by repeated invasions from the steppe lands. Walls—such as the Roman *limes* or the Great Wall of China—were monuments of the civilized world's futile attempt to contain the encroaching and often unknown peoples from Inner Asia. When the hordes of Inner Asia broke through, they did bring death and destruction with a terrible swiftness. It was because of such invasions that the peoples of Inner Asia first entered recorded history in some detail and accuracy.

THE HISTORY OF INNER ASIA

The peoples of Inner Asia who lived in the tundra and taiga were widely dispersed in small communities and posed no threat to their neighbors. It was the peoples of the steppes, formed in large tribes with vast herds of sheep, goats, camels, cattle, and horses, who were highly mobile and had the organizational ability to lead military excursions against their sedentary neighbors. When these peoples first appear in historical sources, they come from two great steppe regions: the south Russian (or Pontic) steppe and the Mongolian steppe.

Scythians. The first important Inner Asian people, the Indo-Iranian Scythians, appeared on the south Russian steppe in the eighth century BCE and began to fade out of the historical scene around 175 BCE, although some remnants survived until the third century CE. While little is known about their origin, a detailed description of their mode of life and some remarks on their history are given by Herodotus (c. 480–420 BCE) in book 4 of his *Histories.* The Scythians were the first historically known people to use iron, and having defeated the Cimmerians, they assumed full command of the south Russian steppe. Their greatness as steppe warriors was recognized when Darius I (r. 521–486 BCE), king of Persia, led a campaign against the Scythians north of the Black Sea from 516 to 513. These Scythian mounted archers soon frustrated Darius by seemingly fleeing before him, attacking when and where he least expected, all the while drawing him farther and farther into their land. In the end, Darius was forced to retreat to Persia. This type of warfare and the ability of the skilled horseman to turn and shoot behind him—the Parthian shot—became a trademark of the Inner Asian warrior.

In Persian sources these people were called Saka, and three kinds were enumerated: the Saka beyond the sea, the pointed-hat Saka, and the Saka who revered Hauma. The Scythians of Herodotus lived north of the Black Sea, while the Saka of Persian sources lived beyond the Oxus River (the modern Amu Darya) and south of this area in Iran. The social structure of the Scythians was tripartite: agriculturists, warriors, and priests. They had cities, centers of metallurgy, and a highly developed, stylized animal art.

Animals, particularly horses and cattle, as well as humans were sacrificed as offerings to the gods. Herodotus listed the Scythian gods with what he thought were their Greek equivalents, the supreme deity being Tabiti (Vesta). Images, altars, and temples were used. Scythian soothsayers were called into service when the king was ill; Enarees, womenlike men among the Scythians, practiced divination; elaborate funeral and burial rites, a strong will to protect the tombs of their ancestors, and prescribed ceremonies for oath taking existed. By the late second century BCE, the ethnically and linguistically related nomadic tribes of the Sarmatians began to replace the Scythians, who had reached a degree of civilization perhaps unparalleled by any other Inner Asian empire. [*See also* Scythian Religion *and* Sarmatian Religion.]

Hsiung-nu. On the eastern edge of Inner Asia, the Hsiung-nu were the first clearly identifiable and important steppe people to appear on the borders of China, constantly menacing the frontier with raids that sometimes penetrated deep into Chinese territory. Their center of power was the Mongolian steppe. Appearing in Chinese sources around 230 BCE, an account of the Hsiung-nu was provided by the grand historian of China, Ssu-ma Chʻien (c. 145–86 BCE). By about 56 BCE internal revolts had begun to rack the Hsiung-nu empire and some tribes moved to the west; in 48 CE the Hsiung-nu finally split into two major groups: the Southern Hsiung-nu and the Northern Hsiung-nu. The former continued to be a serious threat to China and finally faded from the historical scene around 400 CE, while the Northern Hsiung-nu remained on the original homeland of the Mongolian steppe. The Northern Hsiung-nu never regained their former power, however, and about 155 CE they were destroyed by another steppe people, the Hsien-pei.

The language of the Hsiung-nu is unknown. Long thought to be Mongol or Turkic, more recent studies seem to indicate that it comprised some elements of the Yenisei branch of the Paleosiberian languages. Since the eighteenth century, it has been popular to equate the Hsiung-nu of the east with the Huns of the west: at best the theory is controversial.

The military power of the Hsiung-nu, like that of the Scythians, lay in their remarkable skill as highly disciplined mounted archers. In fact, Ssu-ma Chʻien considered warfare their main occupation. Made up of numerous tribes, the Hsiung-nu confederation was most highly organized in its relations with foreign states, depending upon the horse for both military superiority and for economic gain. The Chinese set up border markets in an attempt to weaken the Hsiung-nu by supplying them with luxuries and fostering a dependence on Chinese goods. Even though there was a hereditary aristocracy within the Hsiung-nu confederation, internal organization was loose, each tribe having its own pastures. A son would marry his stepmother when his father died; a brother would marry a deceased brother's widow—both practices aimed at preventing the extinction of the clan.

At set times of the year, sacrifices were offered to ancestors, gods, heaven and earth, while auspicious days were chosen for major events, and the stars and moon were consulted for military maneuvers. Burials were elaborate, particularly for the ruler, with many of his concubines and loyal ministers following him in death. Although condemned by the Chinese for lacking in morals, not understanding court ritual, and not showing respect for the aged, the Hsiung-nu had laws, customs, and manners of their own that contradicted the ethnocentric views of the Chinese.

Yüeh-chih, Wu-sun, and Kushans. The Hsiung-nu greatly affected the history of Inner Asia to the west and south of their domains where, in 160 BCE, they inflicted a terrible defeat on the Yüeh-chih, an Indo-European people located on the Chinese border of modern Kansu Province. This caused the Yüeh-chih to divide; the Lesser Yüeh-chih moved to the south while the Greater Yüeh-chih began moving west. As the latter migrated through the Ili River valley, they abandoned the Mongolian steppe to the complete control of the Hsiung-nu, while they themselves displaced the Sai (or Saka) tribes. The majority of the Yüeh-chih continued to move west into the Greek state of Bactria. At about the same time, the Chinese emperor Wu-ti (r. 140–87 BCE) sent Chang Ch'ien to the Greater Yüeh-chih to form an alliance against the Hsiung-nu. Leaving in 139, Chang Ch'ien had to pass through Hsiung-nu territory, where he was detained and held prisoner for more than ten years. Chang Ch'ien's account, made to the Chinese emperor on his return, brought the first real knowledge of the western regions to China, information that would allow China to expand westward and become actively involved in Central Asia. Although his mission to the Yüeh-chih failed, he was sent again in 115 to try to form a different alliance against the Hsiung-nu, this time with the Wu-sun, another people probably of Iranian origin, who accepted the gifts that Chang Ch'ien brought as well as an imperial princess to become the wife of their ruler, but who also refused to cooperate. It was not until the Hsiung-nu empire was disintegrating that the Wu-sun inflicted serious defeats on them.

The Yüeh-chih tribes that settled in Bactria were later united under one tribe, the Kushans, probably in the first century BCE. Besides Bactria, their kingdom included extensive domains in Central Asia and large portions of Northwest India, where centers of Greco-Buddhist art were established at Gandhāra and Mathurā. The Kushan period is extremely controversial, and the dates and order of kings are widely disputed. But it was during the reign of Kaniṣka, a patron of Buddhism, that this Indian religion began to spread into Central Asia and China, heralding a new era for the region. Chinese monks began to travel to India and Sri Lanka to obtain the Buddhist *sūtra*s, passing through Tun-huang, Khotan, and Turfan on the edge of the Tarim Basin, as well as Ferghana and Sogdiana. Most notable are the accounts left by the monks Fa-hsien (traveling from 399 to 413 CE) and Hsüan-tsang (traveling from 629 to 645). Buddhist texts had to be translated into Turkic languages; the routes used by pilgrims were destined to become active trade routes, linking east and west. [*See also* Missions, *article on* Buddhist Missions, *and* Buddhism, *article on* Buddhism in Central Asia.]

Huns. With the appearance of the Huns toward the end of the fourth century CE, a new movement began on the south Russian steppe. Rumors of invasions spreading fear and panic reached Jerome (c. 311–420) in Palestine, where he wrote that these "wolves of the north"—the Huns—"spared neither religion nor rank nor age." It was with this turmoil on the steppe north of the Sea of Azov that the *Völkerwanderung,* or migration of the peoples, began. The name *Hun* first appears in the writings of Ptolemy (fl. second century CE), but later historians of the Huns such as Ammianus Marcellinus (c. 322–400), Priscus (fl. fifth century), and the less reliable Jordanes (fl. sixth century) portray a culture typical of Inner Asian society and very different from Roman civilization. Aided by civil wars in Italy that occupied the Roman army, some Hun tribes had established themselves by 409 on the Roman *limes* and in the Roman province of Pannonia (on the right bank of the Danube). When, in 434, a Hun king named Rua died, he was succeeded by his nephews, Bleda and Attila.

Hun penetration into Europe and the displacing of existing tribes were instrumental in the formation of modern Europe. Aetius, the great fifth-century general and power broker of the Western Roman Empire, provoked some Hun tribes to attack the Burgundians in 437 in order to shatter Germanic power and to strengthen Roman rule in Gaul. The Visigoths, who had been pushed from the east into the Toulouse area, forced the Vandals into Spain and North Africa, an event that caused great consternation to the entire Roman empire. However, Aetius's attempt to use the Huns to defeat the Visigoths failed in 439. Turmoil continued, this time in the Eastern Roman Empire with the Persian decision to attack Byzantium; at the same time, Attila attacked the Byzantines from the north, gaining new treaty concessions. Then in 445 Attila murdered Bleda, thus becoming the sole ruler of the Hun tribes of Pannonia. In the end, a nervous Aetius allied himself with the Visigoths to meet Attila in the Battle of the Catalaunian Plain (451) near Troyes, France, where the Visigoth king Theodoric II lost his life and the Romans withdrew in a battle that left neither Hun nor Roman the victor. With Attila's death in 453, Hun influence on Europe rapidly crumbled.

Where the Huns had originated is unknown, but written sources leave no doubt on their physical appearance, which was clearly mongoloid. No text in the Hun language has been found; archaeological finds from Hun areas remain controversial. What is certain is that despite their impact on the formation of Europe, the Huns never attained the power of the great Inner Asian states such as those of the Türks or the Mongols. [*See also* Hun Religion.]

Hsien-pei and Juan-juan. As already mentioned, the Northern Hsiung-nu state was replaced around 155 CE by that of the Hsien-pei, who probably spoke a Mongol language. Through this victory, the Hsien-pei became the dominant tribal confederacy on the Mongolian steppe. With other nomadic peoples, including the Southern Hsiung-nu and the Wu-huan, they continued attacks on China but were repulsed, particularly by the famous Chinese general Ts'ao Ts'ao. When the Hsien-pei first appeared, during the Wang Mang interregnum (9–23 CE), they had no supreme ruler; unified leadership is not ascribed to them until just before their defeat of the

Hsiung-nu. Oral tradition embellished this first leader, T'an-shih-huai (d. between 178 and 183), with a "miraculous birth," heroic qualities, and the wisdom to be a chief, yet the Hsien-pei failed to create a lasting empire in this fragmented period of steppe history.

From approximately 400 to 550 a new power emerged on the Mongolian steppe: the Juan-juan (or Jou-jan). Their origins are uncertain but future research may clarify their relation to the Hua and to the Avars who appeared in Europe in the fifth century. According to a widely accepted but yet unproven theory, the Juan-juan in the east are identified with the Avars in the west. Personal names, as given in Chinese, do not appear to be either Turkic or Mongol, but it is with the Juan-juan that the title *kaghan* is first used for the ruler. In 546 the last ruler, A-na-kui, was approached by a man named Bumin (T'u-men), whom he called a blacksmith slave, and who had the audacity to request the hand of one of A-na-kui's daughters. He was rudely refused—so the story goes—whereupon Bumin and his followers revolted, overthrew the Juan-juan, and established their own Türk empire.

Türk. The appearance of the Türk—the first Inner Asian people whose language is known and the first also to use with certainty a Turkic idiom—marks a turning point in the history of the steppe. According to Chinese sources they were metallurgists employed by the Juan-juan, but it is not clear whether the revolt led by Bumin (d. 552) was social in character or a minority uprising. After Bumin's death the empire split, one group, led by his son, establishing itself on the Mongolian steppe, while the other group, under the leadership of his brother Ishtemi, ruled over the more western part of the empire. They encountered the Ephthalites (or White Huns) on the borders of Persia. The Türk made an alliance with Sasanid Persia (226–655), encircled and destroyed the Ephthalites, establishing thereby a common border with Persia, but also obtaining control of the lucrative silk trade. Because of its commercial interests—represented mainly by Sogdian merchants—the Western Türk empire then found itself embroiled in the conflict between Persia and Byzantium. Persian attempts to stop silk from reaching Byzantium forced the Türk to go directly to Byzantium by a northern route. It was for this reason that embassies were first exchanged between Türk and Byzantium, opening up entire new horizons for Romans as well as for the Chinese. The first Türk embassy, headed by a Sogdian named Maniakh, reached the court of Justin II (r. 565–578) in 567. The Türk embassy remained in Constantinople, then part returned to the Türk with the Byzantine ambassador Zemarkhos. A later Greek ambassador arrived at a Türk camp at the death of the ruler and witnessed the funeral rites, which included laceration of the faces of the mourners and the sacrifice of horses and servants. The Western Türk empire disintegrated around 659.

The Eastern Türk empire, in a semipermanent state of war with China and plagued by internal dissension, was finally defeated in 630. Chinese rule then lasted until 682 when the Türk revolted and again seized power, forming a second Türk empire that was overthrown in 743 by the revolt of three Turkic tribes: the Basmil, the Karluk, and the Uighur. It was from the period of the second Türk empire that the first indigenous texts from Inner Asia—as stated above, written in a Turkic language—have been found. The most famous of these are funeral-stela inscriptions written in a runiclike alphabet found in the area of the Orkhon River and dedicated to the

Türk ruler, Bilge Kaghan (r. 716–734), his brother Kül Tegin, and the prime minister Tonyuquq. These texts give not only a history of the Türk people but also provide valuable insight into Türk society and customs, including their belief in *tengri* ("heaven, sky"), in the sacred mountain of Ötükän, and in the erection of *balbal* (stone pillars) on the tomb of a warrior inscribed with the name of an enemy he had killed. [*See* Tengri.] Chinese sources recorded three Türk legends of origin quite different from one another: the child raised by a wolf, the child born of the spirit of wind and rain, the child born of the spirit of the lake. Such a multiplicity of ancestral traditions would suggest that the Türk empire was most likely a confederation of tribes of diverse origin.

Avars, Khazars, and Bulgars. The Greek historian Priscus wrote of a migration of peoples taking place from 461 to 465 on the south Russian steppe. An embassy from the Oghur, Onoghur, and Saroghur had arrived in Byzantium, reporting that they had been pushed by the Sabir, who in turn were being displaced by a people in Central Asia called Avar. For almost a century there was no news of them, but in 558 the Avars, now in the Caucasus, sent an embassy to the Byzantine emperor Justinian I (r. 527–565) requesting land in exchange for military protection. Fleeing from the Western Türk, the Avars were given asylum in the Byzantine empire by Justin II, an act that infuriated the Türk, who considered the Avars their own, fugitive subjects. It is a well-documented Inner Asian concept that ruling tribes owned the peoples whom they had conquered. Settled in the Carpathian Basin, the Avars remained there for some two and a half centuries, becoming an effective wedge between the northern and southern Slavs. When they had arrived in the Carpathian Basin, the Avars found two Germanic tribes, the Gepids, whom they destroyed, and the Lombards, who fled and settled in northern Italy. The Avars also menaced the Byzantines and the Franks. In 626 the Avars and the Persians jointly attacked Constantinople and were defeated only when the Byzantine forces destroyed the Persian fleet as it attempted to cross the Bosphorus.

Meanwhile, the south Russian steppe continued to be a place of turmoil. The Turkic-speaking Khazars became increasingly powerful with the weakening of the western Türk, and by the mid-seventh century achieved independence. Christian and Islamic missionaries had already had some influence among the Khazars, but in 740 the Khazar ruler and his entourage adopted Judaism. Not an empire bent on conquest, but practicing a settled, mixed economy based on cattle breeding, agriculture, and trade, the Khazars nevertheless caused some movement on the steppe and prevented Arab and Islamic penetration into eastern Europe. Pushed by the Khazars, the Bulgars (a Turkic-speaking people who had lived on the Pontic steppe from the late fifth century) split around 680. One group, moving north to the Volga-Kama region, was, in 921, visited by an Arab embassy described by one of its members, Ibn Faḍlān, who left an invaluable account of both the Khazars and the Volga Bulgars. A Christian Bulgar prince, Kovrat, and his son Asparukh led other Bulgar tribes, mostly Turkic, to the lower Danube region where Asparukh created a Bulgar state between 679 and 681. Some of the Bulgars settled with the Avars in the Carpathian Basin, but the formation of this Bulgar buffer state between the Avars and Byzantium effectively ended Avar-Byzantine relations by 678. As a result, the Avars led a reasonably quiet life for over a century until they were attacked and greatly weakened (although not defeated) in 791, 795–796, and 803 by Charlemagne. The Avars slowly disappeared over the next eighty years until Hungarian (Magyar) tribes filled the vacuum and maintained the non-Slavic wedge in central Europe. [*See also* Hungarian Religion.]

Uighurs. The final blow to the Türk empire was delivered by the Uighurs who, as we have seen, had been a part of the Türk confederacy. Their language was basically the same as that of the Türk, with some of their texts written in runic script and some in a script borrowed from the Sogdians, one that would become a major script used in Inner Asia. Unlike the Türk, whom they overthrew in 743, the Uighurs often allied themselves with China; thus, during the reign of Mou-yü the Uighurs helped China to quell the An Lu-shan rebellion (755–757). When Mou-yü visited Lo-yang in 762–763, he was converted to Manichaeism, which had been propagated in China by the Sogdians. A description of his conversion appears on the trilingual inscription (in Uighur, Sogdian, and Chinese) of Karabalghasun, the Uighur capital city. When Mou-yü returned home he took Manichaean priests with him and made Manichaeism the state religion. [*See* Manichaeism, *overview article*]. Thus, the Uighurs became the first Inner Asian people to adopt an institutionalized, major religion. Many Uighurs disliked the influence gained by Sogdians in Uighur affairs and an anti-Sogdian faction, led by the uncle of Mou-yü, revolted and killed the kaghan and his family. There followed a succession of rulers embroiled in family intrigues, plagued by assassinations and suicide. Even so, Sogdian and Manichaean influence remained in a kingdom dominated by Buddhism. An Arab traveler, Tamīm ibn Baḥr, visited Karabalghasun in 821 and left an account of what he saw. Of particular interest are his remarks about the flourishing town of Karabalghasun and other small settlements, located in richly cultivated areas. The picture he draws contradicts the stereotyped image of the incompatibility of Inner Asian civilization and urban development. In 840 the Uighurs were attacked by a new Turkic power, the Kirghiz, who lived north and west of the great Mongolian steppe.

Not absorbed into the new ruling Kirghiz confederacy, the Uighurs moved. Some went to China, settling in today's Kansu Province, where some of their descendants can still be found; the majority moved to the Tarim Basin and created a new state centered on the city of Kocho (850–1250), where a sophisticated, multilingual, and multiethnic civilization developed. A cultured leisure class in the refined society supported Buddhism, Manichaeism, the arts and letters, and lavish entertainments. Here, the Uighurs adopted a completely sedentarized life based on agriculture supported by extensive irrigation works. As Kocho was a main stop on the east-west trade route, economic prosperity played a major role in the growth of Uighur civilization. When the Kitans, a Mongol people who overthrew the Kirghiz in 924, offered to let the Uighurs return to their former steppe lands, the Uighurs declined to move, preferring their life in Kocho. In 1250, the kingdom of Kocho voluntarily submitted to the Mongols. Uighur script was adopted by the Mongols and many Uighur scribes became skilled administrators for the Mongols. The famous German Turfan expeditions of 1902–1903, 1904–1905, and 1905–1907, led by A. Grünwedel and Albert von Le Coq, unearthed from the dry sands of the Tarim Basin the glories of the kingdom of Kocho: unparalleled art treasures including Manichaean and Buddhist frescoes and manuscripts in many languages, illuminating the splendor of Uighur civilization.

Mongols. The rise of Mongol power and the domination of the Chinggisid states brought unification to Inner Asia in a way that had not existed since prehistoric times.

Central Asia Before the Mongol Conquest. Arab penetration into Central Asia began in 652 and culminated in the Battle of Talas (751), thus permitting the spread of Islam into Central Asia. Wars with the Uighurs had forced the Karluk west and in 999 they seized Bukhara, an act that brought strong Turkic influence to the region. Farther to the west on the steppe north of the Black and Caspian seas lived the Turkic tribes of the Kipchaks (known also as Cumans or Polovtsy), whose move to these regions is shrouded in mystery. To the south of them, the Oghuz tribes—mentioned in the Orkhon inscriptions—were steadily moving westward, into Anatolia, where they were to form the basis of the Ottoman state.

The Rise of Inner Asian Powers in Manchuria. A mixture of forests rich in game, agricultural land made fertile by abundant rainfall, and pastures suitable for horse and cattle breeding determined the basic economy of Manchuria. The settled way of life also made pig raising an important feature of all Manchurian civilizations. In the fourth century, the Mongol-speaking Kitan began to gain dominance in the region, entering into relations with China in 468, but by the sixth century, they came under Türk domination. A new Kitan rise to power was signalled by their attack and defeat of the Kirghiz ruling over the Mongolian steppe in 924; they then expanded their rule over North China, adopting the Chinese dynastic title of Liao (927–1125). In 1125 Kitan domination was replaced by that of the Jurchen, a Tunguz-speaking Manchurian people who had been Kitan subjects. The Jurchen assumed the Chinese dynastic title of Chin (1125–1234) and maintained their rule over northern China until the Mongol conquest. When the Jurchen moved into North China, some Kitan tribes, with the permission of the Uighurs, moved west across the Tarim Basin through the kingdom of Kocho to Central Asia, where a third Kitan state was founded (after those of Manchuria and China), that of the Karakitai (Black Kitan or Kitai) centered at Balasagun in the Chu River valley.

Chinggis Khan and the Mongol Conquest. Between Central Asia and Manchuria, two major mongolized Turkic tribes, the Naiman and the Kereit, were vying for power in the eleventh century. Both tribes had been strongly influenced by Nestorianism; the conversion of the Kereit around 1000 was related by the Syriac chronicler Bar Hebraeus (fl. thirteenth century). [*See also* Nestorian Church.] The first united Mongol kingdom ended in the late eleventh century, followed by a period of internecine warfare between Mongol tribes and against the neighboring Tatar tribes. It was not until Chinggis (known as Temüjin before he was elected khan) had defeated all of his rivals that a new and powerful Mongol state emerged. These events, chronicled in *The Secret History of the Mongols* (mid-thirteenth century), were only the first shadows of what was to come as the Mongol empire spread over the Eurasian continent.

Chinggis, angered by the Naiman leader Küchlüg, who had defeated the Karakitai in Central Asia, began the great push west, defeating the Naiman in 1218, and then led a punitive campaign against Khorezm aimed at avenging the murder of Mongol envoys. Before Chinggis's death in 1227, Central Asia had been devastated, and the campaigns of the famous Mongol generals Jebe and Sübetei had spilled into Georgia,

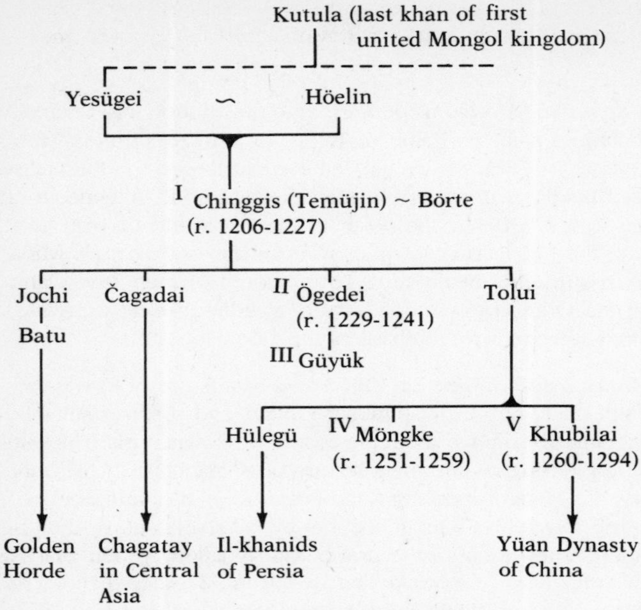

FIGURE 1: **Genealogy of the House of Chinggis**

across the Caucasus, and into Russian territory, where the Russian forces and their Cuman allies were defeated in the Battle of Kalka in the late spring of 1223. The Mongols advanced as far as the city of Bulgar where they were turned back at the very end of the year 1223. With the death of Chinggis, the Mongol empire was to be divided among his four sons. But the eldest son, Jochi, predeceased Chinggis and his appanage of the westernmost Mongols, the so-called Golden Horde, went to his son, Chinggis's grandson, Batu. Of the remaining sons, Čagadai's domains were in Central Asia, Tolui remained on the homeland, and Ögedei was elected great khan in 1229. (See figure 1.) [*See also the biography of Chinggis Khan.*]

The Mongols in Europe. Defeating Bulgar in the winter of 1237–1238, the Mongols then swept into eastern and central Europe with a great offensive begun in the winter of 1239–1240: Kiev fell on 6 December 1240, German forces were defeated at the Battle of Liegnitz on 9 April 1241, and the Hungarian army fell two days later. Suddenly, in 1242, the Mongols withdrew from Europe and returned to the rich pastures of the south Russian steppe. All of Europe now accepted the Mongol threat as real, however, an attitude that opened a period of rapprochement in Mongol-Western relations, begun by Pope Innocent IV (r. 1234–1254) at the Council of Lyons (June 1245). Three groups of papal emissaries were sent to the Mongols: the Dominican Ascelinus, the Dominican Andrew of Longjumeau, and the Franciscan Giovanni da Pian del Carpini, who brought back the first extensive accounts of the Mongols, as did the later Franciscan missionary William of Rubrouck, who journeyed to the Mongols from 1253 to 1255.

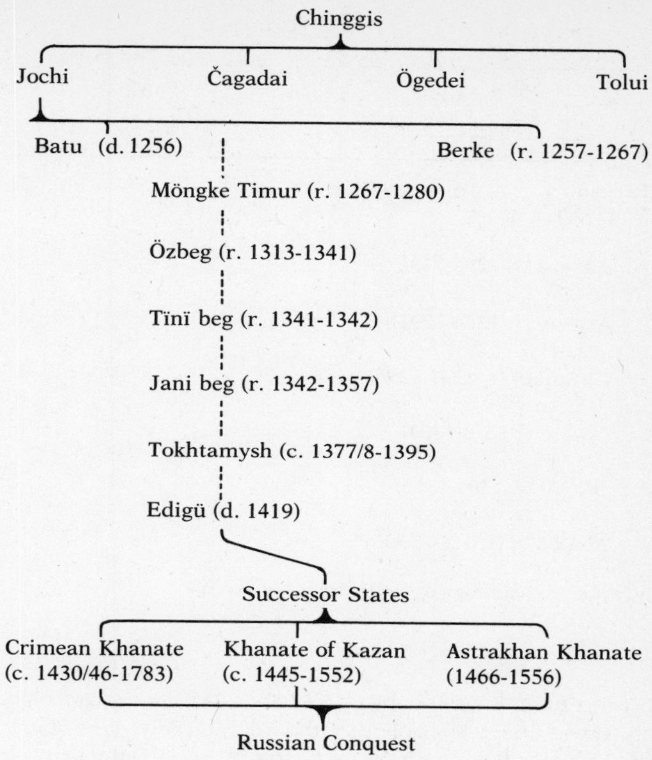

FIGURE 2: Genealogy of the Golden Horde

The Golden Horde and the Il-khanids. With Batu's death in 1256, his brother Berke (r. 1257–1267) became ruler of the Golden Horde. He converted to Islam, thus placing the Golden Horde at odds with the Il-khanids of Persia. The Il-khanids came to power under Hülegü, who sacked Baghdad in 1258 and ended the Abbasid caliphate. The Mamluk sultan Baybars (r. 1259–1277), powerful foe of the Crusaders but also of the Mongols, defeated the Il-khanid forces in the Battle of Ain Jalut (1259), thereby stopping the Mongol conquest of the Arab world. During the reign of the Il-khan Arghun (r. 1284–1291), Buddhism was declared the state religion and close contact was maintained with Europe, particularly with the Vatican and the kings of France and England. Under severe economic pressure, Il-khanid Persia declined and religious tension forced Gazan (r. 1295–1304) to proclaim Islam the official religion. With the death of Abu Saʿīd in 1335, Il-khanid Persia fragmented. (See figure 2.) Meanwhile, the power of the Golden Horde reached its apogee under Özbeg (r. 1313–1341), but attempts to expand its territory brought it into military conflict with ambitious Muscovite princes and the great military leader Timur (Tamarlane; 1336–1405) in Central Asia. Finally, the Golden Horde split into three successor states: the khanates of Kazan, Astrakhan, and the Crimea. (See figure 3.)

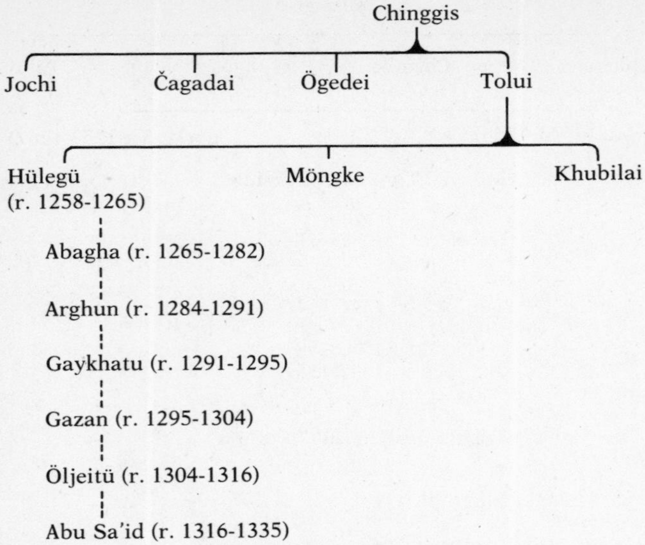

FIGURE 3: **Genealogy of the Il-khanids of Persia**

The Mongols in China. It was Khubilai (r. 1260–1294), the last great Mongol khan, who brought China under Mongol rule (the Yüan dynasty, 1264–1368). With the extended visit of Marco Polo to Khubilai's court (1271–1292) the first reliable information about China came to the West. After the death of Khubilai, Mongol rule in China began to weaken until they were overthrown in 1368 by the Chinese. What remained of Mongol power returned to the steppe where the western Mongols (Oirats, Dzungars, Kalmuks) became a factor in Central Asia, with two successive Oirat states menacing the territory between the western Mongolian steppe and the Caspian Sea from the mid-fifteenth century until their final defeat in 1758 at the hands of the Chinese.

With the decline of the Mongol empire, the patterns of Inner Asian civilization were well established. The development of firearms eliminated the advantages of the Inner Asian warrior: the economic structure of Inner Asia could not technologically advance. The change from land routes to sea routes considerably diminished Inner Asia's role as an intermediary between east and west. Even though the last Chinese dynasty, the Ch'ing (1644–1911) was Manchu, founded by Tunguz-speaking peoples from Manchuria, it rapidly became sinicized, losing much of its Inner Asian character at a very early date. The simultaneous penetration by Russia and China had profoundly changed the structure of Inner Asian civilization. The history of these later periods, not typically Inner Asian, does not shed light on what made the civilization of Central Eurasia unique.

[*See also* Turkic Religions; Mongol Religions; Islam, *article on* Islam in Central Asia; *and* Prehistoric Religions, *article on* The Eurasian Steppes and Inner Asia.]

BIBLIOGRAPHY

The classic definition of Inner Asia can be found in Denis Sinor's "Central Eurasia," in *Orientalism and History,* 2d rev. ed., edited by Denis Sinor (Bloomington, Ind., 1970), pp. 93–119, and expanded in textbook form in his *Inner Asia: History, Civilization, Languages; A Syllabus* (Bloomington, Ind., 1969). Sinor's *Introduction à l'étude de l'Eurasie Centrale* (Wiesbaden, 1963) is the basic bibliographic work for the study of Inner Asia and is invaluable for the author's opinion on research in a field dominated by French, German, Russian, and Hungarian scholarship. Other histories of Inner Asia that can be consulted with profit include René Grousset's *The Empire of the Steppes: A History of Central Asia,* translated by Naomi Walford (New Brunswick, N.J., 1970); Wilhelm Barthold's *Turkestan down to the Mongol Invasion,* 3d ed. (London, 1968); and the collection of essays in the *Handbuch der Orientalistik,* vol. 5.5, *Geschichte Mittelasiens,* under the general editorship of Bertold Spuler (Leiden, 1966). *The Cambridge History of Inner Asia,* under preparation by its editor, Denis Sinor, will bring the scholarship on Inner Asia up to date.

For the art of Inner Asia, Karl Jettmar's *The Art of the Steppes,* translated by Ann E. Keep (New York, 1967), provides an excellent introduction plus ample illustrations both in black and white and in color. The best book on the epic in Inner Asia is Nora K. Chadwick and Victor Zhirmunsky's *Oral Epics of Central Asia* (Cambridge, 1969), but it concerns only the Turkic-speaking peoples.

For a discussion of the early Arab penetration into Inner Asia, which opened the region to Islam, H. A. R. Gibb's *The Arab Conquests in Central Asia* (London, 1923) remains a useful account. In a similar vein, Owen Lattimore's *The Inner Asian Frontiers of China* (New York, 1940) and *Studies in Frontier History: Collected Papers 1928–1958* (Oxford, 1962) are unique in that much of Lattimore's life has been spent in the region.

The most extensive portrayal of the life of the Scythians can be found in Ellis H. Minn's *Scythians and Greeks: A Survey of Ancient History and Archeology on the North Coast of the Euxine from the Danube to the Caucasus* (Cambridge, 1913). The most detailed account of the Huns is J. Otto Maenchen-Helfen's *The World of the Huns: Studies in Their History and Culture,* edited by Max Knight (Berkeley, 1973). Annemarie von Gabain's work on the Uighur kingdom of Kocho, *Das Leben im uigurischen Königreich von Qočo: 850–1250,* in "Veröffentlichungen der Societas Uralo-Altaica," vol. 6 (Wiesbaden, 1973), is unparalleled. There is no good history of the Türk empire, a gap that will be filled by *The Cambridge History of Inner Asia.*

For the Mongols, however, there is an abundance of material. René Grousset's *Conqueror of the World,* translated by Denis Sinor in collaboration with Marian MacKellar (Edinburgh, 1967), is the best book on the life of Chinggis. For the Mongol Il-khans and the Golden Horde, Bertold Spuler's *The Muslim World: A Historical Survey,* vol. 2, *The Mongol Period* (Leiden, 1960); *Die Goldene Horde: Die Mongolen in Russland, 1223–1502,* 2d ed. (Wiesbaden, 1965); and *Die Mongolen in Iran* (Leipzig, 1939) are by far the most useful in this complex period of Mongol history.

12 ISLAM IN CENTRAL ASIA

Alexandre Bennigsen and Fanny E. Bryan

Central Asia (Turkistan) was already an ancient and prosperous center of civilization when penetrated by Islam in the seventh century. Its population, both sedentary and nomadic, was of Iranian stock. For several hundred years its rulers had controlled the two most important trade routes of the ancient world, the Silk Road linking the Mediterranean to China and the Spice Road to India. Despite its location and the resulting prosperity, however, Turkistan had not been the center of a mighty empire: the native principalities were too weak to mount a successful opposition to their more powerful neighbors to the east, north, and west.

Indeed, Central Asia had been invaded and conquered more than once, by the Achaemenid Persians, the Macedonians of Alexander, the Seleucids (who succeeded Alexander), the Sasanids, the Kushans (nomads from the north), the Hephthalites, the Türk (in the sixth century), and finally the Chinese, who had reached the zenith of their political power toward 620 under the T'ang dynasty. The Türk, who made their first appearance in Central Asia around 565, had displaced the Iranian nomads and established an immense empire from the frontiers of China to the confines of Sasanid Persia and Byzantium. On the eve of the Arab invasion, Turkistan was divided into a number of small principalities, the most important of which were the kingdoms of Samarkand, Ferghana, and Khorezm. As a result of its past history, the sedentary civilization of the area presented a unique picture of religious and cultural syncretism. Almost all the major organized religions were to be found there, coexisting in a climate of exceptional tolerance: Zoroastrianism, the religion of the ruling class of Khorezm and Bactria; Buddhism, especially in Bactria, Sogdiana (the capital of Samarkand), and Tokharistan; as well as Nestorian Christianity, Judaism, and Manichaeism among the urban trading communities of the Silk Road. When the Arabs penetrated into Turkistan, the various priesthoods played no part whatsoever in the warfare.

THE BEGINNING OF ISLAMIZATION

In marked contrast to the rapid progress of the Arab conquerors in Iran or North Africa, the expansion of Islam in Transoxiana (Lat., "beyond the Oxus," like the

Arabic name for the same territory, Mā warā'a al-Nahr, "what lies beyond the river") was a slow and lengthy matter. The earliest Arab expeditions beyond the Amu Darya (Oxus River) were motivated by the desire for booty and glory. In the main, religion was of as little importance to them as it was to the defenders of the land. Although the expeditions began in 649, it was not until a century later, after the Arabs' great victory over the Chinese at the battle of the Talas River in 751, that Islam prevailed in Turkistan. At this same time Arab victories over the Turkic nomads on the Syr Darya River (Jaxartes) brought about the final dismemberment of the Turkic khaganate. As a result, a new era of peace and prosperity came to the sedentary town lands of Transoxiana, and the basis was laid for the "Golden Age" of the Samanids in the tenth century.

Legend has it that the first Arab incursion took place under the caliph ʿUthmān (r. 644–656), when 2,700 companions of the Prophet were said to have invaded Ferghana, and Muḥammad ibn Jawr led the companions to their death in battle against the "infidels." In fact, ʿAbd Allāh ibn Amīr, governor of Basra, conquered Merv and Sarakhs in present-day Turkmenistan in 649. Twenty-five years later the first Arab troops crossed the Amu Darya and defeated the ruler of Bukhara; this raid, under ʿUbayd Allāh ibn Ziyād, governor of Khorasan, was followed by several others north of the Amu Darya.

In 676 a cousin of the Prophet, Qutham ibn al-ʿAbbās, is said to have arrived in Samarkand together with Saʿīd ibn ʿUthmān ibn ʿAffān. Qutham became known to the Central Asians as Shah-i Zindah, the "living prince." During the reign of the Abbasids, and probably with their cooperation, Qutham's tomb in Samarkand—whether actual or alleged is not known—became the object of religious pilgrimage, and it is still one of the most holy places in Central Asia.

A successful campaign was waged against Khorezm between 681 and 683 by Salm ibn Ziyād, governor of Khorasan. He later advanced to Samarkand and became the first Arab governor to winter across the Amu Darya.

Other expeditions were conducted across the Amu Darya against Shahr-i Sabz and Tirmidh (Termez) in 697 and again at the turn of the century, but the real conquest of Turkistan began early in the eighth century. During the period between 704 and 715, Qutaybah ibn Muslim, governor of Khorasan, brought the definitive annexation of the lands north of the Amu Darya. He conquered Bukhara, where he built the first mosque (on the site of a former Buddhist temple), and Samarkand. Establishing an Arab garrison at Shāsh (Tashkent), he pressed forward to the north as far as Isfījāb. At his death in 715, Qutaybah was campaigning in Ferghana.

After Qutaybah's death, the Arabs suffered a considerable setback in Transoxiana. In 721 Khojend, the key of the Ferghana Valley, surrendered to them; three years later, however, a Muslim expedition on Ferghana was heavily defeated by the Türk.

Asad ibn ʿAbd Allāh al-Qaṣrī, governor of Khorasan, was the first to fortify the border of the Arab possessions. In 727 he built *ribāṭ*s (stations for cavalry troops) to defend the frontier against the attacks of the Türk. Asad also began the project of converting all the inhabitants of Transoxiana to Islam. Missionaries dispatched to Samarkand initially met with moderate success, but as taxes *(kharāj)* continued to be levied on all those who were formerly liable, a general revolt broke out. The whole of Sogdiana rose against the Arabs, and help was sought from the Türk. In 728, only Samarkand remained in Arab hands, but in 729 the Arabs reestablished their authority over Bukhara as well.

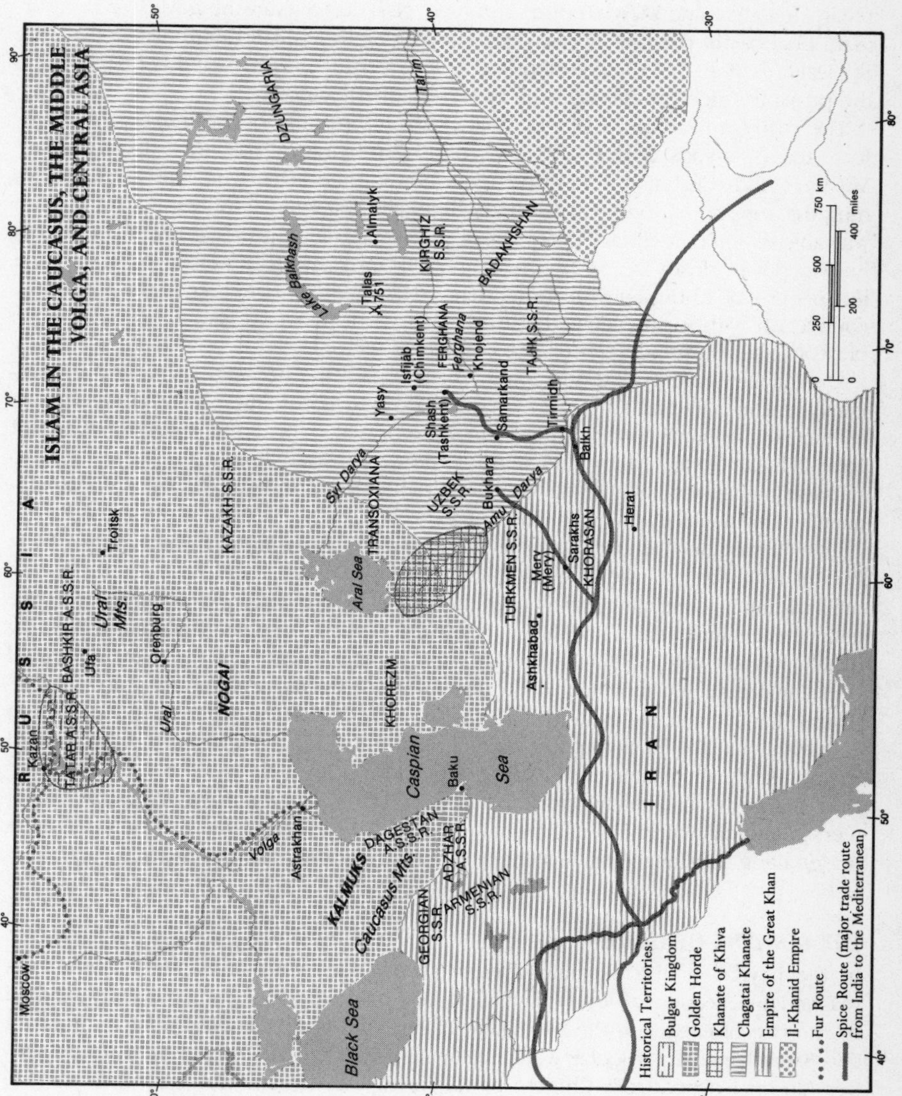
ISLAM IN THE CAUCASUS, THE MIDDLE VOLGA, AND CENTRAL ASIA
Historical Territories:
Bulgar Kingdom
Golden Horde
Khanate of Khiva
Chagatai Khanate
Empire of the Great Khan
Il-Khanid Empire
Fur Route
Spice Route (major trade route from India to the Mediterranean)
R U S S I A
Moscow
Kazan
TATAR A.S.S.R.
BASHKIR A.S.S.R.
Ufa
Ural Mts.
Troitsk
Orenburg
Ural
NOGAI
KAZAKH S.S.R.
Volga
Astrakhan
KALMUKS
Caucasus Mts.
DAGESTAN A.S.S.R.
ADZHAR A.S.S.R.
ARMENIAN S.S.R.
GEORGIAN S.S.R.
Black Sea
Caspian
Sea
Baku
KHOREZM
Aral Sea
TRANSOXIANA
Syr Darya
UZBEK S.S.R.
Bukhara
Amu Darya
TURKMEN S.S.R.
Ashkhabad
Merv (Mery)
Sarakhs
KHORASAN
Herat
Balkh
Tirmidh
Samarkand
Shash (Tashkent)
Yasy
Isfijab (Chimkent)
FERGHANA
Ferghana
Khojend
TAJIK S.S.R.
Talas X 751
KIRGHIZ S.S.R.
BADAKHSHAN
Lake Balkhash
Almalyk
DZUNGARIA
Tarim
I R A N
0 250 500 750 km
0 200 400 miles
90° 80° 70° 60° 50° 40°
50° 40° 30°

For over a decade the Arabs remained on the defensive, losing control of practically all their territories north of the Amu Darya, and in 737 the Turkic khagan was even able to make incursions south of the river. The following year, however, the Arab-Turkic competition for control of Transoxiana came to an end. The Türk were finally defeated, and their empire crumbled. Naṣr ibn Sayyār, the governor of Khorasan, once again pacified Transoxiana and reestablished Arab domination over the Syr Darya region. In 739 he established Arab governors in Shāsh and Fergana to rule the provinces side by side with the native (Iranian) princes.

The real islamization of Central Asia began at the time of the transfer of power from the Umayyads to the Abbasids around 750. A major role was played by Abū Muslim (ʿAbd al-Raḥmān ibn Muslim), an Abbasid missionary who succeeded in winning the support of the local feudal nobility and the rural population. Abū Muslim was able to effect a certain compromise between Islam and local beliefs. Although he was put to death in 755 by the caliph al-Manṣūr, he had a lasting influence on the people of Khorasan and Transoxiana. His memory was constantly revived in connection with various cults that made their appearance in later years, and series of proto-Shīʿī movements were also connected with his name.

During the same period, the T'ang emperor, still the nominal sovereign of Turkistan, sent a powerful Chinese expedition to reestablish his power. The Chinese entered the upper Syr Darya Valley but were heavily defeated in 751 at the Battle of Talas. This victory, led by Abū Muslim's general, Ziyād ibn Ṣāliḥ, put an end to Chinese pretensions of rule in Transoxiana and was soon followed by the final submission and the conversion to Islam of the rulers of the Turkistani principalities.

The islamization of Turkistan was accompanied by a singular renaissance of the Persian language and literature that V. V. Barthold (1956–1962) has called "the cultural triumph of the vanquished over the victors." This triumph was achieved at the end of the ninth century with the foundation of the Iranian Samanid dynasty by Ismāʿīl ibn Aḥmad (r. 892–907). From their capital in Bukhara, the Samanids ruled over the whole of Transoxiana. Ferghana and Khorezm, protected against the shamanist Turkic nomads by a line of frontier posts, were regarded as good Muslim countries, and their native populations began to take part in the battle for the faith against their infidel neighbors. There appeared at this time the first guilds of "warriors for the faith" *(ghuzāt* and *fityān;* sg., *ghāzī, fatā)* composed of urban volunteers. Sedentary Turkistan also began to be used as a base by the first Ṣūfī dervishes undertaking missionary work within the Turkic steppes. [*See* Dervishes.]

THE ROOTING OF ISLAM

In the heyday of the Samanid dynasty (ninth and tenth centuries), Central Asia reached an exceptional level of political, cultural, and economic prosperity marked by the rise of cities and the expansion of international trade and industry. Bukhara and Samarkand in particular were important centers for the manufacture of rag paper (an art learned from Chinese prisoners captured at the Battle of Talas in 751) and textiles. Enterprises in these cities maintained close trade contacts with China, India, the kingdom of Bulgar and the rest of the Muslim world. The brilliant Samanid court made Bukhara one of the capitals of the Muslim world and, with the poet Rūdākī (913–943), the birthplace of Persian literature. The new order of centralized civil and military bureaucracy introduced by the Samanids brought autocratic rule and heavy taxation to their subjects, and their political structure came to supersede completely the old feudal regime of independent princes and landed aristocracy. Even so, the subject population retained some of its warlike habits and continued to carry arms; it was the urban masses who provided the bodies for the "warriors of the faith" defending the frontiers against the raids of the pagan nomads.

It was also under the Samanids that Sunnī Islam of strict orthodoxy was firmly established in Transoxiana. Islamic judges and religious leaders acquired great prestige. Among the most celebrated were Abū Ḥafṣ (d. 832), Abū Manṣūr al-Māturīdī of Samarkand (d. 944), and Abū Bakr al-Qaffāl al-Shāshī (d. 1114). By the end of the ninth century, Bukhara had a solid reputation as one of the main centers of Islamic theology.

The Early Spread of Islam. The Samanids were the first Central Asian rulers to conduct raids against the shamanist or Christian Turkic people of the steppes. In 893, under the leadership of Ismāʿīl ibn Aḥmad, the Samanids carried out a successful expedition to Talas and converted the main Nestorian church into a mosque. They also granted lands along the Syr Darya to Turkic settlers who agreed to embrace Islam and to defend the border against their shamanist kin. It was these sedentary people, together with Muslim merchants and the vagabond dervishes, who brought Islam to the steppes.

The Muslim rulers of Khorezm, vassals of the Samanids, and the merchants from Gurganj played the same missionary role vis-à-vis the steppes of the Lower Volga and the faraway Bulgar. But the Samanids never tried to mount a systematic religious propaganda campaign, nor did they attempt to convert the Turkic nomads by force. As Barthold points out, "The success of the Muslim trade was not always accompanied by the success of Islam as a religion. Muslims who traveled for commercial purposes did not get involved in religious propaganda" (*Four Studies on Central Asia,* vol. 1, p. 19). It was through example rather than through persuasion or force that Islam was spread among the nomads.

Thus, in the second half of the tenth century (955), Satuk Bughra Khan, the Karakhanid ruler, embraced Islam. The year 960 is considered to be the date of the first conversion of an entire Turkic horde (200,000 tents strong), without any mention of a "holy war." In 977, Sebüktigin, the Turkic slave who founded the Ghaznavid dynasty, was already a Muslim. In 980, Seljuk, the chief of a Türkmen tribe, crossed the lower reaches of the Syr Darya and became a Muslim.

Numerous non-Muslim colonies survived in Turkistan. Barthold remarks that Central Asian Christians and Manichaeans profited more in their proselytizing activities from the success of Muslim trade than did the Muslims themselves. In fact, the Christians and Manichaeans made their most important gains in Inner Asia (including Sinkiang and Mongolia) under Muslim rule during the tenth and eleventh centuries.

At the time of the Samanids, there were Nestorian Christian communities to the south of the Syr Darya on the border between the cultivated lands and the steppes; Nestorian communities were also to be found in and around Samarkand and Merv (the seat of a Nestorian bishopric). Monophysite Christians were numerous in Khorezm, and there were Jewish trading colonies and Manichaean communities in Samarkand, Bukhara, and Balkh. Traces of Zoroastrianism were to be found around Bukhara and in Khorezm. In the tenth century, a Zoroastrian temple was still in existence at Ramush in the neighborhood of Bukhara. At the periodic fairs held in the city of Bukhara, idols (probably Buddhist figures) were freely sold. Although all Buddhist temples were destroyed in the ninth and early tenth centuries, it is probable that heathen, Buddhist, or dualist beliefs persisted in the countryside. Indeed, these beliefs have survived to the present. Within Sufism, for example, the cult of saints includes some barely distinguished Zoroastrian or Buddhist deities.

At the end of the Samanid period, the northern frontier of Islam coincided broadly with the limits of the cultivated land: Islam did not penetrate deeply into the steppes. Even so, the Muslim base was sufficiently widespread that there was no important incursion of Turkic shamanists from the steppes into Transoxiana after 904. At that time, the invaders were driven back, and from then until the era of the Kara-Khitay, all the nomadic invaders entering Transoxiana from the steppes were already Muslim.

The eastern provinces of Wakhan, Shughnan, Darwaz, and Rushan were politically subject to the Muslims but were populated by shamanists. The city of Jarm in Badakhshan marked the extreme limit of Muslim dominion. Farther north, in the eastern part of the Ferghana valley, the city of Osh (formerly a Zoroastrian center) was a fortified frontier *ribāṭ*.

Ṣūfī Influence. As early as the tenth century, Central Asian Islam had acquired features that distinguished it from Islam in the neighboring regions. The most important of these features was the Ṣūfī *ṭarīqah* (lit., "way"; brotherhood). As early as the ninth century, Abū ʿAbd Allāh Muḥammad ibn Karrām (806–869), a native of Sistan, founded the Karrāmīyah, a mystical sect that spread throughout Transoxiana, including Ferghana, Merv, and Samarkand, and lasted until the Mongol domination. Its adepts practiced pietism and extreme asceticism and were responsible for the conversion of a large number of Zoroastrians and Christians.

Another characteristic aspect of Central Asian Islam was the cult of saints, which combined the veneration of authentic *ghāzī*s and more or less historical Ṣūfī shaykhs with various pre-Islamic beliefs, including the ancestor cult and Zoroastrian or Buddhist deities. Holy places were particularly numerous in the Ferghana Valley near the border of the *dār al-Islām.* Among the most venerated was the tomb of the prophet Ayyūb (Job) near the city of Jalālābād; the tomb was known in the tenth century. Also important were the burial place of the legendary 2,700 companions of the Prophet in Ferghana; the *mazār* ("tomb") of Imam ʿAbd Allāh, the grandson of Imam Ḥusayn, in the city of Kokand; the tomb of Qutaybah ibn Muslim near the village of Kakh; and the tomb of the Ṣūfī shaykh Ḥakīm Abū ʿAbd Allāh Muḥammad ibn ʿAlī al-Tirmidhī in the city of Tirmidh.

With the fall of the Samanids in 1005, the Iranians were replaced by the Turkic dynasties—Karakhanids, Ghaznavids, Khwarizm-shahs, and Seljuks—but this change neither modified the profile of Central Asian Islam nor interrupted the development of Iranian culture. The general economic progress of the country continued as well. The new conquerors either were already Muslim when they crossed the fortified borderline or, as in the case of the Seljuks, embraced Islam as soon as they penetrated into the sedentary territory. They imitated the model of the Samanid court, protecting the frontiers against their barbarian brethren (Türk) or cousins (Mongols).

The new rulers were rapidly "iranized" and became zealous Muslims, allowing all recollection of their pre-Islamic past to fade. Their old Uighur alphabet was abandoned in favor of the Arabic script. Persian and Arabic became the only official languages of the court. All elements of earlier cultures—Manichaean, Chinese, Buddhist, and Nestorian Christian—were forgotten.

During the eleventh and twelfth centuries the brilliant literature flourishing in Central Asia was based exclusively on Muslim and Persian patterns. Among the distinguished scholars, writers, and philosophers of the era were the poet Abū Bakr Muḥammad ibn al-ʿAbbās al-Khwārizmī; the historian Maḥmūd al-Kāshghari, who gave a detailed account of the Turkic tribes and dialects of the Karakhanid kingdom in his *Dīwān lughāt al-Turk;* the Khorezmian Abū al-Rayḥān al-Bīrūnī; the philosopher Abū Sahl al-Masīḥī; Abū ʿAlī ibn Sīnā (Avicenna) from Khorezm, who wrote in Persian and in Arabic; and the great poet Firdawsī at the court of Maḥmūd of Ghaznah. [*See the biographies of al-Bīrūnī and Ibn Sīnā.*]

The Turkic rulers, especially the Karakhanids, were distinguished by great piety, but contrary to their Samanid ancestors, they honored Ṣūfī shaykhs and ascetics more than they honored representatives of the dogmatic religion. During their reign (and especially between 1131 and 1141 under Maḥmūd II ibn Sulaymān), several expeditions were undertaken against the shamanist nomads (Kipchaks) in order to impose Islam by force of arms, although more important in the spread of Islam was the preaching of the Ṣūfī missionaries in the Kipchak steppe.

The twelfth century was marked by the transformation of loose Ṣūfī communities into closely knit, well-organized brotherhoods with formal initiation rites. Two native *ṭarīqah*s were particularly active. The Kubrawīyah *ṭarīqah* in Khorezm was founded by Najm al-Dīn Kubrā (born in Khiva in 1145 and killed in Urgench in 1220 by the Mongols). The Yasawīyah *ṭarīqah* had a great influence in both eastern and western Turkistan and in the adjacent steppes. It was founded by the Turkic poet and mystic Aḥmad Yasawī (born in Isfījāb, present-day Chimkent, and died in 1166 in Yasy, present-day Turkistan in southern Kazakhstan). The Yasawīyah spread throughout Transoxiana, to Khorezm and as far as Bulgar. Its success was partly due to the fact that the brotherhood incorporated into its doctrine certain pre-Islamic (shamanistic) religious practices such as the "loud" *dhikr,* a vocal prayer ceremony in remembrance *(dhikr)* of God. [*See* Dhikr.]

THE PERIOD OF DISASTERS

On 9 September 1141, the army of the Seljuk sultan Sanjar was routed in the Qaṭvān steppe to the north of Samarkand. The new invaders were the Kara-Khitay, a federation of Mongol tribes who had ruled northern China. The defeat by the Kara-Khitay was the greatest disaster ever suffered by the Muslims. Not only were as many as thirty thousand men said to have been killed, but the defeat had been inflicted by "infidels." All of Turkistan had been subjected to the power of a non-Muslim people. Kara-Khitay rule was not exceedingly harsh (especially compared with the Mongol invasion of the next century), but for the first time, a major sector of Islam was challenged by a rival ideology of equal or even superior military and political might. All Muslim chronicles of the time reflect the utter horror of the Islamic world in the face of this new and unexpected development. Indeed, the episode even became known in western Europe.

The Kara-Khitay in Central Asia. Kara-Khitay rule in northern China lasted from 916 to 1125, when their kingdom was overrun by the Jurchens, a Manchu people, and the remaining Kara-Khitay moved westward. The Kara-Khitay had been strongly influenced by Chinese culture and probably used Chinese as their official administrative language. There were some Nestorian Christians and Confucians among them, but the great majority were Buddhists who were particularly unyielding to Islam. The first Kara-Khitay ruler *(gür-khan),* Yeh-lü Ta-shih, was Buddhist; his son and successor had a Nestorian Christian name, Yi-lieh (Elie). The Kara-Khitay penetrated into the steppes of present-day Kazakhstan in 1130; crossing the Syr Darya several years later, they inflicted a heavy defeat on the Karakhanid ruler near Khojent in 1136. Their victory at Qaṭvān in 1141 made them the masters of the whole of Central Asia with the exception of Khorezm.

Even Buddhist domination did not moderate the expansion of Islam, however. Instead, the brief period of peace established by the Kara-Khitay rule permitted Muslim merchants, Ṣūfī preachers, and men of learning to spread Islam farther north and east into the steppes. During the twelfth century, the Turkic rulers of the Ili valley and Almaligh became Muslim, and, according to legend, the Qādirīyah brotherhood began to penetrate into Turkistan.

The situation of Islam grew worse when the Kara-Khitay emperor was deposed by Küchlüg, head of the Mongol Naiman tribe, in 1211. Originally a Nestorian Christian like the majority of his tribe, Küchlüg later became "pagan" (probably Buddhist). He was an open enemy of the Muslims, and under his rule—for the first, and the last, time since Islam was introduced into Central Asia—the religion of the Prophet suffered persecution. Public Muslim worship was suppressed. Muslims were forced to embrace Christianity, to become "idolaters," or at the very least to exchange their Muslim clothing for the Chinese garb of the Kara-Khitay.

Central Asia Under the Mongols. In the autumn of 1219, Mongol vanguards appeared in Central Asia. Less than two years later they had conquered Turkistan, Afghanistan, and the Caucasus. Chinggis Khan was tolerant in religious matters and had no personal animosity against Islam. Muslims, chiefly merchants, were his trusted counselors. Under his reign, Muslims and all other religious groups enjoyed complete religious freedom. His son and successor, Ögedei, was also kindly disposed toward Muslims and gave preference to Islam over other religions. Nonetheless, the destruction and slaughter wreaked on the major cities were so overwhelming that the Mongol conqueror became the symbol of the deadliest danger ever to threaten Islam. The brilliant Muslim civilization of Transoxiana and Khorezm suffered a major setback. For a century Turkistan was put under the administration of yet another "infidel" power. The first Mongol ruler of Turkistan (with the exception of Khorezm, which fell within the province of the Golden Horde) was Chinggis Khan's son Chaghatai. Unlike his father, he was personally hostile to Islam and rigorously punished the observance of certain Islamic prescriptions that infringed on Mongol law, such as performing ablutions in running water or slaughtering an animal by cutting its throat. Chaghatai died in 1241. The majority of his successors remained shamanists. Several, such as Khan Alu-ghu (1259–1266), were strongly inimical to Islam, while others were tolerant in religious matters, although some were more or less influenced by Buddhism or Nestorian Christianity.

This was an unhappy period for Central Asian Islam. A state religion for centuries, it had lost its predominant position and was obliged to share its prestige with other religions, including the hated Buddhism—the creed of the despised idolaters (Pers., *būt-parast*). In the thirteenth and fourteenth centuries there was an upsurge of Nestorian Christianity in Central Asia. Christians were allowed free rein to propagate their faith and to build churches. Orthodox Christians (Alans, Khazars, and Russians) are mentioned by late thirteenth-century European travelers in Urgench, and in 1329 Pope John XXII sent a Catholic bishop to Samarkand, a city where Christians were predominant, according to a Chinese source. There was a Nestorian bishop in Kashgar.

Even more significant was the deep change that took place within Central Asian Islam. The decline of urban culture was followed by the decline of the old Arab-Iranian Muslim religious establishment that had been deeply rooted in city life. Under the Mongols, Islam ceased to be the religion of the ruling elites and became the religion of the rural masses, both sedentary and nomadic.

In the early fourteenth century, according to Barthold, the Mongol rulers of the Chaghatai *ulus* ("appanage") made a decisive step toward the adoption of traditional Islamic culture, if not yet of Islam as a religion. The khan Kebek (1318–1326) renounced the nomadism of his ancestors and took up residence in Transoxiana; although he remained shamanist, he protected the Muslims. His brother and successor, Tarmashirin (1326–1344), was converted to Islam and maintained a climate of great religious tolerance.

Mongol rule witnessed the further development of the Ṣūfī *ṭarīqah* in Central Asia. The Kubrawīyah spread throughout Khorezm; the Yasawīyah was dominant in the Ferghana Valley and among the southern Türkmen tribes; the Qādirīyah developed mainly in the cities of Transoxiana. J. Spencer Trimingham has noted in *The Sufi Orders of Islam* that

> *during this period, the Ṣūfis became for the people the representatives of religion in a new way. . . . The shrine [of the holy* murshid*], not the mosque, became the symbol of Islam. The shrine, the dervish house, and the circle of* dhikr*-reciters became the outer forms of living religion for Iranians, Turks, and Tatars alike.*

THE VICTORY OF ISLAM AND THE ERA OF DECADENCE

The character of Central Asian Islam changed once more in the fifteenth and sixteenth centuries under the Timurid dynasty and its Shaybanid successors. Though Timur followed the Mongol state and military traditions, Islam and Islamic culture were, as Barthold remarks, "cleverly exploited to justify his actions and enhance the splendour of his throne. . . ."

The great conqueror enjoyed the full support of the Muslim upper classes, the religious leaders, and the nomadic aristocracy, whose zeal for Islam was moderate. Timur was also supported by the Iranian population of the Transoxianan cities, those merchants and craftsmen who were more religious than the nomadic Turks. Timur himself was a pious Muslim and was personally interested in deepening the hold of Islam among the superficially islamized rural population and among the nomads. It was during Timur's reign that all traces of non-Muslim religion, with the exception of Bukharan Jews, disappeared from Central Asia. Among the first to disappear were the Nestorian Christians, so powerful under the Čagadai Mongols.

The Ṭarīqahs. Ṣūfī brotherhoods played a dominant role in the expansion and intensification of Islam in Central Asia. They were active during Timur's reign and those of his successors. At this point the Naqshbandīyah and the Yasawīyah were particularly active.

The Naqshbandī *ṭarīqah* was founded in Bukhara by Muḥammad ibn Bahā' al-Dīn Naqshband al-Bukhārī (1317–1389). It is a highly intellectual order, practicing the silent *dhikr.* Although the order is mystical, it is permanently involved in worldly affairs, a dual character symbolized in the two well-known Naqshbandī rules: "Khalvat dar anjoman" ("Solitude in the society") and "Dast be-kār dil bā Yār" ("The hand at work and the heart with the Friend").

The Naqshbandīyah rapidly gained immense prestige throughout Central Asia on every social level. It penetrated the upper echelons among the administrative and military elite of the Timurid state, and also became a major factor on the popular level among the craftsmen of the cities. The tomb of the founder of the *ṭarīqah,* located in a village near Bukhara, is still one of the most popular centers of pilgrimage in Turkistan.

The adepts of the Yasawīyah, meanwhile, were active in spreading the teachings of Islam among the Turkic nomads. Ṣūfī saints whose cults were connected to the national traditions of nomads were particularly important for Timur. Significantly, Timur himself built the mausoleum of the order's founder, Shaykh Aḥmad Yasawī, who had been especially active among the nomads.

Under the Timurids, urban life in Central Asia experienced a new era of economic prosperity and cultural development. Samarkand under Ulugh Beg (1409–1449) and Herat under Ḥusayn Bāyqarā (1469–1509) were brilliant centers of intellectual activity. In Herat, Central Asian poetry, especially in Turkic and Persian, reached its peak with Mīr ʿAlī Shīr Navā'ī, who wrote mainly in Čagadai Turkic, and ʿAbd al-Raḥmān Jāmī, the last of the great Persian poets, both of whom belonged to the Naqshbandī *ṭarīqah.* Against the background of this last Golden Age of Turkistan, it is difficult to agree with those historians (including Barthold) who characterize the era of Ulugh Beg by the emergence of "religious reaction," personified by the Naqshbandī *murshid* Khoja Aḥrār (1404–1490). [*See also* Ṭarīqah.]

Later Dynasties. The sweeping Uzbek conquest of Central Asia in the early sixteenth century did not stop its cultural progress. The Shaybanid rulers, unlike their Mongol ancestors in the thirteenth century, were not "barbarians"; that is to say, they were already Muslims when they crossed the borders of Khorezm. Moreover, they protected the borderlands of Central Asia against their nomadic brethren; ʿAbd Allāh Khan (1559–1598), for example, led several expeditions into the interior of the steppes. Under their rule, their capital, Bukhara, and also Balkh became centers of cultural and social life. The Shaybanid khans, especially ʿUbayd Allāh (d. 1539), were regarded as ideal rulers in the spirit of Muslim piety. This was also true of the Astrakhanids (or Janids), another Chinggisid dynasty that succeeded the Shaybanids in the seventeenth century. They were great builders and protectors of the arts and literature, and a rich historical literature developed in Turkistan under their rule.

By the early sixteenth century, however, the first signs of decline were in evidence. One of the main reasons for the decline was the discovery and development of maritime routes between western Europe, India, and China, which rapidly undermined the Inner Asian caravan trade. By the eighteenth century the area had drifted into an era of economic, political, and finally cultural and intellectual decadence.

The emergence of the Safavid Shīʿī power in Iran and the conquest of Astrakhan by the Muscovites in 1556 established major barriers to the north and south of the Caspian Sea. As a result, the Sunnī world was cut into two parts, and the eastern Turkic peoples of Central Asia were permanently isolated from their brethren in the Ottoman empire to the west.

Finally, in the seventeenth and eighteenth centuries Central Asia suffered one of the most tragic disasters that had ever befallen Muslim Turkistan: the invasion of the "barbarians" from Inner Asia. This incursion, which was particularly detrimental to the northern areas, began in the early years of the seventeenth century, when a full tribe from western Mongolia, the Torgut Mongols, left Dzungaria. Crossing Central Asia from northeast to southwest, they settled in 1613 in the southern Volga region, where they took the name of Kalmuks. Militant Buddhists and adversaries of Islam, they remained an alien, hostile body in the midst of a Muslim Turkic environment.

For a century and a half the Volga Kalmuks and their cousins, the Oirats (who had remained in Dzungaria), systematically raided Central Asia. In contrast to the Mongols of Chinggis Khan, neither the Kalmuks nor the Oirats had the slightest intention of settling in Turkistan. Their interest was confined to plundering and destroying their hated enemies, and their expeditions brought all the ferocity of a religious war, a "Buddhist crusade." The imprint of horror they left behind them virtually erased the memory of all previous invaders, including the Kara-Khitay and the Mongols.

Salvation came to the Muslims only after 1757, when the Oirat kingdom of Dzungaria was finally destroyed by the Manchu armies. But the long struggle against the Buddhists had laid waste Central Asia, ruining its cities and breaking its unity. Toward the end of the eighteenth century three new Turkic dynasties were founded: the Mangit in Bukhara, the Qungrat in Khiva, and the Ming in the Ferghana Valley. However, none of them was strong enough to reunify Turkistan or to protect it from an exterior danger. When the last invaders, the Russians, appeared in Central Asia they encountered only a minimal resistance.

RUSSIAN AND SOVIET DOMINATION

Once the Kalmuk and Dzungarian assault had reduced the mighty Turkic (Kazakh and Nogai) Muslim hordes to a state of total impotence, the Russian vanguard moving south from western Siberia was not only unopposed but welcomed. The Kazakh hordes, unable to resist the superior military power of the Oirats, invoked Russian help and asked for protection. After the destruction of the Dzungarians in the middle of the eighteenth century, there were no rivals to Russian rule. Nominal protection was gradually turned into virtual possession, and direct Russian administration displaced the old feudal systems exercised by the native rulers. All revolts led by the feudal aristocracy against the Russians were crushed, and by the middle of the nineteenth century, the power of the Kazakh khans had been liquidated.

In the Kazakh steppes, the Russians did not try to assimilate the natives. Instead, they adopted a policy that tended to favor the development of a purely Kazakh national, modernist, and secular culture. They hoped to turn such a structure to their own advantage, by setting the superficially islamized Kazakh nomadic nobility against the Tatar merchants and Turkistani clerics who represented Muslim civilization. Notwithstanding a few instances of spectacular success, by and large, this strategy met with failure, and the number of "westernized" Kazakhs remained limited. During the second half of the nineteenth century Islam, brought simultaneously by the Tatar reformers known as *jadid*s and the conservative Bukhara clerics, became more deeply rooted among the nomadic masses. [*See also* Modernism, *article on* Islamic Modernism.]

The Russian advance into Turkistan south of the Syr Darya began as soon as the Caucasian Wars were over in 1859 and met with only sporadic resistance. The three native principalities of Bukhara, Kokand, and Khiva, which had long ago lost their economic and political power, were unable if not unwilling to oppose the overwhelming might of the tsarist empire. Even so, it required half a century of military operations to complete the conquest, beginning in 1855 with the occupation of Chimkent and ending in 1900 with the occupation of the eastern part of the Pamirs. The khanate of Kokand was suppressed, and its territory was placed under direct Russian military administration as the governate general of Turkistan. Bukhara and Khiva became Russian protectorates.

In Turkistan, a country of overpopulated oases, rural colonization was impossible. Consequently, Russian presence remained minimal. There were a few officials and military garrisons, creating "white" colonies in quarters specially built for them. The natives were not considered Russian "citizens" and were not drafted into military service. Russians and Muslims formed distinct communities, coexisting but not mixing with each other. Central Asia as a whole was likewise cut off from any other outside influence. The aim of this simple strategy was to preserve the most archaic forms of Islamic culture in Central Asia. Proselytizing by the Russian Orthodox church was strictly prohibited, and the Tatar modernist *(jadid)* teachers were banned as well. In their place, Qur'anic schools, both *maktab*s and *madrasah*s, of the most conservative *(qadim)* type were favored by the Russians and protected from any modernist influence.

By fostering social, intellectual, and political backwardness, the Russian overlords sought to reduce the possibility of organized national resistance, and their strategy was partly successful. On the eve of the 1917 Russian Revolution, Turkistan was without a doubt one of the most conservative and least advanced areas of the entire Muslim world. But in spite of this limited "success," the dream of keeping the immense territory of Central Asia isolated and "protected" from all external influences was an illusion. Foreign influences—Tatar, Turkish, and Iranian—inevitably penetrated the territory, and while they were of diverse character, ranging from revolutionary to conservative, the common factor among all of them was Islam. As it turned out, these disparate ideas played an important role in the cultural and political awakening of Turkistan at the turn of the twentieth century.

In the same way, the attempts of the Russian authorities to win over the sympathies of the Muslim religious scholars *('ulamā')* were only partly successful. The Turkistani *'ulamā'* remained influential and prosperous through the maintenance of religious endowments. They did not participate in anti-Russian movements after the conquest; indeed, until the 1917 Revolution they remained politically inactive. But at the same time, the equally influential Ṣūfī brotherhoods, especially the militant Naqshbandīyah, played a leading role in virtually all uprisings against Russian rule. Particularly important were the Andijan revolt of 1898 led by a Naqshbandī, the *ishān* (shaykh) Madali, and the resistance of the Tekke Türkmen tribe at Gök-Tepe in 1861, led by another Naqshbandī shaykh, Kurban Murat. However, the Central Asian Naqshbandīyah did not succeed in transforming their revolts into a full-scale "holy war" on the model of the Caucasian Wars.

The 1917 Revolution and the Civil War provided Central Asian Muslims with an opportunity to shake off Russian rule. In 1918 a popular guerrilla movement started in the Ferghana Valley and spread to almost all of Turkistan. The revolt, known as the Basmachi movement (from Uzbek *basmach,* "bandit"), lasted for ten years and was finally crushed in 1928 after a long and difficult struggle. Like the earlier Naqshbandī revolts, the Basmachi movement did not have the characteristics of a holy war. Nonetheless, it was an attempt not only to regain independence but also to protect the purity and the glory of the faith. The Russian Bolsheviks were both alien and infidel rulers and "people without religion" *(bī-dīn).* Although it was not a holy war, Ṣūfī shaykhs and adepts, Naqshbandī and Yasawī, were numbered among the guerrilla fighters.

ISLAM IN CENTRAL ASIA TODAY

According to the 1979 Soviet census, the total Muslim population of Central Asia had reached 29 million, including about 27 million natives and about 2 million immigrants from the Caucasus, the Middle Volga, and the Urals. Crimean Tatars and Transcaucasian Turkic peoples (deportees rather than immigrants), and the remnants of former deportees, the Chechen and Ingush, probably constituted a little less than a million people. By early 1983 the total figure was estimated to have risen to nearly 32 million.

The Turkic peoples (native and immigrants) make up the overwhelming majority (around 90 percent) of the population. Non-Turkic peoples include the Tajiks, the Ironis (descendants of Persian prisoners taken in the seventeenth and eighteenth centuries), the Pamirians, the Chinese Muslims, or Dungans (immigrants of 1856), and an unknown number of Muslim gypsies.

The great majority of Central Asian Muslims are Sunnīs of the Ḥanafī rite. Non-Sunnīs include both Ismāʿīlī and Twelver Shīʿah. The Ismāʿīlīyah, numbering roughly 60,000 to 100,000, are made up of Pamirians in the Gorno-Badakhshan Autonomous Region; their ancestors were converted to Ismāʿīlī Shiism in the eleventh century by the poet-philosopher Naṣīr-i Khusraw. The Twelvers include about 30,000 Ironis, approximately 20,000 Baluchis, and an unknown number (perhaps as many as 100,000) of Uzbeks and Tajiks. The Twelvers are scattered throughout the cities of Samarkand, Urgench, Tashkent, Ashkhabad, Bukhara, and Merv.

Administration. Sunnī Islam in Central Asia is endowed with an official administration, the Muslim Spiritual Board of Central Asia and Kazakhstan, created by the Soviets in 1943. Its headquarters are located in Tashkent. The Twelvers are placed under the authority of the Shaykh al-Islām of Baku. There is no officially recognized authority for the Ismāʿīlīyah.

The spiritual board of Tashkent has under its control all the registered clerics (e.g., *imām-khaṭīb,* muezzin) who alone are permitted to perform religious rites; these probably number less than 1,000. The number of working mosques is estimated at 150 to 200. It is believed that there are 4 mosques in Turkmenistan, 39 in

Tajikistan, and probably about 100 in Uzbekistan. The greatest concentration of mosques is found in the cities of Uzbekistan, in southern Kirghizia (the eastern part of the Ferghana Valley), and in southern Kazakhstan along the Syr Darya Valley.

The U.S.S.R. is not only a secular state but is also officially an atheistic state; hence the church (mosque) is totally separated from the state and from the school. Religious activity outside the official working mosque is strictly forbidden. There are no *waqf*s ("endowments") to administer and no religious courts. Although religious education is banned from Soviet schools, two *madrasah*s administered by the Tashkent Spiritual Board are permitted to train Muslim clerics. One of these, Mīr-i ʿArab in Bukhara, is geared toward intermediate instruction, while the other, Imām Ismāʿīl al-Bukhārī in Tashkent, serves the higher level. The total number of students was estimated at about sixty in the 1980s. After graduation, the best students are sent to al-Azhar University in Egypt or to the Qarawīyīn in Morocco.

All religious publications are forbidden, with the exception of a quarterly periodical published by the Spiritual Board of Tashkent. This quarterly, *Muslims of the Soviet East,* appears in five languages: Arabic, Uzbek in Arabic script, Persian, English, and French. Significantly, there is no Russian edition, nor is there one in modern Uzbek; in other words, the periodical is only for foreign consumption, not for a domestic readership.

Faced with these restrictions, the official Islamic establishment appears to be unable to satisfy the spiritual needs of the population. Its meager resources have been dwarfed by the unrelenting and massive antireligious propaganda campaign to which the population has been subjected since 1928. Despite the inadequacies of official Islam and the ever-present propaganda, however, Soviet sociological surveys conducted in the Central Asian republics in the 1970s revealed that the level of the religious feeling of the Muslim population there was astonishingly high. According to these data, the "believers" constituted some 80 percent of the total population. Within the population, about 20 percent were "believers by conviction" (referred to as "fanatics" in Soviet literature); approximately 10 percent were "believers by tradition"; about 20 percent were "hesitants"; and roughly 30 percent were "unbelievers, who, even so, perform essential religious and custom rites." The "atheists" accounted for the remaining 20 percent of the population, but even among that group, the majority performed the three religious rites of circumcision, marriage, and burial that, to the population, represent adherence to Islam. By contrast, among former Christians in the U.S.S.R. about 80 percent were identified as atheists.

Ṣūfī Organizations. In large part, the strength of Islam is due to the intense activity of the Ṣūfī brotherhoods. After a long period of decline in the nineteenth century, the Ṣūfī brotherhoods gained new prestige from the example of the Basmachi movement. Since the beginning of Soviet rule, Ṣūfī organizations have effectively replaced the official Islamic establishment. They have maintained a network of clandestine houses of prayer and Qur'anic schools (especially around the numerous holy places), and in the absence of "registered" clerics, their adepts are performing the religious rites. In fact, the level of the religious feeling is exceptionally high in those areas where official Islam has been weakened to the brink of total disappearance. Such is the case of the Türkmen Republic, where only four mosques have survived but the Ṣūfī brotherhoods are especially active. According to all Soviet surveys, Turkmenistan is the most religious territory of all Central Asia.

The Ṣūfī *ṭarīqahs* are especially active in the formerly nomadic areas, where the traditional infrastructure of tribes and clans has been preserved and the extended family or the clan serves as the basis for the *ṭarīqah.* One of these areas includes Turkmenistan and southern Kirghizia (in the eastern part of the Ferghana Valley); another consists of southern Kazakhstan and Tajikistan.

Four brotherhoods are prominent today in Central Asia: the Naqshbandīyah, the Yasawīyah, the Qādirīyah, and the Kubrawīyah. But in practice, the distinctions among the orders tend to disappear, and there are many examples of adepts belonging simultaneously to two or more *ṭarīqahs*.

The Naqshbandīyah is influential in the cities of Central Asia and in the rural areas of Turkmenistan, northern Uzbekistan, Karakalpakistan, in the Ferghana Valley, and in western Tajikistan. It is still the largest and probably the most popular Ṣūfī brotherhood of Central Asia.

The Yasawīyah is dominant in the Syr Darya area and in the Ferghana Valley. Until the 1917 Revolution the adepts of this brotherhood were involved in secular affairs, but in the 1920s many of the Yasawīyah took an active part in the Basmachi movement. Following the defeat and repression of the Basmachis, the Yasawīyah gave birth to a new sub-*ṭarīqah,* centered in the Ferghana Valley, the order of the "Hairy Ishan" (Kirghiz, *Chachtuu Eshander*), which was a highly politicized secret organization. Soviet sources accuse the "Hairy Ishan" adepts of sabotaging the regime, of fanaticism, and of political terrorism.

The Qādirīyah is probably the second largest Ṣūfī order in the U.S.S.R. Founded in Baghdad in the twelfth century, it was introduced into Central Asia in the thirteenth, but as the more dynamic Naqshbandīyah expanded in the fifteenth and sixteenth centuries, the influence of the Qādirīyah declined. Around 1850, the Qādirīyah was brought to the northern Caucasus by a Dagestani, Kunta Haji Kishiev. After Kishiev died in a Russian prison, his *ṭarīqah* was divided into three sub-orders: Bammat Giray, Batal Haji, and Chim Mirza. In 1943, the deported northern Caucasian Chechen and Ingush brought the Qādirīyah back to Central Asia. In the 1950s the Chim Mirza brotherhood gave birth to a fourth Qādirī sub-*ṭarīqah,* Vis (Uways) Haji, which is the most puritanical of all the Ṣūfī orders. Its adepts practice rigorous endogamy within the brotherhood.

After the rehabilitation of the deported Caucasians in the late 1950s and their return to their homeland, the four Qādirī branches continued to survive in Central Asia. Vis Haji, with its followers concentrated in Kirghizia and southern Kazakhstan, seems to devote the most effort to proselytizing activities. The Kubrawīyah is apparently in the process of being absorbed by the Naqshbandīyah. It survives only in the Aral Sea area (northern Turkistan and Karakalpakistan).

All the Ṣūfī brotherhoods in Central Asia are conservative, traditionalist societies. Although they are clandestine, they are not really closed; indeed, they are involved in an unlawful (from the Soviet standpoint) but active religious proselytism. Their role in the preservation of Islam as a faith, as a way of life, and as an "ideology" has been and still is of capital importance. Without their day-by-day missionary work it is probable that the Muslim republics would have been swept off by a wave of atheism. The role of "preserver of Islam" played by the Ṣūfī brotherhoods under the Soviet regime may be compared to the similar role played by the same *ṭarīqahs* during the dark age of the Mongol invasion. But the role of the conservative Ṣūfī organizations is not limited to the preservation of religious belief and cult observance. For example, the Ṣūfī brotherhoods have also become the focal point of traditional opposition to the Russian presence.

[*For a survey of the Central Asian context into which Islam was introduced, see* Buddhism, *article on* Buddhism in Central Asia; Inner Asian Religions; *and* Shamanism, *article on* Siberian and Inner Asian Shamanism.]

BIBLIOGRAPHY

There is no special monograph on the religious history of Central Asia since its conquest by the Arabs. Information concerning the history of Islam is scattered in all of the historical works on Central Asia. Among the most important are the following.

Barthold, V. V. *Istoriia kul'turnoi zhizni Turkestana.* Leningrad, 1927.

Barthold, V. V. *Four Studies on the History of Central Asia.* 3 vols. Leiden, 1956–1962.

Barthold, V. V. *Turkestan down to the Mongol Invasion.* 2d ed. London, 1958. A classic, basic reference work.

Bennigsen, Alexandre, and Chantal Lemercier-Quelquejay. *Islam in the Soviet Union.* New York, 1961.

D'Ohsson, Mouradja. *Histoire des Mongols depuis Tchinguiz-Khan jusqu'à Timour bey ou Tamerlan.* 4 vols. Amsterdam, 1834–1835.

Grousset, René. *L'empire des steppes: Attila, Gengis-Khan, Tamerlan.* Paris, 1939.

Hayit, Baymirza. *Turkestan im 20. Jahrhundert.* Darmstadt, 1956.

Holdsworth, M. *Turkestan in the Nineteenth Century.* London, 1959.

Howorth, Henry H. *History of the Mongols from the Ninth to the Nineteenth Century.* 4 vols. 1876–1888; reprint, New York, 1927.

Klimovich, Liutsian I. *Islam v tsarskoi Rossii.* Moscow, 1936. A biased but well-informed Soviet work on Islam in the nineteenth century.

Rakowska-Harmstone, Teresa. *Russia and Nationalism in Central Asia: The Case of Tadzhikistan.* Baltimore, 1970.

Rywkin, Michael. *Moscow's Muslim Challenge.* New York, 1982.

Togan, A. Zeki Velidi. *Bugünkü Türkistan ve yakın tarihi.* Istanbul, 1947. A basic reference work on Turkistan under Russian rule.

Wheeler, Geoffrey. *The Modern History of Soviet Central Asia.* London, 1964.

THREE
EAST ASIA

13 CHINESE RELIGION

Daniel L. Overmyer

Traditional Chinese religious institutions and activities flourish today in Taiwan, Hong Kong, Singapore, and in some overseas communities, as well as in parts of China. These activities are the products of continuous historical development from prehistoric times. In that period the area of present-day China was inhabited by a large number of tribal groups. In around 5000 BCE several of these tribes developed agriculture and began to live in small villages surrounded by their fields. Domesticated plants and animals included millet, rice, dogs, pigs, goats, sheep, cattle, and silkworms. The physical characteristics of these early agriculturalists were similar to those of modern Chinese. The archaeological record indicates gradual development toward more complex technology and social stratification. By the late Neolithic period (beginning around 3200 BCE) there were well-developed local cultures in several areas that were to become centers of Chinese civilization later, including the southeast coast, the southwest, the Yangtze River valley, the northeast, and the northern plains. The interaction of these cultures eventually led to the rise of literate, bronze-working civilizations in the north, the Hsia (before 1500 BCE) and Shang (c. 1500–1050 BCE). The existence of the Hsia kingdom is attested in early historical sources that have otherwise been shown to accord with archaeological discoveries. However, archaeologists are still debating which sites can be confidently assigned to the Hsia. The Shang has been archaeologically verified, beginning with the excavation of one of its capitals in 1928.

There is some evidence for prehistoric religious activities, particularly for a cult of the dead, who were often buried in segregated cemeteries, supine, with heads toward a single cardinal direction. In some sites houses and circles of white stones are associated with clusters of graves, while in others wine goblets and pig jaws are scattered on ledges near the top of the pit, perhaps indicating a farewell feast. In the Wei River area, secondary burial was practiced, with bones from single graves collected and reburied with those of from twenty to eighty others. Grave offerings are found in almost all primary burials, with quantity and variety depending on the status of the deceased; tools, pottery vessels, objects of jade and turquoise, dogs, and, in some cases, human beings. Bodies and faces were often painted with red ochre, a symbol of life. All of these practices indicate belief in afterlife and the prehistoric beginnings of ancestor worship. Other evidence for prehistoric religion includes deer buried in fields and divination through reading cracks in the dried shoulder bones of sheep or deer. This form of divination, attested in what is now northeast China by 3560–3240 BCE, is the direct antecedent of similar practices in historical times. Buried deer suggest offerings to the power of the soil, a common practice in later periods.

Early Historical Period

The early historical period (Shang and Chou kingdoms) saw the development of many of the social and religious horizons that continue to this day to be associated with the Chinese. Although obvious links with the earlier period persist, it is with the emergence of these kingdoms that the religious history of the Chinese properly begins.

THE SHANG

The formation of the Shang kingdom was due to technological innovation such as bronze casting, and to the development of new forms of social and administrative control. Extant evidence provides information about the religion of the Shang aristocracy, characterized in the first place by elaborate graves and ceremonial objects for the dead. Grave offerings include decapitated human beings, horses, dogs, large numbers of bronze vessels, and objects of jade, stone, and shell. Some tombs were equipped with chariots hitched to horses. These tomb offerings indicate a belief that afterlife for members of the royal clan was similar to that of their present existence, but in another realm, perhaps in a heaven presided over by the Shang high god Shang-ti, the "Lord on High."

There are two other material sources for our understanding of Shang religion: inscriptions on oracle bones and in bronze sacrificial vessels. From these we learn that the most common objects of petition and inquiry were the ancestors of aristocratic clans. These deified ancestors were believed to have powers of healing and fertility in their own right, but also could serve as intermediaries between their living descendants and more powerful gods of natural forces and Shang-ti. Ancestors were ranked by title and seniority, with those longest dead having the widest authority. Since they could bring harm as well as aid to their descendants, it was necessary to propitiate the ancestors to ward off their anger as well as to bring their blessing. Nature deities named in the inscriptions personify the powers of rivers, mountains, rain, wind, and other natural phenomena. Shang-ti, whose authority exceeded that of the most exalted royal ancestor, served as a source of unity and order. [*See* Shang-ti.]

To contact these sacred powers the Shang practiced divination and sacrificial rituals, usually closely related to each other. In divination, small pits were bored in the backs of turtle plastrons or the shoulder bones of oxen or sheep. Heated bronze rods or thorns were placed in these impressions, causing the bones to crack with a popping sound. Diviners then interpreted the pattern of the cracks on the face of the bone to determine yes or no answers to petitions. The subjects of divination include weather, warfare, illness, administrative decisions, harvests, and other practical issues. Among the divination questions are those inquiring about sacrifices to ancestors and deities. Sacrifices to spirits residing above consisted essentially of burning flesh and grain on open air altars. Spirits of the earth were offered libations of fermented liquors, and those of bodies of water, precious objects such as jade. Sacrificial animals included cattle, dogs, sheep, and human beings.

One may presume that these sacrifices were accompanied by petitions addressed to the deity specifying what was desired in return. There is an emphasis on precision in sacrifice; the correct objects offered in the right way were believed to obligate the spirits to respond. Thus, in Shang sacrifice we already see the principle of reciprocity, which has remained a fundamental patten of interaction throughout the history of Chinese religions. Shang concerns for divination, hierarchical structure, and balanced polarities also anticipated later developments.

THE CHOU

There are many references in Shang oracle bone texts to a people called Chou who lived west of the Shang center, in the area of modern Shensi Province. The Chou, who were considered to be an important tributary state, were at first culturally and technologically inferior to the Shang, but learned rapidly and by the eleventh century BCE challenged the Shang for political supremacy. The final Chou conquest took place in about 1050 BCE. Remnants of the Shang royal line were allowed to continue their ancestral practices in the small state of Sung.

The religious activities of the early Chou aristocracy were focused on their ancestors, who were believed to reside in a celestial court presided over by T'ien, "Heaven," the Chou high god, similar to Shang-ti in scope and function. These ancestors had power to influence the prosperity of their descendants, their fertility, health, and longevity. Through ritual equation with deities of natural forces the ancestors could also influence the productivity of clan lands. In addition, royal ancestors served as intermediaries between their descendants and T'ien [*See* T'ien.]

Ancestral rituals took the form of great feasts in which the deceased was represented by an impersonator, usually a grandson or nephew. In these feasts the sharing of food and drink confirmed vows of mutual fidelity and aid. The most important ancestor worshiped was Hou Chi, who was both legendary founder of the ruling house and the patron of agriculture. As was true for the Shang, Chou rituals were also directed toward symbols of natural power such as mountains and rivers; most significant natural phenomena were deified and reverenced. The proper time and mode of such rituals were determined in part by divination, which in the Chou involved both cracking bones and turtle shells and the manipulation of dried plant stalks of different lengths. Divination was also employed in military campaigns, the interpretation of dreams, the siting of cities, and in many other situations involving important decisions.

Chou-dynasty diviners eventually produced a text to support and codify their work, the *I ching* (Classic of Change), which classifies human situations by means of sixty-four sets of six horizontal lines (hexagrams), broken and unbroken. The broken line sets represent *k'un*, the female force that completes, while those with solid lines represent *ch'ien*, the male force that initiates; all of experience is a combination of these polarities, in unending cycles of change. Through ritual manipulation, dried plant stalks are arranged in sets with numerical values corresponding to lines in the hexagrams. One thereby obtains a hexagram that reflects one's present situation;

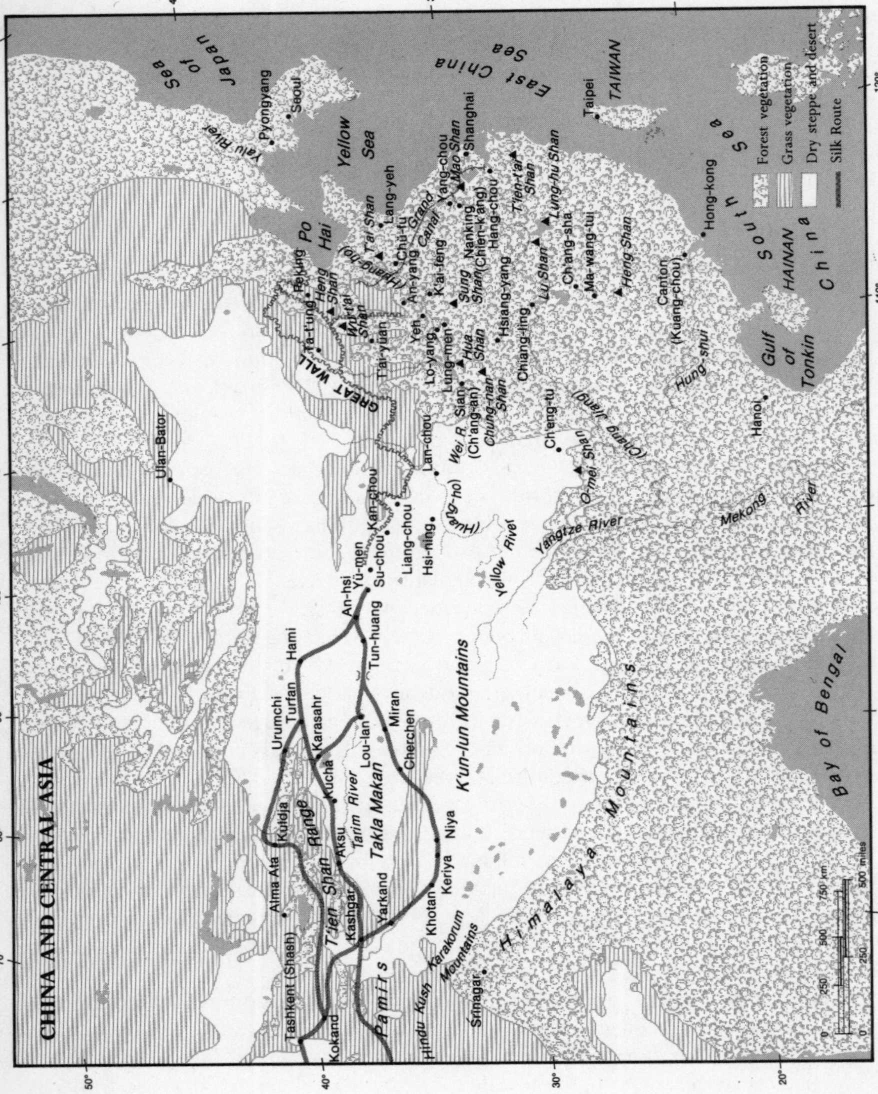
CHINA AND CENTRAL ASIA
Forest vegetation
Grass vegetation
Dry steppe and desert
Silk Route
Sea of Japan
Yellow Sea
East China Sea
South China Sea
Po Hai
Gulf of Tonkin
Bay of Bengal
TAIWAN
HAINAN
GREAT WALL
Grand Canal
Takla Makan
K'un-lun Mountains
Himalaya Mountains
T'ien Shan Range
Pamirs
Hindu Kush
Karakorum Mountains
Yangtze River
Yellow River
Mekong River
Tarim River
Wei R.
Yalu River
Ulan-Bator
Peking
Pyongyang
Seoul
Shanghai
Nanking (Chien-k'ang)
Hang-chou
Yang-chou
Lo-yang
Lung-men
Sian (Ch'ang-an)
Lan-chou
Tun-huang
Yü-men
An-hsi
Kan-chou
Su-chou
Liang-chou
Hsi-ning
Hami
Turfan
Urumchi
Karasahr
Kucha
Aksu
Kashgar
Yarkand
Khotan
Keriya
Niya
Cherchen
Miran
Lou-lan
Kuldja
Alma Ata
Tashkent (Shash)
Kokand
Srinagar
Ch'eng-tu
Chiang-ling
Ch'ang-sha
Hsiang-yang
Canton (Kuang-chou)
Hong-kong
Hanoi
Taipei
T'ai-yüan
Ta-t'ung
Wu-t'ai Shan
Heng Shan
T'ai Shan
Sung Shan
Hua Shan
Chung-nan Shan
O-mei Shan
Lu Shan
Lung-hu Shan
Mao Shan
T'ien-t'ai Shan
Heng Shan
Ma-wang-tui
Chu-fu
Lang-yeh
An-yang
K'ai-feng
Yen

additional line changes indicate the structures of the immediate future. Contemplation of these hexagrams clarifies decisions and provides warning or encouragement.

The *I ching* is essentially a book of wisdom for personal and administrative guidance, used since at least the seventh century BCE. However, from the sixth century BCE on commentaries were written to amplify the earliest level of the text and by the first century CE there were ten such levels of exposition, some quite philosophical in tone. The *Classic of Change* was believed to reflect the structure of cosmic movement, and hence became an object of reverent contemplation in itself. Its earliest levels antedated all the philosophical schools, so it belonged to none, though the Confucians later claimed it as a classic. The polarity of *ch'ien* and *k'un* provided a model for that of *yang* and *yin*, first discussed in the fourth century BCE. The *I ching*'s sometimes obscure formulations gave impetus to philosophical speculations throughout the later history of Chinese thought.

A third focus of Chou worship, in addition to ancestors and nature gods, was the *she*, a sacred earth mound located in the capital of each state and in at least some villages. The state *she* represented the sacred powers of the earth available to a particular domain, and so was offered libations upon such important occasions in the life of the state as the birth of a prince, ascension to rule, and military campaigns. Beside the earth mound stood a sacred tree, a symbol of its connection to the powers of the sky.

The early Chou aristocracy carried out sacrificial rituals to mark the seasons of the year and promote the success of farming. These sacrifices, performed in ancestral temples, were offered both to the high god T'ien and to ancestors. These and other Chou rituals were elaborate dramatic performances involving music, dancing, and archery, concluding with feasts in which much wine was consumed.

The most distinctive early Chou contribution to the history of Chinese religions was the theory of *t'ien-ming*, the "mandate of Heaven," first employed to justify the Chou conquest of the Shang. According to this theory, Heaven as a high god wills order and peace for human society. This divine order is to be administered by pious kings who care for their subjects on Heaven's behalf. These kings, called *t'ien-tzu*, "son of Heaven," are granted divine authority to rule, but only so long as they rule well. If they become indolent, corrupt, and cruel, the "mandate of Heaven" can be transferred to another line. This process can take a long time and involve many warnings to the ruler in the form of natural calamities and popular unrest. Those who heed such warnings can repent and rehabilitate their rule; otherwise, the mandate can be claimed by one who promises to restore righteous administration. In practice it is the victors who claim the mandate, as did the founding Chou kings, on the grounds of the alleged indolence and impiety of the last Shang ruler.

The idea of the mandate of Heaven has gripped the Chinese political imagination ever since. It became the basis for the legitimacy of dynasties, the judgment of autocracy, and the moral right of rebellion. This status it owed in part to its support by Confucius and his school, who saw the mandate of Heaven as the foundation of political morality. In sum, early Chou religion was robust and positive in spirit, a spirit that foreshadowed the confident reciprocity of Chinese rituals in later periods, as well as the positive view of human moral potential characteristic of the tradition as a whole.

The early Chou political and social synthesis began to deteriorate in the eighth century as competing local states moved toward political, military, and ritual independence. Within them, rulers from clans originally enfeoffed by Chou kings also lost their power, which reverted to competing local families. This breakdown of hereditary authority led to new social mobility, with status increasingly awarded for military valor and administrative ability, regardless of aristocratic background. There is some evidence that even peasants could move about in search of more just rulers. These political and social changes were accompanied by an increase in the number and size of cities, and in the circulation of goods between states.

Changes in religion accompanied those in economy and society. Although many older rituals were continued, they became more elaborate and were focused on the ancestors of the rulers of the states rather than on those of the Chou kings.

Social change and widespread civil turmoil and suffering led some in this era to question the power of the gods. In theory, the loss of a state was ultimately due to ritual negligence by the ruler, while the victors were supposed to provide for sacrifices to the ancestors of the vanquished. But in practice, many gods charged with protection were deemed to have failed while their desecrators flourished. In the *Shih ching* (Book of Poetry, c. 600 BCE) there are even verses that question the justice of Heaven itself. In any event, by the sixth century a more rationalistic perspective developed in the minds of some, accompanied by a turning away from gods and spirits to the problems of human society and governance.

Confucius. It was in this context that Chinese philosophy was born, in the teachings of Confucius (c. 551–479 BCE). Confucius (the latinate form of K'ung Fu-tzu, or Master K'ung) was the son of an obscure family in the small state of Lu, a state in which the old Chou cultural traditions were strong but that was buffeted both by repeated invasions and by local power struggles. Confucius's goal was the restoration of the ethical standards, just rule, and legitimate government of the early Chou period as he understood them. To this end he sought public office himself and exhorted the rulers of his day. He also gathered a small group of disciples whom he taught to become *chün-tzu* ("superior men"), men of ethical sensitivity and historical wisdom who could administer benevolent government. In the process he initiated a new level of ethical awareness in Chinese culture and a new form of education, education in what he believed were universal principles for mature humanity and civilization. He assumed that the criteria for holding office were intelligence and high moral principles, not hereditary status, and so further undermined the Chou feudal system that was crumbling around him.

Confucius began a long Chinese tradition of ethical reform in the name of apparently reactionary principles. Statements recorded by his disciples show that in crisis situations the master emphasized that he had a mission from Heaven to restore social harmony. His models for such restoration were the founding kings of the Chou dynasty as described in the ancient *Book of Poetry*, kings who ruled with reverence toward their ancestors and kindness toward their people, ever fearful of losing Heaven's approval. These models had mythic force for Confucius, who saw himself as their embodiment in his own age.

All of Confucius's ethical teachings were intended to describe the "way" *(tao)* of the superior man, a way originating in the will of Heaven for its people. At its best, the inner character of such persons was to be formed by *jen* ("perfect co-humanity"), an ultimately transcendental quality that Confucius believed he had never attained. The actions of an ethically aware person were to be carried out in a balanced way in accord with refined social custom *(li)*. [*See* Li.] Confucius's teachings reveal a religious consciousness that was restrained, philosophical, and prophetic; it is thus not surprising to learn that he did not participate in the exorcism and divination common in his day, nor speculate on the nature of lesser deities and spirits, although he did support veneration of ancestors. At this point his attitude is expressed in the statement, "reverence deities and ancestral spirits, but keep them at a distance." So it was that he directed the attention of his disciples away from questions of deities and afterlife toward the situation of human beings in the world. [*See the biography of Confucius.*]

By the fourth and third centuries BCE the end result of Confucius's gentle skepticism was a psychological interpretation of religion in his own school and the absence of any theological discussion by the formative thinkers of other traditions such as the individualists and the theorists of administrative laws and methods (Legalists). But in the culture at large religious beliefs and activities continued unabated; divination and rituals accompanied every significant activity, and a quest for personal immortality was gaining momentum. There was one well-known philosopher who expressed this common concern for religion quite directly, Mo-tzu (fifth century BCE), a thinker from a lower middle-class artisan background.

Mo-tzu. Mo-tzu was a thorough-going utilitarian who taught that the fundamental criterion of value was practical benefit to all. He was from Confucius's home state of Lu, and educated in the emerging Confucian tradition, but turned against what he perceived to be its elitism and wasteful concern with elaborate rituals. In his ethical teaching Mo-tzu reinterpreted along utilitarian lines earlier principles such as righteousness and filial reverence, centered on the theme of universal love without familial and social distinctions. He also attracted a group of disciples whom he sent out to serve in various states in an attempt to implement his teachings.

For the history of Chinese religions the most significant aspect of Mo-tzu's thought is his concern to provide theological sanctions for his views. For Mo-tzu, T'ien, or Heaven, is an active creator god whose will or mandate extends to everyone; what Heaven wills is love, prosperity, and peace for all. Heaven is the ultimate ruler of the whole world; T'ien sees all, rewards the good, and punishes the evil. In this task it is aided by a multitude of lesser spirits who are also intelligent and vital and who serve as messengers between T'ien and human beings. Mo-tzu advocates that since this is the nature of divine reality, religious reverence should be encouraged by the state as a sanction for moral order.

To protect himself from intellectual skeptics Mo-tzu at one point allows that even if deities and spirits do not exist communal worship still has social value. Although his whole attempt to argue for belief in Heaven on utilitarian grounds could be understood as a last stand for traditional religion within a changing philosophical world, there is no reason to doubt that Mo-tzu himself believed in the gods. [*See* Moism *and the biography of Mo-tzu.*]

The fourth century BCE was a period of incessant civil war on the one hand and great philosophical diversity on the other. A variety of thinkers arose, each propounding a cure for the ills of the age, most seeking to establish their views by training disciples and attaining office. Some advocated moral reform through education, others authoritarian government, *laissez faire* administration, rationalized bureaucracy, agricultural communes, rule in accord with the powers of nature, or individual self-fulfillment. Religious concerns were not paramount for these thinkers; indeed, for some they do not appear at all. The two traditions of this period that do warrant discussion here are the Confucian, represented by Meng-tzu (Mencius, c. 371–289 BCE), and that of the mystically inclined individualists, traditionally known as the Taoists.

Meng-tzu. Meng-tzu (or Meng K'e) was a teacher and would-be administrator from the small state of Tsou who amplified Confucius's teachings and placed them on a much firmer philosophical and literary base. Meng-tzu was concerned to prepare his disciples for enlightened and compassionate public service, beginning with provision for the physical needs of the people. He believed that only when their material livelihood is secure can the people be guided to higher moral awareness. This hope for moral transformation is grounded in Meng-tzu's conviction that human nature is potentially good. What is needed are rulers who nourish this potential as "fathers and mothers of the people." These teachings Meng-tzu expounded courageously before despotic kings whose inclinations were otherwise.

Specifically religious concerns are muted in Meng-tzu's teachings, but can be discerned in the deeper assumptions of his work. The first of these is that *t'ien,* or Heaven, is an expression of the underlying moral structure of the world, so that in the long run "those who accord with Heaven are preserved, and those who oppose Heaven are destroyed." Heaven's will is known through the assent or disapproval of the people. The second theme in Meng-tzu's teaching that might be understood as a religious "ultimate concern" is the above-mentioned belief that the human mind possesses an innate potential for moral awareness, a potential bestowed by Heaven at birth, so that "to understand human nature is to understand Heaven." Meng-tzu represents a further humanization of the Confucian tradition, and his emphasis on the powers of human nature within did much to shape the religious sensibilities of Chinese philosophy. At this point he is in accord with Chuang-tzu and helped prepare the way for similar emphases in Ch'an (Jpn., Zen) Buddhism and Neo-Confucianism. As had Confucius, Meng-tzu assumed that ancestor veneration was a basic requirement of civilized life, but neither thinker emphasized such veneration as much as did later texts like the *Hsiao ching*, the Classic of Filial Piety (third century BCE). [*See the biography of Meng-tzu.*]

Hsün-tzu. The third most important Confucian philosopher before the Han dynasty (202 BCE–220 CE) was Hsün-tzu (Hsün Ch'ing, d. 215 BCE), a scholar from the state of Chao who held offices for a time in the larger states of Ch'i and Ch'u. Hsün-tzu's thought was influenced by several of the traditions that had developed before his time, including those of the Logicians, Taoists, and Authoritarians (Legalists). Hsün-tzu agreed with the Authoritarian emphasis on the need for strong centralized rule and a strict penal code. He also shared their low estimate of human nature, which in his view tended toward selfishness and competition. Nonetheless, Hsün-tzu believed that human attitudes and behavior are perfectible by dint of much discipline and effort, so his differences with Meng-tzu on this point are those of degree.

Hsün-tzu's chief contribution was his reinterpretation of *t'ien* as the order of nature, an order that has no consciousness and is not directly related to human concerns. This interpretation is parallel to the views of the *Lao-tzu (Tao-te ching)* and

Chuang-tzu texts concerning the cosmic "Way" (Tao). Hsün-tzu was concerned to separate the roles of heaven, earth, and man, with human attention directed toward ethics, administration, and culture. In this context rituals such as funeral rites are valuable channels for emotions, but have no objective referent; their role is social, not theological. Ignorant "petty people" who literally believe in the efficacy of rain dances and divination are to be pitied; for the gentleman such activities are "cultural adornment."

Hsün-tzu thus gave impetus to the skeptical tradition in Chinese thought that began before Confucius and was reinforced by later thinkers such as Wang Ch'ung (c. 27– 96 CE). Hsün-tzu's teachings at this point provided a theoretical basis for a rough bifurcation between elite and popular attitudes toward religion and for sporadic attempts to suppress "excessive cults." Hsün-tzu's epistemology also set up the intellectual framework for a critique of heresy, conceived of as inventing words and titles beyond those employed by general consensus and sanctioned by the state. These themes had important implications for the remainder of Chinese history, including official attitudes toward religion today. [*See the biography of Hsün-tzu.*]

Early Taoist Thought. The earliest writings concerned to direct attention toward the mysterious cosmic "Way" that underlies all things are the first seven chapters of the extant *Chuang-tzu*, a text attributed to a philosopher-poet named Chuang Chou of the fourth century BCE. Chuang Chou was convinced that the world in its natural state is peaceful and harmonious, a state exemplified by the growth of plants and the activities of animals. Disorder is due to human aggression and manipulation, a tendency that finds as much expression in Confucian and Moist moralizing as in cruel punishments and warfare. Such moralizing in turn is rooted in a false confidence in words, words that debators use to express their own limited points of view and thus to dichotomize our understanding of the world. Indeed, all perspectives are limited and relative, conditioned by the interests and anxieties of species, social positions, and individuals. The answer to this problem is to understand and affirm the relativity of views, and thus harmonize them all. This the sage does by perceiving the constant rhythms of change within all life and identifying with them. In his view all dichotomies are unified; hence there is no need for struggle and competition. The sage intuits the Tao within and behind all things, and takes its all-embracing perspective as his own. [*See the biography of Chuang-tzu.*]

The other major early book devoted to discussing the Tao behind all things is the early third-century BCE *Tao-te ching* (The Way and Its Inner Power), also known as the *Lao-tzu*, after its eponymous "author," Lao Tan. The *Tao-te ching* discusses the Way in more direct, metaphysical terms than does the *Chuang-tzu*, all the while protesting that such discussion is ultimately futile. Here we are told that the Tao is the source of all things, "the mother of the universe," the ineffable cosmic womb out of which all emerges. The Tao also "works in the world," guiding all things in harmonious development and interaction. As both source and order of the world the Tao serves as a model for enlightened rulers who gain power by staying in the background and letting their people live spontaneously in response to their own needs. The Tao is the vital force of life perceived at its utmost depth; it works mysteriously and imperceptibly and yet there is nothing it does not accomplish. Its symbols are water rather than rock, valleys rather than hills, the female rather than the male. Although its perspective is profound, its author intended this book to be a handbook of wise and successful living, living characterized by a natural, spontaneous action that does not prematurely wear itself out. [*See* Tao and Te.]

The *Chuang-tzu* and *Lao-tzu* were the sources of a persistent tradition of naturalistic mysticism in the history of Chinese religions. They were the inspiration for much poetry, romantic philosophy, and meditation, all intended as a corrective for the bustle and competition of life, a means to peace of mind, and a clarification and broadening of perspective.

There are several passages in these books that describe the enlightened person as living peacefully and long because he does not waste his vital powers on needless contention and aggression. In the *Tao-te ching*, for example, we are told that "He who knows when to stop is free from danger; therefore he can long endure" (chap. 44), and that one who is "a good preserver of his life" cannot be harmed, "because in him there is no room for death" (chap. 50). Although in some passages of the *Chuang-tzu* an enlightened perspective leads to acceptance of death, a few others provide poetic visions of immortals, those who have transcended death by merging with the Tao. These indications of immortality provided the chief point of contact between these books and those who sought immortality by more direct means, including later practitioners of Taoist religion.

The Quest for Immortality. An explicit concern for long life *(shou)* had already appeared on early Chou bronzes and in poems in the *Book of Poetry*. Beginning in the eighth century BCE we find terms expressing a hope for immortality, such as "no death," "transcending the world," and "becoming an immortal." By the fourth century BCE there is evidence of an active quest for immortality through a variety of means, including exercises imitating the movements of long-lived animals, diets enforcing abstinence from grains, the use of food vessels inscribed with characters indicating longevity, the ingestion of herbs and chemicals, and petitions for the aid of immortals residing in mountains or distant paradises. It was in this context that Chinese alchemy began. The alchemical quest became the most dramatic form of the struggle against death, growing in popularity during the Ch'in (221–207 BCE) and Western Han (202 BCE–9 CE) dynasties.

The goal of all these practices was to return the body to its original state of purity and power with its *yin* (quiescent, dark, feminine) and *yang* (active, bright, masculine) forces vital and in proper balance. [*See also* Yin-yang Wu-hsing.] The fact that some of the compounds used were poisonous did not deter the experimenters; those who died were believed by devotees to have transferred themselves to another plane of existence, that of the immortals *(hsien)*. [*See* Hsien.] All this effort and expense were considered necessary because in ancient China the person was understood to be a psycho-physical whole, composed throughout of one vital substance, *ch'i*, in different modes and densities. [*See* Ch'i.] The focal points of physical and mental energy were discussed respectively as the *p'o* and *hun*, which are often translated as "souls," but which cannot exist for long separately, or apart from the body. The intelligent mode, *hun*, can exist in an ancestral tablet as long as it is ritually remembered by its descendants, and the *p'o* in some texts is understood to descend to a murky realm underground, the Yellow Springs. These forms of continuation after death were perceived by some to be tenuous and limited, so they attempted to make the entire person/body immortal by transforming its substance. There was no doctrine of an eternal soul to fall back on as in India or the Hellenistic world, so the only alternative was physical immortality. In China this tradition continued to develop through the Eastern (Latter) Han dynasty (25–220 CE) and produced texts of its own full of recipes, techniques, and moral exhortations. As such, it became one of the major sources of the Taoist religion that emerged in the second century CE. [*See also* Alchemy, *article on* Chinese Alchemy, *and* Soul, *article on* Chinese Concepts.]

Spirit Mediums. The other important expression of Chinese religious consciousness before the Han dynasty was shamanism, which most commonly took the form of deities and spirits possessing receptive human beings. Spirit mediums both female and male are mentioned in discussions of early Chou religion as participants in court rituals, responsible for invoking the descent of the gods, praying and dancing for rain, and for ceremonial sweeping to exorcise harmful forces. They were a subordinate level of officially accepted ritual performers, mostly women, who spoke on behalf of the gods to arrange for sacrifices. In conditions of extreme drought they could be exposed to the sun as an inducement to rain. Female mediums were called *wu*, a word etymologically related to that for dancing; male mediums were called *hsi*. In the state of Ch'u, south of the center of Chou culture, there were shamans believed able to practice "magic flight," that is, to send their souls on journeys to distant realms of deities and immortals. [*See also* Flight.]

Han historical sources indicate that by the third century BCE there were shamans all over China, many of whom were invited by emperors to set up shrines in the capital. This was done in part to consolidate imperial control, but also to make available fresh sources of sacred power to support the state and heal illness. Sporadic attempts were also made by officials to suppress shamanism. These began as early as 99 BCE and continued in efforts to reform court rituals in 31-30 BCE, and to change local practices involving human sacrifice in 25 CE. However, it is clear that shamanism was well established among the people and continued to have formal influence at court until the fifth century CE. Shamans were occasionally employed by rulers to call up the spirits of royal ancestors and consorts and incidents of court support continued into the eleventh century. Owing in part to the revival of Confucianism in that period, in 1023 a sweeping edict was issued that all shamans be returned to agricultural life and their shrines be destroyed. Thus, the gradual confucianization of the Chinese elite led to the suppression of shamanism at that level, but it continued to flourish among the people, where its activities can still be observed in China, Taiwan, and other Chinese communities. [*See also* Shamanism, *overview article*.]

The Beginnings of Empire

In the fifth century BCE the disintegration of the Chou feudal and social order quickened under the pressure of incessant civil wars. The larger states formed alliances and maneuvered for power, seeking hegemony over the others, aiming to reunify the area of Chou culture by force alone. In 256 BCE the state of Ch'in, under the influence of a ruthlessly applied ideology of laws and punishments suggested in the fourth century BCE by Shang Yang, one of the founders of the Authoritarian school, eliminated the last Chou king and then finished off its remaining rivals. Finally, in 221 the state of Ch'in became the empire of Ch'in (221–207 BCE), and its ruler took a new title, "First Emperor of Ch'in" (Ch'in Shih-huang-ti). With this step China as a semicontinental state was born. There were many periods of division and strife later, but the new level of unification achieved by the Ch'in was never forgotten, and became the goal of all later dynasties.

The Ch'in emperors attempted to rule all of China by the standards long developed in their own area; laws, measurements, written characters, wheel tracks, thought, and so forth were all to be unified. Local traditions and loyalties were still strong, however, and Ch'in rule remained precarious. After the emperor died in 209 he was replaced by a son who proved unequal to the task. Rebellions that broke out in that year severely undermined Ch'in authority and by 206 one of the rebel leaders, a village head named Liu Pang, had assumed *de facto* control of state administration. In 202 Liu Pang was proclaimed emperor of a new dynasty, the Han (202 BCE–220 CE), built upon Ch'in foundations but destined to last, with one interregnum, for over four hundred years.

THE CH'IN

The Ch'in was noteworthy both for its suppression of philosophy and its encouragement of religion. The Authoritarian (Legalist) tradition dominant in the state of Ch'in had long been hostile to the Confucians and Moists, with their emphasis on ethical sanctions for rule. For the Authoritarians the only proper standard of conduct was the law, applied by officials concerned with nothing else, whose personal views were irrelevant as long as they performed their task. The only sanctions the state needed were power and effective organization. Not long after Ch'in became an empire it attempted to silence all criticism based on the assumption of inner standards of righteousness that were deemed to transcend political power and circumstance. In 213 BCE the court made it a capital offence to discuss Confucian books and principles and ordered that all books in private collections be burned, save those dealing with medicine, divination, and agriculture, as well as texts of the Authoritarian school. In this campaign, several scores of scholars were executed, and a number of philosophical schools were eliminated as coherent traditions, including the Moists and the Dialecticians. In the early Han dynasty both Taoist philosophy and Confucianism revived, and Authoritarianism continued to be in evidence in practice if not in theory, but the golden age of Chinese philosophy was over. A unified empire demanded unified thought, a dominant orthodoxy enforced by the state. From this perspective variety was a threat, and furthermore, there were no independent states left to serve as sanctuaries for different schools. To be sure, China continued to produce excellent scholars and philosophers, and Buddhism contributed an important body of new material, but most of the issues debated in later Chinese philosophy had already been articulated before the Han. The task of philosophy was now understood to be the refinement and application of old teachings, not the development of new ones. [*See also* Legalism *and the biography of Han Fei-tzu.*]

Ch'in policy toward religion, by contrast, encouraged a variety of practices to support the state. To pay homage to the sacred powers of the realm and to consolidate his control, the First Emperor included worship at local shrines in his extensive tours. Representatives of regional cults, many of them spirit mediums, were brought to the court, there to perform rituals at altars set up for their respective deities. The Ch'in expanded the late Chou tendency to exalt deities of natural forces; over one hundred temples to such nature deities were established in the capital alone, devoted to the sun, moon, planets, several constellations, and stars associated with wind, rain, and long life. The nation was divided into sacred regions presided over by twelve mountains and four major rivers, with many lesser holy places to be worshiped both by the people and the emperor. Elaborate sacrifices of horses, rams, bulls, and a variety of foodstuffs were regularly offered at the major sites, presided over by officials with titles such as Grand Sacrificer and Grand Diviner. Important deities were correlated with the Five Phases *(wu-hsing),* the modes of interaction of natural forces, the better to personify and control these powers.

A distinctive feature of Ch'in religion was sacrifices to four "Supreme Emperors" responsible for natural powers in each of the four quarters. Only the Emperor could worship these deities, a limitation true as well for two new rites he developed in 219, the *feng* and *shan* sacrifices. These were performed on sacred Mount T'ai to symbolize that the ruler had been invested with power by Heaven itself. Another driving force behind Ch'in encouragement of religious activities was the first Emperor's personal quest for immortality. We are told that in this quest he sent groups of young people across the China Sea to look for such islands of the immortals as P'eng-lai.

THE HAN

The defeat of Ch'in forces in the civil wars leading up to the founding of the Han dynasty deposed Authoritarian political thought along with the second and last Ch'in emperor. It took several decades for the new Han dynasty to consolidate its power. Since the Authoritarians had developed the most detailed policies for administering an empire, many of these policies were followed in practice in modified form.

Some early Han scholars and emperors attempted to ameliorate royal power with a revival of Confucian concern for the people and Taoist principles of noninterference *(wu-wei).* For example, a palace counselor named Chia I (200–168 BCE) echoed Meng-tzu in his emphasis that the people are the basis of the state, the purpose of which should be to make them prosperous and happy, so as to gain their approval. A similar point of view is presented in more Taoist form in the *Huai-nan–tzu*, a book presented to the throne in 139 BCE by a prince of the Liu clan who had convened a variety of scholars in his court. This book discusses the world as a fundamentally harmonious system of resonating roles and influences. The ruler's job is to guide it, as an experienced charioteer guides his team. [*See the biography of Liu An.*]

Both Chia I and the *Huai-nan–tzu* assume that the rhythms that order society and government emanate from the cosmic Tao. The ruler's task is to discover and reinforce these rhythms for the benefit of all. This understanding of a Taoist "art of rulership" is rooted in the intuitions of the *Lao-tzu* and *Chuang-tzu*, but in the early Han was expressed in more detail in the writings of the Huang-Lao tradition, the school of the Yellow Emperor and Lao-tzu. Scholars have known of this school for centuries, but its texts had long disappeared, to be rediscovered only in 1973 at Ma-wang-tui, in a tomb sealed in 168 BCE. Four books appended to one of the Ma-wang-tui *Lao-tzu* texts are considered products of the Huang-Lao school, which is here concerned with the Tao as the creative source of both nature and man, their patterns of order, and the ontological basis of law and administration. Here we see an attempt to apply Taoist philosophical principles to the ordering of society by blending them with Legalist ideas. [*See also* Huang-lao Chün.]

However, the oldest and most widely established of the early Han philosophical schools was the Confucian, and the Confucians survived the Ch'in suppression rather well. Numbers of their books escaped the flames of 213 BCE, and those that did not were reconstructed or written anew, with little but the old titles intact. In the third century BCE scholars such as Hsün-tzu had already incorporated the best thought of their day into fundamentally Confucian expositions that advocated a strong centralized state and an ethical teaching enforced by law. This expanded interpretation of Confucius's teachings served his followers well in the early Han. They occupied the middle ground between authoritarianism and Taoist *laissez-faire*. There was room in their perspective for political power, criminal law, advocacy of benevolent rule, moral suasion, religious rituals, and personal ethical development, all supported by a three-century tradition of training disciples to study sacred texts and emulate the models they provided. In addition, by the second century BCE Confucian scholars such as Tung Chung-shu (c. 179–104 BCE) incorporated into their teaching the theories of Tsou Yen and the "Naturalists," who in the fourth century BCE had taught that the world is an interrelated organic whole that operates according to such cosmic principles as *yin* and *yang*. [*See the biography of Tsou Yen*.] The *Huai-nan-tzu* had already given this material a Taoist interpretation, stressing the natural resonance between all aspects of the universe. In the hands of Tung Chung-shu this understanding became an elaborate statement of the relationship of society and nature, with an emphasis on natural justification for hierarchical social roles, focused on that of the ruler. [*See the biography of Tung Chung-shu*.]

Tung Chung-shu provided a more detailed cosmological basis for Confucian ethical and social teachings and made it clear that only a unified state could serve as a channel for cosmic forces and sanctions. Tung was recognized as the leading scholar of the realm, and became spokesman for the official class. At his urging, in 136 BCE the Confucian classics were made the prescribed texts studied at the imperial academy. Texts of other schools including the Taoist theories of administration noted above, were excluded. This meant in effect that Tung Chung-shu's version of Confucianism became the official state teaching, a status it retained throughout the Han dynasty. So it was that the humble scholar of Lu, dead for over three hundred years, was exalted as patron saint of the imperial system, a position he retained until 1911. State-supported temples were established in Confucius's name in cities all over the land, and his home at Ch'ü-fu became a national shrine. In these temples, spirit tablets of the master and his disciples (replaced by images from 720–1530) were venerated in elaborate and formal rituals. As the generations passed, the tablets of the most influential scholars of the age came to be placed in these temples as well, by imperial decree, and so the cult of Confucius became the ritual focus of the scholar-official class. [*See also* Confucian Thought, *article on* The State Cult.]

Han state rituals were based upon those of Ch'in, but were greatly expanded and more elaborate. The first emperor, Kao-tsu, instituted the worship of a star god believed to be associated with Hou Chi, the legendary founder of the Chou royal line. Temples for this deity were built in administrative centers around the realm, where officials were also instructed to worship gods of local mountains and rivers. Kao-tsu brought shamans to the palace and set up shrines for sacrifices to their regional deities. He also promoted the worship of his own ancestors; at his death temples in his honor were built in commanderies throughout the empire.

These efforts to institute an imperial religious system supported by officials at all levels were energetically continued by Emperor Wu, during whose fifty-four-year reign (140–87 BCE) the foundations of imperial state religion were established for Chinese history into the twentieth century. The emperor's religious activities were in turn supported by the philosophy of Tung Chung-shu, with its emphasis on the central cosmic role of the ruler. Emperor Wu revived the *chiao* or suburban sacrifice at the winter solstice to express imperial support for the revival of life forces. [*See* Chiao.] He also began to worship T'ai-i, the "Great Supreme One," a star deity most noble in the heavens, an exalted version of a Chou god. T'ai-i was coequal with Heaven and earth, a symbol of both cosmic power and the emperor's status. In the period 112–110 BCE Emperor Wu renewed the *feng* and *shan* sacrifices at Mount T'ai, the sacred mountain of the east, a key place of direct communication with Heaven for the sake of the whole realm. In 109 BCE he ordered that a *ming-t'ang* ("hall of light") be built at the foot of Mount T'ai as a temple where all the major deities of China could assemble and be worshiped. Emperor Wu also toured the realm, sacrificing at important shrines along the way, all to express his religious convictions and assert his authority.

Detailed instructions for these Han rituals were provided by handbooks of ritual and etiquette such as the *Li chi* (Record of Rites), compiled in the second century BCE but including earlier material as well. Here we find descriptions of royal rituals to be performed at the solstices and the onset of the seasons, as well as instructions for such matters as the initiation of young men and the veneration of ancestors. The emphasis throughout is on the intimate correlations of nature and society, so that social custom is given cosmic justification. The *Li chi* complements Tung Chung-shu's philosophy by extending similar understandings to the social life of the literate elite. In this context periodic rituals served as concentrated reminders of the cosmic basis of the whole cultural and political order. Thus did the imperial ruling class express its piety and solidify its position.

It should be noted, however, that the old Chou concept of the "mandate of Heaven" continued to influence Han political thought in a form elaborated and attenuated at the same time. Particularly in the writings of Tung Chung-shu, evidence for divine approval or disapproval of the ruler was discerned in "natural" phenomena interpreted as portents. In accord with this belief, officials were appointed to record and interpret portents and to suggest appropriate responses, such as changes in ritual procedure and the proclamation of amnesties. The developing tradition of political portents recognized the importance of divine sanctions but provided a range of calibrated responses that enabled rulers to adjust their policies rather than face the prospect of rejection by Heaven. The "mandate of Heaven" in its earlier and starker form was evoked chiefly as justification for rebellion in periods of dynastic decay. Nonetheless, portent theory in the hands of a conscientious official could be used in attempts to check or ameliorate royal despotism, and hence was an aspect of the state religious system that could challenge political power as well as support it.

The Han emperor Wu devoted much effort to attaining immortality, as had his Ch'in predecessor. As before, shamans and specialists in immortality potions were brought to court, and expeditions were sent off to look for the dwelling places of those who had defeated death. The search for immortality became quite popular among those who had the money and literacy to engage in it. In part this was due to the transformation of the Yellow Emperor (Huang-ti) into the patron deity of immortality, the earliest popular saving deity of this type in China. This transformation, fostered by "technique specialists" *(fang-shih)* at Emperor Wu's court, included stories that the Yellow Emperor had ascended to Heaven with his whole retinue, including a harem of over seventy. [*See* Fang-shih *and* Huang-ti.]

A more common expression of hope for some sort of continuity after death may be seen in tombs of Han aristocrats and officials, many of which were built as sturdy brick replicas of houses or offices, complete with wooden and ceramic utensils, attendants, and animals, as well as food, drugs, clothing, jade, bamboo books, and other precious objects. To a large extent this may be seen as a modification of Shang and Chou traditions. However, in a few recently excavated Han tombs there were tightly sealed coffins filled with an embalming fluid in which even the skin and flesh of the bodies have been preserved. An elaborate silk banner has been found on top of one of these coffins, painted with a design evidently intended to guide the occupant to a paradise of the immortals, perhaps that of the Queen Mother of the West.

Another destination for the dead was an underworld that was a Han elaboration of the old legend of the Yellow Springs, a shadowy place beneath the earth referred to as early as the eighth century BCE. From the Han period, there are tomb documents by which living officials transferred the dead in their jurisdiction to those of their counterparts in the underworld. There are also references to a realm of the dead inside Mount T'ai. The god of this mountain keeps registers of the lifespans of all, and death may be referred to as "to return to the Eastern Peak." By the third and fourth centuries CE it was believed that there was a subterranean kingdom within Mount T'ai, where judges decided the fate of the dead. These alternative beliefs represent the state of Chinese understandings of afterlife before Buddhist impact. [*See* Afterlife, *article on* Chinese Concepts.]

What came to be called the Former Han dynasty ended in 8 CE when the throne was occupied by a prime minister named Wang Mang (r. 9–23 CE), who established a Hsin ("new") dynasty that was to last for fourteen years. Wang's chief contribution to the history of Chinese religions was his active promotion of prognostication as a way of understanding the intimate relationship between Heaven and the court. In 25 CE Liu Hsiu (r. 25–57), a member of the Han royal line, led a successful attack on Wang Mang and reestablished the (Latter) Han dynasty. Like Wang Mang, he actively supported prognostication at court, despite the criticism of rationalist scholars such as Huan T'an (43 BCE–28 CE), who argued that strange phenomena were a matter of coincidence and natural causes rather than messages from Heaven.

A related development was controversy between two movements within Confucian scholarly circles, the so-called New Text school of the Former Han, and a later rationalistic reaction against it, the Old Text school. The New Text school developed out of Tung Chung-shu's concern with portents. Its followers wrote new commentaries on the classics that praised Confucius as a supernormal being who predicted the future hundreds of years beyond his time. By the end of the first century BCE this interpretation of the sage in mythological terms was vigorously resisted by an Old Text school that advocated a more restrained and historical approach. These two traditions coexisted throughout the remainder of the Han dynasty, with the New Text scholars receiving the most imperial support through the first century CE. After

Huan T'an the best known rationalist was Wang Ch'ung, whose *Lun-heng* (Balanced Inquiries) fiercely criticizes religious opinions of his day, including prognostication and belief in spirits of the dead. Although Wang Ch'ung was not well known by his contemporaries, his thought was rediscovered in the third century and established as a key contribution to the skeptical tradition in Chinese philosophy. [*See the biography of Wang Ch'ung.*] An important religious legacy of the New Text school was the exalted interpretation of Confucius as a semidivine being, which was echoed in later popular religion. Its concern with portents and numerology also influenced Taoism.

We have noted the appearance of the Yellow Emperor as a divine patron of immortality, and as a representative of a new type of personified saving deity with power over a whole area of activity. In the latter half of the Han dynasty the number and popularity of such deities increased, beginning with the cult of the Queen Mother of the West (Hsi Wang Mu). She was associated with the K'un-lun mountains in the northwest where she presided over a palace and received a royal visitor, King Mu of the Chou dynasty, whom she predicted would be able to avoid death.

In 3 BCE Hsi Wang Mu's promise of immortality to all became the central belief of an ecstatic popular cult in her name that swept across North China. Although this movement abated in a few months, the Queen Mother herself is commonly portrayed in Latter Han iconography. K'un-lun is described as the center pillar of the world, from where she controls cosmic powers and the gift of immortality. This goddess has continued to have an important role in Chinese religion until the present day. [*See* Hsi Wang Mu.]

Mountain-dwelling immortals constituted another source of personal deities in this period. These beings were believed to descend to aid the ruler in times of crisis, sometimes with instructions from the Celestial Emperor (T'ien-ti), sometimes themselves identified with the "perfect ruler" who would restore peace to the world. By the second century CE the most important of these figures was Lao-tzu, the legendary author of the *Tao-te ching*, who appears as a deity called Huang-lao Chün (Yellow Lord Lao) or T'ai-shang Lao-chün (Most High Lord Lao). [*See* Huang-lao Chün.) By this time Lao-tzu had been portrayed for centuries in popular legend as a mysterious wise man who disappeared without a trace. We have seen that the book in his name contains passages that could be interpreted as support for the immortality cult, and by the first century he was referred to as an immortal himself. In an inscription of 165 CE Lao-tzu is described as a creator deity, equal in status to the sun, moon, and stars. A contemporary text assures his devotees that he has manifested himself many times in order to save mankind, that he will select those who believe in him to escape the troubles of the age, and that he will "shake the Han reign." [*See the biography of Lao-tzu.*] It is this messianic theme that provided the religious impetus for two large popular religious movements in the late second century CE that were important sources of later Taoist religion and the popular sectarian tradition. These movements were the T'ien-shih Tao (Way of the Celestial Master) in the west and the T'ai-p'ing Tao (Way of Great Peace and Prosperity) in the north.

The Way of the Celestial Master established a theocratic state in the area of modern Szechwan Province with an organization modeled in part on Han local administration. Its leader, Chang Lu, ruled through officers, both religious and administrative in function, who presided over a number of distinctive rituals. These included reciting the *Lao-tzu*, penance to heal illness, and the construction of huts in which free food was offered to passers-by. Converts were required to contribute five pecks of rice, from which the movement gained the popular name of "The Way of Five Pecks of Rice" (Wu-tou-mi Tao). In 215 Chang Lu submitted to a Han warlord (Ts'ao Ts'ao) whose son founded the new state of Wei in 220. The sect itself was allowed to continue its activities and taught that Wei had simply inherited divine authority from the Celestial Master Chang and his line. By the fourth century the Celestial Masters developed more elaborate collective rituals of repentance, retrospective salvation of ancestors, and the strengthening of vital forces through sexual intercourse. [*See the biographies of Chang Tao-ling and Chang Lu.*]

We know less about the practices of the Way of Great Peace because it was destroyed as a coherent tradition in the aftermath of a massive uprising in 184 CE. Its leader, also named Chang (Chang Chüeh, d. 184 CE), proclaimed that the divine mandate for the Han rule, here symbolized by the phase wood (green), had expired, to be replaced by the phase earth, for which the color is yellow. Chang Chüeh's forces thus wore yellow cloths as symbols of their destiny, and hence the movement came to be called the Yellow Turbans. The Han court commissioned local governors to put down the uprising, which was soon suppressed with much bloodshed, although remnants of the Yellow Turbans continued to exist until the end of the century. [*See the biography of Chang Chüeh.*]

The Yellow Turbans are better understood as a parallel to the Celestial Master sect rather than as connected to it, although the two movements shared some beliefs and practices, particularly healing through confession of sins. The Way of Great Peace employed a scripture known as the *T'ai-p'ing ching* (Classic of Great Peace), which emphasizes the cyclical renewal of life in the *chia-tzu* year, the beginning of the sixty-year cycle. Both sects were utopian, but the Yellow Turbans represent a more eschatological orientation. In retrospect, both of these groups appear as attempts to reconstruct at a local level the Han cosmic and political synthesis that was collapsing around them, with priests taking the place of imperial officials.

The most important legacy of the late Han popular religious movements was their belief in personified divine beings concerned to aid humankind, a belief supported by new texts, rituals, and forms of leadership and organization. This belief was given impetus by the expectation that a bearer of collective salvation was about to appear in order to initiate a new time of peace, prosperity, and long life. From the third century on this hope was focused on a figure called Li Hung, in whose name several local movements appeared, some involving armed uprisings. This eschatological orientation was an important dimension of early Taoism, which at first understood itself as a new revelation, intended to supplant popular cults with their bloody sacrifices and spirit mediums.

In addition to such organized movements as the Yellow Turbans, Han popular religion included cults of local sacred objects such as trees, rocks, and streams, belief that spirits of the dead have consciousness and can roam about, and a lively sense of the power of omens and fate. By the third century there are references to propitiation of the spirits of persons who died violent deaths, with offerings of animal flesh presided over by spirit mediums.

Feng-shui ("wind and water"), or geomancy, also developed during the Han as a ritual expression of the *yin/yang* and five-phases worldview. It is the art of locating graves, buildings, and cities in auspicious places where there is a concentration of the vital energies *(ch'i)* of earth and sky. It is believed that the dead in graves so located will bless their descendants. The earliest extant *feng-shui* texts are attributed to famous diviners of the third and fourth centuries. Chinese religion was thus developed at a number of levels by the time Buddhism arrived, although Buddhism offered several fresh interpretations of morality, personal destiny, and the fate of the dead.

The Period of Disunion

By the time the first Buddhist monks and texts appeared in China around the first century CE, the Han dynasty was already in decline. At court, rival factions competed for imperial favor, and in the provinces restless governors moved toward independence. Political and military fragmentation was hastened by the campaigns against the Yellow Turban uprising, after which a whole series of adventurers arose to attack each other and take over territory. In the first decade of the third century three major power centers emerged in the north, southeast, and southwest, with that in the north controlling the last Han emperor and ruling in his name. By 222 these three centers each had declared themselves states, and China entered a period of political division that was to last until late in the sixth century. In this time of relatively weak central government control, powerful local clans emerged to claim hereditary power over their areas.

THE BEGINNINGS OF BUDDHISM IN CHINA

With the gradual expansion of Buddhism, under the patronage of the Kushan rulers, into the oasis states of Central Asia, and with the corresponding expansion of Chinese influence into this same region, it became inevitable that Buddhism would be introduced into East Asia. Over a thousand-year period from the beginning of the common era until the close of the first millennium the opportunities for cultural exchange with South and West Asia afforded by the so-called Silk Route nourished a vibrant East Asian Buddhist tradition, one that began with earnest imitation of its Indian antecedents and culminated in the great independent systems of thought that characterize the fully developed tradition: Hua-yen, T'ien-t'ai, Ching-t'u, and Ch'an.

From about 100 BCE on it would have been relatively easy for Buddhist ideas and practices to come to China with foreign merchants, but the first reliable notice of it in Chinese sources is dated 65 CE. In a royal edict of that year we are told that a prince administering a city in what is now northern Kiangsu Province "recites the subtle words of Huang-Lao, and respectfully performs the gentle sacrifices to the Buddha." He was encouraged to "entertain *upāsakas* and *śramaṇas*," Buddhist lay devotees and initiates. In 148 CE the first of several foreign monks, An Shih-kao, settled in Lo-yang, the capital of the Latter Han. Over the next forty years he and other scholars translated about thirty Buddhist scriptures into Chinese, most of them from pre-Mahāyāna traditions, emphasizing meditation and moral principles. However, by about 185 three Mahāyāna Prajñāpāramitā (Perfect Wisdom) texts were translated as well.

A memorial dated 166, approving Buddhist "purity," "emptiness," nonviolence, and control of sensual desires, further informs us that in that year the emperor performed a joint sacrifice to Lao-tzu and the Buddha. In 193/194 a local warlord in what is now Kiangsu erected a Buddhist temple that could hold more than three thousand people. It contained a bronze Buddha image before which offerings were made and scriptures were read. During ceremonies in honor of the Buddha's birthday thousands came to participate, watch, and enjoy free food and wine. Thus, by the end of the second century there were at least two centers of Buddhist activity, Lo-yang in the north and an area in the southeast. At court Buddhist symbols were used in essentially Taoist rituals, but in the scriptures the novelty and difference of Buddhism were made clear in crude vernacular translations. Such novelty appears in injunctions to eliminate desires, to love all beings equally, without special preference for one's family, and to regard the body as transitory and doomed to decay, rather than an arena for seeking immortality.

Although early sources mention terms for various clerical ranks, rules for monastic life were transmitted in a haphazard and incomplete fashion. Monks and nuns lived in cloisters that cannot properly be called monasteries until a few centuries later. Meanwhile, leadership of the Chinese clergy was provided first by Central Asian monks, then by naturalized Chinese of foreign descent, and by the fourth century, by Chinese themselves. Nuns are first mentioned in that century as well.

The movement of Buddhism to China, one of the great cultural interactions of history, was slow and fortuitous, carried out almost entirely at a private level. The basic reason for its eventual acceptance throughout Chinese society was that it offered several religious and social advantages unavailable to the same extent in China before. These included a full-time religious vocation for both men and women in an organization largely independent of family and state, a clear promise of life after death at various levels, and developed conceptions of paradise and purgatory, connected to life through the results of intentional actions *(karman)*. In addition, Buddhism offered the worship of heroic saviors in image form, supported by scriptures that told of their wisdom and compassion. For ordinary folk there were egalitarian moral principles, promises of healing and protection from harmful forces, and simple means of devotion; for intellectuals there were sophisticated philosophy and the challenge of attaining new states of consciousness in meditation, all of this expounded by a relatively educated clergy who recruited, organized, translated, and preached.

In the early fourth century North China was invaded by the Hsiung-nu, who sacked Lo-yang in 311 and Ch'ang-an in 316. Thousands of elite families fled south below the Yangtze River, where a series of short-lived Chinese dynasties held off further invasions. In the North a succession of kingdoms of Inner Asian background rose and fell, most of which supported Buddhism because of its religious appeal and its non-Chinese origins. The forms of Buddhism that developed here emphasized ritual, ideological support for the state, magic protection, and meditation.

It was in the South, however, that Buddhism first became a part of Chinese intellectual history. The Han imperial Confucian synthesis had collapsed with the dynasty, a collapse that encouraged a quest for new philosophical alternatives. Representatives of these alternatives found support in aristocratic clans, which competed with each other in part through philosophical debates. These debates, called *ch'ing-t'an*, or "pure conversation," revived and refined a tradition that had been widespread hundreds of years before in the period of the so-called One Hundred Schools, a tradition with precise rules of definition and criteria for victory. By the mid-third century these debates revolved around two basic perspectives, that of the "conservative moralists"*(ming-chiao)* and that of those advocating "spontaneous naturalism" *(tzu-jan)*. By the early fourth century Buddhist monks were involved in these debates, supported by sympathetic clans, advocating a middle ground between the conservatives and libertarians, spiritual freedom based on ethical discipline. Although Buddhism was still imperfectly understood, it had gained a vital foothold.

Chinese intellectuals first attempted to understand Buddhism through its apparent similarities to certain beliefs and practices of Taoism and the immortality cult. Thus, *bodhisattvas* and Buddhas were correlated with sages and immortals, meditation with circulation of the vital fluids, and *nirvāṇa* with *wu-wei*, spontaneous and purposeless action. However, Indian Buddhism and traditional Chinese thought have very different understandings of life and the world. Buddhist thought is primarily psychological and epistemological, concerned with liberation from *saṃsāra*, the world perceived as a realm of suffering, impermanence, and death. For the Chinese, on the other hand, nature and society are fundamentally good; our task is to harmonize with the positive forces of nature, and enlightenment consists of identifying with these forces, rather than in being freed from them. The interaction of these worldviews led Chinese Buddhists to interpret psychological concepts in cosmological directions. For example, the key Mahāyāna term "emptiness" *(śūnyatā)* refers primarily to a radically objective and neutral mode of perception, which accepts the impermanence and change of things without trying to control them with human concepts and values. Indeed, the first discussions of this term used it as a logical tool to destroy false confidence in philosophical and religious concepts, particularly earlier Buddhist ones. They are mutually contradictory, refer to nothing substantial, and hence are "empty." In China, however, "emptiness" immediately evoked discussion about the origin and nature of the phenomenal world. "Emptiness" was equated with "non-being," *(pen-wu, wu),* the fecund source of existence. As their understanding of Buddhism deepened, Chinese thinkers became more aware of the epistemological force of the term "emptiness," but continued to see it primarily as a problem in interpreting the world itself.

Buddhist thought was already well developed and complexly differentiated before it reached China. The Chinese knew of it only through scriptures haphazardly collected, in translations of varying accuracy, for very few Chinese learned Sanskrit. Since all the *sūtras* claimed to be preached by the Buddha himself, they were accepted as such, with discrepancies among them explained as deriving from the different situations and capacities of listeners prevailing when a particular text was preached. In practice, this meant that the Chinese had to select from a vast range of data those themes that made the most sense in their pre-existing worldview. For example, as the tradition develops we find emphases on simplicity and directness, the universal potential for enlightenment, and the Buddha mind as source of the cosmos, all of them prepared for in indigenous thought and practice. The most important early Chinese Buddhist philosophers, organizers, and translators were Tao-an (312–385), Hui-yüan (334–417), and Kumārajīva (334–413), each of whom contributed substantially to the growth of the young church. Tao-an was known principally for his organizational and exegetical skills and for the catalog of Buddhist scriptures he compiled. His disciple Hui-yüan, one of the most learned clerics in South China, gathered a large community of monks around him and inaugurated a cult to Amitābha. Kumārajīva, the most important and prolific of the early translators, was responsible for the transmission of the Mādyamika (San-lun) tradition to China. His lectures on Buddhist scripture in Ch'ang-an established a sound doctrinal basis for Mahāyāna thought in the Middle Kingdom. Another formative early figure was Tao-sheng (d. 434 CE), a student of Kumārajīva. He is known for his emphasis on the positive nature of *nirvāṇa*, his conviction that even non-believers have the potential for salvation, and his teaching of instantaneous enlightenment. These themes helped lay the foundation of Ch'an (Jpn., Zen) later on. [*See the biographies of Tao-an, Hui-yüan, Kumārajīva, and Tao-sheng.*]

The history of monastic Buddhism was closely tied to state attitudes and policies, which ranged from outright suppression to complete support, as in the case of Emperor Wu of the Liang dynasty (r. 502–549), who abolished Taoist temples and built Buddhist ones, and three times entered a monastery himself as a lay servitor. [*See the biography of Liang Wu-ti.*] However, by the fifth century Buddhism was becoming well established among people of all classes, who, to gain karmic merit, donated land and goods, took lay vows, served in monasteries, and established a variety of voluntary associations to copy scriptures, provide vegetarian food for monks and nuns, and carve Buddha images. The most important image-carving projects were at Yün-kang in Shansi and Lung-men in Honan, where huge figures, chiefly those of Śākyamuni and Maitreya, were cut into cliffs and caves. Such major projects of course also involved large-scale official and clerical support.

It was in the fifth century as well that Chinese Buddhist eschatology developed, based in part on predictions attributed to the Buddha that a few hundred years after his entry into *nirvāṇa* the *dharma* would lose its vigor, morals decline, and ignorant, corrupt monks and nuns appear. In addition, from its inception in the second century Taoism had proclaimed itself to be the manifestation of a new age of cosmic vitality, supported by pious devotees, "seed people." A combination of these motifs led to the composition in China of Buddhist scriptures saying that since the end of the age had come, more intense morality and piety were required of those who wished to be saved. These texts also promised aid from saving *bodhisattva*s such as Maitreya, the next Buddha-to-be. In some cases the apocalyptic vision of these texts inspired militant utopian movements, led by monks, but with lay membership. By the early seventh century a few of these groups were involved in armed uprisings in the name of Maitreya, which led eventually to a decline in official support for his cult, although he remained important in popular sectarian eschatology. [*See also* Millenarianism, *article on* Chinese Millenarian Movements, *and* Maitreya.]

The first important school of Buddhist thought developed in China was the T'ien-t'ai, founded by the monk Chih-i (538–597). This school is noted for its synthesis of earlier Buddhist traditions into one system, divided into five periods of development according to stages in the Buddha's teaching. According to T'ien-t'ai, the Buddha's teachings culminated in his exposition of the *Lotus Sutra*, in which all approaches are unified. Chih-i also systematized the theory and practice of Mahāyāna meditation. His most important philosophical contribution was his affirmation of the absolute Buddha mind as the source and substance of all phenomena. In Chih-i's teaching the old Mādhyamika logical destruction of dualities is replaced by a positive emphasis on their identity in a common source. So, in impeccably Buddhist language, he was able to justify the phenomenal world, and thus to provide an intellectual foundation for much of the later development of Buddhism in China. [*See* T'ien-t'ai *and the biography of Chih-i.*]

In 581 China was reunified by the Sui dynasty (581–618) after three and a half centuries of political fragmentation. The Sui founder supported Buddhism, particularly the T'ien-t'ai school, as a unifying ideology shared by many of his subjects in both North and South. After four decades of rule the Sui was overthrown in a series of rebellions, to be replaced by the T'ang (618–907). Although the new dynasty tended to give more official support to Confucianism and Taoism, Buddhism continued to grow at every level of society, and reached the high point of its development in China during the next two centuries.

THE RISE OF TAOIST RELIGION

Taoism is China's own indigenous higher religion, characterized by the fourth century by a literate and self-perpetuating priesthood, a pantheon of celestial deities, complex rituals, and revealed scriptures in classical Chinese. Although the first elements of this tradition appeared in the second century popular movements discussed above, the tradition underwent futher development at the hands of gentry scholars versed in philosophy, ethical teachings, and alchemy. These scholars saw themselves as formulators of a new, more refined religion superior to the popular cults around them. In retrospect, this movement appears as a reformulation of ideas from the *Lao-tzu* and *Chuang-tzu*, elements of the old state religion, together with those of the immortality cult and some local traditions, combined in a new system led by priests who, though not officials, claimed celestial prerogatives.

Taoism is fundamentally a religion of *ch'i*, the vital breath out of which nature, gods, and humans evolve. The source and order of this vital substance is the Tao, the ultimate power of life in the universe. The gods are personified manifestations of *ch'i*, symbolizing astral powers of the cosmos and organs of the human body with which they are correlated. Under the conditions of existence *ch'i* becomes stale and worn out, so it must be renewed through ritual processes that restore its primal vitality. These rituals consist essentially of visualizing and calling down the cosmic gods to reestablish their contact with their bodily correlates. In this way the adept ingests divine power and so recharges his bodily forces for healing, rejuvenation, and long life. Invocations to the gods are accompanied by exercises, massage, abstinence from grains (expressions of the dark *yin* power of the earth), and taking alchemical elixirs. Accomplished practice can bring about immortality through preparing the embryo of a new self that escapes the body at death. Taoist masters can release their cosmic power through ritual actions that revive the life forces of the community around them.

All branches of Taoism eventually traced their origin to a new revelation from the Most High Lord Lao to Chang Tao-ling, the grandfather of Chang Lu, in 142 CE, establishing him as "Celestial Master." He was empowered to perform rituals and write talismans that distributed this new manifestation of the Tao for the salvation of humankind. Salvation was available to those who repented of their sins, believed in the Tao, and pledged allegiance to their Taoist master. The master in turn established an alliance between the gods and the devotee, who then wore at the waist a list (register) of the names of the gods to be called on for protection. The register also served as a passport to heaven at death. Taoist ritual consists essentially of the periodic renewal of these alliances by confession, visualization, petition, and the offering of incense and sacred documents. Taoist texts are concerned throughout for moral discipline and orderly ritual and organization.

When the Celestial Master sect was officially recognized by the state of Wei (220–266) in the early third century its leadership was established in the capital, Lo-yang, north and east of the old sect base area in modern Szechwan. In the North remnants of the Yellow Turbans still survived, and before long the teachings and rituals of these two similar traditions blended together. A tension remained, however, between those who saw secular authority as a manifestation of the Way and those determined to bring in a new era of peace and prosperity by militant activity. Uprisings led by charismatic figures who claimed long life and healing powers occurred in different areas throughout the fourth century and later.

Meanwhile, in the southeast another tradition emerged that was to contribute to Taoism, a tradition concerned with alchemy, the use of herbs and minerals to attain immortality. Its chief literary expression was the *Pao-p'u–tzu* (The Master Who Preserves Simplicity) written by Ko Hung in about 320. Ko Hung collected a large number of recipes and legends of the immortals, intended to show how the body can be transformed by the ingestion of gold and other chemicals and by the inner circulation of the vital force *(ch'i),* special diets, and sexual techniques, all reinforced by moral dedication. Ko Hung's concerns were supported by members of the old aristocracy of the state of Wu (222–280) whose families had moved south during the Latter Han period. [*See the biography of Ko Hung*.]

When the northern state of Chin was conquered by the Hsiung-nu in 316, thousands of Chin gentry and officials moved south, bringing the Celestial Master sect with them. The eventual result was a blending of Celestial Master concern for priestly adminstration and collective rituals with the more individualistic and esoteric alchemical traditions of the southeast. Between the years 364 and 370 a young man named Yang Hsi claimed to receive revelations from "perfected ones" (exalted immortals) from the Heaven of Supreme Purity (Shang-ch'ing). These deities directed Yang to make transcripts and deliver them to Hsü Mi (303–373), an official of the Eastern Chin state (317–420) with whom he was associated. Yang Hsi believed his new revelations to be from celestial regions more exalted than those evoked by the Celestial Master sect and Ko Hung. The Perfected Ones rewrote and corrected earlier texts in poetic language, reformulated sexual rites as symbols of spiritual union, and taught new methods of inner cultivation and alchemy. These teachings were all presented in an eschatological context, as the salvation of an elect people in a time of chaos. They prophesied that a "lord of the Way, [a] sage who is to come" would descend in 392. Then the wicked would be eliminated and a purified terrestrial kingdom established, ruled over by such pious devotees as Hsü Mi, now perceived as a priest and future celestial official. It is perhaps not accidental that these promises were made to members of the old southern aristocracy whose status had recently been threatened by the newcomers from the north. [*See* Chen-jen.]

Hsü Mi and one of his sons had retired to Mao Shan, a mountain near the Eastern Chin capital (modern Nanking); hence the texts they received and transcribed came to be called those of a Mao-shan "school." In the next century another southern scholar, T'ao Hung-ching (456–536), collected all the remaining manuscripts from Yang Hsi and the Hsü family and edited them as the *Chen-kao* (Declarations of the Perfected). With this the Mao-shan/Shang-ch'ing scriptures were established as a foundation stone of the emerging Taoist canon. [*See the biography of T'ao Hung-ching*.]

In the meantime another member of Ko Hung's clan had written a scripture in about 397, the *Ling-pao ching* (Classic of the Sacred Jewel), which he claimed had been revealed to him by the spirit of an early third-century ancestor. This text exalted "celestial worthies" *(t'ien-tsun),* who were worshiped in elaborate collective rituals directed by priests in outdoor arenas. The *Ling-pao ching* established another strand of Taoist mythology and practice that was also codified in the South during the fifth century. Its rituals replaced those of the Celestial Master tradition, while remaining indebted to them. Ling-pao texts were collected and edited by Lu Hsiu-ching (406–477), who wrote on Taoist history and ritual. [*See the biography of Lu Hsiu-ching.*]

Taoism was active in the North as well, in the Northern Wei kingdom (386–534), which established Taoist offices at court in 400. In 415 and 423 a scholar named K'ou Ch'ien-chih (d. 448) claimed to have received direct revelations from Lord Lao while he was living on a sacred mountain. The resulting scriptures directed K'ou to reform the Celestial Master tradition; renounce popular cults, messianic uprisings, and sexual rituals; and support the court as a Taoist kingdom on earth. K'ou was introduced to the Wei ruler by a sympathetic official named Ts'ui Hao (d. 450) in 424 and was promptly appointed to the office of "Erudite of Transcendent Beings." The next year he was proclaimed Celestial Master, and his teachings "promulgated throughout the realm." For the next two decades K'ou and Ts'ui cooperated to promote Taoism at the court. As a result, in 440 the king accepted the title Perfect Ruler of Great Peace, and during the period 444 to 446 proscribed Buddhism and local "excessive cults." Although Ts'ui Hao was eventually discredited and Buddhism established as the state religion by a new ruler in 452, the years of official support for Taoism clarified its legitimacy and political potential as an alternative to Confucianism and Buddhism. Although it continued to develop new schools and scriptural traditions, the basic shape of Taoism for the rest of Chinese history was thus established by the fifth century. [*See the biography of K'ou Ch'ien-chih.*]

The Consolidation of Empire: Seventh to Fourteenth Century

The Chinese religious traditions that were to continue throughout the rest of imperial history all reached maturity during the T'ang (618–907) and Sung (960–1279) periods. These traditions included Buddhism, Taoism, Neo-Confucianism, Islam, and popular religion in both its village and sectarian forms. It was in these centuries as well that other foreign religions were practiced for a time in China, particularly Manichaeism and Nestorian Christianity. Rituals performed by the emperor and his officials continued to be elaborated, with many debates over the proper form and location of altars and types of sacrifices to be offered. During the T'ang dynasty, cults devoted to the spirits of local founders and protectors were established in many cities. These city gods *(ch'eng-huang-shen)* were eventually brought into the ranks of deities to whom official worship was due.

MANICHAEISM, NESTORIAN CHRISTIANITY, AND ISLAM

The area of the T'ang dynasty rivaled that of the Han, with western boundaries extending far into Central Asia. This expansion encouraged a revival of foreign trade and cultural contacts. Among the new foreign influences were not only Buddhist monks and scriptures but also the representatives of other religions. There is evidence for Zoroastrianism in China by the early sixth century, a result of contacts between China and Persia that originated in the second century BCE and were renewed in an exchange of envoys with the Northern Wei court in 455 and around 470. [*See* Zoroastrianism.]

A foreign tradition with more important influence on the history of Chinese religions was Manichaeism, a dynamic missionary religion teaching ultimate cosmic dualism founded by a Persian named Mani (216–277?). The first certain reference to Manichaeism in a Chinese source is dated 694, although it may have been present about two decades earlier. As was true with Zoroastrianism, Manichaeism in its early centuries in China was primarily practiced by foreigners, although its leaders soon composed catechisms and texts in Chinese stressing the congruence of their teachings with Buddhism and Taoism. In 755 a Chinese military commander named An Lu-shan led a powerful rebellion that the T'ang court was able to put down only with the help of foreign support. One of these allies was the Uighur, from a kingdom based in what is now northern Mongolia. In 762 a Uighur army liberated Lo-yang from rebel forces, and there a Uighur kaghan was converted to Manichaeism. The result was new prestige and more temples for the religion in China.

However, in 840 the Uighurs were defeated by the Kirghiz, with the result that the Chinese turned on the religion of their former allies, destroyed its temples, and expelled or executed its priests. Nonetheless, at least one Manichaean leader managed to escape to Ch'üan-chou in Fukien Province on the southeast coast. In Fukien the Manichaeans flourished as a popular sect until the fourteenth century, characterized by their distinctive teachings, communal living, vegetarian diet, and nonviolence. They were called the Ming-chiao ("religion of light"). They disappeared as a coherent tradition as a result of renewed persecutions during the early Ming dynasty (1368–1644). Several Manichaean texts were incorporated into the Taoist and Buddhist canons, and it is likely that Manichaean lay sects provided models for similar organizations that evolved out of Buddhism later. Manichaean dualism and demon exorcism may have reinforced similar themes in Taoism and Buddhism as they were understood at the popular level. [*See* Manichaeism, *overview article*.]

According to a stone inscription erected in Sian (Ch'ang-an) in 781, the first Nestorian missionary reached China in 635 and taught about the creation of the world, the fall of humankind, and the birth and teaching of the Messiah. The ethics and rituals described are recognizably Christian. Chinese edicts of 638 and 745 refer to Nestorianism, which appears to have been confined to foreign communities in large cities on major trade routes. In 845 Nestorianism was proscribed along with Buddhism and other religions of non-Chinese origin, but it revived in China during the period of Mongol rule in the thirteenth and fourteenth centuries. In 1289 the court established an office to supervise Christians, and a 1330 source claims that there were more than thirty thousand Nestorians in China, some of them wealthy and in high positions, no doubt a result of the Mongol policy of ruling China in part with officials of foreign origin. In this period the church was most active in eastern cities such as Hangchow and Yangchow. The Nestorians were expelled from China with the defeat of the Mongols in the mid-fourteenth century, and no active practitioners were found by the Jesuits when they arrived about two hundred years later. So the first Christian contact with China expired, leaving no demonstrable influence on Chinese religion and culture. [*See* Nestorianism.]

The Chinese first learned of Islam in 638 from an emissary of the last Sasanid king of Persia, who was seeking their aid against invading Arab armies. This the Chinese refused, but a number of Persian refugees were admitted a few years later after the Sasanid defeat and allowed to practice their Zoroastrian faith. In the early eighth century Arab armies moved into Central Asia, and in 713 ambassadors of Caliph Walīd were received at court in Ch'ang-an, even though they refused to prostrate themselves before the emperor. However, in 751 a Chinese army far to the west was defeated in the Battle of Talas by a combination of Central Asian states with Arab support. This defeat led to the replacement of Chinese influence in Central Asia with that of the Arabs and the decline of Buddhism in that area in favor of Islam. In 756 another caliph sent Arab mercenaries to aid the Chinese court against An Lu-shan; when the war ended many of these mercenaries remained, forming the beginning of Islamic presence in China, which by the late twentieth century totaled about thirty million people, one of the five basic constituencies of the People's Republic. The eighth-century Arab population was augmented by Muslim merchants who settled in Chinese coastal cities, for a time dominating the sea trade with India and Southeast Asia.

The major influx of Muslim peoples occurred during the Yüan dynasty (1271–1368) when the land routes across Central Asia were secure and the Mongols brought in large numbers of their non-Chinese subjects to help administer China. It was in this period that Islam spread all over China and established major population bases in the western provinces of Yunnan and Kansu. Here their numbers increased through marriage with Chinese women and adoption of non-Muslim children, all converted to Islam. Although the result was a dilution of Arab physical characteristics, the use of the Chinese language, and the adoption of some Chinese social customs, for most the Islamic core remained. Muslims did not accept such dominant Chinese traditions as ancestor worship and pork eating, and kept their own festival calendar. In part this resistance was due to the tenacity of their beliefs, in part to the fact that their numbers, mosques, and essentially lay organization permitted mutual support.

Muslims in China have always been predominantly Sunnī, but in the sixteenth century Sufism reached China through Central Asia. By the late seventeenth century Ṣūfī brotherhoods began a reform movement that advocated increased use of Arabic and a rejection of certain Chinese practices that had infiltrated Islam, such as burning incense at funerals. Sufism also emphasized ecstatic personal experience of Allāh, the veneration of saints, and the imminent return of the Mahdi, who would bring a new age, this last theme due to Shīʿī influence as well.

These reformist beliefs, coupled with increased Chinese pressure on Islam as a whole, led eventually to a powerful uprising in Yunnan between 1855–1873, an uprising allowed to develop momentum because of old ethnic tensions in the area and the distraction of the Chinese court with the contemporary Taiping Rebellion (1851–1864). The Yunnan rebellion was eventually put down by a combination of Chinese and loyalist Muslim forces, and the Muslims resumed their role as a powerful minority in China, called the Hui people.

The chief role of Islam in China was as the religion of this minority group, although in some twentieth-century popular texts it is recognized as one of the "five religions" whose teachings are now blended into a new synthetic revelation, along with Confucianism, Taoism, Buddhism, and Christianity. In historical terms its chief impact was to sharply reduce Chinese contact with India and Central Asia after the eighth century, and thus to cut off the vital flow of new texts and ideas to Chinese Buddhism.

T'ANG BUDDHISM

The first T'ang emperor, Kao-tsu (r. 618–626) approved of a plan to limit both Taoist and Buddhist temples. His son T'ai-tsung (r. 626–649) agreed with the Taoist contention that the imperial family was descended from Lao-tzu, whose legendary surname was also Li; however, T'ai-tsung also erected Buddhist shrines on battlefields and ordered monks to recite scriptures for the stability of the empire. Buddhist philosophical schools in this period were matters of both belief and imperial adornment, so, to replace the T'ien-t'ai school, now discredited on account of its association with the Sui dynasty, the T'ang court turned first to the Fa-hsiang, or Idealist school, the Indian teaching of "consciousness-only." [*See* Yogācāra.] Some texts of this tradition had been translated earlier by Paramārtha (499–569), but it came to be thoroughly understood in China only after the return of the pilgrim Hsüan-tsang in 645. Hsüan-tsang was welcomed at court and provided with twenty-three scholar-monks from all over China to assist in translating the books he had brought back from India. The emperor wrote a preface for the translation of one major Vijñānavāda text, and his policy of imperial support was continued by his son Kao-tsung.(r. 649–683). [*See the biography of Hsüan-tsang.*]

However, the complex psychological analysis of the Vijñānavāda school, coupled with its emphasis that some beings are doomed by their nature to eternal rebirth, were not in harmony with the Chinese worldview, which had been better represented by T'ien-t'ai. Hence, when imperial support declined at Kao-tsung's death in 683, the fortunes of the Fa-hsiang school declined as well, despite the excellent scholarship of Hsüan-tsang's disciple K'uei-chi (632–682). [*See the biography of K'uei-chi.*] At the intellectual level it was replaced in popularity by the Hua-yen ("flower garland") school as formulated by the monk Fa-tsang (643–712). This school, based on a *sūtra* of the same name (Skt., *Avataṃsaka*), taught the emptiness and interpenetration of all phenomena in a way consonant with old Chinese assumptions. Furthermore, in Hua-yen teaching the unity and integration of all things is symbolized by a Buddha called Vairocana who presides over his Pure Land in the center of an infinite universe. [*See* Mahāvairocana.] However dialectically such a symbol might be understood by Buddhist scholars, at a political and popular level it was appropriated more literally as a Buddhist creator deity. [*See* Hua-yen *and the biography of Fa-tsang.*]

It is no accident that the Hua-yen school was first actively supported by Empress Wu Chao (Wu Tse-t'ien, r. 690–705) who took over the throne from her sons to set up her own dynasty, the Chou. Since Confucianism did not allow for female rulers, Empress Wu, being a devout Buddhist, sought for supporting ideologies in that tradition, including not only Hua-yen but also predictions in obscure texts that the Buddha had prophesied that several hundred years after his death a woman would rule over a world empire. Monks in Wu-Tse-t'ien's entourage equated her with this empress and further asserted that she was a manifestation of the future Buddha Maitreya.

When Empress Wu abdicated in 705 her son continued to support the Hua-yen school, continuing the tradition of close relationship between the court and Buddhist philosophical schools. However, during this period Buddhism continued to grow in popularity among all classes of people. Thousands of monasteries and shrines were built, supported by donations of land, grain, cloth, and precious metals, and by convict workers, the poor, and serfs bound to donated lands. Tens of thousands of persons became monks or nuns, elaborate rituals were performed, feasts provided, and sermons preached in both monastery and marketplace. Buddhist observances such as the Lantern Festival, the Buddha's birthday, and All Souls Day became universally practiced, while pious lay societies multiplied for carving images and inscriptions and disseminating scriptures. Wealthy monasteries became centers of money lending, milling, and medical care, as well as hostels for travelers and retreats for scholars and officials. In high literature the purity of monks and monasteries was admired, while in popular stories *karman*, rebirth, and purgatory became truths simply assumed. The state made sporadic attempts to control this exuberance through licensing monasteries, instituting examinations for monks, and issuing ordination certificates, but state control was limited and "unofficial" Buddhist practices continued to flourish.

An important factor in this popularity was the rise of two more simple and direct forms of Chinese Buddhism, much less complex than the exegetical and philosophical schools that were dominant earlier. These were the Pure Land (Ching-t'u) school, devoted to rebirth in Amitābha's paradise, and the Ch'an ("meditation") school, which promised enlightenment in this life to those with sufficient dedication. These traditions were universalist and nonhierarchical in principle, yet came to have coherent teachings and organizations of their own appealing to a wide range of people. Both should be understood as products of gradual evolution in the seventh and eighth centuries, as a positive selection from earlier teachings, particularly T'ien-t'ai, and as a reformist reaction against the secularization of the T'ang monastic establishment.

By the third century CE texts describing various "pure realms" or "Buddha lands" had been translated into Chinese, and some monks began to meditate on the best known of these "lands," the Western Paradise of the Buddha Amitābha. [*See* Pure and Impure Lands *and* Amitābha.] In the fourth century Chih Tun (314–366) made an image of Amitābha and vowed to be reborn in his paradise, as did Hui-yüan in 402. [*See the biography of Hui-yüan.*] These early efforts concentrated on visualization of Buddha realms in states of meditative trance. [*See* Nien-fo.] However, in two Pure Land *sūtras* describing Amitābha and his realm devotees are assured that through a combination of ethical living and concentration on the Buddha they will be reborn at death in his realm, owing to a vow he had made aeons ago to create out of the boundless merit he had accumulated on the long path to Buddhahood a haven for sentient beings. This promise eventually led some monks to preach devotion to Amitābha as an easier way to salvation, available to all, through a combination of sincere thinking on the Buddha and the invocation of his name in faith. To strengthen their proclamation, these monks argued that in fact Amitābha's Pure Land was at a high level, beyond *saṃsāra*, and thus functionally equivalent to *nirvāṇa* for those less philosophically inclined.

Philosophers of the fifth and sixth centuries such as Seng-chao and Chih-i discussed the Pure Land concept as part of larger systems of thought, but the first monk to devote his life to proclaiming devotion to Amitābha as the chief means of salvation for the whole of society was T'an-luan (476–542), a monk from North China where there had long been an emphasis on the practical implementation of Buddhism. T'an-luan organized devotional associations whose members both contemplated the Buddha and orally recited his name. It was in the fifth and sixth centuries as well that many Chinese Buddhist thinkers became convinced that the final period of Buddhist teaching for this world cycle was about to begin, a period (called in Chinese *mo-fa*, the Latter Days of the Law) in which the capacity for understanding Buddhism had so declined that only simple and direct means of communication would suffice. [*See* Mappō *and the biographies of Seng-chao and T'an-luan.*]

The next important preacher to base his teachings solely on Amitābha and his Pure Land was Tao-ch'o (562–645). It was he and his disciple Shan-tao (613–681) who firmly established the Pure Land movement and came to be looked upon as founding patriarchs of the tradition. Although both of these men advocated oral recitation of Amitābha's name as the chief means to deliverance, such recitation was to be done in a concentrated and devout state of mind and was to be accompanied by confession of sins and the chanting of *sūtras*. They and their followers also organized recitation assemblies and composed manuals for congregational worship. Owing to their efforts, Pure Land devotion became the most popular form of Buddhism in China, from whence it was taken to Japan in the ninth century. Pure Land teachings supported the validity of lay piety as no Buddhist school had before, and hence both made possible the spread of Buddhism throughout the population and furthered the development of independent societies and sects outside the monasteries. [*See* Ching-t'u *and the biographies of Tao-ch'o and Shan-tao.*]

The last movement within orthodox Buddhism in China to emerge as an independent tradition was Ch'an (Jpn., Zen), characterized by its concentration on direct means of individual enlightenment, chiefly meditation. Such enlightenment has always been the primary goal of Buddhism, so in a sense Ch'an began as a reform movement seeking to recover the experiential origins of its tradition. Such a reform appeared all the more necessary in the face of the material success of T'ang Buddhism, with its ornate rituals, complex philosophies, and close relationships with the state. Ch'an evolved out of the resonances of Mahāyāna Buddhism with the individualist, mystical, and iconoclastic strand of Chinese culture, represented chiefly by the philosophy of the *Lao-tzu* and *Chuang-tzu*. This philosophy had long advocated individual identification with the ineffable foundations of being, which cannot be grasped in words or limited by the perspectives of traditional practice and morality. Such identification brings a new sense of spiritual freedom, affirmation of life, and acceptance of death.

The importance of meditation had long been emphasized in Chinese Buddhism, beginning with Han translations of *sūtras* describing the process. The T'ien-t'ai master Chih-i discussed the stages and positions of meditation in great detail in the sixth century. Thus, it is not surprising that by the seventh century some monks appeared who advocated meditation above all, a simplification parallel to that of the Pure Land tradition.

The first references to a "Ch'an school" appeared in the late eighth century. By that time several branches of this emerging tradition were constructing genealogies going back to Śākyamuni himself; these were intended to establish the priority and authority of their teachings. The genealogy that came to be accepted later claimed a lineage of twenty-eight Indian and seven Chinese patriarchs, the latter beginning with Bodhidharma (c. 461–534), a Central Asian meditation master active in the Northern Wei kingdom. Legends concerning these patriarchs were increasingly elaborated as time passed, but the details of most cannot be verified. [*See the biography of Bodhidharma.*] The first Chinese monk involved whose teachings have survived is Tao-hsin (580–651), who was later claimed to be the fourth patriarch. Tao-hsin specialized in meditation and monastic discipline, and studied for ten years with a disciple of the T'ien-t'ai founder, Chih-i. He is also noted for his concern with image worship and reciting the Buddha's name to calm the mind.

One of Tao-hsin's disciples was Hung-jen (601–674), who also concentrated on meditation and on maintaining "awareness of the mind." His successor was Fa-ju (d. 689), whose spiritual heir in turn was Shen-hsiu (d. 706), who had also studied with Hung-jen. Shen-hsiu was active in North China, where he was invited to court by the Empress Wu and became a famous teacher. In the earliest and most reliable sources Hung-jen, Fa-ju, and Shen-hsiu are described as the fifth, sixth, and seventh Ch'an patriarchs, with Fa-ju eventually omitted and replaced in sixth position by Shen-hsiu. However, in the early eighth century this succession, based in the capitals of Lo-yang and Ch'ang-an in the North (and hence retrospectively referred to as the "Northern school"), was challenged by a monk named Shen-hui (670–762), who had studied for several years with a teacher named Hui-neng (638–713) in a monastery in Kwangtung Province in the South. Shen-hui labored for years to establish a new form of Ch'an, a "Southern school," centered on recognizing the Buddha nature within the self, and thus less concerned with worship, scripture study, and prescribed forms of meditation.

Shen-hui's most lasting achievement was the elevation of his teacher Hui-neng to the status of "sixth patriarch," displacing Shen-hsiu. This achievement was textually established through the composition of a book entitled *The Platform Sutra of the Sixth Patriarch* (platform here means dais) in about 820 by members of Shen-hui's school. Portions of this book are very similar to the teachings of Shen-hui, who did not cite any writings by Hui-neng although he was no doubt influenced by his study with him. In the *Platform Sutra* Hui-neng is portrayed as a brilliant young monk of rustic background who confounds Shen-hsiu and is secretly given charge of the transmission by the fifth patriarch, Hung-jen (601–674). This book teaches instantaneous enlightenment through realization of inner potential, while criticizing gradualist approaches that rely on outer forms such as images and scriptures. As such it is an important source of the Ch'an individualism and iconoclasm well known in the West. [*See the biography of Hui-neng.*]

The Ch'an tradition as a whole, however, has always been characterized by disciplined communal living in monasteries, centered on group meditation. Although the first extant written codes of monastic conduct are dated 1103 or 1104, they refer back to the teachings of Pai-chang Huai-hai (720–814), a monk in the Hui-neng line of transmission. However, the first monks to establish a new style of monastic life based on communal meditation and manual labor were Tao-hsin and Hung-jen in the seventh century. Other characteristics of early Ch'an monasteries were their independent establishment in remote areas, their rejection of a central hall containing images in favor of "Dharma halls" with meditation platforms along the sides, private consultations with abbots, and frequent group discussions. Frugality and shared responsibility for work were also emphasized in order to reduce dependence on outside donations with the reciprocal obligations they involved. In later centuries agricultural labor was reduced as Ch'an became established and received donations of land and goods from wealthy patrons.

By the ninth century Ch'an was widely supported in Chinese society; during the Northern Sung dynasty (960–1127) it was the major form of monastic Buddhism and hence a focal point of institutionalization. In this context Ch'an produced a new type of literature, the "recorded discussions" *(yü-lu)* of patriarchs and abbots with their disciples as they struggled to attain enlightenment. It is these records, codified as "cases" (Chin., *kung-an*; Jpn., *kōan*), that were meditated upon by novices as they sought to experience reality directly. [*See also* Ch'an.]

Although Buddhism flourished at all levels of Chinese society in the T'ang period, an undercurrent of resentment and hostility toward it by Confucians, Taoists, and the state always remained. This hostility came to a head in the mid-ninth century, strongly reinforced by the fact that Buddhist monasteries had accumulated large amounts of precious metals and tax exempt land. From 843 to 845 Emperor Wu-tsung (r. 840–846), an ardent Taoist, issued decrees that led to the destruction of 4,600 monasteries and 40,000 temples and shrines, and the return of 260,500 monks and nuns to lay life. Although this suppression was ended in 846 by Wu-tsung's successor, monastic Buddhism never fully regained its momentum. Nonetheless, Buddhist ideas, values, and rituals continued to permeate Chinese society through the influence of the Ch'an and Pure Land schools, which survived the 845 persecution because of widespread support throughout the country.

T'ANG TAOISM

Taoism continued to develop during the T'ang period, in part because it received more support from some emperors than it had under the Sui. As noted earlier, T'ai-tsung claimed Lao-tzu as a royal ancestor, and in 667 the Emperor Kao-tsung (r. 649–683) conferred on Lao-tzu the title of emperor, thus confirming his status. Empress Wu, Kao-tsung's wife, swung the pendulum of support back to Buddhism, but Taoism was favored in later reigns as well and reached the high point of its political influence in the T'ang with great suppression of non-Chinese religions in the 840s.

The most important Taoist order during the T'ang was that based on Mao Shan in Kiangsu, where temples were built and reconstructed, disciples trained, and scriptures edited. Devotees on Mao Shan studied Shang-ch'ing scriptures, meditated, practiced alchemy, and carried out complex rituals of purgation and cosmic renewal, calling down astral spirits and preparing for immortality among the stars. These activities were presided over by a hierarchical priesthood, led by *fa-shih*, "masters of doctrine," the most prominent of whom came to be considered patriarchs of the school.

TAOISM IN THE SUNG AND YÜAN PERIODS

The destruction of the old T'ang aristocracy in the turmoil of the ninth and tenth centuries helped prepare the way for a more centralized state in the Sung, administered by bureaucrats who were selected through civil service examinations. This in turn contributed to increased social mobility, which was also enhanced by economic growth and diversification, the spread of printing, and a larger number of schools. These factors, combined with innovations in literature, art, philosophy, and religion, have led historians to describe the Sung period as the beginning of early modern China. It was in this period that the basic patterns of life and thought were established for the remainder of imperial history.

During the tenth through thirteenth centuries Taoism developed new schools and texts and became more closely allied with the state. The Sung emperor Chen-tsung (r. 990–1023) bestowed gifts and titles on a number of prominent Taoists, including one named Chang from the old Way of the Celestial Masters, based on Mount Lung-hu in Kiangsi Province. This led to the consolidation of the Cheng-i (Orthodox Unity) sect led by hereditary Celestial Masters. The other official Taoist ordination centers in this period were those at Mao Shan and the Ling-pao center in Kiangsu.

A century later, during the reign of Emperor Hui-tsung (r. 1101–1126), the most famous imperial patron of Taoism, three new Taoist orders appeared, one with a popular base in southeastern Kiangsi, another a revival of Mao-shan teachings, and the third the Shen-hsiao Fa (Rites of the Divine Empyrean), initiated by Lin Ling-su, who was active at court from 1116 to 1119. Lin's teachings were presented in a new, expanded edition of a fourth-century Ling-pao text, the *Tu-jen ching* (Scripture of Salvation). The scripture proclaimed that a new divine emperor would descend to rule in 1112, thus bestowing additional sacred status on Hui-tsung. This liturgical text in sixty-one chapters promises salvation to all in the name of a supreme celestial realm, a theme welcome at a court beset with corruption within and foreign invaders without. The Kiangsi movement, called T'ien-hsin (Heart of Heaven) after a star in Ursa Major, was most concerned with the ritual evocation of astral power to exorcise disease-causing demons, particularly those associated with mental illness. The first edition of its texts was also presented to Hui-tsung in 1116.

In 1126 the Sung capital Kaifeng was captured by the Jurchen, a people from northeastern Manchuria who, with other northern peoples, had long threatened the Sung. As a result the Chinese court moved south across the Yangtze River to establish a new capital in Hang-chou, thus initiating the Southern Sung period (1127–1279). During this period China was once again divided north and south, with the Jurchen ruling the Chin kingdom (1115–1234). It was here in the north that three new Taoist sects appeared, the T'ai-i (Grand Unity), the Ta-tao (Great Way), and the Ch'üan-chen (Total Perfection). The T'ai-i sect gained favor for a time at the Chin court because of its promise of divine healing. Ta-tao disciples worked in the fields, prayed for healing rather than using charms, and did not practice techniques of immortality. Both groups were led by a succession of patriarchs for about two hundred years, but failed to survive the end of the Yüan dynasty. Both included Confucian and Buddhist elements in a Taoist framework.

The Ch'üan-chen sect was founded in similar circumstances by a scholar named Wang Che (1113–1170), but continued to exist into the twentieth century. Wang claimed to have received revelations from two superhuman beings, whereupon he gathered disciples and founded five congregations in northern Shantung. After his death seven of his leading disciples continued to proclaim his teachings across North China. One of them was received at the Chin court in 1187, thus beginning a period of imperial support for the sect that continued into the time of Mongol rule, particularly after another of the founding disciples visited Chinggis Khan at his Central Asian court in 1222. [*See the biography of* Wang Che.]

In its early development the Taoist quest for personal immortality employed a combination of positive ritual techniques: visualization of astral gods and ingestion of their essence, internal circulation and refinement of *ch'i*, massage, eating elixirs of cinnebar and mica, and so forth, all accompanied by taboos and ethical injunctions. By the eleventh century this quest was further internalized, and alchemical potions were reinterpreted as forces within the body, a tendency well expressed in the writings of Chang Po-tuan (983–1082). Under Confucian and Ch'an influence the Ch'üan-chen school "spiritualized" the terminology of these older practices, turning its physiological referents into abstract polarities within the mind, to be unified through meditation. Perhaps in part because of this withdrawal into the mind, Ch'üan-chen was the first Taoist school to base itself in monasteries, although celibacy to maintain and purify one's powers had been practiced by some adepts earlier, and some Taoist monasteries had been established in the sixth century under pressure from the state and the Buddhist example.

The Ch'üan-chen sect reached the height of its influence in the first decades of the thirteenth century, and for a time was favored over Chinese Buddhism by Mongol rulers. Buddhist leaders protested Taoist occupation of their monasteries and eventually regained official support after a series of debates between Taoists and Buddhists at court between 1255 and 1281. After Buddhists were judged the winners, Khubilai Khan ordered that the Taoist canon be burned and Taoist priests returned to lay life or converted to Buddhism. In the fourteenth century the Ch'üan-chen sect merged with a similar tradition from South China, the Chin-tan Tao (Golden Elixer Way) also devoted to attaining immortality through cultivating powers or "elixirs" within the self. The name Ch'üan-chen was retained for the monastic side of this combined tradition, whereas the Chin-tan Tao continued as a popular movement that has produced new scriptures and sects since at least the sixteenth century. The older Taoist schools continued to produce new bodies of texts from the eleventh century on, all claiming divine origin, and powers of healing, exorcism, and support for the state.

THE REVIVAL OF CONFUCIAN PHILOSOPHY

Confucianism had remained a powerful tradition of morality, social custom, and hierarchical status since the fall of the Han, but after the third century it no longer generated fresh philosophical perspectives. There were a few Confucian philosophers such as Wang T'ung (584?–617), Han Yü (768–824), and Li Ao (fl. 798), but from the fourth through the tenth century the best philosophical minds in China were devoted to Buddhism. However, in the eleventh century there appeared a series of thinkers determined to revive Confucianism as a philosophical system. In this task they were inevitably influenced by Buddhist theories of mind, enlightenment, and ethics; indeed, most of these men went through Buddhist and Taoist phases in their early years and were converted to Confucianism later. Nonetheless, at a conscious level they rejected Buddhist "emptiness," asceticism, and monastic life in favor of a positive metaphysics, ordered family life, and concern for social reform. With a few exceptions the leaders of this movement, known in the West as Neo-Confucianism, went through the civil service examination system and held civil or military offices.

The key eleventh century founders of this movement were Chou Tun-i (1017–1073), Shao Yung (1011–1077), Chang Tsai (1020–1077), and his nephews Ch'eng

Hao (1032–1085) and Ch'eng I (1033–1107), who were brothers. In retrospect we can see that Neo-Confucianism split into two general tendencies, the rationalistic and the idealistic, the first more concerned with the ordering principles *(li)* of life and society, the second with awakening the moral consciousness of the mind *(hsin)*. [*See* Hsin.] These tendencies may be found in eleventh century writings, but did not become explicit until a century later in the work of the "study of principle" *(li-hsüeh)* initiated by Chu Hsi (1130–1200) and the "study of mind" *(hsin-hsüeh)* promoted by Lu Hsiang-shan (1139–1193). Interaction between these poles provided the impetus for new syntheses until the seventeenth century, with the "study of mind" best represented by Wang Yang-ming (1472–1529). The most complete system of thought was produced by Chu Hsi, who sought to enhance the source of moral order within by patient investigation of the patterns of organization in society and nature. Chu Hsi's teachings were made the basis of the civil service examinations in 1313, and hence came to have a powerful influence throughout literate society. [*With the exception of Shao Yung, all of the thinkers mentioned above are the subject of independent entries.*]

In the history of Chinese religions, the impact of Neo-Confucianism is evident at different levels. The intellectual and institutional success of this movement among the Chinese elite led many of them away from Buddhism and Taoism, away from any form of sectarian religion, toward a reaffirmation of the values of family, clan, and state. While the elite were still involved in such popular traditions as annual festivals, geomancy, and funeral rituals, the rational and nontheistic orientation of Neo-Confucianism tended to inhibit their participation in ecstatic processions and shamanism. These tendencies meant that after the eleventh century sectarian and popular forms of religion were increasingly denied high level intellectual stimulation and articulation. Indeed, state support for a new Confucian orthodoxy gave fresh impetus to criticism or suppression of other traditions. Another long term impact of Neo-Confucianism was the confucianization of popular values, supported by schools, examinations, distribution of tracts, and lectures in villages. This meant that from the Sung dynasty on the operative ethical principles in society were a combination of Confucian virtues with Buddhist *karman* and compassion, a tendency that became more widespread as the centuries passed.

All of these developments were rooted in the religious dimensions of the Neo-Confucian tradition, which from the beginning was most concerned with the moral transformation of self and society. This transformation was to be carried out through intensive study and discussion, self-examination, and meditation. In the process one could become aware of the patterns of moral order within the mind, an insight that itself became a means of clarifying and establishing this cosmic order within society. So Confucianism became a more active and self-conscious movement than it ever had been before. [*See* Confucian Thought, *article on* NeoConfucianism.]

SUNG BUDDHISM

Sung Buddhist activities were based on the twin foundations of Ch'an and Pure Land, with an increasing emphasis on the compatability of the two. Although the joint practice of meditation and invocation of the Buddha's name had been taught by Chih-i and the Ch'an patriarch Tao-hsin in the sixth and seventh centuries, the first

Ch'an master to openly advocate it after Ch'an was well established was Yen-shou (904–975). This emphasis was continued in the Yüan (1271–1368) and Ming (1368–1644) dynasties, so that by the late traditional period meditation and recitation were commonly employed together in monasteries as two means to the same end of emptying the mind of self-centered thought.

During the Sung dynasty Buddhism physically recovered from the suppression of the ninth century, with tens of thousands of monasteries, large amounts of land, and active support throughout society. By the tenth century the Ch'an school was divided into two main branches, both of which had first appeared earlier, the Lin-chi (Jpn., Rinzai), emphasizing dramatic and unexpected breakthroughs to enlightenment in the midst of everyday activities, and the Ts'ao-tung (Jpn., Sōtō), known for a more gradual approach through seated meditation. [*See the biography of Lin-chi.*] There was some recovery of philosophical studies in Ch'an monasteries, but it did not recapture the intellectual vitality of the T'ang period. However, for the larger history of Chinese religions the most important development in Sung Buddhism was the spread of lay societies devoted to good works and recitation of the Buddha's name. These groups, usually supported by monks and monasteries, ranged in membership from a few score to several thousands, including both men and women, gentry and commoners. In the twelfth century these societies, with their egalitarian outreach and congregational rituals, provided the immediate context for the rise of independent popular sects, which in turn spread throughout China in succeeding centuries. The Sung associations were an organized and doctrinally aware means of spreading Buddhist ideas of salvation, paradise and purgatory, *karman*, and moral values to the population at large, and so contributed to the integration of Buddhism with Chinese culture.

POPULAR RELIGION

The other major tradition that took its early modern shape during the Sung period was popular religion, the religion of the whole population except those who specifically opted out of it, such as orthodox Taoist priests, Buddhist monks, Confucian scholars, and state officials in their public roles. Chou and Han sources note a variety of religious practices current throughout the population, including ancestor worship, sacrifices to spirits of sacred objects and places, belief in ghosts, exorcism, divination, and the activities of spirit mediums. Many of these practices began in prehistoric times and formed the sea out of which more structured and focused traditions gradually emerged, traditions such as the state cult, Confucian philosophy, and Taoist religion. Each of these emerging traditions was associated with social elites who had to define themselves as different from their peasant and artisan surroundings. In the process they came to criticize or even suppress cults active among common folk devoted to local spirits and concerned primarily with efficacious response to immediate needs. Since the Chinese state had always claimed religious prerogatives, the most important factor was official authorization by some level of government. Unauthorized cults were considered "excessive," beyond what elite custom and propriety admitted. Nonetheless, such distinctions were of importance primarily to the more self-conscious supporters of literate alternatives; to their less theologically inclined peers, "popular religion" was a varied set of customs that reflected the way the world was.

Popular religious practices were diffused throughout the social system, based in family, clan, and village, at first devoted only to spirits with limited and local powers. By the Han dynasty personified deities of higher status appeared, along with organized sects such as the Way of the Celestial Masters, with ethical teachings and new myths of creation and world renewal, all reinforced by collective rituals. These developments were produced by literate commoners and minor officials at an intermediate level of education and status, and show remakable resemblance to the first records of such middle-class thought in the writings of Mo-tzu, six hundred years earlier. This level of Chinese religious consciousness was strongly reinforced by Mahāyāna *bodhisattvas*, images, offering rituals, myths of purgatory, and understandings of moral causation. By the fourth century, Taoist writers were developing elaborate mythologies of personified deities and immortals and their roles in a celestial hierarchy.

During the Sung period all these various strands came together to reformulate popular religion as a tradition in its own right, defined by its location in the midst of ordinary social life, its pantheon of personified deities, views of afterlife, demonology, and characteristic specialists and rituals. Its values were still founded on pragmatic reciprocity, but some assurances about life after death were added to promises for aid now.

This popular tradition is based on ancestor veneration and the cult of household gods. [*See also* Ancestors, *article on* Ancestor Cults.] Beyond the household its rituals are performed at shrines for locality gods and at village temples. Temples are residences of the gods, where they are most easily available and ready to accept petitions and offerings of food and incense. Here too, the gods convey messages through simple means of divination, dreams, spirit mediums, and spirit writing. Great bronze incense burners in temple courtyards are the central points of ritual communication, and it is common for local households to fill their own incense burners with ashes from the temple. All families residing in the area of the village are considered members of the temple community.

The deities characteristic of this tradition are human beings deified over time by increasing recognition of their efficacy and status. Having once been human they owe their positions to veneration by the living and hence are constrained by reciprocal relationships with their devotees. They are responsible for specific functions such as providing rain or healing diseases, and under Taoist influence came to be organized in a celestial hierarchy presided over by the Jade Emperor, a deity first officially recognized as such by the Sung emperor Chen-tsung in the beginning of the eleventh century. [*See* Yü-huang.]

Gods are symbols of order, and many of the gods of Taoism and popular religion are equipped with weapons and troops. Such force is necessary because beneath the gods is a vast array of demons, hostile influences that bring disorder, disease, suffering, and death. Although ultimately subject to divine command, and in some cases sent by the gods to punish sinners, these demons are most unruly, and often can be subdued only through repeated invocation and strenuous ritual action. It is in such ritual exorcism that the struggle between gods and demons is most starkly presented. Most demons, or *kuei*, are the spirits of the restless dead who died unjustly, or whose bodies are not properly cared for; they cause disruption to draw attention to their plight. Other demons represent natural forces that can be perceived as hostile, such as mountains and wild animals. Much effort in popular religion is devoted to dealing with these harmful influences.

There are three different types of leadership in this popular tradition—hereditary, selected, and charismatic—although of course in any given situation these types can be mixed. Hereditary leaders include the fathers and mothers of families who carry out ancestor worship in the clan temple and household, and sect leaders who inherit their positions. Hereditary Taoist priests also perform rituals for the community. Village temples, on the other hand, tend to be led by a village elder selected by lot, on a rotating basis. Charismatic leaders include spirit mediums, spirit writers, magicians, and healers, all of whom are defined by the recognition of their ability to bring divine power and wisdom directly to bear on human problems.

Popular religion is also associated with a cycle of annual festivals, funeral rituals, and geomancy *(feng-shui)*. Popular values are sanctioned by revelations from the gods and by belief in purgatory, where one aspect of the soul goes after death, there to be punished for its sins according to the principle of karmic retribution. There are ten courts in purgatory, each presided over by a judge who fits the suffering to the crime. Passage through purgatory can be ameliorated through the transfer of merit money by Buddhist or Taoist rituals. When its guilt has been purged, the soul advances to the tenth court, where the form of its next existence is decided. This mythology is a modification of Buddhist beliefs described in detail in texts first translated in the sixth century.

THE PERIOD OF MONGOL RULE

The Mongols under Chinggis Khan (1167–1227) captured the Chin capital of Yen-ching (modern Peking) in 1215 and established the Yüan dynasty (1271–1368). From China they ruled their vast domain, which extended all the way to central Europe. For the next several decades the "Middle Kingdom" was the eastern end of a world empire, open as never before to foreign influences. In the realm of religion these influences included the Nestorians, papal letters to Khubilai Khan (r. 1260–1298) brought by Nicolo and Marco Polo, a few Franciscan missionaries in the early fourteenth century, and a large number of Tibetan Buddhist monks.

The first Mongol contact with Chinese Buddhism was with Ch'an monks, a few of whom attained influence at court. In the meantime, however, the Mongols were increasingly attracted by the exorcistic and healing rituals of Tantric Buddhism in Tibet, the borders of which they also controlled. In 1260 a Tibetan monk, 'Phags-pa (1235–1280), was named imperial preceptor, and soon after chief of Buddhist affairs. Tibetan monks were appointed as leaders of the *saṃgha* all over China, to some extent reviving the Tantric (Chen-yen) school that flourished briefly in the T'ang. [*See* Chen-yen.]

By the early fourteenth century another form of popular religion appeared, the voluntary association or sect that could be joined by individuals from different families and villages. These sects developed out of lay Buddhist societies in the twelfth century, but their structure owed much to late Han religious associations and their popular Taoist successors, Buddhist eschatological movements from the fifth century on, and Manichaeism. By the Yüan period the sects were characterized by predominantly lay membership and leadership, hierarachical organization, active proselytism, congregational rituals, possession of their own scriptures in the vernacular, and mutual economic support. Their best known antecedent was the White Lotus school, an independent sect founded by a monk named Mao Tzu-yüan (1086–1166). Mao combined simplified T'ien-t'ai teaching with Pure Land practice, invoking Amitābha's saving power with just five recitations of his name. After Mao's death the sect, led by laymen who married, spread across south and east China. In the process it incorporated charms and prognostication texts, and by the fourteenth century branches in Kwangsi and Honan were strongly influenced by Taoist methods of cultivating the internal elixirs. This led to protests from more orthodox leaders of the Pure Land tradition, monks in the east who appealed to the throne that they not be proscribed along with the "heretics." This appeal succeeded, and the monastic branch went on to be considered part of the tradition of the Pure Land school, with Mao Tzu-yüan as a revered patriarch.

The more rustic side of the White Lotus tradition was prohibited three times in the Yüan, but flourished nonetheless, with its own communal organizations and scriptures and a growing emphasis on the presence within it of the future Buddha Maitreya. During the civil wars of the mid-fourteenth century this belief encouraged full-scale uprisings in the name of the new world Maitreya was expected to bring. The Ming founder Chu Yüan-chang (1328–1398) had for a time been an officer in one of the White Lotus armies, but after his victory tried to suppress the sect. It continued to multiply nonetheless, under a variety of names.

The first extant sectarian scriptures, produced in the early sixteenth century, indicate that by that time there were two streams of mythology and belief, one more influenced by Taoism, the other by Buddhism. The Taoist stream incorporated much terminology from the Golden Elixir school (Chin-tan Tao), and was based on the myth of a saving mother goddess, the Eternal Venerable Mother, who is a modified form of the old Han-dynasty Queen Mother of the West, a figure mentioned in Ch'üan-chen teachings as well. The Buddhist stream was initiated by a sectarian reformer named Lo Ch'ing (1443–1527), whose teachings were based on the Ch'an theme of "attaining Buddhahood through seeing one's own nature." Lo criticized the White Lotus and Maitreya sects as being too concerned with outward ritual forms, but later writers in his school incorporated some themes from the Eternal Mother mythology, while other sectarian founders espousing this mythology imitated Lo Ch'ing's example of writing vernacular scriptures to put forth their own views. These scriptures, together with their successors, the popular spirit-writing texts of the nineteenth and twentieth centuries, constitute a fourth major body of Chinese sacred texts, after those of the Confucians, Buddhists, and Taoists.

The number of popular religious sects increased rapidly during the sixteenth and seventeenth centuries, all part of the same general tradition but with different founders, lines of transmission, texts, and ritual variations. Such groups had been illegal since the Yüan and some resisted prosecution with armed force or attempted to establish their own safe areas. In a few cases sect leaders organized major attempts to overthrow the government and put their own emperor on the throne, to rule over a utopian world in which time and society would be renewed. However, for the most part the sects simply provided a congregational alternative to village popular religion, an alternative that offered mutual support and assurance and promised means of going directly to paradise at death without passing through purgatory.

Popular religious sects were active on the China mainland until the start of the Cultural Revolution in 1966, and they continue to multiply in Taiwan, where they can be legally registered as branches of Taoism. Since the late nineteenth century most sectarian scriptures have been composed by spirit writing, direct revelation from a variety of gods and culture heroes.

Ming and Ch'ing Religion

Mongol rule began to deteriorate in the early fourteenth century, due to struggles between tribal factions at court, the decline of military power, and the devolution of central authority to local warlords, bandit groups, and sectarian movements. After twenty years of civil war Chu Yüan-chang, from a poor peasant family, defeated all his rivals and reestablished a Chinese imperial house, the Ming dynasty (1368–1644). Chu (Ming T'ai-tsu, r. 1368–1398) was an energetic ruler of strong personal religious beliefs who revised imperial rituals, promulgated strict laws against a variety of popular practices and sects, and recruited Taoist priests to direct court ceremonies. For him the mandate of Heaven was a living force that had established him in a long line of sacred emperors; his ancestors were deemed powerful intermediaries with Shang-ti. He elaborated and reinforced the responsibility of government officials to offer regular sacrifices to deities of fertility, natural forces, and cities, and to the spirits of heroes and abandoned ghosts.

MING DYNASTY

Under the Ming, such factors as the diversification of the agricultural base and the monetization of the economy had an impact on religious life; there were more excess funds for building temples and printing scriptures, and more rich peasants, merchants, and artisans with energy to invest in popular religion, both village and sectarian. Sectarian scriptures appeared as part of the same movement that produced new vernacular literature of all types, morality books to inculcate Neo-Confucian values, and new forms and audiences for popular operas. More than ever before the late Ming was a time of economic and cultural initiatives from the population at large, as one might expect in a period of increasing competition for recources by small entrepreneurs. These tendencies continued to gain momentum in the Ch'ing period.

Ming Buddhism showed the impact of these economic and cultural factors, particularly in eastern China where during the sixteenth century reforming monks such as Yün-ch'i Chu-hung (1535–1615) organized lay societies, wrote morality books that quantified the merit points for good deeds, and affirmed Confucian values within a Buddhist framework. Chu-hung combined Pure Land and Ch'an practice and preached spiritual progress through sparing animals from slaughter and captivity. The integration of Buddhism into Chinese society was furthered as well by government approval of a class of teaching monks, ordained with official certificates, whose role was to perform rituals for the people. [*See the biography of Chu-hung.*]

Buddhism also had a synergetic relationship with the form of Neo-Confucianism dominant in the late Ming, Wang Yang-ming's "study of mind." On the one hand, Ch'an individualism and seeking enlightenment within influenced Wang and his disciples; on the other hand, official acceptance of Wang's school gave indirect support to the forms of Buddhism associated with it, such as the teachings of Chu-hung and Han-shan Te-ch'ing (1546–1623).

Taoism was supported by emperors throughout the Ming, with Taoist priests appointed as officials in charge of rituals and composing hymns and messages to the gods. The Ch'üan-chen sect continued to do well, with its monastic base and emphasis on attaining immortality through developing "internal elixirs." Its meditation methods also influenced those of some of Wang Yang-ming's followers, such as Wang Chi (1497–1582). However, it was the Cheng-i sect led by hereditary Celestial Masters that had the most official support during the Ming and hence was able to consolidate its position as the standard of orthodox Taoism. Cheng-i influence is evident in scriptures composed during this period, many of which trace their lineage back to the first Celestial Master and bear imprimaturs from his successors. The forty-third-generation master was given charge of compiling a new Taoist canon in 1406, a task completed between 1444 and 1445. It is this edition that is still in use today.

By the seventeenth century, Confucian philosophy entered a more nationalistic and materialist phase, but the scholar-official class as a whole remained involved in a variety of private religious practices beyond their official ritual responsibilities. These included not only the study of Taoism and Buddhism but the use of spirit-writing séances and prayers to Wen-ch'ang, the god of scholars and literature, for help in passing examinations. Ming T'ai-tsu had proclaimed that each of the "three teachings" of Confucianism, Buddhism, and Taoism had an important role to play, which encouraged synthetic tendencies present since the beginnings of Buddhism in China. In the sixteenth century a Confucian scholar named Lin Chao-en (1517–1598) from Fukien took these tendencies a step further by building a middle-class religious sect in which Confucian teachings were explicitly supported by those of Buddhism and Taoism. Lin was known as "Master of the Three Teachings," the patron saint of what became a popular movement with temples still extant in Singapore and Malaysia in the mid-twentieth century. This tendency to incorporate Confucianism into a sectarian religion was echoed by Chang Chi-tsung (d. 1866) who established a fortified community in Shantung, and by K'ang Yu-wei (1858–1927) at the end of imperial history. Confucian oriented spirit-writing cults also flourished in the late nineteenth and early twentieth centuries, supported by middle level military and civil officials. These cults produced tracts and scriptures of their own. [*See the biography of K'ang Yu-wei.*]

During the sixteenth century Christian missionaries tried for the third time to establish their faith in China, this time a more successful effort by Italian Jesuits. In 1583 two Italian Jesuits, Michael Ruggerius and Matteo Ricci, were allowed to stay in Chao-ch'ing in Kwangtung Province. By their knowledge of science, mathematics, and geography they impressed some of the local scholars and officials; Ricci eventually became court astronomer in Peking. He also made converts of several high officials, so that by 1605 there were 200 Chinese Christians. For the next several decades the Jesuit mission prospered, led by priests given responsibility for the sensitive task of establishing the imperial calendar. In 1663 the number of converts had grown to about one hundred thousand. The high point of this early Roman Catholic mission effort came during the reign of the K'ang-hsi emperor (r. 1662–1722), who, while not a convert, had a lively curiosity about European knowledge. [*See also* Jesuits *and the biography of Ricci.*]

Nonetheless, Chinese suspicions remained, and the mission was threatened from within by rivalries between orders and European nations. In particular, there was contention over Jesuit acceptance of veneration for ancestors and Confucius. In 1645 a Franciscan obtained a papal prohibition of such practices, and this "rites controversy" intensified in the ensuing decades. The Inquisition forbade the Jesuit approach in 1704, but the Jesuits kept on resisting until papal bulls were issued against them in 1715 and 1742. K'ang-hsi had sided with the Jesuits, but in the end their influence was weakened and their ministry made less adaptable to Chinese traditions. There were anti-Christian persecutions in several places throughout the mid-eighteenth century; however, some Christian communities remained, as did a few European astronomers at court. There were several more attempts at suppression in the early nineteenth century, with the result that by 1810 there were only thirty-one European missionaries left, with eighty Chinese priests, but church membership remained at about two hundred thousand.

The first Protestant missionary to reach China was Robert Morrison, sent by the London Missionary Society to Canton in 1807. He and another missionary made their first Chinese convert in 1814 and completed translating the Bible in 1819. From then on increasing numbers of Protestant missionaries arrived from other European countries and the United States. [*See the biography of Morrison.*]

Christian impact on the wider world of Chinese religions has traditionally been negligible, although there is some indication that scholars such as Fang I-chih (1611–1671) were influenced by European learning and thus helped prepare the way for the practical emphases of Ch'ing Confucianism. Chu-hung and Ricci had engaged in written debate over theories of God and rebirth, and even the K'ang-hsi emperor was involved in such discussions later, but there was no acceptance of Christian ideas and practices by Chinese who did not convert. This is true at the popular level as well, where in some areas Chinese sectarians responded positively to both Roman Catholic and Protestant missionaries. Christians and the sectarians were often persecuted together, and shared concerns for congregational ritual, vernacular scriptures, and a compassionate creator deity. Yet nineteenth century sectarian texts betray few traces of Christian influence, and even when Jesus speaks in later spirit-writing books it is as a supporter of Chinese values.

CH'ING DYNASTY

The Manchus, a tribal confederation related to the Jurchen, had established their own state in the northeast in 1616 and named it Ch'ing in 1636. As their power grew, they sporadically attacked North China and absorbed much Chinese political and cultural influence. In 1644 a Ch'ing army was invited into China by the Ming court to save Peking from Chinese rebels. The Manchus not only conquered Peking but stayed to rule for the next 268 years. In public policy the Manchus were strong supporters of Confucianism, and relied heavily on the support of Chinese officials. Most religious developments during the Ch'ing were continuations of Ming traditions, with the exception of Protestant Christianity and the Taiping movement it helped stimulate.

Before their conquest of China the Manchus had learned of Tibetan or Lamaist Buddhism through the Mongols, and had a special sense of relationship to a *bodhisattva* much venerated in Tibet, Mañjuśrī. [*See* Mañjuśrī.] Nurhachi (1559–1626), the founder of the Manchu kingdom, was considered an incarnation of Mañjuśrī. After 1644 the Manchus continued to patronize Lamaism, which had been supported to some extent in the Ming as well, in part to stay in touch with the dominant religion of Tibet and the Mongols. In 1652 the Dalai Lama was invited to visit Peking, and in the early eighteenth century his successors were put under a Ch'ing protectorate.

Early Ch'ing emperors were interested in Ch'an Buddhism as well. The Yung-cheng emperor (r. 1723–1735) published a book on Ch'an in 1732 and ordered the reprinting of the Buddhist canon, a task completed in 1738. He also supported the printing of a Tibetan edition of the canon, and his successor, Ch'ien-lung (r. 1736–1795) sponsored the translation of this voluminous body of texts into Manchu. The Pure Land tradition continued to be the form of Buddhism most supported by the people. The most active Taoist schools were the monastic Ch'üan-chen and the Cheng-i, more concerned with public rituals of exorcism and renewal, carried on by a married priesthood. However, Taoism no longer received court support. Despite repeated cycles of rebellions and persecutions, popular sects continued to thrive, although after the Eight Trigrams uprising in 1813 repression was so severe that production of sectarian scripture texts declined in favor of oral transmission, a tendency operative among some earlier groups as well.

The most significant innovation in Ch'ing religion was the teachings of the T'ai-p'ing T'ien-kuo (Celestial Kingdom of Great Peace and Prosperity), which combined motifs from Christianity, shamanism, and popular sectarian beliefs. The Taiping movement was begun by Hung Hsiu-ch'üan (1814–1864), a would-be Confucian scholar who first was given Christian tracts in 1836. After failing civil service examinations several times, Hung claimed to have had a vision in which it was revealed that Hung was the younger brother of Jesus Christ, commissioned to be a new messiah. Hung proclaimed a new kingdom upon earth, to be characterized by theocratic rule, enforcement of the ten commandments, the brotherhood of all, equality of the sexes, and redistribution of land. Hung and other Taiping leaders were effective preachers who wrote books, edicts, and tracts proclaiming their teachings and regulations and providing prayers and hymns for congregational worship. They forbade ancestor veneration and the worship of Buddhas and Taoist and popular deities. Wherever the Taipings went they destroyed images and temples. They rejected geomancy and divination and established a new calendar free of the old festivals and concerns for inauspicious days.

In the late 1840s Hung Hsiu-ch'üan organized a group called the God Worshipers Society with many poor and disaffected among its members. They moved to active military rebellion in 1851, with Hung taking the title "Celestial King" of the new utopian regime. Within two years they captured Nanking. Here they established their capital and sent armies north and west, involving all of China in civil war as they went. Although the Ch'ing government was slow to respond, in 1864 Nanking was retaken by imperial forces and the remaining Taiping forces slaughtered or dispersed. For all of the power of this movement, Taiping teachings and practices had no positive effect on the history of Chinese religions after this time, while all the indigenous traditions resumed and rebuilt. [*See* T'ai-p'ing.]

The End of Empire and Postimperial China

In the late nineteenth century some Chinese intellectuals began to incorporate into their thought new ideas from Western science, philosophy, and literature, but the trend in religion was toward reaffirmation of Chinese values. Even the reforming philosopher K'ang Yu-wei tried to build a new cult of Confucius, while at the popular level spirit-writing sects proliferated. In 1899 a vast antiforeign movement began in North China, loosely called the Boxer Rebellion because of its martial arts practices. The ideology of this movement was based on popular religion and spirit mediumship, and many Boxer groups attacked Christian missions in the name of Chinese gods. This uprising was put down in 1900 by a combination of Chinese and foreign armies, after the latter had captured Peking.

The Ch'ing government attempted a number of belated reforms, but in 1911 it collapsed from internal decay, foreign pressure, and military uprisings. Some Chinese intellectuals, free to invest their energies in new ideas and political forms, avidly studied and translated Western writings, including those of Marxism. One result of this westernization and secularization was attacks on Confucianism and other Chinese traditions, a situation exacerbated by recurrent civil wars that led to the destruction or occupation of thousands of temples. However, these new ideas were most influential in the larger cities; the majority of Chinese continued popular religious practices as before. Many temples and monasteries survived, and there were attempts to revive Buddhist thought and monastic discipline, particularly by the monks Yin-kuang (1861–1940) and T'ai-hsü (1889–1947). [*See the biography of T'ai-hsü.*]

Since 1949 Chinese religions have increasingly prospered in Taiwan, particularly at the popular level, where the people have more surplus funds and freedom of belief than ever before. Many new temples have been built, sects established, and scriptures and periodicals published. The same can be said for Chinese popular religion in Hong Kong and Singapore. The Taoist priesthood is active in Taiwan, supported by the presence of hereditary Celestial Masters from the mainland who provide ordinations and legitimacy. Buddhist monasteries and publishing houses are also doing well in Taiwan and Hong Kong, though lay Buddhist sects have always been more influential among the people in these areas.

The constitution of the People's Republic establishes the freedom both to support and oppose religion, although in practice religious activities of all types declined there after 1949, particularly during the Cultural Revolution of 1966 to 1969. In general religion has been depicted along Marxist lines as "feudal superstition" that must be rejected by those seeking to build a new China. Nonetheless, many religious activities continued until the Cultural Revolution, even those of the long proscribed popular sects. The Cultural Revolution, encouraged by Mao Tse-tung and his teachings, was a massive attack on old traditions, including not only religion, but education, art, and established bureaucracies. In the process thousands of religious images were destroyed, temples and churches confiscated, leaders returned to lay life, and books burned. At the same time a new national cult arose, that of Chairman Mao and his thought, involving ecstatic processions, group recitation from Mao's writings, and a variety of quasi-religious ceremonials. These included confessions of sins against the revolution, vows of obedience before portraits of the Chairman, and meals of wild vegetables to recall the bitter days before liberation. Although the frenzy abated, the impetus of the Cultural Revolution continued until Mao's death in 1976, led by a small group, later called "the Gang of Four," centered around his wife. This group was soon deposed, a move followed by liberalization of policy in several areas, including religion. Since 1980 many churches, monasteries, and mosques have reopened, and religious leaders reinstated, in part to establish better relationships with Buddhist, Christian, and Muslim communities in other countries. There has been a limited revival of popular religion in some areas as well, particularly in Fukien province, which has long had close connections with overseas Chinese. Private enterprise and the leasing of land by individual farmers are practices returning to the countryside; these may encourage ancestor worship and traditional forms of divination and funeral rituals, although it seems unlikely that the pantheon of popular gods will reappear. Nonetheless, one should remember that aspects of the Marxist regime may also be but passing phases in a long history, and may not leave much more impact than did Christianity or the Taipings centuries before.

[*For further discussion of the various traditions treated in this article, see* Buddhism, *article on* Buddhism in China; Buddhism, Schools of, *article on* Chinese Buddhism; Taoism; Confucian Thought; *and* Chinese Philosophy. *For a discussion of the influence of the major monotheistic religions on Chinese religion, see* Islam, *article on* Islam in China; Christianity, *article on* Christianity in Asia; *and* Judaism, *article on* Judaism in Asia and Sub-Saharan Africa. *For the influence of Inner Asian civilizations on Chinese thought, see* Inner Asian Religions, Mongol Religions, *and* Buddhism, *article on* Buddhism in Central Asia. *See also* Domestic Observances, *article on* Chinese Practices, *and* Chinese Religious Year.]

BIBLIOGRAPHY

Berling, Judith. *The Syncretic Religion of Lin Chao-en*. New York, 1980. A detailed study of a Confucian religious teacher in the sixteenth century.

Bilsky, Lester James. *The State Religion of Ancient China*. 2 vols. Taipei, 1975. A detailed discussion of official rituals and deities from the Chou through the early Han dynasties.

Bodde, Derk. *Festivals in Classical China. New Year and Other Annual Observances during the Han Dynasty, 206 B.C.–A.D. 220*. Princeton, 1975. The best study in English of annual festivals in their early development.

Boltz, Judith M. "A Survey of Taoist Literature, Tenth to Seventeenth Centuries." Berkeley, 1985. A very helpful discussion of Taoist texts, schools, and writers.

Chan, Wing-tsit, trans. and comp. *A Sourcebook in Chinese Philosophy*. Princeton, 1963. The standard selection of Chinese philosophical texts in translation. Accurate and comprehensive.

Ch'en, Kenneth K. S. *Buddhism in China, A Historical Survey*. Princeton, 1964. Detailed and comprehensive. The best general view of the topic in English. Good bibliography.

Ch'en, Kenneth K. S. *The Chinese Transformation of Buddhism*. Princeton, 1973. An excellent study of how Buddhist values, rituals, and economic activities adapted to the Chinese environment.

Ch'en Kuo-fu. *Tao-tsang yüan-liu k'ao*. 2 vols. Peking, 1983. Still the standard study of the development of the Taoist canon.

Ch'en Yüan. *Nan Sung ch'u Hopei hsin Tao-chiao k'ao*. Peking, 1941. The first detailed study of the topic; includes a discussion of the Ch'üan-chen school.

Dumoulin, Heinrich. *A History of Zen Buddhism*. New York, 1963. The standard history of Ch'an/Zen in English.

Dunne, George H. *Generation of Giants. The Story of the Jesuits in China in the Last Decades of the Ming Dynasty*. Notre Dame, Ind., 1962. The standard treatment of the topic in English, based primarily on European sources.

Elliott, Allan J. A. *Chinese Spirit Medium Cults in Singapore.* London, 1955. Thorough field-work study of spirit medium initiation and rituals.

Fairbank, John K., ed. *The Missionary Enterprise in China and America.* Cambridge, Mass., 1974. One of several books on American Protestant missions in China produced by Professor Fairbank and his students. Treats missionaries in their political and social contexts.

Fukui Kōjun. *Dōkyō no kisoteki kenkyū.* Tokyo, 1952. Pioneering studies of the beginnings and early development of Taoism, the *T'ai-p'ing ching*, and relationships with Buddhism.

Fukui Kōjun, Yamazaki Hiroshi, Kimura Eiichi, and Sakai Tadao, eds. *Dōkyō.* 3 vols. Tokyo, 1983. The most comprehensive discussion of Taoism available. Includes a lavish bibliography.

Fung Yu-lan. *History of Chinese Philosophy.* 2 vols. Translated by Derk Bodde. Princeton, 1952. The most authoritative and comprehensive study of the topic in English.

Groot, J. J. M. de. *The Religious System of China* (1892–1910). 6 vols. Reprint, Taipei, 1964. Massive study, with translations of Chinese texts provided. Particularly good on funeral rituals, *feng-shui*, demonology, and shamanism.

Hsü, Francis L. K. *Under the Ancestors' Shadow: Chinese Culture and Personality.* New York, 1948. A fine study of ancestor cult in its social context.

Israeli, Raphael. *Muslims in China: A Study in Cultural Confrontation.* London, 1978. The only recent book-length study of the topic in English.

Johnson, David. "The City-God Cults of T'ang and Sung China." *Harvard Journal of Asiatic Studies* 45 (December 1985): 363–457. The most thorough and recent study of the topic.

Jordon, David K. *Gods, Ghosts and Ancestors: Folk Religion in a Taiwanese Village* (1972). Reprint, Taipei, 1986. A good anthropological study of village religion. Sensitive and lively discussion.

Jordan, David K. and Daniel L. Overmyer. *The Flying Phoenix: Aspects of Chinese Sectarianism in Taiwan.* Princeton and Taipei, 1986. The first systematic study of modern Chinese popular religious sects.

Kubo Noritada. *Dōkyōshi.* Tokyo, 1977. Rich material on Taoist history, rituals, beliefs, and relationships with popular religion.

Latourette, Kenneth Scott. *A History of Christian Missions in China.* London, 1929. Long the standard authority on the topic.

Li Shih-yü. *Pao-chüan tsung-lu.* The most comprehensive bibliography of popular religious texts, with good introductory discussions.

Lieu, Samuel N. C. *The Religion of Light: An Introduction to the History of Manichaeism in China.* Hong Kong, 1979. A short introduction to the topic, with an excellent bibliography.

Lieu, Samuel N. C. *Manichaeism in the Later Roman Empire and Medieval China.* Manchester, 1985. The most complete modern study of the topic.

Makita Tairyō. *Gikyō kenkyū.* Koyto, 1976. The best study of Buddhist texts written in China, most of them found at Tun-huang.

Maspero, Henri. *Taoism and Chinese Religion* (1971). Translated by Frank A. Kierman. Amherst, Mass., 1981. Maspero was the pioneering Western scholar of Taoist religion; this is a collection of his essays. Those on immortality cultivation and popular religion remain particularly valuable.

Needham, Joseph. *Science and Civilisation in China.* Cambridge, Mass., 1956–. One of the great scholarly projects of the twentieth century. Rich bibliographies. See particularly vol. 2 (1956) on the history of Chinese thought and the classical worldview, and vol. 5, parts 2–5 (1974–) on Taoist immortality practices and alchemy. Comparative analysis throughout.

Noguchi Tetsurō. *Min-dai Byakuren kyōshi no kenkyū*. Tokyo, 1986. The most comprehensive study of popular religious sects during the Ming period (1368–1644), in their historical, economic, and political contexts.

Obuchi Ninji. *Dōkyōshi no kenkyū*. Okayama, 1964. Authoritative study by a Japanese master of the topic.

Ogasawara Senshū. *Chūgoku jōdokyōka no kenkyū*. Kyoto, 1951. A study of the early Pure Land masters Hui-yüan, T'an-luan, Tao-ch'o, and Shan-tao.

Ogasawara Senshū. *Chūgoku kinsei jōdokyōshi no kenkyū*. Kyoto, 1963. Authoritative study of later Pure Land history and beliefs.

Overmyer, Daniel L. *Folk Buddhist Religion: Dissenting Sects in Late Traditional China*. Cambridge, Mass., 1976. A survey of popular religious sects in the Ming and Ch'ing dynasties.

Reischauer, Edwin O. *Ennin's Travels in T'ang China*. New York, 1955. An excellent account of Buddhism and Chinese life during the ninth century, taken from the travel diary of a Japanese monk.

Sakai Tadao. *Chūgoku zensho no kenkyū*. Tokyo, 1960. A pioneering discussion of the long tradition of books for moral exhortation, written and distributed by both literati and commoners.

Sawada Mizuho. *Zōhō Hōkan no kenkyū*. Tokyo, 1975. Along with the work of Li Shih-yü, the major study of Chinese popular religious scriptures (*pao-chüan*), their types and origins.

Schipper, Kristofer. *Le corps taoïste; corps physique—corps social*. Paris, 1982. A fine survey of Taoist history, ritual, and meditation by the first Western scholar to become an initiated Taoist priest and thus gain access to the oral tradition.

Seidel, Anna. "The Image of the Perfect Ruler in Early Taoist Messianism." *History of Religions* 9 (1969–1970): 216–247. An important study of early Taoist eschatology.

Shih, Vincent Y. C. *The Taiping Ideology*. Seattle, 1967. The most detailed study in English of the religious beliefs of this mid-nineteenth century movement.

Sivin, Nathan. *Chinese Alchemy, Preliminary Studies*. Cambridge, Mass., 1968. A now standard study of the topic.

Strickmann, Michel. "The Mao-shan Revelations: Taoism and the Aristocracy." *T'oung pao* 63 (1977): 1–64. Taoist history, fourth and fifth centuries.

Strickmann, Michel. *Le Taoïsme du Mao-Chan. Chronique d'une révélation*. Paris, 1981. A pathbreaking study that reshapes our understanding of Taoist history. Good discussion of important texts.

Strickmann, Michel, ed. *Tantric and Taoist Studies in Honour of R. A. Stein*. 2 vols. Brussels, 1983. Volume two contains several excellent and substantive essays on Taoism.

Suzuki Chūsei. "Sōdai Bukkyō kessha no kenkyū." *Shigaku zasshi* 52 (1941): 65–98, 205–241, 303–333. Important study of the spread of lay Buddhist devotional associations.

T'ang Yung-t'ung. *Han Wei liang Chin Nan-pei-ch'ao fo-chiao shih*. Shanghai, 1938. Long the standard Chinese study of this topic.

Thompson, Laurence G. *Chinese Religion: An Introduction*. 3d ed. Belmont, Calif., 1979. The best one-volume introduction to the topic. Fourth edition in preparation, 1986.

Thompson, Laurence G. *Chinese Religion in Western Languages, A Comprehensive and Classified Bibliography of Publications in English, French and German through 1980*. Tucson, 1985. The only comprehensive bibliography of the subject, organized by topics.

Thompson, Laurence G. *The Chinese Way in Religion*. Belmont, Calif., 1973. A good source book, combining translations of Chinese primary texts with selections from the best scholarly studies.

Tsukamoto Zenryū. *A History of Early Chinese Buddhism: From its Introduction to the Death of Hui-yüan* (1979). 2 vols. Translated by Leon Hurvitz. Tokyo, 1985. By far the most detailed study (1305 pages) of the history of Chinese Buddhism through the early fifth century. Both author and translator are masters of the field.

Ui Hakuju. *Zenshūshi kenkyū*. 3 vols. Tokyo, 1939–1943. The standard Japanese study of the Ch'an school.

Wang Ming. *T'ai-p'ing ching ho-chiao*. Peking, 1960. A work of fundamental importance for the study of the first Taoist scripture produced during the formative period of this tradition in the second century.

Wechsler, Howard J. *Offerings of Jade and Silk: Ritual and Symbol in the Legitimation of the T'ang Dynasty*. New Haven, 1985. The most thorough study in English of medieval Chinese state religion.

Welch, Holmes. *The Practice of Chinese Buddhism, 1900–1950*. Cambridge, Mass., 1967. Thorough study of monastic Buddhism based on interviews with monks.

Welch, Holmes, and Anna Seidel, eds. *Facets of Taoism: Essays in Chinese Religion*. New Haven, 1979. Authoritative essays from the Second International Conference on Taoism, 1972.

Wolf, Arthur P., ed. *Religion and Ritual in Chinese Society*. Stanford, Calif., 1974. An excellent collection of essays by anthropologists, based on fieldwork in Taiwan and Hong Kong on such topics as village temples, shamanism, and the relationship between gods and ghosts. Includes two articles on Taoist ritual.

Yampolsky, Philip B. *The Platform Sutra of the Sixth Patriarch. The Text of the Tun-huang Manuscript, Translated, with Notes*. New York, 1967. The introduction (pp. 1–121) is a reliable guide to modern studies of Ch'an history.

Yanagida Seizan. *Shoki Zenshū shisō no kenkyū*. Kyoto, 1967. Pathbreaking critical study of Ch'an historical legends.

Yang, C. K. *Religion in Chinese Society. A Study of Contemporary Social Functions of Religion and Some of their Historical Factors*. Berkeley, 1961. A classic sociological study, the best and most comprehensive available. Good discussions of relationships between religion and the state, ethical values, diffuse and institutional forms of religious organization.

Yoshioka Yoshitoyo. *Dōkyō to bukkyō*. Tokyo, 1959. Seminal essays on Taoist and Buddhist relations and polemical writings from the Han to the present.

Yoon, Hong-key. *Geomantic Relationships Between Culture and Nature in Korea*. Taipei, 1976. The best study of *fengshui* in English, based on Chinese texts and fieldwork in Korea.

Zürcher, Erik. *The Buddhist Conquest of China*. 2 vols. Leiden, 1959. Excellent, detailed study of the first Chinese attempts to understand Buddhist philosophy.

Zürcher, Erik. "'Prince Moonlight.' Messianism and Eschatology in Early Medieval Chinese Buddhism." *T'oung pao* 68 (1982): 1–75. A pioneering study of fifth-century eschatology, based on Buddhist scriptures composed in China.

14 JAPANESE RELIGION

JOSEPH M. KITAGAWA

Like many other ethnic groups throughout the world, the earliest inhabitants of the Japanese archipelago had from time immemorial their own unique way of viewing the world and the meaning of human existence and their own characteristic rituals for celebrating various events and phases of their individual and corporate life. To them the whole of life was permeated by religious symbols and authenticated by myths. From this tradition an indigenous religious form, which came to be designated as Shintō, or "the way of *kami,*" developed in the early historic period. Many aspects of the archaic tradition have also been preserved as basic features of an unorganized folk religion. Meanwhile, through contacts with Korea and China, Japan came under the impact of religious and cultural influences from the continent of Asia. Invariably, Japanese religion was greatly enriched as it appropriated the concepts, symbols, rituals, and art forms of Confucianism, Taoism, the Yin-yang school, and Buddhism. Although these religious and semireligious systems kept a measure of their own identity, they are by no means to be considered mutually exclusive; to all intents and purposes they became facets of the nebulous but enduring religious tradition that may be referred to as "Japanese religion."

It is worth noting in this connection that the term *shūkyō* ("religion") was not used until the nineteenth century. In Japanese traditions, religious schools are usually referred to as *dō, tō,* or *michi* ("way"), as in Butsudō ("the way of the Buddha") or Shintō ("the way of *kami*"), implying that these are complementary ways or paths within the overarching Japanese religion. Various branches of art were also called *dō* or *michi,* as in *chadō* (also *sadō,* "the way of tea"). This usage reflects the close affinity in Japan between religious and aesthetic traditions.

PREHISTORIC BACKGROUND

The Japanese archipelago lies off the Asian continent, stretching north and south in the western Pacific. In ancient times, however, there were land connections between the continent and the Japanese islands. Animal and human populations thus were able to reach present Japan from different parts of the continent. Although we cannot be certain when and how the first inhabitants migrated to the Japanese islands, general agreement traces Japan's Paleolithic age back to between ten and thirty thousand years ago, when the inhabitants of the islands were primitive hunters and food gatherers who shared the same level and kinds of religious and cultural traits with their counterparts in other regions of the world.

Japan's prehistoric period is divided into two phases, (1) the Jōmon period (*jōmon* literally means "cord pattern," referring to pottery decoration) extending roughly from the fifth or fourth millennium to about 250 BCE, and (2) the Yayoi period (so named because pottery of this period was unearthed in the Yayoi district of present Tokyo) covering roughly the era from 250 BCE to 250 CE. Further subdivisions of both the Jōmon and Yayoi periods, as proposed by various archaeologists, are not relevant for our purpose. Archaeological evidence reveals a gradual development in people's use of fishing and hunting tools, but in the artistic qualities of pottery making and designs and in the living patterns of the Jōmon people we still have few clues regarding their religious outlooks or practices. Thus, we can only infer that the practice of extracting certain teeth, for example, indicates a puberty rite and that female figurines must have been used for fertility cults.

There is no clear-cut date for dividing the Jōmon and the Yayoi periods, because the Yayoi culture emerged in western parts of Japan while the Jōmon culture was still developing in the eastern parts. Nevertheless, the transition between these cultural forms was sufficiently marked so that some scholars even postulate the migration during the early third century BCE of a new ethnic group from outside. Yayoi pottery is more sophisticated in design and manufacturing techniques and more utilitarian than Jōmon ware; Yayoi jugs, jars, and pots were used for cooking as much as for preserving food. Moreover, Yayoi culture was based on rice cultivation, employing a considerable number of hydraulic controls. Evidently, communities were established in places of low altitude, and many farmhouses had raised floors, the space beneath them serving as storehouses for grain. As the Yayoi period coincided with the Ch'in (221–206 BCE) and the Han (206 BCE–220 CE) dynasties in China, and as Chinese political and cultural influence was penetrating the Korean peninsula, some features of continental civilization must have infiltrated into western Japan. This infiltration may account for the development in the Yayoi period of spinning and weaving and the use of iron, bronze, and copper. We can only speculate, however, whether and to what extent new features of the Yayoi culture such as bronze mirrors, bronze bells, dolmens, and funeral urns had religious meaning.

The Ainu Controversy and a Culture-Complex Hypothesis. Although it is safe to assume that migrations of people to the Japanese islands were only insignificant parts of larger movements of archaic peoples from Eurasia to North America, it is extremely difficult to determine the ethnic identity of the first settlers in Japan. In this connection a heated controversy has been carried on in recent decades as to whether or not the Ainu—who have lived on the Hokkaido, Sakhalin, and Kurile islands but who throughout history have never been assimilated into the cultural life of the Japanese—were indeed the original inhabitants of the Japanese islands. Current scholarly opinion holds that the Ainu lived in northern Japan as early as the Jōmon period, but that there has never, at least until the last century, been any significant amount of intermarriage between them and other inhabitants of the Japanese islands. [*See* Ainu Religion.]

Although the exact identity of the Jōmon people still remains unsettled, it is widely assumed that a number of ethnic groups came to the Japanese islands from various

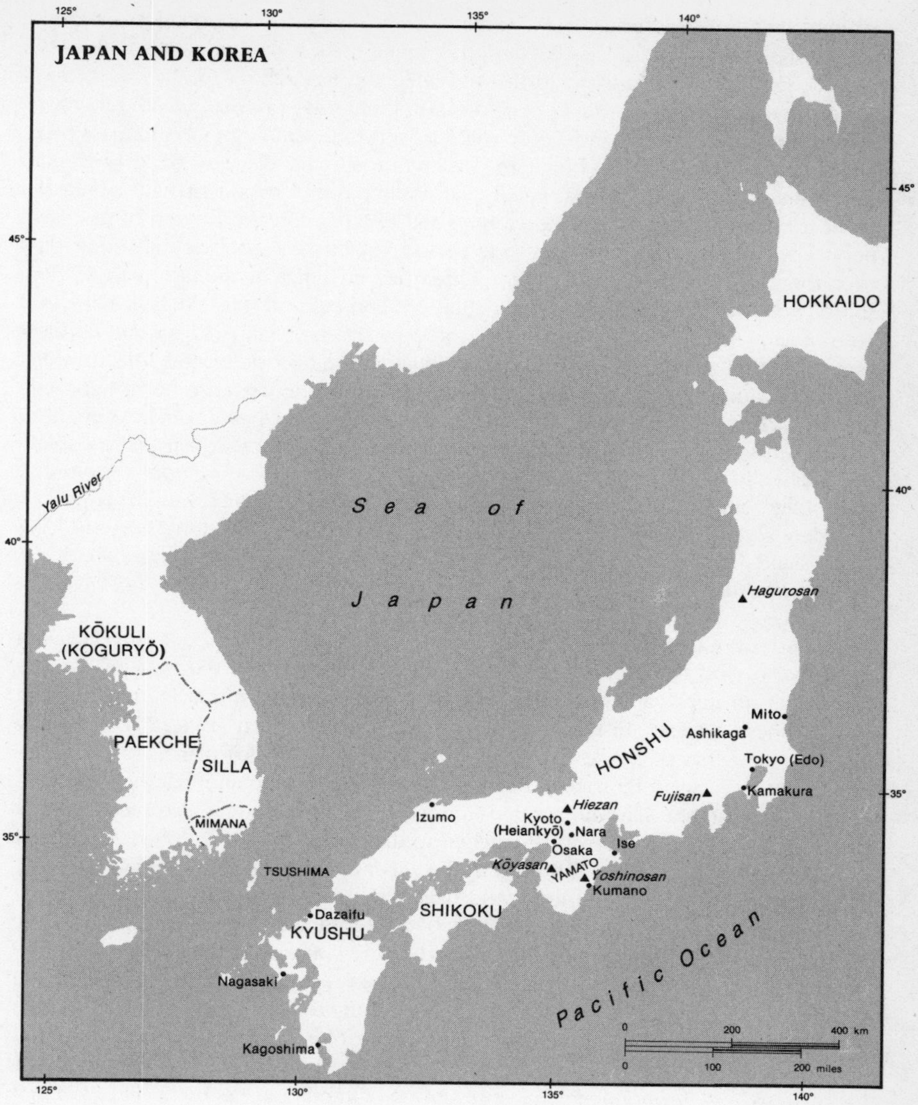

parts of the Asian continent during the prehistoric period, bringing with them various religious and cultural elements. A comprehensive culture-complex hypothesis proposed by Oka Masao in 1933 suggests that there were five major typological components in late prehistoric and early historic Japanese culture, mythology, religion, and social structure. According to Oka, various ethnic groups from South China and Southeast Asia with Melanesian, Austroasian, and Austronesian (Micronesian) cultural and religious traits—the "secret society" system; "horizontal cosmology"; female shamans; mythical motifs of brother-sister deities; initiation rites; cultivation of taro, yam, and rice; and so forth—provided the foundation for the agricultural society and culture of the Yayoi period. A Tunguz group originally from Siberia or Manchuria, on the other hand, contributed a "vertical cosmology," exogamous patrilineal clan system, and the belief in deities *(kami)* who descend from heaven to mountaintops, trees, or pillars. Finally, an Altaic pastoral tribe that had subjugated other tribes in Manchuria and Korea migrated to Japan toward the end of the Yayoi period or the early part of the historic period, establishing itself as the ruling class over the earlier settlers. This group, which had an efficient military organization, shared with the Tunguz group similar religious and cultural traits such as a "vertical cosmology," Siberian type shamanism, and a patriarchal clan *(uji)* system. Its most powerful family emerged as the imperial house in the historic period. Oka carefully avoids the question of the origin and development of the Japanese people and culture in a chronological sense. Although his hypothesis has been criticized by other scholars, his proposal still remains one of the most all-embracing efforts to explain the pluralistic nature of Japanese social structure, culture, and religion. Despite the lack of agreement concerning the details of the culture-complex thus developed, it is widely agreed that by the end of the Yayoi period those who inhabited the Japanese islands had attained a degree of self-consciousness as one people sharing a common culture.

The Yamatai Controversy. One of the age-old controversies regarding Japan in the Yayoi period centers around the geographical location of the state of Yamatai (Yamadai), an important state in the Japanese islands and one that is mentioned in such Chinese dynastic histories as the record of the Eastern (Latter) Han dynasty (25–220) and that of the kingdom of Wei (220–265). We learn from these documents that there were more than one hundred states in Japan and that they acknowledged a hereditary ruler who resided in the state of Yamatai. It is also recorded that the first Japanese emissary was dispatched to the Chinese court in 57 CE. A series of similar diplomatic missions followed in the second and third centuries. These same accounts reveal that during the second half of the second century political turmoil developed in Japan owing to the absence of a ruler. An unmarried female shamanic diviner, Pimiko or Himiko, who "occupied herself with magic and sorcery, bewitching people," then became the ruler, and order was restored. She was offered by the Chinese court the title "Queen of Wo (Wa) Friendly to Wei." Evidently she lived in seclusion in a palace, protected by armed guards. She was attended by a thousand female servants, whereas only a single male, a "younger brother," transmitted her instructions and pronouncements, presumably utterances she made in a state of trance. When she died, a great mound was raised, and a hundred attendants followed her to the grave. After her death a king was placed on the throne, but since the people did not obey him, a young girl of thirteen, Iyo, was made queen, and order was once again restored. From these Chinese records we learn, among other things, that political stability in prehistoric Japan depended heavily on magico-religious authority. The intriguing question still remains, however, whether or not the state of Yamatai was located in the western island of Kyushu, as many scholars now believe, or in the central part of the main island where the so-called Yamato kingdom was established in the early historical period.

EARLY HISTORICAL PERIOD

The early historical period of Japan corresponds to what archaeologists call the Kofun ("tumulus") period (c. 250–600 CE), so named because of the gigantic mausoleums constructed during this period for the deceased of the ruling class in the present Nara and Osaka prefectures. These great tombs are the visible remains of the early Yamato kingdom. It is significant that Japan was not mentioned in Chinese records between the mid-third and the early fifth century. Many scholars conjecture that during this shadowy period, the Yamato kingdom was established in the present Nara Prefecture. Japan also gained a foothold on the southern tip of the Korean peninsula. During the fourth century, according to Korean sources, Japan became an ally of Paekche, one of the Korean states, and Korean artisans and scholars migrated to Japan, introducing new arts and techniques in weaving, ironwork, and irrigation, as well as the Chinese script and Confucian learning. In 391 Japanese expeditionary forces crossed the sea and fought against the north Korean state, Koguryŏ, but were badly defeated. Following the military defeat in Korea, Japan turned to the Chinese court to secure Chinese recognition and support for her claim of suzerainty over Korea. In fact, the *Sung shu* (History of the Liu Sung Dynasty; 420–479) mentions the names of five Japanese rulers who sent emissaries to the Chinese court. During the sixth century Japan continued her effort to restore her influences on the Korean peninsula. In this connection Buddhism was introduced officially from Paekche to the Yamato court in 538 or 552.

Prior to the introduction of Sino-Korean civilization and Buddhism, Japanese religion was not a well-structured institutional system. The early Japanese took it for granted that the world was the Japanese islands where they lived. They also accepted the notion that the natural world was a "given." Thus, they did not look for another order of meaning behind the natural world. Yet their religious outlook had a strong cosmological orientation, so that early Japanese religion might be characterized as a "cosmic" religion. Although the early Japanese did not speculate on the metaphysical meaning of the cosmos, they felt they were an integral part of the cosmos, which to them was a community of living beings, all sharing *kami* (sacred) nature. The term *kami,* a combination of the prefix *ka* and the root *mi,* signifies either a material thing or an embodied spirit possessing divine potency and magical power. The term *kami* thus refers to all beings that are worthy of reverence, including both good and evil beings. Early Japanese religion accepted the plurality of *kami* residing in different beings and objects, but their basic affirmation was the sacrality of the total cosmos. [*See* Kami.]

Equally central to the early Japanese outlook was the notion of *uji* ("lineage group, clan"), which provided the basic framework for social solidarity. Although the *uji* was not based on the strict principle of consanguinity, blood relationship, real or fictitious, was considered essential for communal cohesion. Each *uji* had clansmen *(ujibito),* groups of professional persons *(be)* who were not blood relations of the clansmen, and slaves *(nuhi),* all of whom were ruled by the *uji* chieftain *(uji no kami).* Each *uji* was not only a social, economic, and political unit but also a unit of religious solidarity centering around the *kami* of the *uji (ujigami)* who was attended by the *uji* chieftain. Indeed, sharing the same *kami* was considered more important to communal cohesion than blood relationship.

As far as we can ascertain, the early Japanese religion did not have fixed liturgies. Most religious functions took place either at home or around a sacred tree or sacred rock, in the paddy field, or on the seashore. Because the *uji* group tended to reside in the same locality, the *kami* of the *uji* often incorporated the quality of regional *kami.* Also, there were numerous other spirits that controlled the health, fortune, and longevity of people. They were variously called *mono* ("spiritual entities") or *tama* ("souls") and were believed to be attached to human and other beings or natural things. Equally prevalent was the notion of "sacred visitors" *(marebito)* or ancestral spirits who came from distant places to visit human communities. Celestial bodies (the sun, moon, and stars), meteorological phenomena (wind and storms), and awe-inspiring natural objects (mountaintops, tall trees, forests, the ocean, and rivers) were also considered sacred and thus were venerated. Not surprisingly, then, a variety of persons—fortune-tellers, healers, magicians, sorcerers, and diviners—served as intermediaries to these divine forces.

Religion and Government. The early Yamato kingdom was a confederation of semiautonomous *uji,* each of which owned and ruled its respective members and territories. The Yamato rulers paid tribute to China and in return received a monarchical title from the Chinese imperial court. Within Japan, the Yamato rulers solidified their influence over other *uji* chieftains with their military power and with their claims to genealogical descent from the sun deity. They thus exercised the prerogatives of conferring such court titles as Ō-muraji ("great magnate," conferred upon heads of the hereditary vassal families of the imperial *uji*) and Ō-omi ("chief of chieftains," conferred upon heads of the imperial *uji*'s former rival *uji* that had acknowledged the imperial authority); granting sacred seed at spring festivals to all *uji* groups; and establishing sacred sites for heavenly and earthly *kami,* as well as regulating *matsuri* (rituals) for them. The term *matsuri* has the connotation "to be with," "to attend to the need of," "to entertain," or "to serve" the *kami,* the soul of the deceased, or a person of high status. Prior to a *matsuri,* the participants were expected to purify themselves and to abstain from certain foods and from sexual intercourse. It was understood that the most important duty of the Yamato emperor *(tennō)* was to maintain close contact with the sun deity—who was at once the imperial family's tutelary and ancestral *kami*—and other heavenly and earthly *kami* by attending to their needs and following their will, which was communicated through oracles, dreams, and divinations and which concerned government administration *(matsurigoto).* Thus, in principle, there was no line of demarcation between the sacred and the profane dimensions of life or between religious rituals *(matsuri)* and government administration *(matsurigoto).* Both were the prerogatives of the sovereign, who was by virtue of his solar ancestry the chief priest as well as the supreme political head of the kingdom. The sovereign, in turn, was assisted by hereditary religious functionaries and hereditary ministers of the court. This principle of the unity of religion and government *(saisei-itchi)* remained the foundation of Japanese religion when it later became institutionalized and acquired the designation of Shintō in contradistinction to Butsudō (Buddhism).

Impact of Chinese Civilization and Buddhism on Japanese Religion. With the gradual penetration of Chinese civilization—or, more strictly, Sino-Korean civilization—and Buddhism during the fifth and sixth centuries, Japanese religion was destined to feel the impact of alien ways of viewing the world and interpreting the meaning of human existence. Sensing the need to create a designation for their hitherto unsystematized religious, cultural, and political tradition, the Japanese borrowed two Chinese characters—*shen* (Jpn., *shin*) for *kami,* and *tao* (Jpn., *tō* or *dō*) for "the way." Inevitably, the effort to create almost artificially a religious system out of a nebulous, though all-embracing, way of life left many age-old beliefs and practices out of the new system. Those features that had been left out of Shintō have been preserved in the Japanese folk religious tradition. At any rate, the adoption of the name Shintō only magnified the profound tension between the indigenous Japanese understanding of the meaning of life and the world—authenticated solely by their particular historic experience on the Japanese islands—and the claims of Confucianism and Buddhism that their ways were grounded in universal laws and principles, the Confucian Tao (the Way) and Buddhist Dharma (the Law).

There is little doubt that the introduction of Chinese script and Buddhist images greatly aided the rapid penetration of Chinese civilization and Buddhism. As the Japanese had not developed their own script, the task of adopting the Chinese script, with its highly developed ideographs and phonetic compounds, to Japanese words was a complex one. There were many educated Korean and Chinese immigrants who served as instructors, interpreters, artists, technicians, and scribes for the imperial court and influential *uji* leaders of the growing nation. The Japanese intelligentsia over the course of time learned the use of literary Chinese and for many centuries used it for writing historical and official records. Poets, too, learned to express themselves either in Chinese verse or by utilizing Chinese characters as a form of syllabary for Japanese sounds. The Japanese accepted Chinese as a written, but not a spoken, language. Even so, through this one-sided medium, the Japanese gained access to the rich civilization of China, and Chinese culture became the resource and model for Japan.

Through written media the Japanese came to know the mystical tradition of philosophical Taoism, which enriched the Japanese aesthetic tradition. The Japanese also learned of the Yin-yang school's concepts of the two principles *(yin* and *yang),* the five elements (metal, wood, water, fire, and earth), and the orderly rotation of these elements in the formation of nature, seasons, and the human being. The Yin-yang school thus provided cosmological theories to hitherto nonspeculative Japanese religion. It was also through written Chinese works that Japanese society, which had been based on archaic communal rules and the *uji* system, appropriated certain features of Confucian ethical principles, social and political theories, and legal and educational systems. [*See* Yin-yang Wu-hsing *and* Onmyōdō.]

The introduction of Buddhist art equally revolutionized Japanese religion, which despite its aesthetic sensitivities had never developed artistic images of *kami* in sculpture or painting. Understandably, when Buddhism was officially introduced to the Japanese court in the sixth century it was the Buddha image that became the central issue between the pro- and anti-Buddhist factions in the court. Anti-Buddhist leaders argued that veneration of a "foreign *kami*" would offend the "native *kami.*" After this initial controversy regarding statues of the Buddha, however, the chieftain of the powerful Soga *uji* secured imperial permission to build a temple in order to enshrine Buddha images. Soon, thanks to the energetic advocacy of the Soga, Buddhism was accepted by other aristocratic families, not because the profound meaning of Buddhist law (the Dharma) was appreciated but probably because Buddhist statues were believed to have magical potencies that would bring about mundane benefits. Thus the statues of Shaka (Śākyamuni), Miroku (Maitreya), Yakushi (Bhaiṣajyaguru), Kannon (Avalokiteśvara), and Amida (Amitābha) were venerated almost indiscriminately in the *uji*-based Buddhism of sixth- and early-seventh-century Japan.

Prince Shōtoku. The regency of Prince Shōtoku (573–621), who served under his aunt, Empress Suiko (r. 592–628), marks a new chapter in the history of Japanese religion. By that time the bankruptcy of Japan's Korean policy had resulted in the loss of its foothold on the southern tip of the Korean peninsula, while the powerful Sui dynasty had unified China after centuries of disunity. To protect Japan's survival in the precarious international scene, Shōtoku and his advisers attempted to strengthen the fabric of national community by working out a multireligious policy reconciling the particularistic Japanese religious tradition with the universal principles of Confucianism and Buddhism. Clearly, Shōtoku's mentor was Emperor Wen (r. 581–604) of the Sui dynasty, who unified the races, cultures, and diverse areas of vast China by utilizing Confucianism and Buddhism, and Taoism to a lesser degree, as the arms of the throne, and whose claim to semidivine prerogative was sanctioned and authenticated by various religious symbols.

Shōtoku himself was a pious Buddhist and is reputed to have delivered learned lectures on certain Buddhist scriptures. Yet his policies, as exemplified in the establishment of the Chinese-style "cap-ranks" of twelve grades for court ministers or in the promulgation of the "Seventeen-Article Constitution," represented an indigenous attempt to reconcile Buddhist and Confucian traditions with the native Japanese religious tradition. Shōtoku envisaged a centralized national community under the throne, and he advocated the veneration of Buddhism as the final refuge of all creatures. Moreover, he held the Confucian notion of *li* ("propriety") as the key to right relations among ruler, ministers, and people. [*See* Li.] Shōtoku was convinced that his policy was in keeping with the will of the *kami.* In his edict of 607 he states how his imperial ancestors had venerated the heavenly and earthly *kami* and thus "the winter [*yin,* negative cosmic force] and summer [*yang,* positive cosmic force] elements were kept in harmony, and their creative powers blended together," and he urged his ministers to do the same.

Prince Shōtoku took the initiative in reestablishing diplomatic contact with China by sending an envoy to the Sui court. He also sent a number of talented young scholars and monks to China to study. Although Shōtoku's reform measures remained unfulfilled at his untimely death, the talented youths he sent to China played important roles in the development of Japanese religion and national affairs upon their return. [*See the biography of Shōtoku Taishi.*]

The Ritsuryō Synthesis. Prince Shōtoku's death was followed by a series of bloody power struggles, including the coup d'état of 645, which strengthened the position of the throne. The Taika reforms of 645 and 646 attempted to consolidate the power of the centralized government by such Chinese-style measures as land redistribution, collection of revenues, and a census. During the second half of the seventh century the government, utilizing the talents of those who had studied in China, sponsored the compilation of a written law. Significantly, those penal codes *(ritsu;* Chin., *lü)* and civil statutes *(ryō;* Chin., *ling),* which were modeled after Chinese legal systems, were issued in the name of the emperor as the will of the *kami.* The government structure thus developed during the late seventh century is referred to as the Ritsuryō ("imperial rescript") state. Although the basic principle of the Ritsuryō state was in a sense a logical implementation of Prince Shōtoku's vision, which itself was a synthesis of Buddhist, Confucian, and Japanese traditions, it turned out to be in effect a form of "immanental theocracy," in which the universal principles of Tao and Dharma were domesticated to serve the will of the sovereign, who now was elevated to the status of living or manifest *kami*. [*See* Kingship, *article on* Kingship in East Asia.]

It should be noted in this connection that the government's effort to consolidate the Ritsuryō structure was initially resisted by the former *uji* chieftains and provincial magnates who had residual power in the court. Ironically, after usurping the throne from his nephew, Emperor Temmu (r. 672–686) managed to bring new elements into the rank of court nobility and reorganize the government structure. Emperor Temmu ordered the compilation of two historical writings, the *Kojiki* (Record of Ancient Matters) and the *Nihongi* (or *Nihonshoki,* the Chronicles of Japan), which were completed during the eighth century. Temmu is also credited with canonizing Amaterasu, the sun deity, as the ancestral *kami* and with making her Grand Shrine of Ise the tutelary shrine of the imperial house. [*See* Amaterasu Ōmikami.]

One characteristic policy of the Ritsuryō state was to support and control religions. Thus, the government enforced the Sōniryō (Law Governing Monks and Nuns), which was modeled after a Chinese code, the Law Governing Taoist and Buddhist Priests, of the Yung-hui period (640–655). The government also elevated the Office of Kami Affairs (Kanzukasa) to a full-fledged Department of Kami Affairs (Jingikan), charged with supervising all officially sponsored Shintō shrines and overseeing the registers of the entire Shintō priesthood and other religious corporations. The Jingikan was given equal rank with the Great Council of State (Dajōkan).

NARA PERIOD

During the eighth century Japanese religion reached an important stage of maturity under Chinese and Buddhist inspirations. It was a golden age for the Ritsuryō state and the imperial court. Thanks to the newly acquired Chinese script, the two mythohistorical writings—the *Kojiki* and the *Nihonshoki*—as well as the *Fudoki* (Records of Local Surveys), the *Man'yōshū* (Anthology of Myriad Leaves), and the *Kaifūsō* (Fond Recollection of Poetry) were compiled. Also in this century the Yōrō Ritsuryō (Yōrō Penal and Civil Codes), the legal foundation of the Ritsuryō state, were fixed in writing.

The immanental theocratic principle of the Ritsuryō state undoubtedly was based on the myth of the solar ancestry of the imperial house. Similarly, as mentioned earlier, the compilation of the *Kojiki* and the *Nihonshoki* was ordered by Emperor Temmu in 673 in order to justify his accession to the throne. Thus, although the format of these chronicles was modeled after Chinese dynastic histories, their task was to sort out myths, legends, and historical events in such a way as to establish direct genealogical connections between the contemporary imperial house and the sun deity. With this objective in mind, the chroniclers worked out a smooth transition from the domain of myths, which were classified as the "age of *kami,*" to the "historical" accounts of legendary emperors, who were presumed to be direct ancestors of the imperial house. Although the chronologies in the *Kojiki* and *Nihonshoki* were obviously fabricated, these mytho-historical writings provide a rich source of myths in which the ethos and meaning-structure of early Japanese religion unfold before us. Not surprisingly, these two chronicles came to be regarded as semicanonical scriptures of Shintō.

As important as the chronicles for our understanding of early Japanese religion is the *Man'yōshū,* which betrays amazingly little influence from the continent even though it was compiled two centuries after the introduction of Chinese civilization and Buddhism. In its literary form, the *Man'yōshū* utilized Chinese characters only for their sound value, disregarding their lexical meaning. Many of the poems in this anthology portray an interpenetration of what we now call religious and aesthetic values. The *Man'yōshū* also reveals an enduring feature of Japanese religion, namely, the poet as expert in sacred matters. The poet, as was also true in ancient Greece, was a maker and interpreter of sacral reality, and poems that addressed natural phenomena as *kami* were indeed sacred songs. [*See* Poetry, *article on* Japanese Religious Poetry.]

In contrast to earlier periods, when Korean forms of Buddhism influenced Japan, early eighth-century Japan felt the strong impact of Chinese Buddhism. In 710 the first capital, modeled after the Chinese capital of Ch'ang-an, was established in Nara, which was designed to serve as the religious as well as the political center of the nation. During the Nara period the imperial court was eager to promote Buddhism as the religion best suited for the protection of the state. Accordingly, the government established in every province state-sponsored temples *(kokubunji)* and nunneries *(kokubunniji).* In the capital city the national cathedral, Tōdaiji, was built as the home of the gigantic bronze statue of the Buddha Vairocana. The government sponsored and supported six schools of Chinese Buddhism. Of the six, the Ritsu (Vinaya) school was concerned primarily with monastic disciplines. The other five were more like monastic schools based on different philosophical traditions than sectarian groups. For example, the two Hinayanistic schools—the Kusha (deriving its name from the *Abhidharmakośa*) and the Jōjitsu (deriving its name from the *Satyasiddhi*)—were devoted to cosmological and psychological analysis of elements of the universe, whereas the Sanron (Mādhyamika) school specialized in dialectic analysis of concepts in order to suppress all duality for the sake of gaining perfect wisdom. The Kegon school (deriving its name from the *Avataṃsaka Sūtra*) was a form of cosmotheism, and the Hossō (Yogācāra), probably the most influential system during the Nara period, stressed analysis of the nature of things and a theory of cause. Only those who had taken vows at one of the three official ordination platforms were qualified to be official monks. With government subsidy the monks were able to devote their lives to the study of the doctrinal intricacies of their respective schools, subject, of course, to the Sōniryō. [*See also* Mādhyamika; Yogācāra; *and* Huayen.]

Despite such encouragement and support from the government, Buddhism did not have much impact on the populace. More important were three new religious forms that developed out of the fusion between the Japanese religious heritage and Buddhism.

The first new form was the Nature Wisdom school (Jinenchishū), which sought enlightenment by meditation or austere physical discipline in the mountains and forests. Those who followed the path, including some official monks, affirmed the superiority of enlightenment through nature to the traditional Buddhist disciplines and doctrines. The indigenous Japanese acceptance of the sacrality of nature was thus reaffirmed.

Second, a variety of folk religious leaders, variously called private monks *(shidosō)* and unordained monks *(ubasoku;* from Skt. *upāsaka),* emerged. Many of them were magicians, healers, and shamanic diviners of the mountain districts or the countryside who came under nominal Buddhist influence although they had no formal Buddhist training and had only tenuous connections to Buddhism. Their religious outlook was strongly influenced by the shamanistic folk piety of Japanese religious traditions and Taoism, but they also appropriated many features of Buddhism and taught simple and syncretistic "folk Buddhism" among the lower strata of society. [*See* Hijiri.]

A third new form grew out of the trend toward an interpenetration between, and amalgamation of, Shintō and Buddhism, whereby Shintō shrines found their way into the compound of Buddhist temples and Buddhist chapels were built within the precinct of Shintō shrines. The construction of Tōdaiji was enhanced by the alleged encouragement of the sun deity of the Grand Shrine of Ise and of the *kami* Hachiman of Usa Shrine, Kyushu. In fact, Hachiman was equated with a Buddhist *bodhisattva.* This Shintō-Buddhist amalgamation, which began in the eighth century and later came to be called Ryōbu ("two aspects") Shintō, remained the institutional norm until the late nineteenth century.

Because of the excessive support of religion and culture by the court, which benefited only the aristocracy, the capital of Nara during the second half of the eighth century was doomed by political corruption, ecclesiastical intrigue, and financial bankruptcy. Therefore the capital was moved in 794 from Nara to a remote place and then ten years later to the present Kyoto.

EROSION OF THE RITSURYŌ IDEAL

The new capital in Kyoto, Heiankyō ("capital of peace and tranquillity"), was also modeled after the Chinese capital. Although Kyoto remained the seat of the imperial court until the nineteenth century, the so-called Heian period covers only that time, in the ninth to the twelfth century, when political power was concentrated in the capital. Freed from ecclesiastical interference, the leaders of the Kyoto regime were eager to restore the integrity of the Ritsuryō system, and they forbade the Nara Buddhist schools to move into the new capital. Instead, the imperial court favored, side by side with Shintō, two new Buddhist schools, Tendai (Chin., T'ien-t'ai) and Shingon (Chin., Chen-yen), introduced by Saichō (767–822) and Kūkai (774–835), respectively. Both Saichō and Kūkai had been disillusioned in their youth by the formalism and moral decadence of the Buddhist schools in Nara, both had studied in China, and both were to exert great influence on the further development of Japanese religion.

Saichō, also known by his posthumous name, Dengyō Daishi, established the monastic center of the Tendai school at Mount Hiei, not far from Kyoto, and incorporated the doctrines of the *Saddharmapuṇḍarīka* (Lotus of the Good Law) *Sūtra,* Esoteric (i.e., Tantric) mysticism, Zen (Chin., Ch'an) meditation, and monastic discipline (Vinaya) into his teachings. He was conciliatory to Shintō, and his form of Shintō-Buddhist (Tendai) amalgam came to be known as Sannō Ichijitsu ("one reality") Shintō. Shortly after Saichō's death the Tendai school stressed its Esoteric elements to the extent that it came to be called Taimitsu (Tendai Esoterism). It should be noted that the Tendai monastery at Mount Hiei remained for centuries a most powerful institution and produced many prominent religious figures during the medieval period. [*See also* Tendaishū *and the biography of Saichō.*]

Kūkai, known posthumously as Kōbō Daishi, established the Shingon monastic center at Mount Kōya, not far from present-day Osaka, but also served as the head of the prestigious Tōji (Eastern Temple) in Kyoto. As a result, Kūkai's teachings are often referred to as Tōmitsu (Eastern Esoterism). Kūkai was noted for his unusual erudition. His scheme of the ten stages of spiritual development included teachings from all the major Buddhist schools and also from Hinduism, Confucianism, and Taoism. Moreover, he taught that the essential truth of Esoteric teaching could be revealed in art, thus affirming the mutual penetration of aesthetic and religious experiences. The Shingon school provided the theoretical basis for Ryōbu Shintō, as mentioned earlier. [*See also* Shingonshū *and the biography of Kūkai.*] According to both the Tendai and Shingon traditions of the Shinto-Buddhist amalgam, Shintō *kami* were believed to be manifestations *(suijaku)* of the Buddhas who were the original realities *(honji).* [*See* Honjisuijaku.]

Meanwhile, in an important step toward restoring the Ritsuryō system, the government sponsored the *Shinsen shōjiroku* (New Compilation of the Register of Families), completed in 815. It divided the aristocracy into three arbitrary categories: (1) descendants of heavenly and earthly *kami (shinbetsu),* (2) descendants of imperial and other royal families *(kōbetsu),* and (3) descendants of naturalized Chinese and Koreans *(banbetsu).* The preface to this register acknowledged that provincial records had all been burned. Thus there were no reliable documents. Many commoners then pretended to be scions of noblemen, and children of naturalized Chinese and Koreans claimed to be the descendants of Japanese *kami.* Despite such a frank admission of the impossibility of the task involved, the *Register* presented the genealogies of 1,182 families as an "essential instrument in the hands of the nation."

Nearly a century after the compilation of the *Shinsen shōjiroku* the government undertook the ambitious enterprise of collecting all supplementary rules to previously promulgated edicts and ceremonial rules known during the Engi era (901–922). Of the fifty books that comprise these documents, the *Engishiki,* the first ten are devoted to minute rules and procedures of dealing with various aspects of Shintō, such as festivals, the Grand Shrine of Ise, enthronement ceremonies, ritual prayers *(norito),* and a register of *kami.* Of special importance to the understanding of Japanese religion are the ritual prayers, some of which might be traced back to the mid-sixth century when ritualized recitation of prayers, inspired by the Buddhist example of reciting scriptures (*sūtra*s), developed. [*See* Norito.] The remaining forty books of the *Engishiki* are detailed descriptions of rules and regulations of all the bureaus under the Grand Council of State (Dajōkan), including numerous references to affairs related to Shintō. It is interesting to note that the section on the Bureau of Yin-Yang (Onmyōryō), book 16, mentions the duties of masters and doctors of divination and astrology in reciting the ritual prayers *(saimon)* addressed to heavenly and earthly *kami.* The underlying principle of the *Engishiki,* which epitomized the Ritsuryō ideal, was that the imperial court was the earthly counterpart of the heavenly court. Just as the court of the sun deity included various functionaries, the imperial court included religious and administrative functionaries, and the stylized daily rituals of the court, properly performed, had great bearing on the harmonious blending of the *yin* and *yang* elements in the cosmos as well as on the welfare of the people. The *Engishiki,* which was completed in 927, was not put into effect until 967. When it was finally implemented, the document was no longer taken seriously. This was true not only because the rules of procedures of the *Engishiki* were excessively cumbersome but also because the very ideal of the Ritsuryō system was eroding by that time.

The foundation of the Ritsuryō system was the sacred monarchy, authenticated by the mytho-historical claim that the sun deity had given the mandate to her grandson and his descendants to "reign" and "rule" the world, meaning Japan, in perpetuity. Ironically, during the Heian period the two institutions that were most closely related to the throne, namely, the Fujiwara regency and rule by retired monarchs *(insei),* undercut the structure of the Ritsuryō system.

The regency had been exercised before the ninth century only by members of the royal family and only in times when the reigning monarch needed such assistance. But from the late ninth century to the mideleventh century the nation was actually ruled by the regency of the powerful Fujiwara family. The institutionalization of the regency implied a significant redefinition of the Ritsuryō system by the aristocracy. The aristocratic families acknowledged the sacrality of the throne, but they expected the emperor to "reign" only as the manifest *kami* and not to interfere with the actual operation of the government. The latter was believed to be the prerogative of the aristocratic officials. Moreover, the Fujiwaras, who had managed to marry off their daughters to reigning monarchs, thus claimed added privileges as the titular sovereigns' maternal in-laws.

The custom of rule by retired monarchs began in the eleventh century, when ambitious monarchs abdicated for the purpose of exercising power from behind the throne with the claim that they were still legitimate heads of the patriarchal imperial family. This institution of *insei,* which also compromised the Ritsuryō principle, lost much of its influence by the end of the twelfth century owing to the growth of political power held by warrior families.

The Heian period witnessed the phenomenal growth of wealth and political influence of ecclesiastical institutions, both Shintō and Buddhist, equipped with lucrative manors and armed guards. However, among the lower strata of society, which were neglected by established religious groups, magico-religious beliefs and practices of both indigenous and Chinese origins prevailed. In addition to healers, diviners, sorcerers, and the practitioners of *onmyōdō* (Yin-yang and Taoist magic), mountain ascetics *(shugenja)*—heirs of the shamanistic folk religious leaders of the Nara period—attracted followers in places high and low. In the course of time, mountain ascetics allied themselves with the Tendai and Shingon schools and came to be known as the Tendai-Shugendō and the Shingon-Shugendō, respectively. [*See* Shugendō.] Such literary works as the *Genjimonogatari* (Tale of Genji) by Lady Murasaki and the *Makura no sōshi* (Pillow Book) by Lady Sei-shōnagon also reveal that during this period all calamities, from earthquake, fire, floods, and epidemics to civil wars, were widely believed to have been caused by the vengeance of angry spirits *(goryō).* Some of these spirits were venerated as *kami,* and Shintō shrines were built in their honor. Moreover, festivals for angry spirits *(goryō-e),* with music, dance, wrestling, archery, and horse racing, as well as Shintō, Buddhist, and Yin-yang liturgies, were held in order to pacify the anger of *goryō.*

Frequent occurrences of natural calamities during the Heian period also precipitated the widespread belief that the apocalyptic age of the Latter Days of the Law *(mappō)* predicted in Buddhist scripture was at hand. [*See* Mappō.] This may account for the growing popularity of the Buddha Amida (Skt., Amitābha, the Buddha of Infinite Light, or Amitāyus, the Buddha of Infinite Life), who had vowed to save all sentient beings and had promised rebirth in his Pure Land to the faithful. As we shall see presently, Amida pietism became a powerful spiritual movement in the subsequent period. [*See* Amitābha.]

The Heian period, and the elegant culture it produced, vanished in the late twelfth century in a series of bloody battles involving both courtiers and warriors. Then came a new age dominated by warrior rulers.

RELIGIOUS ETHOS DURING THE KAMAKURA PERIOD

That the nation was "ruled" by warrior-rulers from the thirteenth to the nineteenth century, even though the emperor continued to "reign" throughout these centuries, is a matter of considerable significance for the development of Japanese religion. There were three such feudal warrior regimes (*bakufu* or shogunates): (1) the Kamakura regime (1192–1333), (2) the Ashikaga regime (1338–1573), and (3) the Tokugawa regime (1603–1867). Unlike the Ritsuryō state, with its elaborate penal and civil codes, the warrior rule—at least under the first two regimes—was based on a much simpler legal system. For example, the legislation of the Kamakura regime consisted of only fifty-one pragmatic principles. This allowed established Shintō and Buddhist institutions more freedom than they had under the cumbersome structure of the Ritsuryō state. It also set the stage for the development of new religious movements, many with roots in the folk tradition.

Of course the emergence of warrior rule signified the further weakening of the already battered Ritsuryō ideal. For example, unlike the Fujiwara noblemen and retired monarchs, who had wielded power from within the framework of the imperial court, the Kamakura regime established its own administrative structure consisting of three bureaus—military, administrative, and judiciary. The warriors for the most part were not sophisticated in cultural and religious matters. Many of them, however, combined simple Buddhist piety with devotion to the pre-Buddhist indigenous tutelary *kami* of warrior families rather than those of the imperial Shintō tradition. The cohesion of the warrior society, not unlike the early Yamato confederation of semiautonomous clans, was based on the *uji* and the larger unit of *uji* federation. Accordingly, the tutelary *kami* of warrior families (for example, Hachiman, the *kami* of war of the Minamoto *uji,* founder of the Kamakura regime) escalated in importance. At the same time, the peasantry, artisans, and small merchants, whose living standard improved a little under the Kamakura regime, were attracted to new religious movements that promised an easier path to salvation in the dreaded age of degeneration (*mappō).* On the other hand, the Zen traditions, which had been a part of older Buddhist schools, gained independence under the influence of the Chinese Ch'an movement and quickly found patronage among the Kamakura rulers.

Significantly, all the leaders of new religious movements during this period had begun their careers at the Tendai headquarters at Mount Hiei but had become disillusioned by the empty ceremonialism, scholasticism, and moral corruption that characterized the monastic life of their time. Three of these leaders altered their religious resolutions when they found certitude of salvation in reliance on the compassionate Amida by *nembutsu* (recitation of the Buddha's name). They then became instrumental in the establishment of the three Pure Land (Amida's Western Paradise) traditions. They were Hōnen (Genkū, 1133–1212) of the Jōdo (Pure Land) sect, who is often compared with Martin Luther; Shinran (1173–1262) of the Jōdo Shin (True Pure Land) sect, a disciple of Hōnen, who among other things initiated the tradition of a married priesthood; and Ippen (Chishin, 1239–1289) of the Ji (Time) sect, so named because of its practice of reciting hymns to Amida six times a day. [*See* Jōdoshū; Jōdo Shinshū; *and the biographies of Hōnen, Shinran, and Ippen.*]

On the other hand, Nichiren (1222–1282), founder of the school bearing his name and a charismatic prophet, developed his own interpretation of the *Hokekyō* (Lotus Sutra), the *Saddharmapuṇḍarīka Sūtra,* as the only path toward salvation for the Japanese nation. [*See* Nichirenshū *and the biography of Nichiren.*]

In contrast to the paths of salvation advocated by the Pure Land and Nichiren schools, the experience of enlightenment *(satori)* was stressed by Eisai (Yōsai, 1141–1215), who introduced the Rinzai (Chin., Lin-chi) Zen tradition, and Dōgen (1200–1253), who established the Sōtō (Chin., Ts'ao-tung) Zen tradition. Zen was welcomed by Kamakura leaders partly because it could counterbalance the powerful and wealthy established Buddhist institutions and partly because it was accompanied by other features of Sung Chinese culture, including Neo-Confucian learning. The Zen movement was greatly aided by a number of émigré Ch'an monks who settled in Japan. [*See* Zen *and the biography of Dōgen.*]

Despite the growth of new religious movements, old religious establishments, both Shintō and Buddhist, remained powerful during this period; for example, both gave military support to the royalist cause against the Kamakura regime during the abortive Jōkyū rebellion in 1221. On the other hand, confronted by a national crisis during the Mongol invasions of 1274 and 1281, both Shintō shrines and Buddhist monasteries solidly supported the Kamakura regime by offering prayers and incantations for the protection of Japan.

A short-lived "imperial rule," 1333–1336, followed the decline of the Kamakura regime. This rule aided the Ise Shintō movement, which tried not very successfully to emancipate Shintō from Buddhist and Chinese influences. Ise Shintō influenced the royalist general Kitagatake Chikafusa (1293–1354), author of the *Jinnō shōtōki* (Records of the Legitimate Succession of the Divine Sovereigns). The imperial regime was also instrumental in shifting the centers of Zen and Sung learning, established by the Kamakura regime in the Chinese-style Gozan ("five mountains") temples, to Kyoto. [*See* Gozan Zen.]

ZEN, NEO-CONFUCIANISM, AND KIRISHITAN DURING THE ASHIKAGA PERIOD

Unlike the first feudal regime at Kamakura, the Ashikaga regime established its *bakufu* in Kyoto, the seat of the imperial court. Accordingly, religious and cultural development during the Ashikaga period (1338–1573, also referred to as the Muromachi period) blended various features of warrior and courtier traditions, Zen, and Chinese cultural influences. This blending in turn fostered a closer interpenetration of religious and aesthetic values. All these religious and cultural developments took place at a time when social and political order was threatened not only by a series of bloody power struggles within the *bakufu* but also by famines and epidemics that led to peasant uprisings and, further, by the devastating Ōnin War (1467–1478) that accelerated the erosion of Ashikaga hegemony and the rise of competing daimyo, the so-called *sengoku daimyō* ("feudal lords of warring states"), in the provinces. In this situation, villages and towns developed something analogous to self-rule. Merchants and artisans formed guilds *(za)* that were usually affiliated with established Buddhist temples and Shintō shrines, whereas adherents of Pure Land and Nichiren sects were willing to defend themselves as armed religious societies. Into this complex religious, cultural, social, and political topography, European missionaries of Roman Catholicism, then known as Kirishitan, brought a new gospel of salvation.

Throughout the Ashikaga period established institutions of older Buddhist schools and Shintō (for example, the Tendai monastery at Mount Hiei, the Shingon monastery at Mount Kōya, and the Kasuga shrine at Nara) remained both politically and economically powerful. However, the new religious groups that had begun to attract the lower strata of society during the Kamakura period continued to expand their influence, often competing among themselves. Some of these new religious groups staged a series of armed rebellions—such as Hokke-ikki (uprisings of Nichiren followers) and Ikkō-ikki (uprisings of the True Pure Land followers)—to defend themselves against each other or against oppressive officialdoms. The Order of Mountain Ascetics (Shugendō) also became institutionalized as the eclectic Shugenshū (Shugen sect) and promoted devotional confraternities *(kōsha)* among villagers and townsmen, competing with new religious groups.

Zen and Neo-Confucianism. By far the most influential religious sect during the Ashikaga period was Zen, especially the Rinzai Zen tradition, which became *de facto* the official religion. The first Ashikaga shogun, following the advice of his confidant, Musō Soseki, established a "temple for the peace of the nation" *(ankokuji)* in each province. [*See the biography of Musō Soseki.*] As economic necessity compelled the regime to turn to foreign trade, Soseki's temple, Tenryūji, sent ships to China for this purpose. Many Zen priests served as advisers to administrative offices of the regime. With the rise of the Ming dynasty (1368–1644), which replaced Mongol rule, the third Ashikaga shogun resumed official diplomatic relations with China, again depending heavily on the assistance of Zen priests. After the third shogun regularized two Gozan (the five officially recognized Zen temples) systems, one in Kyoto and the second in Kamakura, Gozan temples served as important financial resources for the regime. Many Zen priests earned reputations as monk-poets or monk-painters, and Gozan temples became centers of cultural and artistic activities.

Zen priests, including émigré Chinese Ch'an monks, also made contributions as transmitters of Neo-Confucianism, a complex philosophical system incorporating not only classical Confucian thought but also features of Buddhist and Taoist traditions that had developed in China during the Sung (960–1127) and Southern Sung (1127–1279) periods. It should be noted that Neo-Confucianism was initially conceived in Japan as a cultural appendage to Zen. Soon, however, many Zen monks upheld the unity of Zen and Neo-Confucian traditions to the extent that the entire teaching staff and students of the Ashikaga Academy, presumably a nonreligious institution devoted to Neo-Confucian learning, were Zen monks. [*See* Confucian Thought, *article on* Neo-Confucianism.]

The combined inspiration of Japanese and Sung Chinese aesthetics, Zen, and Pure Land traditions, coupled with the enthusiastic patronage of shoguns, made possible the growth of a variety of elegant and sophisticated art: painting, calligraphy, *renga* (dialogical poetry or linked verse), stylized *nō* drama, comical *kyōgen* plays, flower arrangement, and the cult of tea. [*See also* Drama, *article on* East Asian Dance and Theater.] Some of these art forms are considered as much the "way" *(dō* or *michi)* as the "ways" of *kami* or the Buddha, implying that they are nonreligious paths to sacral reality.

The Coming of Kirishitan. When the Ōnin War ended in 1478 the Ashikaga regime could no longer control the ambitious provincial daimyo who were consolidating their own territories. By the sixteenth century Portugal was expanding its overseas empire in Asia. The chance arrival of shipwrecked Portuguese merchants at Tanegashima Island, south of Kyushu, in 1543 was followed by the arrival in Kyushu in 1549 of the famous Jesuit Francis Xavier. Although Xavier stayed only two years in Japan, he initiated vigorous proselytizing activities during that time.

The cause of Kirishitan (as Roman Catholicism was then called in Japanese) was greatly aided by a strongman, Oda Nobunaga (1534–1582), who succeeded in taking control of the capital in 1568. Angry that established Buddhist institutions were resisting his scheme of national unification, Nobunaga took harsh measures; he burned the Tendai monastery at Mount Hiei, killed thousands of Ikkō (True Pure Land) followers, and attacked rebellious priests at Mount Kōya in order to destroy their power. At the same time, ostensibly to counteract the residual influence of Buddhism, he encouraged Kirishitan activities. Ironically, this policy was reversed after his death. Nevertheless, by the time Nobunaga was assassinated, 150,000 Japanese Catholics, including several daimyo, were reported to be among the Japanese population.

The initial success of Catholicism in Japan was due to the Jesuits' policy of accommodation. Xavier himself adopted the name *Dainichi* (the Great Sun Buddha, the supreme deity of the Shingon school) as the designation of God; later, however, this was changed to *Deus.* Jesuits also used the Buddhist terms *jōdo* ("pure land") for heaven and *sō* ("monk") for the title *padre.* Moreover, Kirishitan groups followed the general pattern of tightly knit religious societies practiced by the Nichiren and Pure Land groups. Missionaries also followed the common Japanese approach in securing the favor of the ruling class to expedite their evangelistic and philanthropic activities. Conversely, trade-hungry daimyo eagerly befriended missionaries, knowing that the latter had influence over Portuguese traders. In fact, one Christian daimyo donated the port of Nagasaki to the Society of Jesus in 1580 hoping to attract Portuguese ships to the port, which would in turn benefit him. Inevitably, however, Jesuit-inspired missionary work aroused strong opposition not only from anti-Kirishitan daimyo and Buddhist clerics but from jealous Franciscans and other Catholic orders as well. Furthermore, the Portuguese traders who supported the Jesuits were now threatened by the arrival of the Spanish in 1592, via Mexico and the Philippines, and of the Dutch in 1600.

Meanwhile, following the death of Oda Nobunaga, one of his generals, Toyotomi Hideyoshi (1536–1598), endeavored to complete the task of national unification. Determined to eliminate the power of Buddhist institutions, he not only attacked rebellious monastic communities, such as those in Negoro and Saiga, but also conducted a thorough sword hunt in various monastic communities. Hideyoshi was interested in foreign trade, but he took a dim view of Catholicism because of its potential danger to the cause of national unification. He was incensed by what he saw in Nagasaki, a port that was then ruled by the Jesuits and the Portuguese. In

1587 he issued an edict banishing missionaries, but he did not enforce it until 1596 when he heard a rumor that the Spanish monarch was plotting to subjugate Japan with the help of Japanese Christians. Thus in 1597 he had some twenty-six Franciscans and Japanese converts crucified. The following year Hideyoshi himself died in the midst of his abortive invasion of Korea. [*See also* Christianity, *article on* Christianity in Asia.]

THE TOKUGAWA SYNTHESIS

The power struggle that followed the death of Toyotomi Hideyoshi was settled in 1600 in favor of Tokugawa Ieyasu (1542–1616), who established the *bakufu* in 1603 at Edo (present Tokyo). The Tokugawa regime, which was to hold political power until the Meiji restoration in 1867, was more than another feudal regime; it was a comprehensive sixfold order—political, social, legal, philosophical, religious, and moral—with the shogun in its pivotal position.

1. *Political order.* The Tokugawa form of government, usually known as the *baku-han,* was a national administration *(bakufu)* under the shogun combined with local administration by daimyo in their fiefs *(han).*
2. *Social order.* Japan under the Tokugawas was rigidly divided into warrior, farmer, artisan, and merchant classes, plus special categories such as imperial and courtier families and ecclesiastics. Accordingly, one's birth dictated one's status as well as one's duties to nation and family and one's role in social relations.
3. *Legal order.* The Tokugawas formulated a series of administrative and legislative principles as well as rules and regulations *(hatto)* that dictated the boundaries and norms of behavior of various imperial, social, and religious groups.
4. *Philosophical order.* The Tokugawa synthesis was based on the Neo-Confucian principle that the order of Heaven is not transcendental but rather is inherent in the sacrality of nation, family, and social hierarchy.
5. *Religious order.* In sharp contrast to the Ritsuryō system, which was based on a principle of sacred kingship that authenticated the immanental theocratic state as the nation of the *kami,* the Tokugawas looked to the throne in order to add a magico-religious aura to their own version of immanental theocracy. They grounded this notion in what they felt were the natural laws and natural norms implicit in human, social, and political order. It is interesting to note in passing that the first shogun, Ieyasu, was deified as the "Sun God of the East" (Tōshō) and was enshrined as the guardian deity of the Tokugawas at Nikkō. According to the Tokugawas, all religions were to become integral and supportive elements of the Tokugawa synthesis. However, the Tokugawas tolerated no prophetic judgment or critique of the whole system.
6. *Moral order.* Running through the Tokugawa synthesis was a sense of moral order that held the balance of the total system. Its basic formula was simple: the Way of Heaven was the natural norm, and the way of government, following the principle of benevolent rule *(jinsei),* was to actualize this moral order. This demanded something of each person in order to fulfill the true meaning of the relations *(taigi-meibun)* among different status groups. Warriors, for example, were expected to follow Bushidō ("the way of the warrior"). [*See* Bushidō.]

Kirishitan Under Tokugawa Rule. The religious policy of the Tokugawa regime was firmly established by the first shogun, who held that all religious, philosophical, and ethical systems were to uphold and cooperate with the government's objective, namely, the establishment of a harmonious society. Following the eclectic tradition of Japanese religion, which had appropriated various religious symbols and concepts, the first shogun stated in an edict of 1614: "Japan is called the land of the Buddha and not without reason. . . . *Kami* and the Buddha differ in name, but their meaning is one." Accordingly, he surrounded himself with a variety of advisers, including Buddhist clerics and Confucian scholars, and shared their view that the Kirishitan religion could not be incorporated into the framework of Japanese religion and would be detrimental to the cause of social and political harmony. Nevertheless, the Tokugawa regime's initial attitude toward Catholicism was restrained; perhaps this was because the regime did not wish to lose foreign trade by overt anti-Kirishitan measures. But in 1614 the edict banning Kirishitan was issued, followed two years later by a stricter edict. A series of persecutions of missionaries and Japanese converts then took place. Following the familiar pattern of religious uprising (such as Hokke- and Ikkō-ikki), armed farmers, fishermen, warriors, and their women and children, many of whom were Kirishitan followers, rose in revolt in 1637 in Shimabara, Kyushu. When the uprising was quelled, Kirishitan followers were ordered to renounce their faith. If they did not do so, they were tortured to death.

The regime also took the far more drastic measure of "national seclusion" *(sakoku)* when it cut off all trade and other relations with foreign powers (with the exception of the Netherlands). Furthermore, in order to exterminate the forbidden religion of Kirishitan, every family was required to be registered in a Buddhist temple. However, "hidden Kirishitan" groups survived these severe persecutions and have preserved their form of Kirishitan tradition even into the present century.

Buddhism and the Tokugawa Regime. The Tokugawa regime's anti-Kirishitan measures required every Japanese citizen to become, at least nominally, Buddhist. Accordingly, the number of Buddhist temples suddenly increased from 13,037 (the number of temples during the Kamakura period) to 469,934. Under Tokugawa rule a comprehensive parochial system was created, with Buddhist clerics serving as arms of the ruling regime in charge of thought control. In turn, Buddhist temples were tightly controlled by the regime, which tolerated internal doctrinal disputes but not deviation from official policy. Since Buddhist temples were in charge of cemeteries, Buddhism was highly visible to the general populace through burial and memorial services. Understandably, the combination of semiofficial prerogatives and financial security was not conducive to the clerics' spiritual quest. The only new sect that emerged during the Tokugawa period was the Ōbaku sect of Zen, which was introduced from China in the mid-seventeenth century. [*See the biography of Ingen.*]

Confucianism and Shintō. Neo-Confucianism was promoted by Zen Buddhists prior to the Tokugawa period. Thus, that Neo-Confucian scholars were also Zen clerics was taken for granted. Fujiwara Seika (1561–1619) first advocated the independence of Neo-Confucianism from Zen. By his recommendation, Hayashi Razan (1583–1657), one of Seika's disciples, became the Confucian adviser to the first shogun, thus commencing the tradition that members of the Hayashi family served as heads of the official Confucian college, the Shōheikō, under the Tokugawa regime. Not surprisingly, Razan and many Neo-Confucians expressed outspoken anti-Buddhist sentiments, and some Confucian scholars became interested in Shintō. Razan, himself an ardent follower of the Shushi (Chu Hsi) tradition, tried to relate the *ri* (Chin., *li,* "reason, principle") of Neo-Confucianism with Shintō. Another Shushi scholar, Yamazaki Ansai (1618–1682), went so far as to develop a form of Confucian Shintō called Suika Shintō. The Shushi school was acknowledged as the official guiding ideology of the regime and was promoted by powerful members of the Tokugawa family, including the fifth shogun. Especially noteworthy was Tokugawa Mitsukuni (1628–1701), grandson of the first shogun and the daimyo of Mito, who gathered together able scholars, including Chu Shun-shui (1600–1682), an exiled Ming royalist. He thereby initiated the Mito tradition of Confucianism. The *Dainihonshi* (History of Great Japan), produced by Mito scholars, subsequently provided the theoretical basis for the royalist movement.

The second tradition of Neo-Confucianism, Ōyōmeigaku or Yōmeigaku (the school of Wang Yang-ming), held that the individual mind was the manifestation of the universal Mind. This school also attracted such able men as Nakae Tōju (1608–1648) and Kumazawa Banzan (1619–1691). Ōyōmeigaku provided ethical incentives for social reform and became a pseudo-religious system. Quite different from the traditions of Shushi and Ōyōmei was the Kogaku ("ancient learning") tradition, which aspired to return to the classical sources of Confucianism. One of its early advocates, Yamaga Sokō (1622–1685), left a lasting mark on Bushidō, while another scholar of this school, Itō Jinsai (1627–1705), probed the truth of classical Confucianism, rejecting the metaphysical dualism of Chu Hsi.

Throughout the Tokugawa period, Confucian scholars, particularly those of the Shushigaku, Ōyōmeigaku, and Kogaku schools, exerted lasting influence on the warriors-turned-administrators, who took up Confucian ideas on the art of governing and on the modes of conduct that were appropriate for warriors, farmers, and townspeople, respectively. Certainly, such semireligious movements as Shingaku ("mind learning"), initiated by Ishida Baigan (1685–1744), and Hōtoku ("repaying indebtedness"), championed by Ninomiya Sontoku (1787–1856), were greatly indebted to Confucian ethical insights. [*See the biographies of the principal Neo-Confucian thinkers discussed above.*]

Shintō Revival and the Decline of the Tokugawa Regime. With the encouragement of anti-Buddhist Confucianists, especially those of Suika Shintō, Shintō leaders who were overshadowed by their Buddhist counterparts during the early Tokugawa period began to assert themselves. Shintō soon found a new ally in the scholars of Kokugaku ("national learning"), notably Motoori Norinaga (1730–1801), whose monumental study of the *Kojiki* provided a theoretical basis for the Fukko ("return to ancient") Shintō movement. Motoori's junior contemporary, Hirata Atsutane (1776–1843), pushed the cause of Fukko Shintō even further. [*See* Kokugaku *and the biographies of Motoori and Hirata.*] The nationalistic sentiment generated by the leaders of the Shintō revival, National Learning, and pro-Shintō Confucians began to turn against the already weakening Tokugawa regime in favor of the emerging royalist cause. The authority of the regime was threatened further by the demands of Western powers to reopen Japan for trade. Inevitably, the loosening of the shogunate's control resulted in political and social disintegration, which in turn precipitated the emergence of messianic cults from the soil of folk religious traditions. Three important messianic cults developed: Kurozumikyō, founded by Kurozumi Munetada (1780–1850); Konkōkyō, founded by Kawate Bunjirō (1814–1883); and Tenrikyō, founded by Nakayama Miki (1798–1887). [*See* Kurozumikyō; Konkōkyō; *and* Tenrikyō.]

MODERN PERIOD

The checkered development of Japanese religion in the modern period reflects a series of political, social, and cultural changes that have taken place within the Japanese nation. These changes include the toppling of the Tokugawa regime (1867), followed by the restoration of imperial rule under the Meiji emperor (r. 1867–1912); the rising influence of Western thought and civilization as well as Christianity; the Sino-Japanese War (1894–1895); the Russo-Japanese War (1904–1905); the annexation of Korea (1910); World War I, followed by a short-lived "Taishō Democracy"; an economic crisis followed by the rise of militarism in the 1930s; the Japanese invasion of Manchuria and China followed by World War II; Japan's surrender to the Allied forces (1945); the Allied occupation of Japan; and postwar adjustment. The particular path of development of Japanese religion was, of course, most directly affected by the government's religious policies.

Meiji Era. Although the architects of modern Japan welcomed many features of Western civilization, the Meiji regime was determined to restore the ancient principle of the "unity of religion and government" and the immanental theocratic state. The model was the Ritsuryō system of the seventh and eighth centuries. Accordingly, sacred kingship served as the pivot of national policy *(kokutai)*. Thus, while the constitution nominally guaranteed religious freedom and the historic ban against Christianity was lifted, the government created an overarching new religious form called State Shintō, which was designed to supersede all other religious groups. In order to create such a new official religion out of the ancient Japanese religious heritage an edict separating Shintō and Buddhism *(Shin-Butsu hanzen rei)* was issued. The government's feeling was that the Shintō-Buddhist amalgam of the preceding ten centuries was contrary to indigenous religious tradition. After the abortive Taikyō Sempū ("dissemination of the great doctrine") movement and the compulsory registration of Shintō parishioners, the government decided to utilize various other means, especially military training and public education, to promote the sacred "legacy of the *kami* way" *(kannagara):* hence the promulgation of the Imperial Rescript to Soldiers and Sailors (1882) and the Imperial Rescript on Education (1890). Significantly, from 1882 until the end of World War II Shintō priests were prohibited by law from preaching during Shintō ceremonies, although they were responsible—as arms of the government bureaucracy—for the preservation of State Shintō.

Furthermore, in order to keep State Shintō from becoming involved in overtly sectarian activities, the government created between 1882 and 1908 a new category of Kyōha ("sect") Shintō and recognized thirteen such groups, including Kurozumikyō, Konkōkyō, and Tenrikyō, which had emerged in the late Tokugawa period. Like Buddhist sects and Christian denominations, these groups depended on nongovernmental, private initiative for their propagation, organization, and financial support.

Actually, Kyōha Shintō groups have very little in common. Some of them consider themselves genuinely Shintō in beliefs and practices, whereas some of them are marked by strong Confucian features. Still others betray characteristic features of folk religious tradition such as the veneration of sacred mountains, cults of mental and physical purification, utopian beliefs, and faith healing.

Buddhism. Understandably Buddhism was destined to undergo many traumatic experiences in the modern period. The Meiji regime's edict separating Shintō and Buddhism precipitated a popular anti-Buddhist movement that reached its climax around 1871. In various districts temples were destroyed, monks and nuns were laicized, and the parochial system, the legacy of the Tokugawa period, eroded. Moreover, the short-lived Taikyō Sempū movement mobilized Buddhist monks to propagate Taikyō, or government-concocted "Shintō" doctrines. Naturally, faithful Buddhists resented the Shintō-dominated Taikyō movement, and they advocated the principle of religious freedom. Thus, four branches of the True Pure Land sect managed to secure permission to leave the Taikyō movement, and shortly afterward the ill-fated movement itself was abolished. In the meantime, enlightened Buddhist leaders, determined to meet the challenge of Western thought and scholarship, sent able young monks to Western universities. Exposure to European Buddhological scholarship and contacts with other Buddhist traditions in Asia greatly broadened the vista of previously insulated Japanese Buddhists.

The government's grudging decision to succumb to the pressure of Western powers and lift the ban against Christianity was an emotional blow to Buddhism, which had been charged with the task of carrying out the anti-Kirishitan policy of the Tokugawa regime. Thus, many Buddhists, including those who had advocated religious freedom, allied themselves with Shintō, Confucian, and nationalist leaders in an emotional anti-Christian campaign called ***haja kensei*** ("refutation of evil religion and the exaltation of righteous religion"). After the promulgation of the Imperial Rescript on Education in 1890, many Buddhists equated patriotism with nationalism, thus becoming willing defenders and spokesmen of the emperor cult that symbolized the unique national polity ***(kokutai).*** Although many Buddhists had no intention of restoring the historic form of the Shintō-Buddhist amalgam, until the end of World War II they accepted completely Buddhism's subordinate role in the nebulous but overarching super-religion of State Shintō.

Confucianism. Confucians, too, were disappointed by the turn of events during the early days of the Meiji era. It is well to recall that Confucians were the influential guardians of the Tokugawa regime's official ideology but that in latter Tokugawa days many of them cooperated with Shintō and nationalist leaders and prepared the ground for the new Japan. Indeed, Confucianism was an intellectual bridge between the premodern and modern periods. And although the new regime depended heavily on Confucian ethical principles in its formulation of imperial ideology and the principles of sacred national polity, sensitive Confucians felt that those Confucian features had been dissolved into a new overarching framework with heavy imprints of Shintō and National Learning (Kokugaku). Confucians also resented the new regime's policy of organizing the educational system on Western models and welcoming Western learning ***(yōgaku)*** at the expense of, so they felt, traditionally important Confucian learning (Jugaku). After a decade of infatuation with things Western, however, a conservative mood returned, much to the comfort of Confucians. With the promulgation of the Imperial Rescript on Education and the adoption of compulsory "moral teaching" *(shūshin)* in school systems, Confucian values were domesticated and presented as indigenous moral values. The historic Chinese Confucian notion of *wang-tao* ("the way of true kingship") was recast into the framework of *kōdō* ("the imperial way"), and its ethical universalism was transformed into *nihon-shugi* ("Japanese-ism"). As such, "nonreligious" Confucian ethics supported "super-religious" State Shintō until the end of World War II.

Christianity. The appearance—or reappearance, as far as Roman Catholicism was concerned—of Christianity in Japan was due to the convergence of several factors. These included pressures both external and internal, both from Western powers and from enlightened Buddhist leaders who demanded religious freedom. Initially, the Meiji regime, in its eagerness to restore the ancient indigenous polity, arrested over three thousand "hidden Kirishitan" in Kyushu and sent them into exile in various parts of the country. However, foreign ministers strongly advised the Meiji regime, which was then eager to improve its treaties with Western nations, to change its anti-Christian policy. Feeling these pressures, the government lifted its ban against the "forbidden religion." This opened the door to missionary activity by Protestant as well as Roman Catholic and Russian Orthodox churches. From that time until 1945, Christian movements in Japan walked a tightrope between their own religious affirmation and the demands of the nation's inherent immanental theocratic principle.

The meaning of "religious freedom" was stated by Itō Hirobumi (1841–1909), the chief architect of the Meiji Constitution, as follows:

> *No believer in this or that religion has the right to place himself outside the pale of the law of the Empire, on the ground that he is serving his god. . . . Thus, although freedom of religious belief is complete and exempt from all restrictions, so long as manifestations of it are confined to the mind; yet with regard to external matters such as forms of worship and the mode of propagandism, certain necessary restrictions of law or regulations must be provided for, and besides, the general duties of subjects must be observed.*

This understanding of religious freedom was interpreted even more narrowly after the promulgation of the Imperial Rescript on Education; spokesmen of anti-Christian groups stressed that the Christian doctrine of universal love was incompatible with the national virtues of loyalty and filial piety taught explicitly in the Rescript. Some Christian leaders responded by stressing the compatibility of their faith and patriotism. Although a small group of Christian socialists and pacifists protested during the Sino-Japanese and Russo-Japanese wars, most Christians passively supported the war effort.

Another burden that the Christian movement has carried from the Meiji era to the present is its "foreignness." The anti-Kirishitan policy and all-embracing, unified meaning-structure of the Tokugawa synthesis that had lasted over two and a half centuries resulted in an exclusivistic mental attitude among the Japanese populace. A new religion thus found it difficult to penetrate from the outside. However, during the time of infatuation with things Western, curious or iconoclastic youths in urban areas were attracted by Christianity because of its foreignness. As a result, westernized intellectuals, lesser bureaucrats, and technicians became the core of the Christian community. Through them, and through church-related schools and philanthropic activities, the Christian influence made a far greater impact on Japan than many people realize.

Christianity in Japan, however, has also paid a high price for its foreignness. As might be expected, Christian churches in Japan, many of which had close relationships with their respective counterparts in the West, experienced difficult times in the 1930s. Under combined heavy pressure from militarists and Shintō leaders, both the Congregatio de Propanganda Fide in Rome and the National Christian Council of the Protestant Churches in Japan accepted the government's interpretation of State Shintō as "nonreligious." According to their view, obeisance at the State Shintō shrines as a nonreligious, patriotic act could be performed by all Japanese subjects. In 1939 all aspects of religion were placed under strict government control. In 1940 thirty-four Protestant churches were compelled to unite as the "Church of Christ in Japan." This church and the Roman Catholic church remained the only recognized Christian groups during World War II. During the war all religious groups were exploited by the government as ideological weapons. Individual religious leaders who did not cooperate with the government were jailed, intimidated, or tortured. Christians learned the bitter lesson that under the immanental theocratic system created in modern Japan the only religious freedom was, as stated by Itō Hirobumi, "confined to the mind."

Japanese Religion Today. In the modern world the destiny of any nation is as greatly influenced by external events as by domestic events. As far as modern Japan was concerned, such external events as the Chinese Revolution in 1912, World War I, the Russian Revolution, and the worldwide depression intermingled with events at home and propelled Japan to the world stage. Ironically, although World War I benefited the wealthy elite, the economic imbalance it produced drove desperate masses to rice riots and workers to labor strikes. Marxist student organizations were formed, and some serious college students joined the Communist party. Many people in lower social strata, benefiting little from modern civilization or industrial economy and neglected by institutionalized religions, turned to messianic and healing cults of the folk religious tradition. Thus, in spite of the government's determined effort to control religious groups and to prevent the emergence of new religions, it was reported that the number of quasi religions *(ruiji shūkyō)* increased from 98 in 1924 to 414 in 1930 and then to over one thousand in 1935. Many of them experienced harassment, intervention, and persecution by the government, and some of them chose for the sake of survival to affiliate with Buddhist or Kyōha Shintō sects. Important among the quasi-religious groups were Ōmotokyō, founded by Deguchi Nao (1836–1918); Hito no Michi, founded by Miki Tokuharu (1871–1938); and Reiyūkai, founded jointly by Kubo Kakutarō (1890–1944) and Kotani Kimi (1901–1971). After the end of World War II these quasi-religious groups and their spiritual cousins became the so-called new religions *(shinkō shūkyō)*. [*See* New Religions, *article on* New Religions in Japan; Ōmotokyō; *and* Reiyūkai Kyōdan.]

The end of World War II and the Allied occupation of Japan brought full-scale religious freedom, with far-reaching consequences, to Japanese religion. In December 1945 the Occupation force issued the Shintō Directive dismantling the official structure of State Shintō; on New Year's Day 1946 the emperor publicly denied his divinity. Understandably, the loss of the sacral kingship and State Shintō undercut the mytho-historical foundation of Japanese religion that had endured from time immemorial. The new civil code of 1947 effectively abolished the traditional system of interlocking households *(ie seido)* as a legal institution, so that individuals were no longer bound by the religious affiliation of their households. The erosion of family cohesion greatly weakened the Buddhist parish system *(danka)* as well as the Shintō parish systems *(ujiko)*.

The abrogation of the ill-famed Religious Organizations Law (enacted in 1939 and enforced in 1940) also radically altered the religious scene. Assured of religious freedom and separation of religion and state by the Religious Corporations Ordinance, all religious groups (Buddhist, Christian, Shintō—now called Shrine Shintō—and others) began energetic activities. This turn of events made it possible for quasi religions and Buddhist or Sect Shintō splinter groups to become independent. Sect Shintō, which comprised 13 groups before the war, developed into 75 groups by 1949. With the emergence of other new religions the total number of religious groups reached 742 by 1950. However, with the enactment of the Religious Juridical Persons Law (Shūkyō hōjin hō) in 1951, the number was reduced to 379—142 in the Shintō tradition, 169 Buddhist groups, 38 Christian denominations, and 30 miscellaneous groups.

In the immediate postwar period, when many people suffered from uncertainty, poverty, and loss of confidence, many men and women were attracted by what the new religions claimed to offer: mundane happiness, tightly knit religious organizations, healing, and readily accessible earthly deities or divine agents. It is worth noting in this connection that the real prosperity of the new religions in Japan came after the Korean War, with the heavy trend toward urbanization. Not only did the urban population increase significantly, but the entire nation assumed the character of an industrialized society. In this situation some of the new religions, especially two Buddhist groups, namely, Sōka Gakkai and Risshō Kōseikai, gained a large number of followers among the new middle class. Some of these new religions took an active part in political affairs. For example, as early as 1962, Sōka Gakkai scored an impressive success in the elections of the House of Councillors, and its own political wing, Kōmeitō, now enjoys a bargaining power that no other religiously based group has achieved in modern Japanese politics. Other groups have also attempted to gain political influence by campaigning for their favorite candidates for political offices. [*See* Sōka Gakkai *and* Risshō Kōseikai.]

It has not been easy for older Buddhist groups to adjust to the changing social situation, especially since many of them lost their traditional financial support in the immediate postwar period. Also, religious freedom unwittingly fostered schisms among some of them. Nevertheless, the strength of the older Buddhist groups lies in their following among the intelligentsia and the rural population. Japanese Buddhological scholarship deservedly enjoys an international reputation. Japanese Buddhist leaders are taking increasingly active roles in pan-Asian and global Buddhist affairs while at the same time attending to such issues as peace and disarmament at home.

Christian churches, which had experienced hardship and mental anguish before and during World War II, rejoiced over their religious freedom after the war. They showed determination as they confronted many neglected problems, repairing church buildings damaged during the war, regrouping their scattered adherents, and training young leaders for the ministry. However, the popular interest in Christianity that developed in the immediate postwar years waned quickly. Furthermore, the massive support Christian churches expected from abroad never materialized, largely owing to the erosion of missionary incentive among Western churches except in Roman Catholic and fundamentalist groups. Christianity in Japan still suffers from its foreignness, its theological conservatism, and the lack of grass-roots participation in rural areas. On the other hand, church-related educational institutions are growing, and younger Christians are cooperating with other religionists in dealing with social and political issues.

It is difficult to feel the pulse of Japanese religion in the late twentieth century because the external signs are too contradictory. In the midst of their highly technological industrial society, the Japanese people still feel close to nature, still love poetry and the arts, and still observe numerous traditional rituals. A significant part of Japanese religious life continues to focus on family values and on observances performed in the home. [*See* Domestic Observances, *article on* Japanese Practices.] In addition, in spite of high literacy and scientific education, many men and women of high and low social status still subscribe to fortune telling, geomancy, and healing cults. The Japanese are avid global travelers, and yet their world of meaning is still strongly tied to their land, language, custom, and tradition. Furthermore, one is amazed by the quick recovery of Shintō, which smoothly transformed itself from State Shintō to Shrine Shintō almost overnight during the Allied occupation. Millions of pilgrims and worshipers continue to visit large and small Shintō shrines. Understandably, all these contradictory features are difficult for the Japanese to resolve. It may well be that with the redefinition of the once-divine monarchy and the loss of an overarching religious form, the character of the nebulous but deep-rooted Japanese religion has been transformed into a new framework that accommodates a genuine coexistence of different religious forms in the name of religious freedom.

BIBLIOGRAPHY

General Introduction

Anesaki, Masaharu. *History of Japanese Religion.* 2d ed. Rutland, Vt., 1963.

Earhart, H. Byron. *Religion in the Japanese Experience: Sources and Interpretations.* Encino, Calif., 1974.

Hori, Ichirō, ed. *Japanese Religion.* Tokyo and Palo Alto, Calif., 1972.

Kitagawa, Joseph M. *Religion in Japanese History.* New York and London, 1966.

Kitagawa, Joseph M. "The Religions of Japan." In *A Reader's Guide to the Great Religions,* 2d ed., edited by Charles J. Adams, pp. 247–282. New York, 1977. This bibliographic essay includes an appendix listing reference works, published bibliographies, and periodicals relevant to the religions of Japan.

Nakamura, Hajime. *Ways of Thinking of Eastern Peoples: India, China, Tibet, Japan.* Honolulu, 1964.

Sansom, George B. *Japan: A Short Cultural History.* New York, 1931.

Sansom, George B. *A History of Japan.* 3 vols. Stanford, Calif., 1958–1963.

Tsunoda, Ryūsaku, Wm. Theodore de Bary, and Donald Keene, comps. *Sources of Japanese Tradition.* New York and London, 1958.

Prehistoric Background

Groot, Gerard J. *The Prehistory of Japan.* New York, 1951.
Haguenauer, Charles M. *Origines de la civilisation japonaise,* pt. 1. Paris, 1956.
Kidder, Jonathan Edward, Jr. *Japan before Buddhism.* Rev. ed. New York, 1966.
Kitagawa, Joseph M. "Prehistoric Background of Japanese Religion." *History of Religions* 2 (Winter 1963): 292–328.
Komatsu, Isao. *The Japanese People: Origins of the People and the Language.* Tokyo, 1962.
Oka, Masao. "Kulturschichten in Alt-Japan." Ph.D. diss., Vienna University, 1933.

Early Historical Period. Basic textual sources are two mytho-historical writings, *Kojiki,* translated by Donald L. Philippi (Princeton and Tokyo, 1969), and *Nihongi: Chronicles of Japan from the Earliest Times to A.D. 697,* translated by William George Aston (Rutland, Vt., and Tokyo, 1972). Other important textual sources available in English are *The Manyōshū: One Thousand Poems,* translated by the Nippon Gakujutsu Shinkōkai (1940; reprint, New York and London, 1965); *Kogoshūi: Gleanings from Ancient Stories,* translated by Genchi Katō and Hikoshiro Hoshinō, 3d ed. (1926; reprint, New York and London, 1972); and *Izumo Fudoki,* translated by Michiko Y. Aoki (Tokyo, 1971). Regarding the development of the early historic Japanese society and nation, see *Japan in the Chinese Dynastic Histories,* translated and compiled by Ryūsaku Tsunoda, and edited by L. Carrington Goodrich (South Pasadena, Calif., 1951); Robert Karl Reischauer's *Early Japanese History, c. 40 B.C.–A.D. 1167,* 2 vols. (Princeton, 1937); Paul Wheatley and Thomas See's *From Court to Capital* (Chicago and London, 1978); Kan'ichi Asakawa's *The Early Institutional Life of Japan: A Study in the Reform of 645 A.D.*, 2d ed. (New York, 1903); and Richard J. Miller's *Ancient Japanese Nobility: The 'Kabane' Ranking System* (Berkeley and London, 1974).

Historical Period. Most of the books available in Western languages on the historical development of Japanese religion focus on particular religious traditions, primarily Shintō and Buddhism.

For translations of primary texts, see *Norito: A New Translation of the Ancient Japanese Ritual Prayers,* translated by Donald L. Philippi (Tokyo, 1959), and *Engi-Shiki: Procedures of the Engi Era,* 2 vols., translated by Felicia Bock (Tokyo, 1970– 1972), which give us a glimpse of the Shintō foundation of the Ritsuryō state and its immanental theocracy.

Important studies of Shintō are Karl Florenz's *Die historischen Quellen der Shintō-Religion* (Leipzig, 1919); David Clarence Holtom's *The National Faith of Japan* (1938; reprint, New York, 1965); Genchi Katō's *A Study of Shintō* (Tokyo, 1926); and Tsunetsugu Muraoka's *Studies in Shinto Thought,* translated by Delmer M. Brown and James T. Araki (Tokyo, 1964). Holtom's *The Japanese Enthronement Ceremonies* (1928; reprint, Tokyo, 1972) and Robert S. Ellwood, Jr.'s *The Feast of Kingship* (Tokyo, 1973) portray an important aspect of the "Imperial Household" Shintō.

Works on Japanese Buddhism are numerous, including denominational histories, biographies of important Buddhist figures, and expositions of their writings. Among them, those that deal with Japanese Buddhism as a whole are Masaharu Anesaki's *Buddhist Art in Its Relation to Buddhist Ideals, with Special Reference to Buddhism in Japan* (1915; reprint, New York, 1978); Sir Charles Eliot's *Japanese Buddhism,* 2d ed. (London, 1959); Alicia Matsunaga's *The Buddhist Philosophy of Assimilation: The Historical Development of the 'Honji-Suijaku Theory'* (Tokyo, 1969); E. Dale Saunders's *Buddhism in Japan* (Philadelphia, 1964); Emile Steinilber-Oberlin and Kuni Matsuo's *The Buddhist Sects of Japan,* translated by Marc Logé (London, 1938); Marinus Willem de Visser's *Ancient Buddhism in Japan,* 2 vols. (Leiden and Paris, 1935);

and Shōkō Watanabe's *Japanese Buddhism: A Critical Appraisal,* rev. ed. (Tokyo, 1968). On the eclectic Mountain Priesthood, see H. Byron Earhart's *A Religious Study of the Mount Haguro Sect of Shugendō* (Tokyo, 1970).

Books in Western languages on Japanese Confucianism are few and mostly dated. However, mention should be made of Robert Cornell Armstrong's *Light from the East: Studies in Japanese Confucianism* (Tokyo, 1914); Kaibara Ekken's *The Way of Contentment,* translated by Ken Hoshino (1904; reprint, New York, 1913); Olaf G. Lidin's translation of Ogyū Sorai's *Distinguishing the Way: Bendō* (Tokyo, 1970); Warren W. Smith, Jr.'s *Confucianism in Modern Japan* (Tokyo, 1959); and Joseph John Spae's *Itō Jinsai* (1948; reprint, New York, 1967). For the nebulous but persistent influence of Taoism and the Yin-yang school on Japanese religion, see Bernard Frank's *Kata-imi et kata-tagae* (Paris, 1958) and Ivan I. Morris's *The World of the Shining Prince: Court Life in Ancient Japan* (1964; reprint, New York, 1979).

The standard work on Japanese folk religion is Hori Ichirō's *Folk Religion in Japan: Continuity and Change,* edited by Joseph M. Kitagawa and Alan L. Miller (Chicago, 1968). Various aspects of folk religion are discussed in Geoffrey Bownas's *Japanese Rainmaking and Other Folk Practices* (London, 1963), U. A. Casal's *The Five Sacred Festivals of Ancient Japan* (Tokyo, 1967), and Cornelis Ouwehand's *Namazu-e and Their Themes* (Leiden, 1964).

Regarding Christianity in Japan, see Otis Cary's *A History of Christianity in Japan,* 2 vols. (1909; reprint, New York, 1971), and Richard Henry Drummond's *A History of Christianity in Japan* (Grand Rapids, Mich., 1971). On the Catholic church in Japan, see Joseph Jennes's *History of the Catholic Church in Japan: From Its Beginnings to the Early Meiji Period, 1549–1873* (Tokyo, 1973). On its development in the sixteenth and seventeenth centuries, see Charles Ralph Boxer's *The Christian Century in Japan, 1549–1650* (1951; reprint, Berkeley, 1967) and George Elison's *Deus Destroyed* (Cambridge, Mass., 1973). For Protestant Christianity in Japan, see Charles W. Iglehart's *A Century of Protestant Christianity in Japan* (Rutland, Vt., and Tokyo, 1959) and Charles H. Germany's *Protestant Theologies in Modern Japan* (Tokyo, 1965).

The most helpful introduction to Japanese religion in the modern period is *Japanese Religion in the Meiji Era,* edited and compiled by Hideo Kishimoto and translated by John F. Howes (Tokyo, 1956). For the guiding ideologies of the prewar Japanese government, see *Kokutai no Hongi,* edited by Robert King Hall and translated by John Owen Gauntlett (Cambridge, 1949), and Hall's *Shūshin: The Ethics of a Defeated Nation* (New York, 1949). Charles William Hepner's *The Kurozumi Sect of Shintō* (Tokyo, 1935), Delwin B. Schneider's *Konkō kyō: A Japanese Religion* (Tokyo, 1962), and Henry van Straelen's *The Religion of Divine Wisdom* (Tokyo, 1954) discuss the three so-called Sect (Kyōha) Shintō groups. Daniel Clarence Holtom's *Modern Japan and Shintō Nationalism* (Chicago, 1943) deals with the way Shintō was used for political purposes before and during the war.

As to the religious development after World War II, William P. Woodard's *The Allied Occupation of Japan, 1945–1952, and Japanese Religions* (Leiden, 1972) gives us the Occupation army's religious policy and its implications for Japanese religions. Those who want to read of the postwar religious ethos in Japan will find the following works informative: Robert J. Smith's *Ancestor Worship in Contemporary Japan* (Stanford, Calif., 1974), Joseph John Spae's *Japanese Religiosity* (Tokyo, 1971), Fernando M. Basabe, Anzai Shin, and Federico Lanzaco's *Religious Attitudes of Japanese Men* (Tokyo, 1968), and Fernando M. Basabe, Anzai Shin, and Alphonso M. Nebreda's *Japanese Youth Confronts Religion: A Sociological Survey* (Tokyo, 1967). Concerning numerous "new religions" *(shinkō shūkyō),* which have mushroomed since 1945, consult H. Byron Earhart's *The New Religions of Japan: A Bibliography of Western Language Materials,* 2d ed. (Ann Arbor, 1983).

15 KOREAN RELIGION

YIM SUK-JAY, ROGER L. JANELLI, and DAWNHEE YIM JANELLI

Confucianism, Taoism, and Buddhism, often said to be Korea's major religions, all came to Korea from or through China. Another faith, indigenous to Korea, has usually been considered superstition rather than religion because it lacks an explicitly formulated, elaborated, and rationalized body of doctrine. Yet this indigenous creed possesses a rich set of supernatural beliefs, a mythology, and a variety of ritual practices. In recent years, therefore, an increasing number of scholars have come to recognize this folk system of beliefs and rites as another of Korea's major religious traditions.

Little is known about the early history of Korea's indigenous religion. Few Korean records compiled before the latter half of the Koryŏ dynasty (918–1392 CE) survive today. Korea's earliest known myths, recorded in the twelfth and thirteenth centuries, are concerned with the creation of early kingdoms and bear little resemblance to the folk religion and oral mythology collected by folklorists in more recent times.

The importation from China of all three of Korea's elite religious traditions resulted not only from Korea's geographical proximity to the Middle Kingdom but also from the political relationship of these two nations prior to the twentieth century. China's cultural influence on its eastern neighbor began even before the Three Kingdoms period (fourth to seventh century CE); after the unification of the Korean Peninsula, regular exchanges with China continued, as Korea was a tributary state of the Chinese empire. Contacts with othernearby societies, principally Japan, were less frequent; Japanese culture never enjoyed the respect that Koreans held for Chinese civilization.

The three major religious traditions that came to Korea from China arrived more than fifteen hundred years ago and were selected, transformed, and adapted in varying degrees to the social and intellectual conditions prevailing on the Korean Peninsula. As a result, these elite traditions in Korea often differ from their Chinese counterparts. Korean Taoism, for example, is primarily early or philosophical Taoism. Lacking its own priests,temples, and rituals, its ideology is evident chiefly in fortune-telling and geomancy. Human longevity and magical transformations, themes characteristic of later or religious Taoism, are evident in Korean folktales, however. Similarly, Buddhism adapted itself to Korea by absorbing a number of native Korean deities into its pantheon and folk ritual practices into its liturgy. Even the fundamentalist approach to Neo-Confucianism taken by the Chosŏn (Yi) government (1392–1910) did not entirely prevent modifications of its ritual prescriptions to suit indigenous beliefs and social mores.

Affiliation with a traditional Korean religion entailed participation at some of its rites or acceptance of at least part of its ideology rather than exclusive membership in a church organization. As a result, participants at rituals usually include already existing social groups—such as family, village, or extended kinship group—rather than a specially constituted church congregation. Another result has been a religious eclecticism constrained not by feelings of commitment to one faith or sense of contradiction between disparate beliefs but by traditional role expectations of men and women. In many Korean families, men perform ancestor rites and consult geomancers whereas women make offerings to household gods and confer with fortunetellers, but even this gender division of labor is not rigidly observed.

The absence of church congregations not only facilitated eclecticism and adaptation but also allowed significant regional, social, and even interpersonal variations in religious belief and practice. Nowhere is this more evident than in Korea's indigenous folk religion, where the lack of written scripture further encouraged diversity. In the sections below, I identify the most prevalent of the traditional ideas and rites, but variant forms can be found for many of these beliefs and practices.

During the nineteenth century, much of the traditional East Asian world order collapsed, and two major developments in Korean religion soon followed: the rise of Christianity and the emergence of various new religions. Christianity is unique in that it is difficult to characterize as a Korean religion, for the beliefs and rites of its major denominations have apparently not undergone significant indigenization. The adaptation of Christian rites and beliefs occurs readily in several of the new religions, however. These eclectic religious organizations draw upon Christianity as well as traditional Korean faiths in formulating their own respective doctrines and liturgies. Yet the established Christian churches, rather than the new religions, have attracted the larger following in South Korea. (Data on contemporary religion in North Korea are not readily available.) The greater success of Christianity compared with that of the new religions contrasts strikingly with their respective fates in Japan and presents one of the major puzzles of modern Korean religion.

INDIGENOUS FOLK RELIGION

Little can be known with certainty about the history of Korea's indigenous folk religion. Ancient Chinese histories, which occasionally mentioned customs or events in Korea, say nothing about this belief system or its rites. The *Samguk sagi* and the *Samguk yusa,* Korea's earliest histories, compiled in the twelfth and thirteenth centuries, respectively, contain extensive accounts of the Three Kingdoms period but reveal only that people called *mu* existed at that time. The word *mu* is written with the same Chinese character as the first syllable of the Korean word *mudang,* the term used in recent times to designate a ritual specialist of Korea's folk religion; the orthographic correspondence suggests some sort of relationship between the two terms. The early histories do not provide a clear description of the *mu*'s activities or functions, however, and much scholarly effort has been expended trying to interpret the relevant passages.

The earliest source on the rituals of Korea's folk religion appears in the *Tongguk Yi Sangguk chip,* a collection of poems and essays by Yi Kyu-bo (1168–1241). One of his poems describes some folk religious practices only briefly, but the description corresponds with the rites presently performed by *mudang* in Kyŏnggi Province, located in the western-central part of the Korean Peninsula. Historical documents from the Chosŏn dynasty contain frequent references to *mudang* and their activities, but these references are primarily condemnations of *mudang* or legal sanctions against their practices rather than descriptions of ethnographic value. Compiled by Confucian literati, these documents describe *mudang* as charlatans, assess heavy taxes on them in order to hinder their activities, and ascribe them to the lowest class of Chosŏn society. Despite these repressive sanctions, however, Korea's folk religion remained embedded in everyday life. New *mudang* continue to emerge today, and their rites still occur regularly in rural areas and frequently in urban areas as well.

Religious Specialists. Though different regional terms also exist, the term *mudang* is used throughout Korea to designate the specialists of Korea's folk religion. It is usually translated into English as "shaman," but this translation is problematic because several different definitions have been advanced for the term *shaman.* Moreover, there are two types of *mudang*—possessed *(kangsin mu)* and hereditary *(sesŭp mu)*—and only the former fits some of the better-known definitions.

An apparently normal person, usually a woman, begins the process of becoming a *kangsin mu* when she exhibits some of the following symptoms: loss of appetite, the drinking only of water, use of crude language, violent behavior, unintelligible speech, and going off to mountains and subsequently not recalling her activities while there. When normal attempts at treatment fail, these symptoms are interpreted as signs of "spirit illness" *(sinbyŏng),* an illness that can be relieved only by becoming a *mudang.*

A woman who is to become a *kangsin mu* is apprenticed to a senior *mudang* with whom she establishes a spiritual mother-daughter relationship. From her spiritual mother, the novice acquires ritual techniques, a more detailed knowledge of the supernatural, and other lore; by engaging in shamanistic activities in this way, the apprentice's spirit illness is relieved and her abnormal behavior ceases. After a period of apprenticeship, the spiritual mother performs an initiation ritual for the novice, who thereby becomes a full-fledged *mudang.* During the rites she performs throughout her career, various deities or ancestors "descend" or "come" to speak and act through her body. Should the new *mudang* abandon the role for any length of time, her spirit illness would return.

The other mode of recruitment into the profession of *mudang* entails heredity rather than spirit possession. *Mudang* and their families belonged to the lowest social stratum in the Chosŏn dynasty and thus frequently intermarried. A girl born of such a family usually married into another *mudang*'s household and then accompanied her mother-in-law's ritual performances, acquiring the latter's song texts, dances, and other ritual techniques. Unlike *kangsin mu*, *sesŭp mu* did not suffer from spirit illness, did not undergo initiation rites, did not become possessed at rituals, and were never men. A male born into a *sesŭp mu*'s family learned how to sing, play musical instruments, and perform acrobatic feats. With these skills he became an entertainer or assisted at his wife's and mother's rites.

Until recently, possessed and hereditary *mudang* occupied different regions of Korea. The Han River, which flows across the center of Korea, affords a rough dividing line between two of these major regions. To its north, *kangsin mu* prevailed; and to its south, *sesŭp mu* predominated. Cheju-do, Korea's largest island, located off the peninsula's southern coast, constituted a third region. There, both possessed and hereditary *mudang* were common. Today, however, these regional differences are disappearing rapidly and possessed *mudang* prevail everywhere in South Korea.

Pantheon. The pantheon of Korea's folk religion is polytheistic. A variety of gods are available to aid supplicants, bring them good fortune, and help them avoid misfortune. Some of these deities are known only in particular regions, but the following are known throughout Korea and are among those that most often receive rites: Mountain God, Earth God, Dragon King God, Smallpox God, Seven-Star God, God of Luck (Chesŏk), God of the House Site, Kitchen God, and Birth God. These represent only a small fraction of the total pantheon, however. More than three hundred names have been collected, and the number of Korean deities is even greater since several of them are often designated by the same term. A different mountain god exists for each mountain, for example.

Many of the folk deities have particular functions or territorial domains, but unlike the deities of Chinese folk religion, the Korean gods are not believed to be organized into a vast supernatural bureaucracy. Mountain God, for example, has for his domain a mountain's earth, rocks, trees, and landslides; Dragon King God is in charge of a lake, a sea, or a stream, and such activities as fishing and sailing. Similarly, God of the House Beam is charged with a household's prosperity, God of Luck with its property, and Seven-Star God with regulating each member's life span. With a few possible exceptions, each of these deities is autonomous. Indeed, they do not even consult or communicate with each other when carrying out their various functions.

A possible exception to the autonomy of Korean deities is implied by differences in ritual treatment accorded the various supernatural beings. Some are invited by the *mudang* to receive individual rites and food offerings not presented to others. Among the various household gods, for example, the god of the house beam and the god of the house site belong to the former category; the toilet god, the gate god, and the chimney god belong to the latter. The treatment of this latter category is not unlike that given to wandering and hungry ghosts, souls of the dead who have no descendants to care for them. Thus they gather at feasts to obtain a small handout. Some food is strewn about the ground for these supernaturals whenever *mudang* perform rites for the major deities.

The systematic differences in treatment offered to Korean deities imply differences in status and, in turn, authority. Yet even status differences are not expressed explicitly in *mudang*'s songs or articulated by believers. Neither are the deities equal, however. Some are more important than others because their domains cover activities that are particularly significant or frequently undertaken by believers. Perhaps *parallelotheism* is the best term for characterizing the autonomy, lack of hierarchy, and even lack of communication between Korean deities. Like parallel lines, each occupies its own space without meeting the others.

The deities are not thought to be inherently good or evil; whether they are helpful or harmful depends on the circumstances. If they are treated with regular offerings, they bring good fortune; otherwise, they inflict punishment. The god of the house beam, charged with taking care of the household's prosperity, and the god of luck, charged with its property, would seem to be purely helpful or protective deities. But if they are ignored, before long they will inflict poverty on the household. Nor is the smallpox god, who brings the disease to children, an entirely harmful deity. If taken care of properly and given food offerings, this god not only reduces the severity of the illness but may even bring good fortune as well.

The place where the deities reside is not clearly set forth in the indigenous belief system. Apparently the deities do not live in this world but inhabit an upper world, a higher plane than mortals, for the *mudang* invite them to "descend" and informants often say that "they look down on us." Yet the deities do not dwell in any specially designated or sacred area, such as the Mount Olympus of Greek mythology. Some informants say that a mountain god resides in a particular mountain, or a river god in a river; but whenever a *mudang* performs a rite for one of these deities, even at the site of its own domain, the god is invited to come to the rite, which would seem to imply that the god normally dwells elsewhere.

One characteristic of the Korean deities that stands out quite clearly is their dislike of dirt. Before invoking the gods at a major shamanistic rite, a great deal of effort is expended to clean the area where the ritual is to be performed. Dead animals and feces are removed, clean earth spread about, and straw rope used to cordon off the area. The food offerings, decorations, and other material objects used at the rite should be new, purchased on an auspicious date, and bought without haggling over their prices. Ritual participants should wash themselves and not taste the food offerings while they are being prepared. They should also be careful not to allow any spittle, hair, fingernail clippings, or dust to fall into the food. Prohibited from visiting the site of the ritual are people considered ritually "dirty," such as those in mourning, those who recently saw a dead body or attended a funeral, pregnant women, or those who have a swelling of any kind. Finally, the *mudang* usually performs a cleansing rite at the start of a major ritual. *Mudang* say that gods invited to a dirty place would inflict punishment instead of bringing good fortune.

The deities that figure in present-day rites of Korean *mudang* include not only those who originally belonged to Korea's indigenous religion but those who were added after the importation of Buddhism, Taoism, and Confucianism. Typically, these latter gods are thought to be male and have no special activity or function under their control. The indigenous deities, by contrast, are usually thought to be female and charged with major functions. Some of the originally female deities, however, appear to have changed their gender with the passage of time. Although it is far from conclusive, some evidence suggests that female deities were originally the most important in Korea's folk religion and that male deities came to be added as a result of centuries of pervasive Neo-Confucianism and male dominance.

Rituals. The rituals of Korean folk religion, generally known as *kut,* vary greatly in complexity, but three major categories can be identified. The simplest, called a *pison,* consists of no more than rubbing one's hands together to implore the assistance of a deity. The second type is called a *p'uttakkŏri* or *kosa,* depending on whether its purpose is to remove a present misfortune or seek a future benefit. At a *p'uttakkŏri* or *kosa,* food is offered to the deities.

The third and largest type of the major rituals, generally known as a grand *kut,* may involve as many as seven or eight *mudang* and musicians and may last from three to seven days and nights. A grand *kut* is a comprehensive rite offered to all the deities as well as to ancestors and ghosts. Several tables of food offerings are prepared, decorated with paper flowers, and furnished with candles and incense. The rite itself is usually composed of about fifteen to twenty-five sections *(kŏri, sŏk),* each comprising a *mudang*'s song, dance, instrumental music, and dialogue with supernatural beings.

The songs sung by the *mudang,* different for each of the *kut*'s sections, take anywhere from a half hour to three hours to perform. Their texts have been handed down orally, but the songs are not rigidly memorized and sung by rote. Though *mudang* usually adhere to their song's general content and structure, they often add, omit, or rearrange sections, depending on the purposes of the *kut,* the circumstances of the family or village sponsoring it, and other contingencies.

The contents of the *mudang*'s songs reveal much about the ideology of Korean folk religion. Rather than honor deities or thank them for past favors, the songs plead for good fortune or the removal of misfortune. Thus, the gods are perceived not primarily as objects of admiration and respect but as tools with which to satisfy one's desires. Related to this view is the timing of most *kut:* they are more often held when a specific need arises rather than on a regular or periodic basis.

The dialogue between the supernatural beings, speaking through the mouths of the *mudang,* and the persons who sponsor a *kut* is also instructive. Typically, the deities complain that their food offerings are inadequate; the sponsors respond by apologizing for being unable to prepare more, blame their poverty (and, by implication, the deities) for this inability, and promise to present larger offerings in the future if their economic situation improves. The gods then respond by saying that they will accept the offering this time and promise to bring good fortune to the supplicants.

Maintaining or improving the welfare of a household, either through economic aid or by relieving the illness of one of its members, is perhaps the most frequent motive for sponsoring a *kut.* Other common motives are promoting the welfare of a village and leading the soul of a recently deceased family member to the other-world. A special *kut,* held when a child was afflicted with smallpox, was also very common in the past, but the eradication of this disease in Korea has obviated its *kut* as well.

ANCESTOR WORSHIP

The history of Korean ancestor worship is better documented than the history of Korean folk religion, though it too suffers from a paucity of written records before the end of the Koryŏ dynasty (918–1392). Some form of rites for the dead probably existed in prehistoric times, and Buddhism was closely involved with such rites at the time of its importation from China in the fourth century CE. By the end of the Koryŏ dynasty, both Buddhist and *mudang* rites for the dead evidently existed. Such rites can still be seen today, and traces of Buddhist teachings are still evident in Korean funeral customs.

The establishment of the Chosŏn dynasty (1392–1910) brought the adoption of Neo-Confucianism as Korea's official ideology and government efforts to transform ancestor rites to a Neo-Confucian format. Particularly seminal was the *Chu-tzu chia-li,* a ritual manual attributed to the Chinese philosopher Chu Hsi. By the end of the Chosŏn dynasty, Neo-Confucian ancestor rites, with modifications, became generally accepted throughout most of the population. Even today, many Korean households have etiquette books with instructions for ancestor rites derived in some measure from the *Chu-tzu chia-li.*

The Chosŏn dynasty transformation of ideology and ancestor ritual procedures was accompanied by profound changes in Korean family and kinship organization as well as significant alterations in the structure of ancestor ritual obligations. As primogeniture and membership in patrilineal descent groups assumed greater importance toward the middle of the dynasty, women gradually lost their ritual responsibilities and eldest sons assumed a greater role in ancestor worship than any of their siblings.

Rituals. The kind of ritual activity directed toward an ancestor depends largely on the length of time that has elapsed since his or her death. A funeral usually begins with calling out the name of the deceased while setting forth shoes and rice for the death messenger(s) who come to escort the souls of the deceased along a difficult journey to face judgment in the underworld. The remainder of the funeral, during which visitors make condolence calls and the corpse is prepared for burial, usually lasts three days: the day of death, the following day, and the day of burial.

After the funeral is completed, a spirit shrine is erected at the home of the deceased. There his or her soul is said to reside for the duration of the formal mourning period. During this period interaction with the deceased is modeled closely on behavior appropriate toward living elderly parents. For example, portions of daily meals are placed at the spirit shrine, and visitors to the home are brought to the shrine to greet the deceased, just as they would be brought to greet elderly parents.

For the next four generations, ancestors receive rites at the home of their eldest son or subsequent primogeniture descendant (eldest son of the eldest son, etc.) on death anniversaries and holidays. Until recently, wooden ancestor tablets representing four generations of deceased paternal forebears and their wives were kept at the homes where the rites were offered, but in recent decades these have been almost entirely replaced by paper tablets, which are prepared for each ritual and later burned.

After four generations have passed, the primogeniture descendant is relieved of his obligations to offer an ancestor's death-anniversary and holiday rites. In their place, one ritual a year is offered at the ancestor's grave, usually in the fall. These grave rites are financed by a small piece of farmland acquired for this purpose by the ancestor's patrilineal descendants. It is rented out to a cultivator who, in return for its use, provides the food offerings and labor needed for the rite. By this method, the rites can be offered in perpetuity.

One of the striking features of Korean "ancestor" worship is that participants at these rites are not limited to patrilineal descendants of the commemorated ancestor but often include other agnatic kinsmen as well. This is especially true of holiday rites where several patrilineally related men reside together. In such communities, first, second, and even third cousins participate in the rites for each other's fathers, grandfathers, and great-grandfathers as well as in the rite for their common great-great-grandfather.

Not all of the dead receive the same complement of rites. A few famous people, granted the special privilege of permanent ancestor tablets by the Chosŏn government, receive death-anniversary rites perpetually. At the other end of the social scale are those whose descendants are dispersed and unorganized or too poor to provide grave rites for their ancestors beyond four generations. Others, who die without descendants, may receive only holiday rites from their next of kin or no rites at all. For these descendantless dead, rituals other than Neo-Confucian forms may also be offered: a tablet can be made and cared for by priests at a Buddhist temple or by a *mudang* in her shrine.

Even ancestors who receive standard Neo-Confucian rites also receive *mudang* rites. Shortly after death, such a rite may be offered to comfort the soul of the deceased and guide its transition to the otherworld. And most *kut* performed by *mudang* include a section for the benefit of the sponsoring household's deceased relatives. When performed by a *kangsin mu,* it takes the form of a séance.

Ritual attention is given to ancestors on yet other occasions. When a bride first enters her husband's family, for example, she bows before the tablets of the ancestors regularly commemorated by his household. A person's death may be reported to his ancestor, represented by a tablet; or an impending burial may be reported at the grave of the senior ancestor already interred on the same hill or mountain. And visits to ancestors' graves, usually to ensure their maintenance, are often accompanied by offerings of food and wine.

Ideas About the Afterlife. Rites for ancestors take place in three different contexts, each implying a different location for the soul: before ancestor tablets, at graves, and at seances to which ancestors "come" from the otherworld. When pressed, individuals can justify these seemingly disparate practices by reciting the well-known saying that each person has three souls. In other situations, however, this multiplicity of souls is rarely mentioned.

With the exception of *mudang,* few people claim certain knowledge of the afterlife, but some basic ideas are prevalent. In general, the dead are thought to remain in the same condition as they were at the time of death and thus to retain the same need for clothing, shelter, and, especially, food. To meet these needs, sets of clothing are occasionally offered at *mudang* rites, graves are maintained, and food offerings are presented at Neo-Confucian rites. Those without offspring to provide for their needs, those whose offspring are negligent, or those who still retain some other pressing desire from their earthly existence and therefore cannot enter the otherworld are the dead who are most likely to afflict the living with illness or other misfortune in order to draw attention to their plight. Ancestors are generally thought to be benevolent, but when sudden illness or other misfortune arises, some consideration may be given to the possibility that a dead relative or other deceased person may have been the cause.

In cases of affliction, the ritual offering provided to the dead depends in large measure on his or her relationship to the living. Moving or repairing a grave is done only for patrilineal forebears and their wives. Any relative may be offered a Buddhist or *mudang* rite, however, though such rites are normally sponsored by descendants or, in their absence, next of kin. In general, responsibility for care of the dead falls on their closest living relatives, for nearest kin have the greatest obligation toward each other and thus are the most likely targets of retribution if care of the dead is inadequate. A dead stranger, by contrast, can afflict anyone but is given only a small food offering. Dead strangers, like beggars, can demand a small amount of food but not clothing, housing, or a large feast. In other words, obligations to the dead perpetuate obligations between the living.

DIVINATION AND FORTUNE-TELLING

A plethora of methods for fortune-telling and divination are known in Korea. Major differences can be seen in their philosophical foundations, practitioners, and scope, and even in the seriousness with which they are regarded. This section does not provide a systematic examination of all these characteristics for every technique but indicates the range of variation found among the more prevalent methods. Many others also exist, but they are more esoteric and less widely practiced.

Most of the divination practiced by professional fortune-tellers falls into two major categories: spirit divination and horoscope reading. The first is used by possessed *mudang* and possessed diviners. Though the latter, unlike *mudang,* do not perform *kut,* their divination techniques are the same. Speaking through the mouth of either a *mudang* or diviner, a supernatural being makes a revelation about the cause of a present misfortune or predicts a future event or condition. Often the fortune-teller mimics the spirit that is providing the revelation, speaking like a child, for example, when possessed by a dead child.

Mudang and spirit diviners also make predictions by interpreting patterns formed by grains of rice or tossed coins. Or they may have a client randomly select one of five colored flags. These methods, too, can be regarded as forms of spirit divination, for it is generally thought that a supernatural being shapes the patterns or causes a particular flag to be chosen.

Horoscope reading, the other major form of fortune-telling practiced by professional diviners, is especially prevalent in cities. Based on the theory that the time of a person's birth determines the main course of his or her life, horoscope reading utilizes the system of reckoning time according to the sexegenary cycle. Each year, month, day, and two-hour period is designated by one of sixty pairs of Chinese characters; and combining the four pairs associated with a person's year, month, day, and hour of birth yields eight characters. These are translated into predictions according to a variety of complex methods described in several printed manuals. Mastery of these complex methods is said to demand years of study, and their practice is limited to professional fortune-tellers who specialize in them. Since men enjoyed greater opportunities for study and the acquisition of literacy in traditional Korea, it is primarily they who practice horoscope reading. Most spirit diviners, by contrast, are women.

In addition to spirit divination and horoscope reading, professional fortune-telling includes less popular but still widely known methods. Most popular among these are reading hands and facial configurations or determining a person's fate from the number of strokes used to write his or her personal name. Like horoscope reading, these methods rely on learned techniques rather than on spirit possession. They are practiced either by professionals who specialize in them or by horoscope readers who utilize them as auxiliary methods. Any of these professional practitioners may also furnish their clients with charms to ward off present or future misfortunes.

Clients consult fortune-tellers in January in order to learn their fortunes for the coming year, or when a particular problem arises. Most clients are women, and their most frequently asked questions pertain to general marriage prospects, the compatibility of two potential marriage partners, future success in a business venture or college entrance examination, and the cause of a present illness. Married women often pose these questions on behalf of other members of their families, for the fate of any person usually affects the welfare of other members of a household.

Various forms of fortune-telling are also practiced by laymen. Typically, these methods require little specialized knowledge. Consulting the *Tojŏng pigyŏl,* a book of divination compiled by Yi Chi-ham (1545–1567), is one such method. It is especially popular in the month of January. After a person's year, month, and day of birth are each converted into a single digit and the digits are combined, the passage of the *Tojŏng pigyŏl* corresponding to that combined number is consulted. Each of the passages provides a general description of one's prospects for the coming year as well as month-by-month forecasts.

Almanacs are also used by laymen in Korea. Published annually, almanacs give day-by-day instructions regarding the auspiciousness of house repairs, marriages, changing one's residence, cutting down trees, funerals, and burials. Violating these prescriptions invites misfortune, but its nature is not specified by the almanac. Generally, the almanac is taken more seriously than other forms of fortune-telling also practiced by nonprofessionals. As with reading the *Tojŏng pigyŏl,* it is usually men who consult almanacs.

GEOMANCY

Geomancy *(p'ungsu)* is a method of finding propitious locations for houses, villages, Buddhist temples, capital cities, and graves. It is predicated on the belief that the site of a dwelling affects the well-being of its occupants, that of a capital city, the fortunes of its nation or dynasty, and that of a grave, the welfare of its occupant's patrilineal descendants. In actual practice, however, geomancy involves primarily the selection of grave sites.

Geomancy posits that a vital force *(saenggi)* travels under the surface of the earth and that individuals can avert misfortune or induce benefits by erecting their dwelling or burying an ancestor in one of the spots where this force congeals. Geomancy does not explain how the force influences human lives, however. Instead, it relies on analogy. In the case of graves, the bones of an ancestor are likened to the roots of a tree, and descendants are likened to the tree's leaves and branches; nourishing the tree's roots with the subterraneous force causes the leaves and branches to flourish also. The thrust of geomantic theory is not concerned with explaining how its effects are wrought but rather how to find and utilize propitious locations.

A geomantically favorable location is found primarily by examining the topography of the area in question, particularly its surrounding streams and mountains. Because water blocks the vital force, geomantically favorable sites usually have water just below them to restrain the force from flowing past. Wind, on the other hand, disperses the vital force, and thus the surrounding mountains should serve as shields to protect it. The configuration of the local mountains also indicates the strength of the force and the types of consequences that it will yield.

Other factors influencing the vital force are soil conditions, compass directions, and time, as calculated by the sexegenary cycle. For example, vital energy cannot congeal in stone, and too much moisture in the soil causes an ancestor's bones, conduits of the force, to decay. Associated with each compass direction and sexagenary couplet, moreover, is one of the five basic elements (fire, water, wood, metal, earth), and these should all be in harmony. A person born in a year designated by a couplet associated with wood, for example, should not be buried in such a way that his or her corpse is oriented along a direction associated with fire.

Reasoning by analogy is also used to infer the potential effects of a site. A mountain that is circular in shape and has a pointed top is said to resemble the tip of a writing brush, so burying an ancestor there will produce descendants who are good calligraphers or who are successful at passing the civil service examination. Similarly, wells should not be dug in a site shaped like a boat, for that would be analogous to sinking the boat and thereby destroying the site's geomantic benefits.

The methods of interpreting local configurations are so diverse that some feature in the local topography or time and place of burial can usually be found to explain a wide variety of subsequent events. In addition to all of the above considerations, an ancestor's discomfort in a grave site may also be advanced as the reason for that ancestor's inflicting misfortune on his or her descendants. The disparity between this interpretation of geomancy and its more conventional conception as an impersonal mechanism, a disparity noted in anthropological analyses of geomancy in China, is a matter of concern to neither informants nor geomantic manuals.

Known as the "theory of wind and water" *(p'ungsu),* geomancy was originally developed in China (where it was known as *feng-shui*) and later spread to Korea, probably before the end of the Unified Silla dynasty (668–935 CE). Professional Korean geomancers appear to have adopted the Chinese system with little modification and even today use some of the manuals authored by Chinese geomancers. How well the Korean laymen's views match those of the professional, and how well these lay views correspond to those found in China, are matters that have yet to be investigated, however.

CHRISTIANITY

Korea's first known contact with Christianity came during the late sixteenth century. A Jesuit missionary accompanied the Japanese army that invaded Korea at that time, but there is no evidence to indicate that his visit had any influence on Korean religion.

Christianity first had an influence in Korea during the following century, when Korean envoys to the Chinese court in Peking encountered some of the ideas brought there by Jesuit missionaries. A few of these attracted the interest of some noted Korean intellectuals of the seventeenth and eighteenth centuries. By the last quarter of the eighteenth century, a few Korean literati had formed study groups to examine and discuss Catholicism, and a few individuals even announced their conversion to the new religion.

The Chosŏn dynasty court soon viewed Catholicism as a threat to Korea's established social order, primarily because of Catholic opposition to ancestor rites. With Neo-Confucianism its official creed, the Chosŏn court viewed the father-son relationship not only as the basic paradigm for relations between subject and ruler but also as fundamental to the maintenance of social order. Any challenge to filial piety, whether toward living parents or deceased predecessors, had serious political implications. Thus the new religion was officially proscribed by the mid-1780s, and a few executions soon followed. This antipathy toward Catholicism was exacerbated in 1801 by the involvement of some Korean Catholics in an attempt to draw Chinese and Western military forces into Korea in order to ensure freedom for their religion. The incident provoked further persecutions and imprisonment of Catholics. Yet despite bloody, if sporadic, persecutions, Catholicism continued to grow throughout the nineteenth century, largely through the efforts of French missionaries and church officials in Peking.

The growth of Catholicism in Korea was later eclipsed by the successes of Protestant missionaries. Though sustained Protestant missionary efforts began only in the penultimate decade of the nineteenth century, by the mid-1980s Protestants outnumbered Catholics by about four to one in South Korea. Though published statistics vary widely, depending on their sources, Catholics appeared to number about 1.5 million and Protestants about 5.5 million at that time.

The success of Christianity, particularly Protestantism, in South Korea is curious in view of the relative paucity of Christian converts in Japan and China, Korea's closest geographical and cultural neighbors. The success is all the more curious in view of the meager indigenization of Christian ideology and ritual in Korea. As a result, identifying the causes of Christianity's growth has emerged as one of the major issues in the study of Christianity. Three major causes have been advanced thus far: preexisting similarities between Christianity and Korean *mudang* practices, the ability of early Protestant missionaries to establish personal ties with members of the Korean court at the turn of the century, and the missionaries' sympathy toward Korean nationalism during the period of Japanese colonial rule (1910–1945). All of these may be valid, but none explains the remarkable growth of Christianity in South Korea during the 1970s and early 1980s. Wide variations in published statistics notwithstanding, both Catholicism and Protestantism apparently doubled their memberships in South Korea between 1972 and 1981. Perhaps this remarkable growth in recent years was fostered by South Korean industrialization and urbanization, the consequent dispersal of many of the social groups that participated at traditional Korean religious rites, and the widespread importation of nonreligious Western culture as well. Perhaps the growth was also fostered by the Christian churches' increasing involvement in the South Korean human rights movement.

NEW RELIGIONS

Like similar movements elsewhere in the world, Korea's new religions have tended to flourish in times of greatest personal distress and social disorder. The final decades of the Chosŏn dynasty and the years following World War II, during which many of these religions emerged and grew, were periods of especially intense social, economic, and political turmoil. In both eras, moreover, threatened or actual foreign military intervention exacerbated Korea's internal difficulties.

Continued foreign intervention in Korean affairs during the past one hundred years probably explains why nationalism has been a major theme of many new religions. The Eastern Learning (Tonghak) movement, the first of Korea's new religions, was at the forefront of anti-Japanese activities immediately prior to and during Japanese colonial rule. Some present-day new religions teach that Korea will eventually become the most important of the world's nations, or they display the South Korean flag prominently during their services.

In formulating their respective doctrines, the founders of Korea's new religions have most often been men who claimed to have received a supernatural revelation, but their teachings have drawn heavily upon Korea's traditional religions as well as upon Christianity. The particular blend of these sources varies greatly from one faith to the next, however, depending primarily on the personal religious background of their founders. Some groups, such as Wŏn Buddhism, are most similar to established Buddhism; others, such as Sun Myung Moon's Unification Church, draw more heavily upon Christianity.

Though the doctrines of the new religions vary, most are directed toward the resolution of economic or health problems rather than a concern for the afterlife. Many of the new religions offer their followers the promise of utopia on earth. As in Korean folk religion, wealth is not viewed as a hindrance to happiness but rather as a blessing to be actively sought.

After they were founded, many of Korea's new religions exhibited one of two common tendencies. Some grew and became established churches, shifted their emphasis away from magical cures and this-worldly concerns, and developed a rationalized, elaborated, and articulated body of teachings. Such was the fate of the Eastern Learning movement, which is now known as the Religion of the Heavenly Way (Ch'ŏndogyo), and of Sun Myung Moon's Unification Church. [*See* Ch'ŏndogyo *and* Unification Church.] Alternatively, some new religions did not grow but were plagued by continual segmentation, often precipitated by one of their members claiming to have received his or her own revelation and then establishing a separate church.

The total membership of Korea's new religions is difficult to determine with any precision, especially because many of the smaller religions have an ephemeral following. The most up-to-date and apparently accurate statistics, compiled by the South Korean government and as yet disseminated only through newspaper reports, estimates their total membership as of October 1983 at about one million, or about 3 percent of the South Korean population.

[*See also* Shamanism, *overview article, and* Ancestors, *article on* Ancestor Cults.]

BIBLIOGRAPHY

Korean-language scholarship on Korean religion is extensive. A good introduction to the entire field is *Min'gan sinang, chongyo,* "Han'guk minsok taegwan," vol. 3, edited by the Kodae minjok munhwa yŏn'guso (Seoul, 1983). This work covers the entire spectrum of Korean religion, including both folk religions and established faiths. It also contains footnotes that refer to much of the Korean-language scholarship and has a sixty-page English summary.

For the histories of the various Korean religions, much useful information can be found in Ki-baik Lee's *A New History of Korea,* translated by Edward W. Wagner with Edward J. Shultz (Seoul, 1984). Though some of his interpretations are controversial, Lee's work builds on that of several authors and thereby offers the best English-language survey of scholarship by Korean and other historians. Several chapter subsections, each one or two pages in length, chronicle each of the various faiths in different periods of Korean history.

The most comprehensive bibliography of Western-language works on Korean religion has been compiled by Kah-Kyung Cho and included in chapter 4 of *Studies on Korea: A Scholar's Guide,* edited by Han-Kyo Kim (Honolulu, 1980), pp. 120–133. With few exceptions, Cho's bibliography ends at 1970, but his classified listing of more than two hundred entries, many of them annotated, still provides the easiest entry to most of the Western scholarship.

Many of the best works on traditional Korean religion have appeared since 1970. Youngsook Kim Harvey's *Six Korean Women: The Socialization of Shamans* (Saint Paul, 1979) analyzes recruitment to the role of *kangsin mu* by identifying commonalities in their life histories and personalities. Laurel Kendall's *Shamans, Housewives, and Other Restless Spirits* (Honolulu, 1985) focuses on *mudang* rites and beliefs, relating these to the roles and social situations common to Korean women. *The Folk Treasury of Korea,* edited by Chang Duk-soon (Seoul, 1970), includes texts of *mudang*'s myths as well as a few myths from Korean literary sources compiled during the Koryŏ dynasty. *Ancestor Worship and Korean Society* (Stanford, Calif., 1982), by Roger L. Janelli and Dawnhee Yim Janelli, presents a description and analysis of rites for ancestors in terms of Korean family, kin group, and class structure. Alexandre Guillemoz's *Les algues, les anciens, les dieux* (Paris, 1983) surveys the diverse religious beliefs and rites of a single Korean village and points to their structural interrelationships.

Korean fortune-telling and geomancy have attracted far less scholarly attention than *mudang* rites and ancestor worship, but here again the best works have appeared within the past few years. For a brief but very informative survey of fortune-telling methods and topics of inquiry in Seoul, see Barbara Young's essay "City Women and Divination: Signs in Seoul," in *Korean Women: View from the Inner Room,* edited by Laurel Kendall and Mark Peterson (New Haven, Conn., 1983). Dawnhee Yim Janelli's "The Strategies of a Korean Fortuneteller," *Korea Journal* 20 (1980): 8–14, provides a brief description of consultation sessions with a horoscope reader in Seoul and identifies some of the techniques she employed to establish and maintain credibility in the eyes of her clients. For an account of Korean almanacs and their use in rural Korea, see M. Griffin Dix's "The Place of the Almanac in Korean Folk Religion," *Journal of Korean Studies* 2 (1980): 47–70. For a description of Korean geomancy, based on an examination of geomantic manuals, legends about geomancy, and interviews with professional geomancers, see Yoon Hong-key's Ph.D. dissertation, *Geomantic Relationships between Culture and Nature in Korea,* available as number 88 of the "Asian Folklore and Social Life Monograph Series" (Taipei, 1976).

Christianity has not enjoyed the same degree of recent growth in scholarly interest as have traditional Korean religions, and earlier books generally remain the most useful. The standard history of Protestantism in Korea is George L. Paik's *The History of Protestant Missions in Korea, 1832–1910* (1929; 3d ed., Seoul, 1980). For an account of Christianity's growth in terms of its relationships with Korean history and culture, see Spencer J. Palmer's *Korea and Christianity: The Problem of Identification with Tradition,* "Royal Asiatic Society, Korea Branch, Monograph Series," no. 2 (Seoul, 1967).

Among the more recent publications on Korean Christianity, two articles are especially noteworthy. The first is Donald L. Baker's "The Martyrdom of Paul Yun: Western Religion and Eastern Ritual in Eighteenth Century Korea," *Transactions of the Royal Asiatic Society, Korea Branch* 54 (1979): 33–58. Baker's study deals with the introduction of Catholicism into Korea and its perception by both early converts and the central government. The other is Frank Baldwin's "Missionaries and the March First Movement: Can Moral Men Be Neutral?," in *Korea under Japanese Colonial Rule,* edited by Andrew C. Nahm (Kalamazoo, Mich., 1973). Based on an examination of both Japanese and English sources, Baldwin's study depicts the Western missionaries' reluctance to participate in nationalist movements during the Japanese colonial era despite their personal sympathies toward the Korean cause.

Ch'ŏndogyo and the Unification Church have received far more attention than the other Korean new religions. *The New Religions of Korea,* edited by Spencer J. Palmer and published as volume 43 of the *Transactions of the Royal Asiatic Society, Korea Branch* (Seoul, 1967), is a collection of disparate but informative essays that deal with several of these faiths. It is still the best introduction to these religions.

16 BUDDHISM IN KOREA

ROBERT EVANS BUSWELL, JR.

In any examination of the Korean Buddhist tradition, it is essential to recall that in no way was Korea isolated from neighboring regions of Northeast Asia. During its prehistory, Korean culture was most closely akin to that of the seminomadic tribes of the Central and North Asian steppes. From the Warring States period (403–221 BCE) on, however, when refugees from the northern Chinese states of Yen, Ch'i, and Chao immigrated to the peninsula to escape the ravages of the mainland wars, Han civilization began to eclipse that indigenous culture at an ever-increasing pace. It is for this reason that Korean Buddhism must be treated as part and parcel of a larger East Asian Buddhist tradition. Indeed, Korea's later appellation as the "hermit kingdom" notwithstanding, there was in fact an almost organic relationship between the Korean, Chinese, and, during its incipient period, the Japanese Buddhist traditions. Admittedly, the Silk Route afforded China closer ties with the Buddhism of India and Central Asia, and China's overwhelming size, both in territory and population, inevitably led to its domination of the doctrinal trends within East Asian Buddhism. This does not deny, however, that Korean exegetes working on both the peninsula and the Chinese mainland made seminal contributions to the development of what are commonly considered to be distinctively "Chinese" schools of Buddhism, such as T'ien-t'ai, Hua-yen, and Ch'an. At the same time, many Chinese Buddhist theological insights were molded into new forms in Korea, innovations comparable to the Chinese syntheses of Indian and Central Asian Buddhist teachings. Hence, any appraisal of characteristically East Asian developments in the Buddhist tradition cannot neglect to take into account the contributions made by Koreans.

THREE KINGDOMS BUDDHISM (C. LATE FOURTH CENTURY– 668 CE)

According to such traditional Korean historical sources as *Samguk sagi* (Historical Record of the Three Kingdoms), *Haedong kosŭng chŏn* (Biographies of Eminent Korean Monks), and *Samguk yusa* (Memorabilia and Mirabilia of the Three Kingdoms), Buddhism was transmitted to Korea from the Chinese mainland during the (Korean) Three Kingdoms period. The introduction of Buddhism into Korea is presumed to have occurred in 372 CE, when King Fu Chien (r. 357–384) of the Former Ch'in dynasty (351–394) sent a monk-envoy, Shun-tao (Kor., Sundo), to the Koguryŏ court with scriptures and images. Former Ch'in hegemony over the remarkably cosmopolitan region of eastern Turkistan had brought Chinese culture into intimate contact with Indian, Iranian, and Hellenistic civilizations, ultimately engendering a new, sinified form of Buddhism. Fu Chien's defeat, in 370, of the Former Yen state, which had for decades laid siege to Koguryŏ, initiated close ties between Fu Chien and his Koguryŏ contemporary, King Sosurim (r. 371–383). These contacts allowed this vibrant northern Chinese culture, which included the Buddhist religion, to be introduced into Korea. While a paucity of information remains by which we can evaluate the characteristics of the Buddhism of this early period, it is probable that it was characterized by thaumaturgic practices, a symbiotic relationship between the ecclesia and the state, Maitreya worship, and the study of scriptures affiliated with the Mahāyāna branch of Buddhism. A monastery is said to have been erected for Sundo in 376, the first reference to a formal Buddhist institution on Korean soil.

Sundo was followed in 384 by the Serindian monk Maranant'a (*Mālānanda; *Kumārānandin), who is reputed to have come via sea to Paekche from the Chinese state of Eastern Chin (317–420). His enthusiastic reception by the royal court initiated the rapid diffusion of Buddhism throughout the Paekche kingdom. Less than a year after his arrival a monastery had been founded on Mount Han for Maranant'a and the first Korean natives ordained as Buddhist monks. Studies on Buddhist monastic discipline (Vinaya) appear particularly to have flourished in Paekche. In both Koguryŏ and Paekche, there is evidence that such schools as Samnon (Mādhyamika), Sarvāstivādin Abhidharma, Nirvāṇa, Satyasiddhi, and Ch'ŏnt'ae (Chin., T'ien-t'ai) flourished, though few works from this period are now extant. [*These Chinese traditions are reviewed in* Buddhism, Schools of, *article on* Chinese Buddhism.] Of vital importance for the dissemination of Buddhism throughout East Asia, however, was Paekche's nautical skill, which made the kingdom the Phoenicia of medieval East Asia. Over its well-developed sea lanes, Paekche began in 554 to dispatch Buddhist doctrinal specialists, psalmodists, iconographers, and architects to Japan, thus transmitting to the Japanese the rudiments of sinified Buddhist culture and laying the foundation for the rich Buddhist culture of the Asuka and Nara periods. Silla expansion throughout southern Korea also prompted massive emigration of Koreans to Japan (where they were known as *kikajin*), and many of the cultural and technical achievements of early Japan—such as the development of paddy fields, the construction of palaces and temples, and town planning—were direct results of the expertise introduced by these successive waves of emigrants. These advancements ultimately paved the way for Japan's first constitution, purportedly written by Prince Shōtoku in 604, and led to the Taika reform of 646, which initiated a sinified bureaucracy in Japan. [*See also* Buddhism, *article on* Buddhism in Japan.]

It was not until 529, following the martyrdom of Ich'adon (Pak Yŏmch'ok), that Silla, the last of the three kingdoms to consolidate its power, officially embraced Buddhism. Political exigencies were probably the catalyst for the acceptance of Buddhism in Silla. The Silla nobility, who continued their drive for peninsular unification, found strong incentive to embrace Buddhism in an effort to accommodate the newly conquered Koguryŏ and Paekche aristocracy, which had embraced Buddhism long before. The vital role played by the Buddhist religion as a conduit through which Chinese civilization was introduced into Silla closely parallels the sinification of non-Chinese tribes that occurred throughout Chinese history.

Three Kingdoms Buddhism seems to have been a thoroughgoing amalgamation of the foreign religion and indigenous local cults. Autochthonous snake and dragon cults, for example, merged with the Mahāyāna belief in dragons as protectors of the Dharma, forming the unique variety of *hoguk pulgyo* ("state-protection Buddhism") that was thereafter to characterize Korean Buddhism. One of the earliest examples of this amalgamation was the vow of the Silla king Munmu (r. 661– 681) to be reborn as a sea dragon after his death in order to guard his country and its new faith from foreign invasion. Buddhism and the state subsequently evolved a symbiotic relationship in which the monks entreated the Buddhas and *bodhisattvas* to protect the state and the state provided munificent support for the dissemination of the religion throughout the empire. Many of the most visible achievements of the Korean church throughout its history, such as the xylographic carvings of the Buddhist canon undertaken during the succeeding Koryŏ dynasty, were products of this concern with national protection. Buddhist monks also sought to demonstrate correspondences between Korean ancestral heroes and the new religion, thereby accelerating the assimilation of the religion among Koreans. Attempts were made, for example, to prove that Hwanin, the Celestial Emperor, was identical to Śakro Devāṇām Indra (Chesŏk-ch'ŏn), the Indian and Buddhist king of the gods, and that Tan'gun, the progenitor of the Korean race, was the theophany of Śrī Mahādevī (Kilsang-ch'ŏn). Vestiges of the dispensations of previous Buddhas were alleged to have been uncovered in Korea, and the advent of the future Buddha, Maitreya, was prophesied to occur in the south of the peninsula. Modern-day visitors to a Korean monastery will notice on the perimeter of the campus shrines devoted to the mountain god or to the seven stars of the Big Dipper, the presence of which is indicative of the synthesis of common sinified culture with Buddhism. [*For an overview of indigenous Korean religion, see* Korean Religion.]

One of the most prominent institutions of Three Kingdoms Buddhism that is commonly assumed to have been indicative of this interaction between Buddhism and indigenous Korean culture was the Hwarang (Flower Boy) movement. According to the *Samguk sagi,* this movement was instituted around 576 by the Silla king Chinhŭng (r. 540–575), and was patterned upon a more primitive association of shamanesses. The formation of the Hwarang movement is considered to have been part of the expansionist policies of the Silla court, and was intended to instill in the sons of nobility a regard for ethical virtues and an appreciation of refined culture. A later Silla writer relates that they were trained in Confucian filial piety and national loyalty, Taoist quietism, and Buddhist morality. The prominent religious orientation of the Hwarang as related in this and other accounts militates against the popular notion that it was a paramilitary organization. The group aesthetic celebrations—such as singing and dancing out in the open—that are commonly associated with the Hwarang has suggested to a number of scholars the shamanistic activities of initiation journeys and pilgrimages. While the Hwarang's Buddhist affinities are far from certain, their eventual identification with Maitreya assured that tradition would regard the movement as one intended to disseminate the Buddhist faith among Koreans.

UNIFIED SILLA BUDDHISM (668–935)

After the unification of the peninsula under the Silla banner in 668, the fortunes of the new religion expanded on an unprecedented scale. It was during this period that the major schools of scholastic Buddhism that had developed in China were introduced into Korea. The doctrinal teachings that had begun to be imported during the Three Kingdoms period were consolidated during the Unified Silla into five major ideological schools: the Kyeyul-chong, which stressed the study and training in Buddhist monastic discipline (Vinaya); the Yŏlban-chong, which promulgated the teachings of the *Mahāparinirvāṇa Sūtra;* the Pŏpsŏng-chong (Dharma Nature), a uniquely Korean school of Buddhism that stressed a syncretic outlook toward Buddhist doctrine; the Wŏnyung-chong, which was the early Korean branch of the Flower Garland (Kor., Hwaŏm; Chin., Hua-yen) school; and the Pŏpsang-chong, based on the "consciousness-only" *(vijñāptimātratā)* teachings of Yogācāra. Some of the greatest achievements of early Korean philosophy occurred during this period, and such important scholiasts as Wŏnhyo (617–686) and Ŭisang (625–702) forged approaches to Buddhist philosophy that would become the hallmarks of the Korean church from that time onward. Korean exegetes working in China also played major roles in the development of Chinese schools of Buddhism. Both Wŏnhyo and Ŭisang were important vaunt-couriers in the Hua-yen school, as reflected in their influence on the systematizer of the Chinese Hua-yen school, Fa-tsang (643–712). Wŏnch'ŭk (613–696), a close disciple of Hsüan-tsang (d. 664), was a prominent exegete in the Chinese Fa-hsiang school, whose commentaries on such texts as the *Saṃdhinirmocana Sūtra* exerted profound influence on early Tibetan Buddhism. [*See* Hua-yen *and the biographies of Wŏnhyo, Ŭisang, Fa-tsang, and Hsüan-tsang.*]

It was during this era of ardent scholarly activity that one of the most characteristic features of the mature Korean Buddhist tradition developed: that of syncretism. From the inception of Buddhism in East Asia, the religion had formed around a number of disparate scriptural and commentarial traditions that had developed first in India and later in Central Asia. For this reason, the Chinese church became characterized by a loosely-structured sectarianism. The various extremes each of these factional divisions took led to an attempt, begun first in China and considerably refined later in Korea, to see these various approaches, each ostensibly Buddhist yet each so different, in some common light, so as to find some means by which their discordant elements could be reconciled. Certain features of the Korean tradition contributed to the syncretic tendency of the religion. Owing to the smaller size of Korea and its monastic population, there was little hope that Buddhism could continue as a stable and influential force within the religious arena if it was divided into contentious factions. In addition, the constant threat of foreign invasion created the need for a unified, centrally organized ecclesiastical institution. The quest to discover the common denominators in all of these sectarian interpretations—and subsequently to use those unifying elements in order to establish an interdenominational approach *(t'ong pulgyo)* to the religion that could incorporate all elements of Buddhist philosophy and practice—was to inspire the efforts of all major Korean Buddhist philosophers. This attitude prompted the Koreans to evolve what remains one of the most ecumenical traditions of Buddhism to be found anywhere is Asia.

One of the most momentous developments in the history of Korean Buddhism occurred during the Unified Silla period: the introduction of the Ch'an teachings, known in Korea as Sŏn. The earliest transmission of Sŏn to the peninsula is attributed to the monk Pŏmnang (fl. 632–646), a Korean who is said to have trained with the fourth patriarch of the Chinese Ch'an school, Tao-hsin (580–646). While little is known of Pŏmnang's life or thought, there are indications that he attempted to combine the teachings of two distinct Chinese Ch'an lineages—that of Bodhidharma (c.

fifth century), Hui-k'o (487–592), and Seng-ts'an (d. 606) and that of Tao-hsin and Hung-jen (688–761)—with the syncretic *tathāgata-garbha* theory of the *Ta-sheng ch'i-hsin lun* (Awakening of Faith). [*See* Tathāgata-garbha.] A successor in Pŏmnang's lineage eventually founded the Hŭiyang-san school, the oldest of the Korean Sŏn schools. During the eighth and ninth centuries, other Korean adepts returning from the mainland established eight other mountain Sŏn sites, forming what came to be known as the Nine Mountains school of Sŏn (Kusan Sŏnmun). Of these eight, seven were affiliated with the Hung-chou lineage of the Middle Ch'an period, which eventually evolved into the Lin-chi school of the mature Ch'an tradition; one, the Sumisan school, was derived from the lineage of Ch'ing-yüan Hsing-ssu (d. 740), from which developed the Ts'ao-tung school. Korean masters on the mainland, however, also played major roles in the development of Chinese Ch'an. Perhaps the most prominent of these Koreans was the monk Musang, also known as Kim Ho-shang (694?–762), who was regarded as a patriarch of the Pao-t'ang school of the Szechwan region, and was the first Ch'an master known to the Tibetans. Despite the continued traffic of Sŏn adepts between China and Korea, the entrenched position of the scholastic schools within the Korean ecclesia thwarted the propagation of Nine Mountains Sŏn. Continued frustration at their inability to disseminate their message led such Sŏn adherents as Toŭi (d. 825) and Muyŏm (799–888) to attack the scholastic schools directly, leading ultimately to a bifurcation of the Korean Buddhist church into two vociferous factions. [*See also* Ch'an.]

KORYŎ BUDDHISM (937–1392)

The principal contribution of Koryŏ Buddhists to the evolution of the Korean church was the reconciliation they effected between the Sŏn and scholastic schools. It was Ŭich'ŏn (1055–1101) who made the first such attempt, by seeking to combine both the Nine Mountains and scholastic schools into a revived Ch'ŏnt'ae school. [*See the biography of Ŭich'ŏn.*] Ch'ŏnt'ae teachings are known to have been present on the peninsula prior to Ŭich'ŏn's time. A century before, for example, Ch'egwan (d. 971), a renowned Korean Ch'ŏnt'ae adept, had been invited to T'ang China to reintroduce long-lost T'ien-t'ai manuals; during his expatriation Ch'egwan systematized the school's philosophies in his *T'ien-t'ai ssu-chiao i,* one of the most important of Chinese T'ien-t'ai exegetical writings. [*See* T'ien-t'ai.] Ŭich'ŏn's efforts to revitalize the school, however, have led to his being considered the effective founder of its Korean branch. It appears that Ŭich'ŏn regarded the meditative exphasis of the Ch'ŏnt'ae teachings as the ideal vehicle for accommodating the varying concerns of the Sŏn and scholastic schools. Unfortunately, his premature death at the age of forty-six brought a sudden end to his endeavor and left the sectarian scene still more unsettled.

Ŭich'ŏn's efforts were followed some three generations later by those of Chinul (1158–1210), a charismatic Sŏn master who was similarly motivated by a syncretic vision of the unity of Sŏn and the scholastic teachings. Unlike Ŭich'ŏn's scholastic orientation, however, Chinul sought to merge the various Buddhist schools of his time into a new Sŏn school that would synthesize a disparate variety of Buddhist soteriological approaches. Chinul introduced into Korean Sŏn practice the investigation of the "critical phrase" (Kor., *hwadu;* Chin., *hua-t'ou),* better known by the closely synonymous term *kongan* (Chin., *kung-an;* Jpn., *kōan*), as it had been developed in China by Ta-hui Tsung-kao (1089–1163). Chinul then sought to incorporate this investigation into the soteriological scheme of sudden awakening/gradual cultivation taught by Tsung-mi (780–841), and finally to amalgamate this approach to Sŏn with the interpretation of Hwaŏm thought given by Li T'ung-hsüan (635–730). Chinul's synthesis of Sŏn and the scholastic teachings came to be regarded as a distinctively Korean school of Sŏn, called the Chogye-chong. His efforts revitalized the enervated Koryŏ church, and marked the ascendancy of Sŏn thought in the Korean Buddhist tradition. [*See the biographies of Chinul and Tsung-mi.*]

It was Chinul's disciple, Chin'gak Hyesim (1178–1234), who assured the acceptance of *hwadu* practice as the principal meditative technique in Korean Sŏn Buddhism. Following the model of Chinese thinkers of the Sung dynasty (960–1279), Hyesim examined the points of convergence between the three religions of Buddhism, Confucianism, and Taoism. This attempt to extend the embrace of Chinul's syncretic outlook so as to accommodate still other religions was to inspire a series of such investigations by later Korean authors. A Sŏn master of the later Koryŏ period, T'aego Pou (1301–1382), worked prodigiously to merge the remnants of the Nine Mountains Sŏn schools with the new Chogye-chong, and sought to graft onto this ecumenical school the Chinese Lin-chi (Kor., Imje; Jpn., Rinzai) lineage, into which he had received transmission in Yüan-dynasty China. The efforts of these and other teachers assured that the Chogye-chong would remain the predominant school of Korean Buddhism, a position it has retained down to the present.

YI BUDDHISM (1392–1910)

With the advent of the Yi dynasty in 1392 the fortunes of Buddhism began to wane. While the official policies of the Yi dynasty are commonly considered to have been Confucian in orientation, many of the kings continued to give munificent personal support to Buddhism. For example, the founder of the dynasty, Yi T'aejo (r. 1392–1398), appointed the renowned monk, Muhak Chajo (1327–1398), to the official post of preceptor to the royal family *(wangsa),* and the account of T'aejo's reign in the *Yijo sillok* (Veritable Record of the Yi Dynasty) teems with references to his sponsorship of temple construction projects, maigre offerings to monks, and various Buddhist rites. Confucian bureaucrats, however, continued to pressure the throne for stricter selection procedures for Buddhist monks, limits on the number of temples and hermitages, reduction in the number of officially sanctioned sects, and reorganization of the ecclesiastical system, all in order to effect more centralized supervision of the religion. Such policies were formally adopted by T'aejong (r. 1400–1418), the third Yi sovereign, and carried out on a massive scale by his successor, King Sejong (r. 1418–1450). In Sejong's proclamation of 1424, the Chogye, Ch'ŏnt'ae, and Vinaya schools were amalgamated into a single Sŏn (Meditative) school, and the remaining scholastic schools were merged into the Kyo (Doctrinal) school. New regulations were adopted for obtaining monk's certificates, making ordination much more difficult, and many monks already ordained were defrocked. The official ranks of national master *(kuksa)* and royal master *(wangsa)* were abolished. Temple paddy lands and forest properties were confiscated by the state and the legions of serfs retained by the monasteries were drafted into the army. Buddhist temples were no longer permitted within the capital or major cities. It is not surprising that during this dire period, Buddhist activities were as much concerned with the very survival of the tradition as with novel scholarly and meditative endeavors.

During this extremely difficult period in Korean Buddhist history, it is Sŏsan Hyujŏng (1520–1604) who epitomizes the continued Sŏn orientation of the church. Drawing his inspiration from Chinul's earlier vision of the unity of the Sŏn and scholastic schools, Hyujŏng produced a succinct manual of practice, titled the *Sŏn'ga kugam* (Guide to the Sŏn School). His other guides to Confucianism and Taoism were intended to sustain the reconciliation between Buddhism and its rival religions that was begun during the mid-Koryŏ and to outline their many similarities of purpose. Despite all the attempts of Hyujŏng's lineage, however, Buddhism's creative drive continued to wane. [*See also* Confucianism in Korea *and the biography of Hyujŏng.*]

BUDDHISM DURING THE MODERN ERA

Japanese inroads on the peninsula from the late nineteenth century onward presented both new opportunities and new pressures for the Korean Buddhist tradition. Following the ratification of the Korea-Japan treaty of 1876, Japanese Buddhist sects, beginning with the Higashi Honganji sect of Pure Land, began to proselytize among the increasing number of Japanese immigrants resident in Korea, an activity that soon spread to the native Korean populace as well. Remonstrations by Japanese Nichiren missionaries compelled the impotent Yi court in 1895 to lift the centuries-old prohibition against the presence of Buddhist monks in the capital of Seoul. During the same period, a resurgence of Sŏn practice was catalyzed by the Korean Sŏn master Kyŏnghŏ (1857–1912) and his disciples, and successors in his lineage continue to teach today.

After the annexation of Korea in 1910, some Korean monks felt that the fortunes of the religion were dependent upon arranging a merger with a major Japanese sect. Yi Hoe-gwang went so far as to negotiate a combination of the Korean church with the Japanese Sōtō sect, but most Korean Sŏn monks regarded the gradualistic teachings of the Sōtō sect as anathema to the subitist orientation of their own tradition, and managed to block the merger. Another movement threatened to further divide the Buddhist church. As early as 1913, Han Yong-un (1879–1944), the only Buddhist signatory to the 1919 Korean independence declaration and a major literary figure, had shocked his contemporaries by advocating that monks be allowed to marry, a move he felt was necessary if Buddhism were to maintain any viable role in modern secular society. While this position was diametrically opposed to the traditional celibate orientation of the Korean ecclesia, the Japanese colonial government ultimately sustained it in 1926 with its promulgation of new monastic regulations that legalized matrimony for monks. Within a decade, virtually all temple abbots were married, thereby producing a dramatic change in the traditional moral discipline of the Korean church. Other reform movements designed to present Buddhism in a way that would be more relevant to modern concerns arose with increasing frequency. Among the most prominent of these was Wŏn Buddhism, founded in 1916 by Pak Chung-bin (1891–1943), which combined Buddhist teachings with a disparate variety of elements drawn from Confucianism, Taoism, Tonghak, and even Christianity.

After independence in 1945, Korean Buddhism was badly split between two irreconcilable sects. The T'aego-chong, a liberal sect of married monks, had flourished under Japanese patronage and was based principally in the cities where it catered to the lay Buddhist population. The Chogye-chong was a smaller, religiously conservative faction of monks who had managed to maintain their celibacy during the long years of Japanese occupation; their concern was to restore the meditative, scholastic, and disciplinary orientations of traditional Korean Buddhism. Only after years of intense conflict did the Chogye-chong finally win government support for its position in 1954. While litigation continues between the two sects, all of the major monasteries have reverted to its control. Now the predominant sect of Buddhism in Korea, the Chogye-chong has had considerable success in attracting a new generation of lay believers and monastic postulants to the teachings and practices of Buddhism. [*See also* Worship and Cultic Life, *article on* Buddhist Cultic Life in East Asia.]

BIBLIOGRAPHY

It remains difficult for the nonspecialist to find reliable books on Korean Buddhism in Western languages. Some summaries of research by Korean and Japanese scholars have appeared in *Buddhist Culture in Korea,* "Korean Culture Series," vol. 3, edited by Chun Shin-yong (Seoul, 1974). J. H. Kamstra's *Encounter or Syncretism: The Initial Growth of Japanese Buddhism* (Leiden, 1967), part 3, includes a useful survey of Three Kingdoms Buddhism and its influence on early Japan. The biographies of several prominent monks of the early Three Kingdoms period are translated in Peter H. Lee's *Lives of Eminent Korean Monks: The Haedong Kosŭng Chŏn* (Cambridge, Mass., 1969). A liberal rendering of a major Korean hagiographical and doxographical collection dealing with Three Kingdoms Buddhism appears in *Samguk Yusa: Legends and History of the Three Kingdoms of Ancient Korea,* translated by Tae-hung Ha and Grafton K. Mintz (Seoul, 1972). The travelogue of a Korean monk's pilgrimage to India and central Asia has been newly translated by Han Sung Yang, Yün-hua Jan, and Shotarō Iida in *The Hye Ch'o Diary* (Berkeley, 1984). Korean Hwaŏm thought receives some coverage in Steve Odin's *Process Metaphysics and Hua-yen Buddhism: A Critical Study of Cumulative Penetration vs. Interpenetration* (Albany, N.Y., 1982); the appendix includes a translation of Ŭisang's outline of Hwaŏm philosophy. Ch'egwan's survey of Ch'ŏnt'ae philosophy has been translated in David W. Chappell and Masao Ichishima's *T'ien-t'ai Buddhism: An Outline of the Fourfold Teachings* (Honolulu, 1984).

Korean Sŏn Buddhism is covered in my own book *The Korean Approach to Zen: The Collected Works of Chinul* (Honolulu, 1983). My introduction there includes a rather extensive survey of the early history of Korean Buddhism, and particularly the Sŏn tradition, in order to trace the contexts of Chinul's life and thought; specialists may also consult the bibliography of works in Asian languages on Korean Buddhism that appears there. Chinul's contributions to Korean Buddhism have also been examined in Hee-sung Keel's *Chinul: Founder of the Korean Sŏn Tradition* (Berkeley, 1984). A provocative exposition of Korean Sŏn practice appears in Sung Bae Park's *Buddhist Faith and Sudden Enlightenment* (Albany, N.Y., 1983). The principal works of Wŏn Buddhism are translated in Chon Pal-khn's *The Canonical Textbook of Won Buddhism* (Seoul, 1971). A number of seminal literary compositions by Korean Buddhists from all periods are translated in Peter H. Lee's *Anthology of Korean Literature: From Early Times to the Nineteenth Century* (Honolulu, 1981). A representative selection of philosophical and hagiographical writings by Korean Buddhist authors will appear in *Sources of Korean Tradition,* edited by Peter H. Lee (New York, forthcoming). The few Western-language works on Korean Buddhism written up to 1979 are listed in *Studies on Korea: A Scholar's Guide,* edited by Han-Kyo Kim (Honolulu, 1980); see chapter 4, "Philosophy and Religion."

17 ISLAM IN CHINA

MORRIS ROSSABI

Islam arrived in China within a few decades after the death of the prophet Muḥammad. Yet the first Chinese Muslim writings on Islam date from the seventeenth century. The first detailed descriptions of early Islamic history, as well as the first Chinese translations of the Qur'ān, derive from that same era. Most of the earlier accounts derive from the works of Chinese Confucians and focus on the commercial roles of the Muslims without supplying much information on the social and religious life of the Islamic communities. Thus, knowledge of the trends in Chinese Islam before the seventeenth century is fragmentary.

ARRIVAL OF THE MUSLIMS

Discounting the legendary accounts of the arrival of Islam in China, it seems clear that Middle Eastern and Central Asian traders introduced the new religion to the Chinese. By the late seventh century, Muslim merchants had reached China both by land and by sea. The land routes consisted of the old Silk Roads, which had connected China to the West as early as the time of the Roman empire. Winding their way from Persia through Samarkand and Bukhara, the Muslim caravans skirted the Taklamakan Desert either south via Khotan and Keriya or north via Turfan and Hami. They then headed into China proper, often halting at Tun-huang and Lan-chou, and concluded their travels at the capital in Ch'ang-an (modern Sian). China's northwest was thus exposed to the new religion, and some Chinese converted to Islam as early as the eighth century. The sea route was navigated by Arabs and Persians who set forth across the Persian Gulf to the Indian Ocean and eventually docked in the ports of southeast China. The cities of Canton, Hang-chou, and Ch'üan-chou were the principal destinations of these sailors and merchants.

Diplomacy and Warfare. The first official contacts between the Arab rulers and the Chinese court were more bellicose. In 651 and again during the K'ai-yüan era (713–742), the caliphs, through their generals in the field, dispatched at least two embassies to the T'ang dynasty court. When the envoys in the second mission refused to perform the kowtow to the Chinese emperor, the Chinese elite, appalled by this discourteous behavior toward the Son of Heaven, perceived the Arab rulers as foes. The hostilities between the two empires culminated in the 751 battle of the

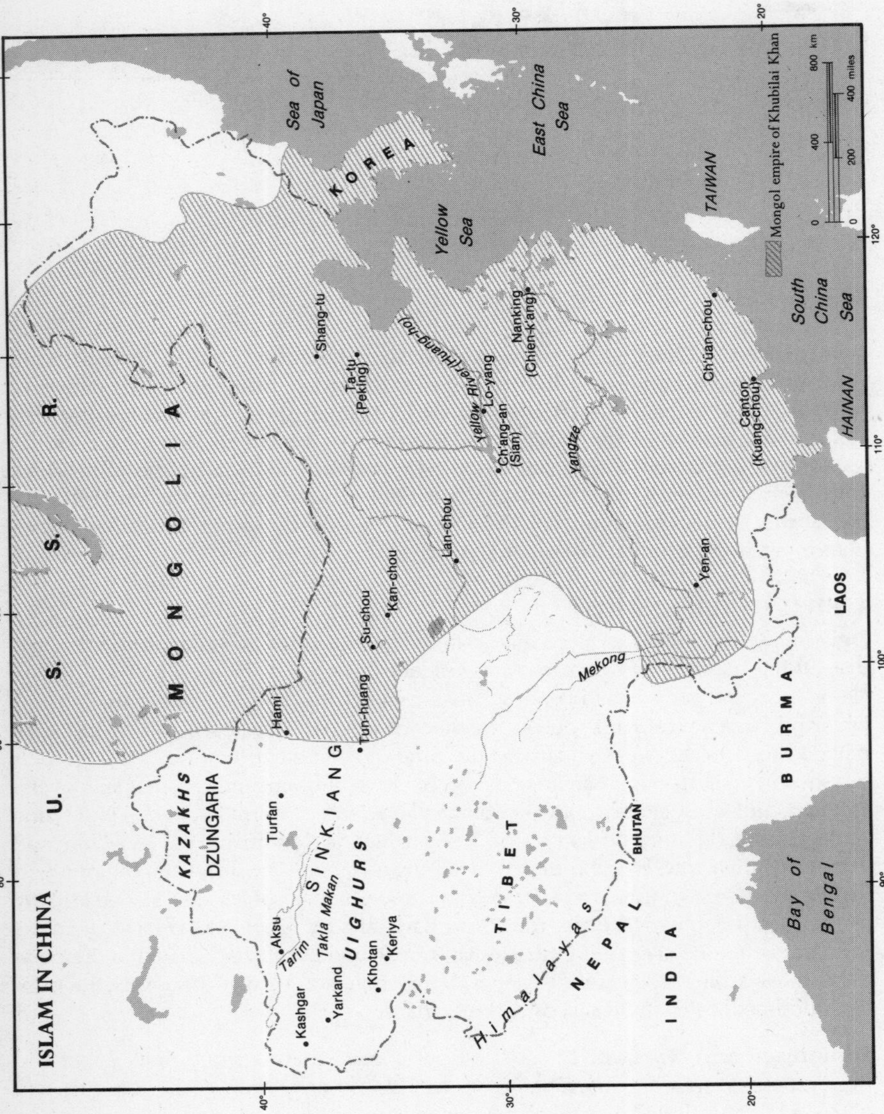
ISLAM IN CHINA
U. S. S. R.
MONGOLIA
KAZAKHS
DZUNGARIA
SINKIANG
UIGHURS
Turfan
Hami
Aksu
Tarim
Takla Makan
Kashgar
Yarkand
Khotan
Keriya
TIBET
Himalayas
NEPAL
INDIA
BHUTAN
BURMA
Bay of Bengal
LAOS
Mekong
Yangtze
Yen-an
Lan-chou
Kan-chou
Su-chou
Tun-huang
Shang-tu
Ta-tu (Peking)
Yellow River (Huang-ho)
Lo-yang
Ch'ang-an (Sian)
Nanking (Chien-k'ang)
Ch'üan-chou
Canton (Kuang-chou)
HAINAN
South China Sea
TAIWAN
Yellow Sea
KOREA
Sea of Japan
East China Sea
Mongol empire of Khubilai Khan
0 400 800 km
0 200 400 miles
80° 90° 100° 110° 120° 130° 140°
40° 30° 20°

Talas River in Central Asia, where an invading Arab army clashed with T'ang troops led by Kao Hsien-chih, a general of Korean descent. The Arabs won the battle but did not capitalize on their victory. Instead, most of them withdrew to return home and take part in the ongoing struggle for power within the Islamic empire, which had recently resulted in the establishment of the Abbasid dynasty (750–1256).

Official hostilities appear to have had scant effects on individual Muslims in China. They were not compelled to leave the country nor were they discriminated against in the Chinese communities where they chose to settle. A few even assisted the T'ang court in quelling a major rebellion: the T'ang dynastic histories report that Arab troops served in the foreign contingents that helped to crush the rebel leader An Lu-shan and to recapture the two capital cities of Ch'ang-an and Lo-yang in 757. The court surely recompensed them for their aid. According to Chinese Muslim tradition, these troops settled in China and became the ancestors of the Muslim communities in central and northwestern China.

The T'ang elite, which had a heightened sense of its own superiority, did not attempt to impose itself upon these Muslims. The Confucian ruling class believed that Chinese civilization was more advanced than any other culture. The sophisticated Chinese language, the carefully devised Confucian ethical principles, and the magnificently planned capital cities could not, in their view, be matched elsewhere. Impressed by China's superiority, foreigners would come to China to be "transformed" or "civilized" *(lai-hua)*. They would be converted into proper Confucian gentlemen and would eventually abandon their own cultural or religious heritage. During this transformation, the Chinese would not actively proselytize; foreigners would, of their own accord, accept and emulate Chinese practices, and until that time, the court would not restrict the foreigners' freedom of religious expression.

Communal Life. As a result of these policies, the Muslim communities prospered, forming virtually self-governing enclaves in their areas of residence. The accounts of contemporary Arab travelers to China confirm the T'ang version of the Muslims' relations with the court. Though the report of Ibn Wahhāb, who reached China and had an audience with the emperor in 815, does not mention the presence of Muslim communities there, the anonymous traveler cited in *Akhbār al-Sīn wa-al-Hind* (Accounts of China and India) offers a description of his coreligionists in southeast China. Reaching China by sea in 851, he provides convincing evidence of the autonomy granted to the Muslim communities. He notes that

> *there is a Mohammedan appointed Judge over those of his religion, by the authority of the Emperor of China, and that he is Judge of all the Mohammedans who resort to those parts. Upon several days he performs the public service with the Mohammedans. . . . The merchants of Irak who trade thither are no way dissatisfied with his conduct or his administration in the post he is invested with, because his actions . . . are conformable to the Koran, and according to Mohammedan jurisprudence.* *(Broomhall, 1910, pp. 47–48)*

He also records, however, that he did not encounter Chinese Muslims; the communities he came across were composed of foreign Muslims residing in China.

The Muslims practiced their religion in China, but it appears that they did not erect a substantial structure as a house of worship during the T'ang period. According to one Muslim tradition, Sayyid [Ibn Abī] Wakkās, identified as a maternal uncle of Muḥammad, built the first mosque in Canton late in the sixth century or early in the seventh century. This chronology is clearly absurd because Muḥammad did not begin to expound the main tenets of Islam until the early seventh century, and his ideas could not have been known in China until the middle or later years of that century. The accounts concerning Sayyid Wakkās appear to be spurious, and the Huai-sheng Mosque and the adjacent Kuang-tʻa minaret in Canton, which he is reputed to have built, doubtless derive from a later period. Similarly, the traditional dates of origin of the Great East Mosque and the Great West Mosque in Sian are questionable. Two stone inscriptions in these mosques, which were said to date from 742, have been shown to be later forgeries, probably originating no earlier than 1300, and the present buildings were either constructed or renovated in the early Ming dynasty (1368–1644). The Muslims may have prayed in small, unpretentious, and unprepossessing halls slowly built up over the years, but the more imposing mosques and minarets are of later origin.

Trade Relations. While it is undeniable that the Muslims enjoyed great leeway in religious practices and self-governance, the Chinese were more hesitant in matters of trade. The court allowed the Arabs and Persians to offer tribute and to trade as long as they abided by Chinese regulations and controls on commerce. The Confucian elite, in theory, considered trade demeaning. Confucian scholars and officials were scornful of mercantile pursuits and considered merchants to be parasites who merely exchanged, rather than produced, goods. Since China was self-sufficient, there was no need, they reasoned, to trade with Muslim merchants, and such trade was permitted only because of the court's compassion, not because of its need for foreign goods. This official view was ingenuous. During the Tʻang, mandarins kept an especially watchful eye on export goods to make sure that the government received its share of the profits. Although the government and its scholars and officials would not admit its value, commerce with the Muslims was lucrative.

Ordinary Chinese were not as unrealistic. Chinese merchants, innkeepers, and even some officials profited from this foreign trade and were grateful for the goods brought by the Muslims. They did not share the official disdain for trade and for the Muslim merchants. Yet inevitably commercial jealousies and disputes created rifts between the Muslim and the Chinese merchants, and animosity toward the Muslims and other foreigners surfaced in a ninth-century rebellion. According to the accounts of the Arab historian Abū Zayd (878–916), the Chinese rebel Huang Chʻao massacred over 100,000 Muslims, Nestorians, and Jews in Canton in 878. The figure that Abū Zayd cites is an exaggeration, but the Chinese dynastic histories confirm the event (which they date to 879, owing to discrepancies between the Chinese and Muslim calendars). Nonetheless, this attack against the Muslims appears to have been an aberration, traceable to economic grievances rather than to religious discrimination, for foreigners generally seem to have been accepted in China.

Knowledge of the religious views and practices of the Islamic community in China is stymied by the attitudes of the Confucian literati, who wrote the principal histories of the time. Feigning a lack of interest in foreigners and foreign lands, they wished to portray foreign practices as infantile and "barbaric" so that the need for sinicization would be obvious. Thus their descriptions emphasized what they believed to be bizarre or exotic or "uncivilized." Similarly, reports on the foreign religions and foreign communities in China were not encouraged.

The Muslims continued to fare well even after the fall of the T'ang dynasty. Overland trade between the Muslim world and China decreased, but the seaborne commerce escalated dramatically. Arab and Persian seafarers arrived at the Chinese court in far greater numbers, bringing with them frankincense, myrrh, and sandalwood, among other commodities. During the Sung dynasty (960–1279), Chao Ju-kua, a superintendent of maritime trade, wrote a lengthy monograph describing the Islamic countries and the products that Muslim merchants imported into China. Toward the end of the dynasty, a Muslim of Arab origin named P'u Shou-keng even became the superintendent of maritime trade in the port of Ch'üan-chou. Yet once again, the Chinese chronicles yield pitifully few details about the religious life and concerns of the Muslims.

ISLAM AND MONGOL RULE

The invasions of the Mongols and the founding of the Mongol Yüan dynasty (1279–1368) brought China into closer contact with the Muslim world and resulted in an influx of Muslims into the Middle Kingdom. The Mongol conquerors did not have the administrative and financial skills to rule the country: they had only recently emerged from nomadic pastoralism and lacked experience in governing a vast sedentary empire. Nor could they rely upon the Chinese to provide the assistance they needed, for the Mongol khans were wary of depending upon the people whom they had just subdued. When Khubilai Khan took power in 1260, he sent Hao Ching to seek a peaceful accommodation with the still-unpacified southern Sung Chinese. Instead the Sung imprisoned the envoy and severed relations with Khubilai. Two years later, a Chinese named Li T'an rebelled against Mongol rule. Understandably enough, Khubilai became ever more suspicious of the Chinese.

Desperate for assistance, Khubilai imported Muslims from various parts of his domain to help govern China. He assigned them to positions in the financial ministries of the government, though a few served in the Bureau of Astronomy and in the army. Many were employed as tax collectors, an occupation that did not endear them to the Chinese. Several Muslims supervised the government monopolies of salt, iron, tea, liquor, bamboo, and other vital commodities, and a few oversaw the foreign trade in the coastal cities of the southeast. These economic activities certainly damaged the Muslim image in the eyes of the Chinese. Khubilai also encouraged Muslims to engage in trade, making them even more vulnerable to Chinese hostility, and he accorded them special privileges, including exemption from regular taxation. The Muslims founded merchant associations, known as *ortaq,* to advance their commercial interests. Contemporary Chinese sources accused the *ortaq* of excesses, evasions, and exploitation. The Chinese histories assert that some of the Muslim merchants compelled soldiers to join and protect them on their travels, forced officials at the postal stations to provide them with lodging, and used improper and illegal methods to force borrowers to repay their loans promptly. These excesses contributed to the development of a negative image of the Muslims.

The Mongols' need for additional revenue imposed further burdens on their Muslim underlings. When Khubilai constructed new capitals in Ta-tu (modern Peking) and Shang-tu (Samuel Taylor Coleridge's "Xanadu"), extended the Grand Canal, and continued his military campaigns in Central Asia, Japan, and Southeast Asia, he turned to his Muslim administrators to raise the required revenue. His finance minister Aḥmad (fl. 1262–1282) imposed new taxes, added to the list of products monopolized by the court, and streamlined the collection of state revenues. Not surprisingly, his success provoked Chinese hostility, and the first serious stirrings of anti-Muslim sentiments surfaced. In this respect, the Muslims were a convenient buffer for the Mongols. Chinese animosity toward the rulers themselves was diverted somewhat to the Muslims, who began to be portrayed in Chinese sources as avaricious and unprincipled.

Yet neither the Mongols nor the Chinese could deny the Muslims' contributions to China. Persian doctors introduced new drugs and new kinds of hospitals. A Muslim architect helped to design the capital city at Ta-tu. In 1267 the Persian astronomer Jamāl al-Dīn built an observatory in the capital and provided new astronomical instruments for China. His successes prompted Khubilai to found an official Institute of Muslim Astronomy in 1271. Ismāʿīl and ʿAlāʾ al-Dīn, two Muslim engineers, constructed weapons to assist the Yüan armies. A Central Asian Muslim named Sayyid Ajall Shams al-Dīn imposed Yüan rule on China's southwestern province of Yunnan, which had been composed of autonomous tribes and kingdoms until the thirteenth century. After the Mongols conquered the region they assigned Sayyid Ajall to bring it into the Chinese orbit. He encouraged the development of an agrarian economy in part by promoting irrigation projects. He also prodded the local people to initiate trade with the rest of China and with the countries to the southwest. As a Muslim, Sayyid Ajall recruited an army composed primarily of his coreligionists, many of whom eventually settled in Yunnan and intermarried with the natives. Most of these families retained their identity as Muslims rather than assimilating into the local or into the Chinese culture, and they became the ancestors of the sizable modern Muslim community of Yunnan.

With the support of their Mongol patrons, it is no wonder then that the Muslims were found in all regions of China. The Muslims had settled in northwest China as early as the T'ang dynasty. Kan-chou, Su-chou, and Yen-an each had separate Muslim quarters, and by 1274 they had built a mosque in Kan-chou. The Muslims had their own leaders, known in Chinese as *ta-shih-man* (from the Persian *dānishmand,* "scholar"), and they maintained relations with their coreligionists in Central Asia. In northern China, Muslims built mosques in Shang-tu and Ta-tu, established their own schools in the province of Hopei, and took part in the horse trade in the province of Shantung. In southwest China, Muslims settled in Szechwan, which lay along the main trade routes to Burma and India. On the southeastern coast, Arabs and Persians continued to trade, and one-third of the thirty-six superintendents of maritime trade in Fukien during the Yüan were Muslims.

The Mongols adopted a *laissez-faire* policy toward the Muslims. In Ch'üan-chou, the community had its own leader, the Shaykh al-Islām (in Chinese, *hui-hui t'ai-shih*), who served as its intermediary with the Mongol authorities. The *qāḍī* ("judge"; in Chinese, *hui-chiao-fa-kuan*) interpreted Muslim laws and principles for the settlement. The Muslim section had its own bazaars, hospitals, and mosque, and many members of the community still spoke Arabic or Persian. The Yüan court generally permitted the Muslims to fast during Ramaḍān, to circumcise male infants, to recite the Qur'ān, and to slaughter animals in their own fashion. The fourteenth-century Arab traveler Ibn Baṭṭūṭah recorded that Muslim musicians in Hang-chou could perform songs in Arabic and Persian. Orchestras composed of three hundred to four hundred men played Middle Eastern music at banquets in his honor.

THE RESTORATION OF NATIVE CHINESE RULE

After the fall of the Mongol dynasty, the native Chinese Ming dynasty (1368–1644) might have been expected to discriminate against the Muslims who had served their oppressors. The court did attempt to restrict or at least regulate relations with the Muslim states, and Chinese officials generally managed to prevent the Muslim envoys from mingling with ordinary Chinese. Yet Ming policy toward the Muslims in China was fairly tolerant. The court employed them as astronomers, calendar makers, and diviners in the Directorate of Astronomy. The Ming emperors also recruited them as envoys, translators, and interpreters. Chinese of Muslim backgrounds became renowned as explorers, philosophers, and military leaders.

Moreover, two of the Ming emperors were attracted by Islam. The Hung-wu emperor (i.e., the emperor of the Hung-wu reign era, 1368–1398), the first Ming ruler, had two Muslim cousins, and some sources claim that his wife was a Muslim as well. Three mosques were built, with imperial approval, during his reign; according to an inscription at one of these mosques,

> *The emperor had proclaimed that each Muslim be given 50* ting *of paper money and 200 bolts of silk and that mosques be built in two places. One* [*was to be built*] *in . . . Nanking, and the other in . . .* [*Hsi-an*] *Sian. . . . If there are dilapidated mosques, restoration is permitted. . . . The administration offices . . . will handle the purchases of all things needed in this restoration. If the transport of materials will involve the passing of ferries and barricades, no one is permitted to stop them.* (*Rossabi, "Muslim Inscriptions," p. 24*)

The Cheng-te emperor (1506–1521), the second of these rulers, surrounded himself with Muslim eunuchs and advisers; he authorized the production of bronzes and porcelains for Muslim patrons, and he welcomed to his court ambassadors from the various Muslim lands. While some Chinese clearly despised and discriminated against the Muslims, and a few of the Ming emperors did not look with favor upon these "outsiders," official court policy encouraged toleration toward them.

Peaceful Coexistence. The Muslims, in turn, abided by court regulations and pursued a policy of peaceful coexistence with the Chinese. They continued to practice their faith but in a way that did not offend the sensibilities of the Chinese. They did not actively proselytize nor were they aggressive or ostentatious in the performance of their religious duties. The Muslim communities in northwest and southwest China were by this time the most numerous, though there were Muslim groups scattered throughout China. Their numbers decreased in southeast China as fewer Arabs and Persians arrived by sea, and with more and more of the newer migrants originating from Turkic Central Asia, Turkic-speaking peoples began to constitute a larger percentage of the Muslims in China.

The Muslims in the northwest and southwest organized themselves in small communities and did not, at least during this period, unite and offer their allegiance to a single leader. The Chinese, pleased by this lack of unity, did not perceive the Muslims as a threat. The Muslims also compromised with Chinese regulations. After a century of the foreign, Mongol rule, the Chinese of the early Ming were determined to compel the foreigners residing in China to accept some Chinese ways. The Muslims thus adopted Chinese dress, erected tablets near their mosques pledging their loyalty to the Chinese emperor, and started to learn the Chinese language; the court demanded that they assume Chinese names as well. But the Ming was to be sorely disappointed in its hopes for their gradual assimilation. The Muslims retained their identity because they had their own leaders, their own educational system, and a strong feeling of their distinctiveness. They lived in separate areas, trained several of their members in Persian or Arabic in order to have access to Islamic texts, and encouraged pilgrimages to Mecca. Each community had its own mosque, which also served as a binding force. Their faith was, in addition, supported by their frequent associations with their coreligionists in Central Asia. In their work as merchants, interpreters, and camel and horse grooms, they had numerous opportunities to meet with Muslims from beyond the Chinese border. Such encounters kept them in touch with the wider Muslim world, enabling them more readily to maintain their faith in a non-Islamic environment.

Some Muslims intermarried with the Chinese. Most of these unions were between Muslim men and Chinese women. Contrary to the Ming court's expectations, however, their children were generally reared as Muslims. The Islamic community also grew as a result of adoptions. Wealthy Muslim families bought or "adopted" young Chinese boys, raised them as Muslims, and thus had mates for their daughters. The court's encouragement of intermarriage and assimilation paradoxically gave rise to Chinese converts to Islam, mostly in the northwest and southwest. These Chinese converts came to be known as "Hui," while the non-Chinese were identified with their ethnic group.

Negative Images. The economic roles of the Muslims as intermediaries reinforced the popular stereotypes about them among the common people. Ordinary Chinese did not resent the Muslims' religious views or customs. They found some of the Muslims' practices (e.g., fasting during Ramaḍān, abstaining from liquor) strange, but they were unfazed by them. In fact, they were so uninterested in investigating these Islamic observances that they failed to distinguish between the Muslims and other religious groups, notably the Jews: they frequently lumped the Muslims and the Jews together because both wrote in "peculiar" scripts and refused to eat pork. Most of their negative images of the Muslims revolved around trade. They described Muslim merchants as not only shrewd but also conniving. Muslim traders could not be trusted. Their avariciousness on occasion led to deception and fraud. They did not even carry out their own religious practices unswervingly; if a specific belief interfered with commercial gain, it would be ignored as they pursued their profits. Chinese anecdotes emphasizing the Muslims' hypocrisy and deception began cropping up during this time, and such disagreeable epithets as *hui-i* ("Muslim barbarians") and *hui-tse* ("Muslim bandits") started to be applied to them.

Despite this developing negative image, the Ming court did not attempt to sever the Muslims' relations with their coreligionists in Central Asia. Mosque communities there, as elsewhere in the Muslim world, guaranteed Muslim travelers a friendly welcome and a place to stay; relations between Muslims in China and Central Asia were further strengthened by the occupations they pursued. Many of the Muslims in northwest China were involved in commerce as merchants, interpreters, postal station attendants, and camel and horse grooms; in short, their livelihood and their very survival was directly linked to trade with fellow Muslims from Central Asia.

REPRESSION AND A MUSLIM RENAISSANCE

The apparent decline of trade with the deterioration of economic conditions in the late sixteenth and early seventeenth centuries was thus devastating to the Muslims of northwest China. The previously profitable caravan trade across Central Asia faced stiff competition from the ocean-going vessels from Europe; Muslim lands such as Persia and Turkey, which had earlier participated in trade, had declined; the expansion of the Russian empire into Central Asia disrupted commerce in that area; and the northwest had suffered from severe droughts. Economic distress led the Muslims to join in the rebellions against the Ming dynasty. Chinese rebel leaders in the northwest had contingents of Muslims in their detachments, and some scholars have even suggested that Li Tzu-ch'eng, one of the two most important rebel leaders, was a Muslim. Li was adopted at the age of ten by an old Muslim woman and was familiar with Islamic practices and beliefs, but it seems unlikely that he converted to Islam. Other rebel leaders, such as Niu Chin-hsing and Ma Shou-ying (also known as Lao Hui-hui or "Old Muslim"), were Chinese Muslims and played a vital role in the early successes of the Muslims in the northwest.

Ch'ing Expansionism. The Manchus, who finally crushed the Ming and established the Ch'ing dynasty (1644–1911), did little to alleviate Muslim discontent and distress. In fact, the Ch'ing exacerbated the Muslims' difficulties with its policies. Contrary to the court's expectations, once again the Muslims did not assimilate. They survived as a distinct minority group and, through intermarriage with the Chinese, had increased in number. Together with their coreligionists in Central Asia, they had proved troublesome in the last years of the previous dynasty. The Ch'ing therefore sought to resolve its Muslim "problem" through an expansionist policy. Assuming that the Muslims of nearby Central Asia were inspiring the Muslims within China to engage in antigovernment activities, the Ch'ing advanced throughout the late seventeenth and eighteenth centuries into Central Asian territories that had never traditionally been part of China. Their first thrust was directed at Dzungaria in the northern region of the modern province of Sinkiang. By 1696, a Ch'ing army had routed the Dzungar Mongols, and the court began to order its forces to move south into the lands of the Muslim Uighur Turks. In 1758, an efficient and ruthless general named Chao-hui imposed Ch'ing rule on the Uighur oases in Central Asia. He occupied the towns of Kashgar, Yarkand, and Aksu in southern Sinkiang. With this military success, the Ch'ing court had now incorporated a new and sizable contingent of Muslims.

The Ch'ing court attempted to promote good relations with the Muslims within China and in the newly subjugated areas in Central Asia. It established an administration with a large measure of local self-rule for the Muslims, and it did not interfere with the Muslims' practice of their faith, though in the 1720s it did impose a temporary moratorium on the construction of mosques. It attempted to foster the economic recovery of the lands in northwest China and Central Asia that had been devastated during the Dzungar wars. Yet these policies were not properly implemented and ultimately backfired. In seeking to promote the economy of the northwestern regions, the Ch'ing court encouraged its Chinese subjects to migrate there to raise grain, fruit, and cotton and to extract the vast mineral and natural resources, including iron, gold, and copper. The Chinese peasants and merchants who moved into the Muslim areas tended to engage in bitter disputes with the local inhabitants and to exploit them, despite the good intentions of the government. Though the Muslim leaders had some degree of autonomy, the officials dispatched by the Ch'ing court still made the most critical decisions, and they often exercised their power in a capricious and oppressive manner. They occasionally imposed onerous taxes and other obligations on the Muslims and sporadically contravened the regulations of the court to impede the Muslims' practice of their religion.

Apologetic Response. The Muslim reaction was predictable. Dissatisfaction with Ch'ing rule grew, and eventually such tensions gave rise to violence and revolts. Starting in the late eighteenth and continuing into the nineteenth century, the Muslims in both northwest and southwest China rebelled against the Ch'ing government. But the precursors to the rebellions were the writings of the Chinese Muslims, provoked by oppression and discrimination to define their faith and to assert their identity in the face of powerful opposition. Only in the seventeenth century had the Chinese Muslims produced their first works on the Islamic religion. Some of the early Muslim writers sought an accommodation with Confucian thought while the later, more radical Muslim authors insisted on a clear distinction between Islam and Confucianism and emphasized a pure, untainted form of Islam.

The Chinese Muslim Wang Tai-yü (1580–1650?) wrote the first important text in Chinese on Islam. As a youth, he had received a Muslim education in a mosque, but as an adult he devoted himself to a study of the Confucian classics. He wrote his principal work, the *Cheng-chiao chen-ch'üan* (Veritable Explanation of the True Religion), in 1642 in order to explain the fundamental tenets of Islam to the Chinese Muslims. By this time, many of the Muslims were Chinese converts who had scant detailed knowledge of Islam. Wang thus tried to expound the Islamic teachings in a style familiar to the Chinese. Using Confucian terminology and argumentation to explicate the major ideas of the foreign religion, he asserted that Confucianism and Islam shared common views with regard to personal virtue, brotherly love, and the ordering of social relationships, as between sovereign and ministers or fathers and sons. Even the dualistic concept of *yin* and *yang* was acceptable to him. He also appropriated the term for the five Confucian virtues of benevolence and wisdom, among others, to signify the five cardinal responsibilities of a Muslim, including the pilgrimage to Mecca and almsgiving. In effect, he appealed to the Chinese Muslims in terms and ideas they understood and showed them that Islam was not unremittingly hostile to Confucianism. The main critique he made of Confucianism was its lack of concern for and its unwillingness to accept monotheism. The concepts of God and of divine intervention were, Wang regretted to point out, omitted in Confucian thought. Yet even on this crucial point of Islamic doctrine he did not fault Confucius, attempting instead to establish some common grounds with that revered Chinese cultural figure. He found some shreds of monotheistic thinking in Confucius's use of the terms *t'ien* (heaven) and *Shang-ti* (God?). Wang clearly did not seek a break with Confucianism; he merely wished to clarify and champion Islamic beliefs.

Liu Chih (1662?–1736?), the most renowned of the Chinese Muslim authors of the late seventeenth and early eighteenth centuries, likewise focused on the similarities between Islam and Confucianism. In his familiarity with the two religions he resembled Wang, but his education was even more encompassing, for he also pursued studies on Buddhism and Taoism. He borrowed Confucian concepts and applied them to his definition of Islam. In his book *T'ien-fang hsing-li* (The Philosophy of Arabia), for example, he wrote that the Confucian term *li* (moral rectitude) was universal; Muslims too, he argued, strove to achieve this goal. In the same book, Liu repeatedly praised some of the Confucian cultural heroes. A contemporary Chinese official was so pleased with Liu's work that he noted in the preface that "although his book explains Islam, in truth it illuminates our Confucianism" (Ford, p. 150).

Liu nonetheless still perceived the Chinese Muslims as his prime audience, and in his books he tried to explain as concisely and simply as possible the main features of the Islamic tradition. In his biography of the Prophet *(Chih-sheng shih-lu),* he wrote a sketch of the life of Muḥammad that gained wide circulation in the Muslim community. Basing himself on his researches in Arabic and Persian sources, he provided a straightforward, clear, and generally accurate account of the career and teachings of the founder of Islam. In *T'ien-fang tien-li* (Laws and Rituals of Islam), he offered a brief description of the basic ceremonies and laws associated with the faith. Though Liu was not a creative, innovative thinker, he undertook considerable research in the preparation of these books. His views accorded with those of the Ḥanafī school of law within Sunnī Islam, the principal mode of belief of most of the Chinese Muslims. Yet also noticeable in his works was a growing reliance on and interest in Sufism, which he employed to seek an accommodation with Confucianism.

The New Teaching. The principal Muslim thinkers of the later eighteenth century, however, were much more hostile to Confucianism. The mid-eighteenth-century repression of Islam by local Chinese officials and by private citizens prompted the development of a more fundamentalist form of Islam. The Chinese Muslim Ma Ming-hsin, a native of Kansu Province in northwest China, was the main exponent of a Ṣūfī order that challenged both Confucianism and the Ch'ing dynasty. After a period of study in the Middle East and Central Asia, Ma returned to China in 1761 to introduce the New Teaching *(Hsin-chiao),* a different form of the Ṣūfī teachings that had reached northwest China as early as the seventeenth century. Like the earlier Ṣūfīs, Ma belonged to the Naqshbandī order and, also like them, stressed a personal, mystical expression of faith. Unlike the earlier Ṣūfīs, who were known as proponents of the so-called Old Teaching *(Lao-chiao),* however, Ma's New Teaching emphasized chanting and a vocal remembrance of God *(dhikr-i jahrī),* a characteristic of the Jahrīyah branch of the Naqshbandīyah, which differed from the more sober form of the Naqshbandīyah in India and Central Asia. The Old Teaching was less rambunctious and more solitary because it entailed a silent remembrance *(dhikr-i khafī)* of God, which was associated with the Khafīyah branch of the Naqshbandīyah, and the leaders of the entrenched Old Teaching viewed Ma as a subversive. He appears to have been a charismatic figure, and he reportedly engaged in faith healing. His disciples and supporters danced, bobbed their heads, chanted, and went into trances in their efforts to achieve union with God. Such public displays offended the leaders of the Old Teaching. His emphasis on the personal relationship between the master (shaykh) and his followers and on worship at the site of tombs of important shaykhs also challenged the Old Teaching hierarchy, which was organized into leading lineages *(men-huan)* with hereditary leaders who controlled landed estates and dominated the commercial networks among the Muslims. They resented the intrusion of Ma's New Teaching because it threatened their political and economic power.

The Ch'ing dynasty was to be even more perturbed by Ma's ideas and activities. He repeatedly denounced any doctrinal or ritual compromises with foreign religions or cults and advocated a return to the pure, untainted form of Islam. From the Ch'ing standpoint, such an uncompromising attitude might contribute to social unrest, and like the leaders of the Old Teaching, the Ch'ing authorities in the northwest perceived Ma to be a subversive. He had already challenged the power of the lineages of the Old Teaching by noting that "since religion belonged to all . . . why should it be made the private possession of one family?" Now Ma was inciting his followers to adopt a hostile stance toward Confucianism and, by extension, toward the Confucian Ch'ing state. The loyalty he demanded from these same followers was also worrisome to the Chinese and Manchu authorities, for the power that thus accrued to him could readily be translated into political authority. The Naqshbandī orders in general and Ma in particular were not hesitant to become embroiled in politics. In fact, Ma's uncompromising attitude necessitated involvement in politics in order to ward off the possibility of being engulfed or even tainted by the Confucian civilization that surrounded the Muslims in China.

MUSLIM REBELLIONS

The ultimate logic of Ma's views was the establishment of a Muslim state along China's borders, and the religious and economic hostilities that separated the Muslims and the Chinese soon resulted in actual rebellions. In 1781, Ma and his fellow Muslim Su Ssu-shih-san led a revolt against the Ch'ing authorities in the province of Kansu. The New Teaching forces were defeated only after the arrival of Ch'ing troops from other provinces. Ma was executed, but Muslim unrest did not wither away. A Muslim religious brotherhood descended from the Central Asian religious leaders known as Khojas, who were associated with the Naqshbandīyah, organized this popular discontent into violent outbreaks with the intent of establishing an autonomous Muslim theocratic state in northwest China. The first result of their efforts was a rebellion in 1784, and the Ch'ing needed an even greater effort to defeat the rebels. After the suppression of the revolt, the Ch'ing proscribed the New Teaching, prohibited the construction of new mosques, and barred the conversion of Chinese Confucians to Islam.

Resentment over these new Ch'ing policies grew and finally flared out into open rebellion. In 1815, a Muslim chieftain of non-Chinese descent named Ḍiyā' al-Dīn led a short-lived rebellion in the modern province of Sinkiang. Five years later, the religious leader Jahāngīr Khoja organized an insurrection against the Ch'ing government. Although he was defeated, the troops sent against him could not annihilate his forces; eight years elapsed before they finally captured him and disbanded his army. Even then his capture did not end China's difficulties in the northwest, for his relative success encouraged other Muslims to challenge Ch'ing rule. In 1832, his brother Khoja Muḥammad Yūsuf attacked several garrisons in Sinkiang before fleeing to the safe haven of western Central Asia. In 1847, seven Khojas from Central Asia led forays into Sinkiang and caused havoc there until the Ch'ing troops forced them to withdraw. One of these Khojas reappeared in 1857 to plague Sinkiang and occupied part of the region for some months.

The most devastating of the rebellions erupted in Shensi in 1862, provoked by a dispute between some Muslims and Chinese over the sale of bamboo poles. The Chinese Muslim Ma Hua-lung, the recognized leader of the New Teaching groups, quickly became a prominent figure. From his base in Kansu, he fostered anti-Ch'ing sentiment and encouraged his followers to seek independence from China. The rebel forces were successful, and within two years most of Shensi and Kansu were no longer under Ch'ing control. But the religious leadership was unable to establish its rule over the rebel troops. Instead a Muslim adventurer-soldier named Yaʿqūb Beg ultimately took charge. His harshness, the corruption of some of his associates, and his increasingly oppressive secret police force alienated his people and disrupted the unity of the Chinese Muslims. The disunity among them enabled the Ch'ing government to move slowly to recapture the northwest. Under the able Chinese general Tso Tsung-t'ang, the Ch'ing gradually reconquered most of Shensi, Kansu, and Sinkiang. In 1877, Yaʿqūb Beg died, and by early in the following year Tso had recovered all of the rebellious lands and had reimposed Ch'ing control.

As a result of these rebellions, Chinese views of the native and foreign Muslims again became increasingly unfavorable. Anecdotes about the Muslims, mostly apocryphal stories, portrayed them as profiteering, insincere, and faintly sinister. The moral of many of the stories was that Muslim merchants could not be trusted. They were avaricious, and crafty to the point of dishonesty. They were false Muslims, practicing their faith only when it suited them. They often ignored the taboos on pork and liquor, finding bizarre rationalizations for their transgressions. Stories such as the following manifested the Muslims' "cruel, evil natures":

> *During the season of the Chinese New Year, Muslims, who do not observe the same festival, invited the Chinese in their caravan to make merry, while they would stand the night watch. After the Chinese were drunk, the Muslims rose up, pulled their tent down on them and beat them to death under it. Then, they threw the bodies into a dry well and made off with the silver.*
>
> *(Lattimore, 1929, pp. 165–166)*

Muslim intermarriage with Chinese and their adoption of Chinese boys perturbed officials. They had counted on the gradual assimilation of foreigners and foreign ideologies. Here they faced a group that not only refused to abandon its religious heritage but gained a following among native Chinese as well.

The negative Chinese image of the Muslims in the late nineteenth and early twentieth centuries contributed to the tensions in western China, where there was much unrest. In the southwestern province of Yunnan, a Muslim rebellion erupted in 1855 and lasted until 1873. During these eighteen years, perhaps as many as five million of the eight million residents of the province died. Neither the Ch'ing victory in Yunnan in 1873 nor its suppression of the northwestern rebellions in 1878 quelled the turbulence in China's western domains. The New Teaching did not perish and continued to clash with the adherents of the Old Teaching. The internal conflicts among the Muslims complicated their relations with the Chinese. In the struggles that broke out after the suppression of the initial Muslim rebellions, Muslims of the

Old Teaching occasionally cooperated with the Chinese against the adherents of the New Teaching. Some even advocated closer collaboration with the Chinese. In 1900, Ma Fu-hsiang, a Muslim warlord from the province of Kansu, urged his own people to integrate into Chinese society and he organized an Assimilationist Group to promote such an integration.

AUTONOMY FOR SINKIANG, 1911–1949

After the fall of the Ch'ing dynasty in 1911, a number of Chinese officials in the Muslim areas sought to ingratiate themselves with the Muslims and to encourage their assimilation into Chinese society. Yang Tseng-hsin, the most important military figure in the northwest, tried to prevent exploitation of the non-Chinese, in particular the Muslims, in his domain in Sinkiang. Maintaining an effective system of controls over the government, he imposed harsh sanctions on those who illegally alienated the Muslims. His economic policies were designed to reduce the tax burden on the Uighurs and Kazakhs, the majority of whom were Muslims, and the Chinese Muslims, now known as the Hui, and to win their support. Many of the Muslims responded to his benevolent policies, and by 1916 the tensions that had bedeviled relations between the Muslims of the northwest and their Chinese rulers had abated. Yang himself was virtually independent of any control of the various governments based in Peking. After the Bolshevik Revolution he became increasingly close to the Soviet Union, further limiting the Peking government's jurisdiction over him.

Yang's death in 1928 ended the somewhat less hostile relationship that had prevailed between the Chinese and the Muslims of Sinkiang. Chin Shu-jen and Sheng Shih-ts'ai, the succeeding warlords who ruled the province until 1943, were less sympathetic to Muslim interests. Instead they sought to reimpose Chinese controls, with scarcely any concern for the Muslims. The native people grew increasingly restive. In the waning years of Sheng's regime, local uprisings broke out and finally led to a full-scale rebellion by the Kazakh chieftain Osman (Usman) Bator. By the mid-1940s, several Muslim groups in Sinkiang were calling for autonomy; in January of 1945, they united to form the Eastern Turkistan Republic, an independent state free of Chinese control.

The Nationalist government of Chiang Kai-shek, which controlled most of China other than Sinkiang from 1928 to 1948, paid lip service to the ideals of equality for the Muslims within its domains. In fact, its policies did not differ significantly from those of many earlier Chinese governments. It still did not respect the Muslims' differences and uniqueness. But it also did not admit that its ultimate goal was the sinicization of the Muslims. Instead the government proclaimed the Muslims one of the five "great peoples" of China, alongside the Han (ethnic Chinese), the Mongols, the Tibetans, and the Manchus. A national flag composed of five symmetrical stripes represented the equality of the five different peoples in Chinese territory. Yet the Nationalists' own prejudices and the activities they sanctioned undermined their efforts to win over the Muslims. Many in the government regarded themselves as superior to the Muslim minorities and considered them lazy, slow, and "inexact." The Nationalists wanted to civilize these "barbarians."

The Muslim communities responded in different ways to the pressures exerted by the warlords in Sinkiang and by the Nationalists in other parts of China. The non-Chinese Muslims of Sinkiang retained their identities, continued to practice their

Islamic faith, and repeatedly sought to establish independent states. The Hui, the Chinese Muslims, were not as separatist. They did not attempt to set up their own autonomous states, nor did they seek to impose barriers between themselves and their Chinese neighbors. Their knowledge of Islamic doctrine was becoming increasingly sketchy. Not only could they not distinguish between Sunnī and Shīʿī forms of Islam, but many had barely any acquaintance with the Qur'ān. Few of the Chinese Muslim communities had members who could read Arabic or Persian. Many of the Hui probably knew more about Confucianism and Buddhism than about the essential features of their own faith. Yet they considered themselves to be different from the Chinese. Although their conceptions of fundamental Islamic beliefs were hazy, they maintained some practices that bolstered their view of their uniqueness and set them apart from the Chinese. Thus they abstained from eating pork, for example, and occasionally practiced circumcision. The fact that they often lived in their own neighborhoods, clustered around a mosque, also promoted greater unity among them.

ISLAM UNDER THE PEOPLE'S REPUBLIC

When the People's Republic of China (PRC) was founded in 1949, the leadership needed to assert its authority over the Muslim areas in the northwest. No Chinese national government had truly governed Sinkiang since 1911, and since 1925, the Muslims of Sinkiang had maintained closer ties with the Soviet Union than with China. The main opposition to PRC rule came from the Sinkiang League for the Protection of Peace and Democracy, a group founded in 1948 and primarily composed of Muslims. After a mysterious airplane crash in 1949 killed many of the leaders of that organization, Burhan and Saifudin, the two succeeding Muslim leaders of non-Chinese origin, worked out an agreement with the government. The final effect of this compact was the creation in 1955 of the Sinkiang Uighur Autonomous Region, which by its name, at least, indicated a greater degree of independence for the Muslims of the region. Saifudin became the first governor of the newly constituted government, another indication of the autonomy pledged to the region by the central authority. In fact, it has imposed numerous controls on the Muslims of the region.

Sinicization and its Limits. Consonant with its attitude toward all religions, the government has been condescending toward the Islamic faith. The traditional Chinese literati had believed that they possessed a unique ideology, Confucianism, and a sophisticated civilization superior to any other in the world. Like their forebears, the Communists have asserted that their unique form of Marxism would enable them to be a more productive and, by implication, superior civilization. Islam is, from this viewpoint, a conservative ideology that could not compete with Marxism. Like the "barbarians" of old, the Muslims need instruction from the Chinese. The state's ultimate goal for the Muslims still appears to be sinicization. Since the Muslims constitute a majority in some areas, particularly in Sinkiang, sinicization has proven difficult.

The government's eagerness to maintain good relations with the Islamic states also impeded sinicization. Some of the Islamic states outside of China had vast petroleum reserves, were located on the crossroads of Asia, Africa, and Europe, and could prove troublesome if they allied themselves with powers hostile to China. A few of their leaders (e.g., Nasser of Egypt, Sukarno of Indonesia) frequently acted as spokesmen for the Third World, a bloc of countries that the Chinese hoped to affect. Influence on the Muslim Middle East might also translate into influence in Africa, another area that the Chinese hoped to sway politically. The government could therefore not afford to impose Chinese culture on the Muslims within their own country. Nor could it appear to discriminate against Islam or to prevent the Muslims from practicing their faith. In effect, its general antireligious sentiments and policies had to be moderated in the case of Islam, for repressive policies would inevitably harm Chinese interests in the Islamic world.

Similarly, good relations with the Muslims were vital for the security of China's northwestern frontiers. The non-Chinese Muslims, including the Uighurs and the Kazakhs, inhabited the border regions adjacent to the U.S.S.R. Across the borders lived Muslims of Turkish background who shared the same language and ethnic derivations as those on the Chinese side. Such a community of interests might make the Muslims of China responsive to Soviet blandishments. With the growing rift between China and the U.S.S.R. after 1956, the Muslims residing along the Sino-Soviet border became increasingly important. Both the Soviet and the Chinese governments attempted to sway the Muslims and to recruit them to their side of the dispute. From the Chinese point of view, a hostile Muslim minority threatened to weaken border defense, increase the danger of Soviet attack, and perhaps even result in territorial losses.

Perhaps equally significant for the Chinese was the economic potentiality of the Muslim regions in the northwest. The mineral resources of these territories are virtually untapped; their lands offer a useful source of animals and animal products, and the so-called Autonomous Regions of Sinkiang and Ninghsia, inhabited mostly by Muslims, are relatively underpopulated and can absorb migrants from the more crowded eastern coast of China. The figures for Muslim population cited by the Chinese are unrealistically low. According to the 1980 estimates by the government, a total of thirteen million Muslims resided in China. Less biased experts on demography estimate that there are forty to fifty million Muslims throughout the country. Nonetheless, the regions in which the Muslims live are sparsely settled and are attractive to Chinese planners who face problems of tremendous overcrowding in most other regions of China.

Conflicting Policies. It is not surprising then that the government has devoted considerable attention to the Muslim minority in China. But its policy toward the Muslims has been inconsistent, alternating between radical and conservative positions. The conservative approach, which was dominant from 1949 to 1957, 1962 to 1965, and again after 1976, emphasized the special characteristics of the Muslims and proposed a cautious, conciliatory policy. The Turkic Muslims were permitted to use their own languages and dialects in the schools and the mass media; the majority of Communist party cadres were recruited from the native peoples, not from Chinese migrants to the Muslim areas; in the Chinese Muslim, or Hui, areas as well, many party members were drawn from the Muslims; the native elites of the pre-1949 period were often granted important positions in local government; and the distinctive customs and practices of the Muslims, even if they occasionally impeded economic development or communization, were neither interfered with nor prohibited. The government, for example, often sidestepped the issue of equal rights for women in the Muslim areas, where Islamic practice accorded women a lesser role and lower status.

The radical approach, which informed government policy during the Great Leap Forward of the late 1950s and the Cultural Revolution from 1966 to 1976, posited that nationality and ethnic distinctions would disappear with the obliteration of class differences and contended that class struggle ought to be the cornerstone of policy toward the Muslims. Communist cadres replaced the traditional Muslim leadership and sometimes displayed scant consideration for Islam. The central government dominated the autonomous regions founded in Muslim areas. Some mosques were closed or destroyed or converted to other uses. The government insisted that the Chinese language be adopted in the schools and employed in the mass media. The Chinese Islamic Association, a quasi-governmental agency, supervised the mosques, decided how many copies of the Qur'ān were printed, and, in effect, controlled the religious hierarchy. The leaders would not permit Muslim customs to interfere with the economic and social changes promoted by the government. They also encouraged and, in fact, ordered non-Muslim Chinese to move into the Muslim regions, including Sinkiang, hoping in this way eventually to outnumber the Muslims in the northwest.

Despite their differences, both the conservatives and the radicals favor the integration and the assimilation of the Muslims into Chinese culture and society. They differ only in the tactics they employ rather than in their objectives: both seek a "common proletarian culture" for the Chinese and the Muslims. One means of promoting the assimilation of the Muslims has been by showing them a "better life," and indeed, the government has raised their living standards: they are better fed, clothed, and sheltered than before 1949 and have greater access to medical care. Yet the Muslims still consider themselves to be different from the rest of the population of China.

The negative images of Muslims entertained by the Chinese majority have exacerbated the difficulties of integration. Visitors to China in the 1980s reported that some Chinese they encountered expressed blatantly anti-Muslim sentiments. These Chinese asserted that only the elderly actually worship in the mosques. They told foreign visitors that religious Muslims sometimes do not abide by the dictates of their faith (e.g., by evading the taboo on liquor). Like the Chinese of earlier dynasties, they expressed the belief that the Muslims would assimilate, as was the case with other minorities such as the Manchus and the Mongols in the nineteenth and twentieth centuries (the Manchus no longer survive as a distinct population in China).

Muslim Response. The Muslims' reactions to government policies since 1949 are difficult to gauge. Independent observers were until the late 1970s excluded from the minority areas. Since 1978, tourists and scholars have been permitted access to the Muslim regions, but they have not been granted sufficient time to observe conditions in these areas. Nor have specialists been allowed to conduct research on the Muslims. Consequently, knowledge of the Muslim communities is meager. Religious currents among the Muslims are even more difficult to fathom. It is impossible at the present time to find out about the various orders of Islam. Some of the Ṣūfī orders and Sunnī institutions that had such a profound influence in the eighteenth and nineteenth centuries probably survive, but reliable accounts of their beliefs and activities are currently unavailable.

In theory, the Muslims ought to be struggling for independence. There is no evidence, however, that the Chinese Muslims or the Uighurs, Kazakhs, and other non-Chinese have sought to rebel and establish their own independent states. Yet the Muslims have expressed their discontent with specific Chinese policies directed at them. In 1958, the Chinese leaders, wishing to hasten basic changes in the Kazakh economy and society, adopted a direct and radical approach to reach their objectives. They founded livestock communes, encouraged the development of agriculture to accompany livestock production, and required the Kazakhs to abandon their nomadic pastoralism for a more sedentary lifestyle. They also urged Chinese colonists to migrate to Sinkiang in order to counter the anticipated opposition of some Kazakhs. These policies heightened Kazakh fears of sinicization and resulted in even greater opposition to the Chinese. The drive toward communization and the arrival of the Chinese colonists alienated many Kazakhs. A few who had contacts with the Kazakhs on the Soviet side of the border were attracted by the higher standard of living enjoyed by their compatriots across the frontier. In 1962, approximately sixty thousand Kazakhs fled to the Soviet Union, a tangible indicator of the unrest and dissatisfaction among one group of Muslims.

Again during the Cultural Revolution of 1966 to 1976, the Muslim regions were turbulent. The government appeared to foster anti-Muslim acts, including the destruction of mosques and the harassment of fervent practitioners of the faith. It sanctioned antireligious propaganda and closed down many mosques. It limited the number of texts of the Qur'ān in circulation and demanded the use of Chinese rather than the native Turkic languages in Sinkiang. The results were predictable: hostilities between the Muslims and the radical Red Guard groups erupted, pitched battles ensued, and heavy casualties were suffered by both sides. Until 1969, the northwestern borderlands were extremely unsettled. After the extreme phase of the Cultural Revolution ended in that year, Chinese pressure on the Muslims abated.

Only since 1976 has the government taken positive steps to help the Muslims. The government provided funds for the rebuilding or restoration of mosques damaged during the Cultural Revolution. In 1980, it reprinted the Qur'ān, and that work was made widely available in mosques throughout the country. Antireligious propaganda was stifled, and the mullahs again came forward to become the leaders of many Muslim communities. Muslims were not prevented from attending services at the mosques. Muslim food stores, pastry shops, and restaurants were found throughout China from Peking and Canton in the east to Lan-chou and Turfan in the west. The government has been taking great pains to preserve, repair, or restore Islamic monuments. Many of the older mosques possess stone tablets on which information about the construction or restoration of the minarets, prayer halls, and grounds is provided. These inscriptions yield precise dates, names of prominent leaders in the Muslim community, regulations concerning the mosques, and the circumstances leading to the building projects. Over the centuries, the weather, natural disasters, and perhaps deliberate defacement have taken their toll. Quite a number of the inscriptions have been damaged and are unreadable. Starting in 1982, the government belatedly began an effort to prevent further damage to these tablets.

Toward the end of the twentieth century, at least, there is no active persecution of the Muslims. The mosques have once again become centers for the Muslim communities. Interest in the history and culture of the Muslims has revived both among the minorities themselves and among the Chinese. It is difficult to predict how long this moderate policy will persist. Similarly, it is difficult to ascertain whether the Muslim community can survive surrounded by a huge Chinese population whose leaders are still bent on the assimilation and sinicization of all foreign groups and religions in China.

The most remarkable aspect of Islam in China has been its ability to survive in the face of pressures to assimilate and occasionally hostile government policies. Its tenaciousness in a culture that has sinicized so many different religions and ethnic groups is truly noteworthy. Not only have the primarily Turkic-speaking Muslims survived, but they have also succeeded in converting numerous Chinese to Islam. The Chinese Muslims, or Hui, have not by and large been highly conversant with the tenets of Islam, but they still perceive themselves to be different from other Chinese and have often identified with the larger Islamic world community. Although the Muslims in China have not made any major contributions to Islamic doctrine, they have deviated from traditional Islam in trying to reconcile their doctrines with Confucian ideology. Yet this deviation has not led to a dramatic abandonment of Islam by the Muslims in China.

BIBLIOGRAPHY

General Works. Useful bibliographies on Islam in China include Claude L. Pickens, Jr.'s *Annotated Bibliography of Literature on Islam in China* (Hankow, 1950), Hajji Yusuf Chang's "A Bibliographical Study of the History of Islam in China" (M.A. thesis, McGill University, 1960), and Mark S. Pratt's "Japanese Materials on Islam in China: A Selected Bibliography" (M.A. thesis, Georgetown University, 1962). These works are now dated and are being superseded by the bibliographies produced by Donald D. Leslie, including "Islam in China to 1800: A Bibliographical Guide," *Abr-Nahrain* 16 (1976): 16–48; *Islamic Literature in Chinese* (Canberra, 1981); and, with Ludmilla Panskaya, *Introduction to Palladii's Chinese Literature of the Muslims* (Canberra, 1977).

The best and most detailed general survey of Islam in China is Tazaka Kōdō's *Chūgoku ni okeru koikyō no denrai to sono kōtsū,* 2 vols. (Tokyo, 1964), but it is primarily a compilation rather than an analytical study. Marshall Broomhall's *Islam in China* (London, 1910) is regrettably out of date, and Raphael Israeli's *Muslims in China: A Study in Cultural Confrontation* (London, 1980) and "Muslims in China," *T'oung pao* 63 (1977): 296–323, offer interpretative studies not totally based on the primary sources.

Historical Studies. Specific studies of the Muslims in the early dynasties include F. S. Drake's "Mohammedanism in the T'ang Dynasty," *Monumenta Serica* 8 (1943): 1–40; *Biography of Huang Ch'ao,* 2d rev. ed., translated by Howard S. Levy (Berkeley, 1961), pp. 113–121; and my own "The Muslims in the Early Yüan Dynasty," in *China under Mongol Rule,* edited by John Langlois (Princeton, 1981), pp. 257–295, and "Muslim and Central Asian Revolts," in *From Ming to Ch'ing,* edited by Jonathan D. Spence and John F. Wills (New Haven, 1979), pp. 169–199. Some prominent Muslims have been accorded fine biographies: for P'u Shou-keng there is Kuwabara Jitsuzo's exhaustive biography in the *Memoirs of the Research Department of the Tōyō Bunko* 2 (1928): 1–79 and 7 (1935): 1–104; for the Ming explorer Cheng Ho, a translation of one account of his travels can be found in *The Overall Survey of the Ocean's Shores,* edited by J. V. G. Mills (Cambridge, 1970); and on the late Ming philosopher Li Chih, two recent studies are Jean-François Billeter's *Li Zhi: Philosophe maudit, 1527–1602* (Geneva, 1979) and Hok-lam Chan's *Li Chih, 1527–1602, in Contemporary Chinese Historiography* (White Plains, N.Y., 1980).

Preliminary studies of the Muslim thinkers and writers of the seventeenth and eighteenth centuries can be found in J. F. Ford's "Some Chinese Muslims of the Seventeenth and Eighteenth Centuries," *Asian Affairs: Journal of the Royal Central Asian Society* 61 (June 1974): 144–156, and Joseph Fletcher's "Central Asian Sufism and Ma Ming-hsin's New Teaching," in *Proceedings of the Fourth East Asian Altaistic Conference,* edited by Ch'en Chieh-hsien (Taipei, 1975), pp. 75–96. An extraordinary analysis of the Muslim order in nineteenth-century China can be found in Joseph Fletcher's "Ch'ing Inner Asia c. 1800" and "The Heyday of the Ch'ing Order in Mongolia, Sinkiang, and Tibet," in *The Cambridge History of China,* vol. 10, *Late Ch'ing, 1800–1911, Part 1,* edited by John K. Fairbank (Cambridge, 1978), pp. 35–306, 351–408. The late nineteenth-century rebellions are covered in Chu Wen-djang's *The Muslim Rebellion in Northwest China, 1862–78* (The Hague, 1966), Immanuel C. Y. Hsü's *The Ili Crisis: A Study of Sino-Russian Diplomacy, 1871–1881* (Oxford, 1965), my own *China and Inner Asia: From 1368 to the Present Day* (London, 1975), and Jonathan N. Lipman's "Ethnicity and Politics in Republican China: The Ma Family Warlords of Gansu," *Modern China* 10 (July 1984): 285–316.

The PRC policy toward the minorities is analyzed in June Teufel Dreyer's *China's Forty Millions* (Cambridge, Mass., 1976). Their attitude and policy toward the Islamic countries is described in Bruce D. Larkin's *China and Africa, 1949–1970* (Berkeley, 1971) and Yitzhak Shichor's *The Middle East in China's Foreign Policy, 1949–1977* (Cambridge, 1979). Studies of the Chinese government's policies in Northwest China include Donald H. McMillen's *Chinese Communist Power and Policy in Xinjiang, 1949–1977* (Boulder, 1979) and George Moseley's *A Sino-Soviet Cultural Frontier: The Ili Kazakh Autonomous Chou* (Cambridge, Mass., 1966). Notable studies of the Muslims in contemporary China and in Taiwan include Barbara L. K. Pillsbury's "Being Female in a Muslim Minority in China," in *Women in the Muslim World,* edited by Lois Beck and Nikki R. Keddie (Cambridge, Mass., 1978); Pillsbury's "Factionalism Observed: Behind the Face of Harmony in a Chinese Community," *China Quarterly* 74 (1978): 241–272; and my "Muslim Inscriptions in China: A Research Note," *Ming Studies* 15 (Fall 1982): 22–26.

CONTRIBUTORS

ALEXANDRE BENNIGSEN, École Pratique des Hautes Études, Collège de France
FANNY E. BRYAN, Urbana, Illinois
ROBERT EVANS BUSWELL, JR., University of California at Los Angeles
COLETTE CAILLAT, Université de Paris III (Sorbonne—Nouvelle)
LUIS O. GÓMEZ, University of Michigan
PETER HARDY, School of Oriental and African Studies, University of London
ALF HILTEBEITEL, George Washington University
DAWNHEE YIM JANELLI, Indiana University
ROGER JANELLI, Indiana University
A. H. JOHNS, Australian National University
JOSEPH M. KITAGAWA, University of Chicago (emeritus)
PER KVAERNE, Universiteit i Oslo
RUTH I. MESERVE, Indiana University
DANIEL L. OVERMYER, University of British Columbia
MORRIS ROSSABI, China Institute in America
KHUSHWANT SINGH, Bombay
DAVID L. SNELLGROVE, School of Oriental and African Studies, University of London (emeritus)
DONALD K. SWEARER, Swarthmore College
YIM SUK-JAY, Seoul

JOSEPH M. KITAGAWA is professor emeritus of the History of Religions at the University of Chicago.